A History of
EUROPE

J M ROBERTS

A History of
EUROPE

J M ROBERTS

First published 1996 by Helicon Publishing Ltd

Copyright © J M Roberts 1996

Maps and chronologies copyright © Helicon Publishing Ltd 1996

Helicon Publishing Ltd
42 Hythe Bridge Street
Oxford OX1 2EP

Set in Electra

Design by Roger Walker/Graham Harmer

Printed in Great Britain by
The Bath Press Ltd, Bath

ISBN 1-85986-178-4

British Cataloguing in Publication Data

A catalogue record for this book is available from the British Library

Papers used by the publisher are natural recyclable products
made from wood grown in sustainable forests. The manufacturing processes of both raw materials and paper conform to
the environmental regulations of the country of origin.

This Edition printed 1996 for TSP

The illustration appearing on the half title and title
page, is Europe in 1883, from a German school
atlas *(Tony Garrett collection)*

Contents

List of maps

List of Chronologies

Foreword

My intention in this book is to provide an outline of the history lying behind Europe. My starting-point was what I said about Europe several years ago in my *History of the World*, and the structure of this book reflects that. Sometimes I have repeated here things I said in that earlier book; when I have not changed my mind about a particular topic and have felt no need to give it more or less attention, I have not hesitated to repeat myself. When my words still strike me as the right ones there seems to be no point in striving for elegant variation. But anyone who has read that book will find in this one much that is new and a different perspective.

My wish has been to write a serviceable guide. 'Europe' is nowadays a very political word, and I did not wish to usurp the role of the politician. Nothing which follows is intended to promote any particular response to the word except one: caution about its meaning. We still do not easily agree even on who are Europeans or (if we think we can answer that question) what it is that they share. The answer must always be 'different things at different times' and such questions demand historical answers. History settled much of the way most Europeans see themselves (though they may not know it), and it is worthwhile to try to discern what it was that left many of them with a sense of shared experience.

It may now be more than ever desirable to try to make sense of the past and measure its present weight. Recent events have shown how we are only too often taken aback by the history erupting (or re-erupting) around us. The past is always lying in ambush, as Ireland shows only too well. It should not be necessary to point that out, but history now gets less attention in the family and at school, than was once the case, and that makes us more vulnerable than in the past. Only a few months ago I read in my newspaper that there are now officers of the Royal Air Force who do not know what the Battle of Britain was. More tragically and bloodily, forgotten history has just helped to give Bosnia five years of misery.

My immediate stimulus to write was an invitation from my publisher, David Attwooll. He must not be thought responsible except in the most formal sense for the selective and personal view set out here, but I am grateful for the opportunity he gave me. Some may think what follows a demonstration of the obstacles to understanding the past implicit in any attempt to tell a story. To describe the past is always to over-simplify it and general history above all is open to adverse criticism on this count. That this is very much a general history will be obvious. Even the last two of the six highly condensed 'Books' which are the sub-divisions of my text, and which move at a slightly more leisurely pace than their predecessors, have each to cover half a century or so. Some readers are bound to be disappointed when they find important topics have been excluded. In three hundred thousand words there is not room for very much of a continent's history.

Sometimes I have tried to condense information in numbers, but I do not want to claim too much for them. Except in very specific instances, historical statistics should be illustrative and indicative rather than grounds for nice calculation. They should not be given too much credence. Even the best are often only close approximations, whose usefulness varies with the uses to which they are put. I have tried to follow trustworthy authorities, but even they have often had to work with imperfect data. Scientists ten years after the event still dispute the number of deaths attributable to the Chernobyl disaster. At a very different level, for all the richness of the statistical material provided so generously by all sorts of 'authorities' (the CIA felt able to say that in July 1991 the population of India was not 850 or even 866 million but exactly 866,351,738!) we would be unwise to reckon that we know within 50 million or so how many human beings are at present alive on earth. The further we go back, too, the shakier, usually, are the sources. The best I can hope to have done is to have used considered estimates to indicate meaningful orders of magnitude and relevant comparisons.

Mrs Julie Gerhardi typed several drafts of this book under fierce pressure and without complaint to me (though what her family may have heard about it, I do not know) and I offer her my most sincere thanks. Anne-Lucie Norton, my editor, endured slings, arrows, vicissitudes and much else, but once again showed me great kindness, consideration and helpfulness in her management of publication; I never take it for granted and thank her warmly for it. I must thank her Helicon colleagues, too, for their more specialised assistance. Above all, I am as grateful as ever for the tolerance and patience shown to me by my family in accepting the imposition of timetables they must often have wished to be very different. Had this book a formal dedication it would have been to a friend who died too soon some years ago: Noel Salter. Even fifty years ago he was a fervent Europhile. He would doubtless have disapproved of much in these pages (and would not have hesitated to say so, for he was never reticent in candid criticism of his friends' views) but I think he would not have been sorry that this book should have been attempted. That makes it a good place to record the affection with which I still remember him more than half a century after we met as schoolboys.

July 1996
J.M.R.

BOOK ONE Heritages

Human beings make history and sometimes do so consciously. They can only do so, nevertheless, with materials they find to hand, the ideas they and others have confidence in, their notions of what is possible, and what impossible - in short, within conditions set by circumstance and the past. The past which shapes what they do can be very old indeed. In the case of modern Europeans, it can be traced back into the vast stretches of geological time which laid down certain physical shapes, particular rocks and soils, special mineral resources (as the discovery of North Sea oil fields within the last thirty years should remind us, a lot can turn on what is under the ground we sit on, or the seabed we sit beside). European history took its own direction because the continent occupied a position and had a particular configuration which were to offer some possibilities and tell against others. To identify Europe as a human fact we have to begin with geography.

If physical structure sets some of the context in which human beings make their history, it is shaped also by past human beings. The most noticeable memorials of human effort and ingenuity are not always among the most influential; for the last two thousand years or so Stonehenge is irrelevant except as a focus of scholarship, wonder and curiosity. In those same years other human creations, though, were of overwhelming importance in shaping the future. They acted (as some do even today) upon the minds of generations, sometimes directing, sometimes inspiring, sometimes confining them, always leaving ineradicable signs of their influence on the history of Europeans and of Europe. They are very hard to describe truthfully, and impossible to summarize; the best that can be attempted here is a sketch which may give an approximate impression of their weight and influence. The most important of them are to be found in ancient Greece, the world the Romans made, early Christianity, and the barbarian incursions into western Europe in the closing centuries of antiquity. Between them, they constituted the foundations of a future Europe.

CHAPTER ONE Bedrock

Geography

Our maps lead us to take certain geographical facts for granted, even if some have not been there very long. Among them is a set of shapes. We can begin to look for Europe when the sub-continent at the western end of the Eurasian landmass had acquired more or less the physical form it has today, about 10,000 years ago. Then, much was already in place which was going to settle a lot of later history and shape millions of lives for thousands of years. The much more remote past of prehistory had left behind a big promontory or peninsula jutting out to the west from Asia, rather as India juts out from it to the south. Except in the east, even its most inland areas were and are not very far from the sea. There are some biggish offshore islands to the north and west (the British Isles) and to the south (Corsica, Sardinia, Sicily, Crete); around them and along the mainland's coasts are dotted hundreds of others which are much smaller. Along those coasts also lie subsidiary, but still large, peninsulas of which the most important are those of Scandinavia, Brittany, Iberia, Italy and Greece. Almost everywhere, too, the shoreline is indented with a multitude of inlets, gulfs and bays, some of them fed by rivers winding hundreds of miles inland.

Geography is very important, but it has been remarked that history is made by the men who control and discover geographical facts. The sea was to be one of the major determinants of a changing Europe and of the lives of those who lived there. The first of them could never have dreamed how important the opportunities offered by access to salt water were to be to those who came after them, thousands of years later. To the south they faced two big and almost enclosed tracts of water, the Black Sea and the Mediterranean in the north; the Baltic is another huge lake. The Atlantic and the North Sea, on the other hand, open on the world. When humans finally learnt how to manage long-distance travel at sea, Europeans would find themselves very favourably placed at the edge of major wind systems and currents which offered good opportunities for getting about the world. Another important oceanic fact was the Gulf Stream, and the warmth it brought to north-western Europe. But the most usual determinant of temperature is latitude — position in relation to the sun – and Europe's latitude, together with plentiful Atlantic rain, meant that most of it has been well-watered and has enjoyed mild weather without major upheaval or change since the retreat of the icefields from southern Scandinavia in about 7000 BC.

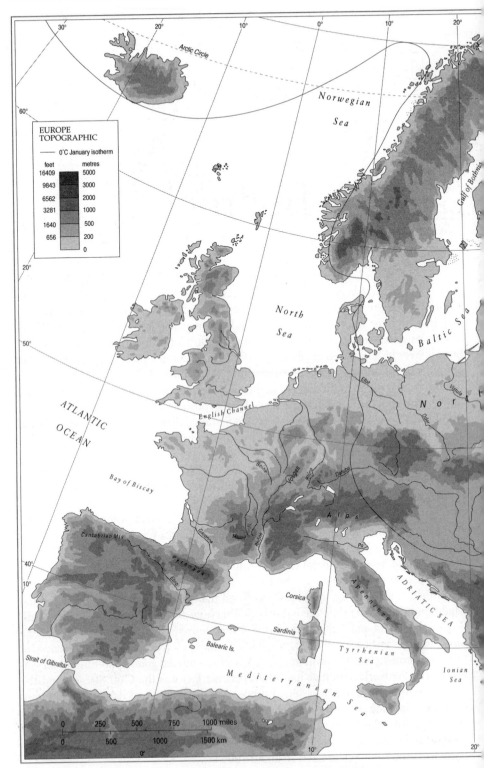

EUROPE
TOPOGRAPHIC

—— 0°C January isotherm

feet	metres
16409	5000
9843	3000
6562	2000
3281	1000
1640	500
656	200
	0

Arctic Circle

Norwegian Sea

Gulf of Bothnia

North Sea

Baltic Sea

ATLANTIC OCEAN

English Channel

Elbe

Oder

Vistula

Nor

Bay of Biscay

Seine

Vosges

Rhine

Danube

Alps

Cantabrian Mts

Pyrenees

Garonne

Massif

Rhône

Po

Ebro

Corsica

Apennines

ADRIATIC SEA

Sardinia

Balearic Is.

Strait of Gibraltar

Tyrrhenian Sea

Ionian Sea

Mediterranean Sea

0	250	500	750	1000 miles
0	500	1000	1500 km	

White Sea

Ural Mountains

E u r o p e a n   P l a i n

Lake

Volga

Ural

Pripet
Marshes

Don

Volga

Dnieper

Don

Carpathians

Prut

Dniester

Sea of Azov

Caspian
Sea

C a u c a s u s

Danube

B a l k a n
Mts

Black Sea

A n a t o l i a

Aegean
Sea

Crete

Cyprus

30°   40°   50°   60°   70°   60°

70°

50°

60°

40°

50°

30°   40°

The northern limit to this moderate climatic zone runs across Scandinavia, whose northern half tails off into a terrain and flora shared with much of the north of what we now call Russia, and distinguished by tundra, forest and, finally, Arctic ice and snow. But most of the rest of Russia, like much of central and eastern Europe, enjoys what is called a 'continental' climate and here, for the first time, we face one of those major, sometimes defining, facts differentiating western and eastern Europe. In Russia, summer and winter temperatures can run to extremes. The other distinctive climatic zone which has had a conditioning influence on Europe's destinies lies to the south. All round the coasts of the Mediterranean basin today's climate is probably less uniform that was once the case. Southern Europe's shores were once much greener than they are today, and so (even more strikingly if we could see them) were those of North Africa, the Levant and the Near East. The biblical cedars of Lebanon came from a country more densely wooded than the modern traveller sees, and North Africa was once a great corn-growing region. Well into historical times, though, the Mediterranean coasts, north and south, were better-watered and more fertile than today. Dessication has gone far to strip the shores of North Africa and the Levant, and the deserts behind them are now much nearer the sea than in ancient times. To the north, the inland margins of what we might call Mediterranean Europe are not so conveniently defined as its shorelines, but one long-significant marker is the northern limit of olive cultivation. 'The first olive tree on the way south marks the beginning of the Mediterranean region' remarks one scholar.[1] Drawn by climate and contour (in Italy it runs along both sides of the central mountain spine, not far from the sea), it has hardly moved in 2,000 years. Europe's first cities all appeared south of it.

Contours and topography have been more stable than climate. The English Channel came and went more than once in prehistoric times, but last appeared again about 8,000 years ago (though only in about 4000 BC did the seas reach their present level). Since then, of course, local topography has often been deliberately changed by humans as more effective technologies became available, and precise coastlines have fluctuated a lot in some places. In particular, the draining of marshlands was to make human settlement possible even in early times, and therefore a human impact on landscape, near the mouths of rivers. Yet the basic physical structure of the continent has altered hardly at all since pre-civilized times.

Internally, its most obvious features are a few spectacular clusters of mountains and numerous river-valleys. The Cantabrian *massif*, the Pyrenees, Alps and Carpathians all rise from land which, over most of Europe except Iberia, tends to slant gently downhill from south to north. Draw a line from, say, Bayonne to Moscow and, there is not much very high ground to be found north of it, except in Scandinavia. Then there are the major river valleys, some making their way over long distances to the Atlantic, North Sea and the Baltic. Especially near their mouths, these have often been so much shaped by human effort that they can no longer be regarded as wholly 'natural' facts. Among those of Iberia, the Douro, Tagus and Guadiana quickly become unsuitable for navigation not far from their mouths and wind through narrow valleys and high ground to the central plateaux; the Guadalquivir was in Roman times mainly marsh; drainage and deepening for a time allowed Seville to be a great port, but it is now silted up close to

---

[1] F. Braudel, *The Mediterranean and the Mediterranean World in the Age of Philip II* (London, 1972), I, p. 168.

the sea, and only the Ebro, Spain's river outlet to the Mediterranean, but rising near the Atlantic coast, provides a broad valley into the interior.

None of these rivers has had the historic importance of the Rhône, Rhine, Po and (longest of them) Danube, all of which rise close to one another, collecting their headwaters from the Alps. To the east, the Elbe, Oder and Vistula all rise within a 100 miles of Vienna, itself on the Danube. Finally, in Russia can be found some of the longest rivers of the continent: into the Black Sea flow the Dniester and the Dnieper, and into the Caspian the Volga.

For the most part the European coasts of the Mediterranean have narrow plains behind them, and then steeply rising mountains. These long offered few easy routes inland. The most obvious were the gaps provided by the upper reaches of the Garonne and Aude in south-western France, by the Rhône valley, and by the Vardar valley in Greece. It would be a long time before the passes of the Alps (the lowest, the Brenner, is just over 4,500 feet) or their slightly easier neighbours at the head of the Adriatic and in the Balkans could be exploited. The Danube valley, and those of the Save and Drave which opened routes both to northern Italy and round the northern side of the Alps, were easier but longer. Europe was harder to get into from the south than from the north and east; Mediterranean coast-dwellers tended to look sideways along their coasts, rather than over their shoulders at the mountains behind them. But their position, together with a shared climate, would make contact with others around the sea natural and likely (though it was to be a long time before voyages could be made that were other than coastal or not dominated by seasonal winds).

Its river-valleys gave Europe (to some extent, even in prehistoric times), some of its major north-south routes of internal communication. East-west movement was to be eased in due course by other geographical features, but this was only to become clear much later. The melting ice had left behind fertile soil for trees. In the so-called 'Boreal' climatic phase which followed the retreat of the glaciers, Europe must quickly (in terms of prehistoric timescales) have been covered by dense forest, difficult to penetrate or cross. In glades and, later, clearings, small groups of human beings could long live in virtual isolation. Clearing these vast woodlands was to take the efforts of many generations. The Romans began to drive roads through them, but major clearances only came slowly and well into the Christian era. In a sense they have never stopped, though in modern times some Europeans have started to plant trees again (Great Britain now has twice as much woodland as at the beginning of this century). Conscious, though piecemeal and gradual, deforestation was the first systematic application of human effort to overcoming the determinism of the European environment. Once the green blanket was thinned, another of the continent's dominating topographical features could then appear: the great northern plain which stretches across it, broadening out from relatively narrow beginnings in France and the Low Countries to spread fanlike across Germany, Poland, the Baltic lands and Russia, petering out at last in the foothills of the Urals and the Caucasus. It was to prove a great two-way corridor. Migrants would come along it westwards under the influence of mysterious pressures (dessication and overpopulation are among the favoured hypotheses) originating in Asia. Later, western Europeans would trek eastward across the same plains, colonizing and breaking in potential agricultural land.

Here we stumble again on a problem suggested already by climatic facts and which will in one way or another crop up through the whole of this book: where does Europe end in the east? A famous nineteenth-century statesman and Chancellor of the Habsburg empire, the Rhinelander, Count Klaus Metternich, was clear; he took the view that Asia began not far from his office windows in Vienna. There is something to be said for that, but it is a view based on history rather than topography. It is not easily defensible (or much use) until much later than prehistoric times. To decide where prehistoric Europe can be said to end, whether geographically or climatically, is in fact bound to be somewhat arbitrary (ethnically it is impossible). There is no natural line demarcating Europe from the rest of the Eurasian landmass which gives an outline so definite as that provided by its coasts further west. The physical continent will therefore be treated in these pages without more ado as including Russia west of the Urals and up to the mountains of the Caucasus.

That makes a total area of about 9,500,000 square kilometres, rather more than twice as big as India, Pakistan and Bangladesh together, and about the same size as the United States. Within it, great economic potential awaited exploitation. In aboriginal times, humans began that exploitation with scavenging, and then hunting and gathering. Since the end of the Pleistocene (the name given to the last phase of prehistory which ends with the receding of the great ice sheets) humans have been continuously, if at first only slightly, at work altering the European environment in which they lived. Only gradually, though, could they come to use fully the fundamental resource, the soil itself.

Europeans live on a large portion of that part of the world's land surface which is naturally suited to cultivation without irrigation, chemical, biological or major engineering input. Most of it is at relatively low altitudes, though the boundary of cultivatable land tends to move higher up the hill sides and mountains as one goes south. This resource was to be slowly but steadily taken in hand by clearance and better management as time went by, a major historical achievement. Later still, when Europeans had so grown in numbers that food had to be imported for them, they looked outside, to supplies from the huge natural granaries of the American prairies or the livestock ranges of the pampas and the Antipodes; in this sense, history was to increase Europe's natural resource area. But Europe had major advantages from the start. After the last Ice Age the environment was always favourable to agriculture — once that had been invented. In Europe, as elsewhere, the appearance of agriculture was crucial. Meanwhile, some Europeans were fishermen long before there were European farmers; they began the exploitation of another huge natural resource, the wealth of the fishing grounds offshore.

Humanity has followed many routes to civilization. There are no immutable courses or worldwide linear progressions in social development. Similar favourable conditions do not always throw up the same forms of society or sustain the same rapidity of cultural development. It seems likely that the collective efforts to manage effective irrigation and flood control which were needed in the great river-valleys of Mesopotamia, Egypt and north-western India stimulated rapid social and political evolution; the peoples who lived there may have had to organize themselves for large-scale works simply in order to survive. In early Europe, on the other hand, bands of a few families could get along, scratching a living from hunting, fishing and a primitive agriculture, with no need for complex governmental or social arrangements to regulate their small numbers. They hardly inhabited a rustic paradise, but they got by, even if it meant later arrival at civilization than elsewhere.

The earliest Europeans

How or when human beings came to be in Europe at all has been and still is much discussed by archaeologists and prehistorians. Fortunately, the questions do not affect European history and need not detain us. We can begin as the last Ice Age drew to an end about 10,000 years ago, when humans of the species *Homo sapiens sapiens* had long been established there. Their ancestors 20,000 or 30,000 years earlier have been identified as already physiologically 'modern' human beings, modern above all in the size of their brains, and in that respect like other members of their species in other continents. In the last stage of prehistory, aboriginal Europeans shared genetically with human beings to be found all over the rest of the world an intellectual capacity which gave humans a unique, innate power to modify their environment and shape their own manner of living, and an innate psychological dualism. This distinguishes humanity and still troubles it. Whatever their physiological or other roots, the presence of both a determining and instinctual emotional legacy from the past, and the power of rational thought which can loosen and limit that legacy's grip are still with us. Europeans were not in those respects special.

Other more visibly evolved human qualities, though, had begun even 10,000 years ago to mark off the story of humanity in Europe and make it different from that story in other parts of the world. For example, well before 10000 BC it was settled that the first Europeans would not be dark-skinned. In what is called the Upper Palaeolithic, the period down to the close of the last Ice Age, humans living in Europe were already physiologically distinctive, with skin pigmentations and particular distributions of subcutaneous fat which made them look different from humans established in other parts of the world. They would have been facially different from modern Europeans, too. Centuries of dietary change and a technology which reduced the need to use teeth as tools would pass before the edge-to-edge bite would virtually disappear and there would follow consequential changes in the shape of the jaw. Speculation about other genetically transmitted characteristics and capacities is unfruitful (which is just as well, for some find it alarming) in the present stage of our knowledge.

Cultural and technological influences come second only to the genetic in making possible successful survival and a growing mastery of nature. *Homo sapiens* all round the world mastered and passed down from generation to generation many important skills already discovered and much refined even before the last Ice Age began. They must have made it easier to survive the challenge it presented. Human beings had long had the power of speech and the knowledge of how to make fire. When drills were first used to make it we do not know, but whenever that happened, it was probably the first application of rotary motion by humans. The same technique was later applied to make bore holes needed to fit stone axe-heads to their shafts; a bow-string drive and an abrasive were utilized to do so. In less distant times humans in Europe (and elsewhere) had added to the stone technologies available for hundreds of thousands of years skills by making tools of horn and bone, and so had a comparatively specialized tool-kit (including, for example, harpoons and needles) with which to grapple with food-gathering and cold weather. They had also produced the first man-made material by mixing clay and powdered bone.

About the mental operations of the earliest Europeans, it is easier to speculate than to speak with confidence. Almost certainly they had some mysterious beliefs about their relationship with the natural world. Some argue that these are expressed in the first surviving works of art, the great cave-paintings, little figurines, pictures etched on bone or ivory implements and geometrically decorated pebbles from many European sites. Whether and how these were shared between any of the particular small groups in which they lived, is impossible to say. Social organization is even more obscure when the curtain rises on these people than is their thinking. It appears that the survivors of the Ice Ages at first went on as before, living mainly in the caves which had been refuges from the cold, getting their living by hunting and fishing, and wearing rudimentary clothes made of animal skins sometimes decorated with beads of bone. Their societies may well have been nearly isolated from one another, for there were very few human beings about. One estimate is that as the ice melted away perhaps 250,000 of a total human population 'approaching the 4,000,000 mark' lived in Europe in 7500 BC.[2]

The Neolithic and agricultural revolutions

Linear developments are usually hard to trace in prehistory. Its evidence is often accumulated from scattered sites where it was left at different times and it is sometimes necessary to make jumps of some thousands of years in a chain of reasoning from it. At this point a fairly short jump will do. It is tempting to think that the last great glaciation had given such a setback to humanity in the northern lands that Europe's inhabitants fell behind culturally and that their slower cultural evolution than that of other humans — as evidenced by the fact that agriculture made its first appearances elsewhere — shows this. However this may be, it is indisputable that one very important marker of a general acceleration of cultural evolution comes with what has been called the 'Neolithic revolution', a term which is in some ways unsatisfactorily precise. When first used in the nineteenth century it referred only to stone tools. This was appropriate in so far as improved stone tools — skin-scrapers, chisels and 'hand-axes' (cutting tools without shafts) — provide most of the early evidence for this major development. At its widest, though, 'Neolithic' has been used to cover not only the shaping and polishing of stone implements to a high finish, but the coming of pottery, weaving, the first metalworking and, above all, agriculture. Not all of these have to be present for prehistorians to use the term 'Neolithic'. Nor do they appear in any regular chronological succession.

Agriculture — the growing of food — was what really mattered. It released the brake on population growth which had held down hunter-gatherer populations, dependent and parasitic as they were on herds of game. As food supplies became more assured, humans were liberated from the need to follow wildlife about, could live more settled lives, could locate themselves in villages of built dwellings. The storing of food, moreover, eased the way to specialization of functions. The underlying demographic growth meanwhile seems clear: by 2000 BC, there may well have been about 5,000,000 Europeans.

Agriculture is thus the pre-condition of civilization; it makes it possible to provide for people who do something other than continuously rummage for food. How it came into being is a matter of speculation. It has been suggested that it may have arisen as a positive response to population pressure (rather than coming into being 'naturally' and then serving as a stimulus to growth). Whatever may have happened in any particular

---

[2] C. McEvedy and R. Jones, *Atlas of world population history*, London, 1978, pp.14,19.

area, it is now apparent that by about 4000 BC primitive farming was going on all over Europe, even if not continuously and contiguously. About 2,000 years later, new cereal crops appear (perhaps from the Near East) and they must have speeded up the advance towards a general participation of Europeans in the west and on the Mediterranean coasts in an agricultural way of life. What could be grown, raised or domesticated was largely a matter of local climate, indigenous vegetation and fauna, but technology helped, too. A great change in ancient agriculture came about with the introduction of iron tools, whose performance was much superior to those made of horn, bone or wood and so greatly increased the productivity of land and labour. They came later to Europe, though, than elsewhere.

Europe's earliest neolithic sites have been found in Greece and the Balkans. By 5600 BC pottery was being made in Macedonia. Locations in the south-eastern parts of the continent were long thought to be very suggestive. Perhaps — some still think certainly — a process of learning from more advanced cultures in mainland Asia was going on around the Aegean and is the main explanation of civilization's appearance in Europe. But other views have been given much greater force by recent developments in archaeological techniques, notably that of radio-carbon dating. Argument about such matters has excited ghosts of long-past debates to walk again. It might be thought that issues of where culture 'came from' are beside the point here, and that exaggerated attention has been given to them in the past, but implications have been and still sometimes are drawn from them about the nature of cultural exchanges in general. Later we shall encounter in historical times undeniably external cultural influences which came to bear very powerfully on Europeans; it is probably helpful to have as realistic a view as possible of what can be said about the receptive element on which influences from the outside played, even in ancient times.

Specialists now tend no longer to accept assertions that all prehistoric cultural and technical advance must have arisen either wholly by spontaneous localized discovery or wholly by diffusion from one source. The broad tendency of the chronologies recently provided by radio-carbon dating weakens the case for what have been called 'diffusionist' theories that technical and cultural innovation always spread outwards from a few key zones. Perhaps such views should always have been treated as implausible; there are obvious examples of both patterns of change in different parts of the world. Agriculture may first have appeared in south-east Asia, in about 10000 BC; in Central America it clearly emerges again in a very different setting and independently 5,000 or so years later. Aurochs, the beasts from which modern cattle descend, appear to have been domesticated by 6000 BC in Crete. This was on an island and why the technique appeared there we do not know. In mainland Europe agriculture could have been the outcome of local and empirical innovation as well as learnt from outside. Conversely, this does not imply that important developments always had both origins. Certain technological skills may well have passed into Europe from Anatolia, the Levant and Near East. One inferential argument for this was a chronological sequence of neolithic sites which seemed to match a slow advance of the relevant skills up the Danube valley, their eventual arrival in the Low Countries somewhere in the fifth millenium BC, and in Scandinavia and the British Isles during the next few centuries. This also seems to fit the pattern set by a line of the light soils (loess) which could be easily tilled with primitive tools, and sometimes with those set by other routes, too. Relative ease of access from outside was bound to be important. The earliest neolithic settlements in France seem to have been in the south, probably established by migrants following the coasts; from them the characteristics of the development can be traced to Switzerland.

These are suggestive facts in support of hypotheses of diffusion. But many new techniques were evolving at the same time and it is not easy to say where any first appeared; what we have is the outcome. Textiles and basket-work have left remains in the Swiss sites. By about 3000 BC people in the Danube valley were building big huts which showed the effects earlier than elsewhere of local innovation; warmer and drier lands might build in mud-brick, but the 'long houses' of Central European peoples used framing made from the timber plentifully available there. They even arrived at the pitched roof, so much better suited to northern weather than the flat roofs of the Mediterranean and Near East.

Metallurgy was important in Europe at a very early date. Copper was the first widely-used metal. Objects made of it by hammering were available in the Near East around 7000 BC, but soon after 5000 BC, it was being mined in the Balkans. This is earlier than the first evidence of its use in the Aegean. Such early dating, challenged though it can still be to within a few centuries, helps to explain why, once the discovery was made that both tin and copper could be found in Europe (both were needed to make bronze) metallurgy appears to advance more rapidly there than elsewhere. The archaeological record reveals a much more rapid evolution of tools and weapons than in the Middle East. No doubt it owed something not only to the availability of European ore, but to the presence of plentiful wood for use as fuel in smelting. It no longer seems likely, then, that Europe's prehistoric peoples made major technological advances in metallurgical skills only by borrowing from centres of civilization further east. Asia would have fundamental and indispensable contributions to make to the civilizing of Europe through its urbanism, technology, literacy, religious and scientific thought, but the older civilizations were not the source of all effective efforts to exploit the continent's potential. Nor were metals all that underlay it. There were other mineral resources whose importance would often appear only much later, well into the historical era. Not for a long time would there be the technology available to exploit, for instance, Europe's position on the northern hemisphere's long coal belt which runs from Appalachia to China, far less the other fossil fuel deposits which lay in oil and natural gas fields under its land surface and around its coasts. The continent's energy sources had to await the coming of technology to tap them; water was harnessed first as direct motive power and then much later as a means of making electricity, another and more easily distributed form of energy.

Migrants and immigrants

By 4000 BC over most of Europe we are well into the era of Neolithic cultures. The peoples who then unwittingly occupied the European treasure-house have been identified as belonging to what were once termed 'Caucasian' stocks which had spread into Europe and Iran from southern Russia long before the appearance of the first civilizations in Mesopotamia and Egypt. For the next few thousand years they and their successors in western and central Europe would be under continuing pressure from other newcomers further east, though it is important to remember that for most of the time this would not have been very apparent to any of them. It is very hard to visualize such pressure as a process on the ground. The numbers involved must have been small in any particular instance, and no-one was in a position to know what was going on as a whole or to make relevant comparisons. For a long time, settlement was fitful. A particular woodland clearing could not have been exploited continuously for more than a few years since primitive agriculture demanded that the land be allowed to recover after a while. That meant moving on to another easily-worked patch. Under such conditions not much of a demographic threat was likely to have been felt by those objectively 'under pressure' from long-term trends even if small groups occasionally came into conflict. No doubt hunter-gatherers would have found their activities restricted by changes in the distribution of fauna and flora which followed the establishment of farming cultures, but with so much land available, any consciousness of collective danger must have been tiny. Hunting cultures must long have survived alongside communities undergoing the full transformations of the neolithic all over Europe.

The majority of newcomers (or perhaps we should say 'latecomers') from the east spoke languages of a family later called 'Indo-European', a linguistic term with none of the genetic or ethnic meaning people have sometimes given it in the last couple of centuries. All but a few of the languages now spoken in Europe, as well as many spoken in Asia, the Americas, South Africa and Australasia (thanks, in the last three cases, to European migration) belong to this linguistic group. By about 2000 BC there had appeared sub-divisions among these peoples sufficiently marked in the archaeological record for some of them to stand out with a little more individuality. Among some enterprising and vigorous stocks penetrating western Europe a little later were two which have been termed, respectively, the 'Beaker' and 'Battle-axe' peoples (because of the easily recognizable special features of things they left in their graves). They are thought to have been warrior-predators, hailing from both ends of the continent, from Russia and from Iberia, to form mixed cultures which were among the first northern and central European aristocratic and warrior societies. From these were to come the 'Celtic' peoples who would cross the sea in the west to enter the British Isles, and (much later), in the east, move into Anatolia (boats go back some way; one dugout found in Denmark has been dated to about 7000 BC).

The Celts have long been given pride of place in accounts of ancient Europe, mainly because they were the first of the northern peoples to be written about (though only after 500 BC or so) by literate observers. They still dominated much of Europe in early classical times. Technologically advanced (they had wheeled transport and had evolved a plough of their own by the time the Romans came across them), they were also accomplished metal-workers who produced beautiful works of art, and memorably formidable warriors. With the battle-axe comes the first incontrovertible evidence of Europeans fighting one another. Early neolithic villages show no signs of defensive building and earlier neolithic Europe seems to have been a peaceful place, no doubt because it was still so empty.

But the Celts take us ahead of the story. To the east and north there were already in the second millenium BC other important groups of Indo-European-speaking peoples, notably the forefathers of the future Slavs, and those of the Teutonic peoples in Scandinavia and Russia. Further north still were the ancestors of the Finns, who did not speak an Indo-European tongue, while crammed into western Britain, Iberia and the Breton peninsula were remnants of the 'first' Europeans. Much remains to be discovered before this crude picture can be improved, but it indicates the elements of a groundplan of a future Europe.

Mentalities

For a long time none of these peoples mattered much to the outside world. It could not for a long time easily get at them. There is almost no written evidence (the literacy which actually shaped Europe — though possibly not literacy itself — came to it from outside, as it came much later to sub-Saharan Africa) and we can only guess at the thinking of pre-civilised Europeans from the material remains they have left behind. To more advanced peoples further east that thinking appears not to have been of much interest for a long time. European lands were of concern only as places from which commodities prized in the cities of the Levant and Aegean could be obtained — metal, amber, pretty stones. But such goods were important enough to stimulate exchange which led to trade (if that is the word) and specialized manufacturing. More was sometimes involved than simple two-way barter. Amber has been found which came originally from the Baltic, from which it was taken to Britain where it was worked into new forms and was then sent on, to end up in mainland Greece. This has been thought to have been very important in explaining Europe's development before civilization and, indeed, by some to have produced something which they are willing to describe as the first 'European' culture.

By 2000 BC metal-working was spread widely through Europe; mining and smelting were going on in Greece and southern Spain, as well as in the Balkans. There was a widespread use of bronze, the alloy of copper and tin which was much superior to pure copper for tools and weapons, and had come to displace it over nearer Asia as well as Europe. Ore or smelted metal was by then being brought long distances to Europe's primitive Sheffields and Essens, tiny as such places must have been. Copper and tin were already beginning to shape routes by which outsiders penetrated the sub-continent, and to influence its coastal and river navigation.

Besides a developing (and varied) skill in metal-working, another body of evidence has been claimed to show even more conclusively that a truly independent civilization

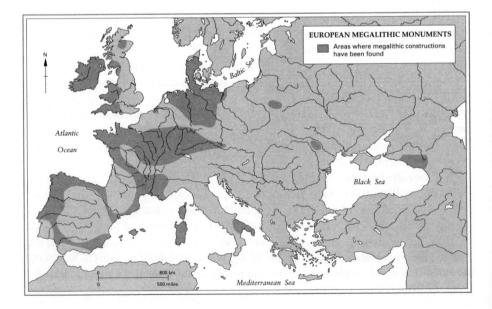

EUROPEAN MEGALITHIC MONUMENTS
Areas where megalithic constructions have been found

existed in ancient Europe before the coming of literacy. A huge arc of thousands of stone monuments called 'megaliths' (a word deriving from the Greek for 'large stone') stretches from Malta, Sardinia and Corsica, westward around the Iberian peninsula to Brittany, the British Isles and Scandinavia. The arrangement and use of very large stones in building is not peculiar to Europe, but our present knowledge suggests that such skills were employed in Europe earlier than in any other continent. The oldest examples, dating from about 4000 BC and early in the Neolithic era, are chamber tombs in Spain and Brittany which antedate by more than a 1,000 years the earliest Egyptian pyramids. The huge carved blocks of Malta's mysterious temples also seem to have been in place by 3000 BC, well before anything similar is found in the Near East. Apart from the megaliths used to roof, line or simply mark tombs, there are others on the mainland laid out in rows, sometimes running for miles across the country, or grouped in patterns, sometimes like groves of trees. The largest are very big indeed, notably the fifty-ton monster blocks which must have been brought long distances to Stonehenge, the elaborate site in southern England whose completion is now dated to about 2000 BC.

How and where the megalithic sites came to be built, why they formed the patterns they did and what were their purposes are questions which have attracted much scholarship (and perhaps even more speculation and fantasy). The presence of many of them (especially tombs) near the coasts was once thought to mean that they could be explained as examples of pure diffusion; they were seen as the work of primitive peoples acting under the guidance of itinerant master-masons and engineers from older centres of civilization where the management of large architectural and building developments was already common — rather as Spanish friars in the sixteenth century set about stimulating and organizing Mexican Indians to build churches and missions in the European style. But recent datings have undermined this once-plausible hypothesis. Stonehenge cannot be shown to depend on the Near East or the Aegean for its builders.

Some argue that some of the more elaborately laid-out megalithic sites (Stonehenge, in particular) were giant clocks, calendars or observatories, aligned to the rising and setting of the sun, moon or stars at major moments of the astronomical year. The alignment of some of them certainly makes it seem likely that careful observation of celestial objects took place before they were sited, though in the absence of written record it is hard to believe it reached the level of detail and precision achieved by the astronomers of Mesopotamia. By analogy with what we know of other cultures — in Central America, for example — it is tempting also to believe that some of the megalithic sites were connected in some way with assemblies for religious celebrations or the manipulation of supernatural powers; perhaps the builders of Stonehenge could claim to control weather and, through it, the harvest. But we do not actually know. Nor do we know whether such ideas (if they existed) were widely shared or were the preoccupation solely of a small elite which could intimidate, coerce, bribe or persuade others to work for it. What is clear is that since no wheeled carts were available (for none could have been built with axles sturdy enough to stand up to the strains of moving the huge masses required) there must have existed in northern and western Europe a social capacity to organize work in stone at least approaching in scale — even if not in the fineness of its finish — the monumental building of the Near East. Yet the builders had no means of recording why such efforts were undertaken, nor can we do more than hypothesize about the existence of social institutions which made them possible.

It is best to be cautious. The monuments do not have to form part of any unified scheme, single social process or continuous surge of activity. The Malta temples are not necessarily related to the tombs of western France and Brittany, even if they precede them in time. All the great megalithic sites may be the work of distinct and fairly isolated cultures, similar in their origins in a few relatively small and simple societies of agriculturalists, some more developed than others, with motives and occasions on which to act which were quite independent of one another. This would be compatible with, in some places, sporadic external influence and occasional imitation. What seems undeniable is that much of Europe's agriculture, its engineering and architecture (if that is indeed an appropriate word) arose, like that of Central America, independently of the outside world. It provides strong evidence that there existed over much of Europe societies of some hundreds of people with social disciplines and institutions strong enough to carry through long-term schemes (they would have required too much distraction from the demands of agriculture to be completed quickly) of major technical difficulty.

Whatever the ultimate explanations, and huge as the achievements of the megalith-builders were, the potential of their societies for future development was limited. Before the Christian era, the energies and creativity of the northern European peoples seem to have been mainly taken up in getting a living and grappling with their environment. It would need for its full exploitation technological resources long to be unavailable. With the exception, perhaps, of its metallurgical potential, northern Europe at the end of prehistory looks somewhat like parts of Africa in later times, a place interesting to scholars for its own sake, but ultimately dependent on, and needing to be stimulated and changed by external forces and powers before it could advance into history. Europe was as yet only a passive contributor to world development, as a source of materials wanted elsewhere. Greed and growing knowledge were always likely to suck in interested enquirers and entrepreneurs from more advanced cultures, but it was to be a slow business learning from them. In the case of northern and western Europe, regular institutionalized contact with such outsiders began only shortly before the Christian era. If those who lived there in those days felt uneasiness, hesitation, uncertainty or simply incomprehension when confronted by the emissaries of more advanced civilizations, then that, too, suggests parallels and similarities in other parts of the world hundreds of years later. Yet 'real' civilization had by then taken root elsewhere in Europe, around and along its southern sea-coasts.

Early Aegean civilization

1000 BC is an arbitrary, but easily remembered and useful date, a helpful marker; one important stage in Europe's evolution is clearly already over by then, that of effective isolation from any but occasional cultural influences from the outside. Well before the end of the second millenium BC, indeed, there had been growing and sometimes intimate intercourse between Mediterranean Europe, Asia and Egypt. It was then that the break-through towards Europe's civilized future began, south of the olive line, along the Mediterranean coasts and scattered over its islands; there, the seeds of the future were already sprouting.

A famous description of the Mediterranean calls it a 'complex of seas'.[3] One of

---

[3] Braudel, I, p.23.

them, the Aegean, was of particular importance as a meeting-place of cultures. Within it a multitude of islands and short sea-crossings made communication much easier than in the northern hinterlands. The Aegean was a cultural collector and distributor; influences flowing into it could quickly circulate around it. Before long they were escaping into the western Mediterranean and Black Sea, too. Only in the winter months was sea-travel very difficult. Unsurprisingly, commerce flourished and languages spread in so favourable a setting. True, virtually all the inhabited areas of the Aegean grew sufficient food for their own needs and for some centuries only specialized goods were exchanged. The same sort of basis for civilized life, indeed, tended to appear all round the Mediterranean, one based on the growing of wheat, barley, olives and wine, and crystallized in the little towns which were the first shoots of European urbanism.

Two especially important long-term influences stand out. The first was long thought to explain virtually everything that mattered which was going on: the impact of Near Eastern and Egyptian civilization, already evident early in the second millenium. Crete was the Aegean island nearest to Egypt. Already before 2000 BC it had towns built of stone and brick, where metal-workers and jewel-makers were at work for a presumably leisured elite. These differentiated and well-developed societies may well have appeared spontaneously (though they would have had to have obtained their metal ore from outside). We do not know when a foreign influence was first felt in Crete. In due course, though, a civilization (to which a British archaeologist gave the name 'Minoan' after a legendary king of the island) appeared there. It had the major accepted characteristics of true civilization: monumental building, complex social organization and literacy. Its influence came to be felt in the next few centuries all round the Aegean and helped to spread further the effect of skills and styles by then obviously introduced to Crete from abroad. This society survived for some 600 years, and to it we owe the earliest European writing, found on tablets used for administration or accounting. Clay-tablets had long been in use on mainland Asia for administrative archives. That is where Cretans may have got the idea, as they may have got architectural ideas from Egypt.

Economically, Minoa long prospered, rich in its agriculture; in 6000 BC or so wheat had been grown near the site of Knossos and the ancestors of modern cattle were already domesticated in the island. The European cultivation of the olive and the vine may well have begun there and came to flourish. Cretans also raised sheep which furnished wool for export. The island has even been seen early in the second millenium BC as the seat of a trading empire, engaging in complex diplomacy with foreign powers, and exercising some kind of maritime hegemony. Yet an end came to the great days of Minoan civilization, at least so far as any Aegean primacy was concerned, in about 1500 BC. It seems likely that a major earthquake and eruption at Thera, another Aegean island, then brought about the destruction of its great palace centre at Knossos. Soon after that, there is evidence of the arrival of invaders from Greece and of a remarkable new fact: the introduction of the first language from mainland Europe. This is revealed by the administrative tablets; after 1450 BC or thereabouts they began to be written in a different script, and scholarly decipherment has now revealed it as a form of Greek. The recently-arrived rulers evidently took over Minoan administrative techniques, but (as it were) wrote up their files in their own language. Such archives have also been found at mainland settlements in southern Greece, the Peloponnese, notably at a place called Mycenae. Meanwhile, the palace complexes in Crete were rebuilt and some sort of polity centred on Knossos survived. Seemingly it finally went under at the hands of other invaders from the mainland of Greece or other Aegean islands in the fourteenth century.

This indicates the second over-arching fact long shaping developments in the Aegean in the second millenium BC; while there is plentiful evidence of techniques moving north and west from the region, there was also movement, prolonged if intermittent, of iron-using peoples speaking Indo-European languages down into the Aegean from the north and north-east. One of these, the Hittites, had by 2000 BC pushed down into Thessaly, and then crossed to Anatolia to establish an empire there. Others had followed them but had gone on from Thessaly in the second millenium to Attica and the Peloponnese. Among them were the first Greek-speakers.

These warrior peoples, the Achaeans, as they came to be called, already in possession of the techniques of chariot warfare, settled in fortified strongholds on sites which were sometimes those of future Greek cities. Athens was one, but the most splendid was at Mycenae, where there remain monuments so impressive that some twentieth-century archaeologists argued that the skills which explain the western megaliths must have originated there. Mycenae seems to have begun to blossom in about 1650 BC. Its tablets of that era show the extension of record-keeping in the service of the government. The Acheans prospered until, in their turn, they were overcome by other conquerors from the north in the closing centuries of the millenium. We might think, perhaps, in terms of tribal war chiefs sweeping aside the first tentative European essays in bureaucracy. From this turmoil there was in the end to emerge another Aegean civilization, and civilized Greece itself. In the Mycenean colonies (which often replaced Minoan trading posts) evidence has been found of literacy, elaborate building, palatial arts such as gem-cutting, pottery made on the wheel, skills which were evidently all firmly established on the mainland. Under the stimulus of Minoan prestige or example (one can only guess at the exact relationships at work) other Achaean statelets had taken them up, as evidence from administrative tablets shows. Mycenae itself had been enough of a power to merit attention in the diplomatic records of the Hittites, far away in Anatolia. Thus by 1400 BC the basis was there for a new civilized achievement, if it could survive the fresh inflow of barbarism.

One raid which showed the vigour of the Achaeans passed into legend as the Siege of Troy, and mobilized forces from many cities and islands. It probably occurred in about 1200 BC. This seems to have been one of the last great Achaean successes. Soon after, the major Mycenean centres were destroyed. A cultural relapse is evident. From it was eventually to emerge a new Greece, broken up into units which seem to be based on the kinship groups of the most recent arrivals, but an obscure era spoken of by scholars as the 'Dark Ages' first intervenes, and of that it is difficult to speak with confidence.

On the eve of those Dark Ages it is sensible to recall once more the great disparities of human development which have always been present between different societies even at close quarters with one another. Such differences have only begun to disappear in this century, and though that change can be noted worldwide, huge cultural obstacles can still survive even modern communications. The cultural variety of prehistory lingered a long time in Europe itself. It can be observed in late classical antiquity and even, in isolated places, in the Middle Ages. In the Dark Age of the Aegean, in about the year 1000 BC, nevertheless, much that was to form the Europe we know had already begun to take shape. There had spread over the region peoples distinct from one another but sharing languages of a common origin. Metallurgical and farming techniques able to maintain populations much increased since Neolithic times (and able to provide subsistence for both technical specialists and for ruling elites) could be found there — and, indeed, over some of the continent to the north. Internal communications were good enough to permit just a little long-distance economic and cultural exchange; a wide region was now in contact with the Aegean region which was to be so vital to the future. Geographically, continental Europe was now fruitfully in touch with mature civilization elsewhere. What was going to be made of such potential would now depend on its peoples.

CHAPTER TWO Ancient Greece

The importance of the classical past

The past is never a simple influence. Even when its effect seems most obvious and direct, it works on us in many ways, through the circumstances it creates, the material culture it leaves behind, its physical relics and articulated doctrines and ideas, its superstitions and errors, its teaching and propaganda, its example for good or ill, the picture we have of it. The Aegean world after 1000 BC or so, even given the setbacks caused by new folk-movements, was itself going to be shaped by the weight of what had come down to it through Minoa, perhaps rooted ultimately in Egypt and Mesopotamia, as well as reminiscences and tales harking back to Mycenae, Greek speech written down in a semitic alphabet from the Levant and a technology able to provide iron tools and weapons and the management of major building undertakings. This was an inheritance through classical antiquity, these, in due time, were all to play their part, too, however distantly, in the making of a Europe unimaginable at that time.

The past also exercises its influence in a different way, through ideas and myths which those who come later come to hold about it, and from which they learn. Often, these shape the goals to which later men come to believe they should aspire, and illustrate what should be avoided. Such influences, like more direct inheritances from the past, are not always very apparent, nor always clear to those who hold them. They may well be most influential when they are not examined, but are taken for granted and not dragged into the light for scrutiny. They can matter immensely, because they define and set limits on what men and women can or cannot do at particular moments in history just as decisively as the circumstances which are inherited and have to be endured.

The factual awareness of the past of anyone living in Europe in the early years of the first millenium BC, though, would have been tiny or non-existent. Even their circumstantial and physical heritage would have been very small – the scatter of megaliths, many of them, possibly, already no longer still related to their first purposes by those who used them, some established tracks (and no paved road anywhere) and a few places of sacredness or exchange where they might meet those who lived in different and equally narrow environments. Occasionally there may have been some awareness that there were, elsewhere, people who were very different, some with names perhaps recalled in the songs of bards. Such fragments are about all that we can predicate as a recognizable inheritance from the human past. What we now know about that time, nonetheless, can justify us in putting down a few historical markers of our own to iden-

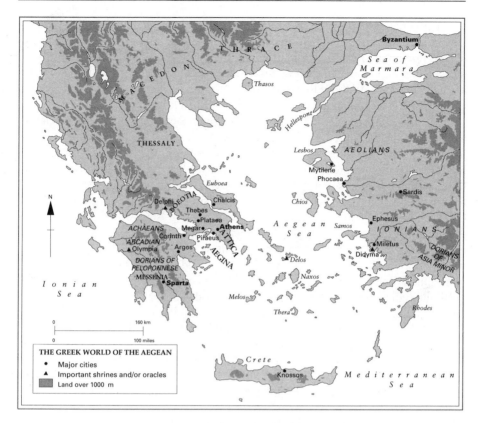

THE GREEK WORLD OF THE AEGEAN
• Major cities
▲ Important shrines and/or oracles
▬ Land over 1000 m

tify what was important, or the onset of an era which we can now recognize to have been of cardinal and enduring importance in shaping Europe and its future.

The beginning of the story is still in the Aegean, and for its first few centuries the focus remains there. On the Aegean coasts and islands there evolved a civilization not only of outstanding importance in its time and geographical setting, but unique in the primacy and density of its impact on a tradition of culture in which we still live. Libraries have been devoted to it, yet its story can only be sketched here, briefly and inadequately. Chronologically speaking, it can be regarded as an identifiable historical entity from about 800 to about 300 BC, and it was the creation of Greeks. It was to elaborate, evolve and spread even in that time from its Aegean cradle to the whole Mediterranean, throwing up new institutions and discarding old ones as it did. Yet its character and many of its characteristics remained recognizable and unmistakable. It was always eclectic and adventurous and changed much in time, in part because it continued to take the impress of new influences which came to bear on it.

About Greek civilization we know a great deal. Besides leaving a huge archaeological and monumental legacy, there is also a richness of written material unequalled and unprecedented in any earlier civilization through which to approach it. But for a long time most of the literary sources for Greece itself were passed on indirectly through channels established by others. This is why the appearance by 300 BC of a new historical entity, Rome, its own culture deeply influenced by Greece, is also a major fact of European history. A distinctive people in central Italy, much influenced from the outset by contact with Greece, was to build a world-order in western Asia, the Mediter-ranean, western Europe, and North Africa which was the first ever to cover the whole region. Roman political predominance, and the boundaries it laid down would be of incalculable importance in shaping future ideas of Europe, and transmitting to it the legacies of Greece. Without Rome and the opportunities its great cities presented, the Greek past and its influence might have been confined to the Near East.

Still more important, without Roman predominance, a new religious revelation which was to be the supreme defining influence on Europe's later character could not have taken root and prospered as it did. Some of those who adhered to it were so impressed by their awareness of what Rome meant that they saw her discharging a supernatural task, as a part of that revelation itself. That Rome in time became Chris-tian made possible (for hundreds of years) a Christian Mediterranean and then a Christian Europe. Without Rome the religious vision of Israel would have remained that of an isolated self-defined people, largely confined to the Levant and the Jewish communities scattered through its ports and those of the Mediterranean. In the long run, the variety of Judaism we call Christianity would not have become a world reli-gion without Rome. Through the Greek and Latin languages the Jewish myths and the possibilities they suggested were to flow into a world which, at the time of Christ's cru-cifixion, was a political unity. For centuries, men struggled to find a place in that unity for the Judaic beliefs of what most Greeks would have considered a 'barbarian' culture. When they succeeded, the beliefs which were (said St Paul) 'to the Greeks foolishness' had been put into Greek (few non-Jews read Hebrew) and had taken fresh colour and meaning from that language and the culture it carried. For a 1,000 years, educated Europeans would read their religion's sacred writings and doctrines in Greek or Latin.

These were facts of such historical importance that it is easy to understand why Europe so long remained profoundly conscious of its classical roots. But that outcome also owes much to the enormously successful self-projection of the ancients. Our pic-ture of ancient Greece and its continuing and real influence, came to us mainly through the Greek and Latin writers who provided so much of the syllabus (other than the Bible) which was taken up into later European culture. What is more, they set what for a long time were unquestioningly accepted as criteria by which to judge human life. This is an implication of the word 'classical': the classical is the source of standards by which subsequent achievements can be measured.

Such a way of thinking has, of course, its own subtle dangers and entrapments; the assumptions underlying it take it for granted that there can be criteria applicable to all humanity, all cultures, and that they should be universally recognized because univer-sally valid, and that is not a fashionable view at the end of the twentieth century. We should remember, too, that other cultures have had their own classical eras which gen-erated for them standards honoured by later ages and similarly seen as of universal application. We can also note that the demarcation and definition of classical traditions is always likely to be open to debate. Yet when all this has been said and allowed for, and when sceptical modern scholars have done their spectacular best to qualify and explain the limits of civilization in the Greek and Roman worlds, we are left with a huge mass of cultural facts which down to this day have helped to determine the way in which Europe and the minds of Europeans took shape in history. To understand that, we have to start with the Greeks.

The Greeks

From the Greeks later Europeans were to inherit an immense and indissoluble residue of mental achievement from which our ancestors copied and learnt for centuries, and of which we still make use. Vigorous and restless – even to the point of self-destructiveness – the Greeks passed to the future modes of thought, ideas, ideals and institutions, which take us out of the mysterious uncertainties of the first civilizations and into, as an Oxford scholar once put it, 'a world whose air we can breathe'.[1] 'Legacy' is an over-used and over-familiar historical metaphor, and liable to mislead; even if they can be identified, legacies in the end turn out to be ambiguous and complex. The word suggests something easy to describe, but that is rarely the case. The influence of a civilization is not simple and specific and what the ancient Greeks left to our own is particularly hard to pin down because it is so widely-ramifying, so often concealed. We think, for instance, of philosophers setting out certain ideas and doctrines. Yet philosophic thought itself, the business of reflecting systematically (even on thought itself), was invented by the Greeks, who left us not only specific ideas, but also frameworks within which philosophers can still work. One even in this century described the whole European philosophical tradition as a series of footnotes to the work of the Athenian Plato.[2] Greek philosophy devised many of the structures and categories and much of the language in which issues are still discussed. That is a very deep, but also a very subtle form of influence. When people grumble that some modern philosophy does not look to them much like the real thing, they are often reflecting preconceptions about what it ought to be which have come down to us from the Greeks.

Other examples of the hidden pervasiveness even today of Greek influences in our collective life – in art, politics, science – could be given; they become quite explicit when we go back a few centuries into European history. Even when they come out in misconceptions and misunderstandings (for people often go wrong in trying to follow ancient guidance) the influence almost always turns out to have been deep and effective. In trying to come to grips with so diffuse and powerful a heritage it is best not to hope for too much – and certainly not to seek to draw up precise catalogues or to map intellectual genealogies which cover the whole field.

To return briefly to philosophy, like many other words in modern English, it comes to us from Greek. With those others — 'democracy', 'history', 'politics', are some which are familiar – it has passed in recognizably similar forms into almost all European languages. This is one reason why language is a good place at which to begin. Another is that language was something making the ancient Greeks — 'Hellenes', as they called themselves – self-conscious and linking them in special ways with one another. Whatever individuality and self-assertiveness they might feel and show as Thebans, Corinthians, Spartans or anything else, they all spoke versions of a shared language. It gave them a shared mental world embodied first in an oral and then a written literature; when Greek met Greek they could talk to one another, in a very meaningful sense. They had a pantheon of gods they all held sacred, whatever their local deities and cults. When they met at the games at which all Hellenes might be represented, they were aware of these bonds between them; though they might quarrel fiercely, fighting and ravaging

---

[1] A. Andrews, *Greek Society* (Harmondsworth, 1971), p. 294.
[2] A.N. Whitehead, *Process and Reality*, (Cambridge, 1929), p. 53.

one another's lands, they recognized a common heritage Hellenes did not share with other men. They belonged, they felt, to 'Hellas'.

This was not just an abstract idea, but a psychological and cultural reality. Non-Hellenes, those who did not talk Greek as their native tongue, were lumped together as *barbaraphonoi* — 'barbarians'. Whether Scythians, Persians, Egyptians or anything else, whether they possessed power, skill or wealth or not, barbarians were outside the pale of the Greek-speakers and thus inferior. This distinction was fundamental. It would shape perceptions, psychology and behaviour for centuries after the Greeks had themselves lost control of their world. It came to express something more general than linguistic distinction; it drew attention to a particular level of achievement, or, rather, non-achievement, inferior to that of civilized men. When in the fifth century BC the Greeks fought in two great wars against the Persians they were conscious that for all the wealth and might of the Persian empire (and in spite of the fact that many Greeks fought on its side as mercenaries), they were fighting barbarians. They did not see the Great King's subjects as capable of behaving towards one another as civilized men should, or of running their own affairs; they were not truly free men, as their practice (demeaning and ridiculous in Greek eyes) of kowtowing to their ruler showed. The resonances of this antithesis took a long time to die away and perhaps have not altogether done so. Thousands of years later men would still see the Persian Wars as a conflict not only of Greek and barbarian, but of west and east, of Europe and Asia.

The Greek diaspora

Greek self-consciousness made possible the holding of the first panhellenic games in 776 BC. With that date the ancient Greeks began their chronology. Greeks from all over the Aegean came to these competitions in sports from communities not differing much in their material level of life. They lived by fishing, farming the narrow plains behind coastal settlements, or, more and more, by trading. The first distribution of these little communities had been settled during the Dark Age of the Aegean, after the end of the Mycenean era, when the comings and goings of peoples on the mainland were producing pressures like those which drove the earlier Greek peoples out into the islands and Ionia. Tradition has assigned a particular importance to Athens as a source for the settlement of Greeks in Ionia and the Asian islands, and archaeology does not suggest that tradition is wrong. Athens was not a Dorian city and may have retained more of Mycenean culture in the Dark Ages than other cities. Ionic, the Greek of Asia Minor, was a different dialect from Dorian, which was spoken in the Peloponnese and characteristic of such cities as Sparta and Argos. Between 1200 and 800 BC the new arrivals had fanned out to emerge into the post-settlement age as distinct groups of Dorians, Boetians and others. They spread further the new skills and knowledge flowing about an increasingly cosmopolitan area. The Aegean made them Hellenes. The new setting was very important and counted for more than the past in shaping the future of these peoples. Nowhere on the mainland of Attica and the Peloponnese, for instance, was more than 60 kilometres from the sea. Narrow coastal plains and steep hills encouraged men to look outwards. The Greeks were almost forced to sea.

These Dark Age movements were marked by comings and goings to and fro, and some of the going (from the mainland) was in the direction of established settlements further east, survivals from the Mycenean age. Exchange across the Aegean can never wholly have ceased, even if for a long time it lacked one great simplifier, money. Seventh-century Greeks laboriously transferred iron goods like tripods and spits as a crude kind of currency until, at last, money was invented and the first coins, standard pieces of metal so imprinted as to indicate their content and value, were struck (this invention has long been attributed to the Lydians, a legendarily rich non-Hellenic people living in the north-west of Asia Minor, and there seems to be no good reason to quarrel with that view). This made commerce much easier.

There was also Hellenic colonization. Demographic pressure undoubtedly played a part in it. Growing numbers were bound to press on the supply of food which could be grown in the small and closely confined agricultural lands of the early settlements; this was a spur to emigration and settlement. Hellenes first migrated across and around the Aegean, then on into the Black Sea and the western Mediterranean. In the end, there were more than a 1,000 Greek communities, located first by the chances and opportunities of primitive settlement, and later by trade and politics. When a city grew too big for its resources, or its inhabitants felt that it had done so, a company of emigrants made up of whole families and households would set out to find a suitable place overseas for a new settlement. Suitability was a matter of being able to pursue a Greek way of life with as little change as possible, and given the Mediterranean's shape and climate, this was not usually too difficult. The resulting colony, for all its civic and economic independence preserved a special relation with the founding city, whose offshoot it was and whose ways it tried to preserve. So there grew up the Greek cities scattered round the Mediterranean coasts and islands, as one Greek put it, 'like ants and frogs round a pool', diffusing knowledge of their common language and bringing to bear Greek cultural influences, if only by example, on other peoples.

Some of the most important Greek colonies in the west were founded in Sicily and southern Italy, later called in Latin *Magna Graecia*; 'Great Greece'. Greeks had first gone west in search of commodities, above all metals available in central Italy. Some colonies emerged from trading-posts and ports. Syracuse was the largest and wealthiest of them. Founded by emigrants from Corinth in 733 BC, it had the best harbour in Sicily and in time became a dominating power in the western Mediterranean and one of the greatest and richest cities of the Greek world. Further west, colonies appeared in Corsica at an early date, as well as on the western coasts of central Italy, and in southern France; (one, Massilia, has left behind a name still recognizable as Marseilles). If, as is believed, the Greeks also began the re-shaping of the western European eco-system by introducing the vine to Provence and the Rhône valley, then Greek colonization indeed left a profound legacy of civilization in the West.

With colonies came further expansion of Greek overseas trade and then conflict with competitors. Among the earliest of these were the Phoenicians, an enterprising commercial people from the Levant cities of which the most famous are commemorated in the Old Testament: Tyre and Sidon. In the Phoenician cities (or among the traders who came from them) the Greeks found the semitic original of the alphabet which they took and adapted for their own use. It was later to become the basis of the Latin alphabet now in use in greater or lesser degree everywhere in the world. The Phoenicians competed successfully with the Greeks in Spain, succeeding largely in ousting those who got so far, and also established their own strongholds in Sicily, though they were unable to expel the Greek colonists from that island.

The city-state

There can at first seem to be something disproportionate in the amount of time, energy and ink which has been spent over many centuries in exploring the life of the Greek cities, some of them hardly of a size to merit the dignity of government by an English District Council. Yet such communities could have an intense self-consciousness, a strong sense of identity. Though they could quarrel violently with one another, it was in fact the things which the Greek city-states had in common which for the most part have struck posterity. Physically, few of them took up much space. That had important consequences both for their economic resources and their social life, and any implied similarities between what we call Greek cities and modern cities would be very misleading. Size also contrasted them with contemporary structures in Egypt, Mesopotamia, Persia and the Levant. A large proportion of those men who lived in them could and did take part in some measure of collective consideration and oversight of their shared affairs. Relative wealth (and therefore relative deprivation) no doubt always had important effects, but the rich and poor were less remote from one another in their style of life and patterns of consumption than rich and poor can be today; by later standards, most Greeks lived simply. The better-off among them owned land, but in relatively small parcels.

Most Greek cities had an acropolis or high place on which stood a temple to the patronal deity. This allegiance was important to the city's identity, and was expressed in the physical and architectural dominance of the site. Greeks, though, did not only belong to their cities; they had loyalties to other groups, too, notably those of kin. In early times kinship was often the basis of civic organization and provided its most important sub-units. The significance of tribes would wane, although as late as the fifth century they would still matter as organizational ideas; when they emerged from the tumultuous dark age, the Hellenic communities were for the most part ruled by kings. The next stage came, the evidence suggests, when royal power was gradually eclipsed by that of aristocratic councils, the descendants of warrior forbears who had early acquired land. They could afford the iron arms and armour which were necessary but increasingly costly to the fighting forces of the city. In the seventh century, though, aristocratic councils were often elbowed aside by 'tyrants', a word we have borrowed from the Greeks and still use, but to which a pejorative meaning has been given by time. The Greek tyrants are better seen as strong rather than bad men, and their great age was the seventh century.

The aristocrats would certainly have owned more land than most of the other citizens, though that might not have been much by modern standards. But the poorer peasants had less still. With sometimes only tiny plots and sometimes none they might work for the bigger landlords, perhaps to discharge debts they had contracted. Other residents in the community (but not of it) were slaves and the foreigners or 'metics'; these were excluded from citizenship. There tended to be more metics as the economy ramified and became more elaborate with the growth of exchange and trade between one city and another. By the fifth century BC, mainland Greek cities were importing grain from the western Mediterranean, Egypt and even the Black Sea ports. The other important group outside the citizen body were the women who were not slaves. Greek attitudes towards women changed little between archaic times and the end of the sixth century (or, in some respects, much later). They were of the city only as the appendages of their husbands and male relations, and had no independent status or legal rights. In this respect, their quasi-tutelage made ancient Greece not very different from the rest of the ancient Mediterranean and Near Eastern world.

The most important regulatory force in these little societies was custom and customary law. We hear of law-givers, usually when a need arises to adapt customary patterns to changed circumstances. One, Solon of Athens, left a name which has come to stand for legislators in American newspaper headlines. But it is not easy to be clear until much later about the way new law was made or even how the idea took root that legislation – drawing up and imposing laws – was possible. Aristotle, who gave more reflexion to constitutional questions which has survived than any other Greek, seems to have been against legislation unless it was absolutely necessary. Though, too, we know quite a lot about some cities' constitutional arrangements (Athens above all), there are scores of which we know nothing or have at best only second-hand reports. It is dangerous to talk confidently about the way Greeks ran their public affairs once we move away from specific evidence. The comparative and cultural point, nonetheless, can be made on the basis of the evidence which exists: though they were all male, a much larger proportion of Greeks took part in some way in public life than did their contemporaries in any other ancient civilization. Moreover, they not only shared a government and many common economic interests, but formed also a cultural unity, with a measure of what we should now call ideology, notably in the form of a set of religious beliefs and practices, and some assumptions and ideals. It was expressed in ceremonies, art, processions and the drama which arose out of them – and they were to be important for the future, too.

The Greeks invented politics. The word they used for a city was *polis* and its connexion with our word 'politics' (and with 'political' and 'politician') is obvious. The Greek word, though, had connotations going far beyond those we attach to the word 'city'. It meant not only a sizeable agglomeration of people and buildings, but much that we should indicate by a word like 'community' or have in mind when we think of states or nations. They were autonomous, self-governing societies, with formal and sometimes even elaborate arrangements to assure civic participation. Such arrangements appear to have reached their furthest development in the direction of what we call (again borrowing a Greek word) 'democracy' at Athens in the course of the fifth century. The existence of some sort of periodic general assembly of the citizen body was nevertheless fairly common by 500 BC. In the acts and the deliberations of these assemblies began politics as we know them, the discussion by constitutionally qualified persons of public and collective business and the subsequent making of decisions. The boundaries and patterns of the activities which we call politics are of course ever ill-defined and shifting. But at their heart lies some recognition of a shared, public interest and an area of common concerns about which argument is possible; this the Greeks achieved and it was a big step. They could picture a collective good which ws more than just a following of immemorial custom, or obedience to immutable law, and was something to whose definition the citizen could contribute. When it first appeared, the area open to debate must have been very small, extending only to major and specific acts of policy – a decision, perhaps, for war or peace. Those who could participate would at first have been few; they would have constituted a council, perhaps, or even the court of an individual ruler where competition for favours and power could take place. But such bodies would tend to grow and, more importantly, to reflect growing awareness of interests and the potential weight of others still left outside them. Dimly, in the background, there was a *public*, sometimes appearing in a general assembly of citizens.

Given modern experience, it is tempting to be sceptical about the proposition that participation in politics is a great educational force. Yet educational it is; the demonstration in practice of the fact that public decisions can be made by discussion and argument, even when that argument is conducted by few, marks an advance upon the blind assertion of the weight of tradition, custom or authority. Politics have taken many forms, overt and covert, and have been exploited for many corrupt and wholly private purposes, and their influence has waxed and waned across the centuries almost, at times, to the point of disappearance. They were, though, to prove one of the supreme contributions of the Greeks to civilization. Later, politics spread the Greeks' political idiom around the world in a vocabulary we still use; democracy, oligarchy, tyranny, autocracy are still the common currency of our debate, however we now gloss them.

Conflict in the Greek world

By 500 BC, the rise of commerce and consequent specialization, both between cities and between inhabitants of the same city, had already begun to bring change. In many of the city-states legal and institutional innovations were restricting the power of the traditional ruling classes, the 'aristocrats' or 'better sort' belonging to the landowning families which had dominated early economic life. Although we can only follow the process in one or two places (above all, Athens) such change was frequently accompanied by new provisions for the involvement of a large part or even the whole of the citizen body in the state's affairs. As warfare changed its nature with the coming of more iron (and some steel) weapons, and more ordered and better-drilled formations appeared on the battlefield, citizen-soldiers called *hoplites* were increasingly typical of the city-state armies.

The ground-plan of the Greek world was set by 500 BC. Over mainland Greece, the Aegean, the shores of Asia Minor and even more remote regions such as the Black Sea were scattered hundreds of Greek cities. What lay beyond that world so far as the Greeks knew can be grasped from the writings of one of the two men who have been identified as the fathers of the art and science of history, Herodotus of Halicarnassus, a little town in Asia Minor where he was born in the first half of the fifth century. He spent much of his life travelling and tells us that beyond the edges of the Greek sphere there lay to the north and north-west the little-known territory the Greeks called 'Europa'; about it, though he says little. But there, for the first time in a text, is the name applied to a place. To the north-east, in southern Russia (not a name then used) beyond the straits which led to the Black Sea and the lands of the Golden Fleece, lived barbarians, the Scythians among the most important, trading with the Greeks of the coasts. The southern coasts of the Black Sea were ruled by the Great King, the ruler of Persia, whose territories stretched at their greatest extent from the Gulf to the Mediterranean. In Africa (another as yet unknown name) lay the great kingdom of Egypt, famed for its monuments and wisdom, and to the west of it the kingdom of Libya. Of what lay beyond these lands Herodotus is more fanciful. Yet he was an assiduous and careful historian, interrogating whatever witnesses he could find and travelling far in search of information for which he could vouch by personal observation. Inevitably, though, his enquiries were limited. In any case, for all his universal range of interest, his main preoccupation was firmly tied in time and space to a great central theme, a long struggle between Greece and Persia.

The Greeks fought two great wars against the Persians. The first began in 492 BC, when a Persian army was sent to punish Athens and Eretria for the help they had given to an Ionian revolt against Persian rule. This was followed by a second expedition which ended in Persian defeat at Marathon in 490 BC. A second war ended after three great Greek victories in 480–479 BC and then the Persians went home. Greeks were taught to see them as struggles of civilized men against barbarians, freemen against slaves; yet many Greeks fought in the Persian ranks, for mercenary service abroad was a well-established Greek custom. Yet myth came to obscure such reality. A consciousness of east–west antagonism is a recurrent theme in European history, and some have always seen this contest as its first expression, and one with a moral element to it, the opposition of liberty and servitude. It had an ethnic and geographical component, too, and an Athenian orator and contemporary of Aristotle was already able to trace history backwards and to present the Trojan War as a conflict of Europe and Asia.[3]

The ebbing of the Persian menace opened the way to an age later associated with the greatest achievements of the Greek culture. But this can be misleading. One of the most important achievements of Greek civilization had come as early as the sixth and seventh century, when Greeks in the Ionian cities invented science. Later, partly because of great writers, propaganda and self-esteem, the cultural picture tends to be dominated by Athens and, indeed, the Athenians, encouraged to think of themselves as a model for other Greek cities, came to stand for most of what was later remembered as the 'Greek achievement'. In a major sense, too, that achievement was brief. The city-states did not survive. Even during the Persian wars their rivalries and divisions had been apparent. It has intrigued many historians to speculate on the reasons why the Greeks never overcame their divisions. Within individual cities they brought on a great struggle which in the end broke the power of many of them – Athens, above all – and left them prey to outsiders, the Peloponnesian War.

A brilliant analytical account of much of it was left to posterity by the man who stands with Herodotus as the other founding father of the discipline of history, the Athenian Thucydides. The struggle between Athens and Sparta which was at the heart of it went back to differences between them in the Persian Wars. An open rivalry for alliances with other states became explicit when Athens became the leader of a league of what were, in effect, tributary states in the 470s and 460s. This first led to war in 457. In the following decades domestic politics at Athens complicated inter-state relations further. Athenian democracy threatened the oligarchies of other states, which in consequence looked to Sparta for support. In the end, conflicts merged in two great struggles between 431–421 and 414–404 which are together called the Peloponnesian War. This succession of conflicts in the end fatally weakened the Greek states. Athens and her satellites were militarily defeated and then humiliated at the peace, but all Greece was the real loser. Nor did the quarrels of the city-states cease. A brief Spartan hegemony followed but in the end, the unity of submission and empire was to be imposed upon the Greeks by an external power in the next century.

---

[3] See F. Chabod, *Storia dell 'idea d' Europa*, ed. E. Sestori and A. Saitta (Bari, 1961), p.16. Aristotle himself still distinguishes Europe from Greece (*Politics*, vii, 1327b) and remarks that those who live there 'are full of spirit, but wanting in intelligence and skill' (Jowett's version).

The Greek 'achievement'

There is always a risk in looking in the past for the elements of what came later. Greek civilization was much more varied than what posterity (and there was more than one posterity to select and sieve what survived) came to prize. Yet so remarkable still are the works of the Greek intellectuals and so large have they loomed in shaping later cultures and societies, that it requires effort to penetrate through them to the values of the world from which they emerged. They left plenty of space for irrationality and superstition as well as for reason and intellect. Much of Greek art expresses that. Nor was the whole of the Greek achievement decisively beneficial for the future. Arguments, for example, that slavery was natural because it was in accordance with the way certain humans were constituted were to be for centuries all too persuasive. The Greek subjection of women is to modern eyes another disquieting side of Greek culture less easily ignored than the practice of other societies.

Most Greeks lived in cocoons of tradition, irrationality and superstition; even those who were in a position to understand something of the speculations which were opening new mental worlds rarely welcomed or accepted their implications. A continuing respect was shown to the old public orthodoxies, and in some respects it was reinforced as time went by. It was impiety in late fifth-century Athens, for example, to deny belief in the gods. One philosopher believed that the sun was a red-hot disc; it did not protect him that he had been the friend of the great demagogue Pericles when he said so, and he had to flee. It was at Athens, too, that public opinion was convulsed, on the eve of a great military enterprise, by the mysterious and ominous mutilation of certain public statues, the 'Hermae'. The disasters to the Sicilian expedition which followed were attributed by some to this sacrilege. Popular superstition must have been more typical of Greek community than the presence of distinguished philosophers. Furthermore, Greek thought reflected changes of emphasis and fashion arising from its own dynamism. These sometimes led to dead ends and blind alleys, to exotic and extravagant fantasies. Greek thought is not monolithic, but an historical continuum extending across three or four centuries, in which different elements predominated at different times.

Nonetheless, the heart of the Greek legacy to the future and the way it operated in the long run are not hard to discern. The Greeks made greater advances in submitting nature and human experience to rational, conscious enquiry and control than was made anywhere else in antiquity. They were curious about the world and its inhabitants as no other peoples had ever been; their thinkers were disinclined to relax into indifference or submissive acceptance. In consequence, for all the deep irrationality and superstition which still pervaded their culture, they made a huge stride towards the control of human life by reason, even if we must never forget to qualify such statements. The gods were always in the background. *Nemesis* lay in wait for the man who got above himself and forgot he was only human, or who fancied that the favourable fortune he enjoyed was somehow the reflexion only of his own merits and skill; the sense that the gods had to be propitiated never left most Greeks, even if they were not all able to put it quite like that. St Luke's account of St Paul's encounter at Athens with a shrine to the 'Unknown god' expresses two enduring truths about the Greek mind, its curiosity and superstitious caution.[4] Even the élite among the Greek philosophers appear to have accepted limitations to scepticism which now seem surprising. Old orthodoxies received at least formal respect for most of the time, and sometimes more.[5] Nevertheless when all such relevant facts are duly weighed and placed in the balance, the Greeks presented an unprecedented challenge to mere authority in intellectual matters. After them, the enquiring mind could not, in spite of efforts which continued for the next 2,000 years and more, ever quite be put back in blinkers. The outcome was a great and beneficial myth, that there was no limit to what conscious thought might understand, as well as a technique of intellectual activity and an inspiration.

The beginnings of systematic enquiry

The beliefs that conscious investigation and argument were good and would lead to truth, were coupled by some Greeks with another assumption also of great importance to posterity. This was, that whatever its ultimate foundations and the mysterious forces embodied in them, the natural world and universe were for the most part logical and coherent in their working and could, therefore be investigated by human reason. This assumption lies at the heart of European science, whose story begins in Ionia. In the sixth century BC that part of the Greek world was producing men who speculated about the natural world and the way it worked. These were the true founders of modern science, although their names (or a few of them) are now unremembered except by specialists. All scientific work now done all round the globe, stems from a systemization and institutionalization which took place in early modern Europe, but that rested ultimately on a Greek heritage which had descended to it by both direct and indirect routes.

Why this happened is still obscure, but Ionian science signals a revolution in thought. It crosses a crucial boundary between myth and rationality. That boundary had been approached by earlier men; it can hardly be doubted (for instance) that the practice of architecture by the Egyptians and the knowledge they won empirically of engineering and manipulating materials must have revealed to them something of the mathematics of mensuration. Babylonian astronomers had made important observations in the service of religion, and carefully recorded them. Yet when we confront those Greeks in Asia Minor who first left evidence of their thinking about the natural world, they are already investigating it in a different, more detached way.

The most famous of those whom we now identify as the first Greek scientists, Thales and Anaximander, lived in sixth-century Miletus (a circumstance which may be significant; it was a rich city, and they seem to have been well-enough off to afford the time to think). Both probably owed many of their fundamental cosmological notions as well as much of their data to Babylonian sources; indeed, if science begins with observation, then it is in Babylon that its deepest traceable roots lie. The next stage, though, is the understanding and, therefore, interpretation of what is observed.

---

[4]   *Acts.* xvii.16–33. St Paul was engaged in his second missionary journey (for the first presentation of Christianity in Europe) which can be dated to AD 51–52. St Luke, who is generally and traditionally accepted to be the author of the *Acts of the Apostles*, accompanied St Paul on this journey and remarks of the Athenians that they 'spent their time in nothing else, but either to tell, or to hear some new thing'.

[5]   The philosopher Socrates urged that he owed obedience to the law he was charged with infringing and should not seek to escape its weight when it condemned him. His arguments are set out in the dialogue called *Crito*, of which a convenient translation is available in H. Tredennick, *Plato: the Last Days of Socrates* (Harmondsworth, 1954).

Later comes the manipulative ambition, with the acquisition of the experimental method and, by accretion, better technology. The Ionians soon went beyond whatever they took from Asia and their attempts to replace myth with impersonal explanation are more important and more striking than the specific answers they put forward, which in the end tended to be wrong. This was to be true of later Greek scientists, too. One of them advocated an atomic theory which was 2,000 years and more before its time, but the consensus of the Greek scientific culture settled in favour of a theory of matter which analyzed it into four 'elements' — air, earth, water and fire – mingled in different proportions in different substances. This theory which was to enjoy great success as the basis for western science for 2,000 years, did much to shape its boundaries and possibilities. But the validity of what the Ionians and their successors 'discovered' is less significant than the fundamental break they were making with the past. Their approach was gradually pushing the gods and demons out of the explanation of nature. This did not always meet with approval. Late fifth-century Athens condemned as blasphemous views far less daring than some of those of the Ionians (one of whom had said, strikingly and sceptically, that 'if the ox could paint a picture, his god would look like an ox')[6]. Classical Mediterranean civilization would later lose much of that boldness; not all of those who were to be most influential for the future liked to question accepted ideas.

One of the problems which always arises in examining other cultures is the avoidance of inappropriate terms. Greek categories of thought for example – the way, so to speak, in which they laid out the intellectual map before beginning to think about its individual components in detail – are not our own, though they settled some of them and are often deceptively like them. Some of those we use did not exist for the Greeks and they drew boundaries between fields of enquiry different from those which we take for granted. Often, this is obvious and presents no difficulties; Aristotle, for example, located the management of a household and its estate in a study he called 'politics', and we are not likely to be misled by this. Nonetheless, such classifications and allocations can be confusing in other matters. Yet many of the ways in which the Greeks organized their approach to the cosmos have remained vigorously alive and helpful: philosophers still speak of branches of their study as 'ethics', 'metaphysics', 'logic' — all of them in origin Greek terms and ideas.

Much of the content of Greek speculation was to have a very long life, too. One instance is associated above all with the most famous of all Greek philosophers, the Athenian Plato. An aristocrat, he had turned away from the world of affairs in which he had hoped to take part, disillusioned by the democratic politics of Athens (which, among other things, condemned his revered teacher, Socrates, to death for blasphemy). From Socrates he had derived an 'idealist' approach to ethical questions, and a technique of philosophical enquiry. The Good, he thought, was discoverable by argument and intuition: it was reality. It was the greatest of a series of 'ideas' — Truth, Beauty, Justice were others – which were not ideas in the sense that at any moment they necessarily had shape in anyone's mind (as one might say 'I have an idea about that'), but were real entities, enjoying a real existence in a world fixed and eternal, of which such ideas were the elements. This world of changeless reality, thought Plato, was hidden from us by the senses, which deceive and mislead; reality was immaterial. But it was accessible

---

[6] q. in E.R. Dodds, *The Greeks and the Irrational* (Berkeley and Los Angeles, 1959), p.181.

to the soul, which could understand it by the use of reason. This is the beginning of the long European philosophic tradition called Idealism.

In it and in the ideas of some other Greeks can be found traces of another familiar idea, that man is irreconcilably divided between the soul, of divine origin, and the body, its fleshly prison. Not reconciliation, but the victory of one or another, must be the outcome.[7] This dualism was long to appeal to moral puritans. It was to pass to a world religion, Christianity, with enormous effect long after fifth-century Athens was only a memory. Plato believed that knowledge of the Ideal world of universals and reality could help men to make better arrangements under which to live; conversely, he believed that some arrangements could hinder the acquisition of that knowledge. This way of thinking lay behind the dialogues between Socrates and people who came to argue with him, which Plato wrote down. They were the first textbooks of philosophical thinking. The one we call *The Republic* was the first book in which anyone had ever set out a scheme for a society directed and planned to achieve an ethical goal. It describes an authoritarian state (reminiscent of Sparta) in which marriages would be regulated to produce the best genetic results, families and private property would not exist, culture and the arts would be censored and education carefully supervised. The few who ruled this state would be those of sufficient intellectual and moral stature to fit them for the studies enabling them to realise the just society in practice by apprehending the Ideal world. Like Socrates, Plato held that wisdom was the understanding of reality and eschewing the temptations of appearance. He assumed that to see truth ought to make it impossible not to act in accordance with it. Unlike his teacher, though, he held that for most people education and laws should impose exactly that unexamined life which Socrates had thought not worth living.

Plato was much excited and attracted by mathematics. Some of the roots of his idealism lie here. The numbers which mathematicians thought about seemed to Plato to have something of the unchanging quality which the physical world so manifestly lacked; they possessed both the defined perfection and the abstraction of the Ideas which he believed embodied reality. To other Greek thinkers, too (the famous Pythagoras was one), mathematics had a quasi-mystical appeal, but this was not its only significance in the larger setting of Greek thought. Besides settling most of the arithmetic and geometry on which Europeans were to rely down to the seventeenth century AD (they would get their algebra elsewhere), mathematics profoundly affected the way Greeks interrogated nature. It encouraged the view that the universe was to be understood by mathematical and deductive techniques, rather than by observation and experiment (important though some Greeks thought these). It thus helped to fix astronomy on the wrong lines for a couple of thousand years by providing the basis of a vision of the universe as a system of concentric spheres on which moved sun, moon and planets in a fixed and circular pattern about the earth. Some noted that this did not seem to be the way in which the heavens actually *did* move; nonetheless – to summarize crudely – by introducing more and more refinements into the basic scheme its plausibility was kept going for centuries. (Some introduced in the second century AD by a famous Alexandrian, Ptolemy, were still providing guidance good enough to serve as the basis of oceanic navigation in the age of Colombus.)

---

[7]   See Dodds, p.139.

If the theory of the four elements and the development of astronomy reveal the deductive bias of Greek thought, Greek medicine made more use of empirical method (and Galen and Hippocrates were to live as authorities to future centuries). Yet observation and record, the basic techniques of an empirical approach to the world, in fact loomed much larger in the works of Plato's pupil Aristotle than in his master's, and for good and ill, later philosophical discussion was to be shaped by these two men more deeply than by any others. For all of his distaste for what he saw about him and the prejudice it awoke in him, Plato anticipated almost all the great questions of philosophy, whether they concerned morals, aesthetics, the basis of knowledge, or the nature of mathematics, and he set out his ideas in great works of literature, which were to be read with pleasure. Aristotle, a thinker more comprehensive and balanced, less sceptical of the possibilities of the actual, and less adventurous, never altogether rejected Plato's teaching. Nonetheless he was a great classifier and collector of data (with a special interest in biology). He did not reject sense experience as did Plato, and argued inductively from facts to general laws. His historical influence is as hard to delimit as that of his master's. Aristotle's writings set a framework for the discussion of biology, physics, mathematics, logic, literature and criticism, aesthetics, psychology, ethics and politics in Europe for 2,000 years. He founded a science of deductive logic which was not displaced until the end of the nineteenth century. The Aristotelian approach was elastic and capacious enough eventually to sit easily with both Christian philosophy and Islam. His is a vast achievement.

Aristotle and Plato both thought the city-state was the best conceivable social form, if it could be reformed and purified, but beyond this diverged. For Aristotle the *polis* was by nature and in principle admirable because it could give the beings who made it up the roles naturally appropriate to them; what was needed was reflexion on practical issues that, in most existing states, could lead to happiness. In formulating an answer, he made use of a Greek idea to which his teaching was to give long life, that of the Mean, the idea that excellence lay in a balance between extremes. The empirical facts seemed to confirm this and Aristotle assembled greater quantities of such evidence in a systematic form than any predecessor, it seems; but in stressing the importance of the facts of society and its institutions, he had been anticipated by another Greek invention, that of history.

Attention to the past was not in itself new. Many ancient societies had chronicles or annals purporting to record events. In Greece, though, this was not the route to history. Historical writing in Greek emerged from poetry and the recitation of oral tradition. Amazingly, it quickly reached the highest level in the work of its pioneers and founders, Herodotus and Thucydides. The word *historie* already existed; it meant enquiry. Herodotus gave it the added meaning of enquiry about events in past time, and in putting down the results of his enquiries wrote the first prose work of art to survive in a European language. For the first time, events and facts became the subject of more than a chronicle. Thucydides sought to be more rigorous in his approach to reports of fact and some have thought his intellectual achievement even greater than that of his predecessor, though its austerity throws into stronger relief the charm of Herodotus' work. Thucydides' choice of subject was even more contemporary, and reflected deep personal involvement. He was a member of a leading Athenian family who served as a general in the Peloponnesian War until disgraced for an alleged failure in command. He wanted to discover the causes which had brought his city and Greece into their dreadful plight. He shared with Herodotus a practical motive, thinking (as most later Greek historians were to do) that what he found out would have practical value. The result is one of the most striking pieces of historical analysis ever written, and a model of disinterested judgement. The book takes the story only to 411 BC but is decisive on the central issue: 'the growth of the power of Athens and the alarm which this inspired in Sparta made war inevitable'.[8]

History is thus present at the heart of the literature created by the Greeks at an early stage. That literature is the first complete one in any language. The Jewish Old Testament is almost as comprehensive, but it contains neither drama nor critical history, let alone the lighter *genres*. As for influence, Greek literature was to share with the Christian Bible a primacy in shaping the whole of subsequent western writing. It defined both the major literary forms and the first critical canons by which to judge them.

From the start literature meant more to the Greeks than enjoyment. Poets were seen by the Greeks as teachers, their work suffused with mystical overtones, inspiration, even if there were many styles of poetry. The story begins with Homer, a poet so unchallengaeably central to Greek culture that he was usually referred to simply and anonymously as *the* poet (though some scholars have taken the view that the work attributed to him was written by more than one man, and there is general agreement that it incorporates traditional bardic material). Two great epics bear his name. The *Illiad* narrates an episode in the legendary siege of Troy by the Achaeans. The *Odyssey* tells the story of the wanderings, adventures and heroic deeds of an Achaean captain as he slowly makes his way home after the city had fallen. These great poems came to be regarded by the Greeks as virtually religious texts, providing information about deities, legendary history and historical characters. They provided the Greeks with models of behaviour to be followed or shunned and these were set not only by humans but by divinities. Greek gods and goddesses often behaved in very human ways, for all their great power, and showed very human emotion. They constituted a uniquely humanized pantheon, unlike those of other civilizations.

There is still argument about who Homer was and when 'his' books were first written down. They were copied more frequently than any other Greek literary text and in the form in which they reach us it seems likely that they took shape in Ionia slightly before 700 BC. By the sixth century they had achieved their authoritative standing, and were the staple of Greek education. They were to prove not only the primary documents of Greek self-consciousness, but the foundations of the classical culture which was to shape Europe. Together with the Bible they are the ultimate source of western literature.

Homer supremely illustrates the link Greeks felt existed between literature, religious belief and moral teaching. This underlies the public role of literary art: the greatest Greek poetry passed slowly into the collective and civic area, into, eventually, the public festivals which were to be vehicles of the greatest specimens of Greek literary art, the tragedies. Bard to rhapsodist and rhapsodist to actor is the sequence through which the European theatre came to birth. Everywhere, drama's origins lie in religion and those of the Greek drama are to be found in the ritual of worship, in the dithyramb, the choral song recited at the festivals of Dionysus, together with dance and mime. In 535 BC, we are told, this was the subject of a crucial innovation, when a poet named Thes-

---

[8]   Thucydides, *History of the Peloponnesian War*, trans. R. Crawley (London, Everyman edn., 1945), p.12.

pis added to it an individual actor whose speech was some kind of antiphone to the chorus. Further innovation and more actors followed and within a hundred years we have reached the fifth century and the full, mature theatre of Aeschylus, Sophocles and Euripides, the great age of Greek drama. Of their work thirty-three plays survive. Yet more than 300 different tragedies were performed in the fifth century. In this drama the religious emphasis is still there, not only in the words, but in the occasions at which they would have been performed. There was a firm didactic impulse. More was required of a Greek audience than passive awe or thoughtless abandon. Conscious reflexion was expected.

The great tragedies were sometimes performed in trilogies at civic festivals (one complete trilogy has come down to us) and the audience was already familiar with the stories (often mythological) which they embodied. Yet most Hellenes can never have seen a play by (say) Aeschylus and perhaps only few Athenians did; certainly there would have been far fewer of either than, say, the number of modern Britons who have seen Shakespeare on the stage, let alone television. Nonetheless, those who were not too busy on their farms, or too far away, provided large audiences; the size of theatres indicates that in Athens, for example, it would have been physically possible for more than 10,000 spectators to witness a performance.

Like philosophy (whose audience was, of course, much smaller) drama could be a provocative educational experience. In no other ancient society was the moral and social content of the world scrutinized and reflected upon in the theatre as in Greece. What actors presented there was a revealing emphasis in familiar rites, a new selection from familiar tales, even if some plays went beyond this and, at favourable moments, satirized social pieties. It was not a naturalistic theatre. It displayed the operation of the laws of a heroic, traditional world and their agonizing impact on individuals caught in their working, or in the divergence of divine and human intentions. The plot was familiar, and at is heart lay a recognition of the weight of inexorable law and *nemesis*. Perhaps, in the last resort, this bears testimony to the irrational rather than the rational side of the Greek mind.

The scope of the Athenian theatre broadened as the fifth century went on. Euripides questioned conventional assumptions. Attic comedy developed as a form in its own right, and found in Aristophanes the first great manipulator of men and events for others' amusement. His often political, almost always highly topical, and frequently scurrilous material is among the most striking evidence we possess of the tolerance and freedom of Athenian society. A 100 years later, we have almost reached the modern world in a fashion for plays about the intrigues of slaves and troubled love-affairs. It has not the impact of Sophocles, but it can still amuse and remains a near-miracle, for nothing like it had been there 200 years before.

The rapid growth and elaboration of Greek literature after the age of epic poetry is further evidence of the innate vigour of Greek culture. At the end of the classical age literature still had a growing audience, for Greek was to become both *lingua franca* and an official language over all the Near East and much of the Mediterranean. It was still to throw up masterpieces though it was not to reach again the heights of Athenian tragedy. In the visual arts, too, above all in monumental architecture and the sculpted nude, Greece again set standards for the future. From originally Asian borrowings a wholly original architecture was evolved, the classical style whose elements are still consciously evoked even by the austerities of twentieth-century builders. Within a few hundred years it spread over much of the world from Sicily as far as to India; in this art, too, the Greeks were cultural exporters.

The quantities of high-quality stone to be found in Greece were a help. Its durability is attested by the magnificence of the relics we look at today. Yet there is an illusion in this. The purity and austerity with which fifth-century Athens speaks to us in the Parthenon conceals the way the Greeks would have seen it. The garish statues of gods and goddesses, the paint and ochre and the clutter of monuments, shrines and *stelae* that must have encumbered the Acropolis and obscured the simplicity of its temples have disappeared. A hint of them may be obtainable from the jumble of untidy little shrines cluttered by traders, booths, and the rubbish of superstition on the path up to the Temple of Apollo at Delphi. Misleadingly or not, though, the erosion of time has allowed an astonishing beauty to emerge from the Greek ruins. The interplay of our judgement of the object with standards of judgement which derive ultimately from the object itself is here impossible to allow for. It remains simply true that to have originated an art that has spoken so deeply and powerfully to men's minds across such ages is itself not easily interpreted except as evidence of unsurpassed artistic genius and immense skill in giving it expression.

For the sculptors, the local availability of good stone was an inestimable advantage. The important original influence of oriental, often Egyptian, models once absorbed, Greek sculpture evolved towards greater naturalism. Its supreme subject was the human form, no longer portrayed as a memorial or cult object, but for its own sake. Though, when we visit the museums, we cannot always be sure of the appearance of the finished statues the Greeks saw (these figures were often gilded, painted or decorated with ivory and precious stones), they show a clear evolution. We begin with statues of gods and of young men and women whose identity is usually unknown, simply and symmetrically presented in poses not too far removed from those of Egypt. In the classical figures of the fifth century, naturalism begins to tell in an uneven distribution of weight and the abandonment of the simple frontal stance. Then comes the mature, human style of the fourth century in which the body – and for the first time the female nude – is treated with a new, idealized, naturalism.

An attempt to summarize

Great cultures are more than museums. They cannot be reduced to catalogues. For all its reservation to a minority at its peaks, the achievement and importance of Greece comprehended all sides of life; the politics of the city-state, a tragedy of Sophocles and a statue by Phidias are all organic to it. Intuitively, later ages grasped this, happily ignorant of the vigour with which later historians and scholars would analyse and discriminate between periods and places. But if that intuition was factually questionable, it was fruitful. In the end what Greece was to be thought to be was as important to the world as what she actually was. The Greek experience was to be represented and reconsidered and, in different ways, reborn and re-used, for more than 2,000 years. Even its errors could be creative. All Europe drew interest on the capital Greece laid down, and through Europe the rest of the world has traded on the same account. Once away from the great original determinants of physical geography, climate and resources, the Greek heritage was the first and most fundamental agency which would shape the culture of a new sort of civilization.

Yet it remains too rich and varied to generalize about. What can be seen is that if civilization is advance towards the control of mentality and environment by reason, and the provision of standards we can later recognize as positive contributions to the future, then the Greeks did more for future civilization than any of their predecessors. As part and parcel of one of the great intuitions of all time, that a coherent and logical explanation of things could be found, that the world did not ultimately rest upon the meaningless and arbitrary fiat of gods or demons, they invented philosophical enquiry. Though most Greeks may not have known that and continued to live in a world permeated with irrationality and superstition, this was a revolutionary and beneficial fact. It looked forward to the possibility of societies where such attitudes might be generalized. The Greek challenge to the weight of irrationality tempered its force as it had never been tempered before even if that was not always obvious. For all the subsequent exaggeration and myth-making about it, the liberating effect of this emphasis was to be felt again and again for thousands of years.

CHAPTER THREE The making of the Roman world

Etruscan origins

One of the earliest Italian sites of iron-using peoples was found not far from modern Bologna, at a place called Villanova. Similar cultures have subsequently been named Villanovan by archaeologists and by the eighth century BC similar sites were clearly well-established across central Italy. Some 'Villanovans' were already trading with the Phoenicians and the Greek colonies of the south. Among them were some later to share a more familiar name: Etruscans. Much obscurity still surrounds them. Archaeology tells us more about their culture than about their history or chronology. Different scholars have argued that distinctive Etruscan civilization came into existence at different times, from the tenth to the seventh century BC. They have not even been able to agree about where the Etruscans' ancestors came from, though clearly they were not the first Italians. Whenever and wherever from they came to Italy, they joined there a confusion of peoples, descendants of aboriginal natives and second-millenium Indo-European invaders among them.

In about 1000 BC Villanovans were vigorously exploiting the iron deposits of Elba, off the coast of Tuscany and the area now called Etruria. The iron weapons they provided appear to have made possible an Etruscan hegemony. At its greatest extent this may have covered the whole central peninsula, from the valley of the Po down to Campania. Its organization remains obscure, but Etruria was probably a loose league of cities governed by kings. The Etruscans were literate, using an alphabet derived from Greek which may have been acquired from the cities of *Magna Graecia* (though their writing is not fully understood), and they were relatively rich.

In the sixth century BC the Etruscans had an important bridgehead on the south bank of the river Tiber, in one of a number of the small communities of the Latins, another people long-settled in the Campania. This was to become Rome. It was a focus of important land and water routes, high enough up the Tiber for it to be bridged, but not so high that it could not be reached by sea-going vessels. Through Rome something of the Etruscan legacy was to survive and flow into (and eventually be lost in) the European tradition. Through her Etruscan past Rome also had her first access to the Greek civilization with which she was for centuries to live in contact both by land and sea. Fertilization by Greek influence was perhaps the most important inheritance, but Rome also carried forward many Etruscan institutions. One was the way she organized her people in 'centuries' for military purposes; more superficial but striking instances were her gladiatorial games, civic triumphs and reading of auguries – a consultation of the entrails of sacrifices in order to discern the shape of the future.

Near the end of the sixth century Rome broke away from Etruscan dominion during a revolt of the Latin cities against their masters. Until then, the city had been ruled by Etruscan kings of the house of Tarquinius, the last of whom, tradition later said, was expelled in 509 BC. Whatever the exact date, this was probably about the time at which Etruscan power, over-strained by struggle with the western Greeks, was successfully challenged by other Latin peoples, who thereafter went their own ways. Though the expulsion of the kings was obviously a crucial moment, later Romans liked to look back further still, claiming their city was founded by one Romulus in 753 BC. We need not take this seriously, but the legend of the foster-mother wolf which suckled both Romulus and his twin, Remus, says something more about early Rome's debt to the Etruscans, among whose cults has been traced a special reverence for the wolf.

Macedon and the Hellenistic age

The fifth century BC, the first of the new Roman republic, was also the greatest age of Greece. The Greek world of the western Mediterranean, the world from which the Romans first learnt what civilization was and of which they formed a part, was, for all the splendour of some of its cities or the vigour of Phoenician commerce, nonetheless somewhat marginal to the central sphere of Greek culture, the Aegean and Asia Minor. So it was to remain for another couple of centuries. Though Roman territorial and political expansion began at an early date, it only began to change world history when Rome entered that eastern sphere. Paradoxically, a new and enlarged Hellas had emerged there in the fourth century BC from the decay of the Greek city-states.

Towards the end of the Peloponnesian war a new force had been beginning to make itself felt on the northern edge of the Greek world, the kingdom of Macedon. Its inhabitants spoke Greek and their representatives attended the pan-Hellenistic festivals. Macedon's kings said they were descended from Achilles, the great Achaean hero of the

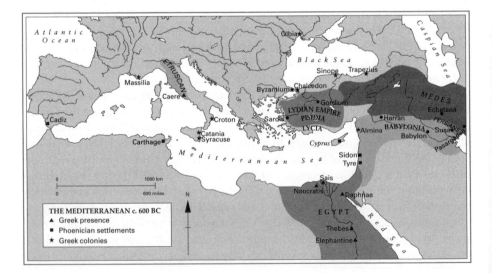

THE MEDITERRANEAN c. 600 BC
▲ Greek presence
■ Phoenician settlements
★ Greek colonies

Illiad and claimed, simply and explicitly, to govern a Greek state and be part of Hellas. But many Greeks disagreed, thinking the Macedonians a barbarous lot, barely civilized, and by no means on a par with the cultivated city-dwellers of the Aegean, Ionia and *Magna Graecia*. Undoubtedly Macedon was a rougher, tougher place than, say, Athens or Corinth; its kings had to manage an aristocracy of mountain chiefs who would prob-ably not have been much impressed by Athenian sophistication. Yet Macedon changed the course of history by giving Greek civilization a huge new extension.

In 359 BC there came to power there an able and ambitious prince - ambitious, among other things, that Macedon should be recognized as Greek. Philip II was at first regent for an infant prince, and then king (after deposing his ward and rightful ruler). Circumstances were in his favour; the Greek states were worn out by their long strug-gles and Persia was troubled by a series of revolts. Macedon was rich in gold; Philip could pay for a strong army, whose later effectiveness owed much to his personal efforts. Pondering Greek military methods while at Thebes in his youth he had decided that the answer to them lay in a new formation, the phalanx of ten ranks of infantry armed with pikes twice as long as ordinary spears. Those who carried them stood slightly apart so that the pikes of men in the rear stuck forward between those in the front ranks. The result was a hedgehog-like array of points, a formidable weapon. To back it up, the Macedonians had armoured cavalry and a siege-train of heavy weapons such as cata-pults. With this army Philip and his son ended the independence of the mainland Greek cities and an era of human history, the age of the *polis*. 335 BC, when Thebes was razed to the ground and its inhabitants enslaved as a penalty for rebellion, will do as a marker both for that and for the opening of an era of rapid and spectacular change.

Alexander the Great

Among Philip's decisions had been to lead the Greeks in a new struggle with Persia, but before he could do this he was assassinated, in 336 BC. Alexander, his son, is one of those historical figures traditionally called 'Great'. The legends which sur-rounded his name led to him being idolized for thousands of years. Though above all a soldier and conqueror, he was also much more. Nonetheless, many of the facts of his life and personality remain obscure. He was a passionate Hellene, who believed Achilles was his ancestor and carried with him on his campaigns a treasured copy of Homer. He had been tutored by Aristotle. He was a brave though sometimes reckless soldier, a shrewd general and a great leader of men. He could behave with sympathy to peoples whose rulers he overthrew. He could also be irascible and violent; it seems he once while drunk killed a friend in a brawl. He may have agreed to his father's murder. What is clear is his decisive impact on world history, from 334 BC, when he crossed Asia to attack the Persians at the head of an army drawn from many Greek states, to die in Babylon (perhaps of typhoid) only thirty-three years old.

Alexander had a staggering record of success. After defeating the Persians in Asia Minor at the battle of Issus in 333 BC (the Greeks sent him their congratulations), he marched through the length of the Persian empire, first southwards through Syria to Egypt, then back north and east to Mesopotamia, pursuing the Persian king Darius III, who was murdered while still on the run. This was the end of the Achaemenid empire, long the great power of the Near East. On went Alexander across Iran and Afghanistan, over the Oxus to Samarkand. He founded a city on the Jaxartes before coming south again, to invade India. 200 kilometres or so beyond the Indus, well into the Punjab, his weary generals made him turn back. A terrible march followed back down the Indus and along the northern coast of the Persian Gulf to Babylon, where he died in 323 BC.

This short life had a significance going far beyond simple conquest. Alexander's 'empire' spread Greek influence where it had never been felt before. He had founded cities (many named after him: there are still several Alexandrias as well as other places whose names disguise his own somewhat more) and he had mixed Greeks and Asians in his army so that it became a more cosmopolitan force. He enlisted young Persian nobles in it and once presided at a mass wedding of 9,000 of his soldiers to eastern women. He himself married Darius' daughter as his second wife (his first was a Bactrian princess). The former officials of the Persian king were kept in post to administer his conquered lands. Alexander even adopted Persian dress (though this did not go down well with his Greek companions; nor did they like it when he made visitors to his court kowtow to him as Persian kings had done).

To overthrow the mightiest empire of the day and end the age of the independent Greek cities were world-shaping deeds, though their full impact was not at once obvious. Many of the most positive results were only to appear after his death, when, in Greek and non-Greek lands alike, the effects would be felt of the Greek ideas and standards he spread far and wide – though not to the western Mediterranean. This is why the words 'Hellenism' and 'Hellenistic' have been coined and applied both to the age which followed his death and to much of the area formerly covered by his empire (roughly speaking, from the Adriatic and Egypt in the west to the mountains of Afghanistan in the east). It did not hold together for long; Alexander left no heir who could take over from him and his generals soon began fighting over the spoils.

The Hellenistic world

It took forty years or so of fighting before the lands of the former empire settled down into a number of kingdoms, each ruled by one of Alexander's generals, or a descendant of one. These men are sometimes referred to as the 'Successors' or *Diadochi*. The richest of their kingdoms was Egypt, where a Macedonian named Ptolemy seized control. After getting hold of Alexander's body he had it buried in a splendid tomb at Alexandria in Egypt; this gave him a special prestige and pre-eminence as its guardian. Ptolemy founded the last Egyptian dynasty of antiquity, which was to rule Egypt until 30 BC (when the last of the Ptolemies, the legendary Cleopatra, died) as well as Palestine, Cyprus and much of Libya.

Yet Egypt was not the biggest of the successor states. Although Alexander's Indian conquests had passed to an Indian king, the descendants of another of his generals, Seleucus, for a time ruled an area running from Afghanistan to the Mediterranean. The Seleucid kingdom was not to remain as big as this. Early in the third century BC a new Hellenistic kingdom of Pergamon appeared in Asia Minor, and in Bactria yet another was founded by Greek soldiers. Macedon itself passed to a new dynasty after invasion by barbarians. Meanwhile the old Greek states, loosely organized from time to time in leagues, continued to moulder away (though some of them had hoped to recover independence at Alexander's death). The difference made to history by these ups and downs and political reorganizations was that from them emerged what Alexander's conquests

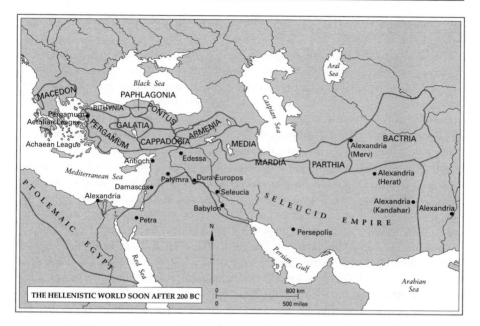

THE HELLENISTIC WORLD SOON AFTER 200 BC

had made possible – a framework within which Greek civilization took root as never before. Greek became the official language of the whole Near East and was widely used as an everyday language, too, in the cities.

There were many new cities, especially in the Seleucid lands. Greek immigrants were encouraged to settle in them. But they were unlike the old city-states of the Aegean. For one thing, they were much bigger. Alexandria in Egypt, Antioch in Syria, and the new capital, Seleucia, near Babylon each grew to nearly 200,000 inhabitants. Nor were they in any sense autonomous. The Seleucids governed through provincial rulers and machinery taken over from the old Persian empire – which fifth-century Greeks had thought a barbarian despotism. The bureaucracies of the successor states drew on ancient traditions of Egypt and Mesopotamia, not those of the *polis*. The *Diadochi* and their successors were given semi-divine honours, like the old Persian kings. In Egypt the Ptolemies revived the old cult of the pharaohs, and the first of them took the title of *Soter*, that is, 'Saviour'.

Still, the cities usually looked Greek. Their buildings were in the Greek tradition, and they had theatres, gymnasia, centres for games and festivals which were much like those of the past. Greek tradition showed in artistic style, too. Perhaps the best known of all Greek statues is that of Aphrodite found on the island of Melos and now in the Louvre at Paris (the '*Vénus de Milo*'), and it is a Hellenistic work. As Greek style and fashion spread, so did Greek culture, though the countryside remained almost untouched by it (Greek was the native tongue of only a minority in any of the successor states, though many city-dwellers came to speak versions of it). Soon Greek literature was being added to by new writers, who found audiences and patrons in an environment which was for a long time one of growing prosperity. Alexander's wars had released an enormous booty in bullion and precious objects which stimulated economic development and made it possible to pay for art, as well as for standing armies and bureaucracies. The Hellenistic world was bigger than the old Greek world, and a broader stage for Greek culture.

At Alexandria in Egypt, and Pergamon in Asia Minor were the two greatest libraries of the ancient world; in Athens the Academy went on. Hellenistic science was another sign of continuity with what had gone before. Alexandria in Egypt was especially pre-eminent in it. Euclid, the man who systematized geometry and gave it a shape which lasted until the nineteenth century, lived there. Archimedes, who invented the windlass and became famous for his untimely death in Sicily, where he was constructing war-machines, as well as for his theoretical discoveries in physics and the legend of the bath which prompted one of them, was probably Euclid's pupil. Among other Alexandrians were the first man to measure the size of the earth and the first to use steam to transmit energy. Aristarchus, from Samos, arrived at the view that the earth moved round the sun, and not vice versa; his idea was rejected by his contemporaries because it did not square with Aristotelian physics, but it was a remarkable achievement. Hellenistic science made notable additions to the human toolkit even if it was held back because there was neither the inclination nor the apparatus to test some theories experimentally and because of the Greek bias towards the mathematical rather than the practical sciences. The existing state of technology may also have made it difficult to make practical use of some ideas (though this view has been contested: some think that the Hellenistic scientists had the means to build a steam-engine had they only conceived it, and Archimedes was a considerable engineer), but the triumphs of Hellenistic science may nonetheless be thought somewhat to offset the loss of a tradition of self-government in politics and of rigorous questioning about the aims of life and the way men should behave. Yet the Hellenistic world produced one important new ethical philosophy, Stoicism. It taught, roughly, that it was men's duty to be virtuous whatever the consequences for themselves. To be virtuous, said the Stoics, consisted above all in obeying the natural laws which ruled the universe and all men, not just Greeks. It was the first attempt to provide a moral philosophy for all humanity. It also produced the first condemnation of slavery, an extraordinary mental leap never achieved by the philosophers of classical Greece. Stoicism was to be influential for centuries among the élite of Rome.

The rise of Roman power

What was later called Hellenistic civilization was a particular selection of the Greek achievement. That was also to be true of the civilization of Rome. She, too, in the end became a Hellenistic successor state. Before this, though, she already had a long history. Her citizens were for centuries to insist on their old republican traditions even when they came to live under what looked much more like a monarchy. This was not without its importance to the later Europe: agreement about civic principles and a certain mythology of republicanism were to be nurtured in the future by what later Europeans thought had gone on in the Roman republic.

In practice, the Roman republic lasted as a reality for more than 450 years and even after that its institutions survived in name. Romans always liked to harp on continuity and their loyal adherence (or others' reprehensible non-adherence) to its good old ways. There was some reality in such claims, much as there is, for example, in those made for the continuity of parliamentary government in Great Britain or for the wisdom of the founding fathers of the United States in agreeing a constitution which still operates successfully. Yet with time came changes. They eroded the institutional and ideological continuities and historians still argue about how to interpret them. For all these changes (or perhaps because of them), though, this did not hinder the making of a Roman Mediterranean and a Roman empire stretching beyond it. Had it done so, the history of the Roman republic might not now matter more to us than the history of Corinth or Thebes.

The physical ruins of Roman empire still provide the most visible signs of what Europe owes to it; literally and figuratively, future Europeans were to live in their shadows. Not only all round the Mediterranean's non-European and European shores, but across the wide tracts of western Europe, the Balkans and Asia Minor, such relics can still be seen. In some places – above all Rome itself – they are very plentiful. It took nearly a 1,000 years of history to put them there, and men goggled and wondered at them for another 1,000 after that. If we no longer look back on the Roman achievement as our ancestors often did, feeling dwarfed by it, we can still be puzzled and even amazed that men could do so much.

Of course, the closer the scrutiny historians give to those mighty remains and the more scrupulous their sifting of the evidence which illuminates Roman ideals and Roman practice, the more we realize that Romans were not, after all, superhuman. The grandeur that was Rome sometimes looks more like tinsel and the virtues its orators proclaimed sound as much like cant as do many political speeches of today. Yet when all is said and done, there remains an astonishing and solid core of creativity. In the end, Rome remade the setting of Greek civilization, and did so in a spirit of self-conscious achievement. Romans who looked back on it when it was later crumbling about them still felt themselves to be Romans like those who had built it up: they were, it is true, though by then in little except the sense that they believed it. Yet that was the most important sense. For all its material impressiveness and occasional grossness, the core of the explanation of the Roman achievement was an idea, the idea of Rome itself, the values it embodied and imposed, the notion of what was one day to be called *romanitas*.

The spread of Roman power already in republican times came to encompass the whole Mediterranean world in a system of domination, a Roman empire which provided a framework and cradle for much still shaping our lives today. The early republic, nonetheless, was preoccupied in the first place with the politics of a city, and then with its relations with its neighbours. The history of its first two centuries or so was studded by violent internal struggles, sometimes arising from the demands of the poorer citizens for a share in the power of the better-off families, the 'patricians'. With time, wealth came to matter more. Patrician status declined, though members of a noble family with two ancestors who had been consuls continued to be eligible for those and other high offices. Patrician families long dominated the Senate, which was the main governmental body, as the inscription carried on many monuments and on the standards of the army indicated: SPQR, the initials of the Latin words for 'the Roman Senate and People'.

Somehow the republic's civic struggles were endured for a long time without mortal damage being caused to it, though its institutions slowly changed as concessions were made to popular forces. Yet, though the poorer citizens won many victories and a bigger share of the spoils of power, Rome never became a democracy in the sense that they ever

SABINI

Tiber

Rome
SAMNIUM
LATIUM

Adriatic Sea

Capua
Neapoli
CAMPANIA
APULIA

LUCANIA
Heraclae
Tarentum

Tyrrhenian Sea

SICILIA
Messina
Catania

Syracuse

Mediterranean Sea

N

0   160 km
0   100 miles

SOUTHERN ITALY 509–272 BC

Land over 1000 m

controlled the government for long. For a long time the typical Roman citizen was a peasant farmer, benefiting from the climate and fertility which have always made Italy a rich country when well-governed, and sometimes when not, and showing the industry and skill often demonstrated by later Italians in exploiting these advantages. On his work rested the early republic; we must not think of the huge metropolis of later centuries, living on imported corn and swollen by huge numbers of immigrants, as typical of Rome's early centuries. For a long time the typical Roman was an independent smallholder. Only with the second century BC did big estates owned by townsmen and relying on slave labour to grow cash crops of grain or olives (for oil) become at all common. To the very end of the story, Romans were to look back sentimentally to the simple days when the republic and Roman virtues were upheld by the free smallholding citizens.

This narrow agricultural base makes it hard to explain the first stage of Roman expansion. It would not be fair to say that Romans were always aggressive and anxious to make conquests. Roman rule (like that of later empires) often spread because of fear rather than greed. Expansion was slow, moreover. Though Rome's territory doubled at the expense of her neighbours in the fifth century, and Roman supremacy then replaced Etruscan in central Italy, this was not the beginning of an uninterrupted story of successful expansion. In 390 BC barbarians from the north called Gauls sacked the city (according to legend, the Capitol to which the Romans had withdrawn was only saved from a surprise attack by the honking of the geese who noticed what was going on). Yet a 150 years later the Romans dominated Italy south of the Arno; all of it by then was ruled either by the republic or by its allies, who were allowed to run their own internal affairs in return for supplying recruits to the Roman army. Their citizens enjoyed the rights of Roman citizens when they came to Rome.

Early Rome had a number of strategic advantages. The city's position was one. Another was the distraction of the Etruscans in struggles with the Greeks and other Latin cities, while Celtic tribes pressed on them from the north. The Romans also had a military system which made the best of their manpower: every male citizen who owned property had to serve in the army if needed. An infantryman had to serve sixteen years under the early republic (though service was not for the whole year, since campaigns started in spring and finished during the autumn). This provided a military machine which became in the next few centuries the finest the world had yet seen, organized in legions of 5,000 and operating, at first, in solid phalanxes with long, pike-like spears. The pool of recruits on which the army drew steadily increased with the obligations of Rome's allies to send contingents to it.

The Roman abolition of Italy was still incomplete, when the republic became involved with powers farther afield. Some of the cities of *Magna Graecia* had called in Pyrrhus, king of Epirus, to help them against the Romans in the early third century BC. He campaigned in the south and Sicily, thinking perhaps of building himself an empire in the west like Alexander's. He won battles, but at such a cost that we still talk of successes which cost more than they are worth as 'Pyrrhic victories'.

The Punic Wars

At one time it looked as if the Ptolemies might want Rome's alliance, but though the first great preoccupations of the Republic outside Italy were to be in Africa, they lay farther west than Egypt. Carthage, on what is now the Tunisian coast, was in origin Phoenician, but became richer than Tyre and Sidon had ever been. It was a great naval power, with outposts in Sicily and Sardinia. At times allied to and at times at war with the Greeks of Sicily, Carthage was a standing menace to western Italy and the trade of its ports. Three 'Punic' (the name comes from the Latin word for Phoenician) wars were fought over a long period by Rome and Carthage. The first made Rome a naval power and ended in 241 BC with the Carthaginians having to give up Sicily after more than twenty years of intermittent fighting, and the appearance of the first Roman 'province' in the west of the island. Mainland Italy was by then all either governed directly as part of the Republic or was formally allied to it. In addition, Rome took control of Corsica and Sardinia. These were the first overseas conquests of the Republic.

Wars are by no means always the most important elements in historic narrative but in this instance it is worthwhile to stick to them as chronological pegs for a little longer. Before the second Punic war (which began in 218 BC) the Carthaginians had established themselves in Spain, settling at 'New Carthage' (the modern Cartagena). The Romans began to be alarmed when Carthaginian power reached the Ebro. An attack on one of the few remaining independent cities on the Spanish coast was followed by the march of a Carthaginian army – complete with elephants – to Italy under Hannibal, the greatest Carthaginian general. Defeat and hard times followed for the Romans. Many of their allies deserted them. But they hung on and in the end recovered their grip. After twelve years in Italy the Carthaginians were starved and driven out. The Roman Senate gave their successful general, Scipio, permission to cross to Africa, and at Zama in 202 BC he defeated Hannibal and broke the back of Rome's only serious rival in the west. This settled the fate of the western Mediterranean. The Carthaginians had to make a crippling peace. But many Romans still feared them mightily. A third Punic war did not break out for a long time – until 149 BC – but it then ended with so complete a defeat for the Carthaginians that their city was destroyed and legend says that ploughs were run over the site where it had stood and salt was sown in its fields. The details seem improbable, but it was the end of Phoenician power in the west.

Empire

By then a Roman empire was in being in fact if not in name. The Po valley had been taken over early in the second century BC and Italy can thereafter be regarded as Roman. The overthrow of Carthage had also meant the end of Syracuse, the last independent Greek state in Sicily, because she had once more allied with the Carthaginians; all Sicily was now Roman. Southern Spain, too, was conquered. Soon slaves and gold from Sicily, Sardinia and Spain were awaking some Romans to the idea that conquest might be profitable. Further east Rome had already begun to dabble in Greek politics, because Macedon had at one time been allied with Carthage. In 200 BC a direct appeal for help against Macedon and the Seleucids was made by Athens and the kingdom of Pergamon. The Romans were by then psychologically ready to become involved in further adventures in the east and they responded.

The second century BC was crucial there. Macedon was overthrown, the Greek cities were reduced to vassalage, and the last king of Pergamon bequeathed his land to Rome in 133 BC. A new Roman province, called Asia and consisting of the western end of Anatolia was set up in the same year. By then northern Spain had been conquered and, southern France (Gallia or Gaul) was soon taken; in the next century northern France followed and then further conquests in the east. The Republic had made the empire.

The impact of this astonishing success story went beyond changes in the map. One effect difficult to assess but very important was the further Hellenization of Roman culture and the spread of Hellenistic civilization to the west. Of course, Rome had owed much to Greece from the earliest times, and even through her Etruscan heritage. With empire and direct involvement in the government and politics of the east, Hellenistic influence became manifold and more suasive. The Romans, like other savage conquerors (Macedonians) whom the Greeks had culturally taken captive, had looked to Greeks like another set of barbarians: it was symbolic that Archimedes had been struck down by a Roman soldier who did not know who he was as he was pondering geometrical problems in the sands. The Romans now took to Hellenistic ways with enthusiasm, though. The luxury of the baths which were to become so exemplary of Roman civilization, came from the east. The first Roman literature was translated Greek drama: the first comedies in Latin imitated Greek models. Hellenistic artwork flowed westward to Roman collections and found imitators there. The education of the upper-class Roman boys from this time customarily incorporated the study of the Greek classics, the literary expression of a culture they were now taught to respect as the roots of their own. People, too, began to move more: in this new and Roman Hellenistic age they could travel from end to end of the Mediterranean more easily.

Some did not travel willingly: in the middle of the second century BC a 1,000 hostages were sent to Rome by Greek cities. Among them was one, Polybius, who wrote a history of Rome in the years 220–146 BC in the tradition of Thucydides. His theme was Rome's success in overthrowing Carthage and conquering the Hellenistic world; he saw in it a complement to Alexander's work in bringing unity to a huge area and recognized that Roman government offered advantages to its subjects. Power brought peace (the *pax romana*) for longer periods to larger areas of the Mediterranean and Near East than ever before. In spite of growing corruption and violence in politics at home, and bad though some Roman provincial governors may have been, Republican administration imposed order over many peoples. It provided a common law. Many non-Romans benefited and, like Polybius, admired at least some of those who ran the system for their sense of justice, disinterestedness and the civilizing work they did. Romans came to feel proud of this achievement, too; it was part of a self-definition which was forced on them by their confrontation with the full weight of Hellenistic civilization. The practical outcome was decisive for the history of the world. The republic created a political and military framework on a scale which could not be found anywhere west of China, if, indeed, there. Many different cultures could live side by side within it, making their own contributions to the cosmopolitan whole, and all themselves in varying degrees moulded by it.

Celtic Europe

For a long time, Rome's reach did not extend outside the Mediterranean lands and even in Italy only up to the valley of the Po. In that region they encountered 'Gauls' whose forebears had sacked Rome at the beginning of the fourth century. These barbarians were part of a family of peoples spread across northern and western Europe and the higher reaches of the Danube. Their history requires notice, for they reached the highest levels of culture attained by any Europeans outside the Mediterranean world before being conquered by the Romans. These were the Celts, some of whose languages survive on the fringes of western Europe and fragmentarily in other languages.

Skilled iron-workers, the Celts attained levels of technical sophistication and artistic achievement which have left a spectacular legacy in artifacts. The archaeological record shows two early concentrations of settlement, established between the seventh and fifth centuries BC, one in the western Alps and the other a little south of the upper Danube. From a central heartland running northward from these areas to the mouths of the Rhine and Weser, Celtic peoples seem to have spread to the east as well as south and west, without eliminating, though certainly subjugating, those already there. Between 600 and 400 BC they settled in Spain, the British isles and over virtually the whole of what is now France (which became for the Romans '*Gallia*', Gaul, the land of the *Gallii*), and then in the Po valley and Liguria. To the east, they made their way down the Danube. The Greeks called them *Keltoi* and soon after 300 BC Macedonia was suffering from their depredations. Delphi was raided by them. Some of them in the third century went so far as to cross (at the invitation of a local king) to Asia Minor where they settled in what was later known because of them as Galatia.

Though they fought amongst themselves from time to time (and everyone agrees that the Celts were formidable and enthusiastic warriors), and are often distinguishable by tribal names in the Roman accounts (Belgae, Helvetii, Allobroges and many others),

Celts tended to share some physical characteristics (the celebrated Boadicea or Boudicca of Britain is described as red-headed) and an ethnic unity which may have promoted some collective self-consciousness above the level of the tribe. They shared many stylistic and artistic traits, and their horned helmets, long swords and shields testify to their craftsmen's skill as well as to the ferocity of their fighting-men. But they had no knowledge of writing until the fifth century. Perhaps in compensation, they have been thought to show remarkable powers of oral memory. Latin writers tell us they lived in towns (*civitates*), which seems surprising, under kingly rulers. They could not, certainly, evolve politically as a nation united enough to stand up to the legions of the Roman republic. After some indecisive encounters in the third century in north Italy, the Celts were brought to heel in the next. *Gallia Narbonense*, a part of southern France, became a Roman province in 121 BC and forty years later the Celts of Liguria and north Italy were incorporated in the Roman sphere as the province of *Gallia Cisalpina* (Gaul-this-side-of-the-Alps).

Republican decay

The great achievements of the republic had their costs. Some were paid, inevitably, by the conquered, sometimes in slavery, always in taxation. But the republic itself paid a price for foreign conquests, too. This was not quickly apparent. The Romans liked to congratulate themselves for following what they called *mos maiorum* – 'the ways of our ancestors'. They were fond of old traditions and liked to keep alive old ways of doing things. Roman religion was in large measure a matter of making sure that ancient ceremonies were kept up and carried out in the proper manner. Even when doing something new, the Romans liked to wrap it up in antique packaging. The names and forms of many republican institutions – and the delusion that the state was a republic and not a monarchy – endured long after they ceased to be appropriate.

Roman citizenship is the best example. All were men and to begin with almost all were peasants. They had the right to vote and seek justice before the courts, and the duty of serving in the army. Three important changes came about as the centuries went by. In the first place, rights of citizenship were gradually given to many people outside the original Roman territories. Next, the Punic Wars impoverished the Italian peasant. Conscription took Roman soldiers away for longer from their homesteads and families, who often fell into poverty as a result (the second war did enormous damage in the Italian countryside). When peace at last returned, many former smallholders could not make a living. On the other hand, men who had made money out of the wars began to buy up land to farm it in big estates. Slaves (part of the booty of conquest) were sometimes used to work them. The citizen-peasant tended to drift to the city to find a living there as best he could. He was on the way to being what the Romans called a 'proletarian' – someone whose only contribution to the state was to breed children. Both these changes affected politics. More poor citizens meant more votes to be bought by politicians anxious to get into positions giving them a chance to get at the rich prizes offered by conquest abroad. Politics thus came to be about the Senate's powers of patronage – in choosing governors for new provinces, or tax-gatherers from the 'knightly' class (*equites*). Such patronage became more valuable as time passed.

War favoured a third change: the army became more and more a full-time professional force, no longer one of citizens armed and brigaded for emergencies. There ceased to be a property qualification for service. If the propertyless could serve, sufficient volunteers would come forward (they were willing to serve for pay), so that conscription now became hardly necessary. True, for some time the recruit still had to be a citizen, but in the end non-citizens were allowed to join up. They then received citizenship as a reward for their service. Gradually, in these ways, the Roman army grew apart from the republic. Its famed legions became permanent organizations, whose soldiers increasingly felt loyalty to their comrades and their generals. From the first century BC each legion carried 'eagles' – standards which symbolized the honour and unity of the legion, part religious idol and part regimental colour. Against this background, the shadow of warlord rule began to lengthen in the last century of the republic.

Impoverished citizens with votes to be bought; opportunities for politicians to get at wealth on a huge scale in the new territories to which they could be appointed as governors and generals; an army which was unbeatable (or almost) in the field and more and more loyal to itself and its leaders than the Senate – these were slow but crucial political developments, and they went on for nearly two centuries, transforming the state under the surface even though much about it still looked the same. It was a muted revolution. Meanwhile Romans were obviously getting richer. This was not just a matter of the loot and slaves available as a result of conquest to those in the right place at the right time; the urban poor also benefited. When new provinces could be taxed, taxation ceased at home. Expensive 'games' were put on to amuse the masses. Some new wealth also went into the beautifying of Rome and other Italian cities, sometimes reflecting other changes as contact became more common with the east and the Greek cities whose cultural past educated Romans were brought up to respect. New fashions and standards came to the west, too, as the process of Hellenization spread farther.

Civil war

In the first century BC, the empire continued to expand. In 58 BC the Romans annexed Cyprus. A year earlier, a young politician called Julius Caesar had been chosen consul. A little later he took command of the Roman army in (transalpine) Gaul and in the next few years finished off the independence of its Celtic peoples (he also led two reconnaissance expeditions across the Channel to the island Romans called Britannia, but did not stay there). These can be regarded as the last additions to the republican empire. By 50 BC all the northern coast of the Mediterranean, all France and the Low Countries, all Spain and Portugal, a substantial chunk of the southern Black Sea coast and much of modern Tunisia and Libya were under Roman rule. While this had been going on, though, the disorder of Roman politics had broken out in civil war.

Why the republic should have collapsed in the end has already been suggested. The way things happened nonetheless owed much to individuals and to chance – as historic change often does. The extension of citizenship to virtually the whole of Italy made nonsense of the idea that the Roman popular assemblies (which only met at Rome) still had the last word. More wars in the east threw up yet more war-lords with political ambitions at home. Emergencies in Africa and southern France (the Roman Gaul) led to the granting of exceptional powers to generals who were politicians at home, and they used them against their political opponents as well as the republic's enemies. Rome became a dangerous place – to political intrigue and corruption were now added

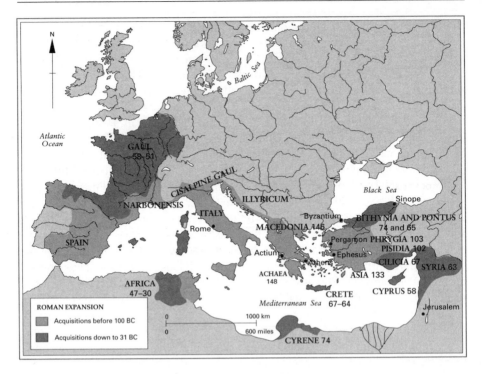

the murder of political rivals and mob violence. People began to fear the emergence of a dictator, though it was not clear where he was to come from.

Somewhat unexpectedly it turned out the be the conqueror of Gaul. Seven years there had given Julius Caesar three great advantages; he was away from Rome while other people were blamed for increasing disorder, violence and corruption; he became enormously rich; and he won the loyalty of the best-trained and most experienced of the Roman armies. His soldiers felt that he would look after them, assuring them pay, promotion and victory.

Caesar has always been a fascinating figure. He has been seen both as a hero and as a villain, and his reputation has swung about. He did not have a very long career at the top, and it finished at the hands of his enemies, yet few have questioned his abilities. By writing his own accounts of his successful campaigns in some of the best Latin of his day, he helped to manufacture and sustain a belief in his powers. So persuasive was his prose that he has been said to have 'invented' the Germans as an ethnic entity. He had great qualities of leadership, cool-headedness and determined patience. Though by Roman standards not very cruel, he was ruthless. Whatever his aims and the morality of what he did, he was no worse than most other politicians of his day and showed himself better than some of them.

In January 49 BC Caesar struck. Claiming to be defending the republic from its enemies, he crossed the river Rubicon, the border of his province – an illegal act – and marched on Rome with his army. For four years he fought a civil war in Africa, Spain and Egypt, chasing opponents who had armies which they might use against him. He crushed opposition by force but also won over former enemies by mildness after success. Victorious, he carefully organized political support in the Senate and was made dictator for life. But by now some Romans feared that Caesar might re-establish a monarchy in the centralizing oriental style. The cant of republicanism served his enemies; in the end they came together and in 44 BC he was murdered.

In form, the republic was still there. But Caesar's changes in the direction of centralized power were left intact. Problems could not be solved by putting the political clock back. Within a couple of years his great-nephew and adopted heir, Octavian, hunted down the politicians who had murdered him and they, too, were dead. Caesar was proclaimed a god. Octavian then fought another civil war which took him as far afield as Egypt (it was duly annexed as a province, after the legendary suicides of Anthony and Cleopatra). When he returned to Rome supported by the loyalty of his old soldiers (and those of his great-uncle), he used his power to get the Senate to provide a cloak of republican respectability for everything he did. He was, formally speaking, only *imperator* – a title meaning he commanded soldiers in the field – but he went on being elected consul, the most important of the republic's executive officers, year after year. In due course he was given the honorary title of *Augustus* and it is as Caesar Augustus that he has gone down in history. His power grew as more and more offices and honours were given to him, though he never ceased to insist that this was all within the old republican framework. He was *princeps* – first citizen – not king. In reality, though, Augustus increasingly relied on the power given him by his grip on the army (he organized the first regiment specially raised to serve in the capital itself, the Praetorian Guard) and on a bureaucracy of paid civil servants. He intended to be succeeded by a kinsman. He could not do better than an adopted stepson (his own child was a daughter) but five Caesars in a row became *imperator* and *princeps* after him. And, after he died in AD 14, Augustus, too, was declared a god. Thus the centuries-old domination of Rome by a relatively small class of politicians ended with the triumph of one of its leading families.

The Caesars were not to enjoy an untroubled ascendancy, but they launched what we know as the Roman empire. The state was now on a new course. It would be ruled in future by monarchs, though they would depend on, and therefore need to please, the army. The empire (as we may now call it) was to bring great achievements and would spread Roman rule even farther, before it too failed in the end. Augustus went to his grave remembered as the great bringer of peace and restorer of old Roman ways. But none of the three Caesars who followed his immediate successor, Tiberius, died a natural death – and some have thought that Tiberius did not either.

The Jews and the Roman empire

In the last years of Augustus' reign, an event took place of which, if historical importance is measured by impact on numbers of people, we can safely say that none in ancient times and perhaps none in the whole of human history is so important. This was the birth of the Jew whose name has passed into history as Jesus. We can be fairly certain this was in Nazareth, in Palestine, and slightly less sure when it happened, though 6 BC seems the most likely date.

His special importance to Christians is that he was believed to be divine. At (literally) a more mundane level it is not necessary to say so much in order to establish his importance. The whole of human history since his time shows it. Quite simply, those later calling themselves Christians – the followers of Jesus – were to change the world.

So far as Europe was concerned, they did more to shape its history than any other single identifiable group of men and women. To find something which has had an impact comparable to that of Christianity we have to look not to single events but to big processes like industrialization, or the great forces of prehistoric times like climate which set the stage for history. Agreement about the scale of Christianity's historical consequences, though, has never impeded violent disagreement about who Jesus was and about what he was trying to do. What can be seen easily enough is that his teaching had much greater impact than that of other holy men of his age because his followers saw him crucified and yet believed he later rose again from the dead. We are what we are and Europe is what it is today because a handful of Palestinian Jews bore witness to these things.

The Jews were an oriental people who had come to be and to feel distinctive, quite unlike others living in the Near East. To understand Jesus, we must, however briefly, take account of their unique religious vision, which he shared. Jews had long believed in one God only, a deity immanent and universal whose nature had been revealed to them, his Chosen People. No image might be made of him and his law was to be obeyed. Ritual practices which set the Jews apart from other peoples were part of that law. Even more distinctive in shaping the Jews was their historical experience, which they saw as a revelation of God's intervention. The traditional history of the Jews was a story of a 1,000 years of wandering, suffering and exile, with occasional periods of prosperity and peaceful residence in the Holy Land God ordained them to inherit. Heroic and divinely-guided leaders, patriarchs and prophets, soldiers and judges dominate this epic story. But suffering predominated in it, and pious Jews waited patiently for the coming of the Messiah, when at last their sufferings would end.

This wonderful story and exemplar of the weight of historical experience can be for our purposes taken up at a late stage, in the sixth century BC, when a Babylonian conqueror destroyed the Jews' cult centre, the great temple at Jerusalem, and carried off many of them to exile in Mesopotamia. The prophets who led some of the Jews back from exile in 538 BC (after the Persians had overthrown Babylon) made sure the temple was rebuilt and preached a more exact and narrow observation of the Jewish law, in order to set Jews still more clearly apart from other peoples, the 'gentiles'. Though some Jews took to Hellenistic ways when Palestine passed under Seleucid rule, they belonged to an upper-class minority; they were often distrusted and disliked by the people, who clung unquestioningly to their tradition – and indeed became even more tenacious of it. There was a great Jewish revolt (168–164 BC) against what we may call Hellenization. After this Seleucid kings treated the Jews cautiously.

Seleucid rule of Palestine ended in 143 BC. There followed a period of independence for about eighty years, and then Judaea was taken by Rome. 2,000 years were to pass before there was again to be an independent Jewish state in the Middle East. But the freedom of movement and trade offered first by the Hellenistic states and then by the rule of Rome had spread Jews all round the Mediterranean coasts. At Rome itself there may have been 50,000 of them, and there was a large Jewish population in Egypt at Alexandria. This was the 'Dispersion' (*diaspora*). By the time of Augustus, fewer Jews lived in Judaea than in the rest of the Roman empire. There were others still farther afield, settled in Arabia and Mesopotamia, and even in the ports of western India.

A few gentiles were attracted to Judaism (some even to conversion) by its moral code, by religious ceremonies which centred round reading the scriptures and did not need shrines or priests, and above all because it promised human salvation. The Jewish view of history was clear and inspiring; the Jewish people would be refined in the fire for the Day of Judgement, but would then be gathered to salvation. It is difficult to see why this should have awoken resentment. Yet relations between Jews and their neighbours were often strained. Sectarian riots were not uncommon and troubled the Roman authorities. Popular prejudices were easily aroused by Jewish distinctiveness and success.

In AD 26 a new Roman 'procurator' or governor, Pontius Pilate, was appointed at a bad moment in the history of Syria, the province of which Judaea was a part. It was especially disturbed. Above all, the Jews hated the Roman occupiers and their tax-gatherers, but Syrian and Palestinian Jews also hated one another (as well as their Greek and non-Jewish Syrian neighbours). There were important sectarian divisions among them. Some of them belonged to a sect called Zealots who were in a sense a nationalist movement. Many Jews were waiting for the early appearance of a 'Messiah', anointed by God, and a descendant of the line of David, the most glamorous of the heroes of the Old Testament, who would take them forward to victory – whether military or symbolic there was much disagreement.

Jesus of Nazareth

Jesus had grown up amid such expectations. He was about thirty when Pilate took up his commission. Jesus knew himself to be a holy man and his teaching and the miracles reported of him had awoken great local excitement. Of his life we have the Gospels as a record, accounts written down after his death by followers, on the basis of the memories of those who had known him. The Gospels were written to show that they were right in thinking him a unique person – the Messiah – though what that meant was to be disputed. They make it clear that Jesus was wholly orthodox in his own religious observances, adhering to the practices of Judaism, but incurring the hostility of its religious leaders by his preaching and teaching, which emphasized the inadequacy of formulaic observance by itself to change men's lives.

The uniqueness of Jesus was soon convincingly demonstrated for his followers by what happened at and immediately after the end of his life. Charged with blasphemy by the Jewish religious leaders, he was taken before the Roman governor. Anxious to avoid further communal strife in a troubled city, Pilate bent the letter of the law somewhat and allowed him to be condemned. So Jesus was crucified, probably in AD 33. Soon afterwards his disciples believed that he had risen from the dead, that they had met him and talked to him after that, that they had seen him ascend into heaven and that he had left them again only to return soon, when he would sit at the right hand of God to judge all men at the end of time.

Whatever may be thought of the Gospel records, it cannot plausibly be maintained that they were written by men who did not believe these things, nor that they did not write down what they were told by men and women who believed they had seen some of them with their own eyes. Clearly, too, Jesus' life was not so successful in a worldly sense that his teaching was likely to survive because of the impact of his ethical message alone. He had, it is true, especially attracted many of the poor and outcast, as well as Jews who felt that their traditions or the forms of behaviour into which they had hardened were no longer wholly satisfactory. But these successes would have died with him had his disciples not believed that he had conquered death itself and that those who were saved by being baptized as his followers would also overcome death and live for ever after God's judgement. Before a century had passed, this message was being preached throughout the whole civilized world united and sheltered by the Roman empire.

St Paul

Thus a new Jewish sect (for that was what the earliest followers of Jesus were) came to spread, at first in the Jewish communities of the empire. Christianity (a word taken from the Greek name soon given to Jesus – the 'Christ' or 'anointed one') thus acquired its first geographical diffusion. Soon, though, Jesus was preached also to the gentiles. This was the decision of the council of Christians (the word was by then beginning to be used of his followers) held at Jerusalem in AD 49. Besides those who had known him personally (Jesus' brother James and his disciple, Peter, among them) there may also have been present a Hellenized Jew from Tarsus, one Saul. After Jesus himself, he is the most important figure in the history of Christianity and is remembered as St Paul. Many gentiles were already interested in the new teaching, but it was Paul's missionary work in a series of voyages and journeys over most of the eastern Mediterranean, and the decision of the Jerusalem Council at his urging that gentiles should not be asked to conform to the Jewish law – that is, accept the full rigour of the Jewish religion, and show it by undergoing circumcision and practising dietary restraints – which released what was to become the most successful of world religions from the Jewish cradle which sheltered its infancy.

Christianity was never simply the creation of a great Judaic teacher; it was made – or, rather, made itself. It was a historical artifact. It now began to emerge from Jewish society, and came through Paul to distinguish itself from the world of Jewish ideas. So far as we know, Jesus' own doctrinal teaching at no time ventured beyond the intellectual world of the law and the prophets; he was evidently scrupulous in his own religious observances. Paul, a Greek-speaker and an educated man, put his understanding of Jesus' message into Greek and, in the process, into the language and ideas of the Greek intellectual world. Greek ideas of the distinction between soul and body, of the links between the visible and material and the invisible and spiritual, flowed into his preaching. He outraged orthodox Jews by seeing in Jesus a manifestation of God himself; such an idea could have no place within Judaism. But this was the doctrine which would be preached to the world by the Christian churches. It can be argued that Paul was the first of the conscious makers of Christianity. Most of the theology of the Christian Church has its roots in his interpretation of Jesus' teaching. The *Acts of the Apostles* provide ample evidence of the uproar it could cause.

Paul had seized an opportunity. The world was at peace, protected by Roman government and law; men could travel easily and securely about it except for natural hazards (like the shipwreck which Paul himself suffered), while the widespread Greek language made communication of ideas easy, too. Thus Christianity was launched on its huge career of expansion within a half-century of the crucifixion. It is not surprising that Christians soon began to think that the Roman empire itself was somehow created by God to make the spreading of the truth possible. Some came to believe it was divinely intended to further Christianity. As time passed another and more sinister idea began to take root, too: that it was not the Romans, after all, but the Jews who had actually killed Jesus.

Almost the last thing we hear of Paul is that when he was accused by the Jewish leaders at Jerusalem of sedition and profanation of the temple, he used his rights as a Roman citizen to appeal in AD 60 from the judgement of the governor of Caesarea to the emperor at Rome. To the capital he made his way to await trial. What happened to him after that we do not know, though early Christian tradition said he was martyred at Rome in AD 67. Whether he was or was not, he had by then made his own place in history.

CHAPTER FOUR Imperial Rome and world history

Establishing the empire

The major Roman contribution to civilization was the empire itself. Much of its history, like its nomenclature, was only to evolve gradually and in an unplanned way; as under the working Republic, institutions and ideas changed gradually and some-times almost unnoticed in the short term. It was a long time before *imperator* meant the man at the top of the empire. Its nature and government were nonetheless in outstanding degree the creation of Octavian. As Caesar Augustus, he gave his name to an age and left an adjective to posterity. Significantly, more representations of him than of any other Roman emperor have come down to us; he was a master of public relations. Formally, he was only the first of Rome's citizens. Popular and senatorial elections continued under him, though he said who was to be elected.

In the century after Augustus' death there were twelve emperors; Nero was the last of the four related to him or his family, and he died in AD 68. The empire then dissolved in civil war; within the year four emperors were proclaimed. This was the first instance of what was to become a recurrent phenomenon: when an emperor could not assure a peaceful takeover for his successor, real power would prove to lie with the army. There might even be more than one army in question; provincial garrisons would sometimes support different candidates, or the Praetorian Guard on the spot at Rome might itself have the last word. The Senate would go on formally appointing the first magistrate of 'the Republic', but could only manoeuvre and intrigue; in the last resort it could not defeat the soldiers. As for the emperors themselves, provided they kept the soldiers with them, their personal characters and abilities would decide what they could do.

In the end a good emperor emerged from the 'Year of the Four Emperors'; Vespasian's worst fault seems to have been stinginess. No aristocrat (his grandfather had been a centurion turned tax-collector), he was nonetheless a distinguished soldier. The old Roman families had now clearly lost their grip on power, but Vespasian's family – the Flavians – were not able to keep a hereditary succession going for long, either. Second-century emperors went back to Augustus' solution of adopting heirs. Under the four 'Antonine' emperors, the empire had almost a century of good and quiet government (AD 98–190), which later seemed a golden age. Three of them were Spaniards, one was a Greek. Now the empire did not belong to the Italians either, let alone the Romans. Nor did the imperial office remain unchanged. As its prestige grew, emperors less and less resembled the chief magistrates, and more and more looked like oriental kings, different in kind from their subjects. Indeed, dead emperors were soon seen as gods. Julius Caesar and Augustus were the first to be deified. With Vespasian's son, though, the process of deification began while he was still alive. Particularly in the east, altars on which sacrifices had been made to the Republic or Senate were re-allocated to the emperor as time went by.

More cosmopolitan at the top, the empire meanwhile went on mixing up its peoples at the bottom. The romanization of leading families in the provinces went ahead steadily. Young Gauls, Syrians, Africans and Illyrians all learnt Latin and Greek, wore clothes like those of the Romans and learnt to think of *romanitas* – the Roman heritage – as something to be proud of. Meanwhile the civil servants and army held the framework together, respecting local feeling so long as the taxes came in regularly. When a decree gave the rights of citizenship to all free subjects of the empire in AD 212, this was the logical outcome of a long process of assimilation. By then even senators were sometimes non-Italian by birth. To be 'Roman' was by then not to have been born in a particular place, but to belong to a particular civilization.

That is entangled with the question of the material reality of imperial government and administration, of what the empire was to its subjects. As a historical and working fact, it was an organism whose origins lay in the search to enrich some by exploiting others. To begin with, the some who benefited were a relatively few influential men living in Italy; later their numbers grew and at the peak of the system the whole of Rome and its people could have been said to be parasitic on the empire. The actual structure stemmed from the acquisition of new territory (sometimes haphazard, sometimes to safeguard other territory already seized) and exploiting it. There was in the early stages of the process not much reflection about what benefits imperial power over non-Romans might bring to them. Empire was more naked in those days. Its most obvious impositions or benefits, according to your point of view, were order and taxes. Roman governors tended to interfere in other matters only in so far as they eased or hindered the collection of taxes and had lubricant or frictional effects which bore on public order. The army and the governing class were the main instruments in assuring the empire's survival.

The visible expression of the empire and the focus of its civilization were its cities. Spreading round and beyond them were indigenous peoples who might or might not understand Latin, and lived in villages and encampments as they had done immemorially. Among them were scattered, in the settled provinces, the owners of villas and estates; businessmen, Italian exiles who had never gone home after a foreign posting, and retired soldiers. These constituted a store of experienced personnel from among whom magistrates and officials were chosen. Estates were often self-contained so far as the daily lives of those who worked and lived on them was concerned. Their most important link to the rest of the empire was usually through the contribution they made in the raising of cash crops – oil, wheat, wine – which circulated in a Mediterranean economy. Yet the uniformity of the agricultural sector must not be exaggerated. The extent of the empire sheltered enormous contrasts of society and economic activity – inevitably, given its huge contrasts of terrain and climate.

The imperial legacy

Even Romans who sentimentalized over the old republic could take pride in the empire. To provide regular, lawful government over a wider area than ever before, to black, white, brown 'Romans' equally, and to assure to them also peace and prosperity – all this was without precedent and remains the best ground for saying that the Romans did great things. Materially, they left behind great monuments, buildings and works of engineering. Centuries later, men explained Roman ruins as the work of long-departed giants and magicians, so amazing did they find them; an English seventeenth-century antiquarian said that Stonehenge was a Roman temple, because he thought that only the Romans could possibly have built anything so grand. Such mistakes are understandable and revealing. What the Romans left behind in brick, stone and concrete was long unrivalled in western Europe. Though most of it had very practical aims much of it was spectacular. No legion was supposed to camp even for a night without digging itself into a properly planned and defensible camp with ramparts, so that the army got plenty of practice in surveying, engineering and building. Romans created the first big European cities away from the Mediterranean, (though most city-dwellers lived in Mediterranean countries). To service their cities, they provided arenas, baths, drains and freshwater supplies. They liked magnificence and produced some vulgar things, but they were practical, not building anything so inexplicably useless to later non-believing ages as the pyramids, even if some of their tombs were very grand (centuries later, that of the emperor Hadrian in Rome became the papal castle of St Angelo).

Roman technology was efficient but not very novel. They had better tackle than their predecessors (windlasses, cranes and more iron tools), and used a wide range of materials, but most of them were already available; the exception was concrete, which they invented. It made possible building in new shapes. Roman architects were the first to find a better way to hold up broad spans of roof than lines of pillars; they invented the dome supported on vaults. But among the most visible works they left to a future Europe were roads. Often they still define major channels of communication and in one or two places, still carry traffic. A special corps of surveyors kept up the skills which made possible the astonishing accuracy with which they went across hill and vale, and they were usually built by the legions. They gave the empire the communications needed to govern so wide an area, and France her main roads until the eighteenth century. Between the age of the Caesars and that of the steam railway there was no increase in the speed with which messages and goods could be sent overland in Europe, except for marginal improvements in visual signals which were always liable to interruption by bad weather.

Because Roman ruins provided huge quantities of ready-cut stone for later builders, it is now difficult to imagine just how unprecedentedly splendid much of the empire must have looked. Some great single monuments remain in Europe – the Pont du Gard in the south of France; the arena at Nîmes, not far away; the Black Gate at Trier, the aqueduct still bringing water to Segovia, in Spain; or the complex of baths at Bath, in England. At Pompeii, Ostia, and Leptis Magna in Libya whole towns can still be seen. But the astonishing wreckage of imperial Rome itself, sometimes erupting almost at random amid the traffic of a modern capital city, is the greatest monument of all. It was the supreme city (at its greatest, it had a 1,000,000 inhabitants) in a civilization of cities. They stood like islands of Graeco-Roman culture in the aboriginal countrysides. Allowance made for climate, they reflected a pattern of life of remarkable uniformity. Each had its forum, temples, theatre, baths, whether added to old cities, or built as part of the basic plan of those which Rome refounded. Regular grid-patterns were adopted as ground plans. They were run day-to-day by local bigwigs, the *curiales* or city-fathers who at least in the first century enjoyed a very large measure of independence in the conduct of municipal affairs, though later a tighter supervision was imposed on them. Some of them, such as Alexandria or Antioch, or Carthage (which the Romans refounded), grew to a very large size.

The omnipresence of the amphitheatre is a standing reminder of the brutality and coarseness of which Roman society was capable. It is important not to get this out of perspective, just as it is important not to infer too much about 'decadence' from the much-quoted works of would-be Roman moral reformers. Nonetheless, the gladiatorial games and the wild-beast shows were emphatically mass entertainment in a way in which the Greek theatre was not. The Romans institutionalized the least attractive aspects of popular entertainment by building great centres for their shows, and by developing entertainment as a political device; the provision of spectacular games was a way for a rich man to bring to bear his wealth to secure political advancement. The gladiatorial and wild-beast shows were exploitations of cruelty as entertainment on a bigger scale than ever before and unrivalled until twentieth-century cinema and television. Urbanization could deliver mass audiences for them.

The Romans long prided themselves on being tough and hardy, but they also liked comfort. This became more and more evident as experience of the east and the spoils of empire enlarged their opportunities and provided the resources to gratify them. Sometimes they overdid the business of self-indulgence (as the menus of what was served at the great feasts of the rich when big parties were fashionable show). Their acquired enthusiasm for bathing and central heating and their attention to plumbing and sanitation are more easily admired. Elaborate aqueducts brought drinking-water to the cities within which public baths and lavatories looked after outer and inner cleanliness. In private houses, steam-rooms and living-rooms had under-floor heating. Only in the twentieth century did the inhabitants of Britannia again begin to take it for granted that houses should be properly heated.

Away from their architecture, engineering and hydraulics, the Romans were not great technological innovators. They made little contribution to pure science. In agriculture, watermills were just beginning to be introduced towards the end of imperial times; windmills had not by then made an appearance. Muscles, animal and human, remained the main source of energy. It has often been suggested that because they had plenty of slaves the Romans did not need to invent labour-saving machines, but other facts are relevant, too. It was often hard to turn a good idea into practical machinery, given the state of technology. Increasingly, too, the empire's history tended to force rural estates to try to be self-sufficient; they got by on what they could do for themselves, and did not rush to try experiments. Finally, there was no stimulus from outside; China's treasury of technical skill was too far away, and Rome's immediate neighbours had nothing very impressive with which to offer stimulus or challenge to her.

Law and order

The intellectual activity the Romans seem most to have admired is, characteristically, a practical one – the law, and the art of oratory that went with it. Rome did not stimulate philosophers like those of classical Greece who speculated about every branch of experience in an inquisitive way (but neither did anybody else emulate the Greeks, one might note, although Indians did much for mathematics). The Hellenistic philosophers were not such adventurous thinkers as their predecessors, either. Roman culture, nonetheless, could boast some good expounders of Stoic philosophy, a few major historians, and a galaxy of writers of Latin prose and verse, among whom Virgil, the epic poet, became a giant figure in world literature. Moreover, if it is usual to compare the Roman intellectual achievement somewhat slightingly with that of Greece, it should be remembered that for centuries it educated a supply of conspicuously able all-rounders. This suggests that the reliance of Roman culture on conservative ideas and Greek culture had much to be said for it. Roman politicians who reached the top might have to act as administrators, generals, supervisors of building and engineering works, advocates and judges. Rome, especially under the late Republic, produced men in abundance who could do all this. If the government they ran was often harsh and brutal in its enforcement of its laws, those laws were in some respects tolerant and cosmopolitan. Roman rule had some intellectual sophistication about it: it was a later and Christian empire that went back to trying people for blasphemy.

One aspect of Rome's brutalities was shared with all other ancient societies: slavery. As in other empires, it was omnipresent and had so many forms that it is hard to generalize about what it meant. Many slaves earned wages, some bought their freedom and formally Roman slaves had a few rights at law. The growth of large plantation estates probably made life harder for slaves, but it would be hard to say Roman slavery was worse than that of other ancient societies. A few who questioned the institution were very untypical: moralists reconciled themselves to slave-owning as easily as later Christians were to do.

Slavery was a part of the institutional violence on which the *pax romana* rested. Even under the republic, in 73 BC, the suppression of a great slave revolt took three years of military campaigning (and was punished with the crucifixion of 6,000 slaves along the roads from Rome to the south). In some provinces revolt was endemic, but it was always likely to be provoked by bursts of harsh or bad government, as was the famous rebellion of Boadicea in Britain. In one particular instance, that of the Jews, rebellion touched chords not unlike those of later nationalism. The spectacular Jewish record of disobedience and resistance goes back beyond Roman rule to 170 BC, when the 'westernizing' practices of the Hellenistic kingdoms were bitterly resisted. The imperial cult made matters worse. Even Jews who did not mind Roman tax-gatherers and thought that Caesar should have rendered unto him what was Caesar's were bound to draw the line at the blasphemy of sacrifice at his altar. In AD 66 came a great revolt; there were others under Trajan and Hadrian. Jewish communities were powder-barrels. Their liability to explode make it a little easier to understand the unwillingness of the Procurator of Judaea to press hard for the strict observance of the legal rights of an accused man when Jewish leaders demanded his death. Pilate sacrificed Jesus' life to public order, not to ideology.

To Roman magistrates, the peaceful and continuing collection of taxes was more important than the truth or fidelity of religious belief. In normal times, the taxes paid for policing and bureaucracy quite adequately. Yet tax-gatherers were usually hated. Things could be made worse, too, by occasional special exactions – levies in kind, requisitioning, forced recruiting. These had to be borne by an economic base, to which the *pax romana* was essential if its small surpluses were to be secured and its lands spared ravage. For all its idealization, rural life was harsh and laborious, and tax-collectors are never welcome figures.

The Roman peace in the end depended on the army. Roman society and culture were always militaristic, yet the instrument of that militarism changed. From the time of Augustus the army was a regular long-service force in which the ordinary legionary served for twenty years, four in reserve. As time went by he more and more came from the provinces. Surprising as it may seem, given the repute of Roman discipline, volunteers seem to have been plentiful enough.

Christianity and the empire

By the end of the first century AD there were Christian congregations all over the Roman world. For all the achievements of Paul and his colleagues, this probably owed less to deliberate evangelization than to contagion and osmosis within the Jewish communities of the empire. There was no over-arching structure to link Christians in a wider 'Church'. Everyone agreed that the Christians at Jerusalem, whose first generation of leaders had actually known and heard Christ, deserved special respect. But the only links between all Christians were the rites of baptism (the sign of acceptance into the new faith) and the 'eucharist' (the special service which re-enacted and commemorated Christ's last meal with his disciples on the eve of his arrest, trial and crucifixion), and their belief in the risen Christ. Christians usually also believed that the end of the world was at hand, that Jesus would soon return to gather up those faithful to him, and would assure them salvation at the Last Judgement. If that was so, then clearly there was not much to do here and now except watch and pray. Running the churches was not therefore a very complicated business. Still, as they grew in numbers and wealth, there were administrative decisions to be taken, and so there appeared ecclesiastical officers called bishops, presbyters and deacons. As time went on, they took on more sacerdotal roles, overseeing the conduct of worship as well as administration. They would remain the three orders of clergy.

Though Christianity never shed its essential Jewish inheritance – monotheism, the Old Testament books of the Bible, and a view of human destiny as a chosen people's special pilgrimage through history – and though Christian culture remained soaked in ideas and images drawn from the Jewish past, it nonetheless broke with the Jewish people. Jewish Christians had failed to convert their fellow-Jews to their view that the long-awaited Messiah of his people had already come in Jesus, and they could hardly go on attending the synagogue when it was known that they sat at meals with gentiles who were uncircumcised, ate pork, and did not observe other features of the Jewish law. By the end of the second century most Christians were no longer converted Jews.

The Romans long thought of Christians as just another Jewish sect, but the growth of gentile Christianity made them distinctive. Jews, moreover, had been the first to persecute Christians. They had not only demanded the crucifixion of Christ, but had killed the first Christian martyr (St Stephen). They had given St Paul (to many of them a renegade) some of his roughest moments. Some scholars have even blamed Jews at Rome for bringing down on the Christians the first Roman persecution, as scapegoats for a great fire at Rome in AD 64. Legend says that both St Peter and St Paul died in this persecution and many Roman Christians certainly perished horribly in the arena or were burned alive. In AD 66 when a Jewish revolt broke out against the Romans in Palestine, though, Christians did not join in. Jerusalem was taken from the Jews after the revolt whose horrific course and brutal aftermath made Jews even more self-conscious and reliant upon the strict observation of the law, since the temple was again no more. This intensified the difficulties of Jewish Christians.

Roman persecution of Christians, in fact, though sometimes terrible when it came, was occasional and usually local. Christians seem customarily to have enjoyed official toleration until well into the second century AD. Tales were told about them by the suspicious – they were said to practise black magic, cannibalism and incest. Some Romans disliked the way that their religion encouraged Jack (or Joanna) to think himself (or herself) as good as his (or her) master in the eye of God, and therefore to resist the traditional authority of employers, husbands, parents and slave-owners. It was easy for the superstitious to think that tolerating Christians led to natural disasters – the old gods were made angry and so sent famines, floods, plagues, it was argued. But this did not much influence officialdom. Authority only came into overt conflict with Christianity when it began to be noticed that some Christians refused to sacrifice to the emperor and the Roman deities as the laws required. The Romans had come to accept a similar refusal from the Jews: they were a distinct people with customs to be respected. But when most Christians were not Jews why should they not carry out these acts of formal respect like other people? Roman religion was a part of the *res publica*, a matter of ritual whose proper maintenance was good for the state, and whose neglect would bring retribution. For the proletarian this might mean no more than that he should not work on a holiday. Beyond such formal observance there was only superstition and popular cult activity. Roman religion was undemanding, eclectic and cosmopolitan. Christians were persecuted not for being Christian, but for refusing to do something the law commanded. This no doubt also encouraged unofficial persecution; in the second century there were pogroms and harryings of Christians, notably in Gaul.

Yet the second century was also one of significant advance for the Church. The first of the great theologians who laid down the main lines of Christian doctrine so as to distinguish it more and more sharply from other creeds and to make more precise the duties and obligations of Christians belong to this age. Irenaeus, bishop of Lyons, wrote the first great outline of Christian doctrine and was one of those who tried to connect Christian and Greek ideas (and therefore to help separate Christianity from a mass of other oriental cults). All over the Roman world men and women were searching for new ways in religion, and Christianity profited from the eager questing of would-be believers. New ideas spread quickly. By the end of the third century about a tenth of the population of the empire may already have been Christian, one emperor had been Christian (at least nominally), and another seems to have included Jesus Christ among the gods honoured privately in his household. In many places the local authorities were by then used to dealing officially with the local Christian leaders, who were often prominent in their communities, and, as bishops, played a large part in their affairs.

Imperial problems: the east

When the emperor Trajan died, in AD 177, the empire covered an area about half that of the modern United States. Roman territory ran from north-west Spain to the Persian Gulf. The most remote frontier lay for a time on the Caspian (this was when Armenia was part of the empire). In Europe, the big province of Dacia, north of the Danube, had been conquered a few years earlier. Some of these lands (notably those across the Euphrates) had quickly to be given up. Even without them, so huge an area posed big security problems. Though Rome was only in the east threatened by a great power – a state like Rome, capable of putting big armies into the field and carrying out long-term diplomatic and strategic plans – problems elsewhere grew harder to deal with as time passed. Africa was almost the only place which stayed reasonably quiet.

The most enduring problems were in Asia. For centuries the lands called Syria and other parts of the Asian Near East were disputed between great powers. A Roman army had reached the Euphrates in 92 BC. Another (40,000 strong) was destroyed by the Parthians when it crossed the river nearly forty years later. For the next three centuries relations with Parthia troubled Roman rulers. At one time a Parthian empire stretched from Bactria in the east to Babylonia and the Euphrates frontier with Syria (all that was left by that time of the Seleucid kingdom) in the west. It had formidable military resources. In particular Rome and Parthia quarrelled often and long over Armenia, the frontier kingdom east of Anatolia. Each thought of it as falling within its own sphere. In long-prolonged and ding-dong struggles, each side had its victories; once a Roman army actually occupied the Parthian capital. Yet the frontier did not change much. The disputed area was too far away for Rome to be able to hang on to conquests there without great effort and expense, and the problems of the Parthian kings at home were too distracting for them to think of expelling the Roman threat from Asia altogether.

In about AD 225, the last Parthian king was killed by the ruler of Fars, or 'Persia', a man named Ardashir (Greek-speakers called him Artaxerxes). He claimed all lands ruled by Darius, the great king who had led the first Persian invasion of Greece over 700 years earlier. His descendants would make the splendour and grandeur of the Achaemenids live again and were to restore Persian supremacy in much of the Near East. Within a few years he had begun the first of many invasions of Syria and nearly four centuries of Persian struggle with the empire in a new great power duel. The Sassanid emperors (so-named after one of Ardashir's ancestors) were to become Rome's greatest antagonist. They emphasized continuity with the Persian past, while the traditions of Sassanid bureaucracy went back even further, to Assyria and Babylonia, and so did the royal claim to a divine authority. The Sassanid threat was all the more dangerous because it flared up when Rome was threatened elsewhere and troubled at home. Between AD 226 and 379, there were thirty-five Roman emperors, while only nine Sassanid kings ruled in Persia; long reigns and the stability that went with them were advantages. One Sassanid king even took captive one Roman emperor (Valerian, who, poor man, was said to have been skinned alive and stuffed by the Persians, though this may not be true), as well as conquering Armenia and invading Syria and Cappodicia on several occasions. After this there were longer periods of peace between Rome and Persia, but the two great powers never settled down to live easily together and an enduring drain on Roman strength in the east was the result.

Imperial problems: Europe

In Europe west of the Danube the strategic problems were different. Rome faced no great power, but all along the frontier from the Black Sea to the mouths of the Rhine were Germanic peoples. Some of them had been thrown out of their original homelands by the Romans. They could be formidable opponents. Augustus had hoped to extend the empire to the Elbe, but it had become clear that this would not be possible – not least because of a great disaster in AD 9 when three legions were entirely wiped out in the German forests. To deal with the problem presented by the Germanic peoples, an elaborate frontier, the *limes*, as the Romans called it, had been created.

The *limes* was not just meant to show where one government's responsibilities ended and another began, as do boundaries between most states today, but was also intended to protect what lay behind it and to separate two different states of culture. It defined a 'Latin' Europe distinct from a 'barbarian' world (a word the Romans had adopted from the Greeks). On one side of the frontier were Roman order, law, prosperous markets, fine towns – civilization, in short; on the other were tribal society, technical backwardness, illiteracy, barbarism. Of course, complete insulation was impossible; there was always coming and going. Still, the Romans saw the frontier as something they looked out from warily, not as a stage on a journey leading somewhere else. Where possible, they based the *limes* on natural obstacles. Much of it followed the lines of the Rhine and Danube. In the gaps between natural obstacles fortifications were built of turf, timber or sometimes masonry. Along it were dotted permanent legionary camps linked by signal towers and smaller strongpoints. Troops could march quickly from point to point along roads which ran along the frontier. One long stretch of works ran between the upper Rhine and Danube, and another in the Dobrudja ran down to the sea. As a frontier fortification Hadrian's Wall, begun in about AD 122 in northern Britannia, between the Tyne and Solway Firth, remains the most remarkable because the most complete. It was built of stone, eighty Roman miles long (about 120 km), protected on both sides by ditches and connecting sixteen forts. Smaller strongpoints were placed at intervals of a mile, with two turrets between each of them. Its purpose, said Hadrian's biographer, was 'to separate the Romans from the barbarians'. As defences, such barriers were not effective unless properly manned. Twice, once at the end of the second century and once during the fourth, a temporary weakening of the garrison led to Hadrian's Wall being overrun, and incursions of wild Scots and Picts, pillaging and destroying far into the south.

The Rhine frontier, though comparatively short, was guarded by eight legions. By Augustus' day the army was already a long-service force, based on volunteer recruits, more and more of whom were drawn from the provinces. Barbarians served only in specialist units with a local background like the skilled slingers of the Balearic isles, or the heavy cavalry of the Danube provinces. The legions of infantry were the core of Rome's military power. Usually there were twenty-eight of them, about 160,000 men in all, all serving along the frontiers or in distant provinces like Spain and Egypt. To support them there were about as many cavalry, auxiliary and specialist soldiers. As time passed, long duty in the same areas tended to make the legions less mobile. Garrison towns came to house populations of families and other dependants who could not easily move. But the internal network of roads still gave the empire's commanders advantages in marching their forces swiftly from one place to another. Gradually the balance of the army's dispositions was changed to reflect changing strategic needs; by the early third century half the Rhine legions had been withdrawn, while the army on the Danube had been doubled in size.

Soon after AD 200 Germanic peoples were pressing harder and harder on the frontiers, demanding to cross and settle within the empire's own lands. Some were no doubt attracted by order, civilization and wealth. But there were also more fundamental forces at work. Other peoples further east, were being propelled westwards by changes in Central Asia, both natural (such as climate) and political (such as the disturbance by the Han emperors of the Hsing-Nu, a people later to be remembered by Europeans as

Huns). A sort of ethnic shunting was going on. At the end of the line someone was bound to bump into the Roman frontier. One outcome of the adoption of the Rhine boundary in the north was a distinction between different Germanic peoples who were in due course to shape, unwittingly, sub-divisions of a future Europe.

The barbarians' numbers must not be exaggerated: usually they seem only to have been able to put 20,000 or 30,000 men into the field at once. Given its strains and diversions elsewhere, though, even this was too much for the third-century empire. It was impossible to hold them off forever. Appeasement was tried. First some of the Rhenish tribes were allowed to settle in Roman territory (where they were then recruited to help defend the frontier against later arrivals). Then the Goths, another family of peoples, crossed the Danube in 251 (and killed an emperor in battle); five years later the Franks (another group) crossed the Rhine. Yet another, the Alamanni, were soon raiding as far south as Milan, while the Goths went on to Greece and then to harry Italy and Asia Minor from the sea. Trans-danubian Dacia was abandoned in 270.

The third century was thus a terrible time for Rome on the frontiers east and west alike, while at home a new period of civil war and disputed successions had begun. Twenty-two emperors (excluding pretenders) came and went. The last Antonine emperor had been strangled after a palace intrigue in 192 (this had led to another year of four 'emperors') and several third-century emperors were killed by their own troops. One fell in battle to his commander-in-chief (who was then himself slain by the Gauls after one of his officers betrayed him to them). Crushing taxation, economic recession and soaring inflation meanwhile struck at people far removed from these exalted circles; local magnates and moneyed men began to be unwilling to serve as town-councillors and officials when such posts meant that they would have to incur unpopularity by collecting heavier taxes – often in kind, as the monetary crisis grew worse. Cities began to rebuild their defensive walls. They had not been needed under the Antonines, but now even those of Rome were put in order. Towns which had never been fortified were given defences in the second half of the century.

Diocletian

At the end of the century Rome's luck changed; it is difficult to put it otherwise, for once again a succession of able emperors came to the top. The first to turn the tide was an Illyrian, Aurelian, 'Restorer of the Roman empire' as the Senate optimistically called him, though he was murdered as he was about to invade Persia. His successors were, nevertheless, like him, good soldiers. Nearly ten years later, in 284 another Illyrian, Diocletian, came to the throne. He was not only to re-create (at least in appearance) the old power and glory of the empire, but actually to transform the way it operated. Of humble origins, he was very traditionally-minded and had a very exalted view of his role. He took the name 'Jovius' – Jove or Jupiter, the Roman name for the king of the gods, the old Greek Zeus – and seems to have seen himself as a god-like figure, supporting single-handed the civilized world. Diocletian sought practical remedies for the empire's troubles. An attempt to halt inflation by fixing prices and wages, though, was a disaster. His most important step, too, was one whose full implications he may well not have seen: more than any other single man, Diocletian opened the way to splitting the empire in two. Whether without him this outcome, or something like it, was inevitable has been much debated.

Rome had welded together much of Alexander's empire in the Hellenized east with the western Mediterranean Greek world the great conqueror had never visited. For all the (very visible) differences between these heritages, it was only in the difficult third century that incompatibilities between them began to appear. One difficulty was that of giving due attention to the problems of the western provinces when the economic and manpower resources of the richer east were needed against the barbarians and Persians. In AD 285 Diocletian devised if not a solution, a relief. He divided the empire along the line separating the provinces of Pannonia from Dacia, and Africa from Egypt, appointing a co-emperor to the western half who, like himself, bore the title 'Augustus'. Each emperor also had an assistant, nominated as his successor and called a 'Caesar'. The title *princeps* was dropped. Other changes followed. The Senate's small remaining powers disappeared; to be a senator was now only an honorific distinction. The old provinces were divided into smaller units ('dioceses') governed by imperial nominees and administered increasingly by romanized local élites. The army was regrouped and much enlarged; conscription was brought back, and soon there were about a 500,000 men under arms.

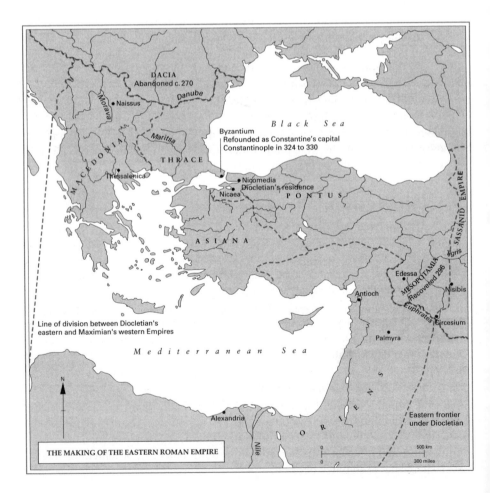

THE MAKING OF THE EASTERN ROMAN EMPIRE

This shake-up helped, but had its own weaknesses. The machinery for assuring a quiet succession of Augusti only worked once, when Diocletian and his colleague abdicated (in AD 305, when Diocletian retired to Split, on the Yugoslav coast, where the ruins of his enormous palace enclose much of the modern town). A bigger army meant more taxation, to be paid for out of a population smaller than early in the previous century. In the long-term, though, a very important step can be seen to have been taken. In spite of further attempts to rule it as a whole, every future emperor had in practice to accept the fact of division. That would not only affect the history of Rome, but would also be significant in the later shaping of Europe.

Another part of the reform effort – and it suggests that people were no longer taking the empire for granted or feeling loyalty to it in quite the same way – was an even greater emphasis on the unique, almost divine authority of the ruler himself. This boded ill for the old Graeco-Roman tradition of religious toleration. The obligation of Christians to sacrifice to the imperial cult was revived. The last general persecution of Christianity was launched by Diocletian in 303. It was not imposed in every part of the empire and did not long outlast his abdication, though kept up a little longer in Egypt and Asia than in the west. By then, paradoxically, Christianity was on the eve of its greatest worldly triumph.

Christian empire

Constantine, son of Diocletian's successor (who only reigned a year) was hailed as emperor by the army at York in 306. He has some claim to have changed world history more than any other emperor. After two decades of civil war he reunited the empire in 324. In that struggle, he had soon decided to see if the Christians' god would help him. There is no reason to doubt Constantine's religious credulity or his sincerity. He seems in any case always to have hankered after a monotheistic creed and for a long time worshipped the sun-god whose cult was associated with that of the emperor. In 312, on the eve of an important battle and as a result of what he believed to be a vision, he had ordered his soldiers to put on their shield a Christian monogram by way of showing respect for the Christians' god. He won the battle. Soon afterwards toleration and imperial favour were re-extended to Christianity. Constantine went on to make gifts to churches, then, to building them. Though his coins still for many years bore the symbol of the sun he gave converts rewards and jobs. One can sense from his acts a man moving only gradually towards personal conversion, but in the end, without formally disavowing the old cults, Constantine declared himself a Christian.

Like many other early Christians, Constantine was not baptized until he was on his deathbed, but in 325 he presided over the first ecumenical council of the Church – one attended by bishops from the whole Christian world, though few from the east – at Nicaea. The main business of this council was the condemnation of the teaching of a theologian from Alexandria, Arius, as heretical. Important as this was, it probably mattered more that Constantine thus founded a tradition that Christian emperors enjoyed a special religious authority. It was to last for over a 1,000 years. Constantine also made another great contribution to the future when he decided to build a new imperial capital on the site of Byzantium, an old Greek colony at the entrance to the Black Sea. He wished to build there a city to rival Rome itself, but one unsullied by pagan religion. It was named Constantinople and remained an imperial capital for a 1,000 years and a focus of European diplomacy for another 500. But it was in making the empire Christian that Constantine shaped the future most deeply. He did not know it, but he was founding Christian Europe. He deserves his title – Constantine 'the Great' – though, as has often been said, because of what he did rather than why he did it, or what he was.

Establishment was an enormous worldly gain for the Church. It was now tied to the glamorous and prestigious tradition of Rome, which would prove a rock to build on in the centuries ahead. Yet, paradoxically, within a century or so, Christians saw the Church not as powerful, but as weak. The faithful saw themselves in a favourite image, as the saving remnant of the chosen, tossing in the Ark, while the storms raged about them. This, of course, is one reason why they were so harsh, intransigent, cruel, uncompromising and – if one may so put it – 'unchristian' to their fellow-men. They lived still in a world of demons and magic, where heresy or paganism threatened those who succumbed to their seductions with eternal torture in hellfire. Their pastors often showed an unpleasant temper, if a heroic one, and it long coloured Christian history.

As so often in great historical decisions, there were ironies in Constantine's choice. In the end and often unwittingly, the Church helped to destroy the pagan classical world. For this reason, the greatest of English historians, Edward Gibbon, saw the story of late antiquity – the era during which the once-great Roman empire crumbled into decay – as the progress of barbarism and superstition.[1] By superstition, he meant Christianity. His paradox is too brilliant a reflexion of his own age and too simple to be true, of course: Christianity preserved much of the Roman past which might otherwise have gone under; it did not merely eradicate things it did not like. Yet Gibbon's sneer is a useful reminder of a great historical fact, the triumph of Christianity; it was the triumph of the once-despised beliefs of a tiny Jewish sect. Christianity now grew within the imperial civilization, not outside it, and became almost unwittingly a great transmitter of a pagan past to the future. Symbolically, Roman bricks were often re-used to build new Christian churches, pagan temples were pillaged to provide materials for them, and sometimes whole buildings were adapted to a new religious use.[2]

Less obviously, Constantine's acts also confirmed the cultural division of east and west. He made it easier still for them to drift apart. The more populous east could feed itself and raise more taxes and recruits; the west grew poorer, its towns slipping into decline. It came to depend on corn from Africa and the Mediterranean islands for its food and, in the end, on barbarian recruits for its defence. Gradually Constantinople came to rival Rome and even surpass it. More important still, distinctions within Christianity helped to separate two zones. The increasingly Latin-speaking west (Greek had declined as an educational influence since its golden age after the Punic Wars, thanks in part to the appearance of a significant Latin literature) had two great Christian communities within it, one Roman (presided over by the bishop, the pope of Rome) and one African. Both diverged increasingly from the Greek-speaking churches of Asia Minor, Syria and Egypt, all of which were more receptive to oriental influences and more influenced by Hellenistic tradition. Nicaea had not stifled Arianism, moreover;

---

[1] Edward Gibbon, *The History of the Decline and Fall of the Roman Empire*, ed. J.B. Bury, IV (London, 1898), p.140.

[2] The earliest temple we know to have been converted in this way to Christian purposes is the Pantheon, which is, in consequence, the only intact building from classical antiquity which today survives in Rome; those who worshipped in it looked after it.

the condemnation ensured it would not prosper in the east, but it spread among the Germanic peoples, where it was to survive until the seventh century.

Decline and fall in the west

Constantine's sons ruled the empire until 361. Soon after, it was divided again between co-emperors. Only once more would east and west be ruled by the same man. This was the emperor Theodosius who in 380 finally forbade the worship of the old pagan gods, thus putting the empire's full force behind Christianity and a break with the old Roman past. But by his day things were already going downhill still faster in the west, and a century later the western empire had, in effect, vanished. Society was not suddenly engulfed, though, as if by earthquake. What disappeared was a machine, the Roman state in the west – or, rather, what remained of it after a long process of delapidation. In the fourth century its administration had been seizing up. More demands were made on dwindling resources; a much enlarged army could not be paid for. New conquests to help pay for defence were inconceivable. As taxes went up, more people left the towns and sought to live self-sufficiently in the country to avoid them. Less money meant a still feebler army, and that meant yet more recourse to barbarian mercenaries – which cost still more money. Concessions to them had to be made just as pressure was building up from a new wave of migrations, which were to effect the last major changes in the European genetic pool before the twentieth century.

It is difficult to be sure of avoiding exaggerating or romanticizing these movements. On the one hand, some of them cannot have been very different from the old prehistoric migrations of tribes and groups of families. On the other, the Vandals crossed to Africa from Spain in the fifth century perhaps 50,000 strong, a major transference in a world much more thinly populated than ours. There may be no 'typical' case. What is

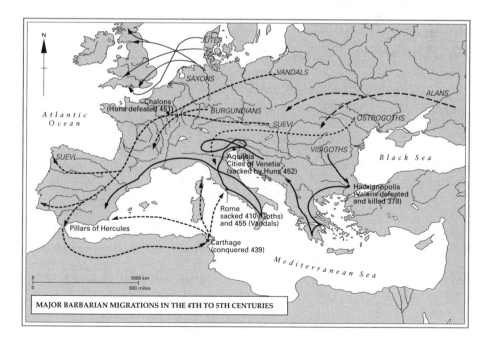

MAJOR BARBARIAN MIGRATIONS IN THE 4TH TO 5TH CENTURIES

MAJOR DATES IN THE LAST CENTURIES OF THE WESTERN EMPIRE

AD 212	Caracalla gives citizenship to virtually all free inhabitants of the empire.
249	First general persecution of Christians begins.
285	Diocletian's ordering of new imperial system: the 'Tetrarchy'.
313	Edict of Milan restores Christian property and freedom of worship.
330	Constantinople dedicated as capital.
376	Goths cross the Danube.
406	Vandals and Suevi cross the Rhine.
409	Vandals, Alans and Suevi invade Spain.
410	Legions withdraw from Britain: sack of Rome by Visigoths.
412–14	Visigoths invade Gaul and Spain.
420	Jutish and Anglo-Saxon landings in Britain.
429–39	Vandals invade North Africa and conquer Carthage.
455	Vandal sack of Rome.
476	Deposition of last western emperor, Romulus Augustulus.

clear is that in the last quarter of the fourth century a particularly nasty nomadic people from Asia, the Huns, had fallen on the Gothic peoples who lived on the Black Sea coast and the lower Danube, beyond the Roman frontier. The Huns were one more (and not the last) of peoples from the steppes of inner Asia who at various times threatened the empire. Their many skills – above all military – and mobility made them formidable opponents and, often levers of world history. Climatic and political changes (where even small disturbances could mean life or death to pastoralists) could set the steppe-dwellers on the move; when this happened, they clashed with those who lived west and south of them. The shunting movements which followed could make history far away, but in the fifth century the Huns themselves penetrated as far west and as far from home as they ever got; all western Europe seemed likely to fall to them.

In the late fourth century, though, the Huns' impact further east on the Gothic peoples had major consequence for the empire. The barbarians pressed to enter imperial territory. In 376, the Visigoths set a precedent; they were allowed to cross the Danube to settle as a distinct people, bringing with them their own laws. When the eastern empire bungled the management of these refugees, the Visigoths turned on it. In 378 they killed an emperor at the battle of Adrianople and soon cut off Constantinople by land from the west as more and more of them flooded into imperial territory. A few years later and the Visigoths were on the move again, but this time towards Italy, until stopped by a Vandal general in the imperial service. From 406 the empire was employing barbarian tribes as 'confederates' (*foederati*, a word which meant barbarians who could not be resisted but who could be persuaded to help). This was the best the western empire could now do for its defence, and soon it was clearly not enough. Titles given to emperors, such as 'Ever-Victorious' and 'Restorer of the World', were signs that things were going badly.[3]

By the time the fifth century opened, a whole world-order seemed to be going under in the west. In 402 the emperor and senate fled to Ravenna, from this time the centre of imperial authority in the west until it disappeared altogether. Barbarian warlords and

---

[3] Peter Brown, *Augustine of Hippo: a biography* (London, 1967), p.25

their followers were soon wandering the length and breadth of the Latin west. In 410 Rome itself was sacked by Goths, an event so appalling that it led to St Augustine, an African bishop and a Father of the Church, to write one of the masterpieces of Christian literature. In *The City of God*, Augustine set out to explain how God could allow such a dreadful thing to happen. Meanwhile, the Visigoths were moving across France, getting as far as Aquitaine before agreeing terms with the emperor, who persuaded them to help him resist another people, the Vandals, who had by then overrun Spain. The Visigoths pushed the Vandals across the Straits of Gibraltar to settle in North Africa, making their capital at Carthage. There they remained, dropping across the Mediterranean in 455 to sack Rome a second time. Terrible as such a raid was, though, the loss of Africa was more serious. The western empire had lost its main source of grain and oil. Its economic base was now shrunk to little more than part of Italy.

Amid such turmoil, it is hard to say exactly when the western empire ceased to be. Names and symbols were, like the Cheshire cat's smile, the last things to go. The Huns were finally turned back from the west at a great battle near Troyes in 451, but the victorious 'Roman' army was made up of Visigoths, Franks, Celts and Burgundians – all barbarians – commanded by a Visigothic king. When in 476 another barbarian ruler deposed the last western emperor, he was addressed by the title 'patrician' by the eastern emperor. For all the forms, the reality was that the western empire as a political structure had by then been replaced by a number of Germanic kingdoms, and the date when the last western emperor died is usually reckoned as merely a line conveniently drawn under the story which began with Augustus.

History, though abhors clean endings. Many of the barbarians (some by this time educated by the Romans) saw themselves as the new custodians of Roman authority. They still looked to the emperor at Constantinople as their ultimate sovereign. By the end of the fifth century many of them had settled down beside the old provincial gentry of Gaul, Spain and Italy, adopting Roman ways; some of them had become Christian. Only in the British Isles did barbarism almost completely obliterate the old Roman past. In about 500, therefore, whatever had happened to the empire, we are not at the end of the story of ancient civilization.

Centuries earlier, when his countrymen overran Greece, a Roman poet had remarked that 'Captive Greece took her wild captor captive'. He had seen that though the Greek states had gone under, the triumphant Romans had been captivated by Greek ways. Something just a little like that happened in the west as the Roman empire came to an end. Rome did not cease to influence history with the disappearance of formal empire in the west. For nearly another 1,000 years an empire calling itself 'Roman' would live on at Constantinople. In the west itself there would still exist even in 1800 something called the 'Holy Roman Empire'. Some Christian clergymen still today wear costume based on that of the Roman gentleman of the second century AD. European universities still use Latin when they wish to add a special solemnity to their ceremonies. Paris, London, Exeter, Cologne, Milan and scores of other towns and cities are all important centres, just as they were in Roman times. Much of the map of Europe has still the shape the Romans gave it by planting their garrisons and building roads. Imperial policy sometimes diverted, sometimes transplanted, barbarian peoples to areas where, unwittingly their settlement was to provide the roots of future nations. European languages are packed with words from Greek and Latin, the tongues through which government and the Bible first came to much of Europe. It was Julius Caesar who took up the suggestion of an Alexandrian Greek that the Egyptian year of 365 days, with an extra day every fourth year, would be better than the complex traditional Roman calendar, and it was under Constantine that the Jewish idea of a Sabbath day of rest once in seven became accepted. And, of course, it is to early Christianity that we owe the distinction of BC and AD on which the whole Christian and most of the non-Christian world still works today (it was a little after 500 that a monk first calculated the date of Christ's birth; he was in error by a few years, but his decision is the root of the western calendar now used round the world).

Such things provide plentiful clues to the extent and variety of the empire's impact. It had, after all, defined the extent of a civilization – or rather, it was to turn out, two civilizations, for it effectively entrenched a division between two separate cultural zones in its western and eastern halves. Above all, the empire gave Christianity first an opportunity and then an establishment which enabled it, centuries later, to join the small number of truly world religions. All these facts shaped the future with unique power.

Nor is even this quite all. Most great civilizations have had classical ages from which they draw the standards by which they assess their own later achievements. Later Europeans sometimes exaggerated what the Greeks and Romans had done, but they found in it criteria. Their inheritance served both as an inspiration and a touchstone of their own performance for centuries to come. Classical antiquity provided a myth, a vision of what civilization could and men ought to be.

Western Europe at the end of antiquity

The history of the western half of Europe has to be taken a little further at this point if its meaning for the future is to be clear. The idea of *romanitas* – of what Roman civilization and the Roman empire had been – lived on. The emperor at Constantinople of whom men might not know much and whose authority might be only vestigial, still held an office nominally the highest available to men; it would be a long time before emperors gave up all claims to territorial sovereignty in the west. Other, new, institutional and ethnic elements were nonetheless also beginning to give western Europe new shape. And there was, finally, the institutional machinery of Catholic Christendom, patchy, thin and brittle though it still might be in its operation, but wielding both the impalpable power religion will always exercise over superstitious minds, and the practical skills of its literate clergy. Between them, these forces played upon a Europe still plastic. They operated over an area which was not exactly co-terminous with the former empire in the west, but one determined basically by the pattern of the Germanic invasions. They settled national identities only to appear centuries later, though there was little about them which hinted at the delineation of future states.

The northernmost Germanic invaders and migrants were the Saxons, Angles and Jutes who were entering the old Roman province of Britannia from the end of the fourth century onwards. There they settled even while Roman rule was still formally intact and operative over the Britons. When the last emperor to be proclaimed there by his soldiers crossed with them to Gaul in 407, Roman rule ended, and the Romano-British and successive waves of newcomers were left to argue out the fate of the islands. At the beginning of the seventh century there had emerged in England a set of seven Germanic (we can call them Anglo-Saxon) kingdoms, fringed by a Celtic world of Irish,

Welsh and Scottish tribes living under their own princes which had hardly been touched by Roman power, even as a menace.

A few of the British lived on in communities keeping to old ways and old tongues, some even as late as the tenth century, but Romano-British civilization soon disappeared more completely than its equivalent anywhere else in the former imperial west. Germanic tongues almost entirely replaced Latin, which was to surge back only with the triumph of Christianity as a language of learning. Of administrative, spiritual or even military continuity (if we except what may be a dim memory of the cavalry-fighting skills of the imperial army in the legend of King Arthur and his knights) there is virtually no trace. There was a Roman physical heritage to the future England in the remains of roads, forts, camps and a few constructions (Hadrian's Wall was the outstanding example) which were to puzzle the Germanic newcomers, who tended to come to the conclusion that they had been the work of giants of superhuman power, but that was all. Whatever Romano-British Christianity had been, it disappeared, the keepers of the faith in these islands retiring for a time to the fastnesses of Celtic Christianity.

The Merovingians

The fate of the former imperial provinces across the Channel was quite different, as, above all, the persistence and often predominance of Latin elements in language suggests. After the Vandals had passed destructively through it, Gaul continued to lie in the shadow of the Visigoths of Aquitaine. Their share in repelling the Huns had given them great importance. To the north-east, beyond the old frontier, were to be found other barbarians who were to begin the positive re-shaping of a new western Europe and have a greater influence on it than any other Germanic tribes. These were the Franks. Their graves reveal them from the outset as a warrior people, divided into a hierarchy of ranks, established in the fourth century in modern Belgium, between the Scheldt and the Meuse, where they became Roman *foederati*. Some of them then moved into Gaul. One group, settled at Tournai, threw up a ruling family subsequently called Merovingians; the third king (if this is the correct word) of this line was Clovis. His is the first great name in the history of the country later named France, after his people.

Clovis became ruler of the western Franks in 481, still formally the emperor's subject. His sway extended far to the west into Gaul and down to the Loire. After being elected king of the eastern Franks, he ruled over a united kingdom of these peoples which straddled the lower Rhine valley and northern France. Clovis then married a Burgundian princess, from another people who had settled in the Rhône valley and the area running south-east to modern Geneva and Besançon. She was a Catholic, though the Burgundians were Arians. At some time after their marriage (traditionally in 496) and after a battlefield conversion which is reminiscent of Constantine's, Clovis himself embraced Catholicism. The step was well-judged and momentous. It gave him the support of the Church, the most important power still surviving from the empire in the barbarian lands, in what it now chose to regard as a religious struggle against Arians and pagans. It also opened the way to friendship with the Roman-Gauls (one day, 'France' would see itself as the 'eldest daughter' of the Church). For the moment, the Frankish kingdom was the nearest thing western Europe could show to a 'successor state', and potentially the heir to Roman supremacy north of the Alps. The emperor in Constantinople named Clovis consul.

Clovis was a considerable war-lord. Though the Burgundians remained politically distinct until after his death, he asserted his power over them, and confined the Visigoths to the Languedoc, Roussillon and Provence of later times. His court moved to Paris, near which Clovis was to be buried, the first Frankish king not to be buried as a barbarian. This, though, was not the start of the continuous history of a capital at Paris. A Germanic kingdom was not what we might call a 'state', but, rather, a heritage, partly of lands, partly of kinship groups. That of Clovis was divided among his sons, to break up again a couple of years later and not to be reunited until 558. Gradually, it settled down in three bits. One came to be called Austrasia, with its capital at Metz and its centre of gravity east of the Rhine; Neustria was the western equivalent and had its capital at Soissons; under the same ruler, but distinct, was the kingdom of Burgundy. Their rulers tended to quarrel over the lands where these regions touched. Here were new coagulations to play a part in the shaping of Europe.

There had in fact begun to appear a Frankish nation which was no longer merely a collection of barbarian warbands, but a group of distinguishable peoples belonging to recognizable political units, speaking Latin vernaculars, and with an emerging class of landowning nobles. Significantly, there was soon written a Christian interpretation of a barbarian people's role in history, the *History of the Franks*, by Gregory, Bishop of Tours, himself a Romano-Gaulish aristocrat. Other peoples would produce similar works (the greatest, perhaps, is that written for the English by the Venerable Bede) which sought to reconcile traditions in which paganism was still strong to Christianity and the civilized heritage. Gregory presented a pessimistic picture of the Franks after the death of his hero Clovis; he thought Frankish rulers had behaved so badly that their kingdom was doomed.

Gothic peoples (Ostrogoths and Visigoths) have left a name and an adjective rich in association to later Europeans. Their ancestors had made their way west from southern Russia. Theodoric, the Ostrogoth king, was recognized by the emperor as ruler of Italy (where he had been called in to fight off other invaders) in 497. He had been brought up at Constantinople until he was eighteen and was the godson of an emperor. His sister was lady-in-waiting to the empress. 'Our royalty is an imitation of yours, a copy of the only empire on earth', he wrote revealingly to the emperor in Constantinople from his capital in Ravenna. On his coins appeared the legend 'Unvanquished Rome' (*Roma invicta*), and when he went to Rome, Theodoric held games in the old style in the circus. Yet he was the only Ostrogoth who was a Roman citizen. His authority might be accepted by the Senate, but his countrymen were merely mercenary soldiers of the empire. To civil offices he appointed Romans, among them his adviser, the philosopher Boethius, who was to be possibly the most important single channel through which the legacy of the classical world passed to medieval Europe (though Theodoric eventually imprisoned and executed him on a charge of treason).

Theodoric maintained good relations with other barbarian peoples (he married Clovis' sister) and enjoyed respect among them. But he did not share his own people's Arian faith, and in the long run religious division told against Ostrogothic power. Unlike the Franks, and in spite of their ruler's example, they were not to ally successfully with the Roman past. After Theodoric's death, the Ostrogoths were in the sixth century expelled from Italy and history by armies from the eastern empire. In the

process, Italy was ruined. Nominal imperial control was briefly restored, but the peninsula was soon again invaded and lost to yet another barbarian people, the Lombards.
The Merovingians, meanwhile seized the former Ostrogoth lands north of the Alps as
part of their support of the Catholic cause against the Arians.

To the west, Clovis had driven the Visigoths virtually out of Gaul, leaving to them
Spain, from which they had themselves driven the Vandals. Other Germanic peoples
were already settled there, too. Spanish terrain presented quite special problems – as it
has continued to do both to invaders and its own governments – and Visigothic rule in
Spain owed more to romanization than it had done in Gaul. The Visigoths – and there
were not so very many of them, less than 100,000 at most – clustered about leaders who
spread out from Old Castile through the provinces; they then quarrelled so much
among themselves that in the sixth century imperial rule was able to re-establish itself
in the south for more than a half-century. Finally, the Visigothic kings turned to
Catholicism. Thus the authority of the Spanish bishops was mobilized behind them
and 587 begins the long tradition of Catholic monarchy in Spain.

What all this adds up to is hard to summarize. The Visigoths, for example, underwent three centuries of evolution between the creation of the kingdom of Toulouse and
the end of their ascendancy in Spain. If their economic life and contemporary technology hardly altered in that long time, mental and institutional forms were undergoing radical, if slow, transformations. This must have been true in all the barbarian
kingdoms. Soon it is not quite right to think of any of them (except, perhaps, the Lombards) in terms of their fifth-century predecessors. The tribes which made them up had
always been minorities, often isolated in alien settings, dependent for their living on
routines long established by the particular environment. They cannot but have been
forced into understandings with the conquered. The passage of their invasions may
have seemed at close quarters like a flood tide, but when it had passed there were often
only tiny, isolated pools of newcomers left behind, here and there replacing the Roman
masters, but often living alongside them and with them. Marriage between Roman and
barbarian was not legal until the sixth century, but that was hardly a check in settler
societies. In Gaul the Franks took up Latin, adding Frankish words to it. By the seventh
century, western European society has already a very different atmosphere from that of
the turbulent fifth.

In some ways, that meant regression. The barbarian past left its imprint. Society in
the old western lands of the empire was long and often irreversibly shaped by Germanic
custom. Its hierarchies were reflected in the characteristic Germanic device for securing public order, the blood feud. Men – and women, cattle, and property of all sorts –
had in the most literal sense their price; wrongs were settled by interesting a whole clan
or family in the outcome if customary compensation were not forthcoming. Yet kings
tended more and more to write down, and thus in a sense 'publish', what such customs
were. Literacy was rare and recording by a scribe on parchment for future consultation
was all that could be envisaged. None the less, in this Germanic world lie the origins of
a jurisprudence one day to be carried across oceans to new cultures of European stock.
The first institution to open the way to this was the acceptance of kingly or collective
power to declare what was to be recorded.

Record-keeping was one of the activities in which barbarians had to seek the skills
of Rome though it was only one form of the respect which so many barbarian rulers
showed for Roman tradition and forms. It was not always easy for them to do so.

Theodoric saw himself as the representative of the emperor but had to avoid irritating his followers, who were easily provoked by any excess of romanization. Perhaps similar considerations weighed with Clovis before his conversion, which was an act of identification with empire as well as with Church. Yet at a level just below such heroic figures, both Frankish and Visigothic noblemen seem sometimes to have taken pleasure in showing themselves the heirs of Rome by writing to one another in Latin and patronizing light literature. There was a tie of social interest, too; Visigothic warriors could find employment in putting down the revolts of peasants who menaced the Romano-Gaulish landowner as well as themselves. Yet so long as Arianism stood in the way, there was a limit to the possible identification of the barbarians with *romanitas*. The Catholic Church, after all, was the supreme imperial relic in the west.

To express it in that way is of course anachronistic. No Christian could have seen things in that light at the end of antiquity. No Christian (or anyone else, for that matter) could then have thought in terms of an alternative to what the empire had sheltered. They could not even think of an alternative to imperial government: it was simply *the* empire, not even qualified as 'Roman', because none other was comparable to it. Even those who dreamed of a Judgement Day which was quickly approaching saw it as one in which earthly powers would fade away and crumble – not as one which would replace one human order, one set of standards, by another. Even educated men knew hardly anything of the worlds of Persia or India, nothing of China. Rome was all they knew. It was what civilization meant. That would continue to be true for a long time to come.

BOOK TWO Christendom

A shorthand way of describing what happened in the thousand years after the end of the old Roman empire in the west is to say that half Christendom then turned into Europe. Ancient heritages, new historical circumstances and new forces all played a part in bringing that about. Sometimes these new forces came from the outside and one of these, Islam, was especially important. Some facts external to western Christendom had a more passive but still important and complex effect, simply by being there – the growing distinctness of the eastern Orthodox world, for example, or the protective cushion so long provided by the eastern empire of Constantinople until it went under to new Asian conquerors in the fifteenth century.

Such forces helped to shape a Europe in the making without anyone foreseeing, far less intending, that outcome; what could be discerned was that western Christendom expanded and came increasingly to think of itself as Christendom. While losing ground across the Mediterranean in North Africa to Islam, the Christian religion had elsewhere expanded into areas unknown to it in the sixth century. It had also developed an elaborate and complex structure of institutions and had much more far-reaching aspirations to regulate lives, and better means to do it. Within Christendom's new space some men had by 1500 also acquired a new collective self-awareness; political units far different from the tribal and kinship forms of barbarian times had come into existence. The wealth to which their peoples had access was unrecognizably different both in scale and in the complexity of the institutions supporting it from anything in the Dark Age west.

The foundations had thus been laid for a new sort of future. Its stage was to be an increasingly integrated world and not one fragmented within self-contained civilizations. Some of those we can begin to call Europeans would be uniquely well-placed to play decisive parts in it and had even begun to think of themselves not only as Christians but as Europeans, too, one of the most remarkable changes of all.

CHAPTER ONE Re-definition

The age of Justinian

Much of the way in which Europe came to be a recognizable entity is a story of things done by non-Europeans, often outside Europe. It was to turn out that the collapse of Roman administration in the west left the eastern half of the empire with nearly a 1,000 years of life before it. Its rulers and their officers went on speaking of themselves as 'Romans' and their own eastern neighbours often called them that, while people in the west came to call them 'Greeks' and to speak of a Greek emperor. That empire in AD 500 actually ruled only half Christendom, the Christian peoples of the east Mediterranean, Asia Minor, Syria and Egypt, but its emperors would go on claiming former west Mediterranean lands and authority over their peoples long after the deposition of their last western colleague in 476. It was not then obvious that they would in the end dominate a core area of civilization no longer integrated with the western half of the old empire and distinctive in its Christianity.

By then, though, crucial developments had already occurred which made the division of Christendom more likely. One had long been operating, the slow shift of imperial attention towards the east which had begun in the third century, and its reinforcement by Constantine's symbolic and world-shaping decisions that a new capital should be built on the Bosphorous and that the empire should embrace Christianity. The second of these was bound to give more weight to the eastern and Greek-speaking provinces where the largest Christian communities of the empire and its oldest and most prestigious churches were to be found. The fifth-century collapse in the west was the next great landmark in the process of differentiation. It left the eastern empire striving to make the best settlement it could with successful barbarians in the west until it could muster the strength to restore its authority. The fiction of a still-united empire was kept alive, but it was not until the accession of a new emperor, Justinian, in 527 that there seemed a chance of making it reality again. His predecessors had not overtly opposed barbarian rule in Italy, and had treated Odoacer, the Hun who deposed the last western emperor, as an independent ruler. Distracted by Persian attacks (a new dynasty, the Sassanids, had replaced the Parthians as the major military threat in the east and established itself there in the third century) and struggling to grapple with barbarians nearer home, in the Balkans, one emperor even gave the title of patrician to the Ostrogoth Theodoric, who had slain Odoacer. Such acts implicitly asserted the claim of imperial authority, but also displayed its hollowness.

Justinian, who boasted that Latin was his native tongue (he came from Illyria) nonetheless hoped still to reunite and restore the old empire, even if it now had to be centred on Constantinople. Contemporaries were struck by the victories his generals began to win in Africa and Italy. They looked forward to a real restoration. No one could really conceive a world without the empire and although it is an exaggeration, it is not a great one, to say that for centuries people were to look around them, wondering where Rome had gone and trying to put something in its place. This is why barbarian kings in the west gladly deferred to Constantinople; clearly, the Roman empire was still going on there. They accepted titles from it; they did not grasp at the purple themselves.

Though almost always at war, Justinian's armies proved to be only occasionally and temporarily victorious. Costly Persian campaigns (and payments to the Persian king) did not lose the empire much ground, but were a grave strategic handicap; lasting recovery in the west, though, eluded it. Belisarius, Justinian's greatest general, destroyed Vandal Africa and then went on to invade Italy and begin a struggle which ended in 554 with the Ostrogoths driven from Rome and the unification once more of all Italy under imperial rule. It was, though, an Italy devastated by the imperial armies. In southern Spain, too, there had been successes; imperial armies exploited rivalry between Visigoths and again set up imperial government in Córdoba. As for the sea, Sicily, Corsica and Sardinia were all re-taken and for a century after Justinian's death, Byzantine ships moved about unmolested in the western as well as the eastern Mediterranean. Yet these re-conquests could not all be held. By the end of the century most of Italy was gone again, this time to the Lombards, another Germanic people and the final extinguishers of imperial power in the peninsula.

In eastern Europe, too, in spite of a vigorous diplomacy of bribery and missionary ideology, Justinian never mastered the barbarian threat. Perhaps there never was a

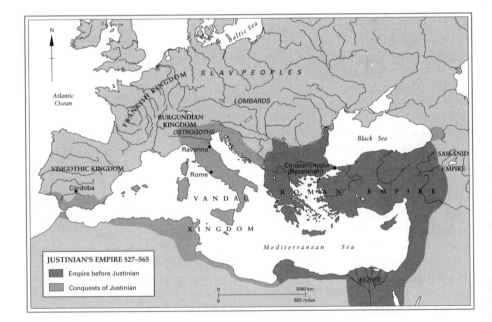

JUSTINIAN'S EMPIRE 527–565

Empire before Justinian

Conquests of Justinian

likelihood that he would. The pressure from behind on migrant peoples moving west and south was great and, besides, they could see great prizes ahead; the barbarians, it was said, having tasted Roman wealth, never forgot the road that led to it. In spite of the emperor's fortress-building, the ancestors of the later Bulgars were at the time of his death already settled in Thrace, and a wedge of barbarian peoples separated west and east Rome by land. Yet, the empire still had a strong hand to play. Its diplomacy built a network of influences among the barbarian peoples beyond the frontier, playing off one against another, bribing princes with tribute, or a title, or an imperial godparent for a baptized child. Above all, there was the impalpable prestige of Rome, to which Justinian's reign was so decisively to add.

Justinian's own contribution to the ultimate division of the empire may have been unintended but was large. For all his admiration for the Roman past, he more than any other emperor made Byzantium the seat of a distinctive political culture. His reign left an indelible print on the regime, ending (at least for his reign) domestic threats to an autocracy which showed itself more and more nakedly. One of its positive aspects was an attack on the huge confusion and complication of Roman law, some of which went back to the early republic. The resulting consolidation of jurisprudence took five years, but was to be used for centuries. At first sight a conservative step, it was actually setting a new course. Immediately effective in the east, in the eleventh century the Roman Law of Justinian was to begin to be accepted as the basis for good jurisprudence in western Europe too. It was powerfully biased towards seeing law as something made by rulers rather than (as in Germanic tradition) handed down in custom. This would appeal to many later princes, though not always to their subjects.

Other decisions weakened old continuities. When Italy was reconquered, Justinian chose to leave its imperial capital at Ravenna. He abolished the Academy of Athens, which had survived from the days of its founder, Plato. He was determined to be a Christian emperor – or, at least, to rule over an empire seen to be Christian – and took away many of the special freedoms enjoyed by Jews, interfering with their calendar and worship and encouraging barbarian kings to persecute them. Long before the cities of western Europe, Constantinople had its ghetto. The old Hellenistic-Roman tradition of religious tolerance was abandoned towards certain Christians, too. Justinian wholeheartedly backed up the Orthodox clergy who had defined and denounced certain doctrines as heresy.

His religious policies in fact promoted the division of Christendom. Justinian could not bring together the Latin Catholics (who more and more looked to the pope of Rome for leadership) and the Greek Orthodox, much as he wanted to do so. The different cultural matrices in which each had been formed always generated a potential for divergence between them. This was an ideological hindrance to imperial reintegration. The western Church would not accept the religious supremacy which he claimed for the imperial office, and demonstrated in enforcement of doctrine, a more important point than might appear at first sight. The arguments about theology which Justinian entered upon with such gusto do not now seem very interesting but there was more to them than an emperor's hobby. The western Church was always to assert that whatever duty might be owed by men to their earthly rulers, only the Church could tell them what their final duty was, for it was owed to God. Church and state in the west would, therefore, have to live together side by side, sometimes amicably, sometimes quarrelling, sometimes one being dominant in practical or political terms, sometimes the other. From this tension would grow liberty. The eastern churches, on the other hand, held that both spiritual and earthly power belonged to the emperor himself. He had the last word in everything, for he was God's viceroy on earth. This was a view of government which was eventually to pass into the autocracy of the Russian tsars ('autocrat' was one Greek title for emperor).

From Justinian's time, the movement towards autocracy was never to be reversed, whatever concessions and weaknesses appeared in practice. Yet his attempts to use his power in administrative and organizational reforms were rarely successful. Given the expense and responsibilities of the empire, it is true that permanent remedies would have been hard to find. One institutional response was a tendency to regiment its citizens. In a tradition of economic regulation which Justinian had inherited, just as peasants were tied to the soil, craftsmen were attached to their hereditary corporations and guilds; even the bureaucracy tended to become hereditary. The resulting rigidity was unlikely to make imperial problems easier to solve. It was coincidentally unfortunate, too, that an exceptionally disastrous series of natural calamities fell on the east at the beginning of the sixth century. Earthquake, famine, plague devastated even the capital itself. The ancient world was a credulous place, but tales of the emperor's capacity to take off his head and then put it on again, or to disappear from sight at will, already suggest that under these strains the mental world of the eastern empire was slipping its moorings in classical civilization.

Justinian's taste for theological disputation also reflected cultural change. But the assertion of what he saw as orthodoxy was unlikely to renew the loyalty to the empire of the Nestorians and Monophysites, heretics who had refused to accept the definitions of the precise relationship of God the Father to God the Son laid down in 451 at a council in Chalcedon. The theology of such deviants mattered less than the fact that they were increasingly identified with linguistic and cultural groups. The empire began to create aggrieved communities – its own Ulsters, as it were. Harrying heretics intensified separatist feeling in parts of Egypt (where the Coptic Church went its own way in opposition to Orthodoxy in the later fifth century) and Syria (where the Monophysites set up a 'Jacobite' church). Both were encouraged and sustained by a numerous and enthusiastic clergy, many of them monks. Some sects and communities, too, had important connexions outside the empire, so that foreign relations were involved. The Nestorians found refuge in Persia. Though they were not heretics, the Jews were influential beyond the frontiers; in Iraq they supported the Persian attacks on the empire and Jewish Arab states in the Red Sea interfered with the empire's trade-routes to India when Jews were persecuted by it.

Justinian's major achievement was neither the religious unity he sought (and never achieved) nor the re-establishment of imperial unity (which he temporarily achieved) but quite a different one, the easing of the path towards the development of a new civilization. After him, Byzantine civilization was really distinct from Roman, even if that was not yet recognized. Its special Christian role and style crystallised under Justinian. The state became a part of the machinery for the salvation of mankind, a task reflected in all it did, and one with a huge propaganda and public relations dimension. It is often impossible to decide whether worldly or otherworldly considerations had priority in imperial policy. Justinian used Christianity and churchmen as a branch of diplomacy, and sent missionaries to convert barbarian princes. The riches and wealth of Constantinople helped to impress the neighbours. His greatest physical monument is still the basilica he built there, the Church of the Holy Wisdom, St Sophia (though its huge dome collapsed once during his reign). For centuries it was the greatest building of Christendom, in which the splendours of the imperial entourage at worship were paraded among silk and gold hangings and a blaze of mosaics and marbles unrivalled anywhere else.

The burdens of empire

Eastern empire inherited from antiquity great territorial responsibilities and unsolved strategic problems. Many had arisen in the long competition with Sassanid Persia, a contest of the two world powers which was an enduring fact of ancient history (which some traced back to the Persian Wars of ancient Greece). Justinian had died in 565 after two great wars which produced no decision. Others followed under his successors. The end came only with the seventh century when a new soldier emperor came to the rescue. In 610 Heraclius, by descent Armenian, succeeded to the purple as the result of an insurrection.

At the moment of his succession, the eastern empire looked sadly stricken. The Italian reconquests of Justinian's reign were gone; peoples from the Volga region, Slavs and Avars, had poured into the Balkans and raided the suburbs of Constantinople itself. But worse was still to come. Almost at once Persian armies invaded Armenia, Cappadocia and Syria, ravaging their cities. They sacked Jerusalem in 615, bearing away its most famous treasure, the alleged relic of the True Cross discovered over two centuries before (legendarily by the only British empress, Helena, mother of the great Constantine). Jews often welcomed the Persians, whose arrival gave them the chance to carry out pogroms of Christians no doubt all the more delectable because the boot had for so long been on the other foot. The next year Persian armies went on to invade Egypt; a year later still, their advance-guards were only a mile from Constantinople. Putting to sea, they even raided Cyprus and seized Rhodes from the empire. The empire of Darius seemed about to be restored just as Byzantium was losing its last possessions to the Visigoths in Spain at the other end of the Mediterranean.

In 626, Heraclius turned the tide. His fleet prevented the Persian army from coming to the support of their Avar allies in an attack on Constantinople. In the following year Heraclius broke into Assyria and Mesopotamia, the old and much disputed heartland of Near Eastern strategy. The Persian army mutinied, Chosroes was murdered and his successor made peace. The great days of Sassanid power were over. The relic of the True Cross came back to Jerusalem. The long duel was, it seemed, at an end.

So, indeed it was, but the focus of world history in the west was to shift to another conflict. The empire's strategic problems had not disappeared. Its lands stretched still along the North African coasts, Egypt, the Levant, Syria, Asia Minor, the far coast of the Black Sea beyond Trebizond, the Crimean shores, and those running from Byzantium itself north to the mouths of the Danube. In Europe there were Thessaly, Macedonia and Dalmatia, a belt of territory across central Italy, and some enclaves in the toe and heel of the peninsula. Finally, there were the islands of Sicily, Corsica and Sardinia. This was a strategist's nightmare, given the empire's potential enemies, and the location of its manpower. When Heraclius died, in 641, it was already clear that he had won only a respite. The story of the next two centuries was to be of the return again and again of waves of invaders.

Changing religious destinies: monasticism

The spiritual life is a universal phenomenon. Nonetheless, its expression in institutions particularizes its forms and expressions. In the early Christian world monasticism was such an institution, vitalizing but also helping to differentiate religious culture east and west. The story begins in about AD 285, when St Antony, a Copt, retired to the Egyptian desert. His act inspired imitation: within a few decades, thousands had followed his example, some of them coming together in communities seeking mutual support in worship, prayer, fasting, meditation, a few to seek more dubious goals. St Antony himself came out of his solitude to lead a group of hermits living under a common rule.

From the Near East, the monastic idea spread to Mediterranean Gaul and the west. There, in the confusion of the fifth century, the ideal of undistracted service to God was especially attractive to many men and women of intellect and character, and there it was to show most clearly its formative power in shaping a civilization. The aspirations of the new religious, male and female, were not always sympathetically understood. People with old-fashioned views, hankering after the old Roman ideal of service to the state, condemned them: they saw them as shirkers, turning their backs on their proper responsibilities to society. Churchmen, too, did not always welcome what they saw as desertion by some of the most zealous among their flocks. Yet many who were to rank among the greatest churchmen of the age became monks. Their communities attracted support and endorsements by landowners (though there were some scandals in grappling with powerful and assertive patrons).

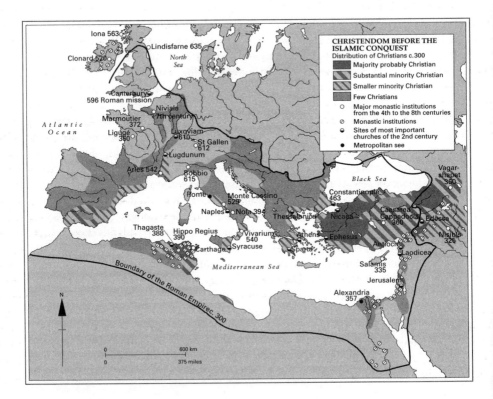

One Italian monk, of whom we know little except his achievement and that he was believed to work miracles, was disturbed and shocked by life at Rome in his youth. In about AD 500 he retired from the world to become a hermit in a cave to the south of the old capital. He was later canonized as St Benedict, and seems never to have been ordained. In 529 he set up a monastery at Monte Cassino in southern Italy, after compiling a new rule for it. The Benedictine Rule was to be a seminal document of western Christianity and western civilization. It directed the attention of the monk to the community, whose abbot was to have complete authority over it. The community's purpose was not to provide solitude for the cultivation or the salvation of individual souls but to worship and live as a group, each individual contributing to its task in an ordered routine of worship, prayer and labour. From the traditional individualism of monasticism St Benedict thus forged a new human instrument and a new ecclesiastical institution. His monks did not seek to mutilate body or spirit. He did not set his sights too high and the Rule could be obeyed by men who loved God. Its success in meeting a need was soon shown by the speed with which Benedictine monasteries appeared all over the west. They became the key sources of missionaries and teaching for the conversion of much of the pagan west. The Celtic Church, founded in Britain by missionaries in the second and third centuries and cut off on the fringe of Europe, clung to the older, eremitical model of the monkish life, but it, too, was in the end to feel the renovating impulse of the Benedictines. They were not only a force in the making of the Latin Church but in the shaping of an as yet inchoate Europe.

Bishops and popes

To realize the possibilities of the new monasticism and to use it effectively there had to be men – and only men could become priests and bishops, even if women became nuns and anchorites – to recognize the opportunity it offered. For a long time, though, ecclesiastics in the west tended not to look to the future, but to identify themselves with what was collapsing; the end of the empire was for many of them the collapse of the world, of their civilization. Almost everywhere in the western empire the Church and her leaders were the only surviving representatives of *romanitas*. People looked to them with superstitious awe. They were often believed to have near-magical power. The bishops were also often men experienced in administration, lettered in an illiterate world, and sometimes drawn from aristocratic families, rich in property. In many places they were the last embodiments of authority. They had to rise to the task before them. Decisively for the future, many did.

For a long time, all western bishops could be called *papa*, a Latin word for 'father', the title today borne by only one of them, the pope of Rome[1]. His diocese was uniquely prestigious, as that of St Peter himself and the guardian of his bones, the place of not only his martyrdom, but of that of St Paul. It was of huge importance in an age when the western Church had much less to connect it directly with the Apostolic age than the churches of Asia. Nonetheless, more is required to explain the Roman papacy's rise to the splendid pre-eminence which it later achieved. It always helped that the bishops of Rome had been the business colleagues of Senate and emperor; the departure of the

---

[1] In 1073, under Pope Gregory VII, the use of the title by any other bishop than that of Rome was prohibited.

imperial court only left their eminence in the city and Italy more obvious. Unpopular and alien civil servants from the eastern, and Greek, empire also helped to turn attention to the papacy as a native, local institution. Rome was, too, a wealthy see at an early date, with an apparatus of government and administrative expertize superior to anything to be found outside the imperial administration itself; no barbarians could compete with it on that ground. It kept better records than others; already in the fifth century papal apologists were exploiting them. The characteristically conservative papal stance, the argument that no new departures are being made but that old positions are being defended, was already in evidence and was wholly sincere; popes did not see themselves as conquerors of new ideological and legal ground; but as men desperately trying to keep the small foothold the Church had so far won.

Already in the fifth century, as the turmoil of the barbarian incursions mounted, the new importance of the Roman papacy could be seen under Leo the Great, whose pontificate began in 440. He vigorously asserted the doctrine that the popes spoke in the name of St Peter and obtained from the emperor a declaration that his decisions had the force of imperial law in the western empire. Leo assumed the title *pontifex maximus* once held by the emperors. It was believed that his personal initiative in going to see Attila, the Hun leader, had staved off Hun attack on Italy. Western bishops who had hitherto resisted claims for Rome's primacy became more willing to accept them in a world turned upside-down by barbarians. For all that, though, Rome under Leo was still part of the state church of the empire, and so it continued to be after 476 (when direct access to imperial authority was made harder by the removal of the seat of imperial authority to Ravenna).

The pope in whom the future papacy is at last clearly revealed was Gregory the Great, who reigned from 590 to 604. He has been called the first medieval pope. He was also the first to have been a monk. A statesman of insight and a Roman aristocrat, loyal to the empire and respectful of the emperor, he nevertheless fully accepted the barbarian context of his reign and the reality of the break with both the classical world and the practical consequence of the ebbing of imperial power. Gregory saw as a part of his duty the launching of the first great missionary venture since the days of St Paul. One target was pagan England, to which he sent Augustine, the first archbishop of Canterbury, in 596. He struggled against the Arian heresy of the barbarian peoples and rejoiced in the conversion of the Visigoths to Catholicism. He was as much concerned with the barbarian kings as with the emperor in whose name he claimed to act, but was also the doughtiest opponent of the Lombards who were the dominant military power in Italy after 568 and the end of the devastating Gothic wars. For help against them he appealed to Constantinople, but also, and much more significantly, to another Germanic people, the Franks. The Lombard invasions necessarily tended to an increase in the political power of the papacy. Not only did they cut Rome off from the imperial 'exarch' at Ravenna but brought new practical problems. Like other bishops in the west who inherited civilian authority, Gregory had to feed his flock and govern it. Slowly, more Italians came to see the pope as successor to imperial Rome as well as to St Peter.

The western Church and the barbarians

Over and above his ability and drive, Gregory was exceptional in another way: he represented something new, even if he could hardly have seen it like that. Christianity had been a part of the classical heritage, from much of which it was now turning away and was becoming more distinct. Significantly, Gregory did not speak Greek; nor did he feel he needed to. There had already begun a transformation in the relations of the western Church with the barbarians. With Gregory, the focus of its story begins to be mainland Europe, not the Mediterranean basin. There were already sown in it the seeds of the future, though not of the near future; for most of the world's people the existence of Europe for the next 1,000 years or so is almost irrelevant. But a Europe of sorts is at last beginning to be discernible, unimaginably different though it was from what was to come. Western barbarian peoples were turning away from their past. The ordered, literate, unhurried life of the Roman provinces had given way to a fragmented society with, encamped in it and living parasitically upon it, a warrior aristocracy and their tribesmen, sometimes integrated with the earlier inhabitants, sometimes not. But changes begin to be observable. Barbarian chiefs called themselves kings and were certainly no longer merely chiefs. In 550 one of them – a Goth – for the first time represented himself on his coins decked in the imperial insignia. Through the impression wrought on their imaginations by the relics of a higher culture, through the efficacy of the idea of Rome itself and through the conscious and unconscious work of the Church, these peoples were on their way to civilization.

If their art had begun to show it, they had brought nothing of high culture with them to compare with what classical antiquity had to offer. Yet the cultural traffic was not all in one direction. The extent to which Christianity, or at least the Church, was still plastic must not be underestimated. The 'christening' of Europe can be exaggerated or thought speedier than it was in reality. Shame and honour, rather than the Ten Commandments, long provided the basic moral concepts of its rulers. Everywhere Christianity had to flow in the channels available to it and they were defined by layers of paganism, Germanic upon Roman upon Celtic. In England, pagan names were used long after Gregory had reconnected the country to Rome. Pagan festivals (midwinter and midsummer days) continued under new names. At least one English king prudently raised altars both to pagan gods and to Christ. The conversion of a king did not mean that his people at once adhered even formally to Christianity; some would still be pagan generations later, as their graves show. But their conservatism presented opportunities as well as obstacles. The Church could utilize the belief in folk magic, or the presence of a holy site which could associate a saint's memory with respect for age-old deities of countryside and forest. Miracles, knowledge of which was assiduously propagated in the saints' lives read aloud to pilgrims at their shrines, were persuasive arguments; men were used to the magical interventions of the old Celtic deities or manifestations of Woden's power. Pagan ritual and spells could be given a Christian cosmetic or twist, as appears to have been the case in the judicial process of ordeal. For most men then, as for most of human history and for recent antiquity, the role of religion in daily life was not the provision of moral guidance or spiritual insight, but the propitiation of the unseen. Only over blood-sacrifice did Christianity unambiguously draw the line between itself and the pagan past; other pagan practice and reminiscence it christened when it could.

It is very easy with hindsight to over-emphasize the extent to which a future even more creative than the classical world was inevitably in the making. The temptation must be resisted. So much might still have gone quite otherwise. Without other challenges which forced them, for example, Justinian's successors might have hung on to the recovered western provinces. Economically, too, the story must be for a long time judged to be touch and go: the precariousness of economic life in Dark Age Europe made it a much poorer place than the Italy of the Antonines. But some irreversible steps had been taken in the Europe west of the Elbe by the seventh century, as perhaps the thinking of Gregory indicates, though in comparison with Byzantium or non-Christian empires it was to be for centuries after the Roman collapse an almost insignificant backwater. Its better-informed inhabitants felt themselves a beleaguered remnant and for a time so they were. They were increasingly cut off from Africa, and their coasts, north and south, were long tormented by raiders and freebooters. To the east lay the pagan lands from which there continued to emerge, sporadically, fresh barbarian hordes. The elements of Europe would be formed in a world western Christians often saw for the most part as hostile. Only the empire ruled from Constantinople might be expected to regard the Christian west benevolently. But it, too came not to do so.

Drifting apart

In 663, Constans II visited Rome, the last eastern emperor to do so until the fifteenth century. The last pope to go to Constantinople (and, coincidentally, the only one who ever bore the name Constantine) did so in 710. Paradoxically, by then already religion had come to be not a uniting but very obviously a divisive force between what was still called the Roman empire and the lands it claimed to rule in the west. In the 900 years of life the empire endured after Justinian this had great distinctive influence as time and circumstance in other ways shaped an eastern civilization and a sister for it in the western part of Christendom.

Scholars have come to call that civilization 'Byzantine'; it is often referred to summarily, like the empire, as 'Byzantium'. There is no clear line to be drawn between it and antiquity, nor between its cultural content and its institutional forms. The imperial office itself showed how smoothly evolution could respect conservatism. Until 800 there was no explicit alternative to the theory that the emperor was the secular ruler of all Christendom although the empire's centre of gravity had long been shifting eastward. When a Frankish king was hailed as an 'emperor' in Rome that year, the uniqueness of the imperial purple of Byzantium was at last challenged, whatever might be thought and said there about the exact status of the new regime. Yet Byzantium continued to cherish the fantasy of universal empire; there would be emperors right to the end. Still theoretically chosen by senate, army and people, they had none the less (and, in some cases, equally theoretically) an absolute authority. While the realities of accession might determine for any particular emperor the actual extent of his power – and sometimes the dynastic succession broke under the strains – he was *autocrat* as a western emperor never was. Respect for legal principle and the vested interests of bureaucracy might muffle the emperor's will in action, but it was always supreme in theory. The heads of the great departments of state were responsible to no one but him. This authority explains the intensity with which Byzantine politics focused at the imperial court, for it was there, and not through corporate and representative institutions such as those slowly evolved in the west, that authority had to be influenced.

Autocracy had its harsh side. *Curiosi* or secret police informers swarmed through the empire. But the nature of the imperial office also laid obligations on the emperor. Crowned by the patriarch of Constantinople, he had the enormous responsibilities, as well as the enormous authority, of God's representative upon earth. The line between lay and ecclesiastical power was always blurred in the east, though in the Byzantine scheme of things there was a continuing pressure upon God's vice-regent to act appropriately, to show *philanthropia*, a love of mankind and of the conduits by which it drew the water of life – orthodoxy and the Church.

Other traditions than the Christian shaped the office, too. Just as pagan emperors had been deified, most of the early Christian emperors were canonized. Byzantine emperors received the ritual prostrations of oriental tradition and the images of them which look down from their mosaics show their heads surrounded by the nimbus in which the last pre-Christian emperors had been depicted, for it was part of the cult of the sun god (some representations of Sassanid rulers have it, too). It was, none the less, above all as a Christian ruler that the emperor justified his authority.

At many other levels the ecclesiastical peculiarities of what came to be called the Orthodox Church marked east off from west. The coalescence of spiritual and lay was important at many levels below the throne. One symbol of it was the retention of a married clergy; the Orthodox priest, for all his presumed holiness, was never to be quite the man set apart whom his western and Catholic colleague later became. Monasticism, too, remained closer to its original forms in the east and the importance of the Holy Man has always been greater there than in the more hierarchically aware Roman Church. Above all, no sacerdotal authority as concentrated as that of the papacy could emerge in the eastern empire. The focus of all authority was the emperor, whose office and responsibility towered above the equally ranked bishops, many of whom came from different national traditions within Orthodoxy. Of course, so far as social regulation went, local variety did not mean that Orthodoxy was more tolerant than the Church of the medieval west. Bad times were always liable to be interpreted as evidence that the emperor had not been doing his Christian duty – which included the harrying of such familiar scapegoats as Jews, heretics and homosexuals.

At another level, distinction from the west was slowly emerging through history. There had been a gradual evaporation of professional contact within the imperial bureaucracy after the division of government east and west, as well as a distinction of style in the way power was used. The Catholic and Orthodox traditions had been on divergent courses from early times, when Latin Christians already felt somewhat estranged by the concessions the Greeks had to make to Syrian and Egyptian practice. Yet such concessions had also kept alive within Christendom a certain polycentrism. Jerusalem, Antioch and Alexandria were the three great patriarchates of the east, other than Constantinople. When, in the seventh century, they fell into non-Christian hands, the polarization of Rome and Constantinople was accentuated and the African tradition came to influence Catholicism more and more. Gradually, too, the Christian world was ceasing to be bilingual; Latin had never been a *lingua franca* in the eastern provinces, and in due time a culturally almost wholly Latin west came to face a culturally Greek east. At the beginning of the seventh century Latin ceased to be the official language of the army and of justice, the two departments of the imperial government where it had held out longest against Greek. That the bureaucracy was Greek-speaking was to be very important and was to have very long-term repercussions for the future of Europe indeed. Although the eastern Church failed to extend its influence in the Levant and Egypt, it was to open a new missionary field among the pagans to the north; when that happened, south-eastern Europe and eventually Russia would owe their evangelizing and their literacy to Constantinople, and that meant – among many other things – that the Slav peoples would take from their teachers a written language based on Greek, and with it much else.

Doctrinal division

The Greeks seem always to have been more disputatious than the Latins; the Hellenistic setting of many of the early Churches favoured speculation, and the eastern churches were always susceptible to traditional influences and even oriental trends. This favoured disagreement and encouraged attempts to impose dogmatic solutions on religious quarrels – which further inflamed dispute. Inevitably, our own secular age finds even the greatest of such quarrels difficult to fathom. We lack a sense of the mental world lying behind them. The issues which divided Aphthartodocetists, Corrupticolists and Theopaschitists (to name a few contesting schools) now seem almost meaningless. It requires an effort to recall that behind the exquisite logic-chopping lay a concern of appalling importance to contemporaries of this quarrel, nothing less than that mankind should be saved from damnation. A further obstacle to understanding arises for a very different reason: theological differences in eastern Christianity often provided symbols and debating forms for questions about politics and society, about the relationship of national and cultural groups to authority. Nonetheless, perhaps this is a little easier to come to terms with; hair-splitting about the secular theology of Marxist-Leninism often provided in this century a language to debate (and sometimes conceal) more practical and actual differences between communists.

Theological and doctrinal difference could affect world history in late antiquity as powerfully as the movements of armies or even peoples. In the slow divergence of the two main Christian traditions it was of enormous importance; divergence may not have originated in theological division, but theological dispute came to help to propel two traditions yet further apart. They created circumstances which make it more and more difficult to decide how or if events might have turned out otherwise. One outstanding example is the debate on Monophysitism. It divided Christians from about the middle of the fifth century, and its significance now seems at first sight puzzling. It originated in an assertion about Christ's nature. Monophysites believed that while on earth, Christ's nature was single and wholly divine, instead of dual (that is, simultaneously both divine and human), as had generally been taught in the early Church. The delicious subtleties of the long debates which accompanied this view can be set aside here. There was an important non-theological setting for the uproar, though. One element in it was the slow crystallization of three Monophysite churches separated from eastern Orthodoxy and Roman Catholicism. The Coptic Church of Egypt and Ethiopia, and the Syrian Jacobite and Armenian churches became, in a way, national churches, embodying and expressing the cultures of particular communities. In trying to reconcile such groups and consolidate the unity of the empire in the face of external threat in the sixth and seventh centuries, the emperors were drawn into the dispute; there was more to it, that is to say, than the personal taste of a Justinian or even the special responsibility of the imperial office first revealed by Constantine's presiding at the Council of Nicaea.

The emperor Heraclius did his best to produce a compromise formula and to reconcile the disputants over Monophysitism. It took the form of a new theological definition soon called Monothelitism. For a short time, agreement on it seemed likely, but in the end it pushed east and west still further apart. Both pope and emperor had been anxious to show a common front when Heraclius had asked the view of Honorius, the successor of Gregory the Great, about the doctrine in the hope of quietening the theological misgivings of the patriarch of Jerusalem. But when Honorius incautiously supported the emperor the anti-Monophysites were so enraged that almost half a century later Honorius achieved the *post mortem* distinction (unusual among popes) of being condemned by an ecumenical council at which even the western representatives joined in the decision. At a crucial moment, though, the sympathies of many eastern churchmen had been alienated still further from the western Church, though formal theological reconciliation again followed in 681.

Byzantium and nearer Asia

The debts of the Byzantine inheritance to Asia were not only a matter of the direct contacts with alien civilizations symbolized by the arrival of Chinese merchandise along the Silk Road, but also of the complexity of the cultural inheritance of the Hellenistic east. Byzantium preserved the prejudice which confused the idea of 'barbarians' with that of peoples who did not speak Greek, and many of its intellectual leaders felt they stood in the tradition of Hellas. Yet the Hellas of which they spoke was one from which the world had long been cut off except through the channels of the Hellenistic east. When we look at that area it is hard to be sure how deep Greek roots went there and how much nourishment they owed to Asiatic sources. The Greek language, for example, seems in Asia Minor to have been used mainly by city-dwellers and to have been little spoken in the countryside. The names of members of the imperial bureaucracy and those of leading families are increasingly drawn from Asia as the centuries go by. Asia was also bound to count for more after losses of territory in the fifth and sixth centuries, which pinned the empire increasingly into a shallow hinterland behind the capital in mainland Europe. Soon, it came to be hemmed in also in Asia Minor, bounded in the north by the Caucasus and in the south by the Taurus. Those who lived on the always permeable border lived in a sort of marcher world between cultures.

This, though, could not but be relevant to Byzantium's role as a great power, a term in many ways anachronistic, and one to be used only figuratively. Yet at the beginning of the seventh century Byzantium's rulers could (because of their historic claims and the inextricable connexion of their state with Christian civilization) have properly claimed, had they wished, that no major decision affecting the destinies of Christian peoples could or should be made without their participation and acquiescence. Such a claim was implicit in the complicated inheritance of an autocratic tradition, in the Roman myth, and in the guardianship of eastern Christianity. At the outset, the empire had huge assets to underpin its power in an ideological and practical unity of government, an accumulation of diplomatic and bureaucratic skills, a great military tradition and enormous prestige. If its commitments could be reduced somewhat, the potential tax and manpower resources should be more than adequate to its essential tasks. Asia Minor was a recruiting ground which relieved the eastern empire of the need to rely upon Germanic barbarians such as were enlisted by the Romans of the west. The imperial armed forces had a notable war-making technology; both the 'Greek fire' which was the secret weapon it used powerfully against ships which might attack the capital, and the huge fortresses as far away as the Euphrates were evidence of it. The situation of Constantinople, too, was a military asset. Its great walls, built in the fifth century, made it hard to attack by land without heavy weapons unlikely to be available to barbarians; at sea the fleet could prevent a landing.

It is a pity that we do not know more about the seventh and eighth centuries (some say that no adequate history of the empire in this disturbed period can be written, so poor are the sources and so skimpy the present state of archaeological knowledge) but one long-run weakening tendency has to be discerned in changes in the empire's social basis. It was always difficult to preserve the smallholding peasantry from the powerful provincial landlords always encroaching on their properties. The law courts would not always protect the small man from them, under economic pressure from inflation as he was, nor from the steady expansion of church estates. But the dimensions of this threat were only to be revealed over centuries. Short-term prospects gave the emperors of the seventh and eighth centuries quite enough to think about. Their story was one of recurrent invasion and continual warfare on many and over-extended fronts. In Europe this brought fighting at times up to the very walls of Constantinople; in Asia it meant wearisome campaigning to dispute the marches of Asia Minor and the desert frontiers of Syria. Persians, Avars, Arabs, Bulgars and Slavs were all to despoil the empire, and in the end the west, too, would prove a menace. The eastern empire's centuries of absorbing punishment which might otherwise have fallen on the west would not save her from Christian predators, too.

Even at its height, then, the appearance of Byzantine power was somewhat misleading. At the beginning of the seventh century, much depended on the factors represented by the slippery word 'prestige'; it was a matter of a penumbra of influences, diplomacy, Christianity and military repute. Its relations to its neighbours might therefore be seen in more than one way; what looks to a later eye like blackmail paid to menacing barbarians by every emperor from Justinian to Basil II could be presented in the Roman tradition of bounty to subject allies and *foederati*. The empire's cosmopolitanism was not necessarily a strength; though masked by official ideology, her peoples' Hellenization was often superficial. Moreover, Byzantium numbered among her allies no great power. In the troubled seventh and eighth centuries her most important friend was the Khanate of Khazaria, a huge and loose agglomeration of nomad tribes which by 600 dominated the other peoples of the Don and Volga valleys and bestrode the Caucasus, the strategic land bridge, barring it to Persians and Arabs for two centuries. At its widest, a Khazar supremacy ran round the Black Sea coast to the Dniester and northwards to include the Upper Volga and Don. Byzantium made great efforts to keep the Khazars' goodwill and seems to have tried without success to convert them to Christianity. What exactly happened is a mystery, but the Khazar leaders, while tolerating Christianity and several other cults, appear to have been converted to Judaism in about 740, possibly as a result of Jewish immigration from Persia after the collapse of the Sassanid empire and perhaps as a conscious diplomatic choice.

The provinces suffered most in the struggle to maintain the empire's great power role. The Persians did appalling damage in the Levant and Asia Minor before their expulsion from Byzantine territory. They have been believed by some scholars to be the real destroyers of the Hellenistic world of great cities; the archaeology is mysterious still, but after Heraclius' victory there are signs that places once great lay in ruins, and that many others reduced to little more than the acropolis which was their core. Population appears to have fallen sharply. It was on this badly shaken structure that there fell a new enemy so ferocious that before Heraclius died virtually all his military successes had been overturned. This was more than a swing of the pendulum. A new fact of world-historical importance had appeared which posed to both eastern and western Christendom a quite new challenge and was in the end to help redefine both of them. This was Islam.

Islam

Immediately, Islam was seen by the eastern empire as a military threat replacing Persia when Persia itself was conquered by Arab armies. But Islam was more than a new fact in great power competition. It was to prove Christianity's only rival as a world religion in its psychological power to animate men, in the vigour and range of its geographical spread, and as a carrier of cultural values.

Islam came from Arabia, a huge region which was in the seventh century for the most part desert, as it still is. It had not always been so. In the early Christian era there had been irrigated land there, the basis of little kingdoms which traded by sea with India, the Persian Gulf and East Africa, prospering by carrying gums and spices up to Egypt, from which they could make their way into the Mediterranean cities and Europe. The great empires, Roman and Persian, had never deeply penetrated the peninsula. But the irrigation system collapsed – we do not know why – the land became desert, migrant tribes moved north from the south Arabian cities and the peoples of the interior reverted to the nomadic, pastoral ways of a more primitive life.

The deepest roots of Islam are the same as those of Christianity, the tribal cultures of the Semitic peoples of the Near East. Like Judaism and Christianity, Islam proclaims that there is only one God. Moslems believe that this is the same God worshipped by Jews and Christians, though they worship him differently. The founder of Islam, the Prophet Muhammad, was born in Arabia at Mecca in about 570, of poor parents who belonged to a minor clan of an important Bedouin tribe. He was soon an orphan. How he grew up, we do not know, but it was at Mecca, an oasis and centre of pilgrimage. It was a place of some resort; Arabs came to it from far away to venerate a black meteoric stone, the Ka'aba, a focus of their pagan religion. Apart from a few who were Jewish or Christian, most Arabs were then polytheists, believing in nature gods, demons and spirits. But oases like Mecca, to which caravans came, and the little ports which were still in touch with the outside world also attracted outsiders and foreigners; some of them had by Muhammad's day brought knowledge of higher religions to Arabia. Some Arabs already revered the god known to them as Allah, and worshipped by Christians and Jews.

Muhammad was struck by signs that something was going wrong among his people. It seems that commerce, population growth and foreign influence had begun to undermine their traditional and tribal arrangements. The old pastoral Arab societies had been organized around blood-ties; nobility, lineage and age were respected by them, not money. Wealth, indeed, did not always go along with noble blood and long years. Here was a social and moral problem. Muhammad began to reflect upon the ways of God to man. One day, as he contemplated in a cave outside Mecca, he heard a voice telling him to set down his vision of the word of God. For the next twenty-two years he spoke prophetically. What his followers wrote down as he did so was put together after his death and became one of the great books of world history, the Koran.

It laid out principles and practices which now unite a brotherhood of believers world-wide. The word 'Islam' means submission, or surrender, and Muhammad saw himself as the mouthpiece through which God made known his will to men. Moslems were to believe that this had in a measure already happened; Muhammad taught that the great prophets of Israel (and Jesus, too) had been true prophets, but he came to feel sure that he was himself the final Prophet, through whom God spoke his last message to mankind. That message set out a belief and a code of behaviour to meet the needs of Muhammad's fellow-Arabs, but it was to prove acceptable to others, too. Its essence was the assertion that no God was to be worshipped but Allah (Islam was uncompromisingly monotheis-tic and one objection Moslems had to Christianity was that they saw it as polytheistic, because it gave the same status to Jesus and the Holy Spirit as to God the Father), and a series of necessary religious observances of which the most important were regular prayer and the avoidance of pollution. This was all that was necessary for salvation.

This was not only a simple but a revolutionary creed. It taught that those who clung to the old gods of Arab society would go to hell – a doctrine likely to provoke opposition until it was established. The emphasis of the supreme importance of a brotherhood among believers was subversive, too, for it cut across blood loyalties. When some of his own kinsmen turned on Muhammad he left Mecca in 622 with about 200 followers and went north to another oasis about 250 miles away; it was to be renamed Medina – 'the city of the Prophet'. There he organized his followers and began to issue regula-tions on practical, daily concerns such as food, drink, marriage, war. On them, Islam was to be built as a distinctive civilization. This migration – the Hegira, as it is called – was the turning-point in the early story of Islam, and has ever since been treated as the beginning of the Moslem calendar still in use all round the world. Breaking with tradi-tional society, Muhammad founded a new sort of community.

He died in 632. Authority to interpret his teaching was inherited by a 'caliph'. The first of those who held this title were all related to the Prophet by blood or marriage. Under them, the tribes of southern Arabia were conquered. Soon fighting spread to the north, to the Arabs of Syria and southern Mesopotamia. Soon, too, the 'patriarchal' caliphs of Muhammad's family were being opposed as exploiters; the caliphate, based on religious and doctrinal authority, seemed in a few years to be degenerating into a sec-ular office. In 661 the last patriarchal caliph was deposed and killed and the office passed to another family, the Umayyad, which held it for nearly a century. By the time they ceded it to other usurpers, though, Islam had remade the map of the Near East and the Mediterranean. Fascinating though it is, the internal political history of Islam can for our purposes now be set aside. What matters here is its expansion and impact, cul-tural as well as military, on the history of Europe.

The Arab conquests

It could hardly have seemed at the outset that Islam's influence would be so great. Like Christianity before it, in its first years the new religion looked pitifully weak in worldly terms. Any sensible outsider at the time of the deaths of Jesus or Muhammad would have thought the prospects of the legacy of either bleak. Whatever the faithful might think, neither sect could then have seemed likely to prosper, let alone become a great force in world history. Yet both did, though in very different ways. The most obvi-ous of these was that Islam was from the start a religion of conquest.

From Medina, Muhammad subdued by force those who had opposed him at Mecca and the tribes nearby; those who submitted were welcomed into the brotherhood of believers which overrode tribal divisions. Yet Islam respected tribalism and the old patriarchal structure in so far as they did not interfere with its own rules. The old dignity of Mecca as a place of pilgrimage was confirmed. Only those who resisted the new faith were driven out of Medina – among them, Arab Jews. Soon after the Prophet's death further military expansion followed. In 633, Arab armies – 'Saracens', as the Byzantines called them – attacked Sassanid and Byzantine territories, startlingly taking on two empires at the same time. It took them five years to take Jerusalem, which remains to this day one of the holy places of Islam, and drive the 'Romans' from Syria. Soon, the Persians lost Mesopotamia to them as well, and Egypt was taken from Byzantium. An Arab Mediterranean fleet was built or commandeered; raids on Cyprus began (the island was later to be divided with the Byzantines) and by 700 Carthage had been seized, the Berbers converted and turned into Arab allies, and the whole coast of North Africa passed into Moslem hands. The Sassanid empire had by then long since collapsed, its last ruler driven out of his capital in 637 to die a few years later after fruitlessly appealing for help to the emperor of China. The Moslems pushed forward as far as Kabul, capital of Afghanistan. At the beginning of the eighth century they invaded India, and established themselves for a while in Sind. At about the same time others crossed the Straits of Gibraltar and pushed into Spain, shattering the old Visigothic kingdom. In 717 they besieged Constantinople for the second time, though unsuccessfully, and had even broken into the Caucasus. This was nearly their military high-watermark. Arab armies won a last great victory over the Chinese high in the Pamirs, in 751, before the Khazars defeated them. A few years before, in 732, exactly a century after Muhammad's death, another Moslem force had been turned back near Poitiers after the deepest penetration they ever made into western Europe. It may have been only a deeply-ranging raid, of which other examples ravaged the west in the next few years. But the tide had turned at last.

One reason for the astonishing record of Arab success was that Byzantium and Sassanid Persia had spent so much time and energy fighting one another and dealing with their other commitments. The Byzantines had Avars and Bulgars to tackle in Europe, the Sassanids too faced invaders from central Asia (of whom the worst were the Huns). It mattered, too, that disaffected Christians irritated by Byzantine government and religious harassment were ready to welcome new masters. Success had been built on success, too: once Persia was out of the way, Byzantium was by the middle of the seventh century the only great power left anywhere west of China to hold off Islam. Nor had the Arabs much to lose; their soldiers were spurred on by the poverty from which they came and the belief that death on the battlefield against the infidel would be followed by entry to paradise. The upshot was a record of conquest which made it look for a time as if Islam might rule the world. That did not happen. No more than Christendom was Islam ever to achieve political unity. The nearest it got to it was under the successive Umayyad and Abassid caliphates. The first ended in 750 when its last head was overthrown by a usurper who prudently rounded off his triumph by a massacre of all the males of the defeated family. This launched the Abassid caliphate under favourable auspices; it soon came to resemble an ordinary dynastic monarchy and as such lasted as a political force until the middle of the tenth century (and, formally, until the thirteenth). Under it Arab civilization reached its greatest heights. Long before then, though the Arab ascendancy had created a non-Arab Islamic world.

An alternative civilization

Cultures often take some of their view of themselves from the suggestions and constraints provided by their neighbours. This was to be true of Europe. By the middle of the eighth century a divided Christendom faced an Islamic civilization which was established in the heart of Spain, dominated the whole North Africa and the Levant as far as the borders of Anatolia and was about to absorb Sicily into a Tunisian empire. And further advances were to follow. This civilization was for centuries the most obvious alternative to Christendom and an anvil on which Christian ideas and attitudes were hammered out.

In early Abassid times, Islamic civilization was still strongly Arab, a fact above all evident in the spread of the Arabic language. The Koran was written in it and through knowledge of that text Arabic was diffused throughout the Islamic world. Indeed, 'Arabic' is a better adjective for Abassid culture and society than 'Arab', for Islam did not take long to shed much of the raw seventh-century style it had brought from the desert. In its early days Arab invaders had tried to keep apart from the peoples they conquered. They left local customs undisturbed – Greek went on being used until the eighth century as the language of government in Damascus – and lived apart as a military caste, supported by taxes levied on the neighbourhood and neither trading or owning land. This separation gave way as conversion to Islam became more frequent. Garrison towns gradually became true cities, and engaged in trade. The Near East began again to be a sphere of cosmopolitan empire; many different traditions could find a place in a culture upheld by the imperial regime ruled from Baghdad, on the Tigris. From a little Christian village, Baghdad became a huge city, rivalling Constantinople, with perhaps 500,000 inhabitants, full of craftsmen and luxuries unknown in the simple lives of the first Arab soldiers of Islam. It was far grander than anything to be found in western Europe. Islamic, Christian, Hellenistic, Jewish, Zoroastrian and even Hindu ideas mingled there, amid traders from many lands who gave Baghdad a prosperity at its height under the legendary Haroun-al-Raschid, supposedly the ruler to whom Scheherazade told her wondrous tales of One Thousand and One Nights. It was potentially a source of immense stimulus to the civilization of Christendom; scholars have seen Abassid culture as the last flowering of Hellenism.

But Islam also long looked threatening; it prompted revulsion as much as envy. This was not merely a matter of theological belief. To Christians and Jews, one of the most striking and abhorrent features of Islam was polygamy (and, indeed some other things in its treatment of women). In principle, though not always in practice, Jewish and Christian women enjoyed more freedom than their Moslem sisters. The most obvious symbol is the veil still worn by women in some Islamic lands. The Koran has, in fact, more to say on the subject of women than on any other social group. Islamic law allowed a man four wives and an unlimited number of concubines who did not share the legal status of the wives. True, the wives were all to be treated equally and each was given a dowry by the husband at the time of marriage which remained her own, arrangements which until very recent times were more favourable to them than was the law in many Christian countries towards Christian wives. On the other hand, a Moslem wife could at any time be divorced by her husband at will, though she might not herself obtain divorce on any grounds at all.

Not just because of such distinctive attitudes, nor only because of local fashions in dress or cuisine, a medieval European traveller would have found Islamic life and culture very different from what he knew at home. For a long time, Islamic painting emphasized calligraphy and intricate design rather than representation, because Islamic teaching forbade the making of likenesses of human forms or faces (only in later Persian and Indian Islamic empires did the miniatures which western eyes now find so appealing appear). In building, too, its architects may have been inspired by a wish to build in a way which would set off the Arab conquerors from the people of the conquered territories. Adopting the Roman invention of the dome, Islam very quickly arrived at a distinctive and attractive style. The first Islamic use of that device was the Dome of the Rock, built at Jerusalem in 691, a shrine sacred to Jew and Moslem alike; Jews believe that on this spot Abraham was ready to sacrifice his son Isaac to God, while Moslems believe that from it the Prophet was miraculously taken up into heaven. Other Islamic domes were soon to follow and today the mosque and its accompanying minaret from which the Faithful are called to prayer are familiar sights in European cities (and all over the world), and not merely in the Islamic lands.

Islam in Europe

Sicily and Spain, unlike other west European countries, were deeply marked by direct Moslem rule and Moslem culture. 652 brought the first Arab expedition to Sicily; just over a half-century later, in 711, a Berber chief, Tariq, crossed the straits between Africa and Spain, to be commemorated in the name of Gibraltar, 'Tariq's mount'. Almost at once there followed the overthrow of the last Visigothic king and the seizure of his capital, Toledo.

Sicily was not a part of Latin Europe when the Arabs arrived. It was still a Byzantine province, Greek in religion, culture, language and government. It was left fairly undisturbed for nearly two centuries after the first Arab incursion before full-scale invasion opened the way to the absorption of the island into the Islamic world. Conquest and settlement proceeded together in the ninth century. In 878, Syracuse, once the greatest city of the western Mediterranean, and the focus of Byzantine power in the island, was stormed and sacked so enthusiastically that it was said that no living creature was left there. But the violence of Moslem conquest (there were only a few last flickers of resistance in the early tenth century) was less important for Sicily's history than the immigration of large numbers of Moslem settlers. They repopulated the countryside, bringing with them lemons and oranges, mulberries and silkworms, cotton and sugar cane, to enrich its agriculture. Sicily was integrated with the prosperous Moslem economy of North Africa, of whose rulers in Tunis it became a political dependency. Christian Sicilians do not seem to have found their government very harsh, and many of them converted to Islam, though others kept to their religion undisturbed when its customs did not infringe Islamic law and social practice. Sicily was once more a prosperous place. Tenth-century Palermo may well have been more populous than any Christian city but Constantinople.

In Spain, meanwhile, Moslem armies had quickly reached the Pyrenees and had driven the rulers of Christian Spain back into the fastnesses of the northern and north-

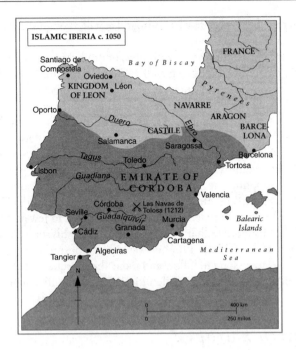

ISLAMIC IBERIA c. 1050

western valleys. In 756, an Umayyad prince who had not accepted the eclipse of his house proclaimed himself *emir*, or governor, of Córdoba (others were soon to imitate him in Morocco and Tunisia). Later, in the tenth century, El-Andalus, as the Arabs called their Spanish lands, acquired its own caliph (until then its rulers remained emirs) though long before that it was politically independent *de facto*. Umayyad Spain was not untroubled. Because Islam had never conquered the whole peninsula there were always Christian kingdoms in northern Iberia willing to help stir the pot of dissidence within Arab Spain, where a fairly tolerant policy towards Christians did not end the danger of revolt. By AD 1000 Christian armies had recovered Catalonia down to the Ebro, and Navarre and Old Castile were back under Christian rule.

Yet El-Andalus prospered. The Umayyads developed their sea-power and contemplated imperial expansion not towards the north, at the further expense of Christendom, but into Africa, at the expense of other Moslem powers, even negotiating for alliance with Byzantium in the process. Ironically, it was only when the caliphate of Córdoba was in decline in the eleventh and twelfth centuries, that Spain's Islamic civilization was to reach its maturity and achieve its greatest beauty in a golden age of creativity which rivalled that of Abbasid Baghdad. It produced great monuments, learned men and philosophers. The 700 mosques of tenth-century Córdoba numbered among them one still arguably the most beautiful building in the world. The learned men and philosophers of Arab Spain were Christendom's guides to the learning and science of the east. For all the bitter struggles over lands and labour resources, Christians and Moslems also passed more material goods to one another in Spain; western Christendom learnt about new agricultural and irrigation techniques and new products, oranges and lemons, sugar. The Arab stamp went very deep, as many students of the later, Christian, Spain have pointed out.

Byzantium's new challengers

The emperors of Heraclius' line included men of ability, but in the seventh century they could do little more than fight doggedly against the Arab tide flowing so strongly against them. After North Africa, Cyprus and Armenia had gone came five years of attacks on Constantinople (673–8); it may have been Greek fire that saved the capital. Before this, in spite of a personal visit to Italy by an emperor, no progress had been made in again recovering Sicily and the Italian territories lost to Arabs and Lombards. Another menace appeared in the last quarter of the century as peoples called Slavs pressed down into Macedonia and Thrace, and others, the Bulgars crossed the Danube.

The century ended with a military revolt which replaced one emperor by another; this suggested that the eastern imperial throne might go the way of the western, becoming the prize of the soldiers. A succession of beastly or incompetent emperors at the beginning of the eighth century let the Bulgars come to the gates of Constantinople and brought about the second siege of the capital by the Arabs in 717. But this, though far from the last appearance of Islam in the Bosphorus, was a true turning-point. There had come to the throne by then one of the most effective Byzantine emperors, the Anatolian Leo III. He had been a provincial official and, after successfully resisting Arab attacks on territory for which he was responsible, he came to the capital to defend it and force the emperor's abdication. His own elevation to the purple followed; it was both popular and warmly welcomed by the clergy. This was the foundation of the Isaurian dynasty, so-called from its place of origin; it was a symptom of the way in which the Greek élites of the eastern Roman empire were gradually transformed into those of Byzantium, the multi-ethnic monarchy. Future emperors were to come not only from Anatolia, but from Syria and the Balkans.

Leo's reign opened a period of recovery, in spite of occasional setbacks. After he cleared Anatolia of the Saracens (as Byzantine Greeks called the Arabs), his son pushed back the frontiers to those of Syria, Mesopotamia and Armenia, where they remained for a time stable. Border raids and skirmishes still went on but marked a relative decline in Arab power. It was true that in the west little recovery could by now be hoped for. Ravenna was lost and only toeholds remained in Italy and, slightly more solidly, in Sicily. But in the east the empire had expanded again from its heartlands in Thrace and Asia Minor and a new chain of 'themes', or administrative districts, was established along the fringe of the Balkan peninsula, too. In the tenth century, Cyprus, Crete and Antioch were all recovered from the caliphate. The struggle for north Syria and the Taurus was kept up and Byzantine forces at one time even crossed the Euphrates. The position in Georgia and Armenia was improved.

Slavs and Bulgars

Yet by then even more formidable problems than hitherto had manifested themselves north of Constantinople. New characters enter the drama of European history. As long before as 2000 BC, there was an ethnic group settled in the eastern Carpathians in which specialists have identified the origins of the peoples now called Slav. Some of them spread slowly east and west for 2,000 years, notably into what is now Russia. In the fifth century AD Slavs also began to move south, into the Balkans. This may reflect pressure from the Avars, an Asiatic people who, after the ebbing of the last Hun invasion of late antiquity formed something of a barrier across the Don, Dnieper and Dniester valleys. Dominating southern Russia and the Ukraine and down to the banks of the Danube, they were courted by Byzantine diplomacy.

Periodically harried by Huns and Avars, Scythians and Goths, the Slavs stuck tenaciously to the lands into which they spread. Their early art shows a willingness to absorb the culture and techniques of others; they learnt from masters whom they outlasted. They also had good fortune: in the seventh century the Khazars in southern Russia and the Bulgars on the lower Danube stood between them and Islam. These strong peoples also helped to channel the slow Slav migration into the Balkans and down to the Aegean. Later it was to run up the Adriatic coast to reach Croatia, Slovenia, Serbia, Moravia and central Europe. By the tenth century Slavs must have been numerically dominant throughout the Balkans.

In this process there emerged the first Slav state, Bulgaria, a paradox, for the Bulgars were not ethnically Slavs. Scholars say they were a Turkic people. Stemming originally from tribes left behind by the Huns, some of them were gradually slavicized by intermarriage and contact with Slavs; these western Bulgars were established on the Danube in the seventh century. They took part with Slav peoples in raids on Byzantium; in 559 they had camped in the suburbs of Constantinople. Like their allies, they were pagans. Byzantium did its best to exploit differences between Bulgar tribes; one of their rulers was baptized, the emperor Heraclius standing godfather. Byzantine help was given to him to drive off the Avars.

Gradually, the Bulgars were diluted by Slav blood and influence. Their distinctive language disappeared. When a Bulgar khanate finally appears at the end of the seventh century, ruling an area roughly equivalent to modern Bulgaria, we can regard it as Slav in language and culture. It is an obscure period of Bulgarian history but an alien body had come into existence in the Balkans on territory long taken for granted as part of the empire, and it was to prove a thorn in the side of Byzantium. Two centuries of struggle with the Bulgars handicapped her attempts at recovery elsewhere. At the beginning of the ninth century they killed an emperor in battle (and made a cup for their king from his skull); it was a long time since an emperor had died campaigning against barbarians.

A turning-point (though hardly for Byzantium) was reached when the Bulgars were converted to Christianity. After a brief period during which, significantly, he dallied with the possibility of playing off Rome against Constantinople, a Bulgarian prince, Boris I, accepted baptism in 865. There was opposition among his people, but from this time Bulgaria was nominally Christian. Whatever diplomatic gain Byzantine statesmen may have looked for (the Roman church had been fishing for Boris' allegiance, too), though, it was far from the end of the Bulgarian problem; conflicts continued. Nonetheless, it is more than a landmark in Bulgarian history; it was a step in another, greater process, the christianizing of the Slav peoples. It was also an indication that this would probably happen from the top downwards, by the conversion of rulers.

No-one knew it, but a great prize, the nature of the future Slav civilization was now to be played for. The game is dominated by two great names. The brothers St Cyril and St Methodius were monks and they are still held in honour in the Orthodox communion. Their missionary work began in Bohemia and Moravia and later was continued in Bulgaria. It must be set in the overall context of Byzantium's ideological diplomacy; Orthodox missionaries cannot neatly be distinguished from diplomatic envoys, and these churchmen would have been hard put to it to recognize a distinction between imperial and Christian service in what they did (Cyril had earlier been on a mission to Khazaria). They achieved much more than the conversion of a dangerous neighbour. In Bohemia they had invented the first Slavic alphabet, Glagolitic, and Cyril's name is commemorated still in the later 'Cyrillic' alphabet which he devised. It was rapidly diffused through the Slav peoples through Church Slavonic, the ancestor of modern Bulgarian. It made possible not only the radiation of Christianity but the crystallization of Slav culture. That culture was potentially open to other influences still, for Byzantium was not the only competitor for Slav allegiance, but in the end eastern Orthodoxy was to be the deepest single influence upon it.

As for the Bulgars, the dangers they presented persisted, perhaps reaching their peak at the beginning of the tenth century. The emperor Basil II, who has gone down in history as *Bulgaroctonos*, the 'slayer of Bulgars', finally destroyed their power at a great battle in 1014 which he followed up by blinding 15,000 of his prisoners and sending them home to encourage their countrymen, led by the fortunate one in a 100 among them whom he left with one eye to lead the rest. The Bulgar ruler is said to have died of shock. Within a few years of that defeat Bulgaria was a Byzantine province, and remained one for over a 150 years, though never successfully assimilated. Shortly afterwards Byzantium made its last conquests when Armenia passed under its rule. With stabilized frontiers on the Danube and the Euphrates, the empire then seemed more solidly established than for centuries.

Religious dispute

The overall story of the empire down to the mid-eleventh century can therefore be read as one of advance and recovery abroad. At home, it was not only one of the great periods of Byzantine culture, but, for the most part (once a period of short reigns and irregular succession was over), it was one of dynastic stability under, first, the Phrygian (820–67) dynasty and then the Macedonian (867–1050). Yet though dangerous waters were successfully navigated, religion remained an almost ever-present source of division and danger and, for one considerable period, deeply damaged imperial authority.

Among the ways in which Orthodoxy came to be very obviously different from Latin and Catholic Christianity was (and still is) the prominent place it gave (and gives) to the display of painted images of the saints, the Blessed Virgin and Jesus Christ himself as objects of veneration by the worshipper and aids to his or her acts of devotion. Icons, as they were called, came to be one of the great devices of Orthodox Christianity for focusing spirituality and teaching. They were already prominent in eastern churches and important in popular devotion by the sixth century. In late antiquity icons had been used widely in the west, too, but to this day they occupy a special place in Orthodox churches where they are displayed in shrines and on special screens to be venerated and contemplated by the believer. More than merely decorative, their arrangement conveys the teachings of the Church and (as one authority has put it) provides 'a point of meeting between heaven and earth', where the faithful amid the icons can feel surrounded by the whole invisible Church, by the departed, the saints and angels, Christ and His mother. It is hardly surprising that something concentrating religious emotion so intensely should have led in paint and mosaic to some of the finest of Byzantine (and, later, Slav) art.

In the eighth century the use of icons came to be questioned (interestingly, just after the caliphate had mounted a campaign against the use of images in Islam, but it cannot be justifiably inferred that the iconoclasts took their ideas from Moslems). Critics of the icons ('iconoclasts' as they were called) denounced them as idols, whose adoration perverted the worship due to God towards the creations of men. They demanded their destruction or expunging and set to work with a will with whitewash, brush and hammer.

Leo III favoured the iconoclasts. Why he did so is still somewhat unclear, but he acted on the advice of the bishops, and Arab onslaughts and coincidental volcanic eruptions were no doubt held to indicate divine disfavour. In 730 an edict forbade the use of images in public worship. A persecution of those who resisted followed but its enforcement was always more marked at Constantinople than in the provinces. The movement reached its peak, persecution becoming fiercest under Constantine V; a council of bishops approved the policy in 754. There were martyrs, particularly among monks, who tended to defend icons more vigorously than did the secular clergy. But the fate of iconoclasm was always in the end dependent on imperial favour or disfavour. It ebbed and flowed in the next century. Under Leo IV and Irene, his widow, persecution was relaxed and the 'iconophiles' recovered ground, though this was followed by renewed persecution. Only in 843, on the first Sunday of Lent, a day still celebrated as a feast of Orthodoxy in the eastern Church, were the icons finally restored.

It is still hard to fathom this undoubtedly important episode. The conversion of Jews and Moslems was said to be made more difficult by Christian respect for images, but that does not take us very far. The dispute certainly cannot be separated from factors external to religion, but the ultimate explanation probably lies in a sense of spiritual precaution, and given the passion often shown in theological controversy in the eastern empire, the debate easily became embittered. It was not, clearly, a matter of artistic merit or aesthetics: Byzantium was not like that. Controversy was driven by the feeling of reformers that the Greeks were falling into idolatry in the extremity of their (relatively recent) devotion to icons. The Arab invasions had been the first rumblings of God's thunder; a pious king, as in the Israel of the Old Testament, could yet save the people from the consequences of sin by breaking the idols. This suited the mentalities of a faith which felt itself at bay. It was notable that iconoclasm was particularly strong in the army. Another suggestive fact is that many icons had represented local saints and holy men; they were replaced by the uniting, simplifying symbols of eucharist and cross, and this says something about a new, monolithic emphasis in Byzantine religion and society observable in other ways from the eighth century onwards. Finally, iconoclasm was also in part an angry response to a tide which had long flowed in favour of the monks who gave prominence to icons in their teaching. As well as a prudent step towards placating an angry God, iconoclasm was a reaction of the centralized authority of emperor and bishops against local pieties, the independence of cities and monasteries, and the cults of holy men.

Iconoclasm had not only offended many in the western Church but showed how far Orthodoxy was now removed from Latin Christianity. The western Church had been moving, too; as its Latin culture established itself among the Germanic peoples converted from Arianism, it drifted further away in spirit from the churches of the Greek east. The iconoclasts had affronted the papacy, which had already condemned Leo's supporters; Rome viewed with alarm the emperor's pretensions to act in spiritual matters. Thus a particular dispute drove deeper divisions already implicit between the two halves of Christendom after cultural differentiation had gone very far. This may seem less surprising if we reflect that it could take two months by sea to go from Byzantium to Italy and that by land Slav peoples soon stood between two Christian zones. Moreover, it was clear by Leo's day that in the west there was only one church as a source of ecclesiastical authority, one doctrinal arbiter, and, increasingly, one focus of ecclesiastical organization, too. The eastern empire had churches, not a universal church. Already in the sixth century the Orthodox churches had denied the universal primacy of the bishop of Rome. When, in 794, a western synod altered the language of the Creed, the eastern churches were outraged by a unilateral decision as well as disputing what it meant.

At another level, too, history was soon to create new division. When the pope crowned a Frankish king 'emperor' in 800 it was a challenge to the Byzantine claim to be the sole legatee of Rome. Distinctions among newly-Christianized, still half-barbarian peoples did not much matter in Constantinople; the Byzantine officials identified as its challenger the Frankish realm. Thereafter all western Europeans were called 'Franks' (a usage which was in the end to spread as far as China). The two empires offended one another's susceptibilities. Again, circumstances often helped. Even the Roman coronation may itself have been in part a response to a woman's assumption of the imperial title at Constantinople; not only was she a woman, but a disreputable one, a mother who had blinded her own son. But the Frankish title was only briefly acknowledged in Byzantium; later emperors in the west were regarded there only as kings. Italy divided the two Christian empires, too, for the lands there still claimed by the eastern empire came to be threatened as much by Franks as they had ever been by Lombards.

Of course the two Christian worlds did not lose touch, even if they could not join forces against the great threat of the age, Islam. In the tenth century, a western emperor took a Byzantine bride and German art was to be influenced by Byzantine themes and style. But it was just the difference of two cultural worlds that made such contacts fruitful, and as the centuries went by, the differences became more and more palpable. The unique splendour and complication of the life of Constantinople, unrivalled in the west, was the most explicit statement of the difference between them. In the imperial city, religious and secular worlds interpenetrated one another. The calendar of the Christian year was inseparable from that of the court; they set the rhythms of an immense theatrical spectacle in which ritual displayed to the people the majesty of the empire. There was some Byzantine secular art, but the art constantly before men's eyes was overwhelmingly religious, expressing the greatness and omnipresence of God, whose vice-regent was the emperor. Ritual sustained the rigid etiquette of a court about which there proliferated intrigue and conspiracy. The public appearance of even the Christian emperor could be like that of the deity in a mystery cult, preceded by the raising of several curtains from behind which he dramatically emerged. This was the apex of an astonishing civilization which showed half the world for perhaps half a millennium what true empire was. When a mission of pagans came to Byzantium from Kiev in 987 to examine its version of the Christian religion as they had examined others, they could report what they had seen in Hagia Sophia had amazed them. 'There God dwells among men', they said.[2] There was no such place in the west.

---

[2] These words are those of the *Russian Primary Chronicle* which probably depended for them on oral tradition. A translation of the relevant passage can be found in G. Vernadsky (ed.) *et al.*, *A Source Book for Russian History from Early Times to 1917* (New Haven, 1972), I, pp.25–26.

CHAPTER TWO The re-shaping of the west

Western Christendom

A re-structured and distinctive western Christendom came into being between AD 500 and 1000. As what seemed to later historians (but seemingly not to contemporaries) the portentous date of the millennium approached, the area we can call by that name had grown to consist of about half the Iberian peninsula, all modern France, Germany as far as the Elbe, Bohemia, Austria, the Italian mainland and England. At its fringes there then lay still semi-barbaric, but officially Christian areas – Ireland and Scotland, and, just at the end of the millennium, the Scandinavian kingdoms. In the tenth century a few men had begun to apply the word 'Europe' to much of this zone; a Spanish chronicle had even spoken of the victors of 732 as 'European'.

Though it had long coasts this region was hemmed in and self-absorbed; the Atlantic was wide open, but no major and lasting advance across it was made once Iceland had been settled by Norwegians, while the western Mediterranean, potentially a highway to other civilizations and their trade, faced in the east an increasingly alien Byzantium and a hostile and long incomprehensible Islamic world to the south. Europeans huddled together under the rule of the warriors they needed for their protection, and grew used to privation rather than opportunity. Yet, in fact, the worst was over by AD 1000, and that date will do, very approximately, as the marker of an epoch. By then external pressures had begun to relax, the lineaments of a later, expanding civilization were apparent and a political geography unimaginable in the year 500 was hardening. Much of the ground-work of future development was in place and Latin Christian culture had already much of its own individual and peculiar character. The eleventh century was to open a new era, one of revolution and adventure for which the centuries often misleadingly called the Dark Ages had provided the raw materials.

One change since the Dark Ages stands out, even if it is hard to define on the map: there had been a cultural and psychological shift away from the Mediterranean, the focus of classical civilization. Between the fifth and eighth centuries, the focus of European history, if the term is permissible, moved to the valley of the Rhine and its tributaries. Decisions made there were increasingly influential. Islam, among other facts, had helped to throw back the west upon this heartland. Another development which was firmly under way, but had still further to go was a gradual advance of Christian settlement to the east. Though far from the end of its expansion by 1000, at least the advance guards of Christian civilization had by then long been pushed out far beyond the old Roman frontier.

The third change was a slackening of external pressure from barbarian peoples. The Magyars crowned a Christian king in the year 1000; the Norsemen who were eventually to provide rulers in England, northern France, southern Italy, Sicily and some of the Aegean had been almost the last wave of Scandinavian expansion, which was in its final phase, while the northern countries from which their forbears had come were actually acquiring their first Christian kings. Even in Spain, western Europe was no longer just a prey. It may often still have been difficult to feel this. Nonetheless, by 1000 she was no longer wholly plastic.

By then there had come into being the geographical and ideological base of a new civilization, one owing much to and preserving much from the past, but distinctive and different from any of the elements which went to its making. Its heart was Christianity. Much of the making of Europe – even on the map – was in the first place the making of the Church, the definition of its geographical scope and its ecclesiastical structures. It often spread by (sometimes rather formal and nominal) conversions of pagan peoples, and was sometimes delimited by Islam, but an emphasis on what we might call demographic or ethnic extension would be in any case misleading. There was much more to early Christian Europe (because there was much more to the Christian life) than just the creation of Christian kingdoms from the amorphous ethnic materials of its barbarian peoples.

Yet, with one of the great success stories of history ahead of them, the leaders of the western Church sometimes felt little confidence about what they had achieved. For most of the long years between the end of the ancient world and even as late as the early twelfth century it was easier for them to feel isolated and embattled. Challenged by pagans, increasingly at odds with, and finally almost cut off from, eastern Orthodoxy except at the highest level (and that intermittently), western Christianity came to show an aggressive intransigence almost as a defensive reflex; it was a sign of its insecurities. It was not threatened merely by enemies without. Within its own sphere the western Church was in the eyes of its leaders often at bay and beleaguered. In the middle of still semi-pagan populations it strove to keep its teaching and practice intact while christening what it could of the cultures with which it had to live, judging as best it could what concessions could be made to local practice or tradition without a fatal compromise of principle. All this had to be done with clergy not many of whom, probably, were men of learning or much discipline, while some were of dubious spirituality.

It is not surprising, then, that churchmen sometimes overlooked circumstances which were on their side. In western Europe they faced no rival faith once Islam was halted; they had to contend only with vestigial paganism and superstition, and these the Church could exploit. The divisions of an age when barbarian peoples had been Arian heretics had been overcome. A lifeline had been maintained to the culture of antiquity, which meant, above all that of Roman letters and what came through them from a more distant past, and churchmen had a monopoly of learning. The great men of this world could be mobilized for religion, too, for they had advantages to gain from the Church's support, even if they would always remain a potential and sometimes were a real threat to its independence. With such advantages and assets, able churchmen were to shape in the end a quite new sort of society, in which the Church's role was one unimaginable at the end of antiquity.

The papacy and the Franks

The Roman papacy is the central and best-documented institution of Christianity and that is one good reason why so much attention has to be given to it (a fact which should provoke reflexion about what we can know about religion in these centuries). Though papal power had alarming ups and downs, the division of the old empire meant that if there was anywhere in the west a leader of the Church and a defender of the interests of religion, it had to be the bishop of Rome. He had no ecclesiastical rival. It was hard to maintain the theory of one Christian empire enclosing all Christian traditions, even while imperial rule lingered on at Ravenna. In 722 Pope Hadrian I ceased to date official papal documents by the regnal year of the emperor at Byzantium, and minted coins in his own name. The last pope who sought imperial ratification from the exarch for his succession was Gregory III, in 731. After Ravenna itself had fallen to a renewed advance by the Lombards in 751, Pope Stephen set out to seek help, but not from Byzantium. No-one wanted to break with the eastern empire, but near-barbarian allies could offer better protection in troubled times.

There were some very bad moments to come in the next two and a half centuries. The Arabs already menaced Italy, and the native Italian magnates became obstreperous in the ebbing of Lombard hegemony. As landowners themselves, the popes were exposed to predators and blackmail. Rome at times had very few cards in its hands and the papacy appeared only to have exchanged one master for another. Its claim to primacy was a matter of the respect due to the guardianship of St Peter's bones and the fact that the see was indisputably the only apostolic one in the west: this was history as much as practical power (though pilgrimage, like modern tourism, was a significant source of revenue). For a long time the popes could hardly govern effectively even within their own domains, for they had neither adequate armed forces nor a civil administration. The successors of St Peter did not welcome confrontations; they had too much to lose.

Outside the Italian peninsula, western Christendom, as it evolved, can conveniently be envisaged in three big divisions. On opposite sides of the Rhine valley lay the elements of a future France and a future Germany. Secondly, there was a west Mediterranean littoral civilization, embracing at first Catalonia, the Languedoc and Provence. With time and recovery from the barbarian centuries, this extended itself further to to embrace all Italy and, in the eleventh century, Sicily. At that time, it still contained most European city life outside El-Andalus. A third Europe can be discerned in the somewhat varied periphery to the west, north-west and north, areas which in so far as they were organized, contained the first Christian states of northern Spain, Germanic England, its independent Celtic and semi-barbarous neighbours, Ireland, Wales and Scotland, and lastly the Scandinavian kingdoms. There were also areas one might allocate to one or another of these three regions, such as Aquitaine, Gascony and sometimes Burgundy.

Historical experience, as well as climate and their ethnic make-up, made these zones different from one another, although they were not internally homogeneous or in any sense united. Nor had their inhabitants any corresponding self-consciousness. Most of them would have had no notion where in the continent they lived; they would certainly have been more interested in differences between them and their neighbours in the next village than of those between one such a region and another. Dimly aware that they were a part of Christendom, very few of them would have had even an approximate conception of what lay in the awful shadows beyond that comforting idea.

The first of these three broad conceptual divisions became the heartland of the medieval west. Under Rome, life in the area so defined had been simpler than that of the Mediterranean coasts. There had been fewer towns than further south and so a less complex economy to run down in the bad centuries; a settlement like Paris was less troubled by the collapse of commerce than, say, Milan. Life was more completely rooted in the soil north of the Alps, and aristocrats were successful warriors turned landowners. Much of this heartland was already dominated by the Frankish peoples in AD 500. From it they began the colonization of Germany, protected the Church and their lands, and hardened and passed on a tradition of kingship rooted in the magical powers of Merovingian rulers.

For centuries, nonetheless, political structures were fragile things, dependent on strong men, for ruling was a personal activity which Frankish ways did not make easier. Though there had been dynastic continuity in the Merovingian line well into the seventh century, a succession of impoverished and therefore feeble kings had to humour and indulge their aristocrats, who warred with one another. Landed wealth could buy power. The family from Austrasia which produced Charles Martel, the soldier who turned the Arabs back at Tours in 732, came to overshadow the Merovingians in the end. Charles helped to launch the conversion of Germany, a considerable mark to have left on European history (St Boniface, the Devon man who became the evangelist of the Germans, said he could not have succeeded without Charles' support) and it confirmed the alliance of the successful house with the Church. Martel's second son, Pepin the Short, was chosen king by the Frankish nobles in 751. It was three years later that Pope Stephen II came to France to look for help, and anointed Pepin king as Samuel had anointed Saul and David. Hadrian I had been the first pope to receive a visit from a Frankish king, and the return visit advertised a Frankish-Roman axis.

Pope Stephen also conferred on Pepin the title of patrician; it was a usurpation of imperial authority, but while the Lombards were terrorizing Rome, it was not the time for legal nicety. The pretensions of the emperor in Constantinople over the west were clearly meaningless (and western churchmen believed, in any case, that he had fallen into heresy). The papacy drew a dividend almost at once on its investment. Pepin defeated the Lombards and in 756 'granted' imperial Ravenna 'to St Peter'. This was the origin of what were later known as the 'Papal States', the beginning of 1,100 years of the Temporal Power enjoyed by the pope over his own dominions as a ruler like other rulers, and a new basis for independence. There was to follow the reform of the Frankish Church, further colonization and missionary conversion in Germany (where wars were waged against the pagan Saxons), the throwing back of the Arabs across the Pyrenees and the conquest of Septimania and Aquitaine. These were big gains for the Catholic Church. Nor did the new magic of anointing benefit only kings. Though it could replace or blur mysteriously with the old Merovingian thaumaturgy and raise kings above common men in more than their material wealth and prowess, the pope gained the subtle implications of authority latent in the power to bestow the sacral oil.

Charlemagne

Pepin, like all Frankish kings, divided his lands at his death. The whole heritage was united again in 771 in his elder son, Charlemagne, who soon became a legend, the greatest of the Carolingians, as his line came to be called. In spite of the difficulties of penetrating the biography of a medieval man, his actions show continuing prepossessions. Charlemagne – Charles Magnus, the 'great Charles' – was more than a traditional Frankish warrior-king who led his people to war and conquered (though he often did that). What was more striking was the seriousness with which he took his Christian role and the promotion of learning and art; he wanted to magnify his kingship by filling his court with evidence of Christian culture.

Territorially, Charlemagne was a great builder. When he rescued the papacy from the Lombards, overthrowing them and becoming their king, their lands, too, passed into the Frankish heritage. In the north, from a baseline running from Mainz to Coblenz his warriors drove east as far as Magdeburg. For thirty years he hammered away in campaigns on the Saxon March to force conversion on its pagans. Fighting against Avars, Wends and Slavs brought him not only treasure but Carinthia, Bohemia and the opening of a route down the Danube to Byzantium. To master the Danes, the Dane March was set up across the Elbe. Early in the ninth century he led his army into Spain and instituted the Spanish March south of the Pyrenees, running down to the Ebro and the Catalonian coast.

Thus he came to rule – though it is by no means clear always what that word might mean – a realm bigger than anything in the west since Rome. Historians have argued ferociously about its reality. Even more fiercely they, like Charlemagne's contemporaries, have argued about one great event: his coronation by the pope on Christmas Day, 800, when he was acclaimed as emperor. 'Most pious Augustus, crowned by God, the great and peace-giving Emperor' ran the chant at the service – but everybody already acknowledged as emperor the one who lived in Constantinople: were there now to be two emperors of a divided Christendom, as in later Roman times? Clearly, an emperor had authority over many peoples; by this title, then, Charlemagne became more than just a ruler of Franks. Perhaps Italy mattered most in explaining it, for among the Italians a link with the imperial past might be a cementing factor as nowhere else. An element of papal gratitude – or expediency – was involved, too; Pope Leo III had just been restored to his capital by Charlemagne's soldiers. Yet Charlemagne is reported to have said that he would not have entered St Peter's had he known what the pope intended to do. He may have disliked the pope's implied arrogation of authority as a maker of emperors. He must have known that to his own people, the Franks, and to many of his northern subjects he was more comprehensible as a traditional Germanic warrior-king than as the successor of the Caesars, yet before long his seal bore the legend *Renovatio Romani imperii*, 'the renewal of the Roman empire', a conscious reconnexion to a great past.

Charlemagne must have expected his coronation to cause irritation at Constantinople. Relations with Byzantium were soon troubled, though the new title was a few years later recognized for a time as valid in the west in return for a concession to Byzantium of sovereignty over Venice, Istria and Dalmatia. With another great state, the Abbasid caliphate, Charlemagne had somewhat formal but not unfriendly relations; Haroun-al-Raschid is said to have given him a cup bearing a portrait of Chosroes I, the Persian king under whom Sassanid power and civilization had been at its height and, more strikingly, an elephant (it is from Frankish sources that we learn of these contacts for they do not seem to have struck the Arab chroniclers as worth mention). The Umayyads of Spain were different; they were near enough to be a threat and to protect the faith from pagans was a part of Christian kingship, so Charlemagne did not court them.

Charlemagne's style of kingship had other expressions. Though he gave its bishops support and protection, the Frankish Church was firmly subordinated to his authority. Charlemagne was only the first, even if he was one of the most high-minded, of several emperors who would make clear to Rome their views of the respective standing of pope and emperor as guardians of religion. He used the Church as an instrument of government, ruling through bishops and presiding in person over Frankish synods. He seems to have hoped to reform both the Frankish Church and the Roman, imposing upon them both the Rule of St Benedict. In such a scheme, for good and ill, lay the seed of later European ideas that Christian kings should be responsible not only for the protection of the Church but for the health of the religious life within their dominions.

Charlemagne strove to beautify the physical setting of his court at Aachen with architecture and decorative treasures, and this too had religious as well as secular importance (we do not know if Charlemagne ever distinguished them). A Frankish court was a primitive thing in comparison with Byzantium – and possibly even in comparison with those of some other early barbarian kingdoms open to influence from a more cultivated world. When Charlemagne's men brought materials and ideas from Ravenna to beautify Aachen, Byzantine artistic style began to move more into north European tradition and classical models began to influence his artists. But the imperial court was also an intellectual centre. From it radiated the impulse to copy texts in a new refined and reformed hand called Carolingian minuscule. This script was to be one of the great instruments of cultural transmission in the west. Charlemagne hoped to use it to supply an authentic copy of the Rule of St Benedict to every monastery in his realm, but the major expression of a new manuscript potential was first evident in the copying of the Bible. This had a more than religious aim. The scriptural story was interpreted as a justification of Carolingian rule; the Old Testament was full of examples of pious and anointed warrior-kings.

The Bible was the major text in the monastic libraries which were beginning to be assembled throughout the Frankish lands, but other texts, too, were copied and diffused for a century after the original impulse had been given at Aachen. This was the core of what modern scholars have called 'the Carolingian Renaissance'. It had none of the pagan connotations of a noun later applied to a revival of learning which focused attention on the classical past, for it was emphatically Christian. Its purpose was the training of the Frankish clergy so as to raise the cultural level of the Church and carry the faith further east (south of the Pyrenees, the problem was not education and conversion, but reconquest). Among the leading men in the beginnings of this transmission of sacred knowledge were the numerous Irishmen and Anglo-Saxons in the palace school at Aachen. One outstanding among them was Alcuin, a cleric from York, a great centre of English learning. His most famous pupil was Charlemagne himself, but he had several others. Besides managing the palace library and writing books of his own he set up a school at Tours, where he became abbot, and began to expound Boethius and Augustine to the men who would govern the Frankish Church in the next generation.

Alcuin's pre-eminence is a striking instance of the shift of cultural gravity in Europe away from the classical world and to the north. But others than he and his countrymen were involved in teaching and copying, and in founding the new monasteries which spread outwards into east and west Frankia; there were Franks, Visigoths, Lombards and Italians among them, too. It was a European task. One of them, a Frankish layman called Einhard (he might be termed the emperor's clerk of works), wrote a life of

Charlemagne. From it we learn human details: the emperor could be garrulous, was a keen hunter, and passionately loved swimming and bathing (the presence of thermal springs explains his choice of Aachen as a residence). He comes to life in Einhard's pages as an aspiring intellectual, too, speaking Latin as well as Frankish, we are told, and understanding Greek. This is made more credible when we hear also of Charlemagne's attempts to write, keeping notebooks under his pillow so that he could do so in bed, 'but' Einhard says, 'although he tried very hard, he had begun too late in life'.

Not only in Einhard's pages, but in oral tradition, there comes down to posterity a vivid picture of a dignified, majestic figure, striving to make the transition from warlord to ruler of a great Christian empire, and enjoying some success in so doing. Charlemagne's physical presence was impressive (he probably towered over most of his entourage), and men came to see in him the image of a kingly soul, gay, just and magnanimous, a heroic paladin of whom poets and minstrels would sing for centuries. His rule was a more majestic spectacle than anything seen to that time in barbarian lands.

When his reign began, Charlemagne's court was still peripatetic, eating its way from estate to estate throughout the year. At the emperor's death, he left a palace and a treasury at Aachen, where he was to be buried. He had been able to reform weights and measures, and had given to Europe the division of the pound of silver into 240 pennies (*denarii*) which was long to serve it well (in the British Isles, for 1,100 years). But his power was personal and hardly institutionalized. He had continually to guard against his noblemen replacing tribal rulers by settling down into hereditary positions of their own; his repeated issuing of 'capitularies' or instructions to his servants was a sure sign that his wishes were often ignored. In the last resort, even Charlemagne could only base effective rule day-to-day on his own domain and its produce and on men close enough to him for supervision. These vassals were bound to him by especially solemn oaths, but even they began to give trouble as he grew older.

The Carolingian heritage

Charlemagne made plans to divide his lands in the usual Frankish way, but he was unfortunate: though five times married and siring eleven children, four of his five sons died before him, so that the inheritance passed undivided to the youngest, Louis the Pious, in 814. With it came the imperial title (which Charlemagne gave to his son) and the papal alliance; two years after his succession the pope crowned Louis. But partition had only been delayed. Charlemagne's successors had neither his authority nor his experience, nor perhaps the same interest in controlling fissiparous forces. Regional loyalties formed around individuals. A series of partitions finally culminated in one in 843 with great consequences, between three of Charlemagne's grandsons, the Treaty of Verdun. A core kingdom of Frankish lands centred on the western side of the Rhine valley and containing Charlemagne's capital, Aachen, went to Lothair, the reigning emperor. Thus it was called Lotharingia and it defied geography; it united Provence, Burgundy, and the region later called Lorraine to the lands between the Scheldt, Meuse, Saône and Rhône. Lothair also got the kingdom of Italy. To the east the lands of Teutonic speech between the Rhine and the German Marches went to Louis the German. Finally, in the west, Gascony, Septimania and Aquitaine, and roughly the rest of modern France outside Lotharingia, went to a half-brother of these two, Charles the Bald. This settlement was not long untroubled, but it was decisive in a very important way; it effectively founded the political distinction of France and Germany whose roots lie respectively in west and east Frankia. Lotharingia had much less linguistic, ethnic, geographical and economic unity than either of these. It was there largely because three sons had to be provided for. Much future Franco-German history was going to be about the way in which the lands between the Rhine, Meuse and Rhône could be divided between neighbours bound to covet them.

No royal house can guarantee a continuous flow of able rulers. Nor can kings for ever buy loyalty by giving away land. Gradually, like their Merovingian predecessors, the Carolingians declined in power. The signs of break-up multiplied, an independent Burgundy re-appeared and people began to dwell on the great days of Charlemagne, a significant symptom of decay and dissatisfaction. The histories of west and east Franks diverged more and more. In the west the Carolingians lasted just over a century after Charles the Bald. By the end of his reign Brittany, Flanders and Aquitaine were to all intents and purposes independent. The west Frankish monarchy started the tenth century in a weak position. In 911 Charles III, unable to expel them, conceded lands in

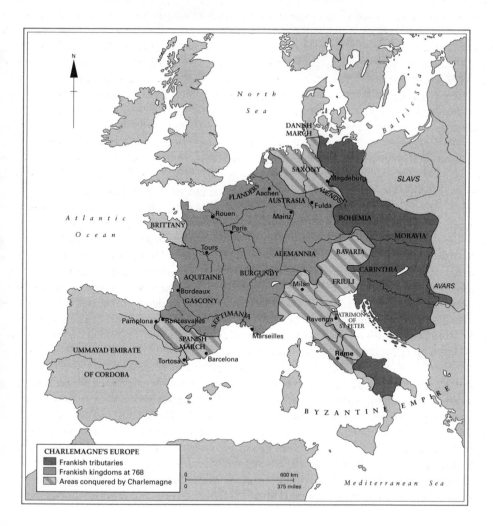

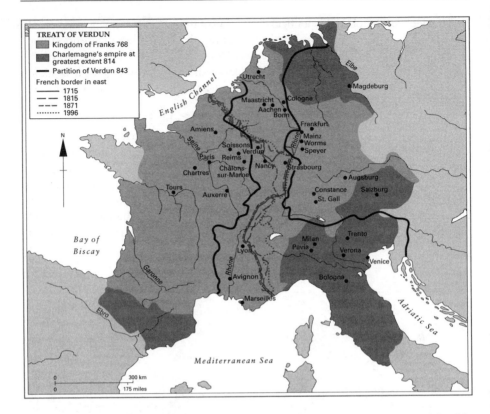

TREATY OF VERDUN
Kingdom of Franks 768
Charlemagne's empire at greatest extent 814
Partition of Verdun 843
French border in east
1715
1815
1871
1996

what was later called Normandy to the leader of Norse arrivals, Rollo. Baptized the following year, Rollo set to work to build the duchy for which he did homage to the Carolingians; his Scandinavian countrymen continued to arrive and settle there until the end of the tenth century, yet soon became French in speech and law. After this, the unity of the West Franks fell even more rapidly apart. From the confusion there emerged a son of a count of Paris who steadily built up his family's power around a domain in the Ile de France, the heart of a future nation. When the last Carolingian ruler of the West Franks died in 987, this man's son, Hugh Capet, was elected king, so opening the history of a royal house which was to rule for nearly 400 years. For the rest, west Frankia dissolved into a dozen or so territorial units ruled by magnates of varying standing and independence.

A new empire

East of the Rhine, the story of the Frankish heritage opens one of the major themes of medieval and early modern history: the long effort to make a reality of the agglomeration which came to be called the 'Holy Roman Empire of the German Nation'. One aspect of this was a centuries-long effort to integrate the east Frankish heritage in Germany with Mediterranean Europe. Geography was one obstacle; Germany's natural outlets lay to the north, down the Oder, Elbe and Weser, and there were formidable mountain barriers to the south. Among other obstacles, there were the consequences in Germany of the repeated division of the Carolingian heritage. After the last east Frank king of that line died in 911, there emerged a political fragmentation which was endured until the nineteenth century. The assertiveness of local magnates combined with stronger tribal loyalties than in the west to produce a half-dozen powerful dukedoms. Slightly surprisingly, Conrad of Franconia, the ruler of one of them, was chosen as king by the others, who wanted a strong leader against the Magyars. The change of dynasty made it advisable to confer some special standing on the new ruler; the bishops therefore anointed Conrad at his coronation (he was the first ruler of the east Franks so to be treated). But it did not work. Conrad was unable to resist the Magyars; he lost and could not win back Lotharingia but strove, with the support of the Church, to exalt his own house and office. The dukes gathered their peoples about them to safeguard their own independence. The four who mattered most were the Saxons, the Bavarians, the Swabians and the Franconians (as the east Franks became known). Regional differences, blood and the natural pretensions of great nobles stamped on Germany a historical pattern which lasted until the nineteenth century; a tug-of-war between central authority and local power was not (as elsewhere) to be resolved in the long run in favour of the centre, though in the tenth century it looked otherwise for a while. Conrad faced ducal rebellion by nominating one of the rebels his successor. The dukes agreed and in 919, Henry 'the Fowler' (as he was called) of Saxony, became king. He and his descendants, the 'Saxon emperors', or Ottonians, ruled the eastern Franks until 1024.

Henry the Fowler had no ecclesiastical coronation. With great family properties behind him and Saxon tribal loyalties on his side he brought the magnates into line by military leadership. He won back Lotharingia from the west Franks, created new Marches on the Elbe after victorious campaigns against the Wends, made Denmark a tributary kingdom and began its conversion, and, finally, defeated the Magyars. This left his son, Otto I, a goodly inheritance of which he made good use. Formally elected, but in truth chosen because he was his father's son, Otto continued his father's work. In 955 he shattered the Magyars at the Lechfeld and ended for ever the danger they had presented. Austria – Charlemagne's *Ostmark* or east March – was recolonized.

Though he faced some opposition, Otto also made the German Church a loyal instrument; it was an advantage of the Saxon emperors that in Germany churchmen tended to look with favour to the monarchy for protection against predatory laymen. A new archiepiscopal province, Magdeburg, was organized to direct the new bishoprics established among Slavs. With Otto ends, it has been said, the period of mere anarchy in central Europe; that may be overstating it, though under him we have the first sense of something we might call Germany. But Otto's ambition did not stop there. He is not remembered as 'the Great' for nothing. In 936 he had been crowned at Aachen, Charlemagne's old capital. Not only did he accept the ecclesiastical service and anointing which his father had avoided, but he afterwards held a coronation banquet at which German dukes served him as his vassals in the old Carolingian style. Fifteen years later he invaded Italy, married the widow of a claimant to the crown of Italy, and assumed it himself. Yet the pope refused him coronation as emperor. Ten years later, in 962, Otto came back to Italy in response to the pope's appeal for help, and this time got his papal coronation. Otto called his empire 'Holy'.

Thus was revived the Roman and the Carolingian ideal of empire. The German and Italian crowns were united again in a structure which (at least in name) would last for nearly a 1,000 years. Yet it was not so extensive an empire as Charlemagne's had been, nor did Otto dominate the papacy as Charlemagne had done. For all his assertiveness Otto was the Church's protector (his brother was an archbishop) who thought he knew what was best for it, but he was not its governor. Nor was the structure of the empire very solid; it rested on the political manipulation of local magnates rather than on administration. It was, nonetheless, impressive and even glamorous. Otto's son, the future Otto II (973–83), married a Byzantine princess. Though he (and his successor

THE MEDIEVAL EMPIRE

Area of East Frankish (German) kingdom under Otto I (c. 950)

Further extension of imperial claims during the 13th century (under Hohenstaufen)

Papal States in the 13th century

Otto III) had to face rebellion when he came to the throne, a fourth hereditary succession had been achieved. Otto III (983–1002) was only three at his accession, but he survived to maintain the tradition of exercising imperial power south of the Alps. This cast something of a shadow at Rome. Otto the Great had engineered the deposition of two popes and the election of two others (one a layman); Otto II removed a usurper (elected by the Romans) and restored the ejected pope; Otto III made a cousin the first German to sit in the chair of St Peter, following him by appointing the first French pope.

Rome seemed to captivate Otto III and he settled down there. Like his father and grandfather, he called himself *augustus* but his seals also bore the legend 'Renewal of Roman empire' – which he equated with Christian empire. Half Greek by birth, he saw himself as a new Constantine. A diptych from a gospel-book painted nearly at the end of the tenth century shows him in state, crowned and orb in hand, receiving the homage of four crowned women: they are Slavonia (Slavic Europe), Germany, Gaul and Rome. His notion of a Europe organized as a hierarchy of kings serving under an emperor was eastern. In this there was megalomania as well as genuine religious conviction; the real basis of Otto's power was his German kingship, not Italy, though it obsessed and detained him. Nevertheless, after his death in 1002, his body was taken to Aachen as he had ordered, to be buried beside Charlemagne.

Otto III left no heir, but the Saxon line was not exhausted; Henry II, elected after a struggle, was a great-grandson of Henry the Fowler. Though crowned at Rome, he was at heart a German ruler, not western emperor. His seal read 'Renewal of the kingdom of the Franks'. Though he made three expeditions to Italy, Henry relied on playing off its factions against one another to control the peninsula. With him the Byzantine style of the Ottonian court began to wane. His attention was focused on pacification and conversion in east Germany.

Italy and Mediterranean Europe

When the eleventh century opened the idea of western empire was still alive and able to beguile rulers, but the Carolingian inheritance had long since crumbled into fragments. It would probably have been agreed that emperors could be expected to make some claims to a vague hegemony over other rulers, and to try to carry out a right and duty to protect the papacy. As for former east Frankia, the idea of Germany barely existed, but the country was a true political universe of its own, even if still inchoate. The curious federal arrangements which were to emerge there would be the main institutional embodiment last refuge of the imperial idea in the west. In France, too, much of a future without the empire was settled, though it could not have been discerned at the time. West Frankia had dissolved into a dozen or so major units over which the suzerainty of the Capetians was for a long time feeble. But they had on their side a centrally placed royal domain, including Paris and the important diocese of Orléans, and the friendship of the Church. These were advantages in the hands of able kings, and able kings would be forthcoming in the next three centuries.

The other major components of the Carolingian heritage had been in Italy. Since the seventh century the peninsula had been evolving away from the possibility of integration with northern Europe and back towards re-emergence as part of a European Mediterranean. Once the Lombard kingdom had been destroyed by Charlemagne, the papacy had no Italian political rival until Carolingian power waned. Then, it had to

---

THE HOLY ROMAN EMPIRE

AD 800	Coronation of Charlemagne.
840–3	Division of Carolingian empire on death of Louis the Pious. Lothair I takes title of emperor (together with Italy and Lotharingia).
955	Battle of Lechfeld: Otto I (the Great) finally removes the Magyar menace with this victory.
966–72	Otto I's third expedition to Italy: deposition of one pope, restoration of another, nomination of a third.
998	Otto III deposes a pope.
1046	Henry III deposes three rival popes and reaffirms right of nomination to the papacy.
1075–1122	Investiture struggle, formally ended by Concordat of Worms.
1125	Elective principle for selection of emperors established with accession of Lothair II.
1138	Hohenstaufen dynasty of emperors begins with Conrad III. Prolonged struggle with papacy follows.
1152–90	Frederick I (Barbarossa) begins use of style 'Holy Roman Empire'.
1183	Peace of Constance (between emperor, pope and Lombard cities) opens way to divergence of Germany and Italy under formal suzerainty of the emperor.
1245	Frederick II deposed by Pope Innocent IV at Synod of Lyons.
1268	Last Hohenstaufen prince murdered.
1356	The 'Golden Bull' of Charles IV settles constitution of the Holy Roman Empire until 1806.

---

face both the rising power of the Italian magnates and the revived ambitions of the Roman aristocracy. The western Church was at its lowest ebb of cohesion and unity in the tenth century, as the Ottonians' treatment of the papacy showed. Yet there was another side to the balance sheet, even if it was slow to reveal its full implications. Pepin's grant would in time form the nucleus of a powerful Italian territorial state, and Leo's coronation of Charlemagne, like Stephen's of Pepin, may have been expedient, but contained a potent seed. In the coronation of emperors there rested veiled claims; it expressed a reality long concealed but easily comprehensible to an age which thought in symbols: the pope conferred the crown and the stamp of God's recognition on the emperor. Perhaps, therefore, he could do so conditionally. Perhaps he could say who was a rightful emperor. When, as often happened, personal weaknesses and succession disputes disrupted kingdoms, Rome could exploit such uncertainties. As time passed, popes withdrew from the imperial coronation ceremony (as from those of English and French kings) the use of the chrism, the specially sacred mixture of oil and balsam for the ordination of priests and the coronation of bishops.

More immediately and practically, the support of powerful kings was used by popes to discipline local churches and advance missionary enterprise in the east. For all the jealousy of local clergy, the Frankish Church felt the change; in the tenth century what the pope said already mattered north of the Alps, too. From the *entente* of the eighth century there emerged gradually the idea that it was for the pope to say what the Church's policy should be and that the bishops of the local churches should not pervert it. A great instrument of standardization was being forged. It was already there in principle, though, when Pepin used his power as a Frankish king to reform his countrymen's church on lines which brought it into step with Rome on questions of ritual and discipline, and further away from Celtic influences.

The balance of advantage and disadvantage long tipped to and fro, the boundaries of effective power exercised by individual popes ebbing and flowing. Significantly, it was after a further sub-division of the Carolingian heritage so that the crown of Italy was separated from Lotharingia that pope Nicholas I pressed his see's claims most successfully. A century before, a famous forgery, the 'Donation of Constantine', purported to show that Constantine had given to the bishop of Rome the former dominion exercised by the empire of Italy; Nicholas addressed kings and emperors as if this theory was accepted in the west. He wrote to them, it was said, 'as though he were lord of the world', reminding them that he could appoint and depose. He used the doctrine of papal primacy against the eastern emperor, too, in supporting an awkward patriarch of Constantinople. This was a peak of pretension which the papacy could not long sustain in practice, for it was soon clear that the application of force at Rome would in fact decide who should enjoy the imperial power the pope claimed to confer (Nicholas' successor, revealingly, was the first pope since the martyrs of the third century to be murdered). Nonetheless, here were signs of a different future ahead.

Of Italy outside the papal territories, the map in 1000 appears messy and confusing, but medieval boundaries did not mean what they mean today. In the north lay a scatter of feudal statelets. Venice already looked promising; for 200 years she had been pushing forward in the Adriatic. She already had Levantine as well as Mediterranean commercial interests. City-state republics existed in the south of the peninsula, at Gaeta, Amalfi, Bari. Across the middle of it ran the pope's territories. Over Italy, though, fell the shadow of Islam. There had been raids as far north as Pisa; emirates appeared for a time at Taranto and Bari in the ninth century and in 902 the Arabs completed the conquest of Sicily, which they were to rule for a century and a half.

The Arabs shaped European destinies further west, too. Not only were they established in Spain, but even in Provence they had more permanent bases (one of them, anticipating a future and somewhat different link, at St Tropez). The coastal peoples had, perforce, a complex relationship with the Arabs, who appeared to them both as free-booters and as traders. Except in Sicily and Spain, though, the Arabs showed little tendency to settle. Southern France and Catalonia were already distinctive. Frankish and Gothic conquest had marked them. Physical memorials of the Roman past were plentiful in both; a Mediterranean agriculture dominated them. Another distinctive characteristic was language. A family of Romance languages appeared in the south, some of which endure to this day. One was Catalan, the language of the Frankish Spanish March created by Charlemagne's conquest and enlarged subsequently by the Counts of Barcelona. In the Iberian peninsula the Catalans for a time shared with a handful of tiny statelets in the Asturias and Navarre the upholding of the Christian cause against Islam. Geography, climate and divisions among the Moslems had helped them to survive in the dangerous eighth century. Then a kingdom of León emerged in the Asturias to take its place beside the kingdom of Navarre. In the tenth century, however, the Christians fell out with one another and the Arabs again made headway. The blackest moment came when a great Arab conqueror, Al-Mansur, took Barcelona, León, and in 998 the shrine of Santiago de Compostela itself, supposedly the burial-place of St James the Apostle. The triumph was not to be long-lived. Here, too, what had already been done to found Christian Europe proved ineradicable. Within a few decades Christian Spain rallied as Islamic Spain fell into disunion, and the reconquest of the peninsula began. In Iberia as elsewhere, the age of expansion which this inaugurated belongs to another historical era, but it would be an age based on the long medieval confrontation with another civilization. For Spain above all, Christianity was to be the crucible of national myth and self-consciousness.

The Viking north

If Christian practice is the test of inclusion in a western Christendom turning itself into Europe, then in AD 1000 it barely included Scandinavia. Not all Scandinavian kings were Christian even then, but long before that time, their pagan peoples had been shaping the history of the offshore islands and northern coasts of the continental mainland. Possibly because of over-population, the Scandinavians had been moving outwards from the eighth century onwards. They had two fine technical instruments, a longboat which oars and sails could both take across seas and up shallow rivers, and a tubbier cargo-carrier which could shelter large families, their goods and animals for six or seven days at sea. In these they struck out across the water for four centuries, to scatter over an area which stretched in the end from Greenland to Kiev. Not all the Norsemen sought the same things. Those who made for Iceland, the Faroes, Orkney and the far west wanted to colonize. The Swedes who penetrated Russia along her rivers were more likely to trade. The Danes did most of the plundering and piracy the Vikings are remembered for. But all these themes wove in and out of one another. No one Norse people had a monopoly of any of them.

Viking colonization was spectacular, given the available resources. Norsemen wholly replaced the Picts in the Orkneys and the Shetlands, from which they extended their rule to the Faroes (previously uninhabited except for a few Irish monks and their sheep) and the Isle of Man. Offshore, their lodgement was more lasting and profound than on the mainland of Scotland and Ireland, where settlement began in the ninth century. Yet the Irish language records their importance in its adoption of Norse words used in commerce, and Dublin, founded by the Vikings and soon an important trading-post, marks it on the Irish map. The most successful colony of all was Iceland, the first European 'new nation' overseas. Irish hermits had got there first, too, and it was not until the end of the ninth century that Vikings came in large numbers. By 930, though, there may have been 10,000 Norse Icelanders, living by farming and fishing, in part for their own subsistence, in part to produce commodities such as salt fish which they might trade. In that year the Icelandic state was founded with an assembly, the *Althing*, which romantic antiquarians later saw as the first European 'parliament'. It was more like a council of the big men of the community than a modern representative body and it followed earlier Norwegian practice, but Iceland's continuous historical record is in this respect a remarkable one, for it continues to meet to this day.

In the tenth centuries, colonies were founded in Greenland; there were Norsemen there for 500 years. Then they disappeared, probably because the settlers were wiped out by Eskimos pushed south by an advance of the ice. Of discovery and settlement further west we can say less. The Sagas and Eddas, the heroic literature of medieval Iceland, tell us of the exploration of 'Vinland', where Norsemen found the wild vine growing, and of the birth of a child there (whose mother subsequently returned to Iceland and went abroad again as a pilgrim to Rome before settling into highly sanctified retirement in her native land). There are good grounds to believe that a settlement discovered in Newfoundland is Norse. But we cannot go much further than this.

In western European tradition, the colonial and mercantile activities of the Vikings were from the start obscured by their horrific impact as marauders. Certainly, they had some very nasty habits (spread-eagling among them) but so did most barbarians. Nor were the Vikings the first people to burn monasteries in Ireland. Some exaggeration must be allowed for, in any case, because our main evidence comes from the pens of churchmen doubly appalled, both as Christians and as victims, by attacks on churches and monasteries; as pagans, of course, Vikings saw no special sanctity in the concentrations of precious metals and food such places so conveniently provided and found them especially attractive targets.

However we qualify, it remains indisputable that the Vikings' impact on northern and western Christendom was very great and very terrifying. They first attacked England in 793, the monastery of Lindisfarne being their victim; though the monastery lived on another eighty years, the attack terrified the ecclesiastical world. Ireland they raided two years later. In the first half of the ninth century the Danes began to harry Frisia and went on doing so year after year, the same towns being plundered again and again. The French coast was then attacked; in 842 Nantes was sacked with a great massacre. Within a few years a Frankish chronicler bewailed that 'the endless flood of Vikings never ceases to grow'. Towns as far inland as Paris, Limoges, Orléans, Tours and Angoulême suffered. Soon Spain came under attack and the Arabs, too, were harassed; in 844 the Vikings stormed Seville. In 859 they raided Nîmes and plundered Pisa, though they suffered heavily at the hands of an Arab fleet on their way home.

At its worst, think some scholars, the Viking onslaught may have come near to destroying civilization in West Frankia; certainly the Vikings helped to shape the differences between a future France and a future Germany, because the East Franks suffered less. In the west Norse ravages threw new responsibilities on local magnates; central and royal control crumbled away and men looked more and more towards their local lord for protection. When Hugh Capet came to the throne, it was very much as *primus inter pares* in a recognizably feudal society, where magnates looked after their own.

Not all efforts to meet the Viking threat failed. Charlemagne and Louis the Pious faced attacks less heavy and persistent than their successors, but they managed to defend vulnerable ports and river-mouths with some effectiveness. The Vikings could be (and were) defeated if drawn into full-scale field engagements and, though there were dramatic exceptions, the main centres of the Christian west were on the whole successfully protected. What could not be stopped were repeated and damaging raids on the coasts. Once the Vikings learnt to avoid pitched battles, the only way to deal with them was to buy them off. Charles the Bald began paying them tribute so that his subjects should be left in peace. This was the first example of what the English called Danegeld.

Anglo-Saxon England

A small group of seven kingdoms had emerged from the Germanic invasions of (or migrations to) Britannia; by the seventh century many Britons of Romano-British descent were living alongside communities of the new settlers, though others had been driven back to the hills of Wales and Scotland. Re-establishing Christianity in the island was largely a matter of the work of missionaries from the Roman mission which had established itself at Canterbury. It competed with the older Celtic Church until 664, a crucial date, when at a synod of churchmen held at Whitby a Northumbrian king pronounced in favour of adopting the date of Easter set by the Roman Church. It was a symbolic choice, determining that the future England would adhere to the Roman traditions, not the Celtic.

The names of the seven kingdoms of the Heptarchy (as the England of the early Germanic settlers is called) were Essex, Wessex, Sussex, Kent, East Anglia, Mercia and Northumbria, all names still used in common speech today. From time to time, one or another of these little states threw up a ruler strong enough to have some sway over the others. Yet none stood up successfully to the wave of Danish attacks from 851 onwards. These led to a Danish occupation of two-thirds of the country before there emerged to lead his subjects against the invaders England's first national hero who is also an historical figure, Alfred the Great, king of Wessex and then of all southern England. As a child of four, Alfred had been taken to Rome by his father and was given consular honours by the pope; the Wessex monarchy was closely linked with Christianity and Europe. One of its kings had served under Charlemagne. Wessex kings defended the faith against paganism as well as against an alien invader.

In 871, the year of his accession (after his brother's death at the hands of the Danes), Alfred inflicted the first decisive defeat on a Danish army in England. Significantly, after being forced to make peace in 878, the Danish king agreed a few years later not only to withdraw from Wessex but to accept conversion as a Christian. This registered that the Danes were in England to stay (and settle in the north) but also that they might be divided from one another. Soon Alfred was leader of the surviving English kings; eventually, none was left but he. He recovered London and when he died in 901 the worst period of Danish raids was over. His descendants were to rule a united country after the re-conquest of the Danelaw, the area of Danish colonization marked to this day by Scandinavian place-names and fashions of speech. The strongholds called 'burghs' which Alfred founded as a part of a new system of national defence by local levies not only gave his successors bases for that conquest, but set much of the pattern of later English urbanization; towns built on their sites are still inhabited today. Finally, with tiny resources, Alfred had also undertaken the cultural and intellectual regeneration of his people. The scholars of his court, like those of Charlemagne, proceeded by way of copying and translation: the Anglo-Saxon nobleman and cleric were intended to learn of Bede and Boethius in their own tongue.

Alfred's innovations were a creative effort of government unique in its day, and opened a great age for England. The shire structure which lasted until 1974 began to take shape under his rule. The Danes were held in a united kingdom through a half-century's turbulence. It was only when ability failed in Alfred's line that the Anglo-Saxon monarchy came to grief and a new Viking offensive took place. Colossal sums of Danegeld were paid until a Danish king (this time a Christian) overthrew the English king and then died, leaving a young son, Cnut (the celebrated Canute), to rule his conquests. Under him England briefly formed part of a great Danish empire (1006–35). A last great Norwegian invasion of England in 1066 was shattered at the battle of Stamford Bridge, just before the descendants of other Norsemen landed to conquer England from the south. By that time, all the Scandinavian monarchies were Christian and Viking culture was being Christianized.

Viking civilization left many evidences of its individuality and strength in both Celtic and continental art. While its institutions survived most visibly in Iceland and other islands, the Scandinavian legacy was strongly marked for centuries in England by language and social patterns. Across the Channel, there was the duchy of Normandy, and a literary heritage to the future. In settled lands, though, the ethnic Norsemen gradually merged with the rest of the population. When the descendants of Rollo and his followers who had settled in France and gave their name to Normandy turned to the conquest of England in 1066 they were really Frenchmen and the warsong they sang at Hastings was about Charlemagne the Frankish paladin. They conquered an England where the men of the Danelaw were by then English. Similarly, far away in the east other Vikings had by then lost their ethnic distinctiveness among the Slavs of Kiev Rus and Muscovy.

The western Church at work

AD 1000 was a date of some significance in Hungarian history: in that year, the Magyar people, once a pagan thorn in the side of Catholic Europe, crowned their first Christian king. Like the conversion of the Scandinavian rulers, such geographical extension of the faith was a huge part of what the Church was doing in these centuries. In the eighth century a great Anglo-Saxon missionary movement whose outstanding figures were St Willibord and St Boniface had launched the evangelizing of Germany. They had asserted the supremacy of Rome; their converts tended therefore to look directly to the throne of St Peter for religious authority, an emphasis which died away in the later phases of central and eastern Europe missionary work, or, rather, became less conspicuous as German emperors and their bishops took their own initiatives. Conversion was combined with conquest and new bishoprics were organized as part of a nascent governmental apparatus, so that such extensions had a political as well as a religious emphasis. To weigh these great successes and judge their historical importance, though, is difficult. It could be thought that even greater success for the Church can be discerned in quite different areas. Religious history must have as its centre belief, and that implies different things for different sorts and conditions of men and women. Yet the story of the Church is liable to be distorted by its records. They provide most of our evidence, but sometimes make it very difficult to see the spirit behind the bureaucracy.

Even the official record makes it clear, though, that the Church uniquely pervaded the whole fabric of society. It had, for instance, almost a monopoly of culture. The classical heritage had been terribly damaged and narrowed by the barbarian invasions and the intransigent other-worldliness of early Christianity: 'What has Athens to do with Jerusalem?' one of the Fathers of the African Church had asked long ago, but such contempt for the classical world had subsided long since. By the tenth century what had been preserved of the classical past had been preserved by the efforts of churchmen, above all by the Benedictines and the copiers of the palace schools who transmitted not only the Bible but Latin compilations of Greek learning. Through their versions of Pliny and Boethius a slender but direct line still connected early medieval western Christendom to Aristotle and Euclid.

Literacy was virtually confined to the clergy. The Romans had been able to post laws on boards in public places and inscribe their records in stone, confident that a sufficient readership was available; far into the Middle Ages, even kings were normally illiterate. The clergy controlled virtually all access to such writing as there was. In a world without universities, only a court or church school offered any access to letters beyond what might be offered, exceptionally, by an individual cleric-tutor. The effect of this on all the arts and intellectual activity was profound; culture was not just related to religion but existed only in the setting of overriding religious assumptions. The idea of 'art for art's sake' could never had made less sense than in the early Middle Ages. History, philosophy, theology, the illumination of manuscripts, all played their part in sustaining a culture above all sacramental. However narrowed it might be, though, the legacy they transmitted, in so far as it was not Jewish, was classical.

Such peaks of generalization are dangerous places, and should prompt us to caution. It is salutary to remember how very little we know or can know directly about what must be regarded both theologically and statistically (if numbers of souls count nowadays) as the most important of all the activities of the Church – the day-to-day business of exhorting, teaching, marrying, baptizing, shriving and praying. Merely as an influence on thought and behaviour, this directly affected more poeple than anything else it did. The religious life of secular clergy and laity was centred about the provision of the major sacraments. Through them, the Church was deploying powers which in those centuries often cannot have been easily distinguished by the faithful from magic. With them it drilled a barbaric world into civilization with great success – and yet we have almost no direct information about how it happened, except at its most dramatic moments, when a spectacular conversion or baptism reveals by the very fact of being recorded that we are in the presence of the untypical.

We know more about Martha's life than Mary's and have better documentation for the economic reality of the medieval Church. It was a great landowner which did not die. It controlled much of society's wealth, therefore, for land was the ultimate resource of all life. The clergy and their dependants were numerous; the Church was the economy's major employer. Their maintenance and the provision of its services (in every sense) rested on the surpluses which only agriculture could produce. Monasteries or cathedral chapters could have very large estates and huge responsibilities; tithes and glebe land directly supported parish clergy, or were appropriated to other ecclesiastical uses. Legacies and gifts to the Church usually took the form of land or direct income from land for particular purposes. Its roots were firmly sunk in the rural economy and this generated a mounting flow of documentation as time went by – charters of entitlement, leases, settlements and, later, accounts of estate management.

Such involvement in the material life of society brought problems with it. Many people were interested in the resources assuring the upkeep of the Church. Its influence and authority over men's minds had often to be deployed in defence of its material interests; after all, with diplomacy and cunning, its mysterious psychological power was all the Church had. Yet material interest could at times push the Church towards conflicts with laymen in which the primary and spiritual tasks of ecclesiastics were in danger of being lost to sight. The questions which arose were complicated. They were often cut across in other ways and at many levels by the interplay of religion with secular circumstance. When for instance, papal authority was eclipsed in the tenth century, and the papal throne became the prey of Italian factions and Ottonian interventions, the day-to-day work of safeguarding Christian interests outside Italy had been left (because it had to be) for the most part to the bishops of the local Churches. They had to pay attention to the powers that were. Seeking the cooperation and help of the secular rulers, they often moved into positions in which they were all but indistinguishable from royal servants. They had to defer to their secular rulers, just as, often, the parish priest had to defer to the lord of the manor. This did not mean bishops did not do much good; but there was a question-mark over their independence.

A recurrent concern about such matters was in the end given focus and energy by a movement of monastic reform in the tenth century which the monks who were its authors had embarked upon as a way of renewing monastic ideals and recalling, where necessary, a degenerate monasticism to its original purposes. These monks, interestingly, found generous support among laymen, who helped them to found new, reformed monastic houses. Most were in the old central Carolingian lands, running down from Belgium to Switzerland, west into Burgundy and east into Franconia. From this area the reform impulse radiated outwards. At the end of the tenth century it began to interest princes and emperors. Their patronage could have intensified the danger of lay intervention in the affairs of the Church but paradoxically made a great recovery of papal independence possible.

The reform movement took its name and much of its impulse from the most celebrated of the new houses, the Burgundian abbey of Cluny, founded in 909 by the duke of Aquitaine. For nearly two and a half centuries Cluny generated religious and ecclesiastical energy. The Cluniac leaders were men of culture, often of noble birth, sprung from the leading families of Burgundy and the West Franks (a fact which helped to widen their influence) and they threw their weight behind the moral and spiritual reform of the Church. Cluniac monks followed a revised Benedictine rule but also evolved something new, a religious order resting not only on a uniform way of life, but on a centrally disciplined organization. Benedictine monasteries had previously been autonomous communities, but the new Cluniac houses were all subordinate to the abbot of Cluny itself; he was the general of an army of (eventually) thousands of monks who only entered their own monasteries after a period of training at the mother house. At the height of Cluny's importance, in the middle of the twelfth century, more than 300 monasteries – some as far away as Palestine – looked to it for direction. It was the greatest ecclesiastical centre and finest church in western Christendom after St Peter's at Rome. From the outset Cluniac monasticism disseminated new practices and ideas throughout the Church, slowly revealing itself as a revolutionary force, above all in the renovation of ideas on the distinction of lay and clerical authority.

Church and State: issues of reform

Seven of the first eight abbots of Cluny were outstanding men: four of them were canonized. They quickly won influence in high places. They advised popes, acted as their legates, served emperors as ambassadors. Leo IX, the pope with whom papal initiative in reform really begins, eagerly promoted Cluniac ideas and ideals; his pontificate marks the beginning of more than two centuries of change and struggle and a revolution in the standing and authority of the papacy, though it ended in a humiliating defeat and imprisonment by the Normans in southern Italy. He spent barely six months of his five years' reign at Rome but moved about from synod to synod in France and Germany, correcting local practice, checking interference with the Church by lay magnates, punishing clerical impropriety, imposing a new pattern of ecclesiastical discipline. Greater standardization of practice followed. Virtually all the issues and aspirations which have come to be lumped together as 'reform', were raised during his pontificate and mixed up with them were concerns over economic and political interest, though under Leo they were not so obviously in question as they were later to become. The western Church began to look more homogeneous. Ironically, this was accompanied by a definitive rupture with Orthodox Christendom in 1054.

Reform was bound to arouse opposition, not least among churchmen themselves. Bishops did not always like papal interference in their affairs; parochial clergy did not always see a need to change established custom (clerical marriage, for example) which did not trouble their flocks for more austere practice. The most spectacular resistance to ecclesiastical reform, though, came in the great quarrel which has gone down in history as the 'Investiture Contest', in which lay power was at issue. The attention given to it – and the issue cropped up in more than one instance – though understandable, has been perhaps slightly disproportionate, even, some would say, misleading. The central episodes lasted only a half-century or so and the outcome was by no means clear-cut. Though implicit in some aspects of the quarrel, the very distinction of Church and State which it raised was in the modern sense still unthinkable to medieval man.

At the heart of things, there was clearly at stake a transcendent theoretical question which did not go away: what was the proper relationship of lay and clerical authority? The specific administrative and legal practices at issue were in fact often the subject of agreement. Many clergy felt more loyalty to their lay rulers than to the pope and sought compromise. The question had a substantial material component which blurred matters: how power and wealth were to be shared within the ruling classes who supplied the personnel of both royal and ecclesiastical government in Germany and Italy, the lands of the Holy Roman Empire. Several countries were touched by similar quarrels – the French in the late eleventh century, the English in the early twelfth – and this indicates the universality of what was at stake.

The most public battle of the struggle was fought just after the election of Pope Gregory VII in 1073. Hildebrand (Gregory's name before his election: hence the adjective 'Hildebrandine' sometimes used of his policies and times) emerges from the records as a far from attractive person, but a pope of great personal and moral courage. He may himself have been a monk at Cluny and he had advised Leo IX and other popes. All his life he fought for the independence and dominance of the papacy within western Christendom. An Italian (but not a Roman) he had played a prominent part in assuring the transfer of papal election to the college of cardinals, and the exclusion from the college of the Roman lay nobility, all before his own pontificate began. When reform became a matter of politics and law rather than morals and manners (as it did during his twelve years' reign) Hildebrand was a man to provoke rather than avoid conflict. He liked decisive action without too nice a regard for possible consequences.

At the core of reform lay the ideal of an independent Church. It could only perform its proper task, Leo and his followers had already thought, if free from lay interference. Their view was that the Church should stand apart from temporal authority, the clergy living lives different from laymen's lives: they should form a distinct society within Christendom, thought the reformers. From this ideal came attacks on simony (the buying of preferment), a campaign against the marriage of priests, and a fierce struggle

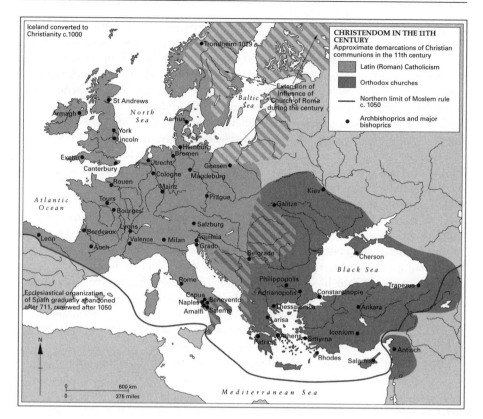

Iceland converted to Christianity c.1000

Trondheim 1029

Extension of Influence of Church of Rome during the century

CHRISTENDOM IN THE 11TH CENTURY
Approximate demarcations of Christian communions in the 11th century

Latin (Roman) Catholicism

Orthodox churches

Northern limit of Moslem rule c. 1050

● Archbishoprics and major bishoprics

St Andrews

Armagh

North Sea

Baltic Sea

York

Lincoln

Hamburg

Bremen

Exeter

Utrecht

Gnesen

Canterbury

Cologne

Magdeburg

Rouen

Mainz

Prague

Atlantic Ocean

Tours

Bourges

Salzburg

Kiev

Galitz

Lyons

Bordeaux

Valence

Milan

Aquileia

Grado

Leon

Auch

Belgrade

Cherson

Black Sea

Ecclesiastical organization of Spain gradually abandoned after 711, renewed after 1050

Rome

Philippopolis

Adrianopolis

Constantinople

Trapezus

Capua

Benevento

Naples

Amalfi

Salerno

Thessalonica

Ankara

Larisa

N

Athens

Smyrna

Iconium

Patras

Rhodes

Salamis

Antioch

0   600 km
0   375 miles

Mediterranean Sea

over the exercise of hitherto uncontested lay interference in appointment and promotion. It was this which gave its name to the long quarrel over lay 'investiture': who rightfully appointed to a vacant bishopric or abbacy, the temporal ruler or the Church? The right was symbolized in the act of the lay ruler 'investing' the bishop-elect with his ring and staff and receiving his homage. It was at stake above all, thought Hildebrand, in the relations of pope and emperor.

Perhaps emperors were bound to find themselves in conflict with the papacy sooner or later, once it ceased to need them against other enemies. Emperors inherited big, if shadowy claims of authority which they could hardly be expected to give up without a struggle. Ways of doing certain things had hardened into accepted custom and tradition. In Germany the Carolingian tradition had subordinated the Church to a royal protection which easily blurred into domination. Within Italy the empire had allies, clients and interests to defend, but both the emperors' practical power over the papacy and their formal authority had declined since the days of the Ottonians and the emperor was left with a theoretical veto and no more in a papal election. Working relationships had deteriorated. Some popes had already begun to dabble in troubled waters by seeking support among the emperor's vassals.

The temperament of Gregory VII would not ease this delicate situation. He took his throne without imperial assent, simply informing the emperor of the fact of his election. Two years later, in 1075, he issued a decree on lay investiture. Curiously, what it actually said has not survived, but its general content is known. He denied any layman the right to invest a cleric with an ecclesiastical office, and affirmed the pope's right to depose lay sovereigns. He further excommunicated some of the emperor's clerical councillors on the grounds that they had been guilty of simony in purchasing their preferment. To cap matters, he summoned the emperor Henry IV to Rome to appear before him and defend himself against charges of misconduct.

Henry was particularly concerned to retain the loyalty of the German bishops, valuing them as an important counter-weight to obstreperous lay magnates. He responded first through the Church itself, getting a German synod to declare Gregory deposed. This earned him a sentence of papal excommunication and deposition, which would have mattered less had he not had powerful enemies in Germany who now had the pope's support. Henry had to give way. To avoid trial before the German bishops presided over by Gregory (who was already on his way to Germany), Henry came in humiliation to Canossa, where he waited in the snow barefoot until Gregory would receive his penance in one of the most dramatic of all confrontations of lay and spiritual authority. At the time, this caused less of a stir than might be thought. The pope's position was too extreme; he went beyond canon law in asserting the revolutionary doctrine that kings were but officers who could be removed when the pope judged them unfit or unworthy. This was almost unthinkably subversive to men whose moral horizons were still so dominated by the idea of the sacredness of oaths of fealty; it was bound to be unacceptable to any king. Gregory had not really won.

Investiture was to run on as an issue for the next fifty years. Gregory lost the sympathy he had won through Henry's bullying. He died in 1083 in exile in the Norman kingdom of southern Italy, after Henry had taken Rome and installed an antipope there. It was not until 1122 that another emperor agreed to a concordat which was seen as a papal victory, though one diplomatically disguised. Yet Gregory had been a true pioneer; his reign had differentiated clerics and laymen as never before and had made unprecedented claims for the distinction and superiority of papal power. More would be heard of them in the next two centuries, when history would carry the Church to a peak of success – worldly and unworldly – unequalled between the age of the Fathers and that of its spread to become a world religion.

CHAPTER THREE Medieval societies

Emerging from antiquity

It is all too easy to generalize misleadingly about the daily life and social relationships of Europeans before modern times. Their essence is diversity within a framework shaped by a few fairly simple facts and constricting material possibilities. Patterns of consumption and the power relationships that mattered were overwhelmingly local. Agricultural possibilities were the ultimate force shaping them, but not the only one.

Economic life in the west at the end of antiquity was at low ebb by comparison with the past, and that meant different things in different places. It was to take a long time to recover. In some areas – notably some once-flourishing Mediterranean cities – it was to suffer further setbacks before recovery came about. In the centuries of imperial decline the old imperial landed class had hung on tenaciously wherever it could. Even during the barbarian centuries, there was probably no great fall in the production of the individual self-sufficient estate. The most developed sections of the economy suffered more. Barter replaced money over most of the west and a money economy emerged again only slowly. The Merovingians began to mint silver, but for a long time there was not much coin – particularly coin of small denominations – about. Spices tended to disappear from ordinary diet, while wine became a costly luxury; most people ate bread and varieties of porridge, and drank beer or water. Scribes turned to parchment, which could be obtained locally, rather than papyrus, now hard to get (this turned out to be an advantage, for minuscule was possible on parchment, as it was not on papyrus, which required large, uneconomical strokes).

These were symptoms of a recession which confirmed the tendency of individual estates to consume their own produce, ruining towns and emptying their markets. The universe of trade disintegrated further from time to time because of war. Commercial activity in the western Mediterranean dwindled when the Vandals cut old trade flows (those, for instance, which supplied grain and olive oil to Italy from Africa) and then again during the seventh century as the Arabs seized the North African coast. Later, it was thanks to the Arabs that trade somewhat revived, sometimes in new forms (one sign was a brisker business in slaves, many of them from eastern Europe, from the Slav peoples who thus gave their name to a whole category of forced labour). Exchange with Byzantium continued and, therefore, the old luxury trade routes from Asia were never wholly stopped, though they tended, because of the generalized poverty of the west, to dwindle. In the north, too, there was flourishing exchange in a few places with the Scandinavians, who were great traders. But this did not impinge on most Europeans.

For the majority, life rested on agriculture, and for a long time subsistence was to be almost all that they could hope for from it. That agriculture was the main concern of the early medieval economy and became for a time less varied in produce and more local in its marketing are some of the few safe generalizations to be made about it. Animal manure or the breaking of new and more fertile ground were the only ways of improving a return on seed and labour itself derisory by modern standards. Only long and laborious husbandry could change this. The animals who lived with the stunted and scurvy-ridden human tenants of the Dark Age landscape were themselves under-nourished and undersized. For fat, the better-off peasant depended upon the pig, or, in the south, on olive oil. Only after centuries do signs appear which suggest the recovery that was slowly under way.

A new agriculture

This recovery changed the economic map of Europe and was the gradual out-come of a number of changes in agricultural technique which made possible greater productivity from land, its primary resource. Broadly speaking, the lands north of the Ebro, Loire and Alps had never formed part in antiquity of what we might (using an anachronistic term) label the 'developed' economic world of the Mediterranean basin. They had never been able to sustain such large populations as the lands further south, principally because they could not produce enough food. Even in the days of Charle-magne, the greater part of France, Germany and England were unusable, covered with forest and waste. The first major rise in productivity had by then begun, though, and it came from the clearance and breaking-in of new land for cultivation. This was con-nected with other, antecedent changes which came together to make available for the first time an effective agriculture of a kind suited to the northern lands of abundant rain-fall and heavy soil. The tools and methods of Mediterranean agriculture had not been able to supply that.

The decisive original contribution has been identified as the adoption in the sixth century among Slav communities of the east and central Europe of a new, heavy, wheeled plough far superior to the simple surface-scratcher hitherto available. Similar ploughs have been detected turning up subsequently in Lombardy in the seventh cen-tury, in the Rhineland in the eighth, and across the Channel in England in the ninth. In their local variations, the new ploughs all brought with them a new capacity. Break-ing into, clearing and cultivating heavy land, speedier working, the preparation of fields for sowing in less time, the abandonment of cross-ploughing such as had previously been necessary, and better draining all followed their appearance. They had other con-sequences in the longer term, too. Because teams of oxen were needed to haul them, the new ploughs favoured bigger fields and a change in their shape (old-fashioned, roughly square, small patches were replaced by long rectangles), and new social practice. Co-operation, agreements and the enforcement of patterns of cultivation all mattered more as common fields took shape, first providing a two-field rotation between cropping and fallow, and then, when beans and peas began to be planted as an alternative to cereals, a system of three fields per village (this seems to have appeared first in the eighth cen-tury). Change in social behaviour was needed to exploit the new possibilities.

There is little chance of measurement, but it is fair to deduce that there was a substantial increase in the production and productivity of northern Europe. Cautious economic historians have been willing to speculate that there might have been a general growth in productivity of the order of 50 per cent between the sixth and tenth centuries. Other technical innovations contributed to that, too. The scythe had been rare in Roman times, but spread now into general use as a much more efficient instrument than the sickle, horse-shoes (especially) and better harness made it possible to use the more responsive and faster traction provided by horses, and the invention of the whipple-tree brought about a modest revolution in transport, because of the larger and better wagons it made possible. All these changes had by the eleventh century brought about an irreversible agricultural revolution in northern Europe, accentuating and underpinning the shift in the dynamic centre of the continent's history from the Mediterranean countries to the north. For the most part the southern lands did not see the same changes; less rainfall made some of them pointless, though there were other new departures. Thus (from Islamic sources) different new crops and techniques made their appearance – rice in the Po valley or Sicily, for example, and intensive vegetable production in southern Spain as Arab irrigation techniques were introduced.

Nowhere did such changes alter the huge and general predominance of agriculture within the economy, of course. Everything depended on it in the end. It was a long time before a new urbanism could show in a thriving town life. Such towns as survived were mainly to be found in Italy, where commercial relations with the outside world had been sporadically kept up even amid the upheavals of first barbarian and then Arab invasions. Elsewhere, towns did not begin much to grow until after 1100; even then, it would be a long time before western Europe could boast any city comparable to the great centres of Islamic and Asian civilization. Almost universally in the non-Mediterranean west the self-sufficient agricultural estate remained for centuries the foundation of the economy. It fed and maintained a population at first almost certainly smaller than the same area had supported in antiquity, though even approximate figures are almost impossible to establish. A series of great plagues had done much demographic damage in the sixth century and there is evidence of little more than a very slow growth of population until the eleventh. But it is hard to believe that growing productivity did not mean rising population. That of the territory covered by the old western Roman empire in Europe may have stood in the year 1000 at about 40,000,000 – getting on for two-thirds of that of the United Kingdom today. Nevertheless, though real income, and consumption levels and life expectancy probably did not vary much across the continent, it must always be remembered that it is misleading to think of *an* early medieval European economy. There were many European economies, with few if any ties between them; they shared little but their poverty.

The social order

In such conditions, possession of land or access to it was more than ever the supreme determinant of the social order. Somehow, slowly, but logically, the great men of western societies, while continuing to be the warriors their ancestors had been when they lived in barbarian tribes, became landowners too. With the dignitaries of the Church and their kings, they were therefore the ruling class; from the possession of land came not only revenue by rent and taxation, but jurisdiction and labour service, too.

Landowners were the lords, and gradually their hereditary status was to loom larger and their prowess and practical skill as warriors was to be less emphasized (though in theory it long persisted) as the distinction that made them noble.

The lands of some of these men were granted to them by a king or great prince. In return they were expected to repay the favour by turning out when required to do him military service. Moreover, administration had to be decentralized after imperial times, barbarian kings did not have the bureaucratic and literate resources to rule directly over great areas. The grant of exploitable economic goods in return for specific obligations of service was therefore very common. This arrangement lay at the heart of what later lawyers and historians, looking back at the European Middle Ages, and greatly exaggerating the coherence, uniformity and extent of what they saw, called 'feudalism'. Many tributaries flowed into this stream. Roman and Germanic custom both favoured the establishment and institutionalizing of dependence in the later days of the empire. In the troubled times of early Merovingian Gaul, men often 'commended' themselves to a great lord; this meant that in return for protection they offered him a special loyalty and service. This was a usage easily assimilated to Germanic custom. Under the Carolingians, the practice began of 'vassals' of kings doing them homage; that is to say, they acknowledged special responsibilities of service to him with distinctive, often public ceremonies. He was their lord; they were his men. The old loyalties of the blood-brotherhood of the warrior-companions of the barbarian chief began to blend with notions of commendation in new moral ideals of loyalty, faithfulness and reciprocal obligation.

As the relationships elaborated, vassals came to have their own vassals and one lord's man might be another man's lord. A chain of obligation and personal service could stretch (in theory) from the king down through his great men and their retainers to the lowest of the free. And, of course, that might produce complicating and conflicting demands. In respect of some of his lands a king could be another king's vassal. At the bottom of society, below the free, were the slaves, more numerous perhaps in southern Europe than in the north and everywhere showing a tendency to evolve marginally upwards in status and to dwindle as a category, becoming serfs – unfree men, born tied to the soil of the manor, but nevertheless, not quite without rights of any kind.

Such a schematic description is likely to be dangerously misleading. Some people later spoke as if the relationship of lord and man could explain the whole of medieval society. This was never so. Though much of the land of Europe was divided into fiefs – the *feuda* from which 'feudalism' takes its name – which were holdings bearing obligation to a lord, much of Italy, Spain and southern France was never 'feudal' in this sense. Especially in southern Europe, the 'mix' of Germanic overlay and Roman background did not always work out in the same way. Such town life as there was survived in Mediterranean lands, too. There were also always freeholders, too, even in the more 'feudal' north, an important class of men, more numerous in some countries than others, who owed no service for their lands but owned them outright. And even where 'feudal' tenures might exist, considerations of honour and status often counted for more in shaping behaviour.

Corporations, too, might be lords or vassals; a tenant might do homage to the abbot of a monastery (or the abbess of a nunnery) for the manor he held of its estates, and a king might have a cathedral chapter or a community of monks as one of his vassals. There was abundant complexity and ambiguity in the feudal 'order'. But the central fact of an exchange of obligations between superior and inferior ran through society.

On the rationalization that lord and man were bound to one another reciprocally rested many of the arrangements of societies of growing complexity. It does more than anything else to make it intelligible to modern eyes, even if it is only one element in a complex picture.

Such arrangements both set much of the tone of medieval society, and settled the way in which many of its resources were distributed. The theory of dependence justified and the realities of power made possible the exaction from the peasant of the wherewithal to maintain the warrior and build his castle. The military function of the system which supported them long remained paramount. Even when personal service in the field was not required, the vassal's undertaking to provide fighting-men (or, later, his money to pay fighting-men) would be. Of the military skills the most esteemed (because it was the most effective) was that of fighting in armour on horse-back. At some point in the seventh or eighth century the stirrup was adopted; from that time the armoured horseman had for the most part his own way on the battlefield until the coming of weapons which could master him. From this technical superiority emerged the knightly class of professional cavalrymen, maintained by the lord either directly or by a grant of a manor to feed them and their horses. They were the source of the warrior aristocracy of the Middle Ages and of European values for centuries to come. Yet for a long time, the boundaries of this class were ill-defined and movement into (and out of) it was common.

Political realities were not always consistent with theory. Some vassals were more easily kept to their obligations than others. The ordinary man probably never saw his king or prince, who might theoretically be the lord of the local magnate, or even the bishop, even though these were the ultimate human authorities set over him. Kings, too, could be threatened or coerced by over-mighty subjects. The causistry of conflicting obligations could be used to justify disobedience – or worse. Even emperors could not do as they liked; the social traditions of Germanic society counted for as much as formal law in determining their real power.

The western country where kings were the most advantageously placed was England, where a central monarchy passed from the Anglo-Saxons who had created it into Norman hands in 1066. But even a weak king had some advantages, if he were pressed. He had, after all, other vassals, not all of whom he need antagonize at once (unless he was very careless); he had a mysterious office, confirmed by the anointing given him by the Church; he was a man set apart by pomp and ceremony. If, in addition, he had large domains of his own, and was careful to keep them – or, better still, enlarge them – he had a good chance of getting his own way.

The beginnings of sustainable growth

From about the year 1000 it is much clearer to the historian that Europeans were beginning to get richer, although slowly. In the twelfth century the evidence shows that important changes had already occurred. In the long run, as a result, more men were to acquire a freedom of choice almost unknown in earlier times; society became more varied and complicated. Slow though it was, this was to prove a many-sided revolution. Wealth was at last beginning to grow faster than population, and in Europe not all the new wealth was squandered by predators (as it was in much of Asia). Improvement by no means occurred everywhere, and it was punctuated by a bad setback in the fourteenth century. Yet the change was decisive, it launched Europe on a unique career of recurring growth lasting to our own day.[1]

The beginnings of this unprecedented trend are just slightly easier to trace and speak confidently about than earlier changes because of one of the most important novelties in the growing variety of the Middle Ages: they are accompanied by just a little more measurement of the dimensions of human life. From these centuries there survives not only a growing flow of commercial record, but the first collections of social and economic facts upon which reasoned estimates can be made. When in 1087 William the Conqueror's officers rode out into England to interrogate its inhabitants and to record its structure and wealth in the Domesday Book, they were unwittingly pointing the way to a new age. Other collections of data, above all for tax purposes, followed in the next few centuries. Thanks to them and to the first accounts (often of monastic estates) which reduce farming and business to quantities, historians can talk with a little more confidence about late medieval society than about earlier times.

For four or five centuries after 1000, for example, although only approximate estimates can be made of population, they are based on more evidence than any earlier estimates. It is unlikely that the errors they contain much distort the overall trend. The 40,000,000 or so people of Europe west of Russia in 1000, appear to grow to 60,000,000 or so in the next two centuries. Further acceleration in the rate of growth then seems to take the total up to a peak of about 73,000,000 in 1300. After this there is indisputable evidence of decline. Europe's total population is thought to have gone down to about 50,000,000 by 1360 and only to have begun again to rise in the fifteenth century, to continue with overall growth uninterrupted ever since.

The location and rate of increase varied, both in the long and short runs. In five centuries the Mediterranean and Balkan lands did not succeed in doubling their populations and by 1450 had relapsed to levels only a little above those of 1000. The same may well have been true of Poland and Hungary. Yet France, England, Germany and Scandinavia probably trebled their populations before 1300 and after bad setbacks still had in 1400 twice as many people as four centuries earlier. Contrasts within countries can be observed sometimes between areas very close to one another, but the general effect is indisputable: population grew overall as never before, but unevenly, the north and west gaining more than the Mediterranean, Balkan and eastern Europe.

The basic explanation lies in food supply, and therefore in further changes in agriculture. More food was obtained, much of it still by bringing more land under cultivation. Europe's great natural advantages included in 1000 large areas of potentially productive agricultural land still mostly wild and forested. They were to be brought into cultivation in the next few centuries with the labour provided by a growing population. Though slowly, the landscape changed. Villages pushed out their fields into the forests. New colonies were sometimes deliberately established by landlords and rulers. The building of a monastery in a remote spot – as many were built – often created a new nucleus of cultivation or stock-raising in an almost empty desert of scrub and trees. Some new land was reclaimed from sea or marsh. In the east, much was won for farming occupation in the colonization of the first German *Drang nach Osten*. Settlement

---

[1]   See the informative and suggestive book by E.L. Jones, *Growth Recurring: Economic Change in World History* (Oxford, 1988).

there was consciously promoted, as it was later to be promoted in North America by the Elizabethans.

By about 1300 the first big increase in the cultivated and grazed area was over, and the breaking-in of fresh land slowed down. There were even signs of over-population. But an increase in productivity had occurred which was never completely lost. In places it may have roughly doubled output. It also owed much to better and better cultivation, the effects of regular fallows and cropping and of the slow enrichment of the soil and the introduction of new crops (grain-growing, though, was still the main business of the cultivator in northern Europe). Cause and effect and hierarchies of influences are difficult to disentangle. Some other forms of innovation are suggestive, too. The first agricultural book-keeping was under way (thanks to monks) and the first manuals of agricultural practice since Roman times appeared in the thirteenth century. More specialized cultivation brought a tendency to employ wage labourers instead of serfs carrying out obligatory work. By 1300 it is likely that most household servants in England were recruited and paid as free labour, as were a third or so of the peasant labour force. The bonds of servitude were relaxing and in some places a money economy was spreading slowly into the countryside. The 'customs' or taxes for protection exacted by some French landlords were being turned into money payments as early as the twelfth century.

Most of the increased wealth, in fact, usually went to the landlord. He (rarely she, for women who owned land were likely to be men's wards) took most of the profits. Most peasants went on living poor and cramped lives, eating coarse bread and various grain-based porridges, seasoned with vegetables and only occasional fish or meat. Calculations suggest the poorest labourer consumed about 2,000 calories daily (approximately the figure calculated for the average daily intake of a Sudanese in 1988), and this had to sustain him for very heavy work. If he grew wheat he did not eat its flour, but sold it, keeping barley or rye for his own food. He had little elbow-room to better himself. Even if his lord's legal grip through bond labour slackened, there were often practical monopolies of mills and carts, which the peasant had to use in order to work the land. 'Customs' were levied on most estates without regard to distinctions between freeholders and tenants; they could hardly be resisted, any more than could the decisions of manorial courts. We tend to see the rural economy through the perspective of the seigniorial estate, though, because that is the route by which so much of the evidence arises. It is important, once again, to remember that no generalization can be absolutely sustained about so richly-varied a continent.

Towns and trade

More cash crops for growing markets gradually changed the self-sufficient manor into a unit producing for sale. It found its markets in the towns, which grew steadily between 1100 and 1300; urban population went up faster than rural in these centuries. This is a complicated phenomenon. The new town life was in part a revival going hand in hand with the revival of trade, in part a reflexion of growing population; their growth came about entirely from migration from the countryside. It is a chicken-and-egg business in more senses than the most obvious. A few new towns grew up around a new castle or a new monastery. Sometimes this led to the establishment of a market. Many towns, especially in eastern Germany, were deliberately settled as colonies. On the whole long-established towns grew bigger – Paris may have had about

80,000 inhabitants in 1340 and Venice, Florence and Genoa were probably comparable – but few were so big. Fourteenth-century Germany had only fifteen towns of more
than 10,000 inhabitants, and London (with about 35,000) was then by far the biggest
city in England. Of the great medieval cities, few except those in the south, many of
them on the coasts, had been important Roman centres (though many in the north, of
course, had, like London and Paris, Roman nuclei). New foundations tended to be
linked distinctively to economic possibilities. They provided markets, or lay on great
trade-routes such as the Meuse and Rhine, or were grouped in an area of specialized
production such as Flanders, where already in the late twelfth century Ypres, Arras and
Ghent were famous as textile centres, or Tuscany, another cloth-producing region.
Wine (one of the first agricultural commodities to loom large in trade between countries) underpinned the early growth of Bordeaux. Ports like Genoa and Bruges often
became the metropolitan centres for maritime regions, providing goods and services to
a sizeable hinterland.

The commercial revival was most conspicuous in Italy, above all, at Venice. In that
great commercial centre banking for the first time separated itself from the changing of
money. By the middle of the twelfth century, whatever the current state of politics,
Europeans (mainly from Italy and Catalonia) were engaged in continuing trade not
only with Byzantium but with the Islamic Mediterranean lands and substantial numbers of their merchants lived in foreign stations. Beyond those limits, an even wider
world was involved. In the early fourteenth century trans-Saharan gold from Mali
began to relieve bullion shortage in Europe. By then, Italian merchants had direct, if
tenuous, contact with central Asia and China. Others sold slaves from Germany and
central Europe to the Arabs of Africa and the Levant, or bought Flemish and English
cloth and took it to Constantinople and the Black Sea. In the thirteenth century the first
voyage was made from Italy to Bruges; before this the Rhine, Rhône and overland
routes had been the only channels of north-south trade. Trade fed on trade and the
northern European fairs drew other merchants from the north-east. The German towns
of the Hansa, the league which controlled the Baltic, provided a new outlet for the textiles of western Europe and the spices of Asia. Others than Italians and Catalans began
to interest themselves in Mediterranean commerce. In 1461 the English, French and
Germans set up a joint consulate at Naples.

In such ways, economic geography changed and a true European economy began
to appear. In Flanders and the Low Countries there grew populations big enough to
stimulate agricultural innovation by making it profitable. Everywhere, towns which
could escape from the cramping monopolies and oligarchies of the earliest manufacturing centres enjoyed new prosperity. One visible result was a great wave of building.
Besides the houses and guildhalls of newly prosperous cities this left a glorious legacy in
Europe's churches, still visible not only in the great cathedrals, but in the scores of magnificent parish churches of little English towns and villages.

Towns are cultural as well as economic engines; they drive and express aspirations
and ways of thinking directed to more than material purposes, and they create new ways
of behaving. Their embellishment by architecture, improvement by the paving of
streets and building of arcades and fountains, their regulated development (by, for
example, what a later age would call 'zoning' to provide for the management by segre-
gation of strangers) and specifications about the dimensions and placing of buildings all
nourished new mentalities, slowly though these took to grow. Safe behind their walls

and strong gates, towns offered a measure of security in a violent world; for all their own histories of riots and mobbings, they provided at times consciously and legally demilitarized areas in a warlike society, where people were forbidden to carry weapons. *Urbanitas* was a word which began in the thirteenth century to be used of city life in a way which carried more meaning than that of simple physical residence in a town – as still does its English successor, 'urbanity'.

Special ceremonies and festivals provided new cement for urban life. For growing numbers of townsfolk, the services they provided were increasingly important. Lay professions crystallized within them. Teachers were drawn to them. Schools appeared, and, later, the student populations from which were to grow the universities. These generated new business, not only for tavern-keepers and the service industries provided by the likes of Mistress Quickly and Doll Tearsheet, but for copyists, scribes and sellers of manuscripts. Occasionally, numerical evidence reveals a growth in literacy. For the first time, significant numbers of boys began to be taught to read, write and cipher, without it being presumed that they would finish as clerks in holy orders. It was claimed that in the early fourteenth century there were between 8,000 and 10,000 children learning to read and write in the schools of Florence and that over a 1,000 were studying in institutions specifically teaching mathematics as a preparation for commerce.[2]

The first citizens of the new age of towns had been barely more than shop-keepers, stall-keepers in the marketplace, or craftsmen selling their own products and skills. It was not long, though, before some among them can be observed engaging in commerce on a larger scale. Some soon commanded capital sufficient to enable them to buy materials which they could then put out to craftsmen for them to turn into goods for sale. Others used the wealth provided by accumulated profits to lend money; in the thirteenth century the practice produced the first European banks. Some townsmen took other roads to economic independence; public scribes and notaries began in the thirteenth century to be identifiable as the members of distinct professions – and their usefulness to the wealthy who had transactions to conduct on parchment or paper gave them opportunities to prosper which were not available to the barber or cobbler. Medieval society in western Europe tended from the twelfth century to produce an increasing number of people, almost always living in towns, who, though ultimately dependent on it, had no direct part in the rural economy but made their living in other ways, some of them anticipated and available in other societies or those of the ancient world, others quite new. In the pursuit of their trades and occupations, some of these men were in some places beginning as early as the eleventh or twelfth centuries to be wealthy on a scale which had not been seen in western Europe since the days of the Roman empire. Some of them, too, were beginning to be skilled in preserving their wealth and in turning it into productive investment.

Technology

Building was the major expression of medieval technology as well as the most visible one. The architecture of a cathedral posed engineering problems as complex as

---

[2] These figures appear in J. Le Goff's excellent introduction to the subject, 'The Town as an Agent of Civilisation c. 1200–c. 1500', which he contributed to C.M. Cipolla (ed.), *The Fontana Economic History of Europe, I. The Middle Ages* (London, 1972), p. 85.

those of a Roman arena or aqueduct; in solving them, the engineer slowly emerged from the medieval craftsman. Medieval technology was not in a modern sense science-based, but drew on accumulated experience and what could be developed from it by trial and error. Its most important achievement was the harnessing of other forms of energy to do the work of muscles and the deployment of muscle-power more effectively and productively when used. Winches, pulleys and inclined planes eased the shifting of heavy loads. Cranes were common by 1500. Technological change may well have mattered most in agriculture, whose productivity it so much increased. It was a sector whose frontiers blurred with other activities where technology made great strides. Growing and better use was being made of wind and water, notably in milling; wind-mills and watermills, first known in Asia, were widely spread in Europe even by 1000. Domesday Book recalls an average of nearly two each for the 3,000 settlements it lists. In later centuries they were put to wider use. Wind usually replaced muscle-power in milling foodstuffs, as it had already done in the north in propelling ships; water was used when possible to provide power for forging (the invention of the crank was of the greatest importance), an essential element in a fifteenth-century surge in Europe's met-allurgical industry which was closely connected with rising demand for artillery, an innovation of the previous century. Water-driven hammers were put to work in fulling and paper-making in the eleventh century and later, once that invention had made its way to Europe from its origins in China. The invention of printing in the fifteenth cen-tury was to give paper-making an importance which may even have surpassed that of new skills in metal-working in Germany and Flanders. Print and paper had their own revolutionary potential, too, and part of it was to make the diffusion of techniques faster and easier in the growing pool of craftsmen and artificers able to use such knowledge. Some innovations were taken over directly from other cultures; the spinning-wheel came to medieval Europe from Asia in the thirteenth century (though the application of a treadle to it to provide drive with the foot seems to.have been a European invention of the sixteenth century).

An era of self-feeding and irreversible technological change had thus begun by 1500. It would have, with time, wider and wider ramifications and display deeper and deeper implications. Its roots were deep. The invention of the cam which made it pos-sible to turn continuing rotary motion into repeated and interrupted action has been traced back as far as the days when Carolingian brewers used it to drive hammers to crush the mash for their beer. The flywheel had appeared in the twelfth century. Weight-driven machinery had evolved so far by the fourteenth century that there was about to be a widespread diffusion of the mechanical clock, with immense and subtle implications for the regulation of life and work. Spectacles – which, because of their vast extension of the period during which a man might expect to use his eyes effectively, have been called the most important invention of the European Middle Ages – had similar far-reaching effect: they launched the craft and industry of optical instrument-making. Armourers developed their skills not only in the manipulation of metal to make better body-armour, but in casting the new guns which entered warfare in the fourteenth century, and in making standardized shot for them. By 1500 there was a European population of craftsmen and technologists of a size and sophistication unimaginable even a couple of centuries earlier. They were at work not only manufac-turing, maintaining and repairing the already considerable stock of European machin-ery, but improving it and inventing new devices, a source of self-grown innovation.

Technology's greatest days in changing manufacture still lay far ahead. But here and there capital had begun to be applied to it by businessmen. Other modernizing technical devices, in any case, were already at work in their affairs. By 1500, Italians had invented much of modern accountancy and new credit instruments for the financing of international trade. The bill of exchange appears in the thirteenth century along with the first bankers. Limited liability was known at Florence in 1408. Marine insurance was available before that. In such novelties, we are at the edge of the age of modern capitalism. Yet though the change from the past was by implication colossal, it is easy to get it out of proportion if we do not recall the scale of the medieval commercial economy. For all the magnificence of its palaces, the goods shipped by medieval Venice in a year would fit comfortably into one modern cargo-carrier of no great size.

The Black Death and after

For centuries, the economy was very fragile. Medieval economic life in the west was never far from the edge of collapse. For all the progress since antiquity medieval agriculture was (by later standards) often startlingly inefficient. It abused the land and exhausted it, putting back into it little except manure. As new land became harder to find, family holdings got smaller. A rural household would have been lucky to farm more than eight acres in 1300. Only in a few places (the Po valley was one) was there much investment in collective irrigation or improvement. Above all, subsistence was vulnerable to weather; two successive bad harvests in the early fourteenth century reduced the population of Ypres by a tenth. Local famine could rarely be offset by imports. Roads had broken down since Roman times, carts were crude and for the most part goods had to be carried by pack horse or mule. Water transport was cheaper and swifter, but could rarely meet the need. Commerce could have its political difficulties, too; new onslaughts by Islamic armies on Byzantium brought a gradual recession in eastern trade in the fifteenth century. Demand was small enough for a very little change to determine the fate of cities; cloth production at Florence and Ypres fell by two-thirds in the fourteenth century.

A plateau of agricultural productivity seems to have been reached by about 1300. Probably available techniques and easily accessible new land for cultivation had by then run out of their potential. Signs of population pressure treading close upon resources have been detected. From this flowed a huge demographic setback in the fourteenth century and then a slow recovery in the next. It is very difficult to generalize, but there was a rapid rise in mortality, not occurring everywhere at the same time, though notable in many places after a series of bad harvests round about 1320. This marked the onset of a slow decline of population which became a disaster with the onset of attacks of epidemic disease. These are often summed up by the name of one of them, the 'Black Death' of 1348–50 and the worst single attack. It was of bubonic plague, but no doubt that masked many other killing diseases which swept Europe with it and in its wake. Europeans died of typhus, influenza and smallpox as well as plague. What is certain is that the outcome was a demographic disaster. In some areas a half or a third of the population may have died; Toulouse was a city of 30,000 in 1335 and a century later only 8,000 lived there. 1,400 once died in three days at Avignon. Over Europe as a whole the total loss has been calculated as a quarter of the population. A papal enquiry put the figure at more than 40,000,000.

There was no universal pattern, but all Europe shuddered under these blows. In extremity, there were signs of collective madness. Pogroms of Jews were a common expression of a search for scapegoats or those thought guilty of spreading the plague; the burning of witches and heretics was another. The European psyche bore the scars of the disasters for the rest of the Middle Ages, whose art in painting, carving and literature is haunted by the imagery of death, judgement and damnation. The fragility of settled order illustrated the precariousness of the balance of food and population. When disease killed enough people, agricultural production fell; then the inhabitants of the towns began to die of famine if they had not already died of plague.

It is scarcely surprising that dislocations and disasters on such a scale should have been accompanied by new and more violent social conflicts. All over Europe the fourteenth and fifteenth centuries brought peasant uprisings. The French *jacquerie* of 1358 which led to over 30,000 deaths and the English Peasants' Revolt of 1381 which for a time captured London were to be especially remembered. The roots of rebellion often lay in the ways in which landlords had increased their demands under the spur of necessity and in the new demands of royal tax collectors. Combined with famine, plague and war they made an always miserable existence intolerable. 'We are made men in the likeness of Christ, but you treat us like savage beasts', was the complaint of the English peasants who rebelled in 1381. Significantly, they appealed to the Christian standards of their civilization; the demands of medieval peasants were often well formulated and effective but it would be anachronistic to see in them a nascent socialism.

Demographic disaster on such a scale paradoxically made things better for some. One obvious and immediate result had been a severe shortage of labour in some places; the pool of permanently under-employed had been brutally dried up and a rise in real wages followed in England, for example. Once the immediate impact of the fourteenth-century disasters had been absorbed, the standard of living of the poor may even have slightly risen, for the price of cereals came down as the market shrank with depopulation. The tendency for the economy, even in the countryside, to move on to a money basis was speeded up by the labour shortage. By the sixteenth century, serf labour and servile status had both receded a long way in western Europe, particularly in England and France, and wage-labour was much more common than three centuries earlier. This weakened the manorial structure and the relationships clustered about it. Landlords had also been suddenly confronted with a drop in their rent incomes in the fourteenth century. In the previous two centuries the better-off had developed more expensive tastes and habits. Now, property-owners suddenly ceased to grow more prosperous. Some landlords adapted. Some could, for example, switch from cultivation which required much labour to sheep-running which required little. Elsewhere, many landlords simply let their poorer land go out of cultivation.

Social change

The results are very hard to pin down, but they stimulated further and faster social change. Medieval life changed dramatically, and sometimes in oddly assorted ways, between the eleventh century and the sixteenth. Even at the end of that age, though, it seems still almost unimaginably remote from our own, recent though its disappearance has been. One sign is the large number of clergy and female religious, who discharged some workaday tasks (as clerks, nurses, social workers) but above all the one of supreme importance: praying for mankind's salvation and making available the sacraments which helped mankind to deserve it. Their position was specially defined by law and it is almost impossible now to grasp how prominently it loomed in the consciousness of medieval society. Lay society's obsession with its own status and hierarchy is another index of its remoteness from our own. Instead of being an individual social atom, so to speak, we might regard medieval European man as the point at which a number of coordinates met. Some of them were set by birth; the most obvious expression of this was the idea of nobility. The aristocratic society defined by blood which was to linger as a reality in a few places as late as the twentieth century was already present in its essentials in the thirteenth. Once the warriors had turned into landowners descent had become more important, because there were inheritances to argue about. One indicator was the rise of the arts of heraldry and genealogy (though they continue mysteriously to prosper in our own day). Another was the appearance of new ranks and titles as distinctions within the nobility ripened. The first English duke was created in 1337, an expression of a European tendency to find ways of singling out the greater magnates from among their peers. Symbolic questions of precedence became of intense interest; rank was at stake. From this rose the dread of disparagement, the loss of status which might follow for a woman from an unequal marriage or for a man from contamination by a lowly occupation. For centuries it was to be assumed that only arms, the Church or the management of his own estates were fit occupations for a nobleman in northern Europe. Trade, above all, was frowned upon except through agents. Even when, centuries later, this barrier gave way, hostility to retail trade was the last thing to be abandoned by those who cared about these things. When a sixteenth-century French king called his Portuguese cousin 'the grocer king' he was being rude as well as witty and no doubt his courtiers enjoyed the sneer.

The values of the nobility were, at bottom, military but had been gradually refined. The outcome was the notions of honour, loyalty, disinterested self-sacrifice which were to be held up for centuries as models (effective or not) to well-born boys and girls. The ideal of chivalry articulated these ideas and softened the harshness of the military code which was its heart: chivalry's function was above all to provide a training and discipline in arms. It was blessed by the Church, which provided religious ceremonies to accompany the bestowal of knighthood with the knight's acknowledgement of Christian duties. One heroic figure who came supremely to embody the notion was the mythological English King Arthur, whose cult spread to many lands. It was to live on in the ideal of the gentleman and gentlemanly conduct, however qualified in practice. Of course, it never worked as it should have done; few great creative myths do. Much of chivalrous practice was a mere mask for appetite. The feudal theory of dependence never worked as it should, either, nor does the vision of democracy. Self-interest could, but did not usually, give way to chivalry, and the pressures of war, and, more fundamentally, economics, were always fragmenting and confusing social obligations. The increasing unreality of the concepts of lord and vassal favoured the growth of kingly power. The coming of a money economy made further inroads, service had increasingly to be paid for in cash, and rents became more important than the services that had gone with them. Some sources of feudal income remained fixed in terms made worthless by changes in real prices. Lawyers evolved devices which enabled new aims to be realized within a 'feudal' structure more and more unreal and worm-eaten.

Medieval nobility had been for a long time very open to new entrants, but it tended to close ranks as time passed. In some places (Venice was an example) attempts were actually made to close for ever access to a ruling caste. Yet from at least the twelfth century European society was everywhere, and not merely in the Italian republics, generating new kinds of wealth and even of power which could not find a place in the old hierarchies and so brought them in question. The most obvious example was the emergence of rich merchants who were more than mere shop-keepers. They often bought land; it was not only the supreme economic investment in a world where there were few secure ones available, but it might open the way to a change of status for which landownership was either a legal or social necessity. In Italy businessmen became the noblemen and rulers of trading and manufacturing cities; so the Medici became the hereditary rulers of Florence. Everywhere, though, such occupations posed a symbolic challenge to a world which had, to begin with, no theoretical place for them. Soon, they evolved their own social forms – guilds, 'mysteries', corporations – which gave new definition to their social role and new satisfaction to burgeoning aspirations to status.

The rise of the merchant class was a function of the growth of towns; merchants were inseparably linked with the most dynamic element in medieval European civilization, the towns and cities which increasingly fostered within their walls so much of the future history of Europe. Though their independence varied greatly in law and practice, there were parallels in other countries to the Italian 'communal' movement of the eleventh and twelfth centuries which for a time successfully held off the powers of both popes and emperors. Towns in the German east were especially independent, which helps to explain the long life of the powerful Hanseatic League of more than a 150 free towns, but there were other free Imperial cities, too. The Flemish towns also tended to enjoy a fair degree of freedom: French and English towns usually had less. Yet kings and lords alike everywhere sought the support of townsmen and their wealth. They gave towns charters and privileges which, like the walls which surrounded the medieval city, were the guarantee as well as the symbol of immunities. The landlords' writ did not run within them and sometimes their anti-feudal implication was even more explicit: villeins, for example, could acquire their freedom in some towns if they lived in them for a year and a day. 'Town air makes men free' said a German proverb. The communes and within them the guilds were associations of free men for a long time isolated in a world unfree. The burgher – the *bourgeois*, the dweller in bourg or borough – was a man who stood up for himself in a universe of dependence, a citizen in the making, as well as a subject.

Much of the history behind this remains obscure because it is the history of obscure men. The untypical wealthiest merchants who became the grandees of the new cities and fought for their corporate privileges are visible enough, but their humbler predecessors are usually not. Before the year 1000, outside a few Italian ports a merchant can have been hardly more than a peddler of exotica and luxuries which the medieval European estate could not provide for itself. A couple of centuries later his successors were the men who would use liquid capital to order the whole business of production for the market, men with a stake in both manufacture and distribution.

In the blossoming of urban life lies buried much which made European history different from that of other continents. Nowhere in the ancient world (except, perhaps, classical Greece), nor in Asia or pre-Columban America, did city life develop the independence, political influence and economic dynamism it came to show in Europe. One reason was the absence of destructively parasitic empires of conquest to eat away at the will to betterment; Europe's enduring political fragmentation usually made rulers more careful of the geese which laid the golden eggs they needed to compete with their rivals. A sack of a city was a noteworthy event in the European Middle Ages; it was the inescapable and recurrent accompaniment of warfare in much of Asia, as the fate of great trading emporia at the hands of the Mongols showed.

It also must have mattered that, for all its obsession with status, Europe had no caste system so implacable as that of India, no ideological homogeneity so intense and stultifying as China's. Even when rich, the city-dwellers of other cultures seem more readily to have acquiesced in their own inferiority. In contrast, the merchant, the craftsman, the lawyer and the doctor had roles in Europe which at an early date made them more than mere hangers-on of landed society. Their society was not quite closed to change and self-advancement; it offered routes to self-improvement other than the warrior's or the court favourite's. Town air made men more equal as well as free, even if some were more equal than others.

It need not surprise us that practical, legal and personal freedom of men was much greater than that of women (though at the bottom of society there were still in 1500 those of both sexes who were legally unfree and some still found themselves enslaved after being born free). Whether they were of noble or common blood, women suffered (by comparison with their menfolk) from major legal and social disabilities, as they have done in every other civilization which has ever existed. Their rights of inheritance were often restricted; they could inherit a fief, for example, but could not enjoy personal lordship, and had to appoint men to carry out the obligations that went with it. In all classes below the highest there was much drudgery to be done by women; but even when the twentieth century began European women in some countries still worked on the land as women do in Africa and Asia today.

Some theoretical elements were contributed to this practical subjection of women by the Church. In part this was because it had traditionally a hostile stance towards sexuality. Its teaching had never been able to find any justification for sex except the reproduction of the species. Woman being seen as the origin of Man's Fall and a standing temptation to concupiscence, the Church threw its weight behind the domination of society by men. Yet there is more to Christian doctrine than this – not least, its assertion that women had souls to be saved. Other societies have, moreover, done more to seclude and oppress women than those of Christendom. The Church long offered women the only respectable alternative to domesticity available until modern times; the history of the female religious is studded with outstanding women of learning, spirituality and administrative gifts. The position of at least a minority of well-born women, too, was marginally bettered by the idealization of women in the chivalric codes of behaviour of the thirteenth and fourteenth centuries, with its nurturing of ideas of romantic love (to become an obsession of later European culture) and the concept of the protection due to a physically weaker sex.

Yet such ideas can have affected very few. Among themselves, medieval European women were more equal before death than would be rich and poor in Asia today (as, of course, were men). Women lived shorter lives than men, it seems, and frequent confinements and a high mortality rate no doubt explain this. Medieval obstetrics remained, as did other branches of medicine, rooted in superstition, custom, Aristotle and Galen; there was nothing better available. But men died young, too. The great teacher and thinker St Thomas Aquinas lived only to forty-seven and philosophy is not nowadays thought to be physically exacting. This was about the age to which a man of twenty in a medieval town might normally expect to survive; he was lucky to have got as far as twenty already and to have escaped the ferocious toll of infant mortality which imposed an average life of thirty-three years or so and a death rate about twice that of modern industrial countries. Judged by the standards of antiquity, so far as they can be grasped, this was by no means bad.

CHAPTER FOUR Frontiers and neighbours

The World's Debate

When the greatest of English historians wrote about the long drawn-out struggles to end the Islamic grip on the Holy Land which are remembered as the Crusades, he chose a striking metaphor: 'the World's Debate'.[1] He deliberately set these dramatic, often squalid, occasionally heroic, episodes in the context of a clash not merely of human ambitions but of civilizations, of a confrontation of ways of living in and ways of seeing the world, both now and hereafter. Gibbon's metaphor can, moreover, be given a wider application. To a major degree, western Europe was defined physically and psychologically by the existence of other, alternative, civilizations – eastern Christian or Byzantine, as well as Islamic – with which it was in physical contact. It was also given a shape, especially to the east, by other forces, not only geographical and topographical, but ethnic and political, whose influence is still felt today. The Middle Ages did not end this process of definition (there was a notable extension of Islamic power in the Mediterranean and south-east still to come in the sixteenth and seventeenth centuries) but carried it a long way forward.

The process of European definition has to be understood, therefore, as much (if not more) as the outcome of historic changes originating outside as inside geographical Europe. Yet in AD 1000 and for a long time afterwards the inhabitants of western Christendom had very little information about where those changes had (or might) come from. Their most learned men knew something about Byzantium, but much less that was reliable even about those parts of the non-Christian world of whose existence they were aware. Their sailors and merchants did not know as much about the physical shape of the globe as the Arabs who traded from China to Africa, or even as much as some of the geographers of antiquity. Medieval maps reflect this; their core and main content was Christendom, of which Jerusalem, where Christ had taught, suffered and died, was usually depicted as the centre. A little was also known by direct contact about the Islamic lands, across land frontiers in Spain and the south of Italy; within Islam, distinctions could be made between Arabs, Berbers, Moors, Egyptians and other peoples with whom Christians traded and fought, but were usually not. In the end, the west's best information about the non-European world came from Christian, but alien, Byzantium, whose trade drew increasing numbers of western Euro-

---

[1] The phrase, capitalized, provides the closing words of Gibbon's fifty-ninth chapter.

peans to its ports, and whose religious affairs sometimes concerned western clergy. Round the rest of the west European periphery, though, where it was not oceanic and therefore ultimately mysterious, contact with alien worlds was still a matter of encounters with primitive and barbarian pagans dreaded as freebooters, but sometimes tolerated for their trade.

Yet though western Europeans could not then have known it, the barbarians who had so long threatened them had largely ceased to be a danger by 1000. The peoples of what are now Poland, Hungary, Denmark and Norway were on the way to Christianization. On the Spanish land frontier with the Arabs, the long roll-back of Islam which is called the Reconquest was about to begin, though it was to take centuries, and even when it was over conscious struggle with Islam elsewhere would go on longer still. The emotional resonances were still to be felt when any substantive threat from Islam had long gone away (and, indeed, when Christendom itself was no longer a reality). Christian armies attracted warriors from many countries for many reasons, but at least well into the seventeenth century, the struggle with Islam drew its unity and fervour from religion. It was the deepest source of European self-consciousness. Catholic Christianity bound men together in a great moral enterprise, and as it did so almost incidentally licensed the predatory appetites of the military class which dominated lay society. In the name of Christ, its members could spoil pagans with clear consciences.

Franks and Greeks

The Normans were in the vanguard. In the eleventh century they took southern Italy and Sicily back from the Saracens, almost incidentally swallowing the last possessions of the eastern empire in the west as well. Like their kinsmen who would follow duke William 'the Conqueror' to England, they wanted land. There were opportunities in Moslem Sicily, which had lost the protection of its North African overlords and had become the prey of the notables of the island who were squabbling with one another. The imperial government at Constantinople had tried to take advantage of this, as did piratical adventurers from Pisa and Genoa. The Normans, though, who had established themselves in southern Italy, had the advantage of papal support; Rome had no wish to see the Greek church firmly re-established in the former Byzantine possessions in the west.

In 1060 the first party of Normans crossed the Straits of Messina but stayed only a few hours. They were soon back. In 1072 one of their leaders, Roger d'Hauteville, was proclaimed 'Count of Sicily'. His followers were few. Of necessity, Roger's administration had to employ Moslem clerks, soldiers, accountants, tax-gatherers. It took decades to overcome the last centres of Moslem resistance and the Normans brought with them little upon which they could rely except their sheer fighting-power, based on the battlefield superiority of the mail-clad cavalryman. They had to conciliate as well as dominate, and sought collaborators among the indigenous population, Moslem and Orthodox Christian alike. The first Norman governor of Palermo took the title of 'emir' and the Christian kingdom (as Sicily became, when the pope confirmed Roger II as king in 1130) had for a century or so a distinctive flavour of mingled traditions, Latin, Greek and Arab. It was not to last, but for a little while the island sheltered societies not only living side by side, but experiencing also some sharing of custom, law, language and culture which has always marked Sicily ever since, firmly and enduringly though it had been attached by the Normans to the history of western Christendom (and therefore to that, later, of Europe).

The burden of defending Christendom against Islam had of course been borne for centuries by the Byzantines, and mainly alone. But that was ignored in the Latin west, of whose expansion into new territories the Normans were exemplars. Unsurprisingly, too, the 'Franks' who were now launching an age of offensive against Islam were seen at Constantinople as just another set of barbarian invaders in spite of their religious allegiance: the final Schism of Orthodox and Catholic churches came in 1054, provoked by papal support for the Normans in south Italy – such support was a usurpation of Byzantine jurisdiction.

In the eleventh century, the eastern empire was still indisputably a great power. Its resources were still great. Though only the capital itself retained the economic importance it had enjoyed before the Arab invasions, when so many of the other great emporia were lost, there was still an important transit commerce in luxury goods from Asia to the west. Constantine's choice of a site had guaranteed Byzantium a great commercial role and stimulation for the artisan industries which provided other exports. This trade, though, like that within the empire, was increasingly in the hands of Franks, above all, Venetians and Genoese.

The economy had been able to support a successful military effort of recovery by the ninth-century emperors. Two centuries later an unfavourable conjuncture once more overtaxed the empire's strength and opened a long era of decline. It began with a fresh burst of internal and personal troubles. Two empresses and a number of short-lived emperors of poor quality weakened control at the centre. Rivalries within the Byzantine ruling class got out of hand; an aristocratic party at court whose roots lay in the provinces struggled with the permanent officials of the higher bureaucracy. In part this reflected also the conflict of a military with an intellectual élite. Unfortunately, the result was the starvation of the army and navy of the funds they needed. They found it impossible to deal with new threats as they appeared. The Normans provided one of these. For the first time, representatives of western Christendom, (or, according to your view, barbarian invaders from the north) appeared as predators on the empire – with the backing of the western Church. To the east, the caliphates with which the emperors had learnt to live had themselves given way to fiercer enemies. In Asia Minor the Turks from central Asia provided a new menace and after a shattering defeat by them in 1071 Asia Minor was virtually lost to the empire, a terrible blow to its fiscal and manpower resources. Elsewhere, a succession of revolts in the eleventh and twelfth centuries in the Balkans had spread widely one of the most powerful of the dissenting movements of medieval Orthodoxy, the Bogomil heresy; it drew upon popular resentments among non-Greeks of the Greek higher clergy and their Byzantinizing ways.

A new dynasty, the Comneni, once again rallied the empire and was to hold the line for over a century until 1185. Norman invaders were pushed back from Greece. A new nomadic threat from south Russia, the Pechenegs, was fought off. It did not prove possible, though, finally to crack the Bulgars or win back Asia Minor. The last emperor of the Comnenus line strangled his predecessor and nephew, evidence of a vigour and ambition also shown by his reforming efforts, which, nonetheless, led to insurrection and his own displacement, torture and murder. The history of Byzantium had by then already become entangled with that of Latin Christendom in a new way, by the crusading movement.

The Crusades

The word 'crusade' is used very loosely nowadays to indicate a public display of enthusiastic support for almost any cause, but it was for a long time conveniently applied almost exclusively to the succession of military expeditions from western Christendom to Syria and Palestine in the twelfth and thirteenth centuries, whose aim was to recover the Holy Places of Syria and Palestine from their Islamic rulers. This is not an exhaustive or complete description. There were many other recognized crusades, but these expeditions long dominated both the European imagination and Europeans' vision of their ancestors' struggle with Islam. Those taking part were assured, on papal authority, of important spiritual benefits; after death, they would enjoy a remission of the time their souls would spend in purgatory, and if they died on crusade they would achieve the status of martyr. Men so assured – even children, on one occasion – kept the Levant in the forefront of the consciousness of western rulers and the Roman Church for more than two centuries. Their efforts were to end fruitlessly, but left profound marks on the eastern empire, the Islamic Near East, and on European society and psychology.

The first and most successful was launched in 1096, and had been promoted at the Council of Clermont by the pope's own preaching, of which news soon spread. Encouraged by the miraculous and apt discovery of the lance which pierced Christ's side as he hung on the cross, the crusaders recaptured Jerusalem, where they celebrated

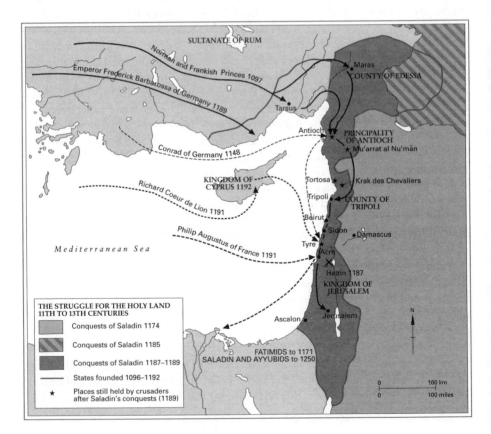

the triumph of the Gospel of Peace by an appalling massacre of their prisoners, women and children included. There followed the creation of what the crusaders came to call 'Outremer', a collection of four statelets in Syria and Palestine (also known as the 'Latin Kingdoms'). They attracted western immigrants bound to their rulers by feudal ties, though never enough of them to meet Outremer's man-power requirements.

The Second Crusade (1147–9), in contrast to the first, *began* with an enthusiastic massacre (of Jews in the Rhineland), but thereafter, though the presence of an emperor and a king of France gave it greater social *éclat* than its predecessor, it was a disaster. It failed to recover Edessa, a city whose loss to the Turks had largely provoked it (though it had a by-product of some importance when an English fleet took Lisbon from the Arabs and the city passed into the hands of the king of Portugal). Then, in 1187, Saladin

---

THE AGE OF THE CRUSADES

The first four Crusades were the most important and together with the liquidation of their creation, Outremer, make what is usually thought of as the Crusading era.

AD 1095	Urban II proclaims the *First Crusade* at the Council of Clermont. It culminated in:
1099	The capture of Jerusalem and foundation of the Latin Kingdoms.
1144	The Seljuk Turks capture the (Christian) city of Edessa, whose fall inspires St Bernard's preaching of a new crusade (1146).
1147–9	The *Second Crusade*, a failure (its only significant outcome was the capture of Lisbon by an English fleet and its transfer to the king of Portugal).
1187	Saladin reconquers Jerusalem for Islam.
1189	Launching of *Third Crusade* which fails to recover Jerusalem, though.
1192	Saladin allows pilgrims access to the Holy Sepulchre.
1202	*Fourth Crusade*, the last of the major Crusades, which culminates in the capture and sack of Constantinople by the crusaders (1204) and establishment of a 'Latin Empire' there.
1212	The so-called 'Children's Crusade'.
1216	The *Fifth Crusade* captures Damietta in Egypt, soon again lost.
1228–9	The emperor Frederick II (excommunicate) undertakes a 'crusade' and recaptures Jerusalem, crowning himself king.
1239–40	'Crusades' by Theobald of Champagne and Richard of Cornwall.
1244	Jerusalem retaken for Islam.
1248–54	Louis IX of France leads a crusade to Egypt where he is taken prisoner, ransomed, and goes on pilgrimage to Jerusalem.
1270	Louis IX's second crusade, against Tunis, where he died.
1281	Acre, the last Frankish foothold in the Levant, falls to Islam.

There were many other expeditions to which the title of 'crusade' was given, sometimes formally. Some were directed against non-Christians (Moorish Spain and the Slav peoples), some against heretics (e.g. the Albigenses), some against monarchs who had offended the papacy. There were also further futile expeditions to the Near East. In 1464 Pius II failed to obtain support for what proved to be a last attempt to mount a further crusade to that region.

recaptured Jerusalem for Islam, a grave setback. The Third Crusade which followed (1189–92) was the most spectacular. A German emperor (drowned in the course of it) and the kings of both England and France took part. They quarrelled and Jerusalem was not recovered. No great monarch answered Innocent III's appeal to go on the next crusade, though many land-hungry magnates did, and it was the most important for the eastern empire. The Venetians financed the expedition, which left in 1202. It was diverted by the deposed pretender to the imperial throne to interfere in the dynastic troubles of Byzantium. This suited the Venetians, who helped to recapture Constantinople for him. Obscure and particular interests then came to operate in the intrigues which followed a terrible sack of the city and the establishment of a 'Latin Empire' at Constantinople. A half-century passed before the Byzantine emperor could return to his capital.

Several more expeditions which were formally and legally crusades set out for the Near East in the thirteenth century, and a German emperor (himself excommunicated) succeeded in re-capturing Jerusalem briefly in 1229, but the movement was ebbing as an independent force. Its religious impulse could still move men, but the first four crusades had shown another, more unpleasant, face of these expeditions. They were the first examples of European overseas imperialism, both in their characteristic mixture of noble and ignoble aims and in their settler colonialism, abortive though it proved. As in Spain, Sicily (where Italian settlers followed the Normans) and on the pagan marches of Germany, western Europeans were pushing forward colonial frontiers; they tried in Syria and Palestine to transplant western institutions to a remote and exotic setting. They also sought to seize lands and goods no longer easily available in the west from the natives and did so with clear consciences because their opponents were infidels who had by conquest installed themselves in Christianity's most sacred shrines. 'Christians are right, pagans are wrong', said a famous medieval poem, *The Song of Roland*, and that probably sums up well enough the average crusader's response to any qualms about what he was doing.

The brief successes of the First Crusade had owed much to a passing phase of weakness and anarchy in the Islamic world. The transplants of the Frankish states and the Latin empire at Constantinople both soon collapsed. But there were permanent results. The Crusades had embittered still further the division of western from eastern Christendom: crusaders had been the first warriors to sack Constantinople. Secondly, they intensified the sense of unbridgeable ideological separation between Islam and Christianity. Subjectively, they not only expressed but helped to forge the special temper of western Christianity, giving it a militant tone and an aggressiveness which would make its missionary work more ruthless and more potent when reinforced by technological superiority.

Nor was the crusading psychology or the formal institution of the crusade itself confined to the Levant. Crusades were proclaimed against other non-Christians (Slav and Prussian pagans, for example) and against heretics (as in the case of the Albigensians of the Languedoc). Crusades were authorized against Christian monarchs who quarrelled with the pope, and even against emperors. As for the future, the roots of a mentality which, when secularized, would energize a world-conquering culture lay in the crusades. As the Reconquest drew to an end the Spanish were already looking to Africa for the battlefields of a new crusade. Soon after that, they would look to the Americas.

The Crusades also affected Europe's history through their contribution to the growth and spread of a new religious institution, the military order of knighthood. It was the most explicit crystallization of militant Christianity, bringing together soldiers committed to fight for the faith by the taking of monastic vows as members of religious orders. Some orders became very rich, with endowments in many countries. The Knights of St John of Jerusalem were for centuries in the forefront of the battles against Islam before they confined themselves to their modern charitable works. The Knights Templar rose to such power and prosperity that a French king feared them and coveted their wealth enough to destroy them; the Spanish orders of Calatrava and Santiago were prominent in the Reconquest. The Teutonic Knights, who had been founded in Palestine in 1190, soldiered in Hungary against the Magyars, before turning to operate in north-eastern Europe, in the Baltic lands, against the heathen Prussians. Their Grand Masters left Palestine in 1291 and set themselves up at Marienburg in 1309; their Christian missionary task, it appears, was by then already stimulating the Knights less than the chance of acquiring estates for themselves.

Eastern Europe and the Slavs

The German frontier of western Christendom, too, was pushed forward by missionary zeal, greed, the lure of land and the stimulus of poverty. The outcome was a change both in the ethnic map and in the culture of the region. The Teutonic Knights were only the spearhead of a Germanic penetration of the Baltic and northern Slav lands, giving new impetus to a tide of men and women which had already flowed for centuries. German expansion eastwards, clearing forest, planting homesteads and villages, founding towns and building fortresses to protect and monasteries and churches to serve them, was as much a huge, slow folk-movement as a planned process. When the Crusades were over, it went steadily forward on the Prussian and Polish marches at the expense of the native peoples, most of whom were pagan. Their despoiling posed little ethical problem. But the Germans were to encounter Christian Slavs as they went further east and into Central Europe. With them there began in the Middle Ages a cultural conflict which persisted down to the twentieth century. In 1941, many Germans were to see 'Barbarossa' (as Hitler's attack on Russia in that year was named in memory of the emperor who died on the Third Crusade) as another stage in a centuries-old civilizing mission in the east.

Though the ground-plan of the Slav peoples of today was established at roughly the same time as that of western Europeans, geography makes for confusion. Slav Europe covers much of that broad and vaguely-defined east European zone where nomadic invasions and the nearness of Asia still left things very fluid long after barbarian society had settled down in the west. In the mountainous central and south-eastern European landmass river valleys channelled the distribution of stocks through the mountains of south-eastern and central Europe. To the north, though still heavily forested, the plains long provided neither obvious natural lodgements nor insuperable barriers to invasion. In its huge spaces, rights were disputed for many centuries. But at the beginning of the thirteenth century there had emerged in the east a number of Slav peoples who would have independent historical futures. For the most part, they have stayed there down to our own day.

There had also come into existence by then a characteristic Slav and Orthodox civilization, though not all Slavs belonged wholly to it; in the end the peoples of Poland and the modern Czech and Slovak republics were to be more closely tied by culture to

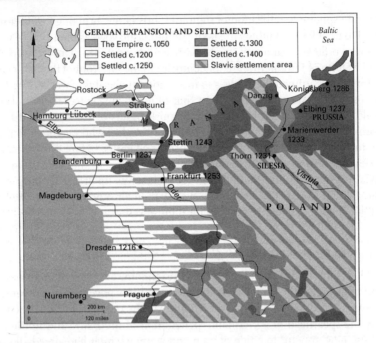

GERMAN EXPANSION AND SETTLEMENT

The Empire c. 1050
Settled c.1200
Settled c.1250
Settled c.1300
Settled c.1400
Slavic settlement area

the west than to the east. The state structures of the Slav world would come and go, but two of them, those evolved by the Poles and Russians, proved particularly tenacious and capable of survival in organized form. They would have much to survive, for the Slav world was at times – notably in the thirteenth and twentieth centuries – under pressure as much from the west as from the east. Western hostility is one reason why the Slav people retained a strong identity of their own, and it was given a special edge by religious difference. Adherence to Orthodox Christianity was to be fundamental to the national identity of some of them.

The legacy of Byzantium – or at least a great and perhaps the most influential part of it – had been secured to the future through the rooting of Orthodox Christianity among the Slavs. With the immense consequences of this, we still live. Had they not been converted to Christianity, the Slav states could not have been seen as part of Europe at all; had they been converted not by the Orthodox but by the Catholics, their history would have shared much more with western Europe. Historians rightly stress all that has made for distinction and separation between Europe east and west. It must never be overlooked, though, that both were Christian. The history of the world would have been immeasurably different if Russia's later emergence had been as an Islamic power.

Kiev Rus

In 860, a few years before the baptism of a Bulgarian ruler announced the formal appearance of the first Christian Slav state, an expedition with 200 ships raided Byzantium. The citizens were terrified. They listened tremblingly in St Sophia to the prayers of the patriarch: his voice might have been that of a western monk invoking divine protection from the sinister longships of the Vikings, and understandably so, for

Vikings in essence these raiders were by origin. But they were known to the Byzantines as Rus (or Rhos) and the raid marks the first sign of a future great power, Russia.

As yet such a power was at best in embryo. There was hardly anything that could be called a state behind the raiders. Their origins lay in an amalgam. Over the centuries Slav peoples had spread across the upper reaches of the river valleys which flow down to the Black Sea. By the eighth century there were enough of them for there to be areas of relatively dense inhabitation on the hills near Kiev. They lived in tribes whose economic and social arrangements remain obscure. We do not know who their native rulers were, but their first towns seem to have been defended stockades, whose garrisons exacted tribute from the surrounding countryside.

On these Slav tribes fell the Norsemen who became their overlords. They combined trade, piracy and colonization, stimulated by land-hunger, and sometimes sold their subjects as slaves in the south. They brought with them formidable fighting power, important commercial techniques, great skills in navigation and seamanship, and, it seems, no women. The Russian rivers, much longer and deeper than the Humber and Seine, gave their longships ways into the country which was their prey. Some went on down the rivers still further south; by 846 we hear of 'Varangians', as they were later called, at Baghdad. One of their many sallies was the attack on Constantinople in 860. They had to contend with the Khazars to the east and may have first settled in Kiev, one of the Khazar tributary districts, but Russian traditional history begins with their establishment in Novgorod, the Holmgardr of Nordic saga. Here, legend said, a prince called Rurik had installed himself with his brothers in about 860. By the end of the century another Varangian prince had taken Kiev and transferred the capital of his people to that town.

The appearance of a new force in the Black Sea area alarmed Byzantium. Characteristically, its response to a new diplomatic problem was cast in ideological terms; there seems to have been an attempt to convert some Rus to Christianity. One ruler may have succumbed. But the Varangians retained their northern paganism – their gods were the savage, unpleasant creatures who have come down to us as Thor and Woden – while their Slav subjects, with whom they were increasingly mingled, had their own gods too, possibly of very ancient Indo-European origins; these different families of deities tended to merge as time passed. Soon there were renewed hostilities. Oleg, a Kiev prince of the early tenth century, once more attacked Constantinople. The Byzantine fleet was away and he is said to have brought his own ships ashore and to have moved them on wheels so as to outflank the blocked entrance to the Golden Horn. However he did it (and whether he did it or not), he was successful in extracting a highly favourable treaty from the empire in 911 which gave the Rus unusual trading privileges. It makes clear the importance of the commercial life of the new principality. Half a century or so after the legendary Rurik, a sort of pagan river-federation centred on Kiev and linking the Baltic to the Black Sea was a reality. When civilization and Christianity came to it, it would be because of the easy access to Byzantium which water gave to the young principality, first designated as 'Rus' in 945. Its unity was then still very loose, its incoherent structure made even less rigid by the custom of dividing an inheritance. Rus princes tended to move around as rulers among the centres of which Kiev and Novgorod were the main ones. Nevertheless, the princes of Kiev became the most important.

During the first half of the tenth century relations between Byzantium and Kiev Rus slowly ripened. Beneath politics and trade a more fundamental re-orientation was taking place. Kiev was relaxing its links with Scandinavia and looking more and more to the south. Varangian pressure seems to have been diminishing (this may have had something to do with the success of Norsemen in finding other lands to exploit further west, notably in what became the duchy of Normandy. Yet it was a long time before there were close ties between Kiev and Byzantium. Imperial diplomacy was cautious and opportunistic, still in the early tenth century as much interested in fishing in troubled waters by negotiating with even wilder peoples as in placating the Rus. The Pechenegs had driven westward the Magyar tribes previously forming a buffer between the Rus and the Khazars and more trouble could be expected there. But Varangian raids on the capital did not come to an end, though there was something of a turning-point when the Rus fleet was driven off successfully in 941. A new treaty followed between the empire and Kiev Rus which significantly reduced the trading privileges granted some thirty years earlier. But a reciprocity of interests was emerging more clearly. Khazaria was in decline and the Byzantines realized that Kiev might be a valuable ally against Bulgaria. Signs of contact multiplied; Varangians appeared in the royal guard at Constantinople and Rus merchants came there more frequently. Some are believed to have been baptized.

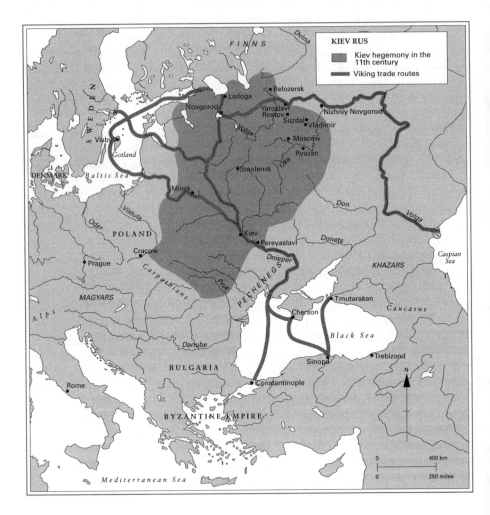

Christianity, though sometimes despising the merchant, has often followed him and his wares. There was already a church in Kiev in 882, which may have served foreign merchants. But nothing seems to have grown from this. There is scanty evidence of Russian Christianity until the middle of the next century. Then, in 945, Olga, the widow of a Kievan prince, assumed the regency on behalf of his successor, her son Sviatoslav. He was the first prince of Kiev to bear a Slav and not a Scandinavian name. Later, in 957, Olga made a state visit to Constantinople. She may before this have been secretly baptized a Christian, but it was then that she was publicly and officially converted, the emperor himself attending the ceremonies in St Sophia. Because of its diplomatic overtones it is difficult to be sure exactly how to understand this event. Olga had, after all, also sent to the west for a bishop, to see what Rome had to offer. Furthermore, there was no immediate practical sequel. Sviatoslav, who reigned from 962 to 972, turned out to be a militant pagan, like other Viking military aristocrats of his time. He clung to the gods of the north and was doubtless confirmed in his belief by his success in raiding Khazar lands (he did less well against the Bulgars, though, and was finally killed by the Pechenegs).

This was a crucial moment. Russia was still Viking, poised between eastern and western Christianity. Islam had been held back at the crucial period by Khazaria, but Russia might have turned to the Latin west. Already the Slavs of Poland had been converted to Rome and German bishoprics had been pushed forward to the east, both in the Baltic coastlands and in Bohemia. The separation, even hostility, of the two great Christian traditions was already a fact, and Russia was a great prize waiting for one of them.

Christian Russia

In 980 a series of dynastic struggles ended with the victorious emergence of the prince who made Russia Christian, Vladimir. It is possible that he had been brought up a Christian, but he showed all the ostentatious paganism which became a Viking warlord. Then he began to enquire of other religions. Legend says that he had their different merits debated before him; Russians treasure the story that Islam was rejected by him because it forbade alcoholic drink. A commission was sent to visit the Christian Churches. The Bulgarians, they reported, smelt. The Germans had nothing to offer. But Constantinople had won their hearts. There, they said in words often to be quoted, 'we did not know whether we were in heaven or on earth. For on earth there is no such splendour or such beauty, and we are at a loss to describe it. We know only that God dwells there among men.'[2] The choice was accordingly made. Around about 986–8 Vladimir accepted Orthodox Christianity for himself and his people.

Whatever his motives, this was a turning-point and Orthodox churchmen have acknowledged it ever since. 'Then the darkness of idolatry began to leave us, and the dawn of orthodoxy arose'[3], said one, eulogizing Vladimir a half-century or so later. Yet for all the zeal Vladimir showed in imposing baptism upon his subjects (by physical force if necessary), it was not only enthusiasm which influenced him.

---

[2] See the words of the *Russian Primary Chronicle* referred to and quoted in part above (p. 105), with the reference cited there.

[3] *Source Book for Russian History…*, I, p. 28

Vladimir had been giving military help to the emperor and now, he was promised a Byzantine princess as a bride, to supplement his collection of allegedly hundreds of concubines. This was an unprecedented recognition of the standing of a prince of Kiev. The emperor's sister was made available; Byzantium needed the Rus alliance against the Bulgars and when things were not going smoothly, Vladimir had put on the pressure by occupying Byzantine possessions in the Crimea. The marriage soon followed. Kiev was worth a nuptial mass to Byzantium, though Vladimir's choice was decisive of much more than diplomacy. 200 years later his countrymen acknowledged this and he was canonized. He had made the first decision which shaped a future Russia.

Tenth-century Kiev Rus may well have had in many ways a richer culture than most of western Europe could then offer. Its towns were trading centres, channelling goods into the Near East where Russian furs and beeswax were prized. This commercial emphasis reflects another difference: in western Europe the self-contained, subsistence economy of the manor had emerged as the institution bearing the strain of the collapse of the classical economic world. Without the western manor, a territorial aristocracy would take longer to emerge in Russian than in Catholic Europe; Russian nobles were still long to remain very much the companions and followers of a war-leader. Some of them opposed Christianity. As in Bulgaria, the adoption of Christianity was above all a political act. It had internal as well as external implications. Though the capital of a Christian principality, Kiev cannot be seen as the centre of a Christian nation. The monarchy and clergy had to assert themselves against a conservative alliance of aristocracy and paganism (which hung on in the north for a long time). Lower down the social scale, the new faith took root only gradually, helped by Bulgarian priests, who brought with them the liturgy of the south Slav Church and the Cyrillic alphabet. This launched Russian literacy. Ecclesiastically, the influence of Byzantium remained strong and the Metropolitan of Kiev was usually appointed by the patriarch of Constantinople.

Kiev became famous for the magnificence of its churches; it was a great time of building and their style showed Greek influence. They were of wood, and few now survive. But a certain artistic primacy can be seen to have accompanied and reflected Kiev's wealth. Its apogee came under Jaroslav 'the Wise', when one western visitor thought it rivalled Constantinople. Russia was then culturally as much in contact with the outside world as she was ever again to be for centuries. Jaroslav exchanged diplomatic missions with Rome and Novgorod received the merchants of the German Hanse. Himself married to a Swedish princess, Jaroslav found husbands for women of his family in kings of Poland, France and Norway. A harried Anglo-Saxon royal family took refuge at his court. Links with western Christendom were never to be so close again. Culturally, too, the first fruits of the Byzantine implantation on Slav culture were being gathered. Educational foundation and legal creation reflected this. From his reign comes also one of the first works of literature in Russia, The Primary Chronicle, an interpretation of Russian history with a political purpose, like much other early Christian history. It sought to provide a Christian argument for the acts of Christian princes, and, specifically, the unification of Russia under Kiev. Significantly, it stressed the country's Slav heritage.

One weakness of Kiev Rus lay in a divisive rule of succession. Though one other eleventh-century prince managed to assert his authority and hold foreign enemies at bay, Kievan supremacy waned after Jaroslav. The northern princedoms showed greater endurance; Moscow and Novgorod emerged, eventually, as the two most important among them, though another 'grand' princedom to match Kiev's was established at Vladimir in the second half of the thirteenth century. In part this shift of the centre of gravity of Russia's history reflects a new threat to the south in the pressure of the Pechenegs, now reaching its peak. It was a momentous change. In these northern states, the beginnings of future trends in Russian government and society can be discerned. Slowly, grants from the princes were transforming the old followers and boon-companions of the warlord kings into a territorial nobility. Even settled peasants began to acquire rights of ownership and inheritance. Many of those who worked the land were slaves, but there was no such pyramid of obligations as constituted the territorial society of the medieval west. Yet these changes unrolled within a culture whose major direction had been settled when Kiev Rus became Christian.

Poland

Another enduring nation which began to crystallize at about the same time is Poland. Its origins lay in a group of Slav tribes who first appear in the records, in the tenth century, struggling against pressure from the Germans in the west. It may well have been politics that dictated the choice in 966 of Christianity as a religion by Poland's first historically recorded ruler, Mieszko I. The choice was not, though, as in Russia's case, the eastern Orthodox Church; Mieszko plumped for Rome. This decision about ecclesiastical authority tied the Poles throughout their history to the Catholic west as Russians were tied to eastern Orthodoxy. It gave the Polish people a particularly difficult historical destiny (often heroically and tragically fulfilled) as a nation Slav by descent and language, but western European in culture and religion, ground between aggressive and fearful powers on both sides. Immediately, it opened a half-century of rapid consolidation for the new state. A vigorous successor began the creation of an administrative system and extended his lands to the Baltic in the north and through Silesia, Moravia and Cracow in the west. One German emperor recognized his sovereignty in 1000 and in 1025 he was crowned king of Poland as Boleslaw I.

Other Slav kingdoms emerged in Bohemia and Moravia which, in spite of the efforts of Orthodox missionaries, had been re-converted to Latin Christianity. By the beginning of the twelfth century, a Christian Slav Europe existed, though it was not a single entity, but divided between the Roman and Orthodox churches, and by geography. Among them, a non-Slav people, the Magyars, was settled in the Danube valley. St Stephen, their greatest king, turned against Orthodoxy and introduced Catholic missionaries; the pope sent him a crown for his coronation in 1001. North and west the Slavs were still under pressure from German settlers. As for the south and east, Byzantium, as the ultimate power sustaining Orthodox Christendom, was in eclipse during the thirteenth century and in 1240 Kiev itself was taken and sacked by the Mongols who followed up their success in the following year by devastating Hungary. It was to be their last incursion to Europe, but that could not be known at the time. The roots of modern eastern Europe go deep into the past, but we must not over-value the degree to which any particular future for the region was fixed before 1300. Much after that date could have taken a different course.

Europe's emerging shape

By 1300 the continent of the Dark Ages of western Christendom had been changed out of recognition. For a long time it must have seemed that the culture of western Europeans could hardly compete – if they had ever wished to do so – in achievement or, it seemed, potential, with that of the eastern empire. Economically, Byzantium had a potential for the sustaining of great military and diplomatic effort unavailable anywhere in the west until long after the Roman collapse. A visitor in the year 1000 would have found western Europe an almost insignificant backwater of civilization in comparison with Byzantium, or, for that matter, with the caliphate, cut off from Africa, challenged and harried still by Islam. It was Byzantium which preserved, even if more and more only in form, the Roman imperial tradition. For centuries, western kings and princes had been little more than warlords to whom men would turn for protection and in fear of something worse. Western Christendom could not for a long time produce any such theoretical justification of lay power as could the eastern empire or the caliphate, while its political unity was for centuries inconceivable.

By the twelfth century, this had already changed. For the first time since antiquity, Christendom had a definition corresponding somewhat to political reality. History had taken a course unpredictable in Justinian's day. All Europe, east and west, outside the Iberian peninsula, was formally Christian; even if paganism survived in the countryside, it was covert and in retreat. At least in aspiration, a second Christian empire bearing the name of Rome had come into being in the west. But the Christian heritages of east and west were different, and were already at work implanting the facts which complicate our modern puzzlings about where Europe might end in the east. What can be seen is that within the sub-continent called 'Europe', two civilized entities were encountering one another as never before. Shaped in the first place by geography and climate, and then by ethnic and linguistic migration, different in their style and culture (though the material life and technological apparatus available to most of their inhabitants were much the same) a western Christendom no longer faced only simple barbarism on its eastern land frontiers, but also another kind of Christian civilization, thinly spread, but distinctive. Notions of boundaries are too simple to be helpful. What was in essence going on was a continuing encounter which was the outcome of the diffusion of two versions of Christianity, of the enduring presence of Byzantium, and of the emergence of the first Slav nations.

By the thirteenth century, the contrasts of western and eastern Christendom were sharper than ever and in each the pace of change had further accelerated. While western Europe had begun to evolve at a more rapid rate both culturally and politically, the eastern lands were (with the exception of Bulgaria) only just being organized in Christian kingdoms and principalities, some distinguished from others by their religious allegiance to Rome or Constantinople, but yet linked in complex ways and for the most part sharing ethnic and linguistic ties. Somewhere among them or beyond them it is again tempting to try to draw a European boundary. But it would be unwise to do so. One could neither be drawn to general agreement, nor clearly or completely. Material life might be somewhat different in, say, Bohemia and Bulgaria, but it was nowhere near so different as it was to become, and contrasts between daily life in Catholic Lithuania and Orthodox Muscovy, for example, would have loomed far less large than the religious distinction between them.

A *psychological frontier*

If Greeks and Latins were consciously distinct, though, and the thinking men among them (which meant, for the most part, the clergy) were especially aware of it, they were nonetheless both Christian. They shared something neither of them shared with Moslems. Islam confronted both of them as an alien reality. There is a certain oddity about this. For all the recurrent outbreaks of hostility, Mediterranean Europe had for centuries continued to have transactions with Moslems and Islam – and not merely in a commercial sense. In the crusading lands, western Europeans had found things to admire and covet other than their Levantine concubines. Some of them took up luxuries not to be found at home, such as silk clothes, perfumes and a new cuisine. A few acquired the habit of bathing more frequently, but this may not have been help-ful in encouraging cleanliness at home in the west, because it added the taint of reli-gious infidelity to a practice already frowned upon because of the association there of bath-houses with sexual licence.

The most continuous intercourse between significant numbers of people from the two civilizations occurred and the greatest opportunity for mutual exchange, cross-fer-tilization and understanding of one another existed in Spain and Sicily. The eventual disappearance in both countries of what a nineteenth-century historian called by a Spanish word, *convivencia* - by which he meant a mutual practical and social tolerance of one another's ways by peoples of different ethnic and religious communities living side by side – has prompted much speculation and possibly even more sentimental regret about lost opportunities.

Both may be beside the point. There are difficulties in interpreting what the *de facto* toleration of aliens and alien communities in the Middle Ages actually meant; certainly it would be anachronistic to interpret it as expressing anything like the modern notion of tolerance. Under Moslem rule, it is true, it was easier for Moslems, Christian and Jews to live side-by-side without disturbance than in Christian lands. Not much more than fiscal disabilities were laid on the older and (in Islamic eyes) errant faiths; their adherents after all worshipped the same God and shared the teaching of some of his prophets. The reverse was not true. The replacement of Moslem by Christian rule seems always in the end to have provoked conflict, especially if accompanied by the implantation of new Christian settlers. Attitudes changed and hardened with time, too: the militant Christianity of the Spanish Reconquest or the crusading era was intransi-gent in a new way. Moslems, too, had their attitudes hardened by the behaviour of the crusaders in the Levant.

Nonetheless, Alfonso VI of Castile, the king who took back Toledo from Islam to become again the Christian capital it had been in Visigothic times, was also proud to be 'king of three religions', and at his court Christian, Moslem and Jewish scholars debated and worked together. Revealingly, his wife and many of his entourage seem strongly to have disapproved. A German emperor, Frederick II, had at his court in thirteenth-cen-tury Sicily Jewish and Arab astrologers and physicians, and kept a harem in the Moslem style. But Frederick, *stupor mundi* as he was called, was always suspect to Christians as an infidel himself (perhaps a wizard); moreover, the impression of tolerance has to be balanced against the fact that he was the ruler under whom Moslem Sicily finally dis-appeared. By his day, Sicily had for a long time ceased to display the apparent social tol-erance which Norman rule had so long left undisturbed. Frederick himself expelled the last Moslems from the island as rebels in the 1220s, re-locating them in Apulia; there were only about 20,000 of them by then – less than a tenth of the number when the Normans had arrived, five per cent of the population instead of fifty. There had been popular pogroms for a long time. Intentionally or not, Sicily was an early example of 'ethnic cleansing' – by conversion, intermarriage, displacement by Christian immigration and, finally, deportation – and the creation of a new, Latin, society.

Significantly, Arabic has left no such rich linguistic deposit in Sicilian and southern Italian language as in Castilian (from which many words of Arabic origin were to pass into other European languages). El-Andalus was for a long time one of the richest parts of a greater Islamic world, as Sicily never was, containing some of the most splendid cities of a civilization of unrivalled geographical extent. In the tenth century, the caliphate of Córdoba may well have been the most powerful state in western Europe, and to its capital (and to Seville, Granada and Toledo) came scholars and intellectuals from all over the Christian and Islamic worlds. The Jews, whose communities were spread through both worlds, often had a special role as communicators and translators between two cultures.

Ideas were generated and developed in Spain which were to be of huge importance in enriching the culture of Christendom. The activity of translating texts was of the first importance: Greek, Persian and Indian science made their way through Arabic into Latin and western Christendom's classical tradition was reconnected in a new way to the ancient world through the Arabic texts of Hellenistic writers hitherto unavailable. In the twelfth century, direct translation from Greek began. Euclid's mathematics, the medicine of Aristotle, Galen and Hippocrates, new interpretations of Greek thought (above all, of Aristotle, thanks to the work of the Cordoban sage, Averroes) all reached the intellectuals of western Christendom by this route. Many more practical and technical transfers also came through Spain. Arab physicians had built up a better body of therapeutic, anatomical and pharmacological knowledge than anything available in Christendom. Besides the special practice of Arab agriculture, which left a permanent mark on the Spanish landscape, Arab cartographical and navigational skills and a knowledge of Ptolemy's astronomy (which Europeans would find a satisfactory basis for cosmology until the sixteenth century), the astrolabe, the use of the decimal point and much else all came to Europe through Islam. It has been claimed, too, that the invention of perspective in art, which was to change European painting, came from thirteenth-century Arab Spain.

To no other civilization did Europe owe so much in the Middle Ages as to Islam. For all their dramatic and exotic interest, reports of the travels of a Marco Polo or the missionary wanderings of friars in central Asia did little to change the west. The quantity of goods exchanged with other parts of the world was still tiny, even in 1500. Europe it is true, took from the Far East (through the eastern empire) the arts of making silk; paper, though made in China in the second century AD, took until the thirteenth to arrive in Europe by way of Islamic Spain. Few innovative ideas reached Europe from Asia, in fact, unless like Indian mathematics they had undergone refinement in the Arabic crucible. Given the permeability of Islamic culture, it seems less likely that this was because Islam was an insulating and selective barrier between Europe and the Orient than because China and India could not make their impact felt across such huge distances. Communications had been no more difficult in antiquity, but they had not done so then, either.

Even when interchange with it was operating most fruitfully, though, the Islamic world was fragmenting. There were disasters in the Near East. In the tenth century, Moslem Spain's own greatest days as a military and political force were drawing to a close. Its last great surge of energy came at the end of the tenth century. Soon afterwards, though, El-Andalus fell into division; the next significant milestone of the retreat of Islamic power was the loss of Toledo.

By then the Islamic phenomenon had made an indelible impression in the west. Yet it was one-sided. For all the exchanges between learned men and the benefits they brought to Christendom, pagans were still wrong, disliked and feared. Ordinary men – including ordinary clergy – remained deeply ignorant of Islam, and for that reason all the clearer about the black-and-white certainties of their prejudices. Nor were Europeans whom we may suppose raised by education above the rank-and-file of society always better informed. It has been pointed out that there is no evidence before 1100 that anyone in northern Europe had even heard of Muhammad, or that any Latin translation of the Koran existed until 1143[4]. Such negative facts, as well as the self-interest of soldiers of fortune and land-hungry squires shaped Europe's longterm views of the major alien civilization with which it was in direct contact for hundreds of years. Indirectly, therefore, they shaped Europeans' views of themselves.

---

[4] R. Southern, *Western Views of Islam in the Middle Ages* (Cambridge, Mass., 1962), pp. 15,28.

CHAPTER FIVE The civilization of the Middle Ages

The identification of an idea

'Medieval', 'medievalist', 'medievalism' are all words invented in the nine-teenth century as useful applications of the idea of the 'Middle Ages', in English an already familiar eighteenth-century phrase. It had been preceded in a singular form, 'Middle Age' (a usage still favoured by the French) as a rendering of a number of earlier Latin expressions in which the common element always present was the idea of a tract of time identifiable because standing between two eras, one embodying an ancient, classical, pre-Christian world, one that of the contemporary who used the phrase. This idea was already frequently employed in the fifteenth and sixteenth centuries; one use of a version of it has been found as early as 1464.[1]

Such phrases, obviously, are not self-contained; they are in fact incomprehensible unless we know some other facts. They designate something at first sight very vague, and need to be anchored in time (and, for that matter in place) before we know what they mean. They refer to an unspecified number of centuries distinguished only by coming between others, and we are entitled to ask 'between what? after what? in the middle of what?' Most people who read this book are likely to know the answers to such questions, approximately at least, before they open it, but only because the phrase 'Middle Ages' has come to be taken for granted; has come to carry with it certain assumptions and presuppositions – among them, that they apply to European history. But they were not there when men started to talk about *medium aevum* or *media aetas*, or coined other phrases as they cast about to express what they wanted to say. There was a time when the Middle Ages was a new idea, an invention, in fact.

Some have traced its kernel back to St Augustine, who began his *City of God* in the aftermath of the sack of Rome. This gave him a starting-point for a new, post-classical era, but no closing date (he assumed that would come with judgement day and the opening of eternity, when all history would come to an end). At the end of the fifteenth century a book of history was published which illustrates that by then it was possible to envisage a new era, begun at the end of classical antiquity, and drawn to a close in their own age, and deserving to be considered as whole.[2] Before this, though, some have

---

1 On this topic see the still helpful note by G.S. Gordon, 'Medium Aevum and the Middle Age', *S.P.E. Tract no. XXI* (Oxford, 1925). He suggested a probable first recorded use of 'Middle Age' in 1611.

2 410–1440 was the period chosen by Biondo, the author of this book (usually referred to for short as his *'Decades'*) which was first printed in Venice in 1483 and reprinted several times within the next few years.

seen in the Italian poet and scholar Petrarch the first man to write as if he saw himself on a historical cusp between two ages, feeling himself at the junction of two eras which we have learnt to call (though he could never have done) medieval and modern.

Quite soon the time came when such a distinction was thought to indicate a qualitative change. Some learned men began to seek to recapture antiquity long cut off from them, an age when, they thought, men had done and made great things. They sensed in themselves and their own time a rebirth and quickening of civilization and came to believe that great things were being done once more. But between two periods of creativity they often saw only a void defined ostensibly by its position between other ages, but in itself dull, uninteresting and barbaric. A negative view, that little importance needed to be attached to these centuries, whose only interest lay in the illuminating contrast they supplied to the more interesting ages they followed and preceded, came to be shared by many thoughtful men. It received forceful and notable expression in 1620 in the writing of the seventeenth-century savant, parasite and royal servant, Francis Bacon, sometime Lord Chancellor of England, a man who came, with reason, to be regarded as one of the founders of modern intellectual activity. As he put it, out of twenty-five centuries in which men had been in search of knowledge, real advance had only been achieved in six – and those of the Middle Ages were not numbered among those. Bacon was sure that neither the Arabs nor the Schoolmen had contributed anything to the increase of knowledge, and had indeed probably diminished it.[3]

Of course, such views were distortions (and some might say this summary is itself a caricature of them). Yet as recently as a couple of centuries ago, when the Middle Ages were thought of as a whole it was still often with contempt, as an era of 'Gothic' darkness. Then came a great change. Men started to idealize those lost centuries as vigorously as their forebears had ignored them. Europeans began to fill out their picture of the past with historical novels about chivalry, their countryside with mock baronial castles inhabited by cotton-spinners and stockbrokers, and their cities with 'neo-Gothic' churches. This was a part of what has been called the Romantic movement. More important, a huge effort of scholarship was brought to bear on medieval records in one of the great intellectual enterprises of modern Europe, the rise of modern historical scholarship. This was a great improvement, but still left barriers to understanding, some of which are still with us. Men came to idealize the unity of medieval Christian civilization in the west and the seeming stability of its life, but in so doing blurred the huge variety within it.

It remains hard to understand the European Middle Ages. One crude judgement, though, looks plausible and can be risked. The centuries between the end of antiquity and the year 1000 or so can be regarded as an age of foundation. Certain great markers then laid out patterns of the future, even if change came slowly and its staying power was still uncertain. In the eleventh century, a quickening of pace can be sensed. New developments became discernible. As time passes, it becomes clear that they are opening the way to something quite different. An age of adventure and revolution was under way. It was to go on increasingly evidently until European history merged with the first age of global history.

This has posed problems: we have had to think again about when the Middle Ages 'end'. In many parts of Europe, they were still going strong institutionally at the end of

---

[3]   *Bacon's Novum Organum*, ed. T. Fowler (Oxford, 1878), pp. 266–7.

the eighteenth century, in Russia, in the nineteenth. In 1800, Europe's first trans-planted offshoot had just come into politically independent existence across the Atlantic, but many and probably most Americans, like millions of Europeans, then still took for granted a supernatural, theocentric view of life. Many held traditional reli-gious views, just as medieval men and women 500 years earlier. Many Europeans still then lived lives materially much like those of their medieval forebears. On the other hand, in some countries the Middle Ages were long past, in reality if not quite in appearance, and in others medieval institutions had disappeared or were crumbling, taking unquestioned traditions of authority with them. In some countries, something we can recognize as the modern world had indeed already been appearing by 1500.

The Church

To understand medieval Europe, the place to begin is the Church. If Europe was anything it was Christian. By 'the Church', Christians traditionally mean the whole body of the faithful, lay and cleric alike, alive and dead. So far as the living were con-cerned, the medieval Church was the same thing as European society. Its comprehen-siveness registered a great success story. Explicit, official paganism had disappeared from the map between the Atlantic coasts of Spain and the eastern boundaries of Poland. In that area unbelief was unavowable and only a few – Jews, visitors and slaves – stood apart from the huge body of Christian people, who, at various levels of under-standing, shared or said they shared Christian beliefs. Moreover, there had been a great qualitative as well as a quantitative change since the Dark Ages. The religious beliefs of Christians provided for hundreds of years the springs of a whole civilization, unthreat-ened in any serious way by division or by alternative mythologies. Christianity had come to define Europe's purpose and to give its life a transcendent goal. It was the way in which Europeans first became conscious of themselves as members of a larger but particular society.

Nowadays, non-Christians are likely to think of 'the Church' as a collection of ecclesiastical institutions, the formal structures and organizations (and even buildings) which maintain the life of worship and discipline of the believer. In this sense, too, whatever qualifications and ambiguities hung about them the Roman Church could boast a great practical achievement. From a backwater of ecclesiastical life in late antiq-uity, it had emerged to become by 1500 the possessor and focus of huge power and influence. For a 1,000 years it had zig-zagged its way towards a new independence and importance in public life. It had given a new temper to Christian living. Since 1000 Christian religious life had become more disciplined, more aggressive and also more rigid: some doctrine and liturgical practice now taken for granted was only adopted when half the Christian era was already over. Above all, the Church had come to pos-sess in a transformed papacy a central institution giving it a coherence and strength it had long lacked.

Hildebrand's immediate successors had acted less dramatically than he had done, but they, too, had gone on pressing papal claims to papal advantage. Urban II used the First Crusade to become a diplomatic leader of lay monarchs; they looked to him, not the emperor. He also built up the Church's administrative machine; under him there emerged the *curia*, a Roman bureaucracy corresponding to the household administra-tions of the English and French kings. Through it the papal grip on the Church itself was steadily strengthened. In 1123, a historic date, the first ecumenical council in the west was held at Rome, in the Lateran palace, and its decrees were promulgated in the pope's own name. And all the time, papal jurisprudence and jurisdiction were grinding away; more and more legal disputes found their way from the local church courts to papal judges, whether resident at Rome, or sitting locally. As the investiture contest receded, secular princes other than the German emperors showed themselves on the whole well-disposed to Rome, even if a spectacular quarrel in England over the question of clerical privilege and immunity from the law of the land had led to the murder of an archbishop of Canterbury. But on the whole, the large legal immunities of clergy were not much challenged in their day-to-day working. Prestige, dogma, political skill, administrative pressure, judicial practice and the control of more and more benefices gradually laid foundations upon which ambitious popes might hope to build the papal monarchy implicit in the ideas of Hildebrand.

In 1195 a canon lawyer became pope. Innocent III was the first pope to call himself 'Vicar of Christ'. Under his pontificate papal pretensions reached a new theoretical height, yet, he did not go quite so far as Hildebrand had done in claiming an absolute plenitude of temporal power everywhere in western Christendom, (though he did say that the papacy had by its authority transferred the empire from the Greeks to the Franks). Nonetheless, he claimed the right to interfere in secular matters as the earthly supervisor of the moral conduct of lay rulers, as well as that of conferring authority on the elected emperor through the bestowing of his blessing and the act of coronation. Within the Church Innocent was limited by little but the capacity of the bureaucratic machine through which he had to operate. He often used his power in support of ecclesiastical reform, and much remained which required his attention. Clerical celibacy gradually became more usual, widespread and ultimately the norm. Among new practices which were imposed on the Church by 1215 – the year of the fourth Lateran council which was the climax of Innocent's reign – was that of frequent individual confession, a powerful instrument of control in a religiously-minded and anxiety-ridden society. By then, too, the cup had been withdrawn from the laity at the mass and the doctrine of transubstantiation, that by a mystical process the body and blood of Christ were actually present in the bread and wine used in the communion service, was imposed by the same council.

Monastic reform and papal autocracy were wedded to intellectual effort in the final christianizing of Europe in the central Middle Ages. This achievement was made visible in stone by the deployment of a new wealth in architecture. For centuries, the European landscape would be dominated, as a result, by church towers or spires rising above little towns. Until the twelfth century most of the greatest buildings of the Church had been monastic; then there began the building of the astonishing series of cathedrals, especially in northern France and England, which remains one of the great glories of European art and constituted the major architecture of the Middle Ages. There was great popular enthusiasm, it seems, for these huge investments, though it is difficult to penetrate to the mental attitudes behind them. Analogies might be sought in the feeling of twentieth-century enthusiasts for space exploration, but this would omit the supernatural dimension of these great buildings. They were both offerings to God and an essential part of the instrumentation of evangelism and education on earth. About their huge naves and aisles moved processions of relics and the crowds of pilgrims who had come to see them, sometimes from hundreds of miles away. Their windows were filled with the images of the biblical story which was the core of European culture; their façades were covered with the didactic representations of the fate awaiting just and unjust. Christianity achieved in these great buildings a new self-representation, a new publicity and collectiveness. Its full impact on the imagination of medieval Europeans is hard to grasp unless we remember how much greater was the contrast its splendour presented to the reality of everyday life than any imaginable today. And that it had no competition.

Innovation and heresy

The power and penetration of organized Christianity and the growth in the resources and authority of the papacy, were reinforced in the early thirteenth century by the foundation of two new religious orders, the mendicant Franciscans and Dominicans; in England they came to be called respectively the Grey and Black Friars, from the colours of their habits. The Franciscans were true revolutionaries: their founder, St Francis of Assisi, left his family to lead a life of poverty among the sick, the needy and the leprous. The followers he soon gathered about him eagerly took up a life lived in imitation of Christ's poverty and humility. They had at first no formal organization and Francis was never a priest, but Innocent III shrewdly seized the opportunity of patronizing this potentially divisive impulse. Instead of letting it escape from control he bade the Franciscans elect a Superior through whom the new fraternity would be kept in obedience to the Holy See. It provided a potential counter-weight to local episcopal authority because the friars could preach without the licence of the bishop of the diocese. The older monastic orders recognized a danger and opposed the Franciscans, but the friars prospered, despite internal quarrels, and were always to remain peculiarly the evangelists of the poor and the mission field.

The Dominicans, or Order of Preachers, were given a narrower and more consciously defined goal. St Dominic, their founder, was a Castilian priest who had ministered in the Languedoc to heretics, the Albigensians. From his companions grew a new organisation; when he died in 1221 his little band of seventeen followers had become an order of over 500 friars. Like the Franciscans, they were mendicants vowed to poverty, and like them, too, they threw themselves into missionary work. But their major impact was intellectual; they became a force in a new institution of great importance, just emerged, the university.

Churchmen had persecuted heretics since the fourth century. Yet their first condemnation by a pope did not come until 1184. Only under Innocent III did persecution come to be the duty of Catholic kings. The Albigensians were certainly not Catholic, and there is some doubt whether they should really be regarded even as Christian heretics, for their beliefs reflect doctrines like those of the Manicheans against whom Augustine had written. They were dualists, seeing the world as a battlefield of absolutely good and evil principles (some of them rejected all material creation as evil). Like those of many later heretics, heterodox religious views were taken to imply aberration or at least nonconformity in social and moral practices. After several missions had failed to convert them, Innocent III seems to have decided to persecute the Albigensians when a papal legate in the Languedoc was murdered, and in 1209 a crusade was launched against them. For ten years it attracted many laymen (especially from northern France) because of the chance it offered for a quick grab at the lands and homes of the Albigensians, but it also marked a great innovation: the joining of State and Church in western Christendom to crush by force dissent which might place either in danger. Persecution was for a long time effective, though never completely so. A new instrument was set up especially to combat heresy, the Inquisition, and in it Dominicans played a notable part. They were given in 1233 the task of extirpating the last survivals of the Albigensian heresy, and this they achieved with complete success.

Tolerance and intolerance are words whose proper application to the medieval world is never easy; there is a danger of misunderstanding the co-existence of such facts as the extension to the foreigner or immigrant of a limited immunity from demands made on Christians, and the ferocious pursuit of heresy. In judging the theory and practice of medieval intolerance it must be remembered that the danger in which society was felt to stand from heresy was appalling: if error went unchecked, its members might face everlasting torment. Yet persecution did not prevent the appearance of new heresies again and again in the next three centuries. Heresy expressed real needs and genuine religious impulse. It was, in one sense, an exposure of a hollow core in the spectacular success of the Church. Heretics were living evidence of dissatisfaction with the victorious outcome of a long and often heroic battle. But other, non-heretical critics also had their disappointments. Arguments for the plenitude of papal power provoked counter-attack: it had long been said by some ecclesiastics, and not only by laymen, that the Church had a sphere of clearly defined activity and that it did not extend to meddling in secular affairs. Such thinking became more appealing as time went by and men became more conscious of membership of national communities and their claims. Much more was to be heard of such things in the fourteenth and fifteenth centuries. Other criticisms had different roots. Even the Albigensians seem to have won support because of the contrast between the austere lives of their most fervent adherents and the worldliness of many parish clergy.

Yet there were plenty of men who confidently insisted on the Church's power (and duty) to put failures and shortcomings right. They faced an increasingly visible problem, though, a gigantic paradox which would not go away. As it grew in power and wealth, the medieval Church deployed lands, tithes and taxes in the service of a magnificent hierarchy whose worldly greatness reflected the glory of God and whose lavish cathedrals, great monastic churches, splendid liturgies, learned foundations and libraries embodied the devotion and sacrifices of the faithful. Yet the point of all this power and grandeur was to preach a faith at whose heart lay the glorification of poverty and humility and the superiority of things not of this world. The *Magnificat*, one of the greatest of Christian hymns, gloried in the putting down of the mighty from their seats and the exalting of the humble and meek; the Church after seemed not to be very good at either.

As time went by, ecclesiastical worldliness drew mounting criticism. It was not just a matter of a few ecclesiastical magnates lolling back upon the cushion of privilege and endowment to gratify their appetites and neglect their flocks. There was a more subtle corruption inherent in power. The defence of the faith had become identified with the triumph of an institution; the Church had acquired an increasingly bureaucratic and legalistic face. The point was not new. It was said as early as the twelfth century that there were too many ecclesiastical lawyers, and the papacy itself was the focus of criticism over it. At the end of the pontificate of Innocent III the Church of comfort and sacraments often seemed obscured behind the granite face of centralization. The proper claims of religion were being confused with the assertiveness of an ecclesiastical monarchy. It was difficult to keep the government of the Church in the hands of men of spiritual stature; Martha pushed Mary aside, as administrative and legal gifts were increasingly needed to run a machine which tended to generate its own purposes. Some argued, that a higher authority than that of the pope and an instrument of purification might be found in an ecumenical council.

Would-be reformers took heart in 1294 when a hermit of renowned piety was elected pope. But their hopes were quickly dashed when Celestine V was forced within a few weeks to resign, seemingly unable to impose his reforming wishes on the *curia*. His successor was Boniface VIII, who has been called the last medieval pope. Boniface embodied all the pretensions of the papacy at its most political and its most arrogant. He, too, was a lawyer, and by temperament far from a man of outstanding spirituality. He quarrelled violently with the kings of England and, especially, France. In the Jubilee of 1300 he had two swords carried before him to symbolize his possession of temporal as well as spiritual power. Two years later, in a notorious Bull, *Unam Sanctam*, he asserted that a belief in the sovereignty of the pope over every human being was necessary to salvation.

Under Boniface the long tensions with kings came to a head in armed conflict. Nearly a 100 years before, Innocent III had laid England under interdict in order to bring its King John to heel; this terrifying sentence deprived the English of any administration of the sacraments while the king remained unrepentant and unreconciled. Men and women could not have their children baptized or obtain absolution for their own sins, and these should have been fearful deprivations in a believing age. John had been forced to yield. A century later, things had changed. Bishops and their clergy were often estranged from Rome, whose pretensions had undermined their authority, too. They could sympathize with a stirring national sense of opposition to the papacy. When the kings of France and England rejected Boniface's authority they found churchmen to support them and resentful Italian noblemen to fight for them. In 1303 some of them (in French pay) pursued the old pope to his native city and there seized him with, it was said, appalling physical indignity. His fellow-townsmen released Boniface and he did not (like Celestine, whom he had put in prison) die in confinement, but die he did, no doubt partly of shock, a few weeks later.

This was only the beginning. A bad time lay ahead for the papacy and, some would claim, for the Church itself. For over four centuries it was now to face recurrent and mounting waves of hostility which, though often heroically confronted, ended in Christianity itself being called into question for the first time by educated men. Even by the end of Boniface's reign, the legal claims he had made were almost beside the point; no one stirred to avenge him. Spiritual failure was now increasingly to draw fire; in the near future the papacy was to be condemned more for standing in the way of religious reform than for claiming too much of kings. It was for failures in their traditional religious task that churchmen were now to be criticized. Yet there were still significant limits to this. The notion of autonomous, self-justified criticism was still unthinkable in the Middle Ages, and no-one thought anyone could do without the Church: what was sought was a reformed Church.

In 1309, a French pope brought the papal *curia* to Avignon, a town belonging to the crown of Naples (from which Clement VI would buy it in 1348) but overshadowed by the French kings whose lands surrounded it. There was to be a preponderance of French cardinals during the papal residence at Avignon, which lasted until 1377. The English and Germans soon said the popes had become the tool of the French kings. They took steps against their assertion of authority in their own lands. The imperial electors declared that their vote required no approval or confirmation by the pope and that the imperial power came from God alone.

The residence of the popes at Avignon has passed into history as 'the Babylonian captivity' because of the alleged subservience to the French monarchy. The building of a huge new palace was a symbol of the popes' decision to stay away from Rome, and its luxury a sign of their growing worldliness. The papal court, of unexampled magnificence, was attended by a splendid train of servitors and administrators paid for by ecclesiastical taxation and misappropriation. Unfortunately, when the fourteenth century brought hard times, a much reduced population was asked to pay more for a more costly (and, some said, extravagant) papacy. Centralization continued to breed corruption – the abuse of the papal rights to appoint to vacant benefices was an obvious instance – and accusations of simony and pluralism had more and more plausibility. The personal conduct of the higher clergy was often very obviously at variance with apostolic ideals. Even among the Franciscans, some, the so-called 'spirituals', broke out in protest that they should take more seriously their founder's rule of poverty when more relaxed colleagues refused to give up the wealth which had come to their order. Theological issues became entangled with this dispute. Soon, some friars were preaching that Avignon was Babylon, the scarlet whore of the Apocalypse, and that the papacy's overthrow was at hand, while one pope, asserting that Christ himself had respected property, condemned the ideal of apostolic poverty and unleashed the Inquisition against the 'spirituals'. They were burned for their preachings, but not before they had been heard sympathetically by some laymen.

The Great Schism

Exile in Avignon thus fed a popular anti-clericalism and anti-papalism alongside and different from the exasperation of kings against priests who would not accept their jurisdiction. Many clergy, too, felt that rich abbeys and worldly bishops were a danger sign, and that the Church had become corrupted. This was the irony that tainted the legacy of Hildebrand. Criticism rose and when the papacy returned to Rome in 1377, it was ill-placed to face the greatest scandal in the history of the Church. Secular monarchs set on having quasi-national churches they could control in their own realms, and the college of twenty or so cardinals anxious to maintain their own revenues and position, together brought about the election of two popes. This began the 'Great Schism'. For thirty years two popes, one at Rome and one at Avignon (elected by the French cardinals alone), simultaneously claimed the headship of the Church. At one point, there was even a third contender. As the schism wore on, criticism became more and more virulent. 'Antichrist' was a favourite term of abuse for the claimants to the patrimony of St Peter. Schism was complicated by the involvement of secular rivalries, too. For the Avignon pope, broadly, there stood as allies France, Scotland, Aragon and Milan; the Roman was supported by England, the German emperors, Naples and Flanders.

For a time, an ecumenical or general council of the Church was the instrument to which reformers looked for a way out. To return to the days of the apostles and the

Fathers for the means to put the papal house in order appeared indeed to many Catholics as good sense. Unfortunately, the conciliar movement did not turn out well. Four councils were held. The first (at Pisa in 1409) struck out boldly; but by deposing both sitting popes and choosing another it created three pretenders to the chair of St Peter. Then, when the newly-chosen pope soon died, another was elected whose choice was said to be tainted by simony (the first John XXIII, now no longer recognized as a pope and the victim of one of Gibbon's most searing judgements). The council of Constance (1414–18), though he had summoned it, removed him, got one of his competitors to abdicate and then deposed the third pretender. At last there could now be a fresh start; the schism itself was over. In 1417 a new pope was elected, Martin V. This was a success, but some people had hoped for more; they had sought reform, from which the council had been diverted. Instead it had devoted its time to heresy, and support for reform dwindled once the unity of the papacy was restored. After another council (Siena, 1423-4) had been dissolved by Martin V for urging reform ('that the Supreme Pontiff should be called to account was perilous', he declared), the last met at Basle (1431–49), but was clearly ineffective long before its dissolution. The conciliar movement had not achieved what so many desired.

The principle that there existed an alternative source of authority in a Council was henceforth always regarded with suspicion at Rome. Within a few years it was declared heresy to appeal from the pope to a general council. Yet though the papacy had maintained its superiority, its victory was only partial; secular rulers had reaped the benefits of anti-papal feeling in new freedoms for national Churches. The Church had not risen to the level of the crisis. One result would be a more decisive movement for reform three-quarters of a century later. As for Rome's moral authority, that had clearly not been restored. The papacy now began to look more and more Italian; the last non-Italian pope for four and a half centuries, Hadrian VI (whose three immediate predecessors had all been Italian) died after only a brief reign in 1523. There were to be some dismal popes to come, but they may well have done less damage to the Church than did the evolution of their see towards becoming just one more Italian state.

Heresy, always smouldering, had burst out during the conciliar period. Two outstanding men, Wycliffe and Hus, focused the discontents to which schism gave rise. They were first and foremost reformers, though the Englishman Wycliffe was a teacher and thinker rather than a man of action. Hus, a Bohemian, became the leader of a movement exciting national as well as ecclesiastical issues; he exercised huge influence in Prague as a preacher. He was condemned by the council of Constance for heretical views on predestination and property and burned in 1415. Wycliffe was more fortunate. The great impulse given by him and by Hus flagged as their criticisms were muffled, but they had tapped springs of national anti-papalism destructive of the western Church's unity. Twenty years after Hus' death, Catholics and Hussites were still disputing Bohemia. Meanwhile, fifteenth-century popes had to make further concessions to lay rulers.

Religious zeal still seemed often to bypass the central apparatus of the Church, while fervour manifested itself elsewhere in a continuing flow of mystical writing and new devotional fashions. In movements like the Brethren of the Common Life of the Low Countries, who followed the teachings of the mystic Thomas à Kempis, laymen created practices and forms which could escape clerical management. A new popular susceptibility to religious excitement was notable in the fifteenth century. Art reflected a new obsession with the agony of Christ's Passion; new devotions to saints, a craze for flagellation, outbreaks of dancing frenzy all suggest a heightened excitability. One outstanding and ambiguous example of the appeal and power of a popular preacher was that of Savonarola, a Dominican who became for a time moral dictator of Florence in the 1490s and, when excommunicated by Alexander VI, demanded a general council which should depose the pope. His flock turned against him and he was hanged.

Yet the fifteenth century in retrospect sometimes looks like an ebbing after a big effort which had lasted nearly two centuries, even if that impression risks a grave misunderstanding. One major fact expressed the most important outcome of centuries of struggle; for most people in western Europe Christendom was their world. They sensed this even more consciously so after the collapse of the eastern Christian empire in 1453. Almost the whole of life was defined by religion. The Church was for most men and women the only recorder and authenticator of the greatest moments of their lives – their marriages, their children's births and baptisms – and its assurances comforted them at death. Many of them wholly gave themselves up to religion; a much greater proportion of the population became monks and nuns than is the case today even in the most Catholic countries. And though they might think of withdrawal to the cloister from a hostile everyday, what they left behind them was no secular world such as ours, wholly distinct from and largely indifferent to religion. Religion coloured and suffused that world, too; they turned their backs on sin, not on disbelief.

Learning, charity, administration, justice and huge stretches of economic life all fell quite explicitly within the ambit and regulation of ecclesiastical authority. Even when men criticized or satirized churchmen, they did so in the name of the standards the Church itself provided and with appeals to the knowledge of God's purposes which the Church had given them. Religious myth was not only the deepest spring of a civilization, it pervaded the life of all men. It defined human purpose in terms of a transcendent good, eternal salvation. Outside the Church, the community of all believers, there were only pagans and Jews. The devil – conceived in a most material form – lay in wait for those who strayed from the path of grace. If there were some bishops and even popes among the errant, so much the worse for them. Human frailty could not compromise the religious view of life. God's justice would be shown and He would divide sheep from goats in the Day of Wrath when all things would end. More than any other single fact, religious faith made medieval Europe utterly unlike ours.

New patterns of power

Most people today are used to the idea that the world's surface is divided between impersonal organizations (most of them called 'states') which provide the final public authority for any given area. They are usually thought in some way to represent peoples or nations. But whether they do or not, they are the building blocks from which most of us would construct a political account of our world and the way we see it. This would not have been intelligible in 1000, though 500 years later some of it might have been to some, for much had by then happened which made the political landscape easier to see in such terms. It depended on what sort of an European you were.

Though far from complete by 1500, the process by which the modern sovereign state emerged is one marker which delimits the modern era of history. The realities came first, before the principles and theory of lawyers and political scientists. The roots of those realities lay in the Dark Ages' primitive kingships, charismatic and patrimonial, intensely personal and focused on the king as leader of the war-band. They were cluttered up with obsessive concern over status, 'face' and honour. Kingly activity was resourced by the ruler's own domain, personal service, hospitality and booty. From such roots there grew in time a royal power served by bureaucracies, maintained by better revenue-raising from subjects, aspiring to monopolies (or at least the lion's share) of lay justice, and a stricter demarcation than before over the territories to which the royal authority extended.

This description is crude and over-schematic. But by the thirteenth century, some monarchies had begun to change in ways and directions which give some substance to it. Those of England and France showed it most. The process was to go much further and become much easier to see in the next couple of centuries, when (for a variety of reasons) it was possible for more rulers to exercise more power over those they ruled. Iron cannons were invented in the early fourteenth century; bronze followed, and in the next century big cast-iron guns became available. As this happened, great men no longer felt so ready to brave the challenges of their rulers from behind the walls of their castles. Steel crossbows, (they, too, were costly) gave an advantage to those who could afford them. Many rulers were by 1500 well on the way to monopolizing the legal use of armed force within their realms. They were arguing more, too, about the frontiers they shared, and this expressed more than just an improvement in surveying; there was a change in emphasis within government, from a claim to control persons who had a particular relationship to the ruler to one to control people who lived in a certain area. Territorial was replacing personal dependence.

Over such territorial agglomerations, royal power was increasingly exercised directly through officials who, like weaponry, had to be paid for. A kingship which worked through magnates known to the king, vassals who did much of his work for him in return for his favours and who supported him in the field when his needs went beyond what his own estates could supply, was giving way to royal government carried out by employees, paid for by taxes. More and more usually raised in cash, not kind, taxation was the main concern of royal servants. The parchment of charters and rolls had begun by 1500 to give way to the first trickles and rivulets of what was to become the flood of modern bureaucratic paper.

Such brevity hopelessly blurs an immensely important and complicated change in political realities. It affected, too, every side of life; religion and the sanctions and authority it embodied; the economy, the resources it offered and the social possibilities it opened or closed; ideas and the pressure they exerted on still plastic institutions. But the upshot is not in doubt. Somehow, Europe by 1500 had begun to organize itself in reality, if not always in appearance, differently from the world of the Carolingians and Ottonians. Though personal and local obligations were long to remain overwhelmingly important for most Europeans, society was beginning to be institutionalized in new ways. The relationship of lord and man which, with the contesting claims of pope and emperor, ecclesiastic and layman, in the background, so long seemed to exhaust political thought, gave way to an idea of princely power over all the inhabitants of a domain. In extreme assertions (such as that of Henry VIII of England early in the sixteenth century that a prince knew no external superior save God) it was strikingly new.

Kings and nations

Change did not come about everywhere in the same way or at the same pace. By 1800 France and England would have been for centuries unified in a way that Germany and Italy still were not. But wherever it happened, the centre of the process was often the aggrandizement of royal families. Kings enjoyed great advantages. If they ran their affairs carefully they had a more solid power base in their usually large (and sometimes very large) domains than had noblemen in their smaller estates. The kingly office had a mysterious aura about it, prominently displayed in the solemn circumstances of coronations and anointings. Royal courts and laws could offer a more independent justice than could be got from the local magnates. Kings could therefore appeal not only to the resources of a feudal structure at whose head – or somewhere near it – they might theoretically stand, but also to other forces outside.

One of these, slowly to be revealed as of growing importance, was the sense of nationhood, another idea we take for granted, and we must be careful not to antedate it. No medieval state was national in our sense. Nevertheless, by 1300 subjects of the kings of England and France could sometimes think of themselves as different from aliens. Relevant distinctions could be made between those born within and those born outside the realm, even if some Englishmen might still regard those who lived in the next village as virtually foreigners and even when not all Frenchmen were subjects of the king of France. One symptom was the appearance of national patron saints; churches had been dedicated to him under the Anglo-Saxon kings, but St George only acquired his heroic repute as a dragon-killer in the twelfth century (possibly by confusion with the Greek hero, Perseus). In the fourteenth century his red cross on a white background became a kind of uniform for English soldiers and he was recognized as the official protector of England. Another symptom was the writing of national histories (already foreshadowed by the Dark Age histories of the Germanic peoples) and the discovery of national heroes. In the twelfth century, a Welshman had more or less invented the mythological figure of Arthur, while an Irish chronicler of the same period built up an unhistorical legend of the High King Brian Boru and his defence of Christian Ireland against the Vikings. Above all, there was more vernacular literature. First Spanish and Italian, then French and English began to break through the barrier set about literary creativity by Latin. The ancestors of these tongues are recognizable in twelfth-century romances such as the *Song of Roland* which transformed the defeat of Charlemagne by Pyrennean mountaineers into the glorious stand of his rearguard against the Arabs, or the *Poema de mio Cid*, the epic of a Spanish national hero. With the fourteenth century came Dante, Langland and Chaucer, each of whom wrote in language which we can read without much difficulty.

The immediate impact must not be exaggerated. The most powerful engine of nation-making, the modern state, still lay centuries away, uninvented, inconceivable, and still technically impossible. For centuries yet, family, local community, religion or occupation were still to be the foci of most men's loyalties. Such national institutions as grew among them could only break a little into this conservatism and at moments; in few places was it more than a matter of the king's justice and the king's tax-gatherers – and even in England, in some ways the most nationally conscious of late medieval states, many people might never see either. German emperors had long never even made any claims to an over-arching jurisdiction. The rural parishes and little towns of the Middle Ages, on the other hand, were real communities; in ordinary times they provided quite enough to think about in the way of social responsibilities. We really need another word than 'nationalism' to suggest the occasional and fleeting glimpses of a community of the realm which might once in a while touch a medieval man, or even the irritation which might suddenly burst out in a riot against the presence of foreign workmen or merchants (medieval anti-semitism, of course, had its own special roots).

England and France

England and France were first European kingdoms occupying anything like the same territory as their modern successors. The few thousand Normans who came over from France after the invasion of 1066 did not destroy the Anglo-Saxon monarchy, but adapted it, gave it a new royal line, and England a new ruling class. Their leader, William the Conqueror, gave them lands, keeping more for himself (the royal estates were larger than those of his Anglo-Saxon predecessors), and asserted an ultimate lordship over the rest: he was to be lord of the land. All men held what they held either directly or indirectly of him. So, at least, ran the theory, but it was less important than his legal claim to the throne, the prestige and machinery of the old English monarchy. These raised him decisively above his fellow warriors. The greatest of them became William's earls and barons, the lesser ones among them knights, ruling England at first from the wooden and earth castles which they spread over the length of the land.

The Normans had conquered one of the most civilized Christian societies in Europe, and it went on under the Anglo-Norman kings to show unusual vigour. A few years after the Conquest, English government carried out a huge survey of England for royal purposes, 'Domesday Book'. The evidence for it was taken from juries in every shire and hundred and its minuteness deeply impressed the Anglo-Saxon chronicler who bitterly noted ('it is shameful to record, but did not seem shameful for him to do') that not an ox, cow or pig escaped the notice of William's men. In the next century there was important, rapid and, by comparison with the continent, unusual development in the judicial strength of the Crown. The principle of an over-riding royal justice with an over-arching procedure of appeal was soon in place. Though minorities and weak kings from time to time led to big royal concessions to the magnates in the next three centuries, the essential integrity of the monarchy was not compromised. The constitutional history of England would for 500 years be a history of quarrels about who exercised the authority of the Crown, whether as its holder or in its name. England, of course, was lucky in her separation from possible enemies (except to the north) by water; it was not easy for foreigners to interfere in her domestic politics. The Normans were to remain her last successful invaders.

For a long time, though, the Anglo-Norman kings and their heirs were encumbered by a complex inheritance of possessions and feudal dependencies stretching at its furthest far into south-western France. Like their followers, they long spoke Norman French. The loss of most of their 'Angevin' inheritance (the name came from Anjou) at the beginning of the twelfth century was decisive for France as well as for England. A sense of nationhood was nurtured in each by their quarrels with one another. The Capetians had hung on grimly and successfully to the French crown. From the tenth to the fourteenth century their kings succeeded one another in unbroken hereditary suc-

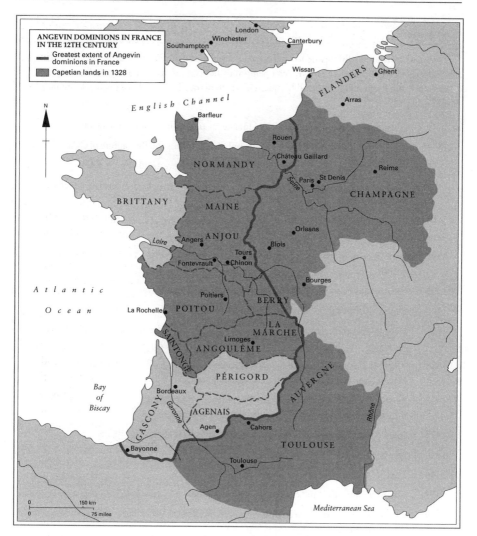

ANGEVIN DOMINIONS IN FRANCE
IN THE 12TH CENTURY
— Greatest extent of Angevin
dominions in France
◼ Capetian lands in 1328

cession. They added to the royal domain new lands but Paris remained their capital, in the heartland of modern France, the cereal-growing area called the Ile de France. For a long time this was the only part of the country commemorating by name its origins in a fragment of the old kingdom of the Franks. The domains of the first Capetians were thus already distinct from other west Carolingian territories, such as Burgundy. By 1300 their vigorous successors had expanded them to include Bourges, Tours, Gisors and Amiens, and had also acquired Normandy and other feudal dependencies from the Plantagenet kings of England; this had greatly reduced the area of France ruled by foreigners.

Yet in the fourteenth century (and later) there were still great fiefs and feudal principalities which make it improper to think of the Capetian kingdom as a monolithic entity. Such unity as it had rested for the most part on the personal tie. During the fourteenth century it was enhanced by an intermittent struggle with England, remembered

THE HUNDRED YEARS WAR

The name conventionally applied to a period of intermittent Anglo-French struggle in pursuit of English claims to the French crown. After performing homage for his lands in Aquitaine to the king of France, the English king, Edward III, quarrelled with his overlord which led to open hostilities and in

1339   Edward III proclaims himself king of France, by right of his mother. There follow:

1340   English victories at Sluys (naval, 1340) and Crécy (1346), and the capture of Calais (1347).

1355–6 Raids by the Black Prince across France from the south-west and French defeat at Poitiers.

1360   Treaty of Brétigny ends first phase of war. Edward given an enlarged, sovereign duchy of Aquitaine.

1369   The French re-open the conflict, the English fleet defeated at La Rochelle (1372) and lose Aquitaine. Steady decline of English position follows.

1399   Deposition of Richard II (married 1396 to daughter of Charles VI of France) renews French hostility.

1405–6 French landing in Wales and attack on English lands in Guienne.

1407   Outbreak of civil war in France, exploited by English.

1415   Henry V re-asserts claim to French throne. Alliance with Burgundy and defeat of French at Agincourt, followed by re-conquest of Normandy (1417–19).

1420   Treaty of Troyes confirms conquest of Normandy, marriage of Henry V to daughter of the king of France and his recognition as regent of France.

1422   Death of both Henry V and Charles VI of France. Infant Henry VI succeeds to the English throne; continuation of war successfully by English until

1429   Intervention of Jeanne d'Arc saves Orléans; Charles VII crowned at Reims.

1430   Henry VI crowned king of France.

1436   Loss of Paris after collapse of Anglo-Burgundian alliance.

1444   Treaty of Tours: England concedes duchy of Maine.

1449   The Treaty of Tours is broken by the English, resulting in the collapse of English resistance under concerted French pressure.

1453   English defeat at Castillon ends English effort to reconquer Gascony; English left with only Calais and the Channel Islands and the struggle peters out in their abortive expeditions of 1474 and 1492.

1558   Loss of Calais to France (but the title of 'King of France' is retained by English kings down to George III – and the French coat of arms is displayed in the *Times* newspaper's device until 1932).

by the misleading name of the Hundred Years War. In fact, English and French were only sporadically at war between 1337 and 1453. Sustained warfare was difficult to keep up; it was too expensive. Formally, what was at stake was the maintenance by the kings of England of territorial and feudal claims on the French side of the Channel; in 1339 Edward III had, through his mother, laid claim to the throne of France itself. There were always specious grounds to start fighting again (as late as the eighteenth century

English kings claimed to be 'kings of France'), and the opportunities war offered to English noblemen for booty and ransom money made it seem a plausible investment to many of them.

For England, these struggles supplied new elements to the infant mythology of nationhood (largely through the great victories won at Crécy in 1346 and Agincourt in 1415) and generated a long-lived distrust of the French. The Hundred Years War was important to the French monarchy because it did something to check feudal fragmentation and broke down somewhat the barriers between Picard and Gascon, Norman and French gentlemen. In the long run, too, French national mythology benefited; its greatest acquisition was the story and example of Joan of Arc (canonized, finally, in 1920, a year when the French republic, too, recognized her patriotic standing by dedicating a secular national holiday to her) whose astonishing career accompanied the tipping of the balance of the long struggle against the English, though few Frenchmen of her day knew she existed. England was the loser in the long run, but one important long-term outcome of the war had followed Crécy; the English seized Calais. It was to be held by them for 200 years. Calais opened Flanders, where a cluster of manufacturing towns was ready to take English wool and later cloth exports, to English trade. Except for Calais, though, England's territorial empire in France had disappeared by 1500. After 1453 French kings had been able to push forward with the consolidation of France undisturbed by the obscure English claims from which the wars had sprung. They could settle down to establish their sovereignty over their rebellious magnates at their leisure – or as best they could. As for England, she once more became almost an island. In each country, war in the long run strengthened the monarchy.

Spain

Spain, too, achieved national unity (though not formally) by the end of the fifteenth century. Spanish nationhood was mythologically underpinned by the Reconquest; the struggle against Islam from the start gave it a quite special flavour. It was to be intimately connected with Christian faith and fervour; the Reconquest was a crusade of men of many tongues and homelands and was driven by all the mixed motives of other such movements. A 100 years after Toledo was recovered Seville was taken by the kingdom of Castile and the great Arab city of Valencia by the crown of Aragon. In 1340, when the last major Arab offensive was defeated, success brought the threat of anarchy as the turbulent nobles of Castile strove to assert themselves. The monarchy took the burghers of the towns into alliance. The establishment of stronger personal rule followed the union of the crowns of Aragon and Castile by the marriage in 1479 of Ferdinand of Aragon and Isabella of Castile. This made easier both the final expulsion of the Moors and the eventual creation of one nation, though the two kingdoms remained formally and legally separate even after the consummation of the Reconquest in 1492, when Granada, the last Moslem capital of Spain, fell to the armies of the 'Catholic Monarchs', *Los Reyes Católicos*, as the title of Ferdinand and Isabella went after 1496. Portugal remained outside the solidifying framework of a new Spain; she clung to an independence often threatened by her powerful neighbour. Otherwise, the Catholic Monarchs ruled the whole peninsula other than the little northern kingdom of Navarre.

Germany and Italy

Few signs of future nationhood were to be found in Italy or Germany in 1500. Potentially, it might seem that the claims of the Holy Roman Emperors were an important and broad base for political power. Yet after 1300 they had lost much of the respect due to their title. A long thirteenth-century dispute between rival emperors was one reason for this. Another was the inability of the emperors to consolidate monarchical authority in their diverse dominions. The last German to march to Rome and force his coronation as emperor did so in 1328, and it proved an abortive effort. Deeply-rooted attitudes and beliefs about the way imperial authority should work, though, probably explain as much as circumstance.

Germany was the heartland of the empire and the crux of the problem. The imperial constitution was a chaos. It was supposed to provide the framework for the affairs of about 400 different states, statelets and notables north of the Alps. There were princes who were the feudal vassals of the emperor but in no other way subordinate to him; dozens of independent imperial cities exercising imperial powers within their territories; the lands of the imperial family, themselves usually scattered and disunited; fifty princes of the Church who ruled in their lands like lay sovereigns; hundreds of minor noblemen – the imperial knights – subject to the emperor as feudal dependants; the Bohemian and Silesian lands which actually belonged to the crown of Hungary (itself outside the empire) and so on and on. This was a terrible mess, though taken for granted.

Much history lay behind it and some of it was negative. One part of the story was the absence in Germany of a tradition or idea of a kingship delegating jurisdiction and declaring law such as (for example) appeared in England. German emperors drew their authority from their positions at the apex of a hierarchy which the ruler presided over rather than commanded, the headship of a polity which he could not regulate but was expected to manage through respect, mediation and diplomacy. Emperors relied as much on personality, style and standing as on power. Within Germany, too, any other focus for authority or nationhood was hard to imagine. There was no capital city, nor any city large enough to grow naturally into predominance. Political and personal circumstance led emperors one after another to devolve more of their authority – and they were in any case elected rulers. In 1356, a document traditionally accepted as a landmark in German constitutional history (though really only a registration of established fact), the Golden Bull, named seven electoral princes who acquired the exercise of almost all the imperial rights in their own lands. Their jurisdiction, for example, was henceforth absolute; no appeals lay from their courts to the emperor.

What persisted in this situation of attenuated imperial power was a mythology of empire rather than its substance. Status itself, though, was still enough to tempt vigorous princes to aspire to the imperial throne. In 1273 the Austrian Habsburg family succeeded in getting one of its princes elected. In the next century and a half, they only managed to win a couple more elections but success lay ahead; after 1438 Habsburgs provided emperors almost without break until the empire came to an end in 1806 (and even then they were to survive another century as the rulers of a different empire). They began with an advantage: as German princes went the Habsburgs were rich. But their most important resources only became available after a marriage in 1477 which duly brought them the inheritance of the duchy of Burgundy, the most affluent of all fifteenth-century European states and one including much of the Netherlands. Other inheritances and marriages would add Hungary and Bohemia to their possessions. *Tu, felix Austria, nube* was a phrase which became famous; 'others make war, but you, o happy Austria, marry'. In the sixteenth-century, for the first time since the thirteenth, it seemed possible that an effective political unity might be imposed not only on the empire but on much of central Europe; family interest in uniting scattered Habsburg territories had a possible instrument to hand in the imperial office.

In Italy, by then, the empire had virtually ceased to matter. All that remained was a title. The struggle to preserve something more had long been tangled with Italian politics: the contestants in feuds which tormented Italian cities called themselves Guelph and Ghibelline the names, originally of the German Welf and Waiblinger families (the last being one of the lordships of the Hohenstaufen dynasty which provided emperors from 1056 to 1254) long after those names ceased to denote, as they once did, allegiance respectively to pope or emperor. After the fourteenth century there was no imperial domain in Italy; emperors hardly went there except for coronation with the Lombard crown. Imperial authority was delegated to 'vicars' who made of their vicariates units almost as independent as the electorates of Germany. Titles were given to these rulers and the areas they ruled, some of which lasted until the nineteenth century; the duchy of Milan was one of the first.

Other Italian states had different origins. Besides the south, where Naples and Sicily finished under the rule of the crown of Aragon, there were the republics, of which Venice, Genoa and Florence slowly emerged as the greatest and longest-lived. Some of these city-states represented the outcome of two trends sometimes interwoven in early Italian history, the 'communal' movement and the rise of commercial wealth. In the tenth and eleventh centuries, in much of north Italy, general assemblies of the citizens with a deceptively democratic look had emerged as effective governments in many towns. They described themselves sometimes as *parliamenta* or, as we might say, town meetings, and represented municipal oligarchies who profited as trade began to pick up from 1100 onwards. In the twelfth century the Lombard cities took the field against the emperor and beat him. Thereafter the Italians north of Rome ran their own internal affairs with considerable freedom from external interference for two or three centuries, though under governments increasingly tending towards hereditary and monarchical arrangements.

A new political structure

By 1500, much which looks like the political ground-plan of modern Europe in the west was in being. On the map, Portugal, Spain, France and England were by then recognizable in their modern form and approximate extent. In Italy and Germany, though, where vernacular language had begun to define nationhood, there was no correspondence between state and nation. The monarchical state, too, though evidently well on the way to becoming the dominant political form west of the Rhine was still far from as substantial as it later became. For all that the Capetians achieved, the kings of France were not (for example) kings in Normandy, but dukes. Different titles stood for differing legal and practical powers in different provinces. There were many such complicated survivals; constitutional relics everywhere cluttered up the idea of the monarchical sovereignty, and they could provide excuses for rebellion. One explanation of the success of Henry VII, the first of the Tudor dynasty, was that by judicious marriage he drew much of the remaining poison from the bitter struggle of great families which had bedevilled the English Crown in the fifteenth-century Wars of the Roses, but there were still English feudal rebellions to come under his successors.

Another institution with a deceptively modern look had also appeared in the fourteenth and fifteenth centuries: the first examples (outside Iceland) of the representative, parliamentary bodies of later nations. One to be in the future the most famous of them all, the English parliament, was well-established by 1500. The origins of such bodies were complex and local. Their powers were usually restricted in so far as they were clear and drew on diverse sources. Germanic tradition laid on a ruler the obligation of taking counsel from his great men and acting on it. The Church, too, was an early exponent of the representative idea, using it, among other things, to obtain taxation for the papacy. There was Italian experience: in the twelfth century representatives from Italian cities were summoned to the diet of the empire. By the end of the thirteenth century few countries had not experienced some summoning of representatives some to attend assemblies called by princes to find new ways of raising taxation. This was the nub of the matter. New resources had to be tapped by the new (and more expensive) state. Once summoned, princes found representative bodies had other advantages. They enabled voices other than those of the magnates to be heard. They provided local information. They had a propaganda value. Townsmen sometimes allied with kings against over-mighty subjects. On their side, the early parliaments (as we may loosely call them) of Europe were discovering that the device had advantages for them, too. In some of them the thought arose that taxation needed consent and that someone other than the nobility had an interest and therefore ought to have a voice in the running of the realm. More would be heard of that particular medieval idea.

CHAPTER SIX New prospects in the east

The Venetian republic

St Mark's, the cathedral church of Venice and the chapel of its Doges, was burned down in the tenth century. It was rebuilt on the model of a basilica in Constantinople planned in the shape of a Greek cross, and the outcome was a supreme example of Byzantine architecture in the west. The style had a certain appropriateness, for the republic was constitutionally and legally, though not effectively, long a dependency of the eastern empire – which, paradoxically, Venice was to play in due course a major role in destroying. Her story long transcended that of a mere Italian state.

Venice was the most successful of the early Italian city-states, long favoured by her detachment from mainland troubles. Her position on a handful of islands in a shallow lagoon, at the head of the Adriatic explains itself and the city's origins: men already fled there in the days of the Huns and Lombards. By 584, when they were officially recognized by the imperial government, twelve little communities existed there and just over a 100 years later the Venetians, as they can by then conveniently be called, chose to rule them a council of twelve tribunes who elected the first doge, or duke, in 697. When Carolingian power began to look menacing, the islanders moved their capital to the island of the Rialto and put themselves formally under the protection of the Byzantine emperor in 810. A few years later, in an act just as important, Venice acquired a patron saint when some merchants brought back form Alexandria in Egypt the body (or what was said to be the body) of St Mark the evangelist.

As the presence of her businessmen in Egypt shows, geography not only had offered the early Venetians security, it also imposed a destiny; Venice, as her citizens delighted later to remember, was wedded to the sea; a great festival whose symbolic climax was the throwing of a ring into the waters of the Adriatic long commemorated it. For a long time, Venetians were forbidden to acquire estates on the mainland and they had perforce turned their energies to trade abroad. Venice soon came to live by overseas trade, the first of western Europe's cities to do so. Even in the eleventh century, the magnificence with which St Mark's was rebuilt showed what this could mean, and there was even greater prosperity ahead. The Venetians worked their way into the markets of Egypt and the Levant (they never showed the qualms expressed by less successful rivals about trafficking with the infidel) and, above all, those of the eastern empire. They won concessions and favours. In return for help against the Normans in the eleventh century, Venetians had been given the right to trade freely throughout the empire and to be

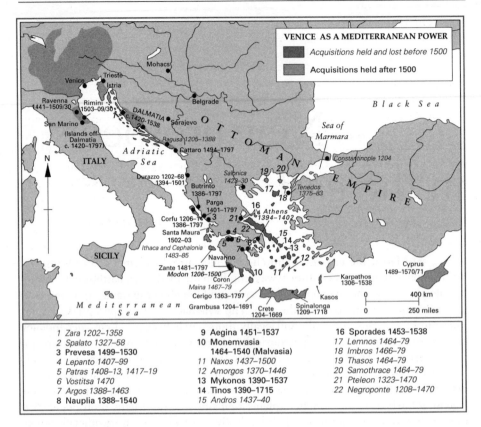

VENICE AS A MEDITERRANEAN POWER
- Acquisitions held and lost before 1500
- Acquisitions held after 1500

Mohacs
Trieste
Istria
Venice
Ravenna 1441–1509/30
Rimini 1503–09/30
DALMATIA c. 1420–1538
Sarajevo
Belgrade
Black Sea
San Marino
(Islands off Dalmatia c. 1420–1797)
Ragusa 1205–1388
Sea of Marmara
ITALY
Adriatic Sea
Cattaro 1494–1797
Constantinople 1204
OTTOMAN EMPIRE
Durazzo 1202–68 1394–1501
Salonica 1423–30
19 20
Butrinto 1386–1797
17
Tenedos 1375–83
18
Parga 1401–1797
16
Corfu 1206–14 1386–1797
3
Athens 1394–1402
21
Santa Maura 1502–03
4 22
15
Ithaca and Cephalonia 1483–85
5 6
7 8 9
14
13
SICILY
Navarino
12
Zante 1481–1797
Modon 1206–1500
Coron
10
11
Cyprus 1489–1570/71
Maina 1467–79
Karpathos 1306–1538
Cerigo 1363–1797
Kasos
0 400 km
Mediterranean Sea
Grambusa 1204–1691
Crete 1204–1669
Spinalonga 1209–1718
0 250 miles

1 Zara 1202–1358	9 Aegina 1451–1537	16 Sporades 1453–1538
2 Spalato 1327–58	10 Monemvasia	17 Lemnos 1464–79
3 Prevesa 1499–1530	1464–1540 (Malvasia)	18 Imbros 1466–79
4 Lepanto 1407–99	11 Naxos 1437–1500	19 Thasos 1464–79
5 Patras 1408–13, 1417–19	12 Amorgos 1370–1446	20 Samothrace 1464–79
6 Vostitsa 1470	13 Mykonos 1390–1537	21 Pteleon 1323–1470
7 Argos 1388–1463	14 Tinos 1390–1715	22 Negroponte 1208–1470
8 Nauplia 1388–1540	15 Andros 1437–40	

treated as subjects of the emperor, not as foreigners. Venetian naval power grew rapidly and, as the Byzantine fleet fell into decline, it was more and more important. It was the Venetians who destroyed the Egyptian fleet in 1123; thereafter they were uncontrollable by their former suzerain.

By then, that the republic was formally the vassal of Byzantium had long ceased to mean anything. It did not matter much even by the tenth century, when Venice had begun to build a maritime and commercial empire. First she acquired the Dalmatian and Istrian coasts of the Adriatic. Next, she came to control the routes of trade to the east (this would become more important as the crusading era opened) and to seize footholds and fortresses in the eastern Mediterranean. The empire itself was an economic host of huge potential for the Adriatic parasite – in the middle of the twelfth century there were said to be 10,000 Venetians living at Constantinople, so important were they there. By 1204 the Cyclades, many of the other Aegean islands, and much of the Black Sea coasts already belonged to them: scores of other communities were to be added to these and Venetianized in the next three centuries. The first commercial and maritime empire since ancient Athens had come into being.

Uneasiness on the part of the imperial government led finally to a breakdown of relations in the twelfth century. First, Venetian privileges were suspended, then a war followed which the Venetians lost. This in part explains why Venice in due course provided transport and financial backing for the Fourth Crusade, which was manipulated in the republic's interest. The major historical outcome was the breaking of the back of Byzantium and the winning for Venice of three-eighths of what they called 'Romania' – the empire. There still lay ahead a bitter and prolonged struggle with the Genoese (leading at times to fighting in Italy itself). In spite of setbacks and losses on the way, it was Venice which in the end left the table with the largest winnings. By 1500, other than her own *Terrafirma*, she had Adriatic possessions on the mainland of Italy at Ravenna, ruled most of the Dalmatian coast and its islands, Corfu and Cephalonia, as well as holding important possessions in the Peloponnese, ports in Crete and other Aegean islands. Finally, she had gained Cyprus and some footholds on the Anatolian coast were still hers. Much of this empire was still there in the seventeenth century and some of it survived until the republic's own extinction in 1797.

1204 and the crippling of Byzantium

In the late eleventh century the Comneni had pushed back the Normans from Greece and fought off another nomad incursion (of the Pechenegs) from southern Russia. They gave the empire a century (1081–1185) of relative security. But they could not recover ground in Asia Minor and had to make important concessions to do what they did, some to their own magnates, some to allies like the Venetians and Genoese. Those to Venice had been especially ominous; her whole *raison d'être* had by then come to be aggrandizement in the eastern Mediterranean and Aegean.

Furthermore, Byzantium, as always, faced other troubles at home. In the twelfth century rebellion became more common. This was doubly threatening at a time when Latin Christendom had entered upon the new enterprise of crusading in the east; from Byzantium, the crusades looked more and more like new barbarian invasions. In the twelfth century the Franks had already left behind four crusading states in the former Byzantine Levant as a reminder of a new rival for power in the Near East. When the Moslem forces rallied under the legendary Saladin, and there was a resurgence of Bulgarian rebellion at the end of the twelfth century, Byzantium faced a crisis.

It was on an already weakened structure, then, that there fell a fatal blow in 1204, when the imperial capital was at last taken and sacked by Christians. The Christian army which had gone east to fight the infidel in a fourth crusade was turned against the empire by the Venetians. It terrorized and pillaged the city (this was when the bronze horses of the Hippodrome were carried off to stand in Venice, as they still do, in front of St Mark's – though now in plastic replica). East and west could not have been more brutally distinguished; the sack was to live in Orthodox memory as a supreme infamy. Contemptuously, the crusaders had enthroned a harlot in the patriarch's seat in St Sophia. The Franks did not see Byzantium as a part of their civilization and some of their churchmen hardly saw it even as a part of Christendom, given a century and a half of schism between the churches. Though they were to abandon Constantinople and the emperors would be restored in 1261 the Franks would not again be cleared from the old Byzantine territories until a new Moslem conqueror came along. In any case, the heart had gone out of Byzantium, though it took two centuries to die. After 1204 she was never again more than a small Balkan state with Asian outposts.

When Constantinople was eventually recovered by an emperor – by Michael Paleologus VIII – it was with the help of a Turkish people from Anatolia, the Osmanlis. Superficially that offered new grounds for hope. The threat of Arab power had by then at last receded; the Latin kingdoms were barely hanging on. Byzantium had once more outlived dangerous enemies. By the standards of Near Eastern empires, it had already had a long run. The old enemy, the Abassid caliphate, had gone under long before, an age of confusion and decline overtaking it in the tenth century. But the caliphate's political decline and the comings and goings of rulers and raiders, did not disturb the foundations of the Islamic societies and cultures which now pervaded the world between the Levant and the Hindu Kush. There, the Christian inheritance of Rome had hung on as a major cultural force only until the eleventh century, bottled up in Asia Minor. After that, Christianity declined in the Near East except in so far as tolerated by a dominant Islam. Acre, the last Christian stronghold in Palestine, fell to the Moslems in 1291.

It may be thought an advantage to the eastern empire that the crucial phase of Mongol aggression was past (though Mongol attacks continued to fall on neighbouring peoples who cushioned Byzantium from them). But there were also new threats. 1204 had permitted the re-establishment of an independent Bulgaria (the 'second Bulgarian empire' as it is sometimes called). Robustly, in the following year, the Bulgarian leader overthrew the Frankish army, too, taking a new, Frankish, emperor prisoner. Byzantine recovery in Europe in the later thirteenth century was also challenged by a Serbian prince with aspirations to empire. He died before he could take Constantinople, but he left the empire with little but the hinterland of the capital and a fragment of Thrace. Against the Serbs, the empire had once more to call on help from the Osmanlis. There was not much for the Palaeologi dynasty to look forward to except a rearguard action, and to prolong it as long as possible.

The Ottomans

In the end, western Asia's confusions were resolved by the emergence of two new Islamic empires. The story of Safavid Persia lies a long way ahead and need not

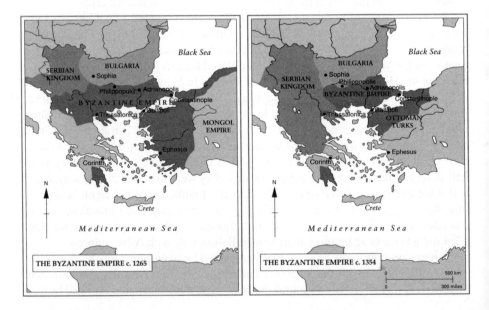

THE BYZANTINE EMPIRE c. 1265

THE BYZANTINE EMPIRE c. 1354

concern us. The other, the Ottoman, based on Anatolia, was to provide the major Islamic influence on Europe and the most obvious threat to it for centuries to come. Its prehistory begins in central Asia. A Turkish 'empire', if that is the right word for a tribal confederation, had once run right across Asia, a web of influence from China to Persia. Chinese, Persian, Indian and Byzantine rulers had all had to take the Turkish khans seriously. The Sassanids allowed Turks to settle within their frontiers in return for help from them, yet like that of other nomadic peoples, Turkish ascendancy proved transient. Arab onslaught shattered its remains in western Asia, and the Turkish story is then obscure until the tenth century, when the Turkish peoples were again on the move as the Abassid caliphate broke up. One Turkish clan, the Seljuks, which had already been converted to Islam, pushed westwards, ending up in Anatolia. At Manzikert in 1071 they inflicted on Byzantium one of the worst defeats of its history. Like many barbarian peoples living on the edges of great centres of civilization, the Seljuks did not seek to destroy the cultures they had learnt to admire, but to share their benefits. Major works of Arabic and Persian literature and scholarship began to be translated into Turkish, and the first true Turkish state now came into being, based on Iran and Anatolia, where the Seljuks called their new province the Sultanate of Rum, since they saw it as part of the inheritance of Rome. The Seljuks began the slow conversion of the once Christian Anatolians to Islam. This helped to touch off the crusades. Turks were less tolerant of Christians and Jews than the Arabs and did more to trouble Christian pilgrims going to the Holy Places.

It was on an internally-divided and already weakened Islamic world that the Mongols fell in the thirteenth century, to bring Islam as near to disaster as it ever came and destroy Seljuk power. Yet though the Mongols destroyed their rulers, they did not eliminate the Turkish settlers of Anatolia. Among these were the Osmanlis, who became known in Europe as the Ottomans. They were to be the last, and finally successful, assailants of Byzantium. They came from the borderlands between the dissolved Abbasid caliphate and the Byzantine empire. Petty princes called *ghazis*, usually Turkish by race, lawless, independent and the inevitable beneficiaries of the ebbing of paramount powers flourished there. One of them was Osman, a Turk of leadership and enterprise, and men gathered to him. His quality is shown by the transformation of the word *ghazi*: it came to mean 'warrior of the faith'. Fanatical frontiersmen, his followers seem to have been distinguished by a certain spiritual *élan*, a military organization somewhat like that of merchant guilds or religious orders in western Europe, and a position on a borderland of cultures, half-Christian, half-Islamic, which must have been provoking and tempting. Whatever its ultimate source, their record of success was to surpass that of Arab or Mongol. They were in the end not only to reassemble under one ruler the territory of the old eastern Roman empire but to add to it far more.

Orkhan, Osman's son, was the first Ottoman to take the title of Sultan. At his death he ruled the strongest of the post-Seljuk states of Asia Minor as well as some European lands (the first Ottoman toehold was established at Gallipoli in 1354). He had been important enough to be three times called upon by Constantinople for help and an emperor's daughter was given to him as a bride. Byzantium had by then already lost Asia Minor to his people and Orkhan's two successors went on to Europe, steadily eating up the Balkans. Their most decisive victory was over a coalition of Serbs, Bosnians and Albanians, at Kossovo in 1389. This was the end of independent Bulgaria and Serbia other than as vassal states. The Ottomans then defeated yet another 'crusade' against them, and followed it by seizing mainland Greece. In 1391 they began their first siege of Constantinople, which they kept up for six years.

Meanwhile, Byzantium stood all but alone. The king of Naples, the Venetians and the Genoese (who by now dominated even the trade of the capital city itself), had given her little respite. Doctrine and ecclesiastical authority still divided Christians east and west. As the fourteenth century wore on, the Greeks had a deepening sense of isolation. They felt abandoned to the infidel. Mercenaries hired from Catalonia themselves attacked Constantinople and set up yet another breakaway state, the Catalan duchy of Athens, in 1311. Occasional victories did not offset the trend. There was occasional civil war within the empire. True to their traditions, the Greeks managed even in such extremity to invest some of these struggles with a theological dimension. On top of all this, the plague in 1347 wiped out much of the empire's population.

The end of Byzantium

In 1400, when the emperor travelled the courts of western Europe to drum up help (a little money was all he got) he ruled only Constantinople, Salonika and the Morea. Significantly, western courts now habitually spoke of him as 'emperor of the Greeks', forgetting he was still titular emperor of the Romans. For a few years, the Ottomans held off because of defeat suffered at the hands of the last great Mongol conqueror, Timur Lang, but they surrounded the capital on all sides. There was another Turkish attack on Constantinople in 1422. The emperor John VIII made a last attempt to overcome the strongest barrier to cooperation with the west when he went in 1439 to the ecumenical council sitting in Florence and there accepted papal primacy and union with Rome. Western Christendom rejoiced; the bells were rung in all the parish churches of England. But the Orthodox east scowled. The council's formula ran headlong against its tradition; too much stood in the way – papal authority, the equality of bishops, ritual and doctrine. The most influential Greek clergy had refused to attend the council; those who did all signed the formula of union except one (he, significantly, was later canonized) but many of them recanted when they went home. 'Better', said one Byzantine dignitary, 'to see in the city the power of the Turkish turban than that of the Latin tiara'. Submission to the pope was for most Greeks a renegade act, a denial of the true Church, whose tradition Orthodoxy had conserved. The emperors were loyal to the agreement but thirteen years passed before they dared to proclaim the union publicly at Constantinople. The only benefit drawn from their submission was the pope's support for a last crusade (which ended in disaster in 1441).

In the end the west and east still could not make common cause. They took different views of the world, and were divided over religion. The infidel was, as yet, in western eyes battering only at the outermost defences. Spain was almost recovered from Islam. France and Germany were absorbed in their own affairs; Venice and Genoa saw their interest might lie as much in conciliation of the Turk as in opposition to him. Even the Russians, harried by the Tatars, a Mongol people, could do little to help Byzantium, cut off as they were from direct contact with her. The imperial city, and little else, was left alone, divided within itself to face the Ottoman's final effort.

The end, when it came, did not disgrace the old empire. The last attack began early in April 1453. After nearly two months, on the evening of 28 May, Roman Catholics and Orthodox alike gathered in St Sophia and the fiction of a united Chris-

tendom was given its last parade. Constantine XI, eightieth emperor since his name-sake, the great first Constantine, took communion and then went out to die fighting (no-one knows exactly how or when). Soon afterwards, the Ottoman sultan entered the city, went straight to St Sophia and there set up a triumphant throne. The church which had been the heart of Orthodoxy became a mosque. Christendom shuddered at the news.

It was a great feat of arms, depleted though the resources of Byzantium were. Mehmet II, named the 'Conqueror', had persisted against all obstacles. He even had seventy ships carried overland to place them behind the imperial squadron guarding the Horn. Among other things he had a Hungarian engineer build him a gigantic cannon whose operation was so cumbersome that it could only be moved by a 100 oxen and fired only seven times a day (the Hungarian's assistance had been turned down by the Christians). In the end, though, Mehmet did better with orthodox meth-ods, driving his soldiers forward ruthlessly, cutting them down if they flinched from the assault and at their hands, finally, nearly 1,500 years of empire came to an end.

Ottoman Europe

Momentous as the victory was, the story of the Ottoman impact on European history cannot be left there. Ottoman empire was to be of unique importance, one of the big differences marking off the history of the eastern half of the continent and the banner of Ottoman triumph was to be raised yet higher. The final absorption of Serbia in 1459 (and soon after, of Bosnia, Herzegovina and Montenegro) was almost at once followed by the conquest of Trebizond; at this remote spot on the south-eastern coast of the Black Sea in 1461 Hellenism and the world of Greek civilization built on the conquests of Alexander the Great gave their last gasp. It marked an epoch as decisively as the fall of Constantinople, which a pope had bewailed as 'the second death of Homer and Plato'. But Ottoman conquest rolled on through the Peloponnese and in the next twenty years into Albania and the Ionian islands. In 1480 the Turks captured the Italian port of Otranto and held it for nearly a year. They took longer to pick up more of the Venetian empire, but at the beginning of the sixteenth century Turkish cavalry were scouting near Vicenza. After conquering Syria and Egypt in 1517, they wiped out the army of the Hungarian king at Mohacs in 1526 in a defeat remembered still as the black day of Hungarian history. Three years later they besieged Vienna for the first time. In 1571 Venetian Cyprus fell to them and nearly a century later Crete. By then they were established deep inside Europe.

Europe's rulers had really only themselves to blame; they had never been (and were never to be) able to unite effectively against the Turks. Byzantium had been left to her fate. 'Who will make the English love the French? Who will unite Genoese and Aragonese?' asked a fifteenth-century pope despairingly; not long after, one of his successors was sounding out the possibilities of Turkish help against France. Yet the challenge had stimulated another sort of response, for even before the fall of Constantinople Portuguese ships were picking their way southwards down the African coast to look for a new route to the spices of the East and, possibly, an African ally to take the Turk in the flank from the south.

Orthodox Christianity survived and the Greek Church was tolerated under Ottoman rule. The heritage of Byzantium was thus in part preserved for its Slav subjects and, indeed, any threat to the supremacy of the patriarch at Constantinople in the Balkans either from the Catholics or from national Orthodox churches disappeared. Outside the former empire, only one important focus of Orthodoxy remained, in Russia. The establishment of the Ottoman empire also briefly sealed off Europe from the Near East and the Black Sea and, therefore, in large measure from the land-routes to Asia, but commercial contacts were flourishing again in the early sixteenth century. Behind the Ottoman frontiers a new multi-racial polity was organized. Mehmet was a man of wide, if volatile, sympathies and later Turks found it hard to understand his forbearance to the infidel. He seems to have wanted a multi-religious society. He brought back Greeks to Constantinople from Trebizond and appointed a new patriarch under whom the Greeks were eventually given a kind of self-government. The Turkish record with Jew and Christian was to prove better than that of Christian Spain towards Jew and Moslem.

Russia

The change 1453 brought to Russia's destiny was momentous. From the twelfth century she had been given a more and more distinctive cultural and institutional shape by her origins and the historical forces playing on her. One was her exposure to the Mongols, whose capture of Kiev in 1240 was a blow to Orthodox Christianity almost as heavy as the sack of Constantinople thirty-six years earlier. They broke the princes of Muscovy who had emerged as successors – with Novgorod – to the former ascendancy of Kiev. With Byzantium in decline and the Germans and Swedes on their backs, Muscovy was for centuries to pay tribute to them and their successors, the Tatars of the Golden Horde, another historical experience sundering Russia from the west, shaping its future political culture. Meanwhile the great expansion of the German east (which would go on through the fourteenth century) had made a new economic, cultural and racial map, and provided a new definition and a new religious frontier to the west. Papal supremacy made the Catholicism of the late medieval period more uncompromising and more unacceptable than ever to Orthodoxy. Moreover, a new political base for a challenge to Orthodoxy, a Roman Catholic but half-Slav state, had emerged in the west. This was the medieval duchy of Lithuania, formed in 1386 in a union by marriage which incorporated the Polish kingdom and covering much of modern Poland, Prussia, the Ukraine and Moldavia. It held Kiev for three centuries. Fortunately for the Russians, the Lithuanians also fought the Germans; it was they who shattered the Teutonic Knights at Tannenberg in 1410.

Tatar domination had its greatest impact in the southern Russian principalities. A new balance within Russia gradually appeared; Novgorod and Moscow had acquired new importance after the eclipse of Kiev, though they had to pay regular tribute to the Tatars in cash, slaves, recruits and labour. Their emissaries, like those of other Russian princes, had to go to the Tatar capital at Sarai on the Volga to make their arrangements with their conquerors. It was a time of dislocation and confusion and the struggle to survive favoured able despots. Muscovy's princes enjoyed Tatar favour because they were effective tax-gatherers. They began to appear the focus of a new centralizing trend. The Church did not resist, and the metropolitan archbishopric of Vladimir was moved to Moscow in the fourteenth century. Harassed though it continued also to be by German and Lithuanians, Muscovy hung on, exploiting, when it could, the divisions within the Golden Horde.

Against this troubled background, the events of 1453 had huge resonance. Churchmen soon came to feel that only a complex and divine purpose could explain such an awful fact as the fall of Constantinople to the infidel. Byzantium, they reasoned, had betrayed its heritage by seeking religious compromise at the Council of Florence (the Council had already led the Russian church to elect its own patriarch, an affront to the one in Constantinople). 'Constantinople has fallen', wrote the Metropolitan of Moscow, 'because it has deserted the true Orthodox faith .... There exists only one true Church on earth, the Church of Russia'. A few decades later, at the beginning of the sixteenth century, a monk could write to the ruler of Muscovy in a quite new tone: 'Thou art the only Christian sovereign in the world, the lord of all faithful Christians .... Two Romes have fallen, but the third stands and a fourth will not be'[1]. It was a deliberate assertion and encouragement of a special role for Muscovy among the Russian states.

The end of Byzantium came at a moment when other historical changes were in fact making Russia's emergence from confusion and Tatar domination possible and even likely. The Golden Horde was rent by dissension while, at the same time, the Lithuanian state was beginning to crumble. These were opportunities. In 1462 a ruler who was capable of exploiting them had come to the throne of Muscovy. Ivan the Great (Ivan III) gave Russia some of the definition and reality England and France had been

---

[1] The celebrated words of the monk Filofei occur in a letter to Basil III and are quoted in G. Vernadsky, *et al.*, eds., *A Source Book for Russian History* (New Haven, 1972), I. p. 156.

moving towards from the twelfth century onwards. Some have seen him as the first national ruler of Russia. He was the first of her rulers to take the title of 'Tsar', a conscious claim to the heritage of the Caesars, the word in which it originated. In 1472 Ivan married the niece of the last Greek emperor. He was called 'autocrat by the grace of God' and adopted the double-headed eagle which was to remain part of the insignia of the Russian rulers until 1917. This gave a further Byzantine colouring to Russian monarchy, which became still more unlike that of western Europe. By 1500 western Europeans already recognized something distinctive in it; Basil III, Ivan's successor, was acknowledged to have a despotic power over his subjects greater than that of any other Christian rulers over theirs. 'They call him the keykeeper and chamberlain of God' wrote a west European visitor to Muscovy[2].

Territorial consolidation was Ivan's major goal. When Muscovy swallowed the republics of Pskov and Novgorod, his authority stretched at least in theory as far as the Urals. The oligarchies which had ruled them were deported, to be replaced by men who held lands from Ivan in return for service. The German merchants of the Hanse who had dominated their trade were expelled, too. After their suzerainty was set aside and another Tatar onslaught on Moscow in 1481 had been beaten off, two invasions of Lithuania gave Ivan much of White Russia and Little Russia in 1503. His successor took Smolensk in 1514.

Much of Europe's future organization seems already discernible by then. In 1500 a centuries-long process of definition and realization was coming to a close. Europe's land limits were now filled up; in the east further advance was blocked by the consolidation of Christian Russia, in the Balkans by the Ottoman empire of Islam, Byzantium's successor. The first, crusading, wave of overseas expansion had aborted and the Ottoman threat forced Europe again onto the defensive in the eastern Mediterranean. Those unhappy states with exposed territories there, such as Venice, had to look after them as best they could. Meanwhile, other Europeans were taking a new look at other, oceanic horizons. A new phase of western Europe's relations with the rest of the world was about to open. It approached it not only as a collection of political and economic potentials, but as the centre of a distinctive civilization whose heart was its religion, its Church the custodian of its culture and the teacher of all men, the vehicle and vessel of civilization itself. That much, it might be said, was shared east and west, but meant very different things in each.

The mind of the west

Since the thirteenth century the burden of recording, teaching and study so long borne by the monks had been shared by friars and, more important still, by a new institution, in which friars sometimes played a big part, the university. It was to prove one of the great European inventions; almost all universities in the world can trace their origins to the models provided by Bologna, Paris and Oxford, the first examples; by 1400 there were fifty-three more. They concentrated and directed intellectual activity and provided education in a new way. One early consequence was the revivifying of the training of the clergy. Already in the middle of the fourteenth century half the English bishops were graduates. But this was not the only reason why universities had been set

---

[2] *Idem.* p. 157.

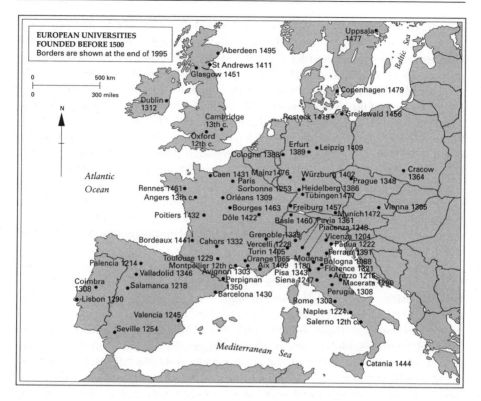

EUROPEAN UNIVERSITIES
FOUNDED BEFORE 1500
Borders are shown at the end of 1995

0   500 km

0   300 miles

N

Atlantic
Ocean

Uppsala 1477

Aberdeen 1495

St Andrews 1411

Glasgow 1451

Dublin 1312

Copenhagen 1479

Cambridge 13th c.

Rostock 1419   Greifswald 1456

Oxford 12th c.

Cologne 1388   Erfurt 1389   Leipzig 1409

Caen 1431   Mainz 1476   Würzburg 1402   Prague 1348   Cracow 1364

Paris   Sorbonne 1253   Heidelberg 1386

Rennes 1461   Orléans 1309   Tübingen 1477

Angers 13th c.

Poitiers 1432   Bourges 1463   Freiburg 1457   Munich 1472   Vienna 1365

Dôle 1422   Basle 1460   Pavia 1361

Piacenza 1248

Grenoble 1339   Vicenza 1204

Bordeaux 1441   Cahors 1332   Vercelli 1228   Pádua 1222

Turin 1405   Ferrara 1391

Palencia 1214   Toulouse 1229   Orange 1365   Modena   Bologna 1088

Montpellier 12th c.   Aix 1409   1180   Florence 1321

Valladolid 1346   Avignon 1303   Pisa 1343   Arezzo 1215

Coimbra 1308   Salamanca 1218   Perpignan 1350   Siena 1247   Macerata 1290

Lisbon 1290   Barcelona 1430   Perugia 1308

Rome 1303

Valencia 1245   Naples 1224

Seville 1254   Salerno 12th c.

Mediterranean Sea

Catania 1444

Baltic Sea

up. The emperor Frederick II founded the university of Naples to supply administrators for his south Italian kingdom; and Walter de Merton founded the first college at Oxford in 1264 with, as one of his purposes, the education of future clerical servants for the crown like himself.

The universities did more, though, than act as development agencies for the training of the administrative cadres society needed in growing numbers. They became major transmitters of information and culture whose origins assured that when laymen came to be educated in substantial numbers, it would be in institutions under the control of the Church and suffused with religion. Their influence was much more than local; they were cosmopolitan, associating men of different nations and language in common interests and shared intellectual activity. Their lectures were given and their disputations conducted in Latin, the language of the church and the lingua franca of educated men until this century (its former pre-eminence is still commemorated in the vestigial Latin of university ceremonies and the names of degrees).

Law, medicine, theology and philosophy all flourished in the universities. The last had all but disappeared into theology in the early medieval period. Then, as direct translation from Greek to Latin began in the twelfth century, European scholars began to be able to read for themselves works of classical philosophy. Texts which became available from Islamic sources were often at first regarded with suspicion. It persisted until well into the thirteenth century, but gradually a search for reconciliation between the classical and Christian accounts of the world got under way. So it came about that the classical heritage was recaptured and rechristened in western Europe. Instead of providing a contrasting and critical approach to the theocentric culture of Christendom it was incorporated. The classical world began to be interpreted as the forerunner of the Christian. Their reintegration was a belated answer – ten centuries late – to that jibing question about what Athens had to do with Jerusalem. In one of the supreme works of art of the Middle Ages – some would judge *the* supreme – the *Divine Comedy* of Dante, the importance of the re-attachment of the world of Christendom to its predecessor is already to be seen. Dante describes his journey through Hell, Purgatory and Paradise, the universe of Christian truth, with the pagan Roman poet Virgil, whose role was much more than decorative; the poet was an authoritative guide to truth, for Dante believed that Virgil had foretold Christ. The classical poet had become a prophet to stand beside those of the Old Testament. Though the notion of a link with antiquity had never quite disappeared (as attempts by enthusiastic chroniclers to link the Franks or the Britons to the descendants of the Trojans had shown) there is in Dante's attitude something marking an epoch, a new and explicit acknowledgement of the classical world by Christian culture.

Virgil was not the only classical figure whose guidance was sought as never before. In part because more became known of him through texts and commentaries drawn from the Islamic world Aristotle came to enjoy a unique prestige. If it could not make him a saint, the Church at least treated him as a kind of prophet. Greater knowledge of his writings provoked, above all in the work of two Dominicans, Albertus Magnus and his pupil Thomas Aquinas, a new intellectual reconciliation and synthesis. The most striking evidence was the remarkable systematic and rationalist achievement of medieval scholasticism, the name given to the intellectual effort to penetrate the meaning of Christian teaching. Its strength lay in its embracing sweep, displayed nowhere more brilliantly than in the uncompleted *Summa Theologica* of Aquinas which has been judged, contrastingly, both its crowning achievement and a brittle synthesis. It was the greatest of the many works through which Christian learning gave the medieval mind a powerful training in logical thinking, even if only a few men, isolated and untypical, could dimly see the possibility of breaking through logic and authority to other ways of understanding the natural world. With all the scholastic clutter which has been alleged of it, the thought of the medieval west was decisive for the shaping of the future European mind. It made possible a change which has usually been seen as very radical, a great revival of humanistic letters from the fourteenth century onwards.

Renaissance

The Renaissance is and was one of those useful myths which help men to master their own bearings and therefore to act more effectively. The word came to be used when some Italians who began to cultivate the study of classical authors, and to invoke explicitly pagan classical ideals, started to think of themselves as part of a 're-birth' of a lost tradition, a 'Renaissance' of classical antiquity. They were formed in the culture which the great changes in Christian civilization from the twelfth century onwards had made possible. To speak of Renaissance is helpful if we keep in mind the limitations of the context in which we use the word; it falsifies history if we take it to imply any cultural break with medieval Christian civilization. In its most concrete sense the word is a label for a blossoming of European art and scholarship between, approximately, the early fourteenth and late sixteenth centuries.

No clear line can be drawn to separate 'Renaissance' from 'Middle Ages', but what can be noticed is a gradual change in high culture. The man and woman in the streets of some cities might eventually be made aware of this change in a new sumptuousness and the new style of some buildings, in the decoration of public places with imitation classical statuary and fountains, in shows and masques celebrating civic acts and so on. But the essence of the Renaissance was change in men's minds, above all in the minds of the scholarly, the intellectuals, the rich and the fashionable.

Though every European country west of Russia experienced this change in some degree (and even Russia could display some of its expressions, in buildings put up by western architects), Italy was above all associated with it. For a century or so, from 1350 to 1450, more scholars, artists, scientists, and poets lived and worked in Italy than anywhere else (many of them came from abroad to do so). Europe went, as it were, to school there. What it learnt was, above all, the superiority of the classical antique. The Renaissance had its roots in the humanism which rediscovered the ancient past. It did this for a long time through Latin; Petrarch had no Greek. By 1500, though, the first of the great Venetian Aldine editions of Greek, as well as Latin, classical texts were available. Although the humanist writers long strove to imitate the style of the Roman Cicero, one of the greatest works of the painter Raphael was his huge *School of Athens*, a glorification of the philosophers of Greece.

Gradually, a change had come about in the way the past was regarded. Men of the sixteenth century, like those of the thirteenth, still often portrayed the great men of antiquity in the garb of their own day (though Raphael did not). Alexander the Great was seen by medieval men as a king like those they knew; Shakespeare's Caesar wears not a toga but doublet and hose. There is no real historical sense in such representations, no awareness of the immense differences between past and present men and things. Instead, history was seen at best as a school of examples. Yet there had been a change in the way the examples were read. Medieval men scrutinized antiquity for the signs of a divine plan, evidence of whose existence once more triumphantly vindicated the teachings of the Church. This was St Augustine's legacy and Dante accepted it. But by 1500 something else was also being discerned in the past, equally unhistorical, but, men felt, more helpful to their age and predicament. Some saw a classical inspiration, possibly even pagan, wholly distinct from the Christian, not just a forerunner of it, and a new attention to classical writings was one result.

The idea of Renaissance is famously and especially linked to innovation in art. Medieval Europe from the twelfth century onwards had already seemed vigorous and creative in a new way. In music, drama and poetry new forms and styles then emerged which can move us still. By the fifteenth century, it is already clear that they are no longer confined to the service of God. Art is becoming autonomous. Its genres are becoming more inclusive, more secular. Renaissance art comes to climax in the late fifteenth and early sixteenth centuries, the age of Raphael (architect as well as painter), Michelangelo (sculptor, painter, architect and poet), Leonardo da Vinci (painter, engineer, architect, scientist and sculptor) – and many others. The Renaissance admired such all-rounders. They expanded mankind's view of human excellence. The eventual consummation of the Renaissance, transcending by far its stylistic innovations, revolutionary though these were, was a sign that the Christian synthesis and the ecclesiastical monopoly of culture were breaking up at last. The slow divergence of classical and Christian mythology was one expression of it; others were the appearance of the

Romance and Provençal love poetry (which owed much to Arabic influence), the deployment of an elaborated Gothic style in secular building (such as the great guild-halls of the new cities of northern Europe), the rise of a vernacular literature for educated laymen, and the secularizing and revolutionary development of education for the élite. Mankind was subtly coming to be seen as of greater potential for earthly achievement than the Church had taught. In Michelangelo's painting of the *Creation of Adam*, the father of the human race is a gigantic and heroic figure, up-staging in power and dramatic effect even his creator, whose finger gives him life.

Printing

Changes of such moment are not easily dated, because acceptance did not always follow rapidly on innovation. In literature, there was a particularly severe physical restriction on what could be done: for a long time there were never enough copies of texts. It was not until well into the sixteenth century that the first edition of Chaucer's complete works was printed and published (though *The Canterbury Tales* were twice printed by Caxton, the first English printer, in the previous century). Even a vernacular text such as *The Canterbury Tales* could not reach a wide public until printing made it possible to copy it in large numbers.

When that happened, the impact of books was vastly magnified and a revolution was under way. The outcome was a new diffusion of knowledge and ideas, dwarfing in scale anything which had occurred since the invention of writing itself. This was a cultural revolution of which all the tendencies so far touched on form parts, but which was something much more than the sum of them and it owes almost everything to the coming of the printed book. That the innovation of scholars and scientist and the facts on which they were based could be diffused more easily than ever before was of outstanding importance.

The technology which brought this about appears to have owed nothing to China (where printing had long been carried out in a different form from that which was to become standard in Europe) except the invention of paper, and that only indirectly. From the fourteenth century good quality paper was being made in Europe from rags. Other elements necessary to the printing revolution were the principle of printing itself (the impressing of images on textiles had been practised in twelfth-century Italy), the use of cast metal for typefaces instead of wood (already used to provide blocks for playing-cards, calendars and religious images), and the availability of oil-based ink. Of these, the key invention was that of movable metal type. The details are obscure. Experiments with wood letters were going on at the beginning of the fifteenth century in Harlem. There seems to be no good reason, though, not to credit the innovation to the man whose name has traditionally been associated with it, Johannes Gutenberg, a diamond polisher of Mainz. In about 1450 he and his colleagues brought the elements of modern printing together for the first time, and in 1455 there appeared what is agreed to be the first true printed book in Europe, the Gutenberg Bible. Twenty years later, William Caxton printed the first book in English, a translation he had himself made.

Gutenberg's own business career collapsed in failure; he was probably under-capitalized and something prophetic of a new age of commerce appears in this. The accumulation of equipment and type was an expensive business and a colleague from whom he borrowed money took him to court for his debts. Judgement went against Guten-berg, who lost his press, so that the Bible, when it appeared, was not his property (hap-pily, the story does not end there; Gutenberg was in the end ennobled by the archbishop of Mainz, in recognition of what he had done). But he had launched the revolution. By 1500, it has been calculated, some 35,000 separate printed editions of books – *incunabula*, as they are called – had been published. This probably means between 15,000,000 and 20,000,000 copies; there may well have been already by then fewer manuscript copies of books in the whole world. In the following century there were between a 150,000 and 200,000 distinguishable editions and perhaps ten times as many copies printed. Such quantitative change merges into the qualitative; the print culture was as different from any earlier one as it is from one which takes radio and tele-vision for granted. One mark of the modern age is that it was the age of print.

It is scarcely surprising that the first printed European book should have been the Bible, the sacred text at the heart of medieval civilization. Through the printing press, knowledge of the scriptures was to be diffused as never before and with incalculable results. In 1450 it would have been very unusual for a parish priest to have easy access to a Bible, let alone to possess one of his own. A century later, it was becoming likely that he owned one, and in 1650 it would have been remarkable if he had not. Gutenberg's text had been that of the Latin Vulgate collected in the sixth century from the transla-tions of St Jerome. The first German Bible was printed in 1466; Italian and French translations followed before the end of the century, but Englishmen had to wait for a printed New Testament in their language until 1526. Into the diffusion of sacred texts – of which the Bible was only the most important – pious laymen and churchmen alike poured resources for fifty to sixty years; presses were even set up in monastic houses. Meanwhile, grammars, histories, and, above all, the classical authors now edited by the humanists also appeared in growing numbers. Another innovation from Italy was the introduction of simpler, clearer typefaces modelled upon the manuscript of Florentine scholars who copied Carolingian minuscule.

The impact of printing could not be contained. The domination of the European consciousness by printed media would be the outcome. With some prescience the pope suggested to bishops in 1501 that the control of printing might be the key to preserving the purity of the faith. But more was involved than any specific threat to doctrine, important as that might be. The nature of the book itself began to change. Once a rare work of art, whose mysterious knowledge was accessible only to a few, it became a tool and artifact for the many. Print was to provide new channels of communication for gov-ernments and a new medium for artists (the diffusion of the pictorial and architectural style in the sixteenth century was much more rapid and widespread than ever before because of the growing availability of the engraved print). It would give a new impetus to the diffusion of technology. A huge demand for literacy and therefore education would be stimulated by it. No single change marks so clearly the ending of one era and the beginning of another.

Re-orientation

Wider diffusion of knowledge – or what was believed to be knowledge – of the past did not have simple, one-way consequences. There were ideas about in the fif-teenth century which were already sapping away (even if only implicitly) at some everyday assumptions of Christian society. This was true even of the deep, uneasy devotional swell of the age which, searching for new answers to spiritual questioning, sometimes also showed a willingness to look for them outside the limits traditionally set by ecclesiastical authority. Heresy had never been blotted out (and had sometimes hardly been contained, when it had been able to find allies in social or political grievance).

One current in fifteenth-century religious life which, nonetheless, was perhaps more profoundly dangerous to the intellectual *status quo* was the movement of learned minds which, for want of a better comprehensive term, is called humanism. It embodied forces which might in the end threaten the roots of the religious outlook itself, though that was not easily discernible for a long time. No man embodied its ideals more obviously in the eyes of contemporaries than the scholar Erasmus of Rotterdam, the first Dutchman to play a leading role in European history. As a loyal Catholic (he was for a time a monk), he hoped for a possible reformation of the Church, a simpler devotion and a purer pastorate. He saw his classical learning not as an end in itself but as the entrance to the supreme study of scripture. His most important book was an edition of the Greek New Testament. The effects of printing a good text of it were, indeed, to be revolutionary, but for all the vigour and wit with which he mocked and teased puffed-up churchmen, and for all the provocation to independent thought which his books and letters provided, Erasmus had no intention of overthrowing religious order. His outlook was grounded in the piety of a fifteenth-century mystical movement in the Low Countries called the *devotio moderna*, rather than pagan antiquity. Subtly and implicitly, though, his scholarly work challenged clerical authority. In the correspondence which he conducted with colleagues the length and breadth of Europe they learnt from him to disentangle their logic and therefore the teaching of the faith from the scholastic mummification of Aristotelian philosophy. In his New Testament translation he made available a new basis for argument about doctrine at a time when the study of Greek was being revived. He also exposed the spuriousness of texts on which bizarre dogmatic structures had been raised. All this he did, moreover, in the age of print.

The weight of the past

It is very hard to measure or say how such changes actually affected the behaviour of Europeans and their ways of thinking, let alone the role they would play in world history. By 1500, there was certainly much to give confidence to the few among them likely to think about such things. Their religion taught them they were a people voyaging in time; they faced prospects made a little more comprehensible and perhaps a little less frightening by contemplation of past perils navigated and awareness of a common goal. As a result Europe was to be the first civilization aware of time not as endless (though perhaps cyclical) pressure, but as continuing change in a certain direction, as progress. The chosen people of the Bible, after all, were *going* somewhere; they were not simply people to whom inexplicable things happened which had to be passively endured. From the simple acceptance of change was before long to spring the will to live in change which is a peculiarity of modern man. Secularized and far away from their origins, such ideas could be very important; the appearance of modern science would soon provide an example. In another sense, too, the Christian heritage was decisive for, after the fall of Byzantium, Europeans believed that they alone (or in effect alone, for there was little sense of what Slav, Nestorian or Coptic Christianity might be) possessed it. It was an encouraging idea. Even with the Ottomans to face, Europe in 1500 was no longer just the beleaguered fortress of the Dark Ages, but a stronghold from which men were beginning to sally forth in counter-attack. Jerusalem had been abandoned to the infidel, Byzantium had fallen. Where should be the new centre of the world?

Deep implications take time to surface. In 1500 there was little to show that the future would belong – for a time at least – to the Europeans. They were not yet modern men and women. We cannot without an effort understand our ancestors of that era, even when they speak Latin, for their Latin has overtones and associations we are bound to miss; it is not only the language of educated men, but the language of religion, and in the half-light of a dawning modernity the weight of that religion remains the best clue to the reality of Europe's first civilization. Religion was the ground and a continual reinforcement of the stability of a culture which we look at almost entirely from an anachronistic perspective, that of change. Except in the shortest term, change was not something most Europeans would have been aware of in the fifteenth century. For all men, the deepest determinant of their lives was still the slow but ever-repeated passage of the seasons, a rhythm which set the pattern of work and leisure, poverty and prosperity, of the routines of home, workshop and study. That remains only vestigially true today; apart from the farmers themselves, in England only MPs, judges and university teachers still work to a year originally divided by the need to get in the harvest. On this rhythm were imposed those of religion. When the harvest was in the Church blessed it and the calendar of the Christian year provided the more detailed timetable to which men lived. Some of it was very old, even pre-Christian; it had been going on for centuries and could hardly be imagined otherwise. It regulated the day for many people; every three hours the religious were called to prayer in thousands of monasteries and convents by the bell of their house, and outside the walls, laymen set the pattern of their day by it, too when they could hear it. Until there were striking clocks, only the bell of the parish church, cathedral or monastery supplemented the sun or the burning of a candle as a record of passing time, and it did so by announcing the hour of another act of worship.

Only in a very special, long perspective can we rightly speak of centuries during which this went on and on as an age of 'revolutionary' changes, though that is what it was. Even the most obvious discontinuities, the growth of a town, an onset of plague, the displacement of one noble family by another, the building of a cathedral or the collapse of a castle, all took place in a remarkably unchanged setting. The fields tilled by English peasants in 1500 were often still those visited by the men who wrote them down in Domesday Book, over 400 years before, and when the king's commissioners went to visit the nuns of Lacock in order to wind up their house in the 1530s, they found, to their amazement, these aristocratic ladies still speaking among themselves the Norman-French commonly used in noble families three centuries earlier.

Such immense inertia must never be forgotten. Only very deep in the humus of this society did there lie, paradoxically, a future. The fundamental Christian dualism of this life and the world to come, the earthly and the heavenly, to which generations had become accustomed was to prove a cultural irritant of great value. It was a vision which could eventually be secularized as a new critical perception, the contrast of what is and what might be, of ideal and actual. Christianity in fact secreted an essence to be utilized against itself, for in the end it would make possible the independent critical stance of the secular mind, a complete break with the world Aquinas and Erasmus knew and shared.

Enterprise

In one way, indeed, the future was in 1500 already appearing. European knowledge of the planet – and therefore of how to use it and exploit it – grew more rapidly in the fifteenth century than ever before. Even in 1400 it had still seemed sensible to see Jerusalem as the centre of the world. Though the Vikings had crossed the Atlantic, men then could still predicate a world which, though spherical (as the Greeks had argued), was made up of three continents, Europe, Asia and Africa, around the shores of one land-locked sea, the Mediterranean. It was just about to become impossible to hold such views.

The route to the future lay across the oceans, because advance in other directions was blocked. Europe's first direct contacts with the East had been by land rather than water. The caravan routes of central Asia were their main channel; goods brought west along them were shipped for the last stage of their journey from the Black Sea or Levant ports. Or, goods were brought up the Red Sea in Arab ships and then carried across land to Egypt where European ships could take them abroad. Elsewhere, those ships rarely ventured far west or south of Morocco until the fifteenth century. Then, a mounting wave of maritime enterprise becomes visible, and with it, the beginnings of true world history. The ships and techniques of long-range navigation needed for oceanic sailing were available from the fourteenth century onwards. They made possible the great effort of exploration which has led to the fifteenth century being called 'the Age of Reconnaissance'.

In ship design there were two crucial changes. One was specific, the adoption of the stern-post rudder; some ships had it by 1300. The other was a more gradual and complex process of improving rigging and sails. A growing maritime trade no doubt spurred such developments. By 1500, the tubby medieval 'cog' of northern Europe, square-rigged with a single sail and mast, was giving way to three-masters with mixed sails. The main mast still carried square-rigging, but more than one sail, while the mizzen-mast had a big lateen sail borrowed from the Mediterranean tradition; the fore mast might carry more square-rigged sails, but also newly invented fore-and-aft jib sails attached to a bowsprit. Together with the lateen sail aft, these made vessels much more manoeuvrable and they could be sailed much closer to the wind. Ships incorporating these changes, small and cramped as they at first were, were safer and faster; they were in essentials already the vessels which would dominate the seas until the coming of steam.

Navigation too had come far since the days of the Vikings. They had been the first Europeans who knew how to sail an oceanic course, using the Pole Star and the sun, whose height above the horizon in northern latitudes at midday had been computed in tables by a tenth-century Irish astronomer. They crossed the Atlantic with this technique by running along a line of latitude and their Scandinavian successors had been able to maintain sea communications with their Greenland and (possibly) North American settlements for centuries. Then there is evidence of two great innovations. In the thirteenth century the compass came to be commonly used in the Mediterranean (it already existed in China, but it is not certain that it was transmitted from Asia to the West or, if it was, how and when). In 1270 there also appears the first reference to a chart being used in a ship on a crusading venture. The next two centuries gave birth to modern geography and exploration. Spurred by the thought of commercial prizes, by missionary zeal and diplomatic possibilities, some princes began to subsidize research. In the fifteenth century princes came to employ their own cartographers and hydrographers. Foremost among them was a brother of the king of Portugal, Prince Henry, 'the Navigator' as English-speaking scholars were later to call him (somewhat misleadingly, for he never navigated anything).

Land-locked by Spain, Portugal was virtually barred from east Mediterranean trade by the experience and ferocity of the Catalans and Italians who jealously guarded it. The Portuguese were almost bound to be propelled into the Atlantic, and had long had experience of its fishing grounds. Their earliest explorations and settlement ventures had been towards the Atlantic islands, and in this Spaniards were engaged, too. By 1339, the first voyage had been made to the Canaries. The Portuguese were already fairly familiar with oceanic waters when Prince Henry began to mount a series of exploratory voyages in another direction. From a mixture of motives, he turned his countrymen southward. Gold and pepper, it was known, were to be found on the other side of the Sahara; perhaps the Portuguese could discover where. Perhaps, too, there was the possibility of finding an ally here to take the Turk in the flank, the legendary Christian prince, Prester John. Certainly there were converts, glory and land to be won for the cross. Henry, for all that he did so much to launch Europe on the great expansion which transformed the globe and created one world, was a medieval man to the soles of his boots. He sought papal authority and approval for his expeditions. When he went crusading in North Africa, he took with him a fragment of the True Cross. Thus the beginnings of the age of discovery lay in government-subsidized research (as we might put it), but also in the world of chivalry and crusade. Henry is an outstanding example of a man who wrought more than he knew or could have intended.

The coast-hugging Portuguese pushed steadily south, some of the bolder among them also reaching out to the Madeiras, where they began to settle in the 1420s. In 1434 one of their captains passed Cape Bojador, an important psychological obstacle whose rounding was Henry's first great triumph; ten years later they reached Cape Verde and established themselves in the Azores. By then they had discovered that the *caravel*, a ship which used the latest rigging, could deal with the head winds and contrary currents of the return voyage by going right out into the Atlantic and sailing a long semi-circular course home. In 1445 they reached Senegal and soon after built the first Portuguese fort in Africa. Henry died in 1460, but by then his countrymen were ready to go on south. In 1473 they crossed the Equator and in 1487 reached the Cape of Good Hope. Ahead lay the Indian Ocean; Arabs had long traded across it and pilots were available. Beyond it lay even richer sources of spices. In 1498 Vasco da Gama picked up an Omani pilot on the east African coast and set off for Asia. In May he dropped anchor off Calicut, on the west coast of India. For the first time, Asia was in direct sea-communication with Europe.

A new world

A few years earlier, a Genoese, remembered by English-speakers as Christopher Columbus, had crossed the Atlantic. The king of Portugal had turned him down but he had succeeded in getting the support of Isabella of Castile for a voyage which, he believed (confidently basing himself on Ptolemy), would take him to Asia by sailing westward. Because of this, a future empire was to fall to the Crown of Castile, though this was one of the least of the momentous consequences to follow. Columbus set sail in 1492 and after 69 days his three little ships made a landfall in the Bahamas. A fortnight later he came to Cuba, which he named Hispaniola, before returning to Spain. The following year he came back to explore the islands known ever since as the West Indies (whose name commemorates Columbus' tenacious belief that he had reached Asia). His confident leap in the dark had changed world history. Without knowing it he had discovered a new world. Unlike the Portuguese navigators who had been bravely, resourcefully and systematically navigating round a continent whose existence (if not its shape and size) was known, to a known destination, Columbus had struck unknown islands at the junction of two whole unknown continents; they were totally unanticipated, and thus truly 'new'. In 1495 the first map showing his discoveries appeared, with Cuba properly marked as an island and not (as Columbus had made his crew swear it was) part of the Asian mainland. He had refused to admit the possibility of the existence of a new continent between Europe and Asia and until his dying day insisted that he had discovered the offshore islands of Asia. A further important step followed in 1502, when

---

THE AGE OF THE MAJOR DISCOVERIES

1445   Portuguese land on Cape Verde Islands.

1455   Papal bull *Pontifex Romanus* recognizes Portuguese monopoly of African exploration.

1460   Death of Prince Henry 'the Navigator'.

1469   Afonso V of Portugal leases a monopoly of West African trade in return for continued exploration.

1479   Spain agrees that Portugal should have monopoly rights in trade with Guinea.

1481   Fort founded at Elmina (in modern Ghana) as base for Portugal's African trade.

1482   Portuguese reach the Congo.

1488   Bartolomeu Diaz rounds Cape of (Good) Hope.

1492   Christopher Columbus reaches the West Indies.

1494   Treaty of Tordesillas giving Spain exclusive rights of exploration west of a line drawn north–south across the Atlantic. Portugal had similar rights east of this line.

1496   First voyage of discovery by Italian John Cabot, commissioned by Henry VII of England.

1497   Cabot reaches Newfoundland on his second voyage.

1498   Vasco Da Gama arrives at Calicut, having discovered the sea route to India.

1499   Under Spanish flag, Florentine Amerigo Vespucci discovers South America.

1500   Portuguese Pedro Alvares Cabral discovers Brazil.

1507   Term 'America' used to denote the New World.

1508   Cabot sets out to find the Northwest Passage.

1513   Balboa crosses the isthmus of Darien to reach the Pacific.

1519   Portuguese Ferdinand Magellan and Juan Sebastian del Cano sail westwards in search of Spice Islands.

1522   Del Cano returns to Spain, having circumnavigated the globe.

an Italian in a Portuguese vessel visiting the coast of what is now Brazil struck southward to sail as far as the river Plate. Amerigo Vespucci's second voyage demonstrated conclusively that a whole continent lay to the south of the first great discoveries. Five years later a German geographer named the new continent in his honour – America – and the name was later applied to the northern continent, too. Not until 1726, though, was it to be demonstrated for certain that it was not joined to Asia in the region of the Bering Straits.

New geographical knowledge quickly changed diplomacy and the relations of states. It was soon recognized that understandings would be needed about European interests in new-found lands. The first treaty over trade outside European waters was made between the rulers of Portugal and Castile in 1479; and soon spheres of influence were being delimited. The pope made a temporary award, based on a division of the world between the two Iberian monarchies along a line a 100 leagues west of the Azores, but this was overtaken by the treaty of Tordesillas in 1494 which gave to Portugal all the lands east of a line of longitude running 370 leagues west of Cape Verde, and to Castile those west of it. In 1500 a Portuguese squadron on the way to the Indian Ocean ran out into the Atlantic to avoid adverse winds and to its surprise struck land which lay east of the treaty line but was not Africa. It was Brazil. Henceforth Portugal would have an American as well as an Asian destiny.

In 1522, thirty years after Columbus' landfall in the Bahamas, another ship sailing west in the service of Spain completed the first voyage round the world. It had set out under the command of a Portuguese, Magellan, who had got as far as the Philippines, where he was killed. By then he had discovered and sailed through the straits named after him and with this voyage and its demonstration that the great oceans were all interconnected, the prologue to the European age can be considered over. Just about a century of discovery and exploration had transformed men's vision of the world and the course of history. From this time nations with access to the Atlantic would have opportunities denied to the land-locked powers of central Europe and the Mediterranean. In the first place this meant Spain and Portugal, but they would be joined and surpassed by France, Holland and, above all, England, a collection of harbours incomparably placed at the centre of the newly enlarged hemisphere, all of them easily accessible from their shallow hinterland, and within easy striking distance of the great European sea routes of the next 200 years.

New visions of the world

New geographical knowledge changed men's minds on many matters besides geography; it led Europeans to see their world in a new way. But a new geography was the starting-point. The maps men now began to draw, for all their limitations, began to show the true structure of the globe. Ptolemy's view of it, virtually forgotten for a 1,000 years, had already included the Canaries, Iceland and Ceylon. In 1400 a Florentine had brought back from Constantinople a copy of his *Geography*. Translation of this text, errors included (Ptolemy believed that the Indian ocean was totally enclosed by land), and the multiplication of copies first in manuscript and then in print (there were six editions between 1477, when it was first printed, and 1500) was a great stimulus to better map-making. The atlas – a collection of engraved and printed maps bound in a book – was invented in the sixteenth century; more men than ever could now consult a picture of their world. With better projections, navigation was simpler, too. Here the great figure was a Dutchman, Gerhard Kremer, who is remembered as Mercator. He was not only the first man to print on a map the word 'America' but the inventor of the projection which is still today the most familiar – one devised as if it were the surface of an unrolled cylinder, with Europe at its centre. This solved the problem of providing a flat surface on which to read direction and courses without distortion, even if it made the calculation of distances harder the further you went north or south. The making of terrestrial and celestial globes was another important consequence of the geographical revolution (Mercator made his first globe in 1541).

A different sort of mental change which came about as a result of the cumulative and systematic nature of this progression, was that European expansion in the next phase of world history would be conscious and directed as it been before only in the age of the Crusades. Europeans had long wanted land and gold; the greed which lay at the heart of enterprise was not new. Nor was the religious zeal which sometimes inspired them and sometimes cloaked their springs of action even from the actors themselves. What had now been added to these inspirations was a growing confidence derived from knowledge and success. Europeans in 1500 were at the beginning of an age in which their energy and confidence would grow seemingly without limit. The world did not come to them, they would go out to it and take it.

This was not at once always clear. In the Mediterranean and Balkans, Europeans would for a long time go on feeling threatened and defensive. The sciences of navigation and seamanship still had far to go – not until the eighteenth century, for example, would there be available a time-keeper accurate enough for very exact sailing – before the risks of exploration notably diminished. But the way was opening to a new relationship between Europe and the rest of the world, and between European countries themselves. A near-complete knowledge of the physical outline of the world and its continents (with the exception of Antarctica) would be available by 1600. Even before this, though, discovery would be followed by conquest. A world revolution was beginning. An equilibrium which had lasted a 1,000 years was dissolving.

The agencies of this dissolution had not existed in AD 1000, let alone AD 500. Yet something we can call at last Europe – a collection of peoples, organized in ways still very unlike our own societies, and still believing things very different from the things most modern Europeans believe – existed by 1500. There were already by then some who could think of 'Europe' and 'Europeans' as meaningful ideas, even if those words still competed with other terms. This self-consciousness and the historical realities behind it had somehow appeared in the previous millenium; the years between AD 500 and 1500 can be accounted the age of creation not only of Europe but of the idea of Europe. The peoples of the continent were then moulded in ways – and into ways – which made some outcomes more likely than others, a few among them inevitable, and others impossible. This was a revolution, no less, even if one of the slowest and most piecemeal in historical times.

BOOK THREE Launching modern history 1500–1800

It is reasonable to guess that when the nineteenth century began, most of the world's inhabitants had no sense of history or historical change. Probably there were more people in Europe with some awareness of it than anywhere else, because Christianity was a uniquely historically-minded religion. But even they had still the reassuring and visible presence of much of the material and institutional past to suggest that little ever changed, and that what did change would do so only very slowly. The weight of that past was still very obvious until almost the very end of the eighteenth century.

Yet the previous three hundred years had brought huge change. The religious unity of medieval Christendom had vanished. With it had gone much more than a particular ecclesiastical arrangement; for centuries that unity provided the central assumptions of Europeans' life and thought. By 1800 many of them thought differently from their sixteenth-century predecessors about heaven and earth, the way nature worked and how it might be used, the way they got their living, their relations with one another and with authority. Their conceptions of world geography had been transformed by new knowledge. Sovereign states had largely replaced the structural confusion of medieval politics and the European map had changed beyond recognition. Some people had even come to the idea (it would have been astonishing in 1500) that progressive improvement was a universal tendency of mankind. Moreover, much of what was left of what was already called the *ancien régime*, solid as it seemed, was mortally stricken and would soon pass away.

All this may be summed up by saying that Europeans had changed the world and that modern history had begun. Launched by Europeans, its revolutionary effects were to spread round the globe. All cultures and civilizations, even if most of their inhabitants still had no inkling of it, were beginning to move away from their separate and self-contained histories towards participation for the first time in world history. This was because of what happened in Europe in these three centuries.

CHAPTER ONE A new age

Modernity and modern history

In 1494, a young Savoyard nobleman set out across the Alps in the service of the king of France, who had just invaded Italy in order to assert his claim to the throne of Naples, far to the south. For Bayard – who was probably not quite twenty years old – this was the beginning of a spectacular career. As a soldier he was often on the losing side; it was not continuous success which built first a European reputation and made him a famous, semi-mythical figure, but his chivalric virtues. A French king sought to be dubbed knight by him because he admired him so much. Once, Bayard defended a bridge single-handed against 200 opponents. When he was made prisoner in Picardy, the English king released him unransomed because of his courage in standing and fighting when his comrades had fled (he too, tried, to persuade Bayard to enter his service, but in vain). When Bayard died in 1524 his historical reputation was assured as the fearless and irreproachable warrior – the *chevalier sans peur et sans reproche*. With the possible exception of Sir Philip Sidney, he is the last man to have won an unquestioned place in the annals of chivalry.

Bayard was a spectacular expression of the way the Middle Ages were still going on in the early sixteenth century – as they were to be still in diminishing areas within it over the next 300 years or so. Attitudes did not change fast. The French kings who led expeditions to Italy set off in the spirit of the knights and paladins of old of whom they had read and heard; in 1520 a spectacular summit meeting in Flanders, the 'Field of the Cloth of Gold', was still run as a medieval social occasion would have been, with tournaments and jousting to provide diversion from the arduous tasks of negotiation and diplomacy. The aims of that diplomacy, too, were still medieval. Kings fought and negotiated for the advancement of personal interests and standing, whether their own or those of their families and dependants, rather than those of the peoples over whom they ruled. As for religious belief, some of those who were at the time carving out the first European empires in the New World sincerely saw themselves as successors to the crusaders as well as to the paladins. Cortes, who won Mexico for the Crown of Castile, always carried on his person an image of the Blessed Virgin, and fought, looted and conquered under a banner signed with the Cross and the historic words *in hoc signum vinces* – 'in this sign shall you conquer'.

Yet even in 1500, an arbitrary date, a new age of history was beginning. New processes had already been launched which, without anyone intending it, were to transform the lives of people round the world, above all and first in Europe. They would give new shape to the institutions, beliefs and behaviour of Europeans, and the relations which they had with other inhabitants of the earth.

Europeans' ventures beyond their own shores had been the most notable early signs; in 1494, the phrase 'New World' for the first time appears in a document, and in print first in 1505.[1] There had just opened, that is to say, an age in which the modern Atlantic world of which Europe was the heart was to emerge. It was to do so as a civilization radically unlike any other, including its own tradition-bound, agrarian-based and geographically-confined predecessor. It was to be innovative and secular-minded, industrial and urban in its material nature, and worldwide in its influence. That outcome was centuries away, but the first stirrings of the unprecedented potential for development and growth which would bring it about had already begun by the sixteenth century.

The boundaries of the first civilization to seek a world role were those of western Christendom. Now, they were beginning to expand, first into the Atlantic (formally, but hardly effectively, demarcated by the Treaty of Tordesillas), and then into the Indian ocean. There would follow the unfolding, at an accelerating rate, of that civilization's role as a shaping force all round the globe. At the same time, the Christian culture which was the source of this process was transformed. The Europe of 1800 already would have been almost unrecognizable to any European alive in 1500. Modern history, in fact, would have begun. The huge changes this implied were to come about very unevenly, both in time and place. Some parts of Europe – England, or the Netherlands, for example, and even France – would change quite rapidly, while in the lives of many Spaniards or Sicilians change would still in 1800 be only marginally evident and sporadically important. But by then the groundwork of a European world hegemony would long have been in place.

One aspect of the onset of modernity is change in men's minds. At one extreme, and perhaps most obviously, this embraced philosophical thinking which, for most educated men, had still appeared in 1500 to be carried on quite satisfactorily within the frameworks provided by the classical ideas adapted and transmitted by medieval Christianity. At another, it embraced more practical affairs: the manipulation of nature, or the ordering and assessment of social and political arrangements, even and of economic relations. This cultural consensus declined as a result of many influences, one of which was western Europe's loss of religious unity in the sixteenth century. But there were others, and they are a part of the modernization which makes 'modern' history distinctive.

People use that term in more than one sense. Some have taken it to be the history that has happened since the 'ancient' history of the Jews, Greeks and Romans; in this sense it is still used as the name of a course of study at Oxford which includes the Middle Ages. But 'modern' history is now distinguished from 'medieval' history, too, and even further refinements are made, as historians have wanted to make distinctions within it. They sometimes speak of an 'early modern' European history. By this, they are drawing our attention to a fact already touched upon. 'Modernization' is a process which has gone forward at different speeds in different European countries (and elsewhere in the world). It did not come to a neat end, completed, in Europe in 1800,

---

[1]   *Mundus novus* was the title of a book published at Florence in that year.

though that is a convenient point to assess its advance, anymore than it had a neat start three centuries earlier. Nor did it always come about by stages occurring in the same order in each country. It had many aspects beyond those intellectual and cultural changes already touched upon. It brought new institutions, new technologies, a new rapidity of social and political change, and much else. It brought a new seed of hope about a better future, a new ability to disregard the past.

Numbers and modernity

We can conveniently begin to explore what modernization meant by recalling a simple and obvious truth: that for most of human history most people's lives have been deeply and cruelly shaped by the fact that they have had little or no choice about the way in which they could provide themselves and their families with shelter and enough to eat. The possibility that things might be otherwise has only recently become conceivable for even a minority (though a large one) of the world's population. It first appeared for any substantial number of people as a result of changes in the economy of early modern Europe, for the most part, west of the Elbe.

Europe in 1500 as a whole imported little food except a few luxuries, and exported virtually none. It is hard to say how much its inhabitants required, because we have only very rough ideas about their numbers, though we may feel more confident of the margins of error in some places than others. Governments had not begun to collect statistics in a systematic way and demography did not exist as a scientific activity. There was strong public feeling against taking censuses, still evident as late as the eighteenth century. Counting people almost always foreshadowed higher taxes; what was more, there were Biblical precedents against such things. Population estimates must therefore be treated with great caution. There exist several for Italy in 1500; scholars still come up with totals of from 5–10,000,000 – a variation of one 100 per cent.

Making the best of such information as we have, it looks as if the total world population in 1500 was about 425,000,000, most of whom lived in Asia. Europe, if we include Russia, may then have had 80,000,000 inhabitants. The setback of the fourteenth century had been grave, but, taking Europe as a whole, it had almost certainly been repaired by then; not all countries, though, were back by 1500 to the levels of, say, 1350. France probably was, and provided western Europe's largest single block of population, with about 16,000,000 inhabitants. She was one of a few countries which had already begun to grow in a new way, with only brief hiccups and setbacks interrupting a continuous slow rise over the long term. This trend was to continue (for changing reasons, as time passed) to the present day. What is more, though there were big differences between countries showing this new trend, virtually all of them grew faster than in earlier times. This began to change the balance between continents. By 1800 there seem to have been about 900,000,000 people in the world, about twice as many as three centuries before, and Europeans almost certainly made up a larger proportion among them. With due qualification, it seems that Europe's eighty millions or so of 1500 had in 1700 become about 140,000,000, and in 1800 slightly less than 200,000,000. At that date, this was likely to have been nearing about a quarter of humanity.

Guessing at population figures is a little less necessary for 1800 than at earlier dates. One reason is an almost continuous and certainly increasing interest shown by Europeans from the seventeenth century onwards in demographic science, and the appearance of a new study, statistics (called 'Political Arithmetic' in England). This led to conscious accumulation of relevant data and marks a notable step in the history of the European mind. It made possible a recognition that at least some of human life could be expressed as a matter of statistical regularities; for all its final inevitability, the age of death had hitherto irresistibly been seen as a matter of awe-inspiring uncertainty. The appearance of life insurance, at the start of what has sometimes been called the 'Age of Reason', signals the potential of such change. It was one expression of the ways in which Europeans would come to accept an increasingly secularized view of their universe. In England an actuarially-based insurance industry was by 1700 demonstrating that some matters hitherto unplannable could now be brought within the scope of conscious and rational consideration. Though a new objectivity in the study of society came to full fruition only very slowly, a growing effectiveness of government helped. Yet only in 1801, over seven centuries after Domesday Book, did a British government hold the first British census;   France had to wait another three-quarters of a century for hers. Before such information became available, demography was still a matter of only relatively solid facts, often based on estimates from small samples, in a sea of guesses and inferences. Nonetheless, we can begin to talk of numbers which are harder than those for earlier times.

The figures available for 1800 indicate the beginnings of an important divergence of population history in much of Europe from that of other parts of the world. In the sixteenth century, it is unlikely that there were such startling disparities between growth rates in Europe and elsewhere as appeared towards the end of it. Even in 1800, though, Europeans died young. A French peasant child in the 1780s had chances of survival and living to adulthood much on a par with those of an Indian peasant in 1900, or of an Italian living under imperial Rome. Females who reached maturity before the eighteenth century tended to die before their menfolk, who often made two or three marriages in a lifetime because they were soon widowers. But there were important regional differences within Europe. West of a line running from the Baltic to the Adriatic married life was often short because people living there tended to make their first marriage later than Europeans in the east; this long made for different population patterns east and west because it offered fewer years for childbearing.[2] Everywhere, though, the wealthier tended to have larger families than the poor; they could afford to feed them properly, even if other factors also affected survival. As for keeping numbers down, abortion and infanticide have been employed in many societies to reduce the number of mouths to be fed, but there is also by 1800 some inferential evidence that some Europeans already sought to restrict their families in other ways. But this remains a mysterious topic; we can say very little with confidence about early birth control in Europe or what the implications might be for the way Europeans thought about their families.

In 1800 (as in 1500) most Europeans lived in a countryside which would have seemed rather empty to modern eyes. Cities were smaller than today's. There were probably a dozen European cities in 1700 with over 100,000 inhabitants. Amsterdam had about 200,000 in the eighteenth century, Paris a 500,000 or so, and since 1500 London had shot up from 120,000 to 700,000 in two centuries. Most towns remained small with populations of less than 10,000, but there were a great many of them.

---

[2]   See J. Hajnal, 'European Marriage Patterns in Perspective', in *Population in History*, ed. D.V. Glass and D.E.C. Eversley (London, 1965).

European population has always been very unevenly distributed. This came to matter more in political terms as time went by. France long remained the largest west European state; she already had about 21,000,000 inhabitants in 1700, when England and Wales had only about 6,000,000. But less reliable estimates for some areas than others combine with boundary changes to make it hard to be sure what we are talking about under the same name at different times. Most countries and regions underwent checks and possibly setbacks to their population growth in a wave of early and mid-seventeenth-century disasters. The Great Plague of London of 1665 is famous, but Spain, Italy and Germany all had bad outbreaks of epidemic disease in the 1630s. Famine was another sporadic and local check; in the middle seventeenth century we hear of cannibalism in Germany. Poor feeding and lowered resistance could quickly lead to disaster when coupled to a bad harvest and, especially, warfare (of which there was plenty, at least before 1700). Famine and disease followed armies about; together they could quickly depopulate a small area[3]. Yet the localization of economic life was also occasionally a protection; a particular town might get off unscathed even in a campaigning zone if it escaped siege or sack, while only a few miles away another was devastated. But their survival was always precarious until population growth began to be overtaken by productivity. The seventeenth century often seems obsessed by hunger.

In the late sixteenth century the obscurely felt pressure of population had produced efforts to stimulate emigration. In the next 200 years Europeans went overseas in large numbers. Modern calculations are that 250,000 British emigrants went to the New World in the seventeenth century, one and a half millions in the next. Considerable numbers of Germans (about 200,000) also went there by 1800, and Frenchmen went to Canada. Perhaps something like 2,000,000 Europeans had by then gone to America north of the Rio Grande. South of it there then lived about 100,000 Spaniards and Portuguese. The promise of land and plenty overseas were not the whole story of the population of the Americas, but came in time to loom larger in settlers' eyes than the old dreams of gold which haunted the first explorers.

A new concern about what was seen as the startling nature of European population growth in the three previous centuries can be gathered from a book published in 1798 by an English clergyman. *The Essay on Population* by Thomas Malthus remains the most influential book ever written on the subject as well as being a symptom of a change in demographic thinking. Though Malthus set out what appeared to be the laws of population growth, his impact on, for example, economic theory and biological science was to be just as important as his contribution to demographic studies. He turned two centuries or so of demographic orthodoxy on its head. It had generally been agreed that a rising population was a sign of prosperity. Kings had sought to increase the number of their subjects not merely because this would mean more taxpayers and soldiers but because a bigger population quickened economic life. It was also an important indicator: larger numbers showed that the economy was providing a living for more people. This view was in its essentials endorsed by no less an authority than the great Adam Smith himself, whose *Wealth of Nations* (a book of even greater influence than that of Malthus), had agreed as recently as 1776 that an increase in population was a good rough test of economic prosperity.

---

[3] For a helpful graph, see that reprinted by G. Parker in his *Europe in Crisis 1598–1648*, (London, 1979), p. 27.

Malthus, though, doused this view with very cold water. Whatever the consequences for society as a whole might be judged to be, he concluded that a rising population sooner or later spelt disaster and suffering for most of its members, the poor. In a famous demonstration he argued that the produce of the earth had finite limits, set by the amount of land available to grow food. This in turn set a limit to population. Yet in the short run population always tended to grow. As it grew, it would press increasingly upon a narrowing margin of subsistence. When this margin was exhausted, famine must follow. The population would then fall until it could be maintained with the food available. This mechanism could only be kept from operating if men and women abstained from having children (and prudence, as they regarded the consequences, might help them by encouraging them to put off marriage) or by such horrors as the natural checks imposed by disease or war. Yet it was not to turn out like that in Europe.

Feeding a larger population

The fundamental fact which told against Malthus was continuing and faster growth in wealth creation, above all in the production of food. This had already been under way for a long time when he wrote. The pre-condition of three centuries of European population growth had been that there was more food to go round, however severe occasional and local shortages might be. Once Europe's productivity began to grow faster than numbers, a major historical break had occurred.

Europe's agricultural output seems to have shown signs of recovery from the effects of the fourteenth century depopulation within the next hundred years. Land which had then been abandoned came back into cultivation. This, though, owed little to innovation. The productivity of land was bound to rise as population collapse led to the abandonment of cultivated but marginal land, while technical improvements were slow in coming and long confined to a few special areas. Medieval ways long lingered on; the use of cash took centuries to penetrate and change the near self-sufficiency of many communities. Yet by 1800, taking Europe as a whole and noting the role of a few leading countries in particular, agriculture was one of the two most progressive economic sectors (commerce was the other). Much more food per head was being grown there than 300 years previously, and that was sustaining a slow but continuing rise of population.

Innovation in agriculture began in orientation towards the market, rather than technical innovation. As a relatively dense population in the neighbourhood created a market and therefore an incentive, innovation often swiftly followed. In the fifteenth century the Low Countries were already leaders in intensive cultivation. Their towns offered markets. Technical improvement in drainage then opened the way to better pasture and to a larger animal population. The towns of the Po valley provided another cluster of markets. They encouraged the introduction of new crops. Rice, for example, an important addition to the European larder, appeared in northern Italy in the fifteenth century (it had done so much earlier in Moslem Spain). Not all new crops enjoyed instant success; it took about two centuries for the potato, which came to Europe from America, to be accepted in England, Germany and France, in spite of its obvious nutritional value (to say nothing of a promotional stress on its qualities as an aphrodisiac and helpfulness in the treatment of warts).

From the Low Countries what was later called agricultural 'improvement' spread slowly abroad, first to England. Among the first results clearly visible there were the enclosing of land for sheep in the sixteenth century, the bringing together of the scattered medieval strips of individual holdings into compact fields, better draining (especially in the Fens), and the making of new land from marsh and sea (as the Dutch had done). These were the foundations for an advance in English farming which would now become continuous and cumulative. The English farmer seemed readier to learn and innovate than those of other countries, though he also had important advantages. It was a literally incalculable benefit that after 1650 there was never again large-scale and protracted warfare on British soil. The farmer had also a growing market for his produce which allowed him to accumulate capital for further improvement. Land-holding was organized so as to bring the benefits of good farming to individuals owning their own land, or to tenants with secure leases. English agriculture was at an earlier date than elsewhere part of an economy in which land came to be treated almost as a commodity like any other. The last important phase in the removal of restraints on its use came in a spate of Enclosure Acts at the end of the eighteenth century (significantly coincident with high prices for grain) which mobilized for private profit the English peasant's traditional rights to pasture, fuel or other economic benefits. One of the most striking contrasts between English and continental agriculture in the early nineteenth century was that the traditional peasant all but disappeared in England. The swarming European rural populations of individuals with some, if minuscule, legal rights, customs and communal usages linking them to the soil had by 1800 no equivalent in England, where wage labourers provided most of the labour force.

Technical progress in English farming, though, was for a long time hit-and-miss. Early breeders of better animals succeeded not because of a knowledge of genetics (there was none) but because they backed hunches. Even so, the results were remarkable. The appearance of livestock changed; the scraggy medieval sheep whose backs resembled, in section, the Gothic arches of the monasteries which bred them, gave way to the fat, square, contented-looking animals familiar today. 'Symmetry, well-covered' was a farmer's toast in eighteenth-century Norfolk. As draining and hedging progressed the big, open medieval fields were replaced by a huge patchwork in the English countryside. Even by 1750, machinery was at work in some of its fields though it does not seem that it made much difference to output until the next century, when larger fields made it easier to use and more productive in relation to cost. Soon after 1800, though, steam engines were driving threshers and drag-line ploughs.

New methods also spread to Germany and the east. Here, where the soil was sometimes poor, it was doubly important to take advantage of every possible way of improving it. What was needed above all to improve productivity in eastern Europe was labour. Landlords therefore resisted all attempts to break up the old manorial disciplines. Serfdom had virtually been replaced by wage-labour in England by 1500, but in the next 200 years, it became more common in Germany and Poland. In the Russia which emerged from Muscovy, too, the serf population grew larger as a proportion of the whole, and new and harsher laws buttressed their masters' control of the peasants. Nor for the first time, nor the last, economic progress went with social injustice; serfdom was a way of making available labour resources which were needed if land was to be made productive, just as forced labour was elsewhere and at many other times. A new distinction between eastern and western Europe was in the making. The former was already socially backward in 1500; as time passed it grew, relatively, more backward, with social and economic structures fundamentally unchanged well into the nineteenth century. In 1800 it was still quite normal for a peasant on an east German estate to be unable to leave it to work elsewhere, or to marry without permission, or to attend to his own patch of garden before he had done work he owed his landlord. In some areas the effects of Ottoman rule had led to depopulation; this was true, for example, of Hungary, so that when it was safely re-acquired for Europe and the Habsburgs in 1699, care was taken to tie the peasants who remained to the land. Nor was labour only due in the field; the serf, his children and womenfolk might have to work for the lord in the house, too. The drive for improvement was not the only reason why serfdom persisted in eastern Europe while disappearing in the west, but it is a part of the explanation. It was very convenient to increase the demands made on your serfs if you wanted to improve your estate. In some places (Poland may have been the worst) the outcome was that peasants were reduced to near-slavery.

Economic change often brings distress and even misery to some, yet it is hard not to accept that the long-term effects were desirable. Above all, agricultural improvement in all its diversity, together with better transport, was to eliminate the recurrent dearths which did so much for so long to check population growth. There were still to be severe shortages in France in the eighteenth century, and in other parts of Europe in the next, but perhaps the last moment when European population seems to have pressed on resources so as to threaten another great calamity like that of the fourteenth century came at the end of the sixteenth century. Then, Italian rulers had to send to buy grain in Danzig and this already indicated a new access to resources through the development of long-distance sea trade. By 1600 some Mediterranean markets had come to depend on the Baltic for the corn for their flour. It was still to be a long time before import would be a certain resource; often it could not operate quickly enough, especially where land transport was required. Yet in the next bad spell, in the middle decades of the following century, England and the Netherlands escaped the worst and thereafter famine and dearth became in Europe local, or at most national, events, gradually succumbing to the increasing availability of imported grain. Bad harvests, it has been said, made France 'one great hospital' in 1708–9, but that was in wartime and after a particularly cold winter. There were notable contrasts, too, for food supply was not the only shaper of demography. In the eighteenth century the population of France still grew faster than production, which meant that the standard of living of many Frenchmen fell at a time on which the English labourer was later to look back – realistically or not – as an age of plenty.

Agriculture provided the first demonstrations of what might be done by even rudimentary science – by experiment, observation, record and experiment again – to increase the control of environment. Improvement favoured the reorganization of land in bigger farms and the reduction of the number of smallholders. A total dependence on wage-labour, and high capital investment in buildings, drainage and machinery in the end followed, but the speed of change must not be exaggerated. Even in England, the onset of 'enclosure', the consolidation for private use of the open fields and common lands of the traditional village, only became general at the end of the eighteenth century and the beginning of the nineteenth. The complete integration of agriculture with the market economy and the treatment of land simply as a commodity like any other had to wait for the nineteenth century. Yet by the eighteenth the way ahead was beginning to appear. In some countries there was visible change in the countryside (and its inhabitants).

England was only the most spectacular example of specialized, regional develop-ment. Technical knowledge spread as time passed and differences of soil and climate were exploited with an awareness of new opportunities in markets. As more grain from the lands south of the Baltic was shipped to western and Mediterranean Europe, there followed growth in shipping, new profits for the old German towns of the league of sea-ports called the 'Hansa', and easier access to the forestry resources of Scandinavia. The appearance and special qualities of animals were different in different places. The Merino sheep (later to spread world-wide) was suited to the dry pastures of Spain: it looked somewhat goat-like to English eyes, but it gave the best wool. Sheep raised on England's greener pastures had coarser fleeces but carried more meat. Such variations meant that levels of well-being and comfort differed from country to country. Foreigners noticed that peasants and craftsmen in seventeenth-century England wore woollen cloth, whereas their continental equivalents made do with coarse linens made from flax.

Many more such differences and distinctions could be listed as Europe's first and basic industry, agriculture, grew into the era of what we may call as we choose, 'Agricul-tural Revolution', 'Improvement', or by any other name. The processes brought mental and cultural changes with them, too. Improvement almost always meant specialization and that meant conscious decision. Individual farmers stopped trying to grow everything and concentrated on the things they could do best, buying their other needs elsewhere. It was also always accompanied by technical betterment. This might mean breaks with the past in the form of new 'rotations' (that is, using fields for different crops each year in such a way as to rest and restore the soil rather than exhaust it), new products (potatoes and maize from America were outstanding examples), new treatments (liming, for example, for the soil), new varieties of familiar crops (special grasses for pasture), new works (building drains and hedges), new machinery (though this came in more slowly), or simply the enclosing of land which was formerly 'common' so as to make it the prop-erty (and therefore the interest) of one man. In the end all these things led to more being extracted from the land, greater production, more food and cheaper clothes – which meant also changes in expectations. It is a phenomenon whose broadest implications escape any summary. The most interesting thing about it is still an unsolved question: why it should have happened first in Europe and nowhere else. There may be a basic explanation in the slow accumulation of wealth and resources – notably displayed in the late medieval towns – which had been going on since the twelfth century. But why did that not happen elsewhere, too – say, in China?

A new commercial world

Even in France and England, the two largest western countries then showing much progress in commerce and manufacture, the agricultural sector still dominated the economy in 1800. Nowhere was anything but a tiny part of the population engaged in an industry unconnected with agriculture. Mining was the only notable exception. Brewers, weavers and dyers all depended on the products of the land. Those who grew crops also span, wove or dealt in commodities for the market. Iron-workers cast and forged for smiths and coopers as well as for soldiers. Apart from agriculture, it is only in the commercial sector that we can observe sweeping change.

Already in the second half of the fifteenth century there had been a visible quick-ening of tempo. Europe had then begun to regain in scale, technique and direction, something like the commercial vigour first displayed in the thirteenth century. Though the great fairs and markets of the Middle Ages still continued into early modern (and even modern) times, and medieval laws on usury and the restrictive practices of guilds remained in force, a whole new commercial world would come into existence by 1800. It was the first stage in the establishment of a worldwide system of exchange which, with two brief twentieth-century exceptions, was from that time to show virtually uninterrupted growth and elaboration down to the present day. Yet its roots lay back beyond 1500, in beginnings, like the trickle of luxury commodities available in the Middle Ages through Byzantium, which only faintly presaged what was to come.

The first significant marker of a new commercial age was a definitive shift of economic gravity from southern to north-western Europe, from the Mediterranean to the Atlantic. One evidence was the eclipse, clear after 1600, of Venice; another was the prosperity of Seville before that date. Some of it can be attributed to the Ottoman advance, some to the Portuguese opening of new routes to Asia, some to American silver, some to political troubles and war which inflicted bad damage on Italy. Other changes can be traced to short-lived but crucial pressures like the Portuguese harassment of Jews which led to so many of them going, taking their commercial skills with them to the Low Countries.

Antwerp was the great commercial success story of the sixteenth century. But the success was brief and collapsed after a few decades in political and economic disaster. In the seventeenth century Amsterdam and London overtook Antwerp, in each case an important seaborne trade based on a well-populated hinterland providing the profits for diversification into manufacturing industry, services and banking. The old banking supremacy of the medieval Italian cities which had invented the bill of exchange passed finally to Holland and London via Flanders and the German bankers of the sixteenth century. The Bank of Amsterdam was already an international economic force in the early seventeenth century and in 1694 the Bank of England was founded. About such institutions clustered other banks and merchant houses undertaking operations of credit and finance. Over the long run, interest rates came down and the bill of exchange became the primary financial instrument of international trade.

So began the rise of paper as a substitute for coin, in domestic as well as in international commerce. In the eighteenth century came the first European paper currencies and the invention of the cheque. Joint stock companies generated another form of negotiable security, their own shares. They were long traded in London coffee-houses, before the London Stock Exchange acquired a name and location in 1773. By 1800 similar institutions existed in many other countries. New schemes for the mobilization of capital and its deployment proliferated in London, Paris and Amsterdam. Lotteries and (at one time) tontines enjoyed a vogue; so did some spectacularly disastrous investment projects, such as the notorious English South Sea 'Bubble', or Law's swindle on the French. But all the time the world was growing more commercial, more used to the idea of employing money to make money, and was supplying itself with the apparatus of modern capitalism.

Rulers grew more interested in these matters. Their predecessors had, of course, always been concerned with wealth and the opportunity of increasing it. Venice had long defended her commerce by diplomatic means and the English had often safeguarded their cloth exports to Flanders by treaty. It was widely accepted that there was only so much profit to go round and that one country could therefore only gain at the expense of others. But it was a long time before diplomacy had continuously to take account of the pursuit of wealth outside Europe. The change to a new set of diplomatic assumptions, if that is the way to put it, began in conflicts over trade with the Spanish empire. It spread rapidly. In the later seventeenth century rulers were paying greater attention to commercial questions and were readier to fight over them. This the English and Dutch did in 1652, so opening a long era during which they, as well as the French and Spanish, went to war again and again over quarrels in which questions of trade were important and sometimes paramount. Governments looked after their merchants (they were, after all, sources of revenue); monopolies and other privileges were given to companies under royal charters. They brought other advantages. Chartered companies could raise capital more easily because they could offer extra security for a return (or so it was argued). In the end they fell into disfavour (they had a last brief revival of favour at the end of the nineteenth century), but while they existed their activities closely involved government in the world of commerce. So, the concerns of businessmen increasingly shaped policy and law.

Oceanic commerce

A developing insurance market was another sign of commercial modernity. The first insurers had been medieval merchants and ship-owners and economic historians still tend to agree that the most impressive structural development in European commerce was its vigorous growth in overseas trade. Mediterranean commerce did not disappear, but declined relatively as against that of the northern seas. In the seventeenth

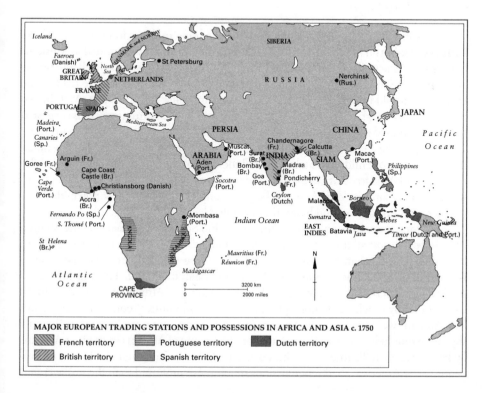

MAJOR EUROPEAN TRADING STATIONS AND POSSESSIONS IN AFRICA AND ASIA c. 1750

century, oceanic commerce was dominated first by the Dutch and then increasingly by their successful rivals, the English. The key to Dutch success lay in origin in the supply of salted herrings to European markets and domination of the important Baltic carrying trade. From its mastery they advanced to become the carriers of Europe. In the later seventeenth century they maintained colonies and trading stations worldwide, especially in the Far East. There they had succeeded the Portuguese in the domination of local maritime commerce; elsewhere they had been obliged to give ground to the English. The Atlantic fishing was the origin of the supremacy of the English at sea. They caught the nutritious and valuable cod on the Newfoundland banks, dried it and salted it ashore, and then sold it for consumption in Mediterranean countries, where fasting on Fridays provided an assured market. Gradually, both Dutch and English broadened and diversified their interests from their origins in specialized markets. Meanwhile, the trade of Spain and Portugal with their transatlantic colonies was important, but closed, at least in theory. Nor was France out of the race; her overseas trade doubled in the first half of the seventeenth century.

Water was almost always cheaper than land carriage and better freight-carrying ships help to explain the slow build-up of an international trade in primary commodities. Shipbuilding itself promoted the market for pitch, flax or timber, staples first of Baltic trade, later important in the economy of North America. The setting of growing colonial empires was more and more important. By 1800 there existed the first global and oceanic economy and an international trading community doing business – and fighting and intriguing for it – around the globe.

Slaving

A striking part of it was a new and thriving trade in slaves from Africa. In 1441 Portuguese sailors had brought home black men they ignorantly described as Moslems but the first African slaves were sold at Lisbon only in 1444. In Europe itself, the taking and selling of slaves had by then much declined (though Europeans were liable to be enslaved and sold into slavery by Arabs and Turks for some centuries yet). Within two or three years though over a 1,000 Africans were sold by the Portuguese. This suggested the profitability of the new traffic, but gives little hint of the scale of what was to come. What was quickly clear was the brutality of the business (the Portuguese quickly noted that the seizure of children usually ensured the docile captivity of the parents) and the complicity of Africans in it. As the demand for slaves went up, and the search for them went deeper inland in West Africa, it became simpler to rely on local potentates who would round up captives and barter them wholesale.

For a long time, Europe and the Portuguese and Spanish settlements in the Atlantic islands took almost all the slaves West Africa supplied. Then came a crucial change. In the mid-sixteenth century African slaves began to be shipped across the Atlantic to Brazil, the Caribbean islands and the North American mainland. This was the beginning of a long period of dramatic growth in populations of African origin in the Americas, with many of whose demographic, economic and political consequences we still live. Africans were not the only slaves in modern history, nor were Europeans the only slavers. Nonetheless, black slavery based on the buying of Africans from other Africans by Portuguese, Englishmen, Dutchmen and Frenchmen, and their sale to other Europeans in the Americas, had repercussions much more profound than the enslavement of Europeans by Ottomans or Africans by Arabs (or by other Africans). Much of the labour which made economic success for Europeans overseas possible was supplied by black slaves. The great majority of them always worked in agriculture or domestic service: black craftsmen or, later, factory workers, remained unusual. Slavery deeply shaped the evolution of American agriculture and, through it, of industry.

The trade was also financially very important. Huge profits were occasionally made – a fact which partly explains the crammed and pestilential holds of the slave-ships in which were confined the human cargoes. They rarely had a death-rate per voyage of less than 10 per cent and sometimes suffered even worse mortality. Yet the view once held that the slave trade's profits provided the capital for European industrialization no longer seems plausible. For two centuries, nonetheless, the trade provoked diplomatic wrangling and even war as nation after nation sought to break into it or monopolize it. Whether economically justified or not, statesmen thought it very important. Though the normal return on capital has been much exaggerated, the expectations of profit made the trade a great and contested prize.

The foundations of an industrial economy

Before 1800, though examples of industrial concentration can be identified in several European countries, manufacturing growth was still largely a matter of the multiplication of small-scale artisan production and its technical elaboration, rather than of radically new methods and organization. This has been sometimes called 'proto-industrialization'. Europe could by 1500 already draw on an enormous pool of skill. Large numbers of craftsmen were already used to investigating new processes and exploring new techniques. Two centuries of gunnery had helped to bring mining and metallurgy to a high pitch. Scientific instruments and mechanical clocks testified to a wide diffusion of expertise in the making of precision goods.

Such advantages shaped the early pattern of the industrial age and were eventually to change an old economic relationship with Asia. For centuries oriental craftsmen had astounded Europeans by their skill. Asian textiles and ceramics had a superiority which lives in our everyday language: china, muslin, calico, shantung are still familiar words. Then, in the fourteenth and fifteenth centuries, supremacy in some forms of craftsmanship began to pass to Europe, notably in mechanical and metallurgical skills. Asian potentates began to seek Europeans who could teach them how to make effective firearms; they even collected mechanical toys which were the commonplaces of European fairs, though this was never enough to pay for the Asian goods Europeans wanted. Such a reversal of roles was based on Europe's accumulation of skills in traditional occupations and their extension into new fields. So much is obvious. What is harder is to see what it was in the European mind which pressed the European craftsman forward and also stimulated the interest of his customers so that a craze for mechanical engineering is as important an aspect of the age of the Renaissance as is the work of its architects and goldsmiths. It did not happen elsewhere with such important consequences.

Early manufacturing areas grew by accretion. The first centres of such European industries as textiles or brewing were bound to be closely related to agriculture. Once established, these old trades tended to attract supporting and specialized crafts. Because English cloth had long been imported to Antwerp, finishing and dyeing establishments appeared there to work up the commodities flowing through the port. In the English countryside, wool merchants unwittingly shaped other industrial potential by putting out to rural spinners and weavers the raw materials they needed. The presence of minerals was another locating factor; mining and metallurgy were the most important industrial activities largely independent of agriculture. But industries could stagnate or even, sometimes, collapse, as happened in Italy. Its medieval industrial pre-eminence disappeared in the sixteenth century while that of the Flemish Low Countries and western and southern Germany – the old Carolingian heartland – lasted another century or so until it began to be clear that England, the Dutch Netherlands and Sweden were the new industrial leaders. In the eighteenth century Russia's extractive industries would add her to this list. By that time, too, what was beginning to be organized science was coming to bear on industrial techniques, and state policy was in some countries shaping industry consciously, as well as unconsciously.

One of the excitements of the eighteenth century is that it produced so many technological and scientific advances which were to come to exercise preponderant and dramatic influence in the later industrialization of Europe and the world. The outstanding example must be steam-power, feeble and crude as were many of its first manifestations. Other innovations – the century brought the first use of a submarine in warfare and, more important, the identification of electricity as a force and the beginnings of technology to tap it – also hint at an immense future. But Europe cannot be regarded as a mechanically industrialized continent in 1800.

The final and indispensable qualification which must be part of any picture of long-term and overall growth is its vulnerability. Dramatic fluctuations could easily occur; even in the nineteenth century, runs on banks and a contraction of demand for manufactured goods big enough to be called a slump could follow harvest failures. This, though, also reflected the growing interdependence and integration of a maturing economy.

Europe in a wider world

Not long after 1500 it began to be noticed that prices were rising in many places with unusual rapidity and persistence. The general effect seems to have been a roughly fourfold rise in European prices in a century, which does not now seem very shocking, but it was unprecedented and bound to have great and grave repercussions. Some landowners reacted by putting up rents and increasing as much as possible the yields from their 'feudal' dues. Some had to sell out. In this sense, inflation made for social mobility (as it still often does). Among the poor, the effects were usually harsh, for the price of agricultural produce went up and money wages did not keep pace. Real wages therefore fell. Almost everywhere in the middle decades of the sixteenth century popular revolts and running disorder reveal both the incomprehensibility and the severity of what was going on. Much ink has been spent by historians on explaining this inflation. It is now clear that it was well under way before American bullion began to arrive in any significant quantity, even if that later aggravated things. Probably the fundamental pressure always came from a population still increasing when the big advances of productivity still lay in the future. The rise in prices continued until the beginning of the seventeenth century, when it showed signs of falling, until a slower increase was resumed around 1700.

The debatable part played by American bullion in the long price rise is nonetheless one among several indicators of the importance to Europe in these centuries of the expanding geographical setting in which all its development has to be understood. American silver changed the prospects of European trade in Asia, by providing a commodity Asians were always willing to accept for their goods. So important was its role that much of it went directly to Asia, from Mexico in the 'Manila galleons', and never reached Europe at all. It is also impossible to envisage the domestic economic history of metropolitan Spain or the Netherlands – or, for that matter, of Europe as a whole – without gold and silver from the New World. It had vast indirect effect, lubricating and capitalizing enterprise of many kinds. But New Worlds stimulated trade in other new commodities, too, as well as changes of magnitude in economic activities long established. Traffic in luxury goods swelled in volume, and some ceased to be luxuries in consequence. New commodities made their appearance in Europe. Coffee seems to have come from Ottoman sources; tea, in growing quantity, direct from China and India. Patterns of consumption not only of individuals, but of manufacturing enterprises – dyers, distillers, weavers and spinners – changed. An accurate assessment of what European economic development owed to extra-European sources and influences in these crucial centuries of expansion is literally incalculable; they touched virtually every process or change already mentioned in this brief survey. Like all other aspects of the life of Europeans, its economics are only to be understood – perhaps as early as 1650 – in an oceanic context.

CHAPTER TWO Society and belief

Social order

Social, political and legal institutions are matters of myth and fiction as well as of concrete reality. One aspect of this is their frequent pretension to permanence, even timelessness. Perhaps, though, we are less likely to be taken in by them than were earlier generations: thanks to our history, we have no faith in the immutability of forms and institutions. Even in 1800, many men and women had. They still believed their places in society to be virtually God-given. They could still do so without difficulty because social change was much muffled and masked by the persistence of old forms. In spite of archaic terminology and thinking, though, much of European society had by then actually been transformed since 1500.

Indeed, traditional rural society had been changing since the central medieval period as agriculture had become in some places more a matter of business than of raising enough to eat on the spot (though by no means only because of that). Forms were usually preserved, and manorial estates and courts, lordship, and quaint dues and fines accruing to the landlord – all that was called the 'feudal system' – were still to be found operating all over continental Europe in the eighteenth century. The forms, though, lacked social reality. 'Feudalism' had survived as an economic device; the *'seigneur'* (to use the usual French term) might not be of noble blood, might never see his tenants, and might draw nothing from his lordship except sums of money which represented his claims on their labour, time and produce. What is more, with the transformation of economic and social reality there had come a growing questioning of them, on many grounds, ethical, practical and economic.

In England, whatever the term might mean, 'feudalism' had ceased to matter long before that. Her noblemen, great though the social authority and economic power some of them enjoyed, had no special legal privilege except the right to be summoned to a parliament (their other legal distinction of being barred from voting in the election of a Member of Parliament left them in that respect like most of the other subjects of King George III). They formed a tiny group; until the end of the eighteenth century the House of Lords had fewer than 200 hereditary members, whose rank and status could only be transmitted to a single heir. For all England's huge inequalities of wealth it had no large class of nobly born men and women enjoying extensive legal privileges and separated as an order from the rest of the population, such as was to be found almost universally elsewhere in Europe. In France there were perhaps a 250,000 nobles on the eve of the Revolution, all with important legal and formal rights; the English peerage could comfortably have been assembled in a small modern cinema.

On the other hand, the collective wealth and social influence of English landowners was immense. Below the peerage stretched an ill-defined class of 'gentlemen', linked at the top to the peers' families and disappearing by 1800 at the other end into the ranks of prosperous farmers and merchants who were eminently respectable but not 'gentlefolk'. The permeability of social divisions promoted cohesion and mobility. Gentlemanly status could be approached by enrichment, by professional distinction, or by personal merit. It was essentially a matter of recognition, of a shared code of behaviour, still reflecting the aristocratic concept of honour, but one civilized by the purging away of its exclusiveness, its legal supports, and many of its gothicisms.

Less striking but nonetheless real contrasts between ruling hierarchies could be drawn everywhere in Europe; not all topdogs behaved or were designated in the same way. England and Scotland were after 1707 part of one United Kingdom, but they were very different in social structure as in other respects. Differences between countries, for all the prevalence of old ideas, were already widening more rapidly by 1700, as new economic forces offered new opportunities and threw up new demands. In some advanced countries personal ties were by then already giving way to market relationships as a way of defining people's rights and expectations, and a vision of society as a collection of corporations which defined the status of their members was being replaced by a more individualist one. Outside England and the United Provinces, though, the replacement of traditional ideas about status and rank by new had barely begun. Figaro, the valet-hero of a notably successful eighteenth-century comedy which Mozart turned into an opera, jibed that his aristocratic master had done nothing to deserve his privileges beyond giving himself the trouble to be born[1]. This was recognized at the time as a subversive observation, but hardly one serious enough to be alarming. Europe was still soaked in the assumptions of aristocracy and was to be for a long time yet. Degrees of exclusivity varied, but the distinction between noble and non-noble remained crucial. Though aristocrats often accused them of doing so, kings found it difficult to ally with commoners against them; kings were aristocrats, too, one monarch said, it was their trade. Only the coming of a great revolution in France in 1789 changed things much, and hardly even then outside that country.

As the nineteenth century began most Europeans still respected noble blood, even if not quite so many people as in 1500 still automatically thought it gave a distinction which ought to be reflected in laws. It had begun to be felt in some quarters that to describe society in terms of orders with legally distinct rights and obligations no longer expressed its reality, and that religion did not necessarily uphold a particular social hierarchy. You could believe still that God made all men and women, and ordered their estate, but also that this need not imply that a fixed unchanging social order was the expression of God's will. Even by 1800 a few religious-minded people thought God rather preferred the rich man who had used God's gifts to make his own way in the world to the one who merely inherited his father's wealth and position. The old formal hierarchies were most criticized in countries where increasing economic mobility, growing urbanism, the rise of a market economy, the appearance of new commercial opportunities and spreading literacy stirred both minds and consciences.

---

[1]   See Act V. sc. iii, Beaumarchais' play, *Le mariage de Figaro*, 1784.

Three contrasting situations stand out. In the agrarian societies of the east the patrimonial relationship remained a reality and had even strengthened. Rulers and landowners who wanted to take advantage of new markets for grain and timber in the growing populations of western and southern Europe found a common interest in tying their peasants more rigorously to the land by law, imposing on them heavier and heavier labour services. This could be observed in Prussia, Poland and Hungary. In Russia serfdom became the very basis of society. It long remained all but unquestioned. Russia was later to prove fertile in the generation of dissidence, but the first serious published criticism of her institutions (and that, by implication) appeared only in 1790, in a celebrated book by the man who has been identified as the first Russian radical, Alexander Radischev, *The Journey from St Petersburg to Moscow* (he was at once condemned to death, though the sentence was commuted to one of exile in Siberia). The Russian ruling class seemed safe from social change. Its members enlarged their privileges in these centuries. The price they paid was endemic peasant revolt with its accompaniments of occasional murder and arson.

In a second group of countries, there was sufficient awareness of tension and a possible clash between the existing order and the economic and social worlds which were coming into being to provoke earlier demands for change. These for a long time proved capable of containment. France was one example, but in some of the German states, Belgium and parts of Italy there were occasional signs of the same sort of critical strain. The third group were those relatively open societies, Great Britain and the United Provinces of the Netherlands (and, across the sea, in the European societies of British North America) where formal definition of status fairly easily gave way to wealth (and even to talent), legal rights were widely diffused, economic opportunity was felt to be widespread, and wage-dependency was marked.

Such crude divisions blur too much, though. Even in the most developed countries much still survived from the past. The towns of England, France and Germany sometimes sheltered the genes of a future new order, but they were for the most part little Barchesters, wrapped in a comfortable provincialism under narrow merchant oligarchies, successful guildsmen or cathedral chapters. Chartres, contentedly rooted in its medieval countryside and medieval ways, its eighteenth-century population still the same size as that five centuries earlier, was part of the same country as Nantes or Bordeaux, thriving, bustling ports in the most dynamic sector of the French economy. Even the nineteenth century would find its immediate forbears unprogressive; if the countries we might now call 'advanced' showed a tendency to move further and faster than others, they could not shake off all their past.

Qualitative differences were nonetheless recognized and commented upon. One great (though cautious) questioner of the status quo, the French critic, Voltaire, was greatly struck by his discovery as a visitor that early eighteenth-century England could esteem and respect a great merchant as much as a nobleman[2]. He blurred important nuances in his admiration of his hosts, yet it is remarkable and true – and a part of the story of the rise of Great Britain to world power – that though the political class which governed eighteenth-century England fiercely reflected and defended the values of landed society, it was also able and vigilant to defend commercial interests. People talked of a political division between the 'moneyed' and the 'landed' interest, and poli-

---

[2]   See his *Lettres philosophiques sur les Anglais*, published in 1734.

tics long remained a matter of disputed places and entrenched prejudices within the landed class, yet commercial interests prospered and were not alienated from established society.

The explanation of different degrees of success and the differences of pace which could be discerned more easily as the centuries passed, has led to much investigation and speculation. Coincidences of social modernization with economic and commercial success were once attributed to change in religion: in the sixteenth century, Great Britain and the Netherlands both ceased to be countries dominated by the Roman Catholic Church. Anti-clericals in the eighteenth century and sociologists in the twentieth sought to explore and exploit this coincidence; Protestantism, it was said, provided an ethic for capitalism. But this causal explanation seemed only briefly plausible. There were too many Catholic capitalists, often successful. France and Spain were still important trading countries in the eighteenth century and for much of it the first seems to have enjoyed much the same rates of growth as Great Britain, though falling behind later. Both these countries had Atlantic access, and were among those which had tended to show economic growth ever since the sixteenth century. Yet a geographical explanation does not go very far, either. Scotland – northern, Protestant and Atlantic – long remained tribal, backward and poor, and many non-Roman Catholic areas of Germany stagnated until well into the nineteenth century.

What is clear is that a divided Europe became more visible as time went by. Some countries were evolving slowly (even before 1800) towards more open social forms while to the east authoritarian governments administered agrarian societies where a minority of landholders enjoyed great powers over a largely tied peasantry, and legal status defined the limits on freedom. Towns did not prosper there as they had done for centuries in the West. They tended to be overtaxed islands in a rural sea, unable because of serfdom to draw from the countryside the labour they needed to prosper. Over great tracts of Poland and Russia, too a money economy barely existed. In Ottoman Europe, other, even more startling, entrants could be found. Much of later European history was implicit in such variety.

Women

Women, too, were treated differently east and west, though in this matter other interesting comparisons can also be made, between Mediterranean Europe and the north, for example. Formally, little change is observable in attitudes towards women anywhere in Europe in these centuries; their legal status usually remained what it had been at the outset and was only questioned right at the end of this period. Nevertheless, there was variety, some surprising: for instance, a Russian woman's property remained her own after marriage, while an Englishwoman's passed to her husband. The practical and actual independence of women and, in particular, of upper-class women, seems to have grown somewhat, too, in the more advanced countries, in however small a degree. Even in the fifteenth century foreigners remarked that Englishwomen enjoyed unusual social freedom and this lead does not seem to have diminished. By the eighteenth century there are signs that in France, too, a well-born woman could have considerable real independence.

This was in part because the eighteenth century brought to a few countries the appearance of a new sort of upper-class life, one with room for other social gatherings than those of a royal court, and one increasingly independent of religious and family ritual. Privacy crept in as an idea focused on the individual, and not merely on the family. In the late seventeenth century men in London began to meet in coffee-houses from which the first clubs were to spring. Soon there appears the *salon*, the social gathering of friends and acquaintances in a lady's drawing room which was especially the creation of the French; some Parisian *salons* were important intellectual centres and show that it had become fashionable for women to show an interest in things of the mind other than religion. When Mme de Pompadour, the mistress of Louis XV, was painted, a book was included in her picture – Montesquieu's sociological treatise, *De l'esprit des lois*. But even women culturally less aspiring than she found that the *salon* and the appearance of a society independent of the court offered real, if limited, chances of escape from the confinement of the family, which, together with religious and professional corporations, had until then been virtually the only structures within which even men could seek social intercourse.

By the end of the eighteenth century western Europe had produced a few female artists and novelists and it was accepted that spinsterhood need not mean retirement to a cloister. How such changes had come about is still not easy to see. In the early years of the century, an English journal, the *Spectator*, already thought it worth while to address itself to women readers as well as men, which suggests that we should look further back than the appearance of the first conscious promoters of feminine interests. Perhaps it helped that the eighteenth century produced an English queen, one Austrian and three Russian empresses, all ruling in their own right, often with success. But it is not possible to speak with confidence. And, of course, such facts did not touch the life of the overwhelming majority of women in even the most advanced societies. No doubt the unquestioned certainties of traditional life weighed most heavily in the primitive villages of Poland or in a southern Spain where Moorish influences had intensified the subordination and seclusion of women, but they were everywhere still heavy in 1800. There had not yet come into being the mass industrial jobs which would provide the first great force prising and splitting imprisoning institutions apart.

The fragmentation of Christendom

For all the rich and varied tapestry of European life already in 1500, it was dominated by one outstanding and unifying fact; outside the Ottoman dominions, Europe was almost completely Christian. Islam was still to extend further into Europe in the wake of the Ottoman armies in the next two centuries, but the Moslems who still lived in Spain in 1500 all but disappeared within a few years (while, in contrast, large Christian populations continued to live their distinctive lives within the Ottoman empire, however attractive conversion to Islam might be made). Some European countries contained small Jewish communities, usually living in their own ghettos under some degree of legal and fiscal disability. Substantial numbers of Jews, though, were only to be found in the borderlands of Poland and Russia, to which their ancestors had fled from persecution in western countries in the Middle Ages.

The most important division between Christians was, as ever, that between the Orthodox churches and the Roman. It sharpened after 1453. In the east, Catholicism gave way to Orthodoxy, and there were borderlands in Hungary, the Ukraine and what was one day to be Yugoslavia where they were somewhat mixed up. Roman Catholic bishoprics could be found as far east as Vilna, and even on the Dniester. But for all the difficulties of churchmen Orthodox and Catholic believers were alike Christian. They shared the same sacraments. They both received a similar teaching which imposed meaning and pattern on the great events of people's lives – birth, marriage, death – from their priests. In Orthodox and Catholic countries alike religion was made visible in villages and towns by large numbers of clergy and other male and female religious. Those they taught and comforted heard the same great stories of the Passion of Christ, of the suffering love of His Mother and of the tribulations and trials of Israel, its patriarchs and heroes; to that degree they shared a religious culture, diluted and tainted by superstition and ignorance and divided by custom and circumstance though it might be.

In the Catholic west, the Church was the only continent-wide institution. In every land, ecclesiastical law operated alongside and distinct from the secular legal system. All universities were governed by churchmen. There was much to cause concern about the Church in 1500, but it was still taken for granted at every level of society, controlling, moulding, setting in familiar grooves and patterns the accidents of each individual's life, watching over him from the cradle to the grave. Religion was so tangled with everyday life that their separation was almost unthinkable. In villages and little towns there might be no other public building than the parish church; people met in it for community business, and for amusement, at 'church-ales' and on feast days (when even dances sometimes took place in it). Yet all this was soon to be changed.

In the early sixteenth century, a great crisis shook western Christianity and destroyed forever the old medieval unity of the faith and the universal authority of the Church. The name later given to it, the 'Protestant Reformation', is misleading; it oversimplifies by implication. Complex and deep-rooted in its origins, the Reformation was hugely varied, rich and far-reaching in its effects and expressions. It was to create (round the world) new churches and cultures founded on the study of the Bible and preaching, which in some of them acquired an importance surpassing that of the sacraments. The lives of millions were to be re-shaped by accustoming them to a new and an intense scrutiny of private conduct and conscience (thus, ironically, achieving something long sought by many Catholic churchmen). A non-celibate clergy reappeared in western Europe. The Reformation slighted or at least called into question virtually every existing ecclesiastical institution. Almost incidentally, it created new political forces which princes could now manipulate for their own ends – often against popes whom they saw simply as princes like themselves – and which sometimes themselves turned against princes.

Those who launched the Reformation would in fact have been horrified had they been able to glimpse the final outcome of what they had done. They were medieval men (for the most part; women are not conspicuous in the story) with medieval minds and they acted on assumptions given them by their upbringing. Believing they were concerned only with unworldly matters, they nonetheless thrust into the arena of politics a mass of new issues; enthusiastic in promoting (often, in imposing) true belief, they destroyed much of the case for uniformity or any imposed faith at all. They opened the way to greater freedom of individual conduct, to tolerance of different religious opinions and to much more separation between the secular and religious in daily life – all things which would have appalled most of them. They blighted a respect for religious authority going back a 1,000 years and destroyed the unity of western Christendom in a way almost incidental to the pursuit of their conscious goals. In short, like the explorers, they helped to launch 'modern history'.

No one could have anticipated such a disaster. At the outset, all that appeared to be involved was yet another dispute over religious authority, another calling in question of the papal claims whose formal and theoretical structure had successfully survived so many challenges. There was nothing new about such disputes. They had deep roots in the past. There was nothing new about demands for ecclesiastical reform, nor about anti-clericalism and cynicism over the bad habits of some clergy. That papacy and *curia* did not necessarily serve the interests of all Christians was not a novel idea in 1500; Hildebrand had known that being mixed up in the everyday world was not always good for the Church. Bishops who played a prominent part in the affairs of their rulers had always been in danger of being too busy to be good shepherds to their flocks. The great Cardinal Wolsey, archbishop of York and favourite of the English king Henry VIII, never visited his see until sent there in disgrace after falling from favour and power, and the popes often seemed to worry too much about their temporal sovereignty. Pluralism – holding many offices and neglecting to perform them while drawing the pay – was another problem the Church had long faced; it did not seem to be able to put it right, but it was probably no worse than in previous centuries.

One enduring problem was that for all the grandeur of the way many bishops and abbots lived, for all the extravagance of the papal court at Rome ('Since God has given us the papacy', one pope is supposed to have said, 'let us enjoy it'), there never seemed to be enough money to go round. One result was that jobs were dished out to reward services. Poverty created other difficulties too. It was unusual for a pope to have to go so far as Sixtus IV, who was finally reduced to pawning the papal tiara, but using juridical and spiritual power to increase papal revenues was an old recourse (and cause of complaint), and it had its roots in the need to find revenue. Money was short in the parishes, too. Priests became more rigorous about collecting tithes – the portion of the parishioner's produce (usually a tenth or twelfth) to which they were entitled. This led to resentment and resistance which tempted churchmen into trying to secure their rights by threatening to refuse the sacraments – to excommunicate - if they did not pay up. This was a serious threat when men believed they might burn in hell for ever as a result. Finally, poverty also contributed to clerical ignorance. The standard of education among the clergy had improved since the twelfth century (this owed much to the universities) but many parish priests in 1500 were hardly less ignorant or superstitious than their parishioners.

There were, therefore, grounds for concern as the sixteenth century opened. But also there was a long tradition of churchmen making efforts to put their house in order. As the fifteenth century went on, some critics – priests among them – had suggested turning back to the Bible for guidance about the way to live a Christian life, since so many of the clergy were obviously not making a very good job of it. They were often labelled 'heretics' and the Church had powerful arms to deal with them. Some of these men (notably Wycliffe and Hus) had strong popular support, and appealed to the patriotic feelings of fellow-countrymen who felt that the papacy was a foreign and unfriendly institution. Some heretics could draw also on social unrest; no Christian could easily overlook what the Bible had to say about the injustices of life. But Lollards and Hussites, harried and chased by the authorities, had never looked likely to pull down the Church.

Luther

Anti-clericalism, heretic speculation, the cupidity of princes, the impulse to reform, humanism – these materials lying about in the early sixteenth century were waiting for a man and an occasion. Both came, and made a religious revolution when in 1517 the unwitting act of a German Augustinian monk, Martin Luther, unleashed the energies which were to fragment a Christian unity intact in the West since the disappearance of the Arians, stimulate a new German national consciousness, and throw a new ideological element into European diplomacy.

Luther was the son of a peasant who had made good and sent his son to university to become a lawyer. A devout and sincere Catholic, impulsive and passionate, at the age of twenty-one Luther became a monk, after an emotional upheaval set off by a thunderstorm which broke on him as he was trudging along the highway. Overcome by terror and a feeling of his own sinfulness which made him sure he was fit only to go to hell were he to be struck by lightning and killed, Luther felt the conviction that God cared for him and would save him. In its suddenness and violence it was like St Paul's conversion on the road to Damascus. Luther's first celebration of Mass was another overwhelming experience, so convinced was he of his personal unworthiness to be a priest. Later he was to believe that Satan appeared to him (indeed, he once threw his ink-pot at the Father of Lies – or so it was said). Luther's nature was such that, when convinced he was right, he was immovable. Germany may have been ripe for Luther, but the Reformation would not have been what it was without him.

Luther lived for most of his life at Wittenberg, a small Saxon town on the Elbe, with a recently-founded university in which he taught. He slowly came to the conclusion that he must preach the Scriptures in a new light, to present God as a forgiving, not a punitive God. The orthodoxy of his views was not in question; he was a celebrated and admired teacher. He had been to Rome, and it was true that he had not liked what he saw there, for the papal city seemed a worldly place and its ecclesiastical rulers no better than they should be. This did not dispose him to feel warmly towards an itinerant Dominican then roaming Saxony as a pedlar of indulgences, certificates whose purchaser, in consideration of payment (which went towards the building of the new and magnificent St Peter's then rising in Rome), was assured that some of the penalties incurred by him for sin would be remitted in the next world. Accounts of this man's preaching were brought to Luther by peasants who had heard him and bought their indulgences. Research has made it clear that what had been said to them was not only misleading but outrageous; the crudity of the transaction infuriated Luther, almost obsessed as he was by the overwhelming seriousness of the transformation necessary in a sinner's life before he could be sure of redemption.

He duly formulated his protests together with some others against certain other practices in a set of ninety-five theses in Latin which were posted (in the tradition of the medieval scholarly disputation) on the door of the castle church in Wittenberg on All Saints' day 1517. He had also sent his theses to the archbishop of Mainz, primate of Germany, who passed them to Rome with a request that Luther be forbidden to preach on this theme. By this time the theses had been put into German. The new information technology ensured their impact; they were printed and circulated everywhere in Germany. So Luther got the debate he sought. Only the protection of his prince, Frederick of Saxony, who, though a fervent Catholic (and believer in indulgences) refused to surrender the most celebrated university professor of his dominions, saved his life. The delay in scotching the chicken of heresy in the egg was fatal. Though Luther's fellow-monks abandoned him, his university did not, and many clergy were drawn to him. Soon the papacy found itself confronted by a widespread and consciously German movement of grievance against Rome. It was sustained and further inflamed by Luther's literary genius and productivity as a pamphlet-writer. Within two years, Luther was being called a Hussite and the Reformation had become a fact of German politics.

Would-be reformers of the Church had often looked to secular rulers for help. Princes tended not to like heretics; their duty was to uphold the true faith. Nevertheless, appeals to lay authority had sometimes opened the way to changes welcomed by reformers and some German rulers now began to show an interest in the religious hubbub. Luther's arguments had rapidly carried him beyond the desirability and grounds of specific reform to the questioning first of papal authority and then of doctrine. The core of his early protests had not been theological, but he now came to reject the Roman view of the eucharist (replacing it with one even more difficult to grasp) and preached that men were justified – that is, set aside for salvation – not by observance of the sacraments only ('works', as this was called), but by faith. Even the Church itself, he said, was therefore not absolutely necessary to salvation. This intensely individualist position struck at the root of traditional teaching. Yet it was known that Erasmus, when asked for his view, would not condemn Luther and thought him to have said much that was good.

In 1520, before a wondering audience, Luther burnt a papal bull condemning him and was excommunicated. He continued to preach and write. Summoned to explain himself before the imperial Diet, he refused to retract his views. Germany seemed on the verge of civil war between his supporters and enemies. After leaving the Diet under a safe-conduct, he disappeared, kidnapped for his own safety by a sympathetic prince. In 1521 the emperor, Charles V, placed him under the Imperial Ban; Luther was now an outlaw and so remained until his death in 1546.

His teaching (by now he had gone on to denounce the practices of confession, absolution and clerical celibacy) won support from those with grievances against tithe-gatherers and ecclesiastical courts, from greedy princes who coveted the Church's wealth and from others driven by circumstance when their own traditional or habitual rivals came out against him. His followers spread his ideas by preaching and by distributing his German translation of the New Testament (it has been said that he dethroned the pope and enthroned the Bible). The German princes entangled Lutheranism in their own complicated relations with the emperor and his vague authority over them. Wars ensued; in them the word 'Protestant' made its appearance.

Nearly forty years after Luther's posting of his thesis in Wittenberg, the imperial Diet of Augsburg in 1555 acknowledged that Germany was irreparably divided into Catholic and Protestant states. It was agreed that the prevailing religion of each state in the empire should be that of its ruler. Nearly ten years after Luther's death, Europe thus institutionalized religious pluralism. It was necessary if an emperor (who saw himself as the defender of universal Catholicism) was to keep the loyalty of Germany's princes. In Catholic and Protestant Germany alike, religion now looked to political authority to uphold it.

The European Reformation

Even in Germany, there was no single Reformation phenomenon. Other varieties of Protestantism soon emerged from the evangelical ferment; Luther had released, without canalizing, a wide range of discontents. He had soon been obliged to distinguish his own teaching from the views of peasants who invoked his name to justify rebellion against their masters. Radicals like the Anabaptists, whose leaders upheld polygamy and communism of property, were persecuted by Catholic and Protestant rulers alike. In Switzerland, another Catholic priest, Ulrich Zwingli had almost at once followed his lead in denouncing indulgences, though soon diverging from Luther on doctrinal questions. The other major expression of Protestantism outside Germany, though, was Calvinism, the creation of the Frenchman, John Calvin. He had formulated his theology while still a young man: the absolute depravity of man after the Fall of Adam and the impossibility of salvation except for those few, the Elect, predestined by God to salvation. It is not easy to understand the success of this gloomy creed. But to its efficacy, the histories not only of Geneva, but of France, England, Scotland, the Dutch Netherlands and British North America were all to bear witness. The crucial step was conviction of membership of the Elect. As the outward signs of this were adherence to the commandments of God and participation in the sacraments, it was less difficult to achieve such conviction than might be imagined.

Geneva, where Calvin finally settled in 1541 was a theocratic state self-governed by believers, and no place for the easy-going. Blasphemy and witchcraft were punished by death; this would not have struck contemporaries as surprising, nor the fact that adultery, too, was a crime (it was in most European countries) but Geneva imposed the death penalty for it. Adulterous women were drowned, men beheaded (an apparent reversal of the normal penal practice of a male-dominated European society where women, considered weaker vessels morally and intellectually, were usually indulged with milder punishments than men). The most severe punishment, though, was reserved for heretics. They were burnt.

From Geneva, where its pastors were trained, the new sect took root in France, where it won converts among the nobility and there were more than 2,000 congregations of Huguenots, as they were called by 1561. In the Netherlands, England and Scotland and, in the end, Germany, Calvinism challenged Lutheranism. It spread also to Poland, Bohemia and Hungary, thus showing a vigour surpassing that of Lutheranism which, except in Scandinavia, was never to be strongly entrenched beyond the German lands which first adopted it.

England: a special case

Lutheranism stirred feelings of German patriotism, but in a way which confirmed national political division. In England, ecclesiastical and religious change of equally momentous but quite different political consequence bound national and confessional history together in a unique way. It arose almost by accident. The second king of the Tudor line, Henry VIII, became entangled with the papacy in 1527 over his wish to dissolve the first of his marriages (there were to be five more) in order to remarry and get an heir, an understandable preoccupation. His wife was a Spanish princess and Charles V's aunt; that posed problems. When the pope declined to help Henry the outcome was a quarrel which led to one of the most remarkable assertions of lay authority in the whole century. With the support of parliament, which obediently passed the required legislation, Henry VIII in 1534 proclaimed himself Head of the Church in England. Doctrinally, he intended no break with the past; he had been, after all, named Defender of the Faith (a title English monarchs still bear) by the pope because of a refutation of Luther from the royal pen. But the assertion of the royal supremacy opened the way to an English Church separate from Rome. A vested interest in the separation was soon provided by a dissolution of monasteries and some other ecclesiastical foundations and the sale of their property to buyers among the aristocracy and gentry. This was of immense importance in digging in England's religious revolution, and for the future history of English society and the English constitution. One effect of this 'Reformation' was that it helped Parliament to survive when medieval representative bodies in other countries were going under before the power of kings. In any case, a kingdom united since Anglo-Saxon times and without provincial assemblies or 'estates' which might rival it gave parliament greater possibilities in focusing national politics than similar bodies elsewhere. A royal mistake helped, too; Henry VIII squandered the opportunity to keep for the crown the mass of property – about a fifth of the land of the whole kingdom – which it held briefly as a result of the dissolutions. Nevertheless, all such imponderables duly weighed, the fact that Henry chose to seek endorsement of his will from the national representative body in creating a national church still seems a crucial decision for the future of monarchy, parliament and nation alike.

Some churchmen sympathetic to new doctrines sought to move the Church in England towards more sharply-defined doctrinal Protestantism in the next reign. Popular reactions were mixed. Some saw this as the satisfaction of old national traditions of dissent from Rome; some resented innovations. From a confused debate and murky politics emerged a literary masterpiece, *The Book of Common Prayer*, and martyrs both Catholic and Protestant. The latter were the first to suffer death, for there was a reversion to papal authority (and the burning of Protestant heretics) under the fourth Tudor, the unfairly named and unhappy Bloody Mary, Henry's daughter by his first wife and England's most tragic queen. By this time, moreover, the question of religion was further entangled with national interest and foreign policy, for Europe divided more and more on religious grounds. In England Protestantism gradually became identified with national feeling.

Wars of the Reformation

Religion could not be kept out of politics but Catholic martyrs died under Elizabeth I (Mary's successor and half-sister) because they were judged traitors, not as heretics. England was less politically divided by religion under her, though, than contemporary Germany and France. There had been intermittent wars and fighting in Germany from 1522 until the Peace of Augsburg. Sixteenth-century France was tormented and torn by Catholic and Calvinist interests, each in essence crystallized in a group of noble clans who fought for power in the nine 'Wars of Religion', which have been distinguished between 1562 and 1598. At times they brought the French monarchy very low; the nobility came near to mastering it. Yet, in the end, aristocratic rivalries benefited a crown which could use one faction against another. Meanwhile, the wretched population of France had to bear the brunt of disorder and devastation.

In 1589 a member of a junior branch of the royal family, Henry, ruler of the little Spanish kingdom of Navarre, became (after the murder of his predecessor) Henry IV of France and inaugurated the Bourbon line whose descendants still claim the French throne. He had been a Protestant, but now accepted Catholicism as the condition of his succession, recognizing the religion most Frenchmen would stand by. The Protestants were given guarantees which left them a state within a state, the possessors of fortified towns where the king's writ did not run; a very old-fashioned sort of solution to the problem, assuring protection by creating immunities. With this settled, Henry and his successors could then turn to the business of re-establishing the authority of a throne badly shaken by assassination and intrigue. But some of his subjects were still far from tamed. Henry has been seen as the first builder of a later 'absolute' monarchy exercising power through a bureaucracy of officials, but that was hardly clear at the time, or under his successor. Real encroachment upon the provincial and local representation bodies whose co-operation or quiescence French kings needed only came with the middle decades of the seventeenth century.

Counter-Reformation

A new virulence was given to religious quarrels by a movement of internal reassessment and innovation within the Roman Church later called the Counter-Reformation. In so far as it was the outcome of ecclesiastical policy, as well as of a changing Catholic psychology and culture, it stemmed from the Council of Trent, a general council summoned by the pope in 1543, and meeting over the next eighteen years. Protestantism's success had forced change on Rome, but Italian and Spanish bishops dominated the Council. Its outcome reflected the fact that Reform challenged Catholicism little in Italy and not at all in Spain. Its decisions became the touchstone of Catholic orthodoxy in doctrine and discipline until the nineteenth century. Remarkably quickly, it helped to change Catholics' outlook and, often, behaviour. It initiated institutional change towards authoritarianism and centralization. Roman Catholicism became more rigid and intransigent or more orderly and better disciplined, according to different points of view. Almost unnoticed, the Council also answered by implication an old question about the headship of Catholic Europe; from this time, it indisputably lay with the pope. Charles V was to turn out to have been the last Holy Roman Emperor to have a papal coronation.

Like that of the Reformation, the significance of the Counter-Reformation went beyond forms and legal principles. Papal authority was not the only source of Catholic reform, nor was merely a structural response to challenge involved. The new spirituality and spontaneous fervour already apparent among the faithful in the fifteenth century was tapped by it, too. It expressed and gave direction to a new devotional intensity and rejuvenated the fervour of laity and clergy alike. The Council made weekly attendance at mass obligatory and regulated baptism and marriage more strictly; it also ended the practice which had detonated the Lutheran explosion, the selling of indulgences. More formally still, the papal Inquisition became the final court of appeal for heresy trials, and an 'Index' of prohibited books was issued for the first time in 1557.

Another potent expression of a new fervour and an institution which was to prove enduring was the invention of a Spaniard, the soldier Ignatius Loyola. Coincidentally and by a curious irony he had been a student at the same Paris college as Calvin in the

early 1530s, though it is not recorded that they ever met. In 1534 he vowed himself to missionary work and as he trained for it devised a rule for a new religious order, the Society of Jesus. In 1540 it was recognized by the pope. The Jesuits, as they came to be called, have had a distinctiveness and importance in the history of the Church akin to that of the early Benedictines or the mendicant friars of the thirteenth century. Their warrior-founder liked to think of them as the militia of the Church, utterly disciplined and completely subordinate to papal authority through their general, who lived in Rome. They were to transform Catholic education and be in the forefront of a renewed missionary effort which carried their members to every part of the world while in Europe their intellectual eminence and political skill gave them influence in high places and in the courts of kings.

Within a few decades the Society of Jesus had come to stand for the Counter-Reformation spirit as did no other institution and its members had come to be the outstanding defenders of revived and Rome-centered Catholicism. Venice, the only state in Catholic Europe which long held out against the waves from Trent (notably, by declining to allow the introduction of the Index to the Republic) significantly replied to a papal interdict laid on its territories in 1605 by expelling the Jesuits. The quarrel with the papacy became entangled with the ambitions of Habsburg Spain, the dominant power in Italy, and therefore with those of Spain's rival, the French monarchy. In the end, diplomacy brought about a settlement safeguarding the Venetians' interests. The most successful advocate of those interests before the public mind of Europe was nevertheless, the republic's own official theologian, the Servite friar Paolo Sarpi. His great polemical work, the *History of the Council of Trent*, (published in Italian in England in 1619) set out a Catholic case against the Counter-Reformation and made it clear that there were at least a few Catholic clergy sympathetic to many of the moral aspirations of the Protestant reformers.

Science: a new force

Reformation and Counter-Reformation were not the only great new facts shaping Europe's intellectual and cultural (or even religious) history in these centuries. Nor were they wholly innovative in their tendency, whatever novel changes followed from them. They still embodied what could be seen as the essentials of a stock of ideas on which Europeans had drawn, ideas for centuries inherited from the classical heritage of Greece and Rome, the social institutions of the barbarian cultures of the Dark Ages, and, of course and above all, from Christianity. Among them, too, lay the germs of modern science. Already identifiable as a new – or renewed – phenomenon in the sixteenth or at least by the seventeenth century, science was to transform European civilization more fundamentally than even religious upheaval, though it took a long time to do so and revealed nothing like its full importance even by 1800.

Science had its deepest effect on society, broadly speaking, in two distinguishable ways. One was by increasingly offering mankind new ways of manipulating the natural world. This, of course, changed ideas about what was possible, given appropriate effort and resources. The other was by providing a flow of facts and ideas which were implicitly deeply subversive; they made questioning of long-held views first possible and then inevitable. That in turn assisted a yet wider subversion: the questioning of the authorities which upheld accepted tradition.

It is no longer so fashionable as it was to identify a sudden scientific 'revolution' in the sixteenth and seventeenth centuries, springing from a similarly over-formulated 'renaissance'. It must be said that some scholarly efforts to avoid any danger of doing so have added little except detail to accounts of the chronology and ways in which a new appreciation of science came about. A new level of activity, and a new outlook can and should certainly be linked to facts observable in earlier centuries, but it is some of the most general such facts which best illustrate the prehistory of modern science. Some were, at their deepest level, the acceptance of commonplaces of medieval Christian culture – the assumption, for example, that the universe was not organized in a random manner, but was ruled by divine and regular law and formed a system stretching down from the stars in their courses to the destiny of the most humble human beings. The

Schoolmen had provided a training of the European intellect – that is to say, of many of its ablest and most speculative minds – in the cultivation of rigorous argument. Artificers had learnt to make instruments which made possible better observations, as the discovery of new stars or of the variation of true from magnetic north by fifteenth-century seamen showed. Other observations on which men began to base new speculation and investigation came from antiquity or other cultures; their sources were as diverse as the exotic and roundabout channels through which often they had passed to Europeans. For all that, though, the invention of modern science was a post-medieval, post-Renaissance and European fact. It embodied at its heart not only the systematic enquiry on a quite new scale which the development of new equipment (at first, and above all, optical) made available, but the advance of the experimental method. Experiment took some time to establish itself as the archetypal form of scientific activity. By the middle of the seventeenth century, though, it was widely advocated as the only way to understand and achieve what one 'natural philosopher' (the term 'scientist' then had not been invented) called 'the management of this great machine of the world'[3] – a phrase itself rich in implication.

The first great achievements of modern science were embodied in the very properly celebrated astronomical and cosmological work of such men as Copernicus, Kepler, and Galileo (whose best-known contribution was a publication which notoriously embodied the argument that what Copernicus had said was true). The detail of their intellectual feats affected laymen less than the often-described outcome, whose importance was soon apparent. This outcome was the impossibility of retaining the world picture embodied in the great synthesis of Aristotle and the Bible which was still in 1600 taken by most educated men to be the best available. Gradually, the work of the cosmologists provided other explanations of the way the universe worked which were more generalized, more coherent with observation (supplied, often, by the newly invented telescope) and less elaborate and dependent on external assumptions than traditional views. This eased the European mind towards new ways of thinking, towards, for example, the proposition that the most general explanation which can be provided for a variety of data is likely to be the most correct especially when sustained by successful prediction of further and confirmatory observation, or by experiment.

Nonetheless, though of revolutionary importance, cosmography had for some time little widespread impact on a wide public; the growing flood of publication about the sixteenth-century voyages of discovery was almost certainly much more noticed. By 1700, though, the application of new views and the experimental method had spread irreversibly to many branches of study and had a place on the mental horizons of most educated men. Even when their minds were not changed by the prospect and they felt they could reject the conclusions of the new science (Spanish universities were still sticking to Aristotle in the eighteenth century), they could hardly ignore it.

By the beginning of the eighteenth century, many natural philosophers were at work, vigorously seeking ways to manipulate nature in the interests of mankind. Nature, nevertheless, then still remained for all but a very few the creation and supreme manifestation of the power of God. Such an assumption was vividly expressed in the life of an Englishman who still remains, in some eyes, the greatest scientist who has ever lived. Isaac Newton was religiously disposed and spent much of his life pondering non-scien-

---

[3] Quoted by C.M. Cipolla, *European Culture and Overseas Expansion* (Harmondsworth, 1970), p. 26.

tific matters, notably a mystical and numerical theology. His scientific work in no way appeared to him incompatible with such speculation, let alone with belief in God. That work, in mathematics and physics above all, was epoch-marking. His explanation of the way the universe worked – for instance, in his celebrated formulation of the idea of gravity – was of enormous integrating power. It set the study of physics on the course which it pursued fruitfully for two centuries. Newton came to exemplify as no-one else the power of the scientist to reveal general laws and so established a model of scientific activity still influential today. Probably his greatest and least conscious achievement in the long run though, was, as his ideas were popularized among a lay public, to win widespread acceptance for the notion that the world is essentially unmysterious, that it is, however wonderful and complicated, rationally explicable.

By Newton's day the patronage of science by public authority as a distinct activity had begun, a sure sign of its new dignity and prestige. The first scientific society, the *Accademia del cimento*, was founded in Florence with grand-ducal patronage in 1657. The English Royal Society received its charter from the king in 1662; a few years later Louis XIV endowed the French Academy of Sciences. Practical motives were at work, too as Charles II's foundation of the Royal Observatory at Greenwich in 1675 illustrated. These were early examples of a growing public interest in and patronage of science which was to become one of the signs of modernization, and to spread throughout Europe in the next century and a half. The *Philosophical Transactions* of the Royal Society – the first scientific journal – began to appear in 1665. By 1800 there can be discerned an international scientific community, as well as national scientific establishments. The achievements of science by that date, included not only the Newtonian cosmology, but the groundwork of modern chemistry, and the first studies of electrical phenomena.

Enlightenment

As the seventeenth century was closing, some people were beginning to express alarm about what was felt as a disturbing scepticism; somewhat unfairly for the reputation of a Hellenistic philosopher who had argued for the impossibility of achieving any certain knowledge, they labelled it 'Pyrrhonism'. Historians have followed them in seeking assiduously for early hints of what came about later – the ebbing of a theocentric world view and its replacement by a secular interpretation of the universe, the decline of established intellectual authority and the emergence of new styles and loyalties – and found them. Yet they were hardly obvious before 1700. A growing awareness of what science could do and what it might promise was not for a long time usually seen as subversive of existing truth, concern over materialism and Pyrrhonism notwithstanding. The example of Newton was impressive. Questions about whether the discovery of new laws of nature necessarily required belief in a law-giver did not trouble many people at first. If fundamental cultural change was already under way it remains difficult to find a summary way of talking about it. A French historian once summed it up as a 'crisis of the European consciousness' and it is hard not to anticipate recognition of what was indeed to come[4]. Yet the conservative weight of the past as the eighteenth century opened was enormous. Unquestionably for the silent majority of millions of illiterate Europeans, superstition counted for more than scepticism. For

---

[4]   P. Hazard, *La crise de la conscience européenne 1680–1715* (Paris, 1935).

decades yet witches would continue to be burnt, judicial torture would be widely used, the practice of medicine would hardly reflect the knowledge gained by the anatomists of the preceding two centuries, and even in France and England many people would continue to believe in the thaumaturgical power of anointed monarchs.

A century later, much of this encumbering weight of the past would have gone. In particular, the minds of the educated would be deeply changed. With due allowance made for differences between nation and nation, region and region, town and country, there were to come to fruition many of the implications of ideas only hinted at or cautiously adumbrated in the seventeenth century. At the risk of gross simplification, one way of characterising the change would be to say that the principles of rational analysis and explanation already visible in science had been extended by 1800 to operate in virtually every sphere of life.

This great transformation has often been summed up as one single and coherent phenomenon, a distorting emphasis. Nevertheless, one word, 'Enlightenment', used by the eighteenth century itself, is still a meaningful indicator. The image of light entered all Europe's main languages: it gave Germans *Aufklärung*, the French *Lumières*, Italians *Illuminismo* and the Spanish spoke of its representatives as *illustrados*. All such words implied that what was going on was above all a process of letting light play upon hitherto dark and obscure ideas, institutions and practices. Many people associated themselves enthusiastically with it, pursuing it with missionary zeal. It became fashionable to be one's own 'philosopher' – which did not mean practising technical philosophy, but thinking for oneself and making up one's own mind. ' Dare to know', suggested one German philosopher; men should escape by the use of reason from self-imposed tutelage.

One outstanding among many who shaped this movement of the European consciousness was the Frenchman Voltaire[5]. He laid the foundations of his private fortune, fame, and independence by being a successful playwright. It was an interesting aspect of his emergence as a writer in another vein that he was soon also noticed by the fashionable world for his popularizing of the ideas of Newton. Whether with admiration or hatred, Voltaire in the end came to be seen all over Europe as the embodiment of Enlightenment attitudes and ideas, and it seems a fair assessment in so far as anyone can be thought to have discharged that role. Claiming to believe in God, and dying (formally, at least) at peace with the Roman Catholic Church, he conducted throughout most of his life a long attack on the evils he believed to flow from clerical authority and obscurantism. He won a deserved reputation for scepticism and irreverence. No social or political revolutionary, he yet condemned much he thought indefensible in contemporary lay society. He sought and rightly believed himself to have achieved a leading position in the culture of the age as its outstanding advocate of the principles of rationalism and humanity. Yet, he said that what he called 'rational philosophy' came to light *before* 1715, at first sight a surprising judgement.

As Voltaire's multifarious interests and writings showed, Enlightenment's achievements and aspirations took many forms. He was himself probably best known for his passionate defence of tolerance and of freedom of expression, though he wrote on many other subjects (including pamphlets on behalf of the crown, in defence of a reforming

---

5 François Marie Arouet took this pen name in his early twenties
6 *The Age of Louis XIV* (Everyman edn., London, n.d.) p.2

French minister against those who resisted him in the name of constitutional rights). Other important Enlightenment figures included the devisors and editors of a great Encyclopedia which was the greatest single cultural artefact left by the age; their aim was to provide useful and practical information while at the same time conveying in their articles ironic comparisons and examples which would lead the reader by deduction or implication towards a rejection of the unreasonableness, obscurantism and brutality the age so much took for granted. It was a huge arsenal of intellectual weaponry for reform of all kinds, a 'war machine' as its editors put it. But all over Europe writers addressed themselves to themes of renovation and reform, of government, penal policy, economic improvement, and urged rulers to use reason to improve the material condition of their subjects.

The Enlightenment aspired to be all-embracing and multifarious. Its implicit programme of perfection was never to be completed. Some have judged this inevitable, whether because of circumstance or its inherent impracticality. Some have argued that it was just as well that this was so, for many 'enlightened' moral and social presuppositions were perverse or self-contradictory (its assertion of individual liberty and its interventionist social engineering, for example). Yet it remains a huge creative episode, whose ramifications, for good and evil, have still fully to be worked out. Its historical impact, though in different ways and at different levels, rivals and perhaps surpasses even that of the Reformation, though in its day it affected far fewer people. It was truly – as the Reformation, made by medieval minds, had not been – the end of the intellectual Middle Ages. The Enlightenment injected into world history impulses towards rationalism and humanitarianism never since eradicated (though sometimes gravely threatened). It gave Europeans a new optimism and a new sense of what they could do. It created the idea of the independent intellectual. It forged principles which were to animate for two centuries reformers and liberals (a word not yet available as a noun in 1800) and which would spread not only throughout Europe but round the world. Most successful ideas (good and bad) of the twentieth century can be traced back to it. Finally, it created a culture believing in the fact of progress.

These very achievements and implications, though, colossal as they are, present a grave danger of imposing a distorted and anachronistic view. The eighteenth century – its heyday – was about much more than the Enlightenment, even if that was its greatest creative achievement. Over most of Europe's geographical extent, Enlightenment scratched only a few shallow marks in institutions or policies. The peasants of the patrimonial estates of eastern Europe, the *latifundia* of southern Italy, the rural slums of Andalucia, or of the Ottoman Balkans never heard the names of Newton or Voltaire – far less those of Montesquieu, Diderot, D'Alembert, Beccaria, Galvani, Kant, Feyjoo, or of any of a hundred and one men whose work changed the thinking of educated Europe. As for countries where there were substantial audiences for 'enlightened' ideas, there also existed in them huge countervailing forces, not only ecclesiastical, clerical and religious in origin, but also historical and institutional – privileged corporations, ancient laws and immunities. Moreover, the Enlightenment's own fermenting effect on the minds of an élite itself helped to blur the outlines of its own messages, as men sought individual expression and satisfaction in irrationalism and mysticism, and cranks and charlatans exploited their longings. The eighteenth century was the century of mesmerism as well as of inoculation; the cautious rationalism and theism of the early freemasons ramified in a few decades into the luxuriant dottiness of mystical and occult

masonry. Such symptoms of irrationalism among the educated ranks of society prefig-
ure the follies of the coming romantic era, many of whose expressions were to be deeply
reactionary and obscurantist. There are few historical phenomena easier to place in a
false perspective than the Enlightenment. The very brilliance and persuasiveness of its
prophets biases us at times towards attributing contemporary influence to them where
they had none, except by provoking reaction.

It is indeed not the long-term importance of Enlightenment but its contemporary
impact that is most dangerously and easily misunderstood. It can encourage a distorted
view of the historical actuality of the age. The assumption that thought should be progressive in its tendency came to birth in the eighteenth century, and it quickly had
important achievements to its credit; a measurable spread of literacy, major scientific
work, the beginning of the conversion of the European mind to the rejection of slavery,
the stirrings of agitation for women's rights, penal and legal reform – to name a few -
cannot but be judged to have helped to make the world a better and happier place. But
we are always in danger of failing to notice the other side of the age, visible even in some
of its reforms. We easily remember the energy of a tsar modernizing Russia's state
machine, or the glitter of the patronage of Voltaire by a Prussian king, but forget the
implications of buttressing autocracy or the growing burdens 'enlightened' rulers laid
on Pomeranian and Polish serfs. It is always worth recalling that among the spectators
who paid large sums for good seats from which to watch the appalling torments
inflicted on Damiens, the would-be assassin of the French king, were ladies of the most
brilliant court in Europe, the social apex of France, the country above all associated
with Enlightenment, whose language gave its ideas international currency. When the
men and women of the early nineteenth century came to look back, in fact, they saw
their parents' and grandparents' Europe as a very conservative, unprogressive structure,
embodying (according to their point of view) a barbarism for the many, or a *douceur de
vie* for the few, which those born later would never know. They saw it as a world looking
backward, not forward, for its sanctions and inspirations. They came to call it the
'*ancien régime*' (the 'old way of running things' might be a colloquial rendering), and it
had proved in their eyes so massive, so strong, so tenacious of the past – whether for
good or ill – that in the end only a unique, unprecedented upheaval had been able to
shatter it.

CHAPTER THREE The political organization of western Europe

Building blocks

The phrase 'international relations' was invented in the eighteenth century by the English philosopher, Jeremy Bentham. It was by then needed to describe a working system of intercourse between the institutions we call 'states', and easily think of as nations. Their consolidation and substantial growth in solidity and effectiveness was notable between 1500 and 1800. In so far as the units of this system were confined to Europe (as, with the exception of the young United States, educated Europeans would have thought them still to be in 1800), they formed something like a society of legal individuals, accepting certain common techniques for handling the business they had with one another, certain standards of behaviour which tempered the operation of unrestrained self-interest, and a certain set of shared ideas and assumptions about values and goals. We must not be too categorical; nothing that was absolutely and universally uniform within it characterized the system even in 1800 except that it was a working system, and that it and its components had not existed in 1500. Then, people would have perhaps been more ready to accept the concept of 'Christendom' as a unifying idea. In the eighteenth century, though, the absence of Christian principle was notable in the business of diplomacy and war. This was a mark of a decline of religion as an ideological motivator. Even before 1800, a different sort of civilized unity was perceived to exist within Europe. 'A philosopher', said Gibbon, 'may be permitted to ... consider Europe as one great republic, whose various inhabitants have attained almost the same level of politeness and cultivation.'[1] Civilization had succeeded religious truth as the content of European cohesion.

Another striking change since 1500 was the acceptance of a general assumption that the world was divided into sovereign states. This lay at the basis of a huge sorting-out in these centuries which gave us much of the present map of Europe. Sixteenth-century Europeans would certainly not have agreed that the world they inhabited could be described as a set of independent areas, each governed by a ruler of its own, and within which one agency was the ultimate owner of the right to use force. Still less could its components be thought to have in any but a few instances any sort of unity which might be called 'national'. This makes political and legal description a complex matter.

---

[1] E. Gibbon, *Decline and Fall* ed. J.C. Bury, IV, p.163 (London, 1898).

In 1500 only four European countries – Spain, Portugal, England and France – already looked on the map somewhat like their modern equivalents. Each had some good natural boundaries, and that was a help. The Pyrenees, the Atlantic and the Mediterranean isolated the Iberian peninsula; once the Moors were defeated, it was not easy for outsiders to interfere there. But within it Portugal had its own king, and Spain, though united under a king and queen, was at that time legally divided into the king-doms of Castile and Aragon, each with its separate laws and customs, while tucked away in the north of the peninsula there was the little independent kingdom of Navarre. As for England, she was still not an island; her kings had conquered Wales long before, but she still had a land frontier with an independent neighbour, Scotland. Though the two kingdoms shared a king after 1603, they were not brought together into one state, 'Great Britain', until 1707 (and even then many of their laws remained different). Ireland, though an island, was until the eighteenth century a conquered province ruled by an English viceroy. In 1500, too, England still held a tiny patch of land around Calais (finally to be lost in 1558) though the French kings were effectively the overlords of most of modern France. Some eastern areas, notably much of Burgundy, Savoy, Alsace and Lorraine, had not yet been brought under their rule, though, and inside their own territories a few little enclaves belonged to foreign rulers; the most notable being Avi-gnon, ruled by the pope.

It was also only in these countries that there could in 1500 be discerned (or con-vincingly depicted) any popular or national sentiment to sustain political unity. Eng-land, a relatively unimportant power, was probably the best example. Insular in psychology, secluded from invasion except in the north, her government was unusually centralized. The Welsh Tudors, whose first king, Henry VII, had ascended the throne in 1485, anxious to assert the unity of the kingdom after a long period of disorder remembered still as the 'Wars of the Roses', consciously associated national interest with that of the dynasty. By the end of the sixteenth century, Shakespeare quite natu-rally used the language of patriotism (and, it may be remarked, said little about religious distinctions). France, too, had by then already come some way further along the road to national cohesion. Valois and Bourbon kings had greater problems than the Tudors. There survived many immunities and privileged enclaves within their territories over which they did not exercise full sovereignty as kings of France. Many of their subjects did not even speak French (nor, of course, did many Welsh subjects of the Tudors speak English, and the only monoglot European nation was Portugal). Nevertheless, France was well on the way to becoming a national state with a national monarchy even in 1500. As for Spain, the history of Reconquest had given her a special sense of national identification with a religious cause, although her two crowns were not united until in 1516 the grandson of the Catholic Monarchs, Charles of Habsburg, became co-ruler with his insane mother as Charles I. He had still carefully to distinguish rights of his two kingdoms (and similar respect for local identity was even more necessary in other parts of the great Habsburg possessions).

Other than in those four countries, national feeling did not count for much in policy-making. Personality, family and dynasty gave such political identity as they pos-sessed to other monarchical states; outside them, and sometimes as enclaves within them, lay hundreds of little fiefdoms, republics and free cities. Finally, the two greatest medieval political institutions, the papacy and the Holy Roman Empire, were still major concerns in the calculations of diplomacy. The first was in part a monarchical state like any other, and visibly so in its agglomeration not only of territory (sometimes detached, but mostly in Italy). The pope also had rights of lordship, jurisdiction and dependency in many other countries. Moreover, however the diplomacy and self-interest of individual popes might make the Papal States look like just one more independent power, they could not but be more than that; the pope in 1500 also still possessed disputed but immense authority as the head of the Universal Church.

The Holy Roman Empire also embodied the medieval past, though sometimes at its most worm-eaten and unreal. Germany, where most of it lay, (people often spoke of the 'Holy Roman Empire of the German Nation'), was a chaos supposedly united under the emperor and his tenants-in-chief, the imperial Diet. Since the Golden Bull seven electors were virtually sovereign in their territories. There were also a 100 princes and more than 50 imperial cities, all independent. Another 300 or so minor statelets and imperial vassals completed the patchwork of the medieval empire. Attempts to reform this confusion and give Germany some measure of national unity had failed; this suited the lesser princes and the cities. All that had emerged was some new administrative machinery.

Given these political entities, European diplomacy in the early sixteenth century was overwhelmingly traditional in its perceptions of what should guide its practitioners: dynasticism, tempered by calculations arising from religion, finance and, in some places more than others, trade. In dealing with these concerns habits had crystallized and institutions had come into being which were long to form the basis of formal diplomacy, a slowly-evolved European invention which was to spread round the world. Rulers had always had to communicate and negotiate with one another. Medieval kings had sent one another heralds, about whom a special ceremonial had grown up and whom special rules protected, or occasional ambassadors for special tasks. After 1500, it slowly became the practice to use in peacetime a device still employed today, a permanently resident ambassador through whom all ordinary business was at least initially transacted and who had the task of keeping his own rulers informed about the country to which he was accredited. The Venetian Republic was the first notable employer of such resident representatives. It is not surprising that a state so dependent on trade, information and regular relationships should have led the way in professional diplomacy. More changes followed and the hazards of the life of earlier emissaries were gradually forgotten as diplomats were given special status protected by privileges and immunities. The nature of treaties and other diplomatic forms also became more precise and regularized. Latin provided a common language for the recording of agreements (though little actual negotiation was done in it). Procedure became more standardized.

These changes came about only slowly, when they were believed to be useful. Strictly speaking, modern professional diplomacy had not even appeared by 1800; ambassadors were then still usually noblemen who could afford to sustain a representative role, not paid civil servants. None the less, professionalization was by then well under way, another sign that a new world of relationships between sovereign states was crystallizing.

Structures and issues

Diplomacy and international relations, fascinating as they can be, do not make for easy reading. They must be about detail and the trees often make it hard to see the wood. Their complexity does not make it easy to discern or set out the general patterns which reveal the importance of what was going on. This is especially true of the three centuries after 1500, when the struggles for advantage in peace and war between European rulers are all the harder to understand because of the very large number of those taking part in them as discrete entities, the ramifications of family trees, and the fragility and brevity of agreed arrangements, thanks to the instability of power relations and the chances of mortality. It is helpful to try to take a preliminary general and long-term view identifying the key events and episodes.

Four major structural changes can be discerned. The first is the seventeenth-century rise of France to hegemony or potential hegemony in Europe, a process involving the eclipse of an earlier Spanish supremacy. As a part of this change, frontiers came to be settled by 1715 in much of western Europe whose main features endured until the nineteenth century. In the background of the French ascendancy was Germany's continuing fragmentation; there was in the end to emerge a rivalry for supremacy between Prussia, a 'new' state, and the Austrian Habsburg empire. It was a further concomitant of this process that the Holy Roman Empire continued its decline into nullity after a last spurt of efforts to re-animate it in the early seventeenth century.

The second big change was the appearance of a new great power in the west, Great Britain (the United Kingdom after 1707). In her emergence, commercial and maritime power played a special part and is connected with the third major theme of these centuries, the creation of the first European overseas empires and the beginnings of overseas conflict between European powers as a result. By 1800 there had been many such conflicts; no continent was untouched by them. The Portuguese and Spaniards led the way; the Dutch, British and French followed (and even the Danes and Prussians dabbled in the game). The most important single long-term consequence of the first age of imperialism was the establishment of the first independent nation of European origin beyond the seas, the United States of America, an outcome in the end much to transcend the consequences for European empires. These empires all had, in varying degree but increasingly, access to power not available to earlier empires – better ships, cannon, signals, administrative techniques, geographical knowledge. But none of them, we should remember, yet had steam, railways or any communications faster than those available to ancient Rome.

The fourth and equally surprising change was the appearance in a century or so after 1660 of a new order in eastern Europe. Against the background of the Ottoman advance to its high-water mark in the south-east and then the beginnings of the long retreat of Ottoman power, two old independent kingdoms, Hungary and Poland, disappeared, and a new great power, Russia, came on to the scene. This, too, much concerned Prussia and Austria. Already by 1800 there could be discerned the 'Eastern Question' which still remains unanswered: what order can or should replace that provided by the Ottoman empire?

Habsburg and Valois

None of these changes was imaginable in 1500 except, perhaps, the emergence of the first oceanic concerns. For the most part, the ambitions and worries of Europe's rulers still for years arose from much more traditional sources. Though one of these rulers, England's Henry VIII, made a bid to become Holy Roman Emperor he was hardly a serious candidate; English monarchs did not usually count for much in the early sixteenth century except when other people were quarrelling among themselves and wanted their help or neutrality. The Valois kings were more important. Their family had ruled France since the fourteenth century and had defeated the English in a long struggle; they cut much grander figures than the *arriviste* Tudors. They had claims to territory (and a throne) in southern Italy, too. In 1500, though, Valois and Tudor alike were outshone (and were indeed going to be long outlasted) by the Austrian Habsburgs, whose ups and downs of fortune would provide much of the story of European diplomacy right down to 1918.

Even in the fourteenth century, the German princes who elected the emperor sometimes chose a Habsburg candidate. After 1438, with only one brief interruption, they did so continuously. In 1500 the emperor Maximilian was head of the family, an ambitious man who at one time thought he might get himself elected pope, for good measure. His first wife was the daughter of one of the richest of medieval princes, the duke of Burgundy, who had left no son to succeed him. The duke's death caused much trouble, and further complicated the map, for fragments of his inheritance passed into many different hands. But before this was achieved there was much quarrelling. One can view many sixteenth-century events as part of a long duel between Valois and Habsburg over the Burgundian inheritance, notably its rich Netherlands provinces (that is, roughly, modern Belgium and Holland). When, in 1519, the Habsburg king of Spain, Charles I, became Holy Roman Emperor as Charles V with the help of heavy bribery, financed by German bankers, and to the discomfiture of his rival, the king of France, he united to the old Habsburg lands the empire of Spain. Charles V was the first man of whom it was said (truthfully) that he ruled an empire on which the sun never set.

It seemed that the Habsburg family might well be on the way to a universal monarchy. Careful marriages among his forbears made Charles the ruler of the furthest-flung territorial empire the world had ever yet seen, to which the imperial title supplied a fitting crown. From his mother he inherited the Spanish kingdoms, the newly discovered Americas and Sicily. From his father came the former Burgundian 'Spanish Netherlands', and from his grandfather the Habsburg lands of Austria and the Tyrol, with Franche-Comté, Alsace and a bundle of claims in Italy. This was the greatest dynastic accumulation of the age. What is more, the crowns of Bohemia and Hungary were held by Charles' brother, Ferdinand, (who was to succeed him as emperor). Habsburg preeminence was the central fact of European politics for most of the sixteenth century. Its real and unreal pretensions are well shown in the list of Charles' titles as he ascended the imperial throne: 'King of the Romans; Emperor-elect; semper Augustus; King of Spain, Sicily, Jerusalem, the Balearic Islands, the Canary Islands, the Indies and the mainland on the far side of the Atlantic; Archduke of Austria; Duke of Burgundy, Brabant, Styria, Carinthia, Carniola, Luxembourg, Limburg, Athens and Patras; Count of Habsburg, Flanders and Tyrol; Count Palatine of Burgundy, Hainault, Pfirt, Roussillon; Landgrave of Alsace; Count of Swabia; Lord of Asia and Africa.'

Leaving out the fictions, this conglomeration fell, for practical purposes into two main blocks. The Spanish inheritance, rich through the possession of the Netherlands and irrigated by a growing flow of bullion from the Americas, and including much of Italy was one. The old Habsburg lands, demanding an active role in central Europe and Germany to maintain the family's pre-eminence there, provided the other. Charles, though, saw from his imperial throne much more than this. He was, indeed, distinctly old-fashioned in his views of his role. Revealingly, he liked to call himself 'God's standard-bearer' and campaigned like a Christian paladin of old against the Turk in Africa, where he still sought some permanent lodgement in continuation of the work of his grandparents, a new extension of the Reconquest. In his own eyes he was still the medieval emperor, much more than one ruler among many, he was leader of Christendom and responsible only to God for his charge. Germany, Spain and Habsburg dynastic interest (the Habsburg family lands were, of course, legally distinct from the Holy Roman Empire of which many of them were not part) were all sacrificed in some degree to Charles' vision of his role. Yet to make a reality of universal empire such as he envisaged was beyond the powers of any man, given sixteenth-century communication and administration. This impossibility was there even before the appearance of the colossal strains imposed on the empire by the Protestant Reformation. Charles, moreover, strove to rule personally. He travelled ceaselessly in pursuit of this futile aim. This paradoxically, may have ensured that no part of his empire (unless it was the Netherlands) felt identified with his house. His aspiration reveals the way in which the medieval world still lived on, and his own anachronism.

The Italian wars

Six years before Charles had been born, in 1494, a new element had been added to Habsburg and Valois rivalry when Charles VIII of France crossed the Alps to claim the throne of Naples. Habsburg-Valois wars in Italy began then and went on intermittently until 1559. But there were many interests caught up in these quarrels. Though one of the most striking geographical unities within Europe, Italy was politically fragmented. Some of it still technically fell within the empire. Most if it was ruled by princely despots, or dependent on external powers. The pope ruled in his own territories. A king of Naples from the house of Aragon ruled the south of the peninsula. Sicily belonged to his Spanish relatives. Venice (still with great overseas possessions), Genoa and Lucca were republics ruled by oligarchs. Milan, the large duchy in the Po valley, was in the hands of the local Sforza family. Florence was theoretically a republic (but from 1509 was in reality a monarchy in the hands of the Medici, a former banking house). In north Italy the dukes of Savoy ruled Piedmont, the other side of the Alps from their own ancestral lands. The divisions of the peninsula made it an attractive prey and family relationships gave outsiders many excuses to dabble in affairs there even if the main theme of European diplomatic history for the first half of the sixteenth century is provided by the rivalry of Habsburg and Valois.

The six so-called 'Italian' wars, more important than they might at first appear, constitute a distinct period in the evolution of the European states system. To Charles V they were a fatal distraction from the German Reformation and also helped drain off the wealth of Spain. To the French, they brought impoverishment and invasion, and to their kings, frustration. In the end, Spain was left dominant in Italy. To Italians the wars brought a variety of disasters. Rome was sacked for the first time since the age of the barbarian invasions (in 1527, by a mutinous imperial army) and the Spanish hegemony which emerged from the wars finally ended the great days of the city republics. Venice, left for the most part to face the Turks alone, watched her empire in the eastern Mediterranean begin to crumble away (Genoa's in the Black Sea had already gone). Perhaps these were good years only for the Ottomans. Both Charles V and his son were defeated in their African enterprises and a great Christian victory at sea off Lepanto in 1571 was only a momentary setback for the Ottomans; three years later they took back Tunis from the Spanish. The struggle and the support of the Habsburg cause in Italy had by then overtaxed the flow of silver to Spain from America. In his last years, Charles V's government was crippled by debt. When he abdicated in 1556, just after the temporary settlement at Augsburg of the religious disputes of Germany, his brother and successor took the Austrian inheritance, while his son, Philip II, a Spaniard born and bred, became ruler of Spain. Charles, though, had been born in the Netherlands and the ceremony which ended the great emperor's reign took place there; he was moved to tears as he left the assembly, leaning on the shoulder of a young nobleman, William of Orange – later to be known as William the Silent. This division of the Habsburg inheritance marks the watershed of European affairs in the 1550s.

The era of Spanish decline

At one time during the Italian wars, the coasts of Italy were raided by French and Turkish ships in concert; the hollowness of the unity of Christendom was revealed by a formal alliance of a French king with the Sultan. Yet religion continued to influence diplomacy, but after the Reformation it did so in a new way. This became clear in what has seemed to many to be the blackest period of Europe's history for centuries. Except for a brief lull early in the seventeenth century, European rulers and their peoples indulged in an orgy of hatred, bigotry, massacre, torture and brutality without parallel until our own day. The dominating facts were the ideological conflict opened by the Counter-Reformation, the paralysis of Germany and, for a long time, of France, by internal religious quarrels, the military pre-eminence of Spain at the outset, the emergence of new centres of power in England, the Dutch Netherlands and Sweden, and the first adumbrations of the overseas conflicts of the next two centuries.

As in later times (but for much longer and much more inextricably) outsiders with their own particular interests got mixed up in a confusion of ideological, political, strategic and economic issues arising from Spain's internal concerns. The roots of the trouble lay in the growth of state power in Spain and the tension it aroused under Philip II. He linked the monarchy anew to a tradition of religious uniformity rooted in the Reconquest and renewed by the Counter-Reformation, which (like the Reformation) could and did strengthen the ambitions of lay rulers to exercise authority over their subjects. Protestant princes sought to protect themselves against resurgent Catholicism; Catholic princes were given new authority and resources by the Church they sought to uphold. A new dependence of religion upon political authority – that is to say, upon organized force – further extended their grip.

In the Spanish kingdoms two forces ran together to create an unimpeachably Catholic monarchy before the Council of Trent ever met. The Reconquest (so recently completed) had been a crusade; the title of the Catholic Monarchs itself proclaimed the identification of a political process with an ideological struggle. Secondly, the Spanish monarchies had the problem of absorbing suddenly great numbers of non-Christian subjects, both Moslem and Jew, who were feared as a potential threat to security in a multi-racial society. The instrument deployed against them was a new Inquisition under the control of the Crown. Established by papal bull in 1478, the Spanish Inquisition began to operate in Castile in 1480. By 1516, the Inquisition was the only institution in Charles' Spanish possessions which exercised authority in all of them, in the Americas, Sicily and Sardinia, as well as in Castile and Aragon. Striking effects already evident had been the expulsion of the Jews and severe regulation of the Moriscoes, converted Moors who stayed in Spain after the expulsion of Islam. Spain's religious unity proved unbreakable by a handful of Lutherans with whom the Inquisition found it easy to deal.

Yet the cost was very heavy. Already under Charles, Spain was, in religion as in her secular life, aspiring to a new kind of centralized, absolutist monarchy. The residues of formal constitutionalism within the peninsula hardly affected this. Spain was a model for Counter-Reformation states elsewhere and one imposed upon much of Europe by force or example in the century after 1558, when the old emperor died after a retirement spent largely in his devotions in a remote monastery in Estremadura. Of all European monarchs who identified himself with the cause of the Counter-Reformation and saw himself as the extirpator of heresy, none was more determined – and bigoted – than his son, Philip II of Spain, husband until her death in 1558 of Mary Tudor and successor to half Charles' empire: Spain, the Indies, Sicily and the Spanish Netherlands. The results of his policies of religious purification in Spain have been variously interpreted. Less open to dispute are the effects in the Spanish Netherlands.

The new Netherlands

What some call the 'Revolt of the Netherlands' and the Dutch the 'Eighty Years' War' has been, like many other an episode in nation-building, a great source of myth-making, some of it conscious. It is misleading to think that, because in the end a very modern sort of society emerged, it was a very 'modern' sort of revolt, dominated by a passionate struggle for religious toleration and national independence. Nothing was less true. The troubles of the Netherlands arose in a very medieval setting, the old Burgundian inheritance of the Spanish Netherlands, seventeen highly differentiated and assorted provinces. Those in the south, where many of the inhabitants spoke French, included the most urbanized part of Europe and the great Flemish commercial centre of Antwerp. They had long been difficult to govern; at one moment in the late fifteenth century the Flemish towns seemed to be trying to turn themselves into independent city-states. The northern provinces were more agricultural and maritime, with inhabitants who showed a peculiarly tenacious feeling for their land, perhaps because since the twelfth century they had been at work recovering much of it from the sea. North and South were to be the later Netherlands and Belgium, an outcome inconceivable in 1554. The provincial representative bodies – the 'estates' – combined in a 'States-General' which could claim to uphold the interests of the provinces as a whole and to which their ruler had more than once turned for help.

Philip's determination to enforce the decrees of the Council of Trent on Protestants in the Netherlands explains some of what followed but the origins of the trouble went deeper. There had been troubles over taxation under his father. As Spanish officials strove to modernize the relations of central government and local authorities, they did so with more up-to-date methods and perhaps less awareness of local sensitivity than the Burgundians had shown (though they had faced revolts and civil war, too). Spain came into conflict first with the noblemen of the southern provinces. As prickly and touchy as other noblemen of the age in defence of their symbolic 'liberties' – that is, privileges and immunities – they felt threatened by a monarch more remote and alien than the great Charles had been. The old emperor, they felt, had understood them (he spoke their language); his son was a Spaniard and did not. The Spanish local commander, the Duke of Alva, they soon argued, was violating local privilege by interfering with local jurisdictions in the pursuit of heretics. Catholic though most of them were, they had a stake in the prosperity of the Flemish cities where Protestantism had taken root and feared the introduction there of the Spanish Inquisition. They voiced their objections to Spanish government in a medieval way, in the Estates of Brabant.

This was soon to turn into something more serious when the brutality of the Spanish army and the leadership of William of Nassau, prince of Orange (nicknamed the 'Silent' because of his legendary care not to allow unguarded anger to escape him when he learnt of his ruler's determination to bring his heretic subjects to heel), united many of the nobles against their lawful ruler, who, they believed was committed to an unprecedented attack on the traditions and public law of the provinces. But there was always a potential rift between them and Calvinist townsmen who had more at stake. Better political tactics by Spanish governors and the victories of the Spanish armies were in the end enough to force it open. As the nobles fell back into line, the Spanish armies defined modern Belgium, without knowing it. The struggle continued in the northern provinces, which remained under the political leadership of William the Silent until his murder in 1584.

Among the Dutch, (as we may conveniently, but inexactly, call them) Protestants were less encumbered than their southern co-religionists had been with the ambiguous dissatisfactions of the nobility. But they, too, were divided even if they used the cry of religious freedom to disguise their divisions. They benefited from a migration northward of Flemish capital and talent. Their enemies faced difficulties; the Spanish army was formidable but could not easily deal with an enemy which retired behind its town walls and surrounded them with water by opening the dykes and flooding the countryside. The Dutch, almost by accident, transferred their main effort to the sea where they could inflict damage on the Spanish on more equal terms. Spanish communications with the Netherlands along the northern sea route were harried by the rebels. It was expensive to maintain a big army in Belgium by the long road up from Spanish Italy and even more expensive when other enemies had to be beaten off. That was soon the case.

The Counter-Reformation had infected international politics with a new ideological element, but is not the only explanation of others' interest and involvement. French kings could not be easy while Spanish armies might invade their realms from Spain, Italy and Flanders at the same time. England was at first sight less concerned. Though she was officially Protestant, it was only in a somewhat particular sense and Philip tried to avoid an outright break with Elizabeth I. He was for a long time unwilling to sacrifice the chance of reasserting the English interests he had won by marriage to Mary Tudor, and thought at first he might best retain them by marrying another English queen. Moreover he was long distracted by campaigns against the Ottomans, to which, like his father, he attached much importance. But national and religious feeling were inflamed in England by Spanish responses to English piracy at the expense of the Spanish empire; as Anglo-Spanish relations decayed in the 1570s and 1580s Elizabeth overtly and covertly helped the Dutch, whom she did not want to see go under, though without enthusiasm for them as rebels. In the end, armed with papal approval for the deposition of Elizabeth, the heretic queen, a great Spanish invasion effort was mounted against England in 1588. 'God blew and they were scattered'; said the inscription on an English commemorative medal; bad weather completed the destruction of the Armada (not a ship on either side was sunk by gunfire). War with Spain went on long after its shattered remnants had limped back to Spanish harbours but a great danger was over, the roots of a naval tradition of enormous future importance had been planted, and a national myth had been born. The English made peace and were not again sucked into continental conflict until the next century.

From the war emerged, almost fortuitously and incidentally, a remarkable new society, a loose federation of seven little states, the United Provinces, under the States-General, Europe's first republic to play a major power role since Venice. They exploited Hispanophobia to forge unity; there was a rumour that Philip II had sentenced everyone in the Netherlands to death (probably less than 4,000 'heretics' actually died). Soon, its citizens discovered a national past (much as decolonized Africans have done in this century) and celebrated the virtues of Germanic tribesmen dimly discernible in Roman accounts of rebellion; relics of such enthusiasm remain in the paintings commissioned by Amsterdam magnates depicting 'Batavian' attacks upon Roman camps (in the era we remember for the work of Rembrandt). The distinctiveness of a new nation thus consciously created is now more interesting than such propagandist mythology. Once survival was assured, the United Provinces enjoyed religious tolerance (a necessity for survival if internal divisions were to be overcome), great civic freedom and provincial independence; Calvinism did not have the upper hand in government. The Provinces came more and more to be ruled by merchants, particularly those of Amsterdam, the chief city of Holland, the richest province, where landed nobility had never counted for as much as the mercantile and urban oligarchy.

England

Later generations came to think they saw a similar linkage of religious and civic freedom in Elizabethan England; this was anachronistic, although comprehensible, given later English history. Elizabeth I had been an incomparable actress-producer of the royal spectacle. When beauty and youth faded, the myths they provoked lived on. In 1603, when she died, she had been queen for forty-five years, the centre of a national cult fed by her own Tudor instinct for welding the dynasty's interest to patriotism, by poets of genius, by mundane devices such as the frequent travel (which kept down her expenses, and put up those of her nobility, with whom she stayed) which made her visible to her people, and by her meanness. Nor did she persecute for religion's sake; she did not, as she put it, want to make 'windows into men's souls'. It is hardly surprising that under her successors the accession day of Good Queen Bess became a festival of patriotic opposition to government. Unhappily or happily, she had no child to whom to bequeath her glamour. She also left an encumbered estate. Like all other rulers of her day, she never had a big enough income. The inheritance of debt she left behind did not help her successor, though her refusal to marry brought him, the indirect heir, to the throne.

James I, the first English king of the Scottish house of Stuart was neither as lacking in judgement as his son nor as unprincipled as his grandsons, but he had little tact and several curious and alien ways. These, as much as more serious defects, encumbered the politics of his reign. In defence of him and his successors, it can be agreed that England's was not the only troubled monarchy in the seventeenth century. There was a roughly contemporaneous crisis of authority in several, curiously paralleled also by an economic recession which seems to have been Europe-wide. The two may have been connected, but it is not easy to be sure what the nature of the connexion was. But an age of unrest and rebellion coincided with a further period of religious wars. No doubt on the continent (though not in England, which stayed out of them) the growing fiscal needs of governments fighting these wars explains some of their domestic strife.

Yet the British kingdoms, ruled by the Stuarts, experienced the most startling, if not the bloodiest, outcomes: regicide and the establishment of the only republic in English history. Historians still argue about where lay the heart of the quarrel and the point of no return in what became armed conflict between a king and his parliament, and whether monarchy was in crisis or simply the victim of circumstance and personality. A crucial moment came in 1640: Charles I then found himself at war with his Scottish subjects and had to call the English to help him. Without new taxation, England could not be defended. But by then some Englishmen were convinced that there existed a royal scheme to overturn the Church by law established from within and to reintroduce covertly the power of Rome. Parliament harried the king's servants (the two most conspicuous, one an archbishop of Canterbury, were sent to the block). Charles decided in 1642 to stand firm and so civil war followed in England. In it he was defeated. The winners were uneasy, as were all men, for if you stepped outside the ancient constitution of King, Lords and Commons, where would things end? Most parties, in different ways, were anxious to defend what they understood to be the constitution, but they disagreed about what that meant. Charles finally threw away his advantage by seeking a foreign invasion in his support (the Scotch fighting for him, this time). Parliament's masters had had enough and Charles was tried and beheaded in 1649. His son went into exile.

In the interregnum which followed, the dominant figure until his death in 1658 was a country gentleman who had risen in the councils of the parliamentary side by his genius as a soldier, Oliver Cromwell. So long as his excellent army stood by him he could dispense with the politicians, but since he could not risk losing the support of his officers his freedom to act was limited. The result was an English republic, the 'Commonwealth', astonishingly fruitful of new constitutional schemes, as Oliver cast about to find a way of governing through parliament without delivering England to intolerant sectarians.

The religious intolerance of some parliamentarians was one expression of the many-sided strain in Protestantism called Puritanism. It had been an ill-defined but identified and growing force in English life since Elizabeth's reign. Its first spokesmen and exponents sought only a particularly close and austere interpretation of religious doctrine and ceremony; there were puritans inside the Anglican Church as well as among the critics who were impatient with it because it kept so much from the Catholic past. By the seventeenth century the epithet 'puritan' also betokened, besides rigid doctrine and disapproval of ritual, austerity of behaviour and a wish to improve that of others in a strongly Calvinistic sense. This meant a minority's imposition of doctrinal and moral puritanism by law not only on conservative and royalist Anglicans, but on dissenting religious minorities – Congregationalists, Baptists, Unitarians – which had found their voices under the Commonwealth. There was nothing politically or religiously democratic about puritans. Those who were of the Elect might freely choose their own elders and act as a self-governing community, but from outside their self-designated circle they looked (and were) an oligarchy claiming to know God's will for others, and therefore all the more unacceptable. A few, untypical minorities, outside the dominant Protestant political establishment, meanwhile threw up more democratic and levelling ideas.

It is still hard to say what was the essence of what some later called the 'English revolution'. Clearly, religion was a big part of it; it was not without cause that the classic English historian of the struggle called it the 'Puritan Revolution'. Extreme Protestantism had been given a chance to have an influence on the national life. As a result it earned the deep dislike of the Church of England and made political England anticlerical for centuries. But religion can hardly exhaust the meaning of these years and a great contemporary historian of the Civil War, Clarendon, spoke instead in his title only of a 'rebellion' – which fitted the constitutional theory of what happened at the Restoration. Others have sought class struggle in these years. Of the (sometimes economically) interested motives of many of those engaged there can be no doubt, but there is no pattern. Still others have seen a struggle between a swollen 'Court', a governmental nexus of bureaucrats, courtiers and politicians, all linked to the system by financial dependence upon it, and 'Country', the local notables who paid for this. But localities often divided; it was one of the tragedies of the Civil War that even families could be split by it. It remains easier to be clear about the outcome than about origins. Circumstance, above all in the way the Scottish factor operated, counted for too much to justify dogmatism.

Unfortunately, once Oliver had died, the institutional bankruptcy of the republic was patent. Englishmen could not agree in sufficient numbers to establish any new order. Most of them, it turned out, preferred to fall back on the old familiar device of monarchy. So the Stuarts were restored in 1660. England took her king back on unspoken conditions. Charles II came home because parliament said he could if he defended the Church of England and the Reformation settlement; revolutionary Puritanism now frightened them as much as Counter-Reformation Catholicism. The struggles of king and parliament were not over, but henceforth the Crown was on the defensive.

The travails of monarchy

Not only rulers, but many other Europeans were shocked by the judicial murder of Charles I as they faced their own political and constitutional troubles. Even if these did not end in the lopping off of kings' heads, though, they were sometimes bloody enough. Over and above food riot and rural disorder, the 'crisis' some historians have seen afflicting Europe in the early seventeenth century had more overtly political manifestations. In Spain, attempts to overcome the provincialism inherent in the formally federal but actually bureaucratic structure of the monarchy led to revolt. Portugal broke away in 1640, after nearly sixty years' subordination to the Spanish crown; there were also unsuccessful but major rebellions in the Basque provinces and in Catalonia, the latter taking twelve years to suppress. In 1647, the Spanish kingdom of Naples erupted. By mid-century, Spain, formally still a great dynastic state, was no longer the dominant European power she had been a 100 years earlier.

France, which had replaced Spain in that role, also had new troubles. They had not ended with the formal settlement of the Huguenot problem in 1598. In 1610 Henry IV, the apostatized Protestant, was assassinated. His son, nine years' old, could not exercise his power and was supervised by a regency for the next five years; he was in fact a focus of quarrels between councillors and advisers for most of his reign. After 1630, the ascendancy of the cardinal Richelieu was to be unshaken, but before it was established, there was another Huguenot rebellion and numerous conspiracies and attempted coups. The cardinal was willing to bribe or negotiate with those whose co-operation was needed to keep taxes flowing to pay for foreign successes. The conscious assertion of royal power by servants of the monarchy had nonetheless contributed to the state's difficulties. In the still overwhelmingly agricultural economy of France, measures to increase the revenue of the monarchy were bound to hurt the poor most. Taxes on the peasant could double and even treble in a few years. Eruptions of popular rebellion, mercilessly repressed, were the result. Some parts of eastern France, too, were devastated by the campaigns of the last phase of the Thirty Years' War, a great struggle for Germany and central Europe. Lorraine and Burgundy were harshly ravaged, the population of some areas declining by a quarter or a third.

The Thirty Years' War

Less a single war than an era of wars, the Thirty Years' War marked the passing of Spanish hegemony in western Europe and its replacement by French. It eventually involved re-opened war between the Dutch and Spanish, the eruption into the affairs of northern Europe of a new power, the Swedish monarchy, and turned finally into a Bourbon-Habsburg conflict. Its immediate origins lay in the attempt of the Habsburg emperor Ferdinand II to rebuild imperial authority in Germany by linking it with the Counter-Reformation. This called in question the Peace of Augsburg and the survival of religious pluralism in Germany. The implications for the Protestant princes were huge. The actual explosion occurred before the imperial election, when in 1618, his Protestant Bohemian subjects rebelled against Ferdinand. Thereafter, circumstance and cross-currents quickly confused the pattern of ideological conflict. There was much that was almost accidental which brought Habsburg and Bourbon to dispute Germany in the seventeenth century as Habsburg and Valois had disputed Italy in the sixteenth. While the unhappy inhabitants of much of central Europe endured the whims and rapacities of quasi-independent warlords, Catholic France, the 'eldest daughter of the Church', under the leadership of a cardinal, joined Dutch Calvinists and Swedish Lutherans in asserting the rights of German princes against the Catholic Habsburgs. Cardinal Richelieu has a better claim than any other man to be the creator of a foreign policy of stirring up trouble beyond the Rhine which was to serve France well for over a century. With him the age of *Realpolitik* and *raison d'état*, of simple, unprincipled assertion of the interest of the sovereign state, has visibly arrived. Religion was all but lost to sight as the miseries of the Thirty Years' War were prolonged until the Peace of Westphalia ended the fighting in 1648.

The peace confirmed and extended (by including Calvinists) the religious pluralism of the empire. It made Sweden a power on the southern coasts of the Baltic and gave her votes in the Imperial Diet. It marked the end of Spanish military supremacy and of the dream of reconstituting the empire of Charles V. It closed an era of Habsburg history. In Germany a new feature had been the interventions of outsiders, Danes, Swedes and French; a period of French ascendancy was beginning in Europe west of the Elbe. This was in several ways a huge registration of change, though still marked by the fading past. It was the end of the era of religious wars in Europe (and that was why, among other things, the pope protested strongly over what was agreed); it was the last time, too, that European statesmen had as one of their main concerns in a general settlement the religious future of their peoples.

On the other hand, in negotiations a century and a half after Columbus, when Spain, Portugal, England, France and Holland all already had important overseas empires, no attention at all was given to a wider world in the peace terms. England was not even represented at either of the centres of negotiations; once the first phase of the war was over, although preoccupied by internal quarrels and her Scotch neighbours, her foreign policy was directed towards ends more extra-European than European. This was why the Commonwealth was led to fight the Protestant Dutch (1652-4). Although Cromwell quickly restored peace, telling the Dutch there was room in the world for both of them to trade, English and Dutch diplomacy was already showing more clearly than that of other nations the influence of commercial and colonial interest. Under his rule, too, England acquired her first overseas colony by conquest from another European state (Spain), Jamaica.

Political thinking and state power

Another sign of the continuing weight of the past at Westphalia was the persistence of concern with dynastic interest. Dynasticism was still the major organizing idea of diplomacy and would long continue to be. Europe's political units were still for the most part ruled by men who saw them less as states than as landed estates, family properties put together gradually by negotiation, aggressiveness, marriage and inheritance – by the same processes and forces, that is to say, by which any non-royal family's property might be built up. Boundaries (which were often very imprecisely drawn) continually changed as this or that portion of an inheritance passed from one ruler to another. The inhabitants had no more say in the matter than might the peasants on a farm which changed hands. Negotiations and treaty-making were monotonously preoccupied with marriages, their possible consequences, good or bad, and the careful establishment and scrutiny of lines of succession. Occasionally the old principles of feudal superiority, fealty and loyalty might still be invoked. This did not mean that there were not also map-making forces strong enough to override such principles, such as the potential of new land for settlement, or the strength of local sentiment. Nevertheless, broadly speaking, most rulers in the sixteenth and seventeenth centuries still saw themselves as the custodians of inherited rights and interests which they had to pass on to others. At the apex of European society, they mirrored and sometimes exaggerated attitudes diffused throughout their societies. The Middle Ages had been fascinated, for good practical reasons, with lineage (and invented an art-form, heraldry, to give it visible expression); the sixteenth and seventeenth centuries were still a great age for genealogists.

Nevertheless, the passage of time weakened old social and political bonds and old ideas. The very invention of the 'feudal' idea as a technical concept was the work of seventeenth-century lawyers, and suggests a need to define something no longer unquestionable. The idea of Christendom, too, though still important in emotional, even subconscious ways, had effectively lost its political reality by 1648. Papal authority had suffered at the hands of national sentiment ever since the Great Schism; that of the Holy Roman emperors had since the fourteenth century been in reality a matter of what individual emperors could achieve. Then had come the Reformation and religious pluralism. Nor did any new unifying principle emerge to re-integrate Christendom. The test case was the Ottoman threat. Christian princes exposed to the Moslem onslaught might appeal to their fellow-Christians for help, popes might still use the rhetoric of crusade, but the reality was that most Christian states followed their own interests, even, if necessary, by allying with the infidel. The era of *raison d'état* and *Realpolitik* was one which consciously subordinated ideological principle to intelligent calculation of the interests of the state. It now seems curious that in an age in which Europeans were inclined more and more to agree that greater distinctions of culture separated them (to their credit, they were sure) from other civilizations than from one another, they paid little attention to institutions (and did nothing to create new ones) which expressed what they had in common. Perhaps, though, it is just in a growing awareness of cultural superiority that the explanation lies. Europe was entering an age of triumphant expansion and did not need shared institutions to tell her so. The institution of the future appeared to be a divisive one for the continent as a whole, the sovereign state.

Its acceptance was, of course, far from complete in the seventeenth century, or until much later. For all the arguments, though, about who should exercise power and a mass of political writing which suggested all sorts of limits on it, there was an implicit advance towards acceptance of the idea of legislative sovereignty – that is, in essence, the idea that there should be within a given area only one ultimate source of law and law-making authority. The state, for all the technical and legal limitations under which it laboured, grew mightily in power between 1500 and 1800. This was sometimes obscured by forms. In the struggles between rulers and subjects which made up so much of Europe's history in these centuries, it is hard always to be sure exactly what was at stake. Some challenged kings on the principle that it would be wrong for any government to have such powers as some rulers claimed; this might be termed the conservative defence of freedom, and it had gone on throughout the Middle Ages. Others allowed that such absolute powers as monarchs sought could properly exist, but were being gathered into the wrong hands; this could be seen as a more modern or liberal argument. Still others simply stuck up for legal privilege and vested interest. In practice, such claims were often inextricably confused, and the confusion itself shows that ideas were in flux.

Much depends upon perception. In the long run and in many continental countries, kings and princes in the end seemed increasingly to be able to get their way. Often in the sixteenth and seventeenth centuries medieval representative institutions lost ground or decayed. The Estates-General of France, the nearest thing to a national representative body in that country, met in 1614 for the last time for a 175 years. Some kings began even in the sixteenth century to enjoy powers which would have frightened medieval barons and burghers. The phenomenon has sometimes been called the rise of 'absolute' monarchy, but that is over-stating it. A host of practical circumstances and checks on royal power might exist which were almost as restricting as medieval immunities had been. The term is, though, just acceptable as an expression of some rulers' aspirations.

The relative practical strength of rulers *vis-à-vis* domestic rivals tended to grow, but at different rates. Spain was in the sixteenth century more 'absolute' than France, to which the term should not really be applied until after 1660. New financial resources gave rulers standing armies and artillery to use against those who could not afford them and they could sometimes ally themselves with local communities or even a growing sense of nationhood in imposing order on the over-mighty nobleman; the late fifteenth century in England and France had already shown that firmer royal government would be accepted if it guaranteed order and peace. There were special forces at work in almost every country. The obligatory sharing of power with great subjects whose status entitled them *de facto* and sometimes *de jure* to office, ceased to weigh so heavily upon some kings as in earlier times. Tudor England's Privy Council was recruited from meritocrats as well as magnates. This example, though, was itself revealing, for it took place in a country uniquely centralized, but one in which the Tudors seized on the existing institution of royal Justices of the Peace to weld local landowners into the structure of royal government.

Government in early modern Europe rested on co-operation as well as coercion. There was no sudden transition to the modern 'state': it took centuries and often old forms. In Tudor England, as in Valois France, noblemen had to be treated with care if they were not to be fatally antagonized. Rebellion was not an exceptional but a continuing fact of life for the sixteenth-century, and when it brought together popular grievance and challenged local interest, it might be fatal. Even if royal troops prevailed in the end, no monarch wanted to be reduced to relying only on force. As a famous motto had it, artillery was the *last* argument of kings. The history of the political turbulence of France right down to the middle of the seventeenth century, or of the effects of antagonizing local interest in England during the same period, or of Habsburg attempts to unify their territories at the expense of local magnates, all show this. Even the United Kingdom faced feudal rebellion (its last) as late as 1745.

Meanwhile, officials and soldiers had to be paid for. One way was to allow officials to charge fees or levy perquisites on those who needed their services. For obvious reasons, this was neither a complete nor a satisfactory answer. Something might also still be done by exploiting royal properties better. But all monarchs, sooner or later, were driven back to seek new taxation and that was a problem few could solve. For three centuries great fertility of imagination was shown in inventing new taxes, but the technical devices required to solve this problem were not to be available even by 1800. Broadly speaking, only consumption (through indirect taxes such as customs and excise, or taxes on sale, or through requiring licences and authorizations to trade which had to be paid for) and real property could be tapped by the tax-gatherer. As consumption taxes bore disproportionately upon the poorest, who spent a larger part of their small disposable income on necessities than the wealthy, they always threatened public order. It was never easy, either, to stop a landowner from passing his property tax burdens along to the man at the bottom of the property pyramid. Taxation, too, was long hindered by immunity; in 1500 it was still generally accepted that there were areas, persons and spheres of action which had special exemptions and privileges which protected them from the fiscal power of rulers. They might be defended by an irrevocable and ancient royal grant (such as were the privileges of many cities), by contractual agreement (such as the English *Magna Carta* was alleged to be), by immemorial custom, or by divine law.

The supreme example was the Church. For all its battles with kings, it had emerged from the Middle Ages with its properties not normally subject to lay taxation, with powers of jurisdiction in its courts over matters inaccessible to royal justice, and a monopoly grip on important social and economic institutions – marriage, for example

– even in Protestant states. A province, or a profession, or a family, too, might enjoy immunities, usually from royal jurisdiction or taxation. Nor was royal status and legal right uniform; the French king was only a duke in Brittany and that made a difference to what he was entitled to do there. Such facts like poor communications, inadequate information or wasteful courts were the realities with which rulers had to live. They could not do other than accept them, even if the future lay with the royal bureaucrats and their files.

CHAPTER FOUR The *ancien régime*

Contrasting monarchies: France and England

Richelieu died before France drew at Westphalia the dividend of a victorious peace on his policies. Before that, further political crisis at the capital under his successors showed that the domestic battle for royal authority was by no means won. The role of defender of the traditional constitution was taken up by special interests, notably the *parlement* of Paris, the corporation of lawyers who sat in and could plead before the first law court of the kingdom. In 1648 this ended in an insurrection in Paris (named the *Fronde*). A compromise settlement was followed after an uneasy interval by a more dangerous second *Fronde* supported by provincial rebels. The lawyers of the *parlement* did not long maintain a united front with the grandees and provincial noblemen who were behind these, and the Huguenots looked to the Crown as a protector. The monarchy survived the crisis, therefore, and in 1660 its position was still essentially intact, even if it had undergone for a time something of an eclipse.

That year, when a young king, Louis XIV, assumed full powers and France emerged from another regency, was to prove a turning-point. France would not be ungovernable again until the 1780s. What was more, she was to show in the next half-century astonishing military and diplomatic strength as the leading continental power. Her king was to become the model for monarchs, embodying a new vision of absolute monarchy and to preside over a golden age of French cultural ascendancy, too.

In the same year, 1660, Charles II returned from exile as king of England and Scotland. In the first, the monarchy had survived an even greater political crisis than that of the *Frondes*, but with an outcome very different from the French. On the one hand, though there were further constitutional troubles ahead and another Stuart king would be deposed in 1688, the country was never again to experience civil war. There came into being at the Restoration a royal standing army, and the last English rebellion (in 1685, when an inadequate pretender led a few thousand deluded yokels to disaster) in no sense seriously menaced the state. The propertied classes dreaded the prospect of renewed civil war and the rule of soldiers. Yet France and England, both to play major roles as great powers in the next century, had solved their problems in very different ways and at different costs to their inhabitants. French taxation laid much heavier burdens on Frenchmen than were borne by the English. For all the Huguenot support of the monarchy in the *Frondes*, too, religious dissent was formidably harried by Louis XIV but (except at the religious extremes) tolerated and even, as time went by, cosseted in England. As for the personal monarchy itself, its powers were notably increased in France while they shrank across the English Channel. Charles II already returned to his realm on unspoken conditions; forty years later his throne was occupied by someone who was in law, too, a ruler by contract.

Such dissimilarities in an age when religious bitterness was still alive for many gave a sharpness to quarrels between the two monarchies which led to further awareness of contrast between them. Yet this, like the rhetoric it generated, masked a shared tendency. In important ways, the effective power of government advanced in each country, though on the basis of quite different constitutional assumptions.

England

England had been in some ways the most obvious candidate among European monarchies for further concentration of monarchic power. Royal justice had run throughout the kingdom (in theory at least) since Anglo-Saxon times. The separation from France with the loss of the Plantagenet heritage had been a benefit to royal power in the long run: it reduced the likelihood of expensive continental military commitments. From the magnates' struggles of the fifteenth century had emerged a dynasty more successful than any of the age, notably, in focusing and canalizing English self-consciousness. Then came the English Reformation, which put the wealth of the monasteries and churches in the hands of a king who was henceforth head of the national church, and could have financed a huge extension of royal power.

Here, though, circumstance pointed in another direction. The Reformation in England was carried out by Act of Parliament. Henry VIII, a potential despot, having conceded parliament's right to legislate on such an important matter, it was more difficult for later kings to act without parliament's support on major issues. More important still, it gave new force to the idea that there might be no limits to legislative authority except those which were psychologically internalized, subjective constraints set by culture and tradition, or the practical ones imposed by circumstance. The implications were for a time obscured by doctrinal issues but after Mary's attempt to revive the old order, her half-sister, Elizabeth I had parliament legislate that she retained the essentials of her father's position; the English Church or Church of England, as it may henceforth be called, claimed to be Catholic in doctrine but was governed by a Royal Supremacy endorsed by an Act of Parliament. England was soon to be at war with a Catholic king of Spain known for his determination to root out heresy in his own lands. This confirmed the identification of the national cause with Protestantism.

These circumstances (and there were others, including those of personality), together with older historical legacies, had much force in shaping constitutional struggle in the seventeenth century so that, for all its violence and confusion, it turned out in the end to have been less about the extent of a legal sovereign's power, than about who should exercise that sovereignty and share the power it conferred. In the eighteenth century only a very few Englishmen would be prepared to assert that there was any limit except practicality to the potential scope of the laws made by the king in Parliament. This conclusion was implicit in the 'Glorious Revolution' of 1688, when England's political class rejected the direct descent of the Stuart male line and pushed James II off the throne. He was believed to be trying to cancel a 150 years of history by making England again a Roman Catholic country; his daughter, Mary, and her consort, the indisputably Protestant but Dutch William of Orange, posed no such danger; they were put on the throne on conditions. England now at last began explicitly to function as a constitutional state. The direction of the nation was henceforth openly shared; its major component lay with a House of Commons dominated by the landowning classes, whose greatest members sat in the House of Lords. The monarchy still kept important powers of its own but its advisers, it soon became clear, had to possess the confidence of the House of Commons. The legislative sovereign, the Crown in Parliament, could do anything by statute. Although something called a 'Bill of Rights' was passed in 1689, it was a statute like any other, open to repeal. No such immunity as still protected privilege in continental countries existed, no human or natural rights not open to legislative change. The English answer to the danger posed by this extraordinary concentration of authority had been to secure, with the threat of revolution if necessary, that authority should only act in accordance with the wishes of the most powerful elements in society.

To Queen Mary's husband, now William III, the major importance of the Glorious Revolution was diplomatic and military: England could be mobilized to defend the independence of the United Provinces against France. There were too many complicated interests at work in them for the Anglo-French wars which followed to be interpreted in merely constitutional or ideological terms. The presence of the Holy Roman Empire, Spain and various German princes in the shifting anti-French coalitions of the next quarter-century would alone make nonsense of any neat contrast between the two sides. Nevertheless, it rightly struck some contemporaries that there was an ideological element buried somewhere in the struggle.

English and Dutch society were indeed more open than that of the France of Louis XIV. They permitted and protected the exercise of different religions. They did not censor the press but left it to be regulated by the laws which protected persons and the state against defamation. They were both governed by oligarchies representing the effective possessors of social and economic power. But, just as the interests of the ruling rich in the Dutch republic often turned out to be the interests of many other people too, so did those of England's rulers. After all, agriculture was England's main industry; what was good for the landlord and the farmer was likely to be good for the country. Nor were other interests – those of bankers and merchants, for example – ignored. They might grumble about policies, but government usually took account of their views. Gradually educated and uneducated Englishmen alike began to feel there was a connexion between some of the advantages they enjoyed – personal freedom, equality before the law, religious toleration, safeguards against absolute monarchy – and the growing wealth of the country. In the eighteenth century many Europeans came to feel Englishmen were freer in their private lives than they. It was less usual to keep Englishmen locked up without trial, for example, than elsewhere, and they did not expect to have their homes entered and searched without a magistrate's warrant. Rank and subservience were very important in English society, but, if a great lord committed a crime, he could be brought before a court like anyone else. All this seemed very strange to continental Europeans and admirable to some of them. Yet it too was largely the consequence of England being ruled by people who wanted to protect themselves and their property and thought the best way to do so was by putting behind such privileges the force of laws which only parliament could change. So, 'constitutionalism' came to be associated with one of the major European powers as something of an ideological fact.

The France of Louis XIV

France was very different and came to stand very obviously at the opposite constitutional pole. Its government's pretensions to authority under Louis XIV reached a climax both in practical and ideological terms, though there remained important limits to both. It is not easy to pin the king's ambitions down in familiar categories; for him personal, dynastic and national standing were not distinguishable. That may be why he became a model for so many European princes. French politics was reduced effectively to courtiership, administration and enforcement; the royal councils, together with the royal agents in the provinces, the *intendants* and military commanders, took account of the existence of the nobility and local immunities, but the reign played havoc with the real independence of political forces hitherto powerful in France. Some later saw the era as in this sense revolutionary; in the second half of the century the frame which Richelieu had first knocked together was at last made secure. Louis XIV tamed his aristocrats. He offered the greatest among them the most glamorous court in Europe and caressed them with honours and pensions, but he never forgot the *Frondes*. His family were excluded from his council, to which were admitted non-noble ministers who were king's men. Above all, local representative bodies were curbed; the provincial 'estates' were managed by royal officials and the *parlements* were restricted to their judicial role. The French Church's independence of Roman authority was asserted, but only to bring it the more securely under the wing of the Most Christian King (one of Louis' titles). Louis was nevertheless determined, whatever the cost, not to be a ruler of heretics; Huguenots (to whose support his family had owed much) who were not exiled were harshly and brutally driven towards conversion.

The coincidence of an end to a period of disorder and the further assertion of French power abroad with a great age of French cultural achievement long made Frenchmen reluctant to recognize the darker sides of the reign of Louis XIV. It was soon called the *Grande Siècle*. Yet he ruled a hierarchical, corporate, theocratic society which, even if up-to-date in methods, looked to the past for its goals, and for its sanctions. Louis at one time hoped to become Holy Roman Emperor; he refused to allow the philosopher Descartes, though a defender of religion, to be given religious burial in France because his ideas were thought dangerous. His government had nasty sides to it, as Huguenot families who had soldiers billeted on them, or peasants reluctant to pay taxes whose villages were visited by a troop of cavalry for a month or so, both knew. Yet Frenchmen rarely resisted. Life may actually have been better than life a few decades previously, in spite of some exceptionally hard years. France was for the most of a long reign, free from invasion. Revealingly, there was a drop in the return expected from investment in land which lasted well into the eighteenth century. These were solid realities behind the glittering façade.

That glitter owed much to Louis himself. France's new European position was won not just by success in war and diplomacy (and by the end of the reign, there had been bad setbacks), but also by royal salesmanship. Louis carried French prestige to a peak at which it was long to remain partly because of the model of monarchy he presented; he was the perfect 'absolute' monarch. Few buildings (or the lives lived in them) can have been so aped and imitated as those of Versailles. In the next century, Europe was studded with miniature reproductions of the huge new palace he built there and its court life. They were models for other would-be *grands monarques* in the decades of stability and continuity which almost everywhere immediately followed the great wars of Louis' reign.

French ascendancy and the balance of power

One way of characterizing the changes of international life in Europe during the reign of Louis XIV is as the gradual eclipse of an Austro-French quarrel (developed from the old Bourbon-Habsburg rivalry) over Europe by a new Anglo-French rivalry which was to last much longer, and assume world-wide dimensions. Such a description is inadequate, and overlooks significant new changes in eastern Europe but it points in the right direction. France enjoyed a huge pre-eminence in continental power and influence in these years. Its bed-rock was the largest population in western Europe (and on this, indeed, French military power was to rest until late in the nineteenth century).

Louis' personal foreign and domestic aims were closely entwined with one another, ideology and the royal temperament. Only for convenience should foreign policy be distinguished from other aspects of his reign. Versailles was not only the gratification of personal taste, but an exercise in a prestige essential to his diplomacy. In order to embellish its gardens, Louis might buy millions of tulip bulbs a year from the Dutch, while despising them as merchants, disapproving of them as republicans, and detesting them as Protestants. He was a legalistic man – kings had to be – and he felt easier when there existed legal claims good enough to give respectability to what he was doing; this was helpful when he sought to give France better frontiers. Thus many considerations shaped a foreign policy of what was later sometimes presented as patriotic aggrandisement. Though in the end it cost his country dearly, it carried France to a pre-eminence from which she was to freewheel through half the eighteenth century, and created a legend to which Frenchmen still look back with nostalgia.

Strategically defensible frontiers for France meant conflict with Spain, which after 1648 still retained the Spanish Netherlands and the Franche-Comté. Victory over Spain opened the way to a war with the Dutch, who at first managed to hold their own, but it ended in 1678 with a peace usually reckoned to be the peak of Louis' achievement in foreign affairs. He now turned to Germany. Besides territorial conquest, he sought the imperial crown. To obtain it he was willing to ally with the Turk. Then came 1688, and the acquisition of England's help by 'Dutch William', the Stadtholder of Holland, when his wife replaced her father on the English throne. From this time Louis had a new and persistent enemy across the Channel. For the first time since the days of Cromwell, England fielded an army on the continent and did so in support of a league of European states (even the pope joined it, though secretly) against Louis. 'King William's war' (also called the 'war of the League of Augsburg'), brought together Spain and Austria, as well as the Protestant states of Europe, to contain the overweening ambition of the French king. In the peace of Ryswick which ended it in 1697 Louis had for the first time to make substantial concessions.

England's new international weight emerged from a confluence of historical forces.

Some were accidental, like the original commitment to Protestantism which became the heart of the nearest thing the country has known to a national political obsession, or the internal disposition of power which emerged from the constitutional struggles of the seventeenth century. Some were more deliberately and purposefully inaugurated, like the resolution of dynastic problems, or that of the land frontier with an independent Scotland, or the more piecemeal changes which brought about the consolidation of commercial and financial strength after the Restoration, so that by 1700 a nation whose rulers had less than forty years earlier gone cap-in-hand to the goldsmiths and merchants of the City of London to borrow money was capable of a sustaining a world-wide war effort and the leadership of a European coalition against France.

These changes were accompanied by the maturing of a new English maritime tradition of sea-power. Geographical position was a part of the story (though France, too, was an Atlantic nation with fine harbours and vigorous and enterprising seamen). Another was the dropping away of Dutch competition as their republic bent under the strain of defending its territory from the French. Cromwell's 'sea-generals' had under the Commonwealth what could be done with a good navy; this encouraged Charles II (and even more his brother) to provide one. They were unusually fortunate; there was at that moment available Samuel Pepys, one of the greatest of English civil servants, able and anxious to help them. By then, the specialization of function between warships and merchantmen had begun to harden, and the notion of a Royal Navy as a regular service had taken root. It was supplemented by privateering, a way of getting sea-power on the cheap, by authorizing private captains and their employers to prey on enemy shipping, keeping the prizes they seized. The first great privateering campaign was fought by the French against the English and Dutch in King William's war. The Royal Navy had meanwhile started to improve its own skills and professionalism. By the end of the century, signalling was formalized and the first Fighting Instructions were issued. The press-gang made an appearance to assure the supply of seamen (the French preferred conscription in their maritime provinces).

By 1700 a decisive point had been passed. The choice of predominance on land or sea had been settled by Louis' dynastic ambitions, and there was no serious settled intention to seek French supremacy at sea, whatever her admirals and sailors might achieve from time to time. The English were never so distracted from oceanic power. Though they fielded a major military effort on the continent between 1701 and 1714, they were not to do so again on such a scale for 200 years; they preferred to keep their continental allies in the field, while retaining command of the surface of the seas so that friendly ships could move in safety and those of an enemy could not. The basis of this was the existence of an unchallengeable battlefleet to neutralize enemy sea-power. For a century, the first aim in any war of British admirals became the early defeat of the enemy's fleet and seizure of command of the sea.

The stabilization of western Europe

In 1700 there died the sickly, feeble-minded Charles II of Spain. Long and elaborate diplomatic preparations had been made for this event. His demise presented great dangers and great opportunities: a huge dynastic inheritance was at stake. Claims arising from marriage alliances in the past meant that the Habsburg emperor and Louis XIV (who had passed his rights in the matter on to his grandson) would have to dispute the matter. But others had interests, too. The English, significantly, wanted to know what would happen to the trade of Spanish America; the Dutch were deeply concerned over the fate of the Spanish Netherlands. The prospect of world and European going undivided either to Bourbon or Habsburg alarmed everybody. As a result, partition treaties providing for arrangements satisfactory to both dynasties had been made. But when Louis accepted on his grandson's behalf the bequest under Charles II's will of the whole Spanish inheritance, the agreements into which he had entered went into the waste-paper basket. A new Grand Alliance of the Emperor, the United Provinces and England (which Louis had offended by recognizing a Stuart Pretender as James III) was soon formed. The War of the Spanish Succession followed. Twelve years' fighting drove Louis to terms in the treaties made in 1713 and 1714 which are called the Peace of Utrecht. By them, the crowns of Spain and France were declared forever incapable of being united. The first Bourbon king of Spain took his place on the Spanish throne, but though he took with Spain the Indies, the Spanish Netherlands went to the emperor as compensation and to provide a tripwire defence for the Dutch against further French aggression. The Habsburgs also profited in Italy. France made concessions overseas to Great Britain. The briefly recognized pretender to the British throne was expelled from France, and Louis acknowledged the right of succession of the Protestant house of Hanover when the last Stuart monarch of England, Queen Anne, should die.

This stabilization of western Europe lasted with only minor adjustments for 75 years. Not everyone liked it (the emperor refused to admit the end of his claim to the throne of Spain) but to a remarkable degree the major definitions of western Europe north of the Alps were to remain as settled in 1713–14. A new Austrian Netherlands occupied much of the same area as modern Belgium (though this was to prove a doubtful asset, an administrative nuisance rather than a strategic advantage), and the United Provinces corresponds to the modern Netherlands. France would henceforth keep Franche-Comté and, until 1871, Alsace and Lorraine, won by Louis XIV. Spain and Portugal after 1714 remained within their present boundaries, still with large colonial empires but without ever again rising out of the second rank of powers. Great Britain, the new force in the west, no longer had to bother as England had done about Scotland since the union of the two countries under a single crown and parliament in 1707. She once more had a personal connexion with the continent after 1714 (when queen Anne died) through her new king, who was also Elector of Hanover.

South of the Alps, the dust took longer to settle. A still disunited Italy underwent another thirty-odd years of uncertainty. Minor representatives of European royal houses shuffled around it from one state to another in attempts to tie up loose ends and seize left-overs of the age of dynastic rivalry. After 1748 only one of the old major ruling families was left in the peninsula, that of Savoy, whose dukes ruled Piedmont on the south side of the Alps and the island of Sardinia. The papal states, together with the decaying republics of Venice, Genoa, Lucca and San Marino, upheld the tattered standard of Italian independence. Foreign rulers were installed in the other Italian states.

Western European political geography was thus set for a long time. This owed much to the need felt by all sensible statesmen to avoid for as long as possible another conflict such as that which had just closed. One of the peace treaties had declared the aim of the signatories to be the security of peace through a balance of power. This practical aim, publicly recognized for the first time, marks an important change in diplomatic thinking. There were pressing motives for such realism; even Great Britain and

France, the only countries capable of sustaining war against other great powers without foreign subsidy, had both been financially stretched. But the end of the War of the Spanish Succession also brought effective settlements of real problems. A new age was opening. Dynasticism was beginning to be pushed into the second rank as a principle of foreign policy in some countries. Some rulers, at least, could no longer separate the interests of their house from those of their nation. Those interests, too, were in some instances now seen as extending far beyond Europe.

Change in eastern Europe

East of the Rhine (and still more east of the Elbe) this was much less true, though great changes had indeed occurred there by 1715. Since the sixteenth century Habsburg Austria and the Polish-Lithuanian kingdom had defended Europe from the Turk on land. At sea, Venice bore the main burden of resistance to Ottoman power, the supreme fact of east European and Mediterranean politics. The phrase 'Eastern Question' had not then been invented but, if it had been, men would have meant by it the problem of defending Europe against Islam, which set the terms of eastern European diplomacy and strategy for more than 200 years. By 1700 the Ottomans' last great effort was spent, though they still had a few conquests to make.

For two centuries after 1453, Venice had been their main European victim. Still rich by comparison with other Italian states, the republic declined, first in military and then in commercial power. In 1479, the Turks took the Ionian islands and imposed an annual charge for trade in the Black Sea. Though Venice turned Cyprus into a major base two years later, that island was in its turn lost in 1571. By 1600, though still (by now thanks to her manufactures) rich, Venice had lost her commercial leadership; first Antwerp and then Amsterdam had replaced her as a centre of exchange. She was no longer a mercantile power at the level of the United Provinces or even England. Ottoman success was then resumed in the second half of the seventeenth century. In 1669 the Venetians had to accept that they had lost Crete.

Hungary had been invaded in 1664; this was the last Ottoman conquest of a European kingdom, but the Ukrainians had soon to acknowledge Turkish suzerainty and the Poles to give up Podolia. In 1683 the second Turkish siege of Vienna began. Europe seemed in its greatest danger for over two centuries. In fact it was not. This was to be the last time Vienna was besieged. The great days of the Ottoman power were over. The effort which began with the conquest of Hungary had been the last big heave.

The Ottoman empire was no longer abreast of the latest military and naval technology, but, more important, its power was badly overstretched; it was pinned down in Asia against Persia as well as in Europe and Africa. The strain was too much for the loose structures of Ottoman government. One vizier pulled things together in the seventeenth century enough to make the last offensives possible. But there were weaknesses in the nature of the empire itself. More a military occupation than a political unity, it was dangerously dependent on subjects whose loyalty it could not win. Although there were always some converts to Islam among them, the customs and institutions of non-Moslem communities, which were ruled through their own authorities, were respected by the Turks. The Greek Orthodox and Armenian Christians, and the Jews each had their own arrangements (the Greeks paid a special poll-tax, for example, and were ruled, ultimately, by their own patriarch in Constantinople). At lower levels, such arrangements as seemed best were made with leaders of local communities for the support of the military machine which was the heart of the Ottoman structure. In the end this bred over-mighty subjects, and pashas feathered their own nests amid incoherence and inefficiency. It gave the subjects, of the sultan no sense of identification with his rule but, rather, alienated them from it as the Ottoman lands in Europe got poorer and poorer.

1683, therefore, was a less dangerous moment than it looked. Symbolically and actually it was the last time that Europe stood on the defensive in her old bastion against Islam. Although the Ottomans would still add to their conquests in the Mediterranean (and, outside Europe, took Kurdistan from Persia – with whom they had hardly ceased to quarrel since 1501 – and sent an army as far south as Aden), the tide of Turkish power would ebb when European powers went over to the attack. Decline would follow almost without interruption until in 1918 the empire had nothing left beyond the immediate European hinterland of Constantinople and the old Ottoman heartland, Anatolia. The relief of Vienna by the King of Poland, John Sobieski, was followed by the liberation of a devastated Hungary, which became part of the Habsburg dominions in 1699. Transylvania, the Bukovina, and most of the Black Sea coasts followed it out of Ottoman control in the eighteenth century.

Poland's troubles

Yet neither the once-great Polish-Lithuanian commonwealth nor the Habsburgs were to be the main beneficiaries of Ottoman decline. The Poles were in fact nearing the end of their own history as an independent nation. A personal union of Lithuania and Poland had been turned into a real union of the two countries too late. In 1572 the last king of the Jagiellon line died without an heir. The throne had become not only theoretically but actually elective. Poland's kings had very little power to balance that of the landowners. They had no standing army to rely on when factions among the gentry or magnates fell back on the practice of armed but constitutional rebellion (`Confederation') to obtain their wishes. In the Diet, the central parliamentary body of the kingdom, a rule of unanimity stood in the way of reform. For a century Polish magnates and foreign kings disputed each election, while their country was under grave and continuing pressure not only from Turks, but from Russians and Swedes. Poland prospered against them only when they were embarrassed elsewhere. In 1660, the last of the Polish coast was given up to the Swedes, who had descended on northern Poland during the Thirty Years' War. Internal divisions had worsened, too; the Counter-Reformation brought religious persecution to the Polish Protestants and there were risings of Cossacks in the Ukraine and continuing serf revolts.

The election as king of the heroic John Sobieski in 1674 was the last which was not the outcome of machinations by foreign rulers. He had won important victories and managed to preside over Poland's curious and highly decentralized medieval constitution. If a geographically ill-defined, religiously divided Poland, ruled by a narrowly selfish rural gentry was to survive, though, more was needed. John Sobieski could do nothing to change social and constitutional fact. The estates of the 1,000,000 or so gentry who were the Polish 'nation' were small and made up less than a tenth of the country's area in 1700. Their proprietors were effectively the clients of a few great families of extraordinary wealth reluctant to surrender their power of getting up confederations and manipulating Diets. The Radziwills owned estates half the size of Ireland and held a court which outshone that of Warsaw; the Potocki estates covered 6,500 square miles (roughly half the area of the Dutch Republic). At the bottom of the pile were the peasants, some of the most miserable in Europe, engaged in unending battle with their landlords who in 1700 still had rights of life and death over them. The towns were powerless. Their total population was only half the size of the gentry class. Yet Prussia and Russia also rested on backward agrarian and feudal infrastructures and they survived; Poland was the only one of the old eastern states to go under completely. The practice of election blocked the emergence of Polish Tudors or Bourbons who could identify their own dynastic instincts of self-aggrandizement with those of the nation. Poland entered the eighteenth century under a foreign king; the Elector of Saxony, chosen to succeed John Sobieski in 1697, was soon deposed by the Swedes, and then put back again on his throne by the Russians, which registered the fact of other changes in the north and east.

The new great power in the east

It now requires an effort to realize how unexpected was the appearance of Russia as a major force of the European age. In 1547 Ivan IV, grandson of Ivan the Great, was crowned. He took the title of 'Tsar of all the Russias', and was the first tsar to do so. The Grand Prince of Muscovy had become an emperor ruling many peoples. In spite of his vigour and ferocity, 'Ivan the Terrible' (as he passed into the historical record) played no significant role in western European affairs (so little-known, indeed, was Russia that even in the next century a French king could write to a tsar, not knowing that he had been dead for ten years). In eastern Europe, things were different. When he came to the throne, Russia was still ill-defined. Though the Ottoman Turks had pushed into south-east Europe, between them and Muscovy lay the Ukraine, the lands of the Cossacks, peoples who fiercely protected their independence. To the east, the Urals provided a theoretical though hardly a realistic frontier.

Russia's rulers have always found it easy to feel isolated in the middle of hostile space. Almost instinctively, they have sought natural frontiers at its edges or a protective glacis of clients. Ivan the Terrible began by consolidating the Russian heartland built by Ivan the Great. Then came penetration of the wilderness of the north. When he came to the throne, Russia had a small Baltic coast and a vast territory stretching up to the White Sea, thinly inhabited by scattered and primitive peoples, but providing a possible route to the west, though a roundabout one. In 1584 the port of Archangel was founded. On the Baltic front Ivan could do little, though he successfully turned on the Tatars after they burned Moscow for the last time in 1571, driving them from Kazan and Astrakhan and winning control of the whole length of the Volga. Muscovite power now reached the Caspian. The other great thrust beginning in his reign was across the Urals, into Siberia. It was less one of conquest than of settlement. The first Russians across the Urals seem to have been political refugees from Novgorod, followed by fleeing serfs and aggrieved Cossacks. By 1600 settlements had been planted 600 miles inside Siberia, with Russian officials who sought to assure the state tribute in furs. The rivers were the key to the region. Within fifty years a man and his goods could travel by river with only three portages from Tobolsk, 300 miles east of the Urals, to the port of Okhotsk, 3,000 miles away. There he would be only 400 miles by sea from Sakhalin, the northernmost of the major islands of the chain which makes up Japan – a sea-pas-

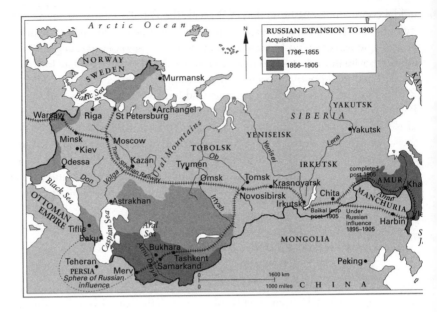

RUSSIAN EXPANSION TO 1905
Acquisitions
1796–1855
1856–1905

sage about as long as that from Land's End to Antwerp. By 1700 there were 200,000 settlers east of the Urals and a treaty on frontier questions had been agreed with the Chinese. Some Russians, we are told, already talked of the conquest of China. The tsars were to be Asian as well as European emperors (in the twentieth century most of the land surface of the empire and its successor states would be in Asia).

This long but steady movement eastward was not much affected by the 'Time of Troubles' which followed Ivan's death. In the west, Russia was still not taken seriously as a European power for most of the seventeenth century. There were moments when an outlet to the Baltic was lost to the Swedish monarchy and when even Moscow was briefly occupied by the Poles. Only in a great war of 1654–67 were Smolensk, Little Russia and the Ukraine recovered from Poland, not to be lost again to invaders until 1812. Maps and treaties now began to have some political reality. By 1700, Russia's south-western frontier ran for most of its length on the western side of the Dnieper, embracing the great historic city of Kiev. The Cossacks who lived on the east bank were given special, semi-autonomous governmental arrangements which were to survive until Soviet times. Most Russian gains had been at the expense of Poland, long preoccupied with fighting off Turk and Swede. But Russian armies joined the Poles in alliance against the Ottomans in 1687; this was a historic moment, too. It posed another version of the classical Eastern Question or, perhaps, revealed another of its dimensions: if Ottoman empire gave way, should anything be done to limit Russian encroachment to the south-west which would almost certainly accelerate further Ottoman decline and perhaps collapse?

As in many other nations, and more evidently than in most, monarchy was the motor of nation-making in Russia. The country had no racial unity to pre-ordain its existence and precious little geographical definition to impose a shape. Though Slav and Orthodox, that was not a unique combination; other Slavs were Orthodox. The growth of the personal domain and power of the tsars was the key to the building of the nation. Under Ivan the Terrible appeared the beginnings of a nobility owing military service in return for their estates, a development of a system employed by the princes of Muscovy to obtain levies to fight the Tatars. It made possible the raising of an army which led a Polish king to warn Elizabeth I of England that if they got hold of western skills the Russians would be unbeatable; the danger was remote, but the warning now seems prescient.

When the last tsar of the house of Rurik died in 1598 the throne was disputed between magnates and Polish interventionists until 1613, when a new family emerged triumphant. Michael Romanov was a weak ruler who lived in the shadow of his dominating father, but his dynasty was to rule Russia for 300 years. His immediate successors fought off rivals and humbled the great ones among them, the boyars, who had attempted to revive a power curbed by Ivan the Terrible. Beyond their ranks the only potential internal rival to the monarchy was the Church. But there would never be an Investiture Contest or a Church and State struggle in Russia. In the seventeenth century the Church was weakened by a schism and in 1667 the patriarch was deprived of his office by the tsar. After this, the Russian Church was structurally and legally subordinated to a lay official. Russia was never to know the conflict of lay and ecclesiastical power which was so creative a force in western Europe, any more than she was to know the stimulus of the coming of religious pluralism in the Reformation.

This made possible the final maturing of autocracy. The tsar retained the semi-sacrosanct authority inherited from Byzantium unlimited by clear legal checks. All institutions within the state except the Church derived from the autocracy and had no independent standing of their own. There was no division of powers between constitutional authorities. In time, a loyal bureaucracy would develop and military goals would remain paramount. Service was owed to the tsar by all his subjects. These qualities were not all present at the start, nor were all of them equally operative and obvious at all times. But they mark tsardom off decisively from western Christian kingship. In old Muscovy, revealingly, the highest official was called by a title which meant 'slave' or 'servant'; at that time, in neighbouring Poland-Lithuania, his opposite number was designated 'citizen'. Even Louis XIV, though he might believe in Divine Right and aspire to unrivalled power, believed also that his wide power was explicitly restricted by rights, by religion, by divinely ordained law. His subjects knew he was an absolute monarch, but they were also sure he was not a despot. Divergent from one another though English and French monarchical practice might be, they both accepted practical and theoretical limitations inconceivable to tsardom; they bore the stamp of a western history Russia had never known. Yet an autocracy which was to be in the west a byword for despotism suited Russia. It seemed to go on doing so, even after the tsars disappeared in 1917. Eighteenth-century sociologists sometimes suggested that big, flat countries favoured despotism. This was over-simple, but there were always latent centrifugal tendencies to be resisted in a country so big as Russia, embracing so many natural regions and so many different peoples.

Peter the Great

In 1682 there came to the throne of Muscovy the tsar who was to make the most memorable use of autocratic power. In one way, Peter I resembled twentieth-century strong men who have striven ruthlessly to drag traditional societies into modernity. Yet he was very much a monarch of his own day, his attention focused on victory in war; Russia was only at peace for one year in his entire reign. His originality, though, lay in seeing that the road to victory in Russia ran through modernizing (not a word which then existed) – and that meant borrowing from western Europe, where modern societies were to be found. Probably in his own mind he did not distinguish the urge to modernize his country from the urge to free his countrymen forever from the fear of their neighbours. His ambition to win a Russian Baltic coast supplied the driving force behind the reforms which would open the way to it. Ascending the throne when he was ten years old, he had grown up in the 'German' quarter of Moscow where foreign merchants and their retinues lived; this may have helped. A celebrated pilgrimage he made to the United Provinces and England in 1697–8 showed his interest in technology. Whatever the exact balance of his motives, his reforms have ever since served as an ideological touchstone; generation after generation of Russians were to look back with awe and ponder what he had done and its meaning for Russia. One of them who thought he knew wrote in the nineteenth century that Peter the Great (as he came to be called) found only a blank page on which he had written the words Europe and Occident. This was an extreme view. Whether they agreed or not, and whether they approved or not of the outcome, by 1800 it was at least clear that what he had done to Russia could not be eradicated.

Peter's territorial achievement was great. He sent expeditions to Kamchatka and the oases of Bokhara and ceased to pay tribute to the Tatars. At the end of his life he seized from Persia much of the Caspian coast (though it was not to remain Russian for long). But his driving ambition was to reach the sea to the west, securing a Baltic outlet and eliminating the Swedish threat. For a while Peter had a Black Sea fleet and annexed Azov, but had to abandon it later because of the distracting priority of a struggle to the death with Sweden. The Great Northern War, as contemporaries termed the final series of conflicts, began in 1700 and lasted until 1721. They arose from the common interest Russia shared with Poland and Denmark in containing the Swedish 'empire' in the southern Baltic coasts. The world recognized that something decisive had happened when in 1709 the Swedish army was destroyed far away from home at Poltava, in the middle of the Ukraine where its leader the Swedish king had sought allies among the Cossacks. The rest of Peter's reign drove home the point. Peace established Russia firmly on the Baltic coast, in Livonia, Estonia and the Karelian isthmus. Sweden's brief days as a great power were over; she had been the first victim of a new one.

Victory opened the way to further Russian contact with the west. In 1703 Peter had already begun to build, on territory captured from the Swedes, the beautiful new city which was for two centuries the capital of Russia, St Petersburg. It was a deliberate break with the past, though Muscovy, of course, had never been completely cut off from Europe. A pope had helped to arrange Ivan the Great's marriage, hoping he would turn to the western Church, and English merchants had made their way there in the sixteenth century. Trade brought to Russia the occasional foreign expert from the west. In the seventeenth century the first permanent embassies from European monarchs had been set up. But there was always a tentative and suspicious response among Russians; as in later times, efforts were made to segregate foreign residents.

Peter threw this tradition aside. He welcomed foreign experts – shipwrights, gunfounders, teachers, clerks, soldiers – and used them to set up schools to teach technical skills. He brought science to Russia, founding an Academy of Sciences; all learning had hitherto been clerical. In administration he tried to institute a bureaucracy selected on grounds of merit. Like later great reformers he did not forget symbolism. Courtiers were ordered to wear European clothes; the old long beards had to be cut back and women were told to appear in public in German fashions. Such psychological shocks were indispensable. Peter was virtually without allies in what he was trying to do and in the end what he achieved had to be driven through by autocratic power and little else. The old Duma of the boyars was abolished and a new senate of appointed men took its place. Those who resisted were ruthlessly broken, but Peter could not so easily dispose of a conservative cast of mind; moreover, he had to work with an administrative machine and communications that would seem inconceivably inadequate to any modern government.

The most striking sign of his success was Russia's new international power. More it is harder to say with confidence. The vast majority of Russians were untouched by educational reforms which only obviously affected technicians and a few among the upper class though by 1800, a fairly westernized higher and court nobility, focused at St Petersburg and largely French-speaking had appeared by then. But its members formed a cultural island in a backward nation and were often resented by the provincial gentry. The masses remained illiterate; the very few who learnt to read did so for the most part at the rudimentary level offered by the teaching of the village priest, often himself only one generation removed from illiteracy.

Social structure marked off Russia more and more. She was to be the last country in Europe to abolish serfdom. The number of serfs had begun to rise in the seventeenth century, when the tsars gratified nobles by giving them land which sometimes already had free peasants settled on it. Debt tied them to their landlords and many of them entered into bondage on the estate to work it off. New laws imposed more and more restrictions on them and legal powers to recapture and restrain serfs were steadily increased. Landlords had a special interest in using such powers after Peter made them responsible for the poll-tax and military conscription. Formally, by the end of the eighteenth century, there was little that a lord could not do to his serfs short of inflicting death on them. Many serfs ran away to Siberia (or even volunteered for the galleys). Society and administration were tied together in Russia more completely than in any western country and the landowners tended to become hereditary civil servants, carrying out tasks for the autocrat.

About half the Russian people were in bondage to their lords in 1800, with many others owing labour services to the Crown and always in danger of being granted away to nobles by it. As new lands were annexed, their populations, too, passed into serfdom. The result was a huge inertia and a great rigidifying of society. By 1800, Russia's greatest problem was already evident; what to do when both economic and political change made serfdom increasingly unjustifiable, but when its scale presented colossal problems of reform. The country faced the legendary problem of the man riding an elephant; it is all right so long as he keeps going but it is hard to get off.

The Russian population nearly doubled in the eighteenth century. About 7,000,000 of the 36,000,000 or so at which it stood at the end came with new territories acquired during it; the rest had accumulated by natural increase. This was rapid growth. Of this population, only about one in twenty-five at most were town-dwellers. Russian soil is by no means rich, and farming methods were poor. It seems unlikely that production ever kept pace with population until the twentieth century though periodic famine and epidemics were the natural restoratives of balance. Yet grain production rose: Russia began to export cereals. More land was brought under cultivation. As was to be the story for much of the imperial era, though, peasant consumption went down and taxes went up. They may well have taken 60 per cent of the peasant's crop already under Peter the Great. Techniques to increase productivity were not available and the growing rigidity of the serf system held back production. Often the typical Russian peasant had no plough, and only a shallow scratching of the soil was possible.

None the less, this agricultural base somehow sustained both the military effort which made Russia a great power, and the first phase of her industrialization. By 1800 she produced more pig-iron and exported more iron ore than any other country in the world. Peter had grasped the importance of Russia's mineral resources, initiated surveys and imported skilled miners to exploit them, and provided serf labour. By way of incentive, the death penalty was prescribed for landlords who concealed mineral deposits on their estates or tried to prevent their use. Communications were developed to allow access to these resources and slowly the centre of Russian industry shifted towards the Urals. Only a few years after Peter's death the Baltic was linked by water to the Caspian.

Manufacturing grew up around the core of extractive mineral and lumber industry which ensured Russia a favourable balance of trade for the whole century. Less than a hundred 'factories' in Peter's reign became more than 3,000 by 1800, though some of them were little more than agglomerations of artisans. After 1754, when internal customs barriers were abolished, Russia was the largest free-trade area in the world. In this, as in the granting of serf labour or of monopolies, the state continued to shape the Russ-ian economy; Russian industry did not emerge from free enterprise, but from regula-tion. This was unavoidable: industrialization ran against the grain of Russian social fact. There might be no internal customs barriers, but nor was there much internal trade except in the local market-place. Most Russians lived in 1800 much as they had done in 1700, within self-sufficient local communities whose artisans supplied the manufactures they needed and of which many hardly emerged into a money economy. Over most of the country labour service, not rent, was the basis of tenure. Foreign trade was still mainly in the hands of foreigners. The grants of serfs needed by industry shows that such stimuli for maintained growth as were effective elsewhere were lacking or insufficient in Russia.

Monarchy and the state in the eighteenth century

Between 1715 and 1740 European governments and society seemed to settle down. There was no important international tension to provoke serious internal change within states. There were no great wars after Utrecht and Nystadt (the peace which ended the Great Northern War). Nor were states struggling to contain ideological divi-sions like those of the seventeenth century. The turbulence of over-mighty noblemen and factious provincialism appeared to have aborted. Economic and social develop-ment was not so rapid as to impose great strain. Apart from Great Britain, the United Provinces, the cantons of Switzerland and the fossil republics of Italy, absolute monar-chy (or monarchy which aspired to absolutism) was the dominant state form, and it remained so for most of the century.

As the years passed, it sometimes took a style which came to be called 'enlightened despotism' – a slippery term, which neither has nor ever had a clear meaning. It reflects the supposed wishes of some rulers to carry out practical reforms and seek state power through innovations influenced by Enlightenment ideas. Such innovations, when effective, were imposed by power and, if sometimes humanitarian, were not politically liberal. They were, nonetheless, often in one sense modern in the way they under-mined traditional social and religious authority, cut across social hierarchies or legal rights. Often explicitly they aspired to concentrate lawmaking power in the state and assert its unchallenged legal sovereignty over subjects treated increasingly as aggregates of individuals rather than as members of a hierarchy of corporations.

It is almost impossible to find an example which in practice perfectly fulfils such a general description. Among Mediterranean and southern countries, for example, Spain, Portugal, Naples, Tuscany, Parma and even the Papal States all at times had min-isters and rulers who sought economic and administrative reform. Some – Portugal and Spain, for instance – turned to such reform as a way to recover lost status as great powers. Some encroached on the powers of the Church, which had hardly undergone any such challenge as Protestant Reformation had brought further north. The involve-ment of one of the smallest of them, Parma, in a quarrel with the papacy led in the end to a notable attack in all the countries whose royal families were connected to the Bour-bons on the right arm of the Counter-Reformation papacy, the Society of Jesus. In 1773 the pope was driven to dissolve the order, a great symbolic act demonstrating not only the strength of advanced anti-clerical principles among Europe's rulers, but that very varied forces might be mobilized behind them even in Catholic Europe.

For all the diffused anti-clericalism of some monarchies, though, it remains true that there was always more appearance than reality to the self-presentation of 'enlightened' rulers. The reality in Poland was a sprawling and ramshackle medieval relic of a kingdom where there was in any case no effective royal power to press home modernization. In three other major eastern states, it is true, Prussia, the Habsburg empire and Russia, the maintenance of a specious façade of up-to-date, modern ideas was at times effective, though what was always really at stake was the mobilization of power. The clue to policy was the need to find money for war (which became more frequent again after 1740), a game always more expensive than even the most lavish attempts to copy Versailles.

Prussia and the Habsburgs

In 1701 the Elector of Brandenburg, with the consent of the emperor (and over the protests of the pope), had taken the title of king; his new kingdom, Prussia, consisted of lands scattered from the Niemen to the west bank of the Rhine. The Hohenzollern family had been electors since 1415, steadily adding to their ancestral domains. Prussia had been united to Brandenburg in the sixteenth century, after the Teutonic Knights had been ousted from it. An elector was converted to Calvinism in 1613, while his subjects remained Lutheran; religious toleration was institutionalized. The 'Great Elector', Frederick William, the creator of the Prussian standing army, had been the first German ruler to check the Swedes, and had so founded the most enduring military tradition in modern European history and won his dynasty further territory. He left to his successor an army 30,000 strong and about a 500,000 subjects. Arms and diplomacy then gave his successor the kingly crown and led to participation in the Grand Alliance against Louis XIV. This imposed new and heavy costs but careful housekeeping and Prussia's remarkable tradition of cheap and efficient administration had again filled the treasury by 1740, when Frederick II came to the throne.

He was yet another eighteenth-century monarch to be remembered as 'Great'. It is difficult to decide whether Frederick was more or less of a moral monster than his brutal father (whom he hated); he was ruthless, malicious, vindictive and completely without scruple. But he was highly intelligent and much more cultivated (he played and composed for the flute) and enjoyed the conversation of clever men. He was also utterly devoted to the interests of his dynasty, the extension of its territories and the magnification of its prestige. He exploited Prussia's assets at the cost of the Habsburgs and the kingdom of Poland, heavy taxation for his own people and their exposure to foreign invasion.

An opportunity to take Silesia from the Habsburgs came in 1740. The emperor Charles VI died that year, and with him expired the direct male line of the family. He left a daughter, Maria Theresa, whose succession he had sought to assure but whose prospects were uncertain. She was to be Frederick's most unforgiving opponent until her death in 1780 and her intense personal dislike for him was fully reciprocated. The general European war 'of the Austrian Succession' which followed his seizure of Silesia left Prussia holding the province, not to be lost in later wars. But the attempt to put another emperor on the throne had been surmounted and in 1745 Maria Theresa's husband had been elected Holy Roman Emperor. Habsburg occupancy of the imperial throne was now to continue until the empire itself expired some sixty years later.

In Frederick's last year he formed a League of German Princes to thwart the attempts of Maria Theresa's son and successor, Joseph II, to acquire the kingdom of Bavaria as a recompense for the loss of Silesia. That episode matters more to European history as a whole than might be expected of a contest for a German province, however rich, or even one for the leadership of the German princes. What was by then already clearly under way was a struggle between Habsburg and Hohenzollern for the mastery of Germany; the dynastic issue remained paramount and was only to be settled in 1866. The Hohenzollerns could appeal to German patriotic sentiment against the Habsburg emperor, many of whose essential interests were non-German. In the long struggle Austria's great handicap was always that she had to be more than a purely German state. The dynasty's lands were diverse in nationality, language, institutions; the emperor was also king of Hungary, duke of Milan, archduke of Austria – to name only a few of his many titles. Moreover, like the Bourbon states, but unlike Russia or Prussia, the Habsburg dominions were overwhelmingly Roman Catholic and the power of the Church was deeply entrenched in them; they included most of those lands outside Spain and Italy where the Counter-Reformation had been most successful. The Church owned huge properties; it was protected by tradition, canon law and papal policy, and it had a monopoly of education.

Yet competition with Prussia drove forward reform in the Habsburg dominions; it was the basic explanation of the emergence of a new bureaucratic structure. When Maria Theresa came to the throne she had no sympathy to reform with 'enlightened' implications, nor did she later warm to new ideas, but her advisers were able to present a persuasive case for changes when it became clear that the Habsburg monarchy would have to struggle for supremacy in Germany with Prussia. Centralization and greater administrative uniformity were essential if the Habsburgs' variegated collection of peoples and territories was to exercise its due weight in European affairs. Once the road to fiscal and administrative reform had been entered upon, it was likely in the end to lead to conflict between Church and State. This came to a climax in the reign of her son and successor, Joseph II, a man who did not share the pieties of his mother and who was alleged to have enlightened views. His reign is especially associated with measures of secularization. Monasteries lost their property, religious appointments were interfered with, the right of sanctuary was removed and education was taken out of the hands of the clergy. Their angry opposition would have mattered less had not Joseph also antagonized the nobilities and their representative bodies to the point of open defiance in Brabant, Hungary and Bohemia. The powerful local estates and diets which opposed his policies effectively paralysed government in many other of Joseph's realms by the end of his reign. By then, though, a new preoccupation had arisen for Austria's rulers.

Russia and the eastern question

Not until 1793 did Russia acquire a common frontier with the Habsburgs. Polish and Ottoman territory for a long time separated them, and Russia had undergone something of an eclipse after Peter the Great's successes. The impetus of innovation was not maintained; there was not a strong enough bureaucracy to keep up the pressure

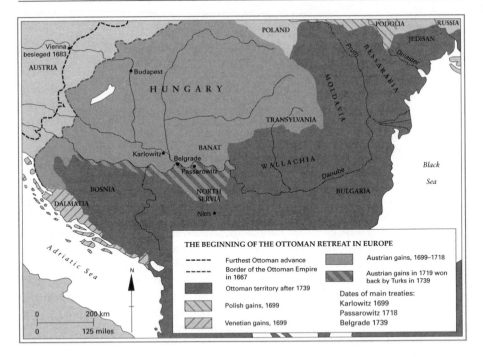

THE BEGINNING OF THE OTTOMAN RETREAT IN EUROPE

- - - - - Furthest Ottoman advance
- - - - - Border of the Ottoman Empire in 1667
Ottoman territory after 1739
Polish gains, 1699
Venetian gains, 1699

Austrian gains, 1699–1718
Austrian gains in 1719 won back by Turks in 1739

Dates of main treaties:
Karlowitz 1699
Passarowitz 1718
Belgrade 1739

once the autocrat's driving power had gone. Symbolically, the court returned to Moscow (to the delight of conservatives). Peter had not named an heir (he had his own son tortured to death) and his successors faced a renewed threat of hostility from the great noble families. Yet factional quarrels could be exploited and the replacement of Peter's grandson in 1730 by his niece, Anna, was something of a recovery for the Crown: government went back to St Petersburg. When she died, her successor and infant grand-nephew was within a year set aside (to be kept in prison until his murder more than twenty years later) in favour of Elizabeth, Peter's daughter, who reigned with the support of those irritated by foreigners until in 1762 a nephew succeeded her but was within barely six months forced to abdicate. The mistress of the overmighty subject who subsequently murdered the deposed tsar was the widow of his victim, a German princess who became Catherine II and was to be called, like Peter, 'the Great'.

The glitter of her reign masked a great deal and took in many of her contemporaries. It almost hid the bloody and dubious route by which she came to the throne (it may well be that she, and not her husband, could have been the victim if she had not struck first). In any case, the circumstances of her accession (like those of her predecessors) showed the weakening of the autocracy since Peter. The first part of her reign was a ticklish business; powerful interests sought to exploit her mistakes and for all her identification with her new country (she had renounced her Lutheran religion to become Orthodox) she was a foreigner. 'I shall perish or reign,' she once said, and reign she did, to great effect, though with less innovating force than Peter. She, too, founded schools and patronized the arts and sciences, but in search of prestige rather than practical effect. Forms were often forward-looking. Close observers were not taken in; the reality was shown by the exile of the young Radischev. Such reforming impulses as Catherine showed perceptibly weakened as the reign went on and foreign considera-

---

THE RETREAT OF OTTOMAN POWER IN EUROPE BEFORE 1800

1683	Ottoman (second) siege of Vienna fails.
1691	Ottomans lose Transylvania to Austria.
1697	Ottomans lose Hungary.
1699	Ottoman losses to Austria confirmed by Peace of Karlowitz.
1716–17	New Austro-Turkish war: Austrians conquer Belgrade.
1718	Austro-Turkish war concluded with Treaty of Passarowitz.
1739	Ottoman recovery in Treaty of Belgrade (Austria gives up Belgrade; Russia agrees not to build a Black Sea fleet).
1768–74	Russian occupation of Moldavia and Wallachia; Ottoman fleet defeated by Russians. Russian conquest of Crimea.
1774	Treaty of Kutchuk Kainarja gives Russia basis for future interference in Ottoman empire.
1787–92	Austria and Russians combine against Ottomans.
1791	Treaty of Sistova restores Belgrade to Ottomans; Austria receives part of Bosnia.
1792	Treaty of Jassy gives Russia frontier on the Dniester.

---

tions distracted her. Ever cautious, she refused to tamper with the powers and privileges of the nobility. She was the landlords' tsarina, giving them greater power over the administration of justice and taking away from their serfs the right to petition against their masters. Only twenty times in Catherine's thirty-four year reign did officials try to restrain landlords abusing their powers over their serfs. The obligation of the nobles to service was abolished in 1762 and a charter of rights was later given to them. Exempt from personal taxation, corporal punishment and billeting, they could be tried (and deprived of their rank) only by their peers, and were given the exclusive right to set up factories and mines. Under Catherine, Russia was trussed more tightly still in the corset of her social structure at a time when other countries were beginning to loosen theirs.

Yet by 1796, when Catherine died, Russia's international position was indeed impressive. There lay the most solid ground of her prestige. She said she had been well treated by Russia, to which she had come 'a poor girl with three or four dresses', but that she had paid her debts with Azov, the Crimea and the Ukraine and 7,000,000 new subjects. The international implications went beyond these (and other) territories themselves. Above all, they made dispute with Austria over the fate of the Ottoman empire more likely. For thirty years or so Russo-Turkish relations had slumbered with only occasional minor eruptions. Then, in 1774, after a successful war with the Ottomans in which a Russian fleet had appeared in the Mediterranean and Catherine's emissaries sought to stir up rebellion among the subjects of the Ottoman empire, a peace treaty was signed in an obscure Bulgarian village called Kutchuk Kainarja. It was one of the most far-reaching of the whole century in its implications. The Turks gave up their suzerainty over the Crimean Tatars (an important loss both materially, because of the military manpower of these descendants of a fragment of the Golden Horde, and morally, because this was the first Islamic people over which the Ottoman empire ceded control), and Russia seized the territory between the Bug and Dnieper, together with an indemnity, and the right to free navigation on the Black Sea and through the straits. The concession to Russia most pregnant with future opportunity was the right she won to take up with the Turks the interests of 'the church to be built in Constantinople and those who serve it'. The Russian government took this to mean it was the guarantor and protector of the rights of the Greek Christian subjects of the Sultan, and had received a blank cheque for interference in Turkish affairs. It was a beginning, not an end. In 1783 Catherine went on to annex the Crimea. Another war with the Turks carried her frontier up to the Dniester. The next obvious boundary ahead was the Pruth, which meets the Danube a 100 miles or so from the Black Sea. The possibility of Russia's installation at the mouth of the Danube now became an Austrian preoccupation.

Polish partition

Elsewhere, another part of the cushion between Habsburg and Romanov was being removed. After the eclipse of Sweden, Russia had effectively had her own way in Poland, usually through a compliant Polish king, while the factions of the magnates and their quarrels blocked the road to reform without which Polish independence would be a fiction (because, without it, effective resistance to Russia was impossible). At one moment a seeming chance of reform was checked by skilful Russian exploitation of religious divisions to produce confederations which speedily reduced Poland to civil war – a situation which paradoxically led to the Turks declaring war on Russia in 1768 in defence of Polish liberties. It was in fact the beginning of the end for Poland. Four years later, in 1772, came the first of three partitions of the country. Russia, Prussia and Austria shared out between them about one-third of Poland's territory and one-half of her inhabitants. Two more partitions followed in 1793 and 1796. Russia in the end absorbed something like 180,000 square miles of Polish territory and 6,000,000 new subjects (though in the next century it would be clear that dissident Poles were by no means an unambiguous gain). Prussia also did well, emerging from the division of booty with more Slav than German subjects. Austria took Galicia. The transformation of eastern Europe outside the Ottoman lands was complete. Independent Poland disappeared for a century and a quarter. The stage was set for the nineteenth century, with no Polish booty left to divert Austria or Russia from the Ottoman succession problem.

Catherine had deployed a strength already visible by her day. Even in the 1730s, a Russian army had been as far west as Neckar; in 1760 another entered Berlin for the first, but not the last, time. A few decades later Russian soldiers were campaigning in Switzerland; after another twenty years, they entered Paris. It was a paradox that such military power rested on so backward a social and economic structure. If this was inherent in what Peter had done, though, it did not mean that the clock could be put back.

New international structures

As the end of the eighteenth century approached, the Ottoman empire was in decline as a serious competitor for power. Prussia's emergence had announced a new age as had done Russia's. The historical role awaiting the Dutch and Swedes had been unimaginable in 1500, but their importance, too, had come and was now gone. By

1800, they were clearly in the second rank. France was still a major player in an age of national states as she had been in the days of sixteenth-century dynastic rivalry; indeed, her power was relatively greater and the peak of her dominance in western Europe was still to come. But she, too, faced a new challenger and one which had already defeated her. From the little English kingdom of 1500, cooped up in an island off the coast of Europe under an upstart dynasty, had emerged a world power. This transcended the old categories of European diplomacy quite as dramatically as had done the appearance of Russia as a great power. During 300 years, the major zones of European conflict and dispute had not only migrated from the old battlegrounds of Italy, the Rhine and the Netherlands, moving from them to central and eastern Germany, the Danube valley, Poland and Carpathia, and the Baltic, but also, the greatest change of all, across oceans. A new age had indeed opened, signalled not only by the remaking of Eastern Europe, but in the first world wars of the modern era, imperial and oceanic in their scope.

Yet in 1800 the Holy Roman Empire was still in place as it had been three centuries earlier, and so was the temporal power of the pope. A descendant of the Capetians was still king of France (though he no longer came from the branch of the family reigning three centuries before and, indeed, was in that year in exile). Most states were still confessional entities. The visible presence of history was still enormous in 1800 (and only ten years earlier it had been even greater). The 'Middle Ages' no more came to a sudden end in political and diplomatic than in other aspects of life. Many Europeans would still have held ideas about social and political organization comprehensible and appropriate 300 years earlier. More and more social facts had been fitted into an old framework as time had gone by. What has been called the 'corporate' organization of society, the grouping of men in bodies with legal privileges which protected their members and defined their status, still prevailed in much of continental Europe outside Russia until almost the end of the eighteenth century.

The weight of such facts further helps to explain the limits of what conscious modernization could do. The government of France itself, the leading nation of the Europe, whose officials and élites were clearly sympathetic to reforming policies and aspirations, confirms this. Obstacles to change had grown even stronger after the death of Louis XIV. Under his great-grandson, Louis XV, (whose reign began in 1714 with another minority), the real influence of the privileged had grown. There was an increasing tendency in the *parlements* to criticize laws which infringed special interest and historic privilege, and to hold them up by procedural devices. There was growing resistance to the idea that there rested in the Crown any right of unrestricted legislative sovereignty. Paradoxically, France was in 1789 the country most associated with the articulation and diffusion of critical and advanced ideas, yet also one of those where it seemed most difficult to put them into practice. As the century wore on, France's international role had imposed heavier and heavier burdens on her finances and the issue of reform tended to crystalize in the issue of finding new tax revenue – an exercise that was bound to bring on conflicts. Onto this rock ran most of the proposals for reform within the French monarchy, and, finally, the monarchy itself.

Wherever modernization was tried, vested historical interest and traditional social structure threw hazards in the way. In the last resort, it was unlikely that monarchical absolutism could have solved this problem anywhere. It could not question prescription and the authority of historic institutions (like nobility) too closely, for this was what monarchy, too, rested upon. Many people thought unrestricted legislative sovereignty seemed able to call too much in question. If historic rights were infringed, would not property be? Only the English ruling class seemed to accept that nothing was in principle outside the sphere of legislative competence without fearing that such a revolutionary idea was actually likely to be used against them. This is an important and necessary qualification of the central fact of three centuries' growth in the power of the state. That power easily reached limits it could not overcome. Even the ablest statesmen had to work with machinery which to any modern bureaucrat would seem woefully inadequate. Though they might mobilize resources greater than their predecessors they had to do so without any significant technical innovations. Communications in 1800 depended just as they had done in 1500 on wind and muscle; the 'telegraph' which came into use in the 1790s was a help, but it was only a semaphore system, worked by pulling ropes, and dependent on clear weather. Though better victualled and organized, armies could move only slightly faster than three centuries earlier. If their weapons had been improved in 300 years, they had not been improved out of recognition. No police force such as exists today existed in any country; only in 1798 was the first income tax imposed (in England). A change in the power of the state was coming about because of changes in ideas and because of the development to greater efficiency of well-known institutions, rather than because of technical advance. In no major state could it even be assumed that all its subjects would understand the language of government, while in none before 1789, except perhaps Great Britain and the United Provinces, were rulers more concerned to protect their subjects from foreigners than themselves from their subjects.

CHAPTER FIVE The world's new shape

A new picture of the world

Mankind may well have been more culturally diverse in 1500 than ever before. But criteria in these matters tend to be subjective and when we talk of 'civilization', 'cultures', 'traditions' it is often hard to agree about what we intend such terms to mean. What can be said is that at the beginning of the modern era the world was made up of a number of distinct zones, within each of which can be discerned powerful, often self-conscious and largely independent cultural traditions which did much to shape the lives of people within their ambits. Chinese civilization dominated one such zone, stretching beyond its original home to take in much of south-east Asia, Korea and even Japan. Another was the world of Islam, for all the cultural and ethnic diversity within it. The differences of western and eastern Christendom have already been emphasized. To a large degree, all these zones lived with no significant interplay between them.

300 years later the patterns set by these zones were still very evident, even if a few changes had by then weakened the invisible walls separating them. Some civilizations contained particular empires which were showing signs of decay; such was the case in the Ottoman Islamic world. The native civilizations of the Americas had collapsed, leaving only vestigial influence behind. Another great change just beginning to be apparent was the technological lead already shown by European civilization over all others. The Chinese had been printing with movable characters and made use of gunpowder before Europeans, but now the technological baton had passed, for the last time before technology became a globally shared phenomenon and a standardizing force worldwide (though no-one could know that).

Such changes imply (and require) transformations in thinking. Some which may have made such changes more likely had been going on in Europe for a long time before 1500, perhaps for four centuries or so. Yet (it must constantly be repeated) much was unchanged still in that year – not least assumptions of religious faith and unity still shared by millions of Europeans. Symbolically, the fact that the Bible, their sacred text, was, thanks to printing, available more widely than before showed as never before that Europe was still Christian. That weighty fact might itself be thought to stand in the way of taking new views of the world, rather than promoting them. But circumstances change the meaning and effects of facts. Since 1453, after all, it had begun to be possible to feel that Europe might perhaps be the only really Christian community in the world (too little was known about Muscovy to take it seriously). It was easier than ever to see it as the centre of the world.

This was part of the background to the phenomenon of the 'Age of Discovery'. It should perhaps now be qualified as the 'European Age of Discovery', for in the fifteenth century and after, few non-Europeans discovered much that was hitherto unknown to them. This is itself a somewhat surprising fact. The Chinese had long had magnetic compasses and had built big ocean-going junks. Arab dhows moved incessantly to and fro across the breadth of the Indian ocean while far away, Pacific islanders made mysterious long voyages in open canoes with great navigational skill. Yet it was Europeans who first united the globe through a succession of enterprises on land and sea only ending with the Arctic and Antarctic expeditions of the twentieth century. Why the Arabs or Chinese did not reach the Americas first cannot be explored here; why Europeans did has to be explained by an accumulation of considerations; it is safest not to give any decisive pre-eminence to a single one of them.

The acquisition of new geographical knowledge of the world outside Europe which was reachable by sea continued to unroll, with exhilarating and disturbing effect. The letter which gave news of what Columbus had found was printed nine times in 1493 alone. The significance of what had happened had quickly been registered by calling what had been found across the Atlantic in the western hemisphere a 'New World'. Discovery encouraged further discoverers and the publication of further exciting accounts of what had been found. A European first saw the Pacific ocean – from the west coast of Mexico – in 1513, six years before Magellan set out to enter it round Cape Horn. Searches for north-west and north-east passages to Asia were under way by mid-century, as well as the penetration of the land-masses of the Americas by explorers and sometimes settlers. Europeans already showed a new confidence and were doing so somewhat in the style of their crusading predecessors. To understand why and how such psychological change came about, it is necessary to look not only inside but outside Europe at the lands Europeans were now discovering. They, too, were the product of long histories, but histories very different from those of their discoverers.

Africa

The first European impact on cultures beyond Europe's own shores was probably in Africa. In classical antiquity, Greeks as traders, soldiers and travellers, Romans as conquerors and governors, and, later, Vandals as migrants and raiders, and many others ventured there, but rarely got far beyond Africa's northern coasts and the Maghreb. Behind this limited region stretched desert, mountain and mystery and, except where Africans were touched after the seventh century AD by the coming of Islam and literacy, barbarism. But the Arab conquests also extinguished much of what had been Christian Africa. An odd survival was provided by Coptic missionaries from Egypt who in the fourth century had converted the Ethiopians, thus eventually creating the only indigenous literate non-Islamic nation on the continent.

The dynamic of non-Islamic Africa's history was to be provided from the fifteenth century onwards increasingly by Europeans, their ambitions, rivalries and discoveries, except on the eastern coasts, where the Arabs' impact was earlier and more lasting. Most of the continent's modern history was to be one of response to what came from the outside – iron-working and new crops from the Near East, Asia, Indonesia and the Americas; steam engines and medicine from nineteenth-century Europe. Such introductions all made it possible to grapple more effectively with African nature. Before their arrival, most of Africa seems almost inert under the huge determinisms of topography, climate and disease, though this is something of an illusion. European interest in the continent, whose extent was then still unknown, was originally excited in medieval times by gold. It flowed into the Mediterranean economy from the caravan routes of the Sahara, but Europeans were not able to reach its source in the fabled trading kingdoms of Ghana and Mali, of which only Arab reports are available. The same was true of East Africa until the nineteenth century, though Arabs had begun a 1,000 years earlier to settle there, calling the region the land of the Zanz (from which was later to come the name of Zanzibar); Arab reports said that its peoples prized iron above gold. It is possible, too, that these peoples had some kind of trading relations with Asia even before Arab times; with whom it is not possible to say, but it may have been with Indonesians like those who colonized Madagascar. The Africans owed them the implantation of new crops from Asia, cloves and bananas among them.

Though most of Africa in 1500 was still untouched by either, Arab and Christian outsiders had by then created on each side of the continent a trade in African slaves. For centuries Arabs had collected columns of black men, women and children from compliant rulers and marched them as slaves either north to the Nile valley and the markets of the Near East, or to the coast, to the dhows which would take them to Arabia, the Gulf, India and even China. The European trade was much more recently established, but one informed estimate says that by 1500 something like 150,000 black slaves had already been taken from Africa by the Portuguese. Others were soon to join them in this lucrative and burgeoning trade, about which better information is available for estimates of its effects than for its Arab equivalent. Together with the interior's inaccessibility to Europeans, slaving settled the distribution of Europe's first footholds in west Africa. The stations established in the first Portuguese voyages south of Cape Verde began the process of acquisition and by 1800 the British, French, Spanish, Dutch and Danes all had their African forts and factories. At the Cape of Good Hope, the first Dutch settlers had also installed themselves in its welcoming climate as Africa's first true European colonists, raising crops and livestock in a viable community. Once past the Cape, the Portuguese, few in number though they were, controlled what European access there was to East Africa from a long, thin line of scattered forts and harbours, running as far north as Aden, at the mouth of the Red Sea, and providing a route to the trade of the Persian Gulf and India.

The Americas

No human connexion between the Americas and any other continent can be demonstrated between the time when the first 'Americans' crossed the Bering Straits and the arrival of the Vikings. The next visitors from overseas were the followers of Columbus. For much longer than Africa, and much more completely, the Americas lived apart, cut off not only from Europe, but from the rest of the world. A few pre-agricultural indigenous peoples survive there even today. While 'Indians' (as Europeans came to call them) practised agriculture in eastern North America before European arrival, others further west then still lived in hunting-and-gathering communities. They would still be following most of their traditional ways in 1800, having by then added to their technology the horses, metal and guns brought by the Europeans. In the extreme west, the great Northern American human museum could even produce coastal peoples who fished or collected their subsistence on the seashore in ways fixed since time immemorial, while, far to the north, Eskimos lived self-sufficiently in an all but intolerable environment.

While the aboriginal cultures of North America continued to grapple with environmental challenge much as in the Stone Age, human culture developed much further to the south of the Rio Grande. A succession of major civilizations appeared in central and south America, linked by a common dependence on maize cultivation and often sharing a pantheon of similar nature gods, though in other ways highly individual. The first Europeans to arrive on the mainland eventually met three major styles of civilization, all with cities, temple-centres, complex beliefs and at least the beginnings of literate communication.

The Mayan civilization of Yucatán, Guatemala and Honduras, not least because of its extraordinary setting, was the most remarkable. Virtually all the great Mayan sites lie in tropical rain-forest, where survival demands big efforts, and human society is under constant attack from animals, insects, climate and disease. Yet the Maya not only maintained themselves for many centuries with only primitive agricultural techniques (they lacked ploughs and metal tools and after burning and clearing land could use it only for a couple of seasons before moving on to another site), but raised stone buildings comparable to those of ancient Egypt. These formed part of great ceremonial complexes, combinations of temples, pyramids, tombs and ritual courts, usually, it seems, permanently inhabited only by priests and their attendants. Religious practice appears to have consisted of the performance of regular acts of intercession and worship in a cycle calculated from a calendar derived from impressively accurate astronomical observation. Through their calendar, enough of Mayan thinking can be grasped to make it evident that this people's religious leaders had rich and complex ideas of time.

Maya civilization passed its peak some centuries before the Europeans arrived and it had gone under as a political entity in about 1460, when its capital was destroyed. The Spanish were its grave-diggers rather than its executioners. They were, in any case, much more amazed and impressed by what they had found further north in the valley of Mexico, the civilization of the Aztecs (now sometimes called the Mexica, though the older name will be used here). The Aztecs had entered the valley in about 1350, settling at the edge of Lake Texcoco and establishing their chief site at a village called Tenochtitlan. In less than two centuries they came to rule the whole of central Mexico. Tenochtitlan grew to become a great city built on a group of islands connected to the lake shores by causeways, (one of them five miles long and able to take eight horsemen abreast, said one of the excited descriptions of it by the Spanish). Its magnificence was said by one observer to exceed that of Rome or Constantinople. It probably contained about a 100,000 inhabitants at the beginning of the sixteenth century and was maintained by tribute from subject peoples. By comparison with European cities, Tenochtitlan was indeed a place of marvels, its wealth abundant and impressive, dominated by temples and huge pyramids. The Aztecs were pictographically literate, skilled in agriculture and the handling of gold, but knew nothing of the plough, iron-working or the wheel. Their central religious rituals – which greatly shocked the Spaniards – included human sacrifice; no less than 20,000 victims were killed at the dedication of the great pyramid of Tenochtitlan. Such holocausts re-enacted a cosmic drama which was the heart of Aztec mythology; it taught that the gods had been obliged to sacrifice themselves to give the sun the blood it needed as food.

When the Spanish arrived the Aztec empire was still expanding. Though not all its subject peoples were completely subdued, Aztec rule already ran from coast to coast under a semi-divine but elected ruler, chosen from a royal family. Its government made heavy demands for labour and military service, but provided an annual subsistence. The central role of sacrifice in the religion of Aztec society, though, demanded a continual flow of victims, usually supplied by prisoners of war. Punitive raids were made on subject tribes at the slightest excuse to secure sacrificial victims. This meant that the empire could not win their loyalty; they were likely to welcome the Aztec collapse when it came. Religion also affected the capacity to respond to the threat from Europeans in other ways, notably in the Aztecs' desire to take prisoners for sacrifice rather than to kill their enemies in battle, and in a belief that one day the great god Quetzalcoatl, white-skinned and bearded, would return from the east (to which he had gone after instructing his people in the arts).

The most distant of the American civilizations encountered by the Europeans lay far to the south, in the Peruvian Andes. It greatly impressed the Spanish and others in Europe who were struck not only by accounts of Peru's immense and obvious wealth in precious metals, but by descriptions of what some said was a uniquely just, efficient and highly complex social system. Some Europeans found this very attractive, in so far as they understood it. It required an almost total subordination of the individual to the collective, and to those who ruled in its name, the Incas, who by the end of the fifteenth century presided over a realm extending from Ecuador to central Chile, their conquest of the coastal areas being the most recent. This was an astonishing feat, given the natural obstacles provided by the Andes. The Inca polity was held together by about 10,000 miles of roads (often bridle-paths at best) passable in all weathers by chains of runners who bore messages either orally or recorded in *quipu*, a code of knots in coloured cords. With this device elaborate records were kept and made possible a despotism based on the control of labour. People were kept where they were needed; removal or marriage outside the local community were not allowed. All produce was state property; in this way agriculturists fed herdsmen and craftsmen and received textiles in exchange (the llama was the all-purpose beast of Andean culture, providing wool as well as transport, milk and meat). There was no commerce. Mining for precious metals and copper resulted in an adornment of Cuzco which amazed the Spaniards when they came to it. Like the Aztecs, the Incas organized and exploited cultural achievements which they found already to hand. They aimed to integrate rather than obliterate and they tolerated the cults of conquered peoples. Their god was the sun but the absence of literary record makes it hard to penetrate the mind of Inca civilization. It obviously shared with the Mexican a capacity to produce beautiful precious objects, and a lack of either a psychological or technological preparation for effective resistance.

The beginnings of European imperialism

'Imperialism' can have many meanings. At its widest and most polemical it has been applied to almost any kind of continuing domination exercised by one group of human beings over another, whether consciously or not. More simply, it can refer to physical possession, the acquisition of territory in foreign lands whether by annexation, or by settlement (or both). It has also meant privileges and immunities: it was in 1536 that the first 'capitulations' were made between the Ottoman government and French merchants to whom they assured not only trading privileges in certain posts and immunity from local judicial power, but the holding of property outside Ottoman control.

With the age of discoveries and new opportunities for overseas conquest, above all for nations with easy access to the Atlantic, the modern age of imperialism as acquisition had begun, and on a quite new scale. By then, landward expansion was virtually at an end in the German east except at the expense of other states, the Reconquest of the Iberian peninsula was drawing to a close, and any dreams of reviving the old crusader states were rapidly fading, given the Ottoman advance in the Mediterranean. So the Portuguese and Spanish and to a lesser extent, the English and French, launched the first great wave of European expansion and European settlement overseas, in which they were later joined by the Dutch. By 1600, the Iberians had achieved most. The Portuguese empire was not one of settlement, but in the east a chain of harbours and forts guarding a trading hegemony stretching from China and Japan to Brazil. The Spanish meanwhile had built up in the Americas the most extensive agglomeration of territory, at least notionally, ever to be acquired by one kingdom (Castile) down to this time. The French and British could by 1600 point only to a few stabs at exploration and settlement in North America (the creation of a French viceroyalty of Canada, Newfoundland and Labrador in the 1540s was mere window-dressing) and a quickly-established and successful tradition of piracy and free-booting at the expense of the Spanish in the western hemisphere. Their major American settlements, like those of the Dutch, were to be made later.

Spanish settlement overseas had begun in the fourteenth century in the Canaries. The Spanish who later went to the Americas – those whom other Spanish called the *conquistadores* (the 'conquerors') – were like their predecessors men of the Middle Ages. They made their appearance in the 1490s first as settlers in the Caribbean islands, but were soon making tentative stabs at the mainland in the area of what was later called Venezuela. In 1513, some of them crossed the isthmus of Panama, settled down, built huts and sowed crops, a sign that they were there to stay. The first mainland Spanish jurisdiction was established in that region. There were by then already many settlers in the Caribbean islands and the first African slaves had been brought there to provide labour. The Americas rapidly grew more and more attractive to poor, land-hungry Spanish squires and soldiers of fortune as more became known about them. Emigration to them began to rise.

The *conquistadores* were hard men. One of them was a half-heroic, half-piratical Spanish officer called Hernan Cortés. In 1518 he left Cuba for Mexico, broke free of his superiors' control by burning his boats, founded the town of Vera Cruz and then led his men inland to the high plateau which was the heart of the country. Within a few months he had conquered the Aztec empire. A few years later, in 1531, Pizarro, another Spaniard (and one even more ruthless than Cortés), marched through the Andes to the Inca capital and destroyed the Inca regime. Thus Mexico and Peru both passed to the Spanish crown, to be added as viceroyalties to the territories already acquired in what is now Venezuela and Central America. The first European overseas territorial empire was born.

Legends about fabulous wealth drew Spaniards like a magnet to the 'Indies'. Yet the motives of those who came were mixed. Undoubtedly, they were more excited by the possibilities of carrying off the treasures of their inhabitants than by any other motive. For a long time men were tirelessly to explore South America, looking for the legendary city the Spanish called 'El Dorado' (the golden place) because of its fabulous wealth. The *conquistadores* and their followers did more than this, though; they established themselves and their civilization, building cities, missions, roads and founding universities. Many of them had from the start sought land for estates to secure their fortunes, or slaves to work the ranches and farms they had built up on the islands. This did not make them gentle to the Indians. Though a few of them might wish to bring the Gospel to the natives, the Christianity of the settlers was the militant Christianity of the Reconquest; it was not a creed respectful of cultural difference. Furthermore, many of the Spanish were sincerely horrified at such practices as the Aztec human sacrifices (however hard it may be for us to understand why men easy with the idea of burning Christian heretics should have been so offended).

The effects on the native populations of the arrival of the Spanish were in fact almost uniformly disastrous. This was not entirely the responsibility of the intruders (unless it is argued that they should not have gone to America at all). The diseases they brought with them (smallpox was the worst) had catastrophic demographic effect, first on the islands and then on the mainland. It was possibly reinforced by the psychological shock of the Spaniards' power and seeming irresistibility. The population collapsed. It has been calculated that the population of Mexico fell by three-quarters in the sixteenth century; that of some Caribbean islands was wiped out altogether. There was soon insufficient labour for the settlers. More than ever, they ruthlessly exploited what there was. Churchmen fought against their cruelties, but could not do much to protect the Indians. It was a usual arrangement to allot to a Spanish settler the labour services of a native community in return for government and protection. As disease and overwork took their toll, royal officials and settlers alike strove to prevent labourers from leaving the plantations where they worked and the system was tightened up even more. Virtually, it was slavery. Over large areas of South America even today the word familiarly used for a peasant is *peón*, the Spanish word for a pawn in a game of chess, the lowest-valued piece on the board.

Populations in the Spanish dominions slowly rebuilt themselves over the next two centuries or so by natural increase and immigration from Europe. The outcome was a number of Ibero-American societies in which upper and middle classes of mainly European blood ruled over predominantly Indian populations. Neither the Spanish nor Portuguese much minded inter-marriage but colonial society respected European blood; the more you had the more likely you were to be fairly well off and powerful. People of predominantly European blood born in the Americas (*creoles* was the Spanish name for them) were the rulers and landlords of the Indian survivors of the old civilizations, almost all of whose spectacular past achievements had disappeared. Many Indians came to speak a kind of Spanish; most in the settled areas became Christian, at least in name. The story of European domination over the natives was much the same in Portuguese Brazil though there had been almost nothing there in the way of civilization to be displaced as in Mexico or Peru. But another special fact shaped that country; so many African slaves were brought to work on its sugar plantations that the cultural heritage of black Africa was soon as important in Brazil as the Indian, and it remains more conspicuous today. As in the Spanish colonies, so in Brazil Christianity was a conspicuous way of implanting European civilization; most of Brazil's oldest buildings are churches. As for other European cultural imports, forms of government and laws, traditions and institutions which went back deep into the European past and had no logical connexion with American conditions at all were taken for granted by Spanish and Portuguese alike. Without much thought, they imposed them. This meant that a system of states on European lines, with institutions and laws like those of Europe would survive in South America when the empires had passed away.

The Ibero-American empires were territorially vast but thinly populated. In 1600 they may have had only about 10,000,000 people between them. In theory at least, by 1700 the Spanish claimed an area running from the River Plate in the south to the Colorado in the north. It included almost the whole length of the Pacific coast from southern Chile to northern California (where San Francisco is only one name among many commemorating Spanish sovereignty), much other territory north of the Rio Grande, as well as Florida. Even in 1800 these northern territories were still very sparsely inhabited, the Spanish presence in them being mainly a matter of only a few mission stations and forts (though some of them were to be the sites of important cities in later times). The rest of 'New Spain' (the northern viceroyalty) consisted of Mexico, which was more thickly settled and the lands of the isthmus. Peru and some of the larger Caribbean islands were by 1800 also centres of fairly large populations, with major cities and many universities. The 'Indies' were governed in theory as sister kingdoms of Castile and Aragon by viceroys, but in practice they had to be run with a fair degree of independence. Yet they were part of a true world-wide empire, linked by way of Acapulco and Panama to the Spanish Philippine islands and Spain itself, and the first such to come into being.

The North American colonies

European empire in North America was never to be as impressive as further south. By 1700, nevertheless, the eastern seaboard of the continent was studded with English settlements. The colony of Virginia (so named in honour of the unmarried Queen Elizabeth I) had been the site of the first unsuccessful attempts in the 1580s to 'plant' Englishmen in America. Further attempts followed, but for a long time North America ran a poor second to the Caribbean in economic attractiveness. In the 1620s English settlers in the West Indies were far more prosperous than their countrymen on the mainland. The seventeenth century nonetheless brought settlement to North America on a scale sufficient in the end for success. By 1700 there were twelve English colonies inhabited by about 400,000 people mainly of British stock. The first settlement to survive had been at Jamestown, in the modern state of Virginia and set up in 1607 (just a year before a French explorer, Champlain, built a small fort at Quebec, and only a few before Dutch settlers appeared on what is now the site of New York City).

Much of North America could be cultivated on European lines. The English, unlike the Spanish and Portuguese, transplanted whole communities – men, women and children – who set to work as farmers. Like the colonies of the ancient Greek cities, such colonies were usually soon substantially independent of the mother country. It was soon discovered that tobacco-raising provided a trading product for export; in the early years of Virginia, tobacco was used instead of money for accounting debts. It was the first of several 'staple' products – cotton, rice, indigo were others – which gave colonists the wherewithal to buy things they wanted from the mother-country. Others came from fishing and its associated activities. Canada never had a product of equal importance; the fur trade could not support a comparable population, and in 1661 there were only about 3,000 French people in Canada.

Individual English colonies developed from the outset on distinctive lines, shaped by settler intention, climate and geography, and the prospects they afforded for staple products. 'New England' (as the northernmost group was soon called) from the start attracted men and women with strong and special religious views, some reflecting Calvinist protestantism; they usually tended to very rigorous ideas about behaviour and disliked ceremony in religious worship (though they were sedulous in inflicting their own forms of address and behaviour in a ritualistic way). They were puritans. Though many of them still thought of themselves as members of the established Church of England when they first came to America, they tended to break away from it when they had 3,000 miles of Atlantic between them and home. They were hardy and enterprising and, with time, prospered. But they were not, usually, a very jolly or agreeable lot (some of those in Massachusetts became very irritated when an immigrant less strait-laced than they set up a maypole). On the whole, New England became known as a place where colonists tended to break most decisively with old ways, while those who had more liking for the customs of the mother country went farther south, to Virginia and the Carolinas.

The puritans who landed in 1620 from the ship *Mayflower* and founded a colony at Plymouth, Massachusetts, were to become legendary as the 'Pilgrim Fathers'. Their story later became a foundation myth of a nation. Their compact of self-government, though, did not mean they were democrats. In Massachusetts government tended to be shared by a narrow circle of the well-to-do and the Calvinist clergy; it was in other colonies – Connecticut, for example, or Rhode Island – that more democratic forms of government appeared. What they all shared was a practical independence. Local autonomy was soon a reality in the Anglo-Saxon colonies, whatever the constitutional arrangements under which they had first been set up. Almost everywhere, the realities of travel in the age of the sailing-ship and horse, and the conditions of the New World, tended to erode the power of English government. The colonies nearly always had some form of representative institution which reflected English parliamentary tradition and practice while France, Portugal and Spain ran systems on more authoritarian lines. No European imperial power, though, ever envisaged independence for their colonists, nor any need to safeguard colonial interests against those of the mother country.

None of the North American colonists encountered and had to deal with complicated or rich native societies. Many North American 'Indians' in the seventeenth century were only just entering the agricultural phase of their existence: their technology was at best Neolithic. They could not impress the new arrivals with high civilization, though they could give valuable practical advice and help to them (the early Massachusetts colonists were actually saved from starvation by Indians giving them food). Unhappily, that did not mean Europeans usually treated them any better. There had soon begun a long-drawn-out conflict which was to end in the virtual extinction of some Indian peoples; the survivors moved further west as time passed. This was one of the costs of the opportunities which English America more and more obviously offered to thousands of poor Europeans. Drawn by such prospects, Germans, Huguenots and Swiss began to arrive at the end of the seventeenth century; the Dutch had been there earlier. Anglo-Saxon North America began to be a 'melting-pot' of different stocks long before 1800.

Europe encounters East Asia

The drive to acquire wealth, the conviction of spiritual supremacy and the innate rectitude of their cause, and the same pressures of rivalry, all operated east of the Cape of Good Hope and west of Acapulco just as they did in the Americas or on the slaving coasts of Africa. But there were important differences in East Asia. It had already been known to Europe for centuries as a source of much-prized commodities, high in value and small in bulk (the outstanding examples were spices), which could be bought or bartered for. Secondly, much of it with which Europeans were in occasional contact was ruled by empires with respectable military resources (including firearms and cannon) and long traditions of settled government. Some were clearly great powers. It was the Chinese empire which had finally stemmed the Arab armies in the east. Thirdly, they could often demonstrate cultural and artistic achievement on a scale psychologically intimidating to Europeans; China went on being an object of European adulation until well into the eighteenth century. Finally, there were a great many Asians and very few Europeans; Europeans tended to succumb to diseases for which they were not prepared, and settlement was rarely an option. The outcome, by and large, was the establishment, in the wake of the Portuguese, of trading rather than colonial empires; scattered depots, usually ports, valuable for the conduct or protection of commerce, and of concessions and treaty or customary rights and privileges were enough to enable European merchants to do business. This for a long time left the mass of Asians unaware of a European presence. Over most of Asia it did not exist; where it did it was peripheral.

Europe and China

This was especially true in relation to Asia's longest-lived world power, China. European contact with it was for a long time limited and intermittent. Commercial connexion in the days of Imperial Rome had been conducted through middlemen and had little cultural impact either way. A few medieval venturers (of whom the most celebrated – and as a reporter of facts possibly the most unreliable – was Marco Polo) who made their way to China by land did little to enrich this fundamentally distant relationship. Only in the sixteenth century, when a permanent European presence in the Far East was first established, did the continuous interplay of Europe and China begin.

China was then ruled by the Ming dynasty. By then the possibility (if it ever existed) of reviving the glories of the Sung emperors, when the Middle Kingdom experienced a surge of economic advance such that scholars now puzzle why Europe and not China led the world into modernity, had ceased to be plausible. There were even some signs of decline. The Ming lost control of important peripheral zones of the empire (one was Malacca, in Malaya, seized by the Portuguese in 1511) and the Mongols raided and burnt the suburbs of Peking. But dynasties had dwindled, gone and come again many times in China without much affecting its enduring place in the world.

In 1516, nearly thirty years before the Mongols' raid, the first ship ever to voyage directly from Europe to China, a Portuguese vessel, sailed up the Pearl river to drop anchor at Canton. This was the beginning of a century or so in which the Portuguese monopolized European commercial contact with China. In the following year their first ambassador arrived. He was not officially received, but the Chinese were used to foreign merchants (Arabs and Persians, for example) and were not hostile. A not unpromising start was then squandered by the piracy, aggressiveness and Christian contempt of the Portuguese for a 'heathen' people. Within a few years we hear of naval engagements and the execution of Portuguese as marauders. They were expelled from Canton as early as 1522. They transferred their activities in 1542 to Ningpo but were again turned out for bad behaviour. In 1557 they were finally allowed to settle down-river in the Canton estuary at Macao under careful restrictions and, soon, behind a barrier wall.

Thus began the history of the first and most enduring European station on Chinese territory. Another dimension was then added to the Sino-European relationship when the first Christian missionaries arrived at Canton in 1575. At the end of the century one of them was permitted to travel to Peking to present his religion. Court and Confucian traditions of tolerance for speculation gave opportunities which were successfully exploited and Jesuits became very influential at the Ming court. In the early seventeenth century Chinese officials began to feel alarmed and they were ordered back to Macao. By then, though, besides the mechanical toys and clocks which the missionaries added to the imperial collections, their scientific and cosmographical learning had begun to interest Chinese intellectuals. The correction of the Chinese calendar, which one Jesuit carried out, was of great importance, for the authenticity of the emperor's sacrifices depended on accurate dating. From the Jesuits the Chinese learnt also to cast heavy cannon, another useful art; some Jesuits served, surprisingly to modern eyes, as artillery instructors. In due course, others produced the first modern map of China.

The last Ming emperor was China's only Christian emperor, baptized under the name Constantine in 1648, and he died in the hands of the Manchu, a people from the north who put their own dynasty, the Ch'ing, on the imperial throne in 1644. Though probably 25,000,000 people perished during the Manchu conquest, recovery was rapid. China's revived power was spectacularly apparent under the emperor K'ang-hsi, who reigned from 1662 to 1722, roughly contemporaneously with Louis XIV of France. The emperor K'ang-hsi, like Louis, was hard-working, scrutinizing with a close eye the details of business; both monarchs, too, refreshed themselves by hunting and other pleasures (though the harem of the eastern ruler was an official one), and both expanded their territories and cultivated the artistic splendour of their monarchy.

A perceptive observer might have found something revealing in the disgrace which in the end overtook the Jesuits (who had returned to favour at K'ang-hsi's court). For more than a century these able men judiciously and discreetly sought to ingratiate themselves with their hosts. To begin with they had not even spoken of religion, but had contented themselves with studying the language. They had worn Chinese dress, which, we are told, created a very good impression. Success followed. Yet the effectiveness of their mission was suddenly paralysed from home; their acceptance of Chinese rites and beliefs and their sinicizing of Christian teaching prompted papal condemnation in 1715 and 1742 of improper flexibility in 'accommodating' Christian teaching to Chinese custom. This was striking: evidently Europeans, unlike all other conquerors of China, would not easily give way to its pull, Europe was not going to prove culturally malleable. In China, Europeans would not adapt to that country as earlier barbarian cultures had adapted. The Manchu Ch'ing confronted an alien culture more challenging than any in the past to present itself. There was a message for Asia and, indeed, the world in this.

Yet when Lord Macartney arrived from England in 1793 to ask for equality of diplomatic representation and free trade, Chinese confidence was intact. The first western advances and encroachments had been successfully rebuffed or contained. In the Chinese world view, all nations paid tribute to the emperor, the possessor of the Mandate of Heaven. The representative of George III could only take back to his master a pat on the back for his 'tribute mission' and encouragement to continue to show devotion and loyalty. The Chinese imperial government was little interested in what it thought of as a remote island, 'cut off from the world by intervening wastes of sea'. Cultural and moral superiority was then as unquestioned a part of the mental world of the educated Chinese as it would be of that of countless European and American missionaries and philanthropists of the next century who unconsciously patronized the people they came to serve. Nearly three centuries of trade with China had failed to reveal any manufactured goods from Europe which the Chinese wanted. European trade with China rested on American silver and the products of other Asian countries. China's rulers thought she had all the materials and skills for the highest civilization and that nothing was to be gained by going beyond the limited trade tolerated at Canton, where in 1800 there were only a thousand or so Europeans.

Japan

The Chinese cultural sphere included the inhabitants of Japan, whose society was, nonetheless, highly distinctive. The first Europeans drawn there were Portuguese, probably in Chinese ships in 1543. Others followed in the next few years in their own ships. Japan was at the time much disturbed by civil conflict, virtually without a central government to undertake the regulation of intercourse with foreigners, and could produce magnates highly interested in competing for foreign trade. Nagasaki, then a little village, was opened to the newcomers in 1570 by one of them who was a zealous Christian. He had already built a church there; in 1549 the first Christian missionary had arrived, the Jesuit Francis Xavier, who was to be canonized in 1622.

Among other things brought by the Portuguese (who virtually monopolized early European trade with Japan) were new food crops – sweet potatoes, maize, sugar cane – and muskets, which the Japanese soon learnt to make. These weapons played an important part in assuring that the baronial wars of Japan came to an end, as did those of medieval Europe, with the emergence of a preponderant power and the start of a period of Japanese history known as the 'great peace', and a new system of military government, the 'shogunate' dominated by one of the leading clans, in the name of the emperor. Soon, it began to see Europeans as a danger, and to seek isolation from all external influences which might provoke change. Christianity had at first been tolerated by the Japanese and even welcomed as something which might tempt traders from outside. In the early seventeenth century the proportion of Japanese Christians in the population was higher than it has ever been since – there were perhaps over 500,000 of them. Christianity's subversive potential was feared by Japan's rulers and a savage persecution began which cost the lives of thousands of Japanese martyrs. It also brought trade with Europe almost to an end. The English left and the Spanish were excluded in the 1620s. After the Portuguese had undergone a similar expulsion they rashly sent an embassy in 1640 to argue the toss; almost all of its members were killed. Japanese had by then been forbidden to go abroad, or to return if they were already there, and the building of large ships was banned. Only the Dutch, who promised not to proselytize and were willing to trample, symbolically, on the cross, kept up Japan's henceforth tiny contact with Europe from a little island in Nagasaki harbour.

Europeans in India

As in China, so in India the Portuguese long made the running for Europeans. Within a few years of Vasco de Gama's arrival at Calicut, his countrymen were installed as traders, and often behaving as pirates. They were soon established at Bombay and on the coast of Gujarat and moved round to found new posts in the Bay of Bengal in the second half of the century. They attracted the occasional hostility of good Moslems because they brought with them pictures and images of Christ, his mother and the saints, which smacked of idolatry. Protestants, when they arrived, were to prove less irritating to local religious feeling.

The first British East India Company was founded on the last day of the sixteenth century. Three years later its first emissary arrived at the court of the Moghul emperor Akbar at Agra (by then, Elizabeth I, who had given the merchants their charter of incorporation, was dead). The historical destinies of England and India were long to entwine with enormous effect on them both and for the world, but at that moment no hint of that could have been sensed. To the English, trade was at that moment less interesting in India than in other parts of Asia. As for Indian consciousness, Akbar's empire was one of the largest in the world, his court one of the most sumptuous. He and his successors ruled over a glorious and spectacular civilization, while Queen Elizabeth's kingdom, barely a great power, even in European terms, was crippled by debt and contained fewer people than modern Calcutta. It could not have seemed important enough for Akbar to try to scotch the serpent of imperialism in the egg.

The Ottomans were at the time using naval power formidably against the Mediterranean Europeans, but the Moghuls never built a fleet. By the second half of the seventeenth century, Indian coastal shipping and even the pilgrim trade to Mecca were already endangered by the Europeans. On land, Europeans had by then been allowed to establish their toeholds and bridgeheads and to add to them. The English won their first west-coast trading concession early in the seventeenth century after beating a Portuguese squadron. Then, in 1639, with the permission of the local ruler, they founded the first settlement of British India at Madras on the coast of the Bay of Bengal. To it they added before the end of the century further stations at Bombay and Calcutta. Their ships maintained the paramountcy in trade won from the Portuguese.

There were also Dutch and Danish settlements in India and a French East India Company founded in 1664 soon established its own, too. A century of conflict lay ahead, mainly between the French and English, but also between Indian rulers entangled by the Europeans, who quickly learnt to play politics among the uncertainties aroused by the decline of Moghul power. By 1700 the English were well aware that much was at stake. An era had begun in which India was increasingly caught up in a history not of her own making. Even humble day-to-day changes embodied this. The Portuguese had introduced chilli, potatoes and tobacco from America well before 1600; maize, pawpaws and pineapples were to follow. The story of isolated or near-isolated Indian civilizations and rulers was over and the sub-continent was potentially available to yet another set of conquerors who waited still in the wings for their cue, as yet ready to play hardly more than bit parts. Unlike early conquerors, Europeans would stay for a long time, and would leave a deeper imprint on it than most of their predecessors.

Trade, empire, diplomacy and war

By 1800 it was accepted that quarrels about trade and territory on the other side of the world were proper concerns of European statesmen. They had become as important in diplomatic calculations as dynastic connexion. It had not been like that three centuries earlier, except in a very few instances (the Venetian and Genoese republics had always been special cases). But a new force had even then been coming into play. Discovery and conquest had already left their first marks on diplomatic negotiations. Without consulting anyone else, the rulers of Portugal and Castile, the first two powers interested in oceanic enterprise, had quickly agreed to divide between them any new lands to be found in any part of the world and had received the pope's permission to annex any not belonging to a Christian prince. After the treaty of Tordesillas of 1494 another, in 1529, drew a line east of the Moluccas which allocated everything on its Pacific side to the Spanish (who soon set themselves up in the Philippines), and Africa, the Indian Ocean and the Spice Islands to the Portuguese.

Such arrangements opened three centuries of growing competition for trade and empire. The discoveries had opened a global battleground to traders and soldiers. Just as Catalans, Venetians, Genoans and others had quarrelled and intrigued over east Mediterranean commerce in the Middle Ages, Spaniards, Portuguese, Dutchmen, English and French now set out in ships, and, as opportunity offered, built forts in far-away places, set up markers proclaiming their rulers' sovereignty, bribed, negotiated with, or fought local potentates in order to assure the trade their possessions gave them, and keep it from interlopers. As one French minister of Louis XIV put it, trade was in the later seventeenth century already a perpetual cause of conflict between European states.

Because few Europeans settled in Asia governments quarrelled less in the Far East (and on the African routes to the East) over the ports and stations – 'factories' was the usual English word – where native traders could meet Europeans and business could be done, and over access to markets. The local rulers had to be respected, and so European enterprise in Asia advanced in its early phases as much by diplomacy and negotiation as by conquest. In the sixteenth century the Portuguese, whose king called himself by the splendid title of 'Lord of the Conquest, Navigation and Commerce of Ethiopia, Arabia, Persia and India', had gone on from India to trade in the Spice Islands and carry goods between Asian countries – Persian carpets to India, cloves from the Moluccas to China, Indian cloth to Siam. They won dominance over their Arab rivals from fortified bases at the entrance to the Red Sea and the Persian Gulf. Much of this was simple robbery and piracy; the Portuguese long treated any non-Christian ship as lawful prize. At the end of the sixteenth century, though, they were beginning to be (sometimes bloodily) elbowed aside by the Dutch who set up an 'East India Company' in Amsterdam in 1602 with the aim of replacing the Portuguese control of the spice trade to Europe – a rich prize. With ruthless skill, the Dutch pushed the Portuguese aside, and then fought bitterly to keep the English out of trade in the Spice Islands. In that, too, they were largely successful. By 1700 they had established a general supremacy over what is now Indonesia while English interest was mainly in India.

What the Dutch, would do for predominance in trade was made clear not only in the East Indies, but in the Caribbean and Brazil, where they engaged great fleets against the Spanish-Portuguese defence of the world's chief producer of sugar, and by their reputed desecration of the cross in order to obtain entry to the trade of Japan. Commerce even brought them into conflict with their old allies, the Protestant English; in 1652 the republican Commonwealth found itself fighting the first of three Anglo-Dutch wars over its decision to restrict imports to England to goods travelling in English ships or those of the country producing the goods. This deliberate attempt to encourage English shipping struck at the heart of Dutch prosperity, its European carrying trade (in particular, that in Baltic goods). The Commonwealth had a good navy and won, but a second round began in 1665, after the English seized New Amsterdam (later to be renamed New York). The Dutch, with the French and Danes as allies, now had the best of it at sea and were able to win at the peace an easing of the English restrictions on imports though the English kept New Amsterdam in exchange for an offshoot at Surinam of the English colony of Barbados. These details were not only important but symptomatic. The Treaty of Breda of 1667 was the first multilateral European peace settlement to say as much about overseas concerns as about European. In the great settlement of 1648 not a word had appeared about non-European matters. At Breda France won recognition of her rights in the uninhabited and uninviting but strategically important territory of Acadia. England got some more islands in return to add to the Commonwealth's acquisition of Jamaica.

It would be tedious to trace the similar diplomatic transactions of the next few decades. A brief third Anglo-Dutch war had virtually no important consequence and did not really belong to a new historical drama now opening, a long competition of England and France worldwide. The War of the Spanish Succession was the first true world war of the modern era, as much about the fate of the Spanish empire as about French power in Europe. Overseas matters loomed larger and larger in British foreign policy after this and European considerations mattered relatively less, in spite of the establishment of a German dynasty on the throne in 1714. British policy remained remarkably consistent, always swinging back to the goals of promoting, sustaining and extending British commerce, whether by seeking to maintain a general peace, by diplomatic pressure or by fighting to maintain privileges or strategical advantage. Not until 1739, though, did two European powers go to war for wholly non-European reasons. In that year, the British government began hostilities with Spain over, in essence, the Spanish abuse of right of search in the Caribbean – or, as the Spanish might have put it, over the steps properly taken to secure the Spanish empire against abuse of the trading privileges granted in 1713, when the British had exacted a limited right to trade in slaves with the Spanish colonies. They had quickly pressed it beyond its intended limits. The outcome in 1739 was the 'War of Jenkins' Ear' – the organ produced in pickle by its owner in the House of Commons, whose sensitive patriotism was inflamed and outraged to hear of his alleged mutilation by a Spanish coastguard. This war was soon caught up with the War of the Austrian Succession, and thereby became an Anglo-French struggle, with a European focus, too.

The peace of 1748 did not much change things territorially, nor did it end fighting in North America, where the French appeared to be trying to cut off the British settlements for ever from the American west by building a chain of forts down the Mississippi valley to settlements at New Orleans planted at the very end of the previous century. The chance of ending the long duel came only in the Seven Years' War. France's commitment to her ally Austria in Europe weakened her ability to fight overseas. Once British resources were allocated accordingly, sweeping victories in North America and India were followed by others in the Caribbean (some, as ever, at the expense of Spain, from which the British also seized the Philippines). When peace was made at Paris in 1763, it did not in fact cripple France and Spain as many Englishmen had wanted. But it almost eliminated French competition in North America, gave it a hard blow in India and completed the piecemeal building of the first British empire. In that year, the whole seaboard of eastern North America and the Gulf Coast as far west as the Mississippi delta was British. Offshore, the Bahamas were the northern outpost of an island chain that ran down through the lesser Antilles to Tobago, and all but enclosed the Caribbean. Within it, Jamaica, Honduras and the Belize coast were British. In Africa there were only a few British posts on the Gold Coast but they protected the lucrative African slave trade. A takeover of the direct government of Bengal from the Moghuls was about to open eighty years of British territorial expansion in India.

Under Louis XIV, any discernment that extra-European interests might matter more than European in diplomacy had barely existed. The world, though was then already undergoing transformation. The days when the fate of a French Huguenot settlement in Florida or the flouting of the vague Spanish claims which was implicit in the Roanoke voyages went unnoticed by European diplomats were already over. The Peace of Paris is a good marker of a new world order. It had replaced that dominated by Spain and Portugal, the only great colonial powers of the sixteenth century; both had long passed their zenith by 1763. It registered the ascendancy of Great Britain in the rivalry with France overseas which had preoccupied her for nearly three-quarters of a century. The duel was not over, and Frenchmen could still be hopeful that they would recover lost ground. Great Britain, none the less, was to be the next great imperial power.

Spain, Portugal and the United Provinces all still held important colonial territories and had left marks on the world map which would endure. With France and Great Britain they had been differentiated by their oceanic history from the landlocked states of central Europe or those of the Mediterranean so important in earlier centuries. Most other states had been slower to recognize how important issues outside Europe might be. Of even these five, Spain had fought enough (first in Italy, then against the Ottomans, and finally for European supremacy in the Thirty Years' War) to squander the treasure of the Indies in the process. In their long duel with the British, the French, too, had always been more liable than their rivals to distraction and the diversion of their resources to continental ends.

Global economic change

One way in which this happened was through changing markets. In 1500, hundreds of more or less self-sufficient economies had existed round the world, some almost side-by-side. Trade sometimes went on between them, but over very long distances commercial ties were few and often intermittent. The Americas and Africa were still almost unknown to Europe; Australasia was entirely so. The change in the next three centuries was immense. A worldwide network of exchange came into being to which even Japan and central Africa were tenuously attached, the former through the tiny Dutch community at Nagasaki, and the second, mysteriously inaccessible and unknown though most of it was, through slaving and the Arab traders.

The first signs of this huge change had been the diversion of Europe's trickle of land-based trade with Asia to the sea-routes established (and long dominated) by the Portuguese, and the start of a flow of precious metals from Spanish America to Europe, and, thence often to Asia, where its silver financed Europe's purchases. This contribution to Asian trade may well have been the main economic importance of the American bullion flow which reached its height early in the seventeenth century. These two great dramatic and obvious developments, though, were in the end eclipsed by the general growth of trade which had followed them. By the mid-seventeenth century, slaves for the Caribbean and Brazil were being taken from west Africa across the Atlantic in ships which then sailed back from the Americas with colonial produce for which growing markets existed in Europe. First Antwerp, then Amsterdam, then London surpassed the old Mediterranean trading cities as centres of intercontinental exchange, largely because of the huge growth of the re-export trade in colonial goods carried by Dutch and English ships and the appetite for salt fish from the Atlantic and North Sea fisheries which would keep safely in Mediterranean climates. Around such central flows of trade there proliferated branches and sub-branches which led to further specializations and ramifications. Shipbuilding, textiles and, later, financial services such as insurance all prospered, sharing in the consequences of the increase in sheer volume of transactions. Eastern trade in the second half of the eighteenth century made up a quarter of the whole of Dutch external commerce and during that century the number of ships sent out by the East India Company from London tripled. These ships, moreover, were of improved design, carried more and were worked by fewer men than those of earlier times.

The material consequences for individual Europeans were slow to appear but were in the end to be very great. European diet remains one of the most varied in the world; for a few Europeans this began to be true in the early modern age, and it was by 1800 true for many more. The coming of tobacco, coffee, tea and sugar alone brought about a revolution in taste, habit and housekeeping. The potato was to change the history of whole countries by sustaining much larger populations. Scores of drugs were added to the European pharmacopoeia. For clothes, cotton became much commoner and silk a little so. The material effects on non-Europeans cannot be the subject of these pages, except in so far as they, in turn, had reciprocal consequences for Europe. It is worth remark, nonetheless, that almost nowhere in the world in the first phase of European expansion can non-Europeans be shown to have benefited. Far from it, they often suffered terribly. This appalling truth is not, though, always something for which blame attaches to the Europeans. In an age with none but the most elementary knowledge of infectious disease, the devastating impact of diseases carried by Europeans could not have been anticipated (and some new diseases – syphilis, for example – travelled home with them, too).

Subjection and domination

The often ruthless exploitation of indigenous people on the other hand, is a different matter. There was a *leitmotiv* of subjection and domination running through well-nigh every instance of Europe's early impact on the rest of the world and the legacies are still detectable today. Colonial societies varied and not all presented the same extremes of brutality and horror. Different environments and different European traditions produced gradations of oppression and exploitation. But all were tainted. The roots of the wealth and civilization of the burghers of the seventeenth-century United Provinces lay, at least in the spice islands and Indonesia, in bloody ground. Long before settlers in North America went west of the Alleghenies, the brief good relations of the first English Virginians with the American Indians had soured; extermination and eviction had begun. In spite of efforts by churchmen and officials to protect them, the natives of Spanish America had for the most part been reduced to peonage. Even churchmen had made determined efforts (for the highest motives) to obliterate their culture. In South Africa the fate of the Hottentot, and in Australia that of the Aborigine, would repeat the lesson that European culture was likely to devastate those whom it touched, unless they had the protection of old and advanced civilizations such as those of India or China and even in those countries, much damage would be done. But it was the settled colonies that showed most clearly the pattern of domination.

The prosperity of many of them in the Americas long depended on the African slave trade, a major fact in the story of Europe's expansion and American civilization. Outlets in the New World settler colonies determined its direction, for the slavers found their most reliable customers in the Caribbean islands and on the American mainland. The Portuguese were soon elbowed out of these markets (and turned to Brazil instead), by the Dutch and Elizabeth I's 'sea-dogs'. In the seventeenth century the Dutch lead had been overtaken by French and English traders who between them sent nine or ten millions of black slaves to the western hemisphere, four-fifths of them after 1700; in the eighteenth century, some 6,000,000 of them crossed the Atlantic. Ports like Bristol and Nantes built their new commercial wealth on slaving. As new lands were opened when black slave labour made it possible to work them, greater production of primary products – notably sugar, and cotton – brought, in turn, great changes in European demand, manufacturing and trading patterns. Ethnically, too, we still live with the results.

What has disappeared and can now never be measured is the human misery involved, not merely in physical hardship (a black who survived the horrible conditions of the voyage might live only a few years on a West Indian plantation) but in the psychological and emotional tragedies of this huge migration. Historians still debate whether slavery 'civilized' blacks in the Americas by bringing them into contact, willy-nilly, with higher cultures, or whether it retarded them in quasi-infantile dependence. The question seems as insoluble as the degree of cruelty involved is incalculable; though the fetters and the whipping-block seem decisive evidence, they were commonplaces of European life, too. Further, a priori, self-interest should have prompted the planters to care for their investment. That it did not always do so, slave rebellions showed. Such rebellions though, were infrequent, a fact which also bears reflexion. It is unlikely that the debate will end.

The African slave trade for a long time awoke few misgivings such as those which had been shown by Spanish churchmen in defence of the American Indians, and the arguments with which some Christians resisted any restriction of the traffic still retain a certain gruesome fascination. European slaves though, were still exploited in the fifteenth century in Mediterranean countries. Venice had a sizeable import of servant girls from the slave-markets of the Balkans and Black Sea ports. Feelings of responsibility and guilt about slavery began to emerge widely only in the eighteenth century and mainly in France and England. One curious expression of it came when the British acquisition of another dependency in 1787, Sierra Leone, was followed by its adoption by philanthropists as a refuge for African slaves freed in England. Helped sometimes by a favourable political and economic conjuncture, the current of public feeling educated by humanitarian thought was to outlaw within another half-century the slave trade and, in the European world, slavery. But that is part of a different story. In the age of the unfolding of European world power, slavery was a huge social and economic fact, and only one expression of the way advanced societies could increasingly dominate weaker ones by force.

Changing the world

Most of the outcome of the creation of a worldwide system of exchange looks at first sight much more benevolent than those of the slave trade. Yet even the food plants which the Portuguese carried from America to Africa in the sixteenth century, so enriching African diet, may also have provoked population growth, and so led to social disruption and upheaval. Plants taken to the Americas founded new industries which made settlement possible there. But that in the end created greater demand for slaves; coffee and sugar were grown with slave labour. Though arable farming by British settlers further north did not require slaves, it intensified the demand for land and added to the pressures driving the colonists into the ancestral hunting-grounds of the American Indians, whom they ruthlessly pushed out of the way. What is more objectively demonstrable is that the lives of future generations still unborn were shaped benevolently by such transplants. Wheat was to make the western hemisphere the granary of European cities. Wine-growing was begun by the Spanish in the Madeiras and South America as early as the sixteenth century (and, happily, continues). When bananas were established in Jamaica, though, or coffee in Java and tea in Ceylon, so was the groundwork of much future politics. All such changes, moreover, would be complicated by variations in demand, as industrialization increased Europe's appetite for old staples such as cotton (in 1760 England imported 2,500,000 pounds of raw cotton – in 1837 the figure was 360,000,000) and sometimes identified new possibilities; the successful transplantation of rubber in the nineteenth century from South America to Malaya, was fraught with great strategic and political significance for the future, though no-one knew it.

It was indeed a continuing and very visible characteristic of the European economic reconstruction of the world that it was so unplanned and casual. It was the amalgam of many individual decisions by comparatively few men. They usually foresaw or could foresee only a tiny part of the consequences of their decisions. Ecology illustrates this; almost the entire menagerie of European domesticated animals was settled in the Americas by 1800, and cattle and horses were to make South America a great meat exporter, as well as providing the muscle-power for development on a new scale. Europeans brought human blood-stock, too. The British in America and the Dutch did not for a long time encourage the mixing of races. Yet in Latin America, Goa and Portuguese Africa the effects of inter-breeding were profound.

Perception and feelings

At some point in these centuries, perhaps about a half way through them, growing knowledge of the non-European world and its products, some of it, perhaps only unconsciously registered, began to change the European mind. Such interplay is very hard to assess. Indicators are often rough and ready – for instance, the very large and growing numbers of books published about discoveries and voyages in both East and West. Oriental studies, one outcome, may be said to have been founded as a science in the seventeenth century, though Europeans only begin to show much knowledge of the anthropologies of other people towards its close. By the early eighteenth century, though, there were signs of an intellectual impact at a deep level. Idyllic descriptions of savages who lived moral lives without the help of Christianity provoked reflexion; an English philosopher, John Locke, used the evidence of other continents to show that men did not share any God-given innate ideas. Reports from China furnished examples for speculation on the relativity of social institutions. Less obviously, the penetration of Chinese literature (much aided by the studies of the Jesuits) revealed a chronology whose length made nonsense of traditional calculations of the date of the Flood described in the Bible as the second beginning of all men. As its pro- ducts became more easily available, China provoked in eighteenth century Europe a craze for oriental styles in furniture, porcelain and dress. As an artistic and intellectual influence this has remained more obvious than the deeper perspective given to the observation of European life by an awareness of different civilizations with different standards elsewhere. The growing knowledge of New and Old worlds accumulated in these centuries was a contribution to Europeans' critical self-examination.

While, though, comparison may have had some disquieting aspects (revealing, for instance, that Europe had, perhaps, less to be proud of in its attitude to other religions than China), exploits such as those of the *conquistadores* continued to feed Europeans' notions of their superiority. The now much-deplored notion of 'Eurocentricity' had still not been identified in 1800, though it was then at least theoretically possible. Europeans had in the previous 300 years come to take a new view of their place in the world. They had added to the latent sense of superiority whose first roots lay in the consciousness of possessing a unique religious revelation a new confidence in and admiration for their civilization. The assessment of Gibbon, informed by his reflexions on antiquity, was not contested; the 'partial events' of such matters as swings in the balance of power, the thought, 'cannot essentially injure our general state of happiness, the system of acts, and laws, and manners which so advantageously distinguish, above the rest of mankind, the Europeans and their colonies'[1]. As the nineteenth century began, experience, they thought, demonstrated that civilization's superiority more clearly than ever. They had acquired a more or less complete knowledge of the shape of the world (which Mercator had taught them to see in a certain way, with Europe at its centre). Continents and countries were increasingly defined in terms of their geographical relations with Europe; common parlance already referred to a 'western hemisphere' and an 'Orient' known to be mysterious. In the eighteenth

---

[1]   *Decline and Fall* (ed. Bury), IV, p. 163. He went on to remark that 'the savage nations of the globe are the common enemies of civilized society…'

century alone, the hitherto unknown continent of Australasia had been added to the world maps, the existence of the Bering Straits had been demonstrated, and Cook and Bougainville had explored another new New World, this time in the Pacific, visiting Tahiti, Samoa, eastern Australia, New Zealand and Hawaii; Cook had even penetrated the Antarctic. The settlement of New South Wales had begun in 1788 with a cargo of a few hundred convicts, followed a few years later by the arrival of the first sheep – the guarantee, as it was to turn out, of the economic future of a new nation of Europeans overseas.

The spread of Christianity

In 1797 the first Christian missionaries landed in Tahiti. A process of unprecedented success in disseminating Christianity from its European heartland had by   then been under way for 250 years. Whatever other blessings or horrors their civilization might bring, there were many Europeans in those centuries (and would be many more later) who believed that the salvation of men's souls was the most precious gift they had to offer the rest of humanity. Impulses to plant the Cross as well as the flags of European rulers in heathen lands, and to reap harvests of souls as well as of sugar or cotton, were there from the start. Paul III, the pope who summoned the Council of Trent, had urged in defence of the American Indians that they were 'not only capable of understanding the Catholic faith, but according to our information, they desire exceedingly to receive it'. His information came from, among others, the friars and monks who had at once enthusiastically followed the Spanish discoverers and settlers to the New World, preaching to and baptizing the native peoples, casting down idols, as well as setting up the first European universities overseas, usually to train priests for further evangelization (the first was founded in San Domingo in 1517). In the next 100 years Roman Catholicism won more converts and spread more widely than ever before in its history. The Jesuit missionaries had begun to work in Goa in 1542 and spread from there through south-east Asia, and on to Japan and Peking. It was also important – as even secular-minded critics of colonialism came to recognize – that in the Americas Spanish churchmen kept alive such notions of trusteeship towards subject peoples as were available to early imperialism, and provided the Indians with such protection as they could from rapacious governments and settlers.

The Protestant churches had lagged behind Counter-Reformation Rome in their concern over native peoples in settlement colonies, as they did in missionary work (the Dutch hardly did any and the English American colonists not only did not seek to convert, but actually enslaved some of their Indian neighbours, only the Quakers of Pennsylvania being laudable exceptions). The great Anglo-Saxon overseas missionary societies did not enter the field until the end of the seventeenth century, and other Protestants were not swift to follow this lead. Furthermore, even in the gift of the Gospel to the world, whenever it at last came, there lay a tragic ambiguity. It, too, was a specifically European export. It had enormously corrosive potential, challenging and undermining as it did traditional structures and ideas, threatening social authority, legal and moral institutions, family and marriage patterns. Missionaries, too, often in spite of themselves, were instruments of the process of domination and subjugation which runs through the story of Europe's intercourse with the rest of the globe.

The beginnings of a European world

Such qualifications of what were, not only in scale but in quality, great European achievements must never be lost to sight. It is not a matter of seeking out historic responsibility or guilt (both implausible ideas and hard to attribute after a few years have gone by) but of recognizing that one of history's useful and cleansing roles is to make each generation remember the immense fallibility of the schemes of mice and men. Another very different sort of qualification has also to be borne in mind at the end of this brief survey of 300 years of startling achievement. Vastly though they had changed the world, and decisively and irreversibly as they had in so many ways advanced its integration and cohesion, what Europeans had done round the globe by 1800 would be far outstripped in the next century. The scale of change was still much smaller than we may be tempted to think if we look only at the general account. Europeans traded and worked all round the world, but for all Europe's crowded Atlantic harbours, the oceanic sea-lanes were often very empty. Even in 1789, the East India Company sent only twenty-one ships to China; the Dutch were permitted only two a year to Japan. Central Asia at that time was still only approachable by the land routes known to Chinghis Khan and, for that matter, with the help of much the same transport as he had. On good days, when the weather was clear, the semaphore arms of the stations which have left the name 'Telegraph Hill' scattered over south England could indeed pass their messages from Plymouth or Portsmouth to the Admiralty in London more swiftly than ever before. On a misty day, though, and over most of Europe, despatch riders using post-horses travelled with their letters no faster than those of Julius Caesar had done. Much of the Russian empire – to take a different yardstick – could hardly be said to be under effective government when Catherine the Great died. Australasia might by then have been discovered and its settlement begun, but the heart of Africa was still impenetrably protected by disease and climate. The age of a true global history was yet to come. Europeans had made a new world by 1800, but it was still incomplete.

BOOK FOUR

The
European age

With Europe's modernization, world history begins to be an intelligible theme. It began first to be visible in economic interconnexions, and then as an emerging political and diplomatic system. In our own day, it has moved into its final phase, as cultural and intellectual integration. No-one planned this, or the way it came about. The process was always untidy, inchoate, and often unconscious. Nor did it happen at the same pace or in the same ways in different parts of the globe. The blood feuds still going on in the Balkans in 1900 contrasted strikingly with life in contemporary Paris or Berlin (and there were men and women in other parts of the world who were still then living in the Stone Age). Nonetheless, European communications, technology and imperial government had already brought about a sharing of many practices and ideas, and were already sapping the strength and influence of old and deeply-entrenched civilized traditions in other continents. In material life, in the spread of institutions and ideologies, the tide had begun to run towards the construction of a world more and more caught up in the same currents and processes. That this was overwhelmingly the outcome of what was done and happened in Europe justifies the description of the nineteenth century as the heart of the 'European age'.

Yet for all the growing power and prestige which Europeans deployed in the world, only from the outside did their society and civilization look coherent and uniform. While they were using their new mastery, consciously or not, to make the world one and impose what they sometimes agreed to be 'European' standards, they continued to fight and quarrel with one another at home, and to emphasize what they saw as profound differences between themselves. These differences were enhanced by rapid but unevenly shared change in Europe itself. Europe, it might be said, was politicized, secularized, individualized and industrialized for the first time. Men and women saw in their own lifetimes greater changes than their ancestors had experienced over several generations. Many of these changes were to go on, too, faster and faster, right through the twentieth century.

CHAPTER ONE New politics

An age of revolution

Much of the nineteenth-century history of Europe is (like that of the eighteenth century) the history of wars and conflict. One reason for this – though far from the only one – was a spread and acceptance of certain new political ideas and institutions throughout the continent. The sovereign state had by 1900 reached its apogee in the esteem of Europeans. Its supremacy as a political institution was virtually unopposed in principle except by anarchists and ultramontanes. Other master-ideas of politics which had by then won unprecedented acceptance as the proper basis for the legitimizing of power and regulating its exercise were those of nationhood and nationalism. Yet another such idea, though less completely successful and still questioned and bitterly resisted in some countries in 1900, was the principle of democracy – the belief in the need, desirability or sometimes simple inevitability of a greater measure of popular participation in public life. Finally, millions of Europeans at the end of the century adhered to a creed whose name had not been invented in 1800: socialism. However unwillingly, even Europe's most reactionary rulers had to accept by 1914 that such ideas were to be taken into account, welcome or not.

In the eighteenth century another political word, 'revolution', had come to have a new meaning. Traditionally it had long been used to mean only a change in the composition of government and not necessarily a violent one. Men could speak of a 'revolution' at a particular court when one minister replaced another. After 1789 this was no longer so. In the nineteenth century the word was often on the lips of politicians and agitated the minds of many. Men came to envisage a new sort of revolution, a true rupture with the past, characterized by violence actual or implied, by limitless possibilities for fundamental change, social, political and economic. What is more, this new way of looking at revolution transcended national boundaries; like the phenomenon it described, it had something universal and general about it. Men who disagreed very much about its desirability could none the less agree that a new sort of revolution was fundamental to the politics of the age.

Not all the political changes in the stormy era of the nineteenth century ought to be lumped together under the rubric of 'revolution' conceived in such terms as these. But we can properly speak of an 'age of revolution'. One reason to do so is that there were within a century or so many more political upheavals than hitherto which were indeed revolutions in a radical and violent sense, even though many of them failed and others brought results far different from those people had been led to expect. In the second place, if we give the term a little more elasticity, and allow it to cover examples of accelerated and fundamental change which go beyond the replacement of one set of rulers by another, then there were many non-violent political transformations in these years which were distinctly revolutionary in their effects.

The first overseas European nation

The first political revolution of a new era of European history occurred outside Europe and well before the eighteenth century was over. This was the dissolution of the first British empire. In 1763, British imperial power in North America had been at its height. Canada having been taken from the French, the old fear of a Mississippi valley cordon of French forts keeping the thirteen colonies out of the American West had blown away. This at once stimulated prophecy that the removal of the French threat might weaken, not strengthen, the British grasp on North America. Of the colonists (who were more numerous than the populations of several sovereign states of Europe), many were not of English descent or native English-speakers, and felt no lively loyalty to the House of Hanover. Their economic interests were not those of the imperial power. The huge distances which separated the colonies from London, too, made it unlikely that a firm grip could be taken of them by British government.

The peace of 1763 rapidly precipitated trouble; new problems at once sprang into view. How was the newly-accessible American West to be organized? What were the colonists to be allowed to do there? How were the new subjects of the Crown in Canada to be treated? An Indian rebellion against pressure from would-be western settlers made action necessary; the imperial government therefore proclaimed the area west of the Alleghenies closed to them. This at once enraged many of its colonial subjects. Further irritation followed as British officials negotiated treaties with the Indians and organized a garrisoned frontier to protect them and the colonists from one another. In the next ten years a hitherto dormant potential for colonial independence matured and came to a head. The pace was set throughout by British initiatives. Grumbles turned first into resistance and then into rebellion. Colonial politicians used provocative British measures to radicalize their followers by telling them that the substantial practical liberty they were used to was in danger. No doubt it made matters worse that good intentions abounded at Westminster; Great Britain enjoyed a succession of ministers in these years whose excellent schemes for reform in colonial matters did much to destroy arrangements previously found workable.

All English ministers were clear about the principle that Americans ought to pay their share of taxes needed to uphold their defence and the common good of the empire, even if they differed about policy. Attempts to impose duties on sugar imported to the colonies or to make revenue stamps obligatory on certain legal documents, though, raised another important question of principle, for these were, as both English politicians and American taxpayers saw, unilateral acts of legislation by the imperial parliament. Hitherto, the usual way of raising revenue in the colonies had been by haggling in their own local assemblies. What was now brought into debate was the legislative sovereignty of the parliament of the United Kingdom over the colonies.

THE AMERICAN REVOLUTION

1763	Peace of Paris ends Seven Years' ('King George's') War.
1764–7	Various revenue measures increase agitation in the colonies.
1773	'Boston Tea Party' symbolises resistance to taxation by Great Britain.
1775	Skirmish at Lexington and first bloodshed of the War of American Independence.
1776	Declaration of Independence signed at Philadelphia.
1777	British defeat at Saratoga. Articles of Confederation propose structure for United States of America to the individual colonies.
1778	France signs treaty of alliance with USA.
1779	Spain enters war against British.
1781	British surrender at Yorktown.
1783	Peace at Paris between Great Britain and USA and recognition of American independence.

When riots, non-importation agreements and angry protest followed, these early measures were withdrawn. London took a different tack, imposing customs duties on the import of certain commodities. These were not internal taxes and the imperial government had always regulated trade, so they seemed more promising. But by now Americans were being told by radical politicians that no taxation at all should be levied by a legislature in which they were not represented. Parliament's authority, not that of the Crown, was under attack. There were more riots and boycotts (though that name had not yet been invented) and, in 1770, in one of those resonating scuffles which stud the history and mythology of decolonization, the 'Boston Massacre', (possibly five) rioters were shot dead by British soldiers.

Once more, the British government retreated. Unfortunately, the issue by now transcended taxation, as the British government saw. As George III put it a little later: 'We must either master them, or totally leave them to themselves'. The issue was focused in one place, though it manifested itself throughout the colonies. By 1773, after the destruction of a cargo of tea by radicals (the 'Boston Tea Party'), the crucial question for the British government was: could Massachusetts be governed?

George III, his ministers and the majority of the House of Commons were agreed that there were to be no more retreats. Coercive legislation was passed to bring Boston to heel. It did not help at this juncture that a humane and sensible measure providing for the future of Canada, the Quebec Act of 1774, stirred up wide feeling in America. Some disliked the protected position it gave to Roman Catholicism (it had been hoped to leave French Canadians as undisturbed as possible by their change of rulers), while others saw its extension of Canadian boundaries south to the Ohio as another obstacle to expansion in the west. In September the same year there met a Continental Congress of delegates from the colonies at Philadelphia. It severed commercial relations with the United Kingdom and demanded the repeal of much existing legislation, including the Quebec Act.

By this time armed conflict was probably unavoidable. The radical colonial politicians had brought out into the open the practical sense of independence already felt by many Americans; the speed with which opinion had evolved seems, in retrospect, astonishing.[1] But it was inconceivable that any eighteenth-century imperial government could have grasped this. The British government was in fact remarkably reluctant to use force until disorder and the intimidation of law-abiding colonials had already gone very far, though it had made it clear that it would not willingly bend on the principles of sovereignty. Circumstances in the end brought on the crisis. In April 1775 a detachment of British soldiers sent to Lexington to seize arms gathered by the colonists of Massachusetts was shot at and there followed the first action of the American revolution. It still took a year more for the colonists' leaders to be convinced that only complete independence from Great Britain would do. When they were, the result was the Declaration of Independence of July 1776, and the debate was transferred to the battlefield.

The British lost the war which followed because of geography, American generalship, the entry of the French to the war to win a return match for the defeat of 1763, and that of the Spanish to tip the balance of naval power. The British were also handicapped because they dared not fight the kind of war which might win military victory by terrorizing the American population and so encouraging those who wished to remain under the British flag to cut off the supplies and freedom of movement which the rebel army enjoyed. Their overriding aim had to be to keep open the way to a conciliatory peace with colonists willing again to accept British rule. In these circumstances, the Bourbon coalition was fatal. The military decision came at last in 1781, when a British army found itself trapped at Yorktown between the Americans on land and a French squadron at sea. Only 7,000 or so men were involved, but their surrender was the worst humiliation yet undergone by British arms and the end of an era of imperial rule. Peace negotiations soon began and two years later, at Paris, a treaty was signed in which Great Britain recognized the independence of the United States of America, whose territory the British negotiators had already agreed should run to the Mississippi (a crucial decision in the shaping of a new nation).

It will be helpful to retain a focus on a far-away continent a moment longer, for all the dwindling in Europe's direct concern with it which followed the Revolution. The appearance of a new state of great potential resources in the western hemisphere was by any standard a revolutionary change. If it was at first seen as something less than this by Europeans, that was because the weaknesses of the new nation were at the time more apparent than its potential. Indeed, it was far from clear that it was a nation at all; the colonies were weak and divided and many expected them to fall to quarrelling or disunion. Their one great and inestimable advantage was their remoteness. They could work out their problems virtually untroubled by foreign intervention, a blessing crucial to much that was to follow. They did so in a half-dozen critical years during which a handful of American politicians took decisions which would shape much of the future history of the world, including, of course, that of Europe.

The United States and European opinion

The discipline of war had led the Americans to agree 'Articles of Confederation' in which appeared the name of the United States of America. Peace brought a

---

[1] One historian remarks that 'What seemed to be only common sense to Thomas Paine, and to most Americans in 1776, would have struck them as uncommon madness a dozen years later' (R. Middlekauff, *The Glorious Cause*, New York, 1982, p. 3).

growing sense that more than these arrangements was needed. The eventual outcome was a constitution which came into effect in 1789. In April that year George Washington, the former commander of the American forces in the war against the British, took the oath of office as the first president of the new republic, the first independent, ex-colonial nation of European stock beyond the seas. Its republicanism was an obvious institutional rupture with Europe. Republics in eighteenth-century Europe were few and by no means flourishing. The history of the old Italian republican city-states was unpromising and less edifying than that of Athens and Rome, with which classically educated Europeans were familiar, yet the ancients, too, were as famous for their faction as for the legendarily admirable morals of some of them. Republicans were few in Europe – although some of them were vociferous – and their nostrums, it was usually thought, were likely to be successful, if at all, only in small states. Observers were not, therefore, sanguine about the prospects for the United States. For this very reason, the new nation's later successes were to have huge effect on received opinion about republican institutions. Soon, Europeans advocating political change would look to republican America for inspiration. So would other rebellious colonial subjects of Europeans.

For all that, the new constitution's deepest roots lay in European (specifically, British) political experience. Besides the absorption of Common Law principles by the jurisprudence of the new state (to be locally refreshed in one part of the country a few years later by French law), the actual arrangement of government followed English constitutional theory in putting a monarch (albeit one elected and uncrowned) at the head of its executive. The founding fathers took the best constitution they knew, purified it and added to it modifications appropriate to American political and social circumstance. They did not emulate the more fashionable alternative principle of government at that time available in contemporary Europe, monarchical absolutism, even in its 'enlightened' form.

One way in which the United States diverged consciously from the British constitutional model was in adherence to the principle of federalism. The former colonies had no wish to set up a new central government to bully them as they believed the government of King George had done. The federal structure provided an answer to the problem of diversity – *e pluribus unum*, as the seal of the new republic proclaimed. As the nineteenth century wore on, federalism would appeal to European liberals. They saw it as a key device for reconciling unity with freedom; for a century and a half British governments found it a great standby in their handling of colonial problems and one new European nation – Germany – would adopt it as a constitutional framework.

The other exemplary principle which was to be influential in Europe was embodied in the first words of the constitution: 'We the People'. They seem to have been included almost casually. Political actuality in some of the American states of 1789 was by no means democratic, and the Fathers of the republic included several who feared and even detested democracy. Nonetheless, the principle of popular sovereignty was there from the start. It was a fundamental departure from British constitutional practice and most European thinking; the adoption of the democratic theory that all governments derive their just powers from the consent of the governed (as it had been put as early as the Declaration of Independence) was a decisive break with prescriptive thinking, even if it by no means solved all problems of political authority. It was something else making the American Revolution a landmark in world history. For generations to come the new United States would become the focus of the aspirations of men longing to be free the world over, 'the world's last, best hope,' as one American said.

These were long-term effects. Immediately, the American impact on European countries other than Great Britain was limited. There were a number of upheavals and disturbances called 'revolutions' in smaller countries (the United Provinces and the Swiss canton of Geneva were the most important) in the 1780s and in them American example was occasionally invoked. But the most conspicuous way in which Americans affected politics in Europe was through individual Frenchmen who had served in the revolutionary wars as allies of the nation in making. Soon lost to sight as it was to be in a torrent of other forces, their inspiration, together with the work of two remarkable men who successively held the post of American ambassador to France, Benjamin Franklin and Thomas Jefferson, played a minor but notable part in the shaping of fashionable French opinion. They helped to make the idea of revolutionary change *à la mode* in the years leading up to the greatest political event of the century, the onset of what is still called in a country of many revolutions *the* French Revolution.

The French Revolution

'Event' is in this case an especially artificial term of historical art, hardly to be applied to anything except one or another of the several distinguishable occurrences which have been argued to be the 'real' beginning of a huge process. The 'French revolution' was a tumultuous, unplanned, unprecedented and hitherto unimaginable cascade of events. What happened was more like the removal of the lid on an overboiling saucepan, or the release of a landslide, than the throwing of a switch. No-one in 1789 (the traditional starting date) anticipated any but a tiny fraction of what was to follow. On the other hand, Frenchmen even in that year were rightly confident that what was happening mattered far beyond France's own frontiers, though not, in the end in the way they had expected. But major change in France was bound to be an international event. The French monarchy was the greatest land-power west of Russia. French intellectual and artistic life set the pace for that of other countries; ideas canvassed in Paris had a European resonance thanks to the universal familiarity of the cultivated and ruling classes with the French language. Many of these ideas showed their effect in the great boiling-over after 1789, even if it was also true that many of those who helped, knowingly or unknowingly, to bring about the Revolution had their eyes fixed on the past in that year, rather than on the future.

One historical fact weighing heavily on the French monarchy in the 1780s arose from the intermittent but long-lived competition with Great Britain. The cost of France's participation in the American revolutionary war against her old rival had made a crushing addition to the monarchy's financial burdens. For no important gain except the humiliation of the British, France had added yet another layer to the huge and accumulating debt piled up by the efforts of her rulers since the 1630s to build and maintain a European supremacy. Attempts to liquidate this debt and cut the monarchy free from its cramping burden were made by a succession of ministers under Louis XVI, the young, somewhat obtuse, but high-principled and well-meaning king who had come to the throne in 1774. None of them succeeded and they only advertised the facts of failure. The spectre of state bankruptcy haunted France by the 1780s.

Social and political institutions stood in the way of tapping the wealth of the better-off: the whole legal structure of France, its privileges, special immunities and prescriptive rights, blocked the way ahead. It was everywhere in continental Europe a visible paradox of eighteenth-century government that theoretically absolute monarchies could not much infringe the mass of liberties and rights which made up essentially medieval constitutions without threatening their own foundations. Yet without clearly seeing this, more Frenchmen were in the 1780s coming to think that France had to transform her governmental and constitutional structure if she was to emerge from her difficulties. Some went further still. They saw in the inability of government to share fiscal burdens equitably between classes an extreme example of a whole range of abuses calling for reform. The issue came to be put in terms of rhetorical polarities: of reason and superstition, of freedom and slavery, of humanitarianism and greed. Above all, such rhetoric tended to concentrate on the symbolic question of legal privilege, the embodiment of inequality. The anger this aroused was focused on the nobility, an immensely diverse and numerous body (there seem to have been between 200,000 and 250,000 males of noble blood in France in 1789). Cultural, economic or social generalization about them is impossible, and they were themselves politically divided, but all noblemen shared a legal status which in varying degree conferred privilege at law.

The natural unwillingness on the part of many of the royal advisers (themselves usually noblemen) and of the king himself to proceed except by agreement with the privileged, appeared to be wearing thin by 1788. Government then recognized that conflict was inevitable but still sought to confine it to legal channels. The nearest thing to a national representative body that France had ever possessed was the Estates General, the body of representatives of nobles, clergy and commoners which had last met in 1614. It was now hoped that this impeccably constitutional body would provide sufficient moral authority to squeeze agreement from the fiscally privileged for the payment of higher taxes. Unfortunately, while this solution aroused great expectations, what the Estates General could legally do was obscure. More than one answer was given. Some radicals said the Estates General could make law for the nation, overriding historic and hitherto unquestioned legal privileges.

The political crisis came to a head amid other strains. France's population had risen since the second quarter of the century at what a later age would think a slow rate, but one still fast enough to outstrip growth in the production of food. This sustained a long-run inflation of food prices which bore painfully upon the poor, that vast majority of rural Frenchmen with little or no land. Given that governments had staved off financial crisis by borrowing or putting up the direct and indirect taxes which fell most heavily on them, and that landlords had sought to protect themselves by holding down wages and putting up rents and dues, their lives had been growing harsher and more miserable for most of the century. On this general impoverishment fell special troubles and afflictions in the late 1780s. Bad harvests, cattle disease, and recession all sapped the precarious health of the economy. As a result, elections to the Estates General in 1789 took place in a very excited and embittered atmosphere. Millions of Frenchmen living in misery and desperate to find a way out of their troubles, were eager to seek out and blame those responsible, and had quite unrealistic and inflated notions of what good the king, whom they trusted, could do for them. Few doubted that the needed changes could easily be carried out by him, once he was informed of his people's wishes and needs.

A complex interplay of governmental impotence, social injustice, economic hardship and reforming aspiration thus brought about the French Revolution. Few either anticipated this outcome or desired it. There was much social injustice in France, but no more than many another eighteenth-century state found it possible to live with. There was a welter of expectant and hopeful advocacy of particular reforms ranging from the abolition of the censorship to the prohibition of immoral and irreligious literature. What did not exist was a party of revolution clearly confronting a party of reaction. These only came into existence after the Estates General had met on 5 May 1789, a date which opened an era in which to be for or against the Revolution became a central political question in most European countries. It was also true that because France was a great power, the diplomatic repercussions were immediate; the Estates General would either (as many foreign diplomats hoped) paralyse her, or would free her from her difficulties to play again a forceful international role.

In the summer of 1789 the Estates General turned itself into a national assembly exercising the nation's sovereignty. Breaking with the assumption that they represented the great medieval divisions of society, the majority of its members claimed to represent all Frenchmen without distinction. They got away with this revolutionary step when rural revolt and Parisian riot frightened a government no longer sure that it could rely upon the army, and conservative deputies were intimidated by peasants pillaging country houses. This led the monarchy first to abandon the privileged classes, and then to concede, unwillingly and uneasily, many other things unenvisaged a few months earlier, but now asked for by the politicians who led the new National Assembly. These concessions created a fairly clear-cut division between those who were for the Revolution and those who were against it; in language to go round the world they were soon called Left and Right (because of where they sat in the assembly).

The main task which the National Assembly set itself was the writing of a constitution. In the process, it revolutionised the whole structure of France. By 1791, when it dispersed, it had nationalized the lands of the Church, abolished what it termed 'the feudal system', ended censorship, created a system of centralized representative government, obliterated the old provincial and local divisions and replaced them with the 'departments' under which Frenchmen still live, instituted equality before the law, and separated the executive from the legislative power. These were only the most remarkable things the Assembly did. Its failures tend to mask this huge achievement which, broadly speaking, removed the legal and institutional checks on the modernization of France. Popular sovereignty, administrative centralization, and the legal equality of all citizens were from this time poles towards which her institutional life always returned.

Many Frenchmen did not like all this; some liked none of it. By 1791 the king had given clear evidence of his own misgivings, the goodwill which had supported him in the early Revolution was gone and he was suspected as an anti-revolutionary. Some noblemen (led by two of the king's brothers) had already disliked enough of what was going on to emigrate. Many more Frenchmen turned against the Revolution when the National Assembly's settlement of Church affairs was called into question. Much in that settlement had appealed to many Frenchmen, churchmen among them, but the pope rejected it and French Catholics then had to decide whether his authority or that of the National Assembly was supreme for them. This created the most important division of revolutionary politics and recreated the centuries-old antagonism of Church and State in new forms.

In 1792 France went to war with Austria and Prussia. The reasons were complicated but many Frenchmen believed that foreign powers wished to intervene to end the Revolution and put the clock back. Some foreign statesmen certainly did. By the summer, as things went badly and shortages and suspicion mounted at home, the king was discredited. A Parisian insurrection overthrew the monarchy and led to the summoning of another assembly to draw up a new and, this time, republican constitution. This body, called the Convention, was to be the centre of French government until 1796. Most of its members held views politically not much more advanced than had their predecessors. They believed in the individual and in the sanctity of property (they prescribed the death penalty for anyone proposing a law to introduce agrarian communism). They allowed some of the poor a small say in affairs by introducing universal adult male suffrage. What distinguished them was that they were willing to go further and to behave with greater ruthlessness in meeting emergencies than earlier French assemblies (especially when frightened by the possibility of defeat); they also sat in a capital city whose mobs were for a long time manipulated by more extreme politicians to push them into measures more radical than they really wanted, and into using very democratic language. Consequently, they frightened the rest of Europe, too. Meanwhile, they ensured the survival of the Revolution.

A symbolic break with the past came in January 1793 when the Convention voted for the execution of the king. The judicial murder of monarchs had hitherto been believed to be an English aberration; now the English were as shocked as the rest of Europe. They, too, now went to war with France, fearing the strategical and commercial result of French success against the Austrians in the Netherlands. But the war looked more and more like an ideological struggle. To win it the French government used increasingly bloodthirsty language and adopted much more violent methods. A new instrument for humane execution, the guillotine (a characteristic product of pre-revolutionary enlightenment, combining as it did technical efficiency with benevolence in the swift, sure death it afforded its victims) became the symbol of the Terror, the name soon given to the period during which the Convention strove by intimidation of its enemies at home to save the Revolution. Some of the Terror was only rhetoric, the hot air of politicians trying to keep up their own spirits and frighten their opponents. In practice it often reflected a jumble of patriotism, practical necessity, muddled idealism, self-interest and petty vengefulness, as old scores were settled in the name of the republic. Something over 35,000, perhaps, died, and many emigrated to avoid danger, but the Parisian guillotine killed only a minority of the victims, most of whom died in the provinces in conditions of civil war and sometimes with arms in their hands. In eighteen months or so the Frenchmen whom contemporaries regarded as monsters killed about as many of their countrymen as would die in ten days of street-fighting and firing-squads in Paris in 1871. Bloodshed drove divisions between Frenchmen even deeper, but it should not be exaggerated. All noblemen lost something in the Revolution, but only a minority of them found it necessary to emigrate. Probably the clergy suffered more, man for man, than the nobility; many priests fled abroad. Yet there were fewer refugees from the Revolution than from the American colonies after 1783.

By 1797, only Great Britain among the powers was still at war with France, the Terror had been left behind, and the republic was ruled by something much more like a parliamentary regime under a constitution whose adoption closed the Convention era in 1796. The Revolution was saved. But it did not seem so. Abroad, the royalists strove to get allies with whom to return and also intrigued with malcontents inside France. The return of the old order was a prospect which few Frenchmen would welcome, though. On the other hand, there were those who argued that the logic of democracy should be pressed further, that there were still great divisions between rich and poor which were as offensive as had been the old distinctions of legally privileged and underprivileged, and that the Parisian radicals should have a greater say in affairs. This was almost as alarming as fears of a restoration of those who had benefited from the Revolution or simply wanted to avoid further bloodshed. Thus pressed from Right and Left, the Directory (as the new regime was called) was in a way in a good position, though it made enemies who found the (somewhat zig-zag) *via media* it followed unacceptable. In the end it was destroyed from within when a group of politicians intrigued with soldiers to overthrow it by *coup d'état* in 1799.

Revolutionary appearance and reality

Ten years after the meeting of the Estates General, France seemed to have broken for ever with the medieval past. So, in many ways, she had. Nearly all the great legal reforms had been legislated, at least in principle, in 1789. The formal abolition of feudalism, legal privilege and theocratic absolutism and the organization of society on individualist and secular foundations were the heart of the 'principles of '89' distilled in a Declaration of the Rights of Man and Citizen which prefaced the constitution of 1791. Legal equality and the legal protection of individual rights, the separation of Church and State and religious toleration were their institutional expression. The derivation of authority from popular sovereignty acting through a unified National Assembly, before whose legislation no privilege of locality or group could stand, was the basis of the jurisprudence which underlay them. It showed both that it could ride out financial storms far worse than those the old monarchy had failed to master (national bankruptcy and the collapse of the currency among them), and that it could carry out administrative change of which enlightened despotism had only dreamed. Other Europeans watched aghast or at least amazed as this powerful legislative engine was employed to overturn and rebuild institutions at every level of French life. Legislative sovereignty was a great instrument of reform, as the enlightened despots had known. Judicial torture came to an end, and so did titular nobility, juridical inequality and the old corporate guilds of French workmen. Incipient trades unionism was scotched in the egg by legislation forbidding association by workers or employers for collective economic ends. In retrospect, the signposts to market society seem pretty plain. Even the old currency based on units in the Carolingian ratios of 1:20:12 (*livres, sous,* and *deniers,* the L.S.D. still used in the United Kingdom in 1970) gave way to a decimal system of *francs* and *centimes,* just as the chaos of old-fashioned weights and measures was (in theory) replaced by the metric system later to become almost universal (in reality, they were to go on being used in rural France well into the nineteenth century).

Great changes are bound to be divisive and men's minds change more slowly than their laws. Peasants, who eagerly welcomed the abolition of feudal dues were much less happy about the disappearance of the common lands and the rights to exploit them from which they had benefited; yet those, too, were part of the 'feudal' order. Such conservatism was especially hard to interpret in religious affairs, yet was very important. The holy vessel kept at Rheims from which the kings of France had been anointed since the Middle Ages was publicly destroyed by the authorities during the Terror; an altar to Reason replaced the Christian one in the cathedral of Notre Dame. Many priests underwent fierce personal persecution and the martyrs of the September Massacres were long remembered. Clearly, a France which could show such horrors was no longer Christian in the traditional sense. Yet though the theocratic monarchy went unmourned by most Frenchmen, the treatment of the Church aroused popular opposition to the Revolution as nothing else had done, the cults of quasi-divinities such as Reason and the Supreme Being which some revolutionaries promoted were a flop, and many would happily welcome the official restoration of the Catholic Church to French life when it eventually came. By then, it had long been restored *de facto* in many parishes by the spontaneous actions of French men and women.

The Revolution abroad

The principles of '89 had at first commanded much admiration and not much explicit condemnation or distrust in other countries. This soon changed, in particular when French governments began to export those principles by propaganda and war. Revolution in France generated debate about what should happen elsewhere. Thus France gave a new politics to Europe. The terms Right and Left have been used internationally almost ever since. 'Liberals' and 'conservatives' (though it was to be a decade or so before those words were used) came into political existence when the French Revolution provided what appeared to be a litmus paper for political attitudes. On one side were republicanism, a wide suffrage, individual rights, free speech and free publication; on the other were order, discipline, a belief in duties rather than rights other than those entrenched in law, the recognition of the social function of hierarchy and a wish to temper market forces by morality.

Some Frenchmen had advocated the acceptance by other nations of their recipes for the settlement of French problems. The forces making for French influence were in this way reinforced by conscious propaganda and missionary effort. This was not entirely arrogant. Pre-industrial European societies had many features in common; all could learn something from France. That the Revolution was of universal, unprecedented significance was, however, not an idea confined to its admirers and supporters. It also lay at the roots of European conservatism. Well before 1789, many of the constituent elements of modern conservative thought were lying about in such phenomena as irritation over the reforming measures of enlightened despotism, clerical resentment of the prestige and secularizing effect of 'enlightened' ideas, and the emotional reaction from fashionable and conscious rationalism which lay at the heart of Romanticism. Such forces were notable in Germany, but it was in England that there appeared the first and in many ways the greatest statement of the conservative, anti-revolutionary argument, the *Reflections on the Revolution in France*, published in 1790 by Edmund Burke. As might easily be inferred from his former role as defender of the rights of the American colonists, this book was far from a mindless defence of privilege. In it a conservative stance shook itself clear of the legalistic defence of institutions and expressed itself in a theory of society as the creation of more than will and reason and as the embodiment of morality. The Revolution, by contrast, was condemned as the expression of the arrogance of the intellect, of arid rationalism, and of pride – to the Christian, deadliest of all the sins.

The new polarization which the Revolution brought to Europe's politics clarified new views of revolution. The old idea that a political revolution was merely a circumstantial break in an essential continuity was replaced by one which took it as radical, comprehensive upheaval, leaving untouched no institution, limitless in principle, and tending, perhaps, even to the subversion of such basic social facts as the family and property. Whether people felt heartened or dismayed by this prospect, in sympathizing with or deploring revolution wherever it occurred, they accepted it as a manifestation of a universal phenomenon. The nineteenth century even came to speak of *the* Revolution as a universally, eternally present force. This was the extreme expression of an ideological form of politics which is by no means dead. There are still those who, broadly speaking, feel that all insurrectionary and subversive movements should, in principle, be approved or condemned without regard to the particular circumstances of cases. This mythology has produced much misery, much liberation. First Europe and then the world which Europe transformed have had to live with those who respond emotionally to it, just as earlier generations had to live with religious enthusiasm. Its survival is yet another testimony to the impact of the French Revolution.

Revolution and European overseas empire

The story of what can be now discerned as 'decolonization' begins with some of the earliest external consequences of the American Revolution; they were to be seen south of the Rio Grande. In contrast to the British in North America, the Spanish had tried to introduce sweeping reforms in their colonies in the eighteenth century. After the Bourbons had replaced the Habsburgs there had been substantial restructuring and, conceded at first reluctantly, relaxations of the closed commercial system. Mediterranean Spain and the colonies both benefited from the ending of the monopoly of colonial trade formerly held by the port of Seville. These changes, nonetheless, did not touch all colonial grievances. There were notable insurrections, some threatening colonial governments and requiring big military efforts to master them. The expedient of raising local militias to do so was double-edged for it gave colonists military experience they might use against Spain. Furthermore the white population was divided; although the division between it and the indigenous Indian peoples was everywhere the most important social distinction in the Spanish possessions, that between *creoles* (Spaniards born in the colonies) and *peninsulares* (Spaniards from Spain) also mattered. The gap between them widened with time. The *creoles* resented their exclusion from the major offices of the imperial system. The success of British North Americans in shaking off imperial rule did not go unnoticed by them.

In an Anglo-Spanish quarrel in 1790 the Spanish monarchy at last formally gave up the remnants of its historic claim to sovereignty throughout the whole of the Americas; it was agreed that the existence of a Spanish settlement in North America only brought with it a right to prohibit trade or settlement by other nations within thirty miles of it. The position north of the Rio Grande was then further defined in a series of wars (one with France in 1793, two more with Great Britain in 1796 and 1805, and finally another with France in 1808) which cost Spain more islands in the Caribbean but, far more important, 'Louisiana', which she transferred to France in 1800. That power then sold the territory so-named (roughly speaking the whole area between the Mississippi and the Rockies) to the United States three years later in what remains the largest real estate deed and the greatest single change in the configuration of the United States in its entire history, since it added to the republic a larger area than its own at that moment. The consequences were to be momentous.

Besides her Central and South American possessions, though, Spain still retained much in the northern continent, both west of the Rocky mountains and south of the Red river. Her power to control and preserve her empire was much weakened when her battlefleet was destroyed by the British in 1805 in the battle off Cape Trafalgar. She could now no longer even maintain communications with her empire without British acquiescence. Three years later, a French invasion of Spain swept the Bourbons aside and put a Frenchman on the throne. Spain's domestic history dissolved into guerrilla war, disorder and weakness, with a shadow government of liberals (the Spanish word *liberales* introduced this political term to European politics) at Cadiz contesting the French puppet regime at Madrid. Some *creoles* judged the moment had come.

In 1810 the South American 'wars of independence' began. There were risings against the colonial governments in New Granada, La Plata and New Spain. They were not at first successful. In Mexico the rebels found they had a racial war on their hands when the Indians turned on all whites. But the government at Cadiz could not prevail nor prevent further outbreaks. British sea-power assured the underpinning of the American enunciation in 1823 of the 'Monroe Doctrine' which declared that the Americas were 'henceforth not to be considered as subjects for future colonization by any European powers' and that intervention in the hemisphere by those powers would be taken to show 'an unfriendly disposition' towards the United States.[2] This pronouncement was prompted in part by Russian interest in the Pacific north-west, as well as by uneasiness about Spanish attempts to recover former colonies. By then a collection of republics had emerged on the South American mainland, forming a second generation of European settler nations abroad to stand alongside the United States, though they were drawn from a very different version of Europe and its institutions. By 1825, when Spanish forces withdrew from Peru, Iberian empire in the western hemisphere was confined to the Caribbean and North America, for the story of the disappearance of European empire in South America (apart from small possessions on the northern coast) includes also the winding-up of Portuguese Brazil. Once again, French invasion of the home territory (in 1807) had been a detonator. The Portuguese Prince Regent left Lisbon for Rio de Janeiro, which thus became the effective capital of the Portuguese empire. When he went back to Portugal as king in 1820, he left behind in Brazil a son, Dom Pedro, as regent, who soon found himself championing Brazilian independence against Portuguese attempts to recover its colony. After a little fighting and being named 'perpetual defender of Brazil' he proclaimed the country's independence and was rewarded by coronation on 1 December 1823 as Pedro I, first and constitutional emperor of Brazil, the only monarchical state left behind by the Europeans in the Americas.

Napoleonic Europe

Although many dates can be argued to 'begin' the French Revolution, to say that a specific date marks the 'end' of it would be nonsense. Its work went on for decades. The year 1799 nonetheless provides an important punctuation mark. The *coup d'état* then swept the Directory away and brought to power Napoleon Bonaparte, a general of the

---

2 The text of President Monroe's message to Congress which set out the 'Doctrine' has been often printed in works of reference. The most important section can conveniently be found in *Speeches and Documents in American History*, ed. Robert Birley, Vol.II: 1818–1865 (Oxford, 1944), pp. 48–53.

republic, who quickly inaugurated a dictatorship which was to last until 1814 and turn international relations upside-down again, remaking the European map in the process. Installed as First Consul of the new regime he was soon to be Emperor of France.

Like many of the leading figures of his age, Bonaparte came young to power. He had already shown exceptional brilliance and ruthlessness as a soldier. His victories combined with a shrewd political sense and a readiness to act in an insubordinate manner to win him a glamorous reputation; in many ways he was an example of the eighteenth-century type of 'the adventurer'. In 1799 he had great personal prestige (won by brilliant generalship and spectacular conquests) and popularity. No one except the defeated politicians much regretted it when he shouldered them aside. Immediately he justified himself by returning to the army, defeating the Austrians (who had again joined in a war against France) and making another victorious peace for France. This removed the threat to the Revolution.

The First Consul's commitment to the Revolution was hardly to be doubted, but what did that mean? He was soon to reinstitute monarchy in France. In 1804 Napoleon

NAPOLEONIC EUROPE

Greatest extent of French direct rule

Satellite states

Confederation of the Rhine boundary, 1806

(as he was called officially after that) proclaimed an empire. It was in no sense a restoration. Indeed, he took care so to affront the exiled Bourbon family (by murdering one of its princes) that any reconciliation with it was inconceivable. He sought popular approval for his empire in a plebiscite and got it. This was a monarchy Frenchmen had voted for; it rested on popular sovereignty, that is, the Revolution. It assumed the consolidation of the Revolution which the Consulate, still formally a republican regime, had begun.

All the great institutional reforms of the 1790s were confirmed or left intact; there was no disturbance of the land sales which had followed the confiscation of Church property, no resurrection of the old craft and professional corporations, no restoration of the old legal system, no questioning of the principle of equality before the law. Some further steps were taken. A codification of law which had long been hoped for by civil servants remains the basis of French jurisprudence to this day. The bringing of this to fruition was the result of Napoleon's own initiative and insistence, though the work was essentially that of the revolutionary legislators who had never been able in the troubled 1790s to perfect the new codes so many Frenchmen had hoped for in 1789. Each department was given an administrative head, the prefect, who was in his powers something like one of the emergency emissaries of the Terror (many former revolutionaries became prefects). In the actual working of imperial government, it is true, the principles of the Revolution were often infringed. Like all other French governments since 1793, Napoleon controlled the press by a punitive censorship, locked up people without trial and in general gave short shrift to the Rights of Man so far as civil liberties were concerned. Judicial torture had been abolished, but Napoleon's secret police continued to make use of it. Representative bodies existed under consulate and empire, but not much attention was paid to them. Yet it seems that this was what Frenchmen wanted, as they had wanted Napoleon's shrewdest recognition of reality, a concordat with the pope which reconciled Catholics to the regime by giving legal recognition to the change in the position of the Church in France.

All in all, this amounted to a great consolidation of the Revolution guaranteed at home by despotism and by military and diplomatic strength abroad. Both were eventually undermined by Napoleon's huge military efforts. These for a time gave France the dominance of Europe; her armies fought their way to Moscow in the east and Portugal in the west and garrisoned the Atlantic and northern coast from Corunna to Stettin. Nevertheless, the cost of this was too great; even ruthless exploitation of occupied countries was not enough for France to sustain a military hegemony indefinitely against the coalition of all the other European countries which Napoleon's arrogant assertion of his power aroused. When he invaded Russia in 1812 and the greatest army he ever led crumbled into ruins in the snows of the winter, he was doomed unless his enemies should fall out with one another. This time they did not. Napoleon always blamed the British, who had been at war with him (and, before him, with the Revolution) with only one short break since 1792. There is something in this; the Anglo-French 'Napoleonic' wars were the last and most important round in a century of rivalry, as well as a war of constitutional monarchy against military dictatorship. It was the Royal Navy (at Aboukir in 1798 and Trafalgar in 1805) which confined Napoleon to Europe, British money which financed the allies when they were ready to come forward, and a British army in the Iberian peninsula which kept alive there from 1809 onwards a front draining French resources and giving hope to other Europeans.

By the beginning of 1814, Napoleon could defend only France. Although he did so at his most brilliant, he could not fight off Russian, Prussian and Austrian armies in the east, and a British invasion in the south-west. At last his generals and ministers were able to set him aside and make peace without a popular outcry, even though this meant allowing back the Bourbons. But it could not by then mean the return of anything else of significance from the years before 1789. The Concordat remained, the departmental system remained, equality before the law remained, the Codes remained, representative institutions remained and could now become more of a reality. The Revolution, in fact, had become part of the established order in France. Napoleon had provided the time, the social peace and the institutions for that to happen. Of the institutions of the Revolution nothing survived except what he had confirmed.

This makes him very different from even the most modernizing monarch of the traditional stamp – and that is odd, because he was often very conservative in his policies. In the end he was a revolutionary despot, whose authority came from the people, both in the formal sense of the plebiscites, and in the more general one that he needed (and for a long time won) their goodwill to keep his armies in the field. Though his coronation robes were carefully embroidered with the bees of Merovingian royalty, he is nearer in style to twentieth-century rulers than to Louis XIV. Yet he shares with him the glamour of carrying French international power to an unprecedented height and because of this both of them have retained the admiration of their countrymen. But again there is an important, and twofold, difference: Napoleon not only dominated Europe as Louis XIV never did, but because of the Revolution his hegemony represented more than mere personal or national supremacy. This fact should not be sentimentalized. The Napoleon who was supposed to be a liberator and great European was the creation of later legend. The most obvious impact he had on Europe between 1800 and 1814 was the bloodshed and upheaval he brought to every corner of it, often as a consequence of megalomania and personal vanity. But there were enormously important side-effects, some intentional, some not. They all added up to the further spread of the principles of the French Revolution.

The new map of Europe

The map showed this best. The patchwork quilt of the European state system of 1789 had already undergone revision before Napoleon took power; French armies in Italy, Switzerland and the United Provinces had set up new satellite republics in those countries (one consequence was an end to the long history of the Venetian republic) in the 1790s. But these had proved non-viable once French support was withdrawn and it was not until French hegemony was re-established under the Consulate that there appeared in some parts of Europe a new organization with enduring consequences. The most important were in west Germany, whose political structure was revolutionized, to open a period of seventy years during which most of the historic polities of Germany would disappear. German territories on the left bank of the Rhine were annexed to France for the whole of the period from 1801 to 1814. By way of a start, on the other side of the Rhine, French reorganization secularized the ecclesiastical states, abolished nearly all the Free Cities, gave extra territory to Prussia, Hanover, Bavaria and Baden to compensate them for losses elsewhere, and abolished the old independent imperial nobility. One implication was a reduction of Catholic and Habsburg influence, and a strengthening of Germany's larger princely states (especially Prussia). The constitution of the Holy Roman Empire was revised, too, to take account of these changes. It survived, though, only until 1806, when another defeat of the Austrians led to the final disappearance of the institutional structure which, however inadequately, had given Germany such political coherence as it had enjoyed since Ottonian times. A Confederation of the Rhine was now set up to provide a third force to balance Prussia and Austria. Thus were triumphantly asserted the national interests of France. Richelieu and Louis XIV would have approved a French frontier on the Rhine with, beyond it, a Germany divided into interests likely to hold one another in check. Yet, after all, the old structure had been a hindrance to German consolidation. No future rearrangement would ever contemplate its resurrection. When, finally, the allies came to settle post-Napoleonic Europe, they too provided for a German Confederation. It was different from Napoleon's in that Prussia and Austria were members of it in so far as their territories lay in Germany, but there was no going back on the fact of consolidation. A complicated structure of over 300 political units in 1789 was reduced to thirty-eight in 1815. These would be reduced further in the next half-century.

Reorganization was less dramatic in Italy and its effects less revolutionary. The Napoleonic system provided in the north and south of the peninsula two large and nominally independent units, while much of it (including the papal states) was formally incorporated in France and organized in departments. None of this structure survived 1815, but neither was there a complete restoration of the old regime. The ancient republics of Genoa and Venice were left in the tombs to which the armies of the Directory had first consigned them, their territory absorbed by bigger states (Genoa by Sardinia, Venice by Austria). Elsewhere in Europe, at the height of Napoleon's power, France had annexed and governed directly a huge block of territory whose coasts ran from the Pyrenees to Denmark in the north and from Catalonia almost without interruption to the boundary between Rome and Naples in the south. Lying detached from it were the Illyrian provinces, composed of former Habsburg and Venetian territory and a large piece of what was until recently Yugoslavia. Satellite states and vassals of varying degrees of real independence, some of them ruled over by members of Napoleon's own family, divided between them the rest of Italy, Switzerland and Germany west of the Elbe. Isolated in the east was another satellite, the 'grand duchy' of Warsaw, which had been created from Russian Poland.

Shared experience

In most of these countries common administrative practice and institutions provided a measure of shared experience of institutions and ideas. The principles of the Revolution hardly reached beyond the Elbe, though (except in the brief Polish experiment), and thus the French Revolution came to be another of those great shaping influences which again and again have helped to differentiate eastern and western Europe. Within the French empire, Germans, Italians, Illyrians, Belgians and Dutch were all governed by the Napoleonic codes and their concepts of family, property, the individual, and public power which were thus generally spread through Europe. They sometimes replaced and sometimes supplemented a chaos of local, customary, Roman and ecclesiastical law. Similarly, the departmental system of the empire imposed a common administrative practice, service in the French armies imposed a common discipline and military regulation, and French weights and measures, based on the decimal system, officially replaced many local scales. One must not exaggerate the practical impact on daily life of Napoleonic administration, but neither must one overlook its innovatory importance. It provided models and inspiration to modernizers in countries beyond the actual limits of French rule. The models were all the more easily assimilated because French officials and technicians worked in many of the satellite states while many nationalities other than French were represented in the Napoleonic service.

The full effect of such changes, though deep and often revolutionary, was modernizing, even if by no means necessarily liberal; the Rights of Man formally followed the Tricolour of the French armies, but so, in practice, did Napoleon's secret police, quartermasters and customs officers. More subtle disturbance deriving from the Napoleonic impact lay also in the reaction and resistance it provoked. In spreading revolutionary principles the French often put a rod in pickle for their own backs. Popular sovereignty lay at the heart of the Revolution and it is an ideal closely linked to that of nationalism. French principles said that peoples ought to govern themselves and that the proper unit in which they should do so was the nation: the revolutionaries had proclaimed their own republic 'one and indivisible' for this reason. Many of their foreign admirers applied this principle to their own countries; manifestly, Italians and Germans did not live in national states, and perhaps they should. Moreover, French Europe was run for the benefit of France; it thus denied the national rights of other Europeans. They saw their agriculture and commerce sacrificed to French economic policy, found they had to serve in the French armies, or to receive from Napoleon French (or quisling) rulers and bureaucrats. When even those who had welcomed the principles of the Revolution felt such things as grievances, it is hardly surprising that those who had never welcomed them at all should resist them. Patriotism was given an immense fillip by the Napoleonic era. Whatever their own governments thought, a few Germans began to see themselves as more than Westphalians or Bavarians, and a few Italians to believe they were more than Romans or Milanese, because they discerned a common interest against France. In Spain and Russia the identification of patriotic resistance with resistance to the Revolution was virtually complete. Though the dynasty Napoleon hoped to found and the empire he set up both proved fragile, he thus changed Europe even by antagonizing people. He unlocked reserves of energy in other countries just as the Revolution had unlocked them in France, and afterwards they could never be quite shut up again. This gave the legacy of the Revolution its maximum effect and was his greatest achievement, whether he desired it or not.

The idea of national sovereignty was central to that legacy. After Revolution it was more widely accepted than ever before that no-one had a right to stand between legitimate sovereign (whether prince, republican oligarchy or democratic parliament) and subject; what now became the matter of argument was what constituted a legitimate sovereign. It was still to take a long time for the idea to win complete acceptance and some people went on finding it very difficult to agree that a government could do anything if it was done in due constitutional form (even something cutting across the laws of God, for example) but by 1815 more Europeans than ever before had come to believe that, provided the authority of the state were in the right hands, there should be no restriction upon its power to make laws, whatever relics of older ideas lingered on. This was an enormous step. In earlier centuries the idea that there might not be rights and rules, legal immunities and chartered freedoms inaccessible to change by subsequent lawmakers, fundamental laws which must and would always be respected, or laws of God which could never be contravened by those of men, would have been social or juridical, as well as theological, blasphemy. Seventeenth-century English politicians and lawyers had floundered about in disagreement as they looked for such 'fundamental' laws of the land, but had agreed some must exist. A century later the leading legal minds of France were doing just the same as the monarchy lurched towards breakdown. In the end, nevertheless, there had emerged in both countries (as, to a greater or lesser degree, in most others) the acceptance of the idea that a sovereign, legally unrestrained, lawmaking power was the characteristic mark of the state, and the idea was spread throughout Europe by the Revolution.

Unconditional abdication after military defeat in 1814 was not quite the end of Napoleon's story. Just under a year later he returned to France from Elba where he had lived in a pensioned exile, and the restored Bourbon regime crumbled at a touch. The allies rallied to overthrow him, and at Waterloo, in Belgium, on 18 June 1815, the threat of a revived French empire was destroyed by the Anglo-Belgian and Prussian armies. Napoleon had frightened the victors once too often. This time they sent him to St Helena, thousands of miles away in the South Atlantic, where he died in 1821. The final fright that he had given them strengthened their determination to make a peace that would avoid any danger of a repetition of the quarter-century of almost continuous war which Europe had undergone in the wake of the Revolution. Napoleon thus continued in this way, too, to shape the history of Europe, by memories of the fear France had inspired under his leadership.

CHAPTER TWO

The world's new rich

Europe's numbers

Including that of the Russian empire (about which reliable historical statistics are not always easy to obtain), the population of Europe more than doubled in the nineteenth century. In round terms, it rose from about 190 to 420 millions, an unprecedented acceleration in its rate of growth. Most of those millions were at birth already likely to live longer than their grandparents and parents had been. Here were obvious signs of a huge increase in Europe's wealth; whether by growing it or importing it, there was more food available to feed the additional mouths, more resources to put into housing them, paving their streets, lighting and warming their dwellings, and providing them in a hundred and one other ways with goods unavailable to the Europeans of 1800, and so making it more likely that they would stay alive. By then, the most fundamental processes building up this wealth had been at work for centuries. Not until the nineteenth century, though, did they open up a truly striking gap between the living standards of Europeans and those of the inhabitants of much of the rest of the globe.

Population increase changed the size of Europe's share of world population. The rest of the human race (outside North America) was adding to its numbers more slowly than Europe, so that Europe's share, a fifth or so of the world total in 1800, rose in a century to become about a quarter of it. This, too, was accomplished while growing numbers of Europeans went to live overseas. In the 1830s, for the first time, more than 100,000 Europeans were emigrating each year; the figure for 1913 would be over a 1,500,000. In population history, long perspectives are useful; between 1840 and 1930 about 50,000,000 Europeans went overseas to other continents.

Different European countries, too, grew at different rates. The United Kingdom got off to the fastest start, its population shooting up from about 10,000,000 in 1800 to 21,000,000 by mid-century; it numbered 36,000,000 in 1900. France began the century with nearly 27,000,000 inhabitants, and finished with just over 40,000,000. Germany (not a united nation in 1800, of course) more than doubled its population to over 50,000,000. In contrast, some of the poorest agrarian regions of eastern Europe had to wait until the 1920s and 1930s for really rapid growth.

This mainly reflects the fact that the chief force driving population growth in the last couple of centuries has been a historically unprecedented fall in death-rates, another consequence – in the broadest sense – of wealth creation. People ceased to die as soon as in former times, and this was first observable in economically developed countries. Roughly speaking, birth-rates in all European countries slightly exceeded death-rates in 1800. Yet in their still largely rural economies, little had by then changed so as to affect the great traditional determinants of human life. By 1850, though, this was no longer true and by the 1880s a continuing fall in mortality was very visible in the most advanced countries. Their death-rates went down from about 35 per thousand inhabitants per year to about 28 in the last two decades of the century (and 50 years later hovered at about 18). More backward European countries still had death-rates of 38 per thousand in 1900 which would drop little in the next fifty years, so that the inequality of Europeans before death was actually increasing, according to where people lived. In the richer west and north, expectation of life was for the most part much higher than in the south and east.

Though falling mortality was the main engine of population growth, other factors were also at work by 1900. Increased opportunity in an age of economic growth led to earlier marriage and rising birth-rates. These had more impact than they would have done in earlier times, because children had improving chances of survival to adulthood. Yet, with the exception of vaccination and inoculation (both introduced and spread widely in the eighteenth century), better medical science or the greater availability of medical services probably did not for a long time make much difference. Doctors were only coming to grips with the great child-killing diseases – diphtheria, scarlet fever, typhoid, whooping cough – in the last quarter of the century, when, indeed and as a result, infant mortality began to decline dramatically. Earlier than this, though, social reformers and public engineers had produced their own significant impact. Better water-supplies, drains and cleaning arrangements for the growing cities had already reduced the incidence, if not the fatality, of disease. By 1900, cholera, a scourge of the 1830s and 1840s, had been virtually eliminated in industrialized countries. No major outbreak of plague occurred in western Europe after 1900, either, even if there were still a few cases in seaports (the United Kingdom's last visitation was in Glasgow in 1911). Such improvements everywhere helped to raise the average age at death; by the second quarter of the twentieth century, the inhabitants of the most economically advanced countries could expect to live two or three times as long as their medieval ancestors.

One important consequence in the nineteenth century was a large number of young people in the population, first in the western and then in eastern European countries (as well as those of European stock overseas), even if their proportionate share would go down as the average age of death rose. Their presence both in society as a whole and in the workforce brought problems, but also new resources of energy, buoyancy and vigour. This somewhat offset the higher numbers living to reach an old age beyond employability. These strained the social mechanisms which had seemed sufficient in earlier times for the maintenance of the old and infirm, inadequate as such provision now appears to have been. By 1914, politicians and social scientists in many countries would be giving much more thought than hitherto to problems of poverty and dependence.

A new abundance

Between 1815 and 1848, and again between 1871 and 1914, Europe outside the Balkans enjoyed unprecedentedly long periods of virtually undisturbed peace.

War, with its accompaniments of disease and the destruction of economic resources (above all of agricultural production) no longer operated a historic check on population growth as always hitherto. Sometimes war had brought famine, too, another great obstacle to sustained demographic growth. But famine and dearth were becoming less usual as the nineteenth century went on; railways and steamships made it easier to import food. Rising populations in many countries were also populations experiencing higher standards of living. A rise in the average age of death reflected the fact that since more mouths were surviving to be fed, there was more food to feed them than in earlier times.

Rural Europe

There was under way one of those very few changes in history so sweeping as to transform the basic conditions of human life. The food-producing revolution, radically transforming though slow in its onset, had beginnings far back in the past. By the eighteenth century European arable farming could already provide about two and a half times the yield on seed normal in the Middle Ages. In the next century even greater improvement was to be seen. Meanwhile, new crops – potatoes, sugar beet – were produced more widely; substantial changes in diet followed. From about 1800, it has been calculated, Europe's agricultural productivity grew at a rate of about one per cent a year, dwarfing all previous advance. More important still, as time passed Europe would be able to tap huge larders in other parts of the world. Both of these changes were aspects of another process, the accelerating investment in productive capacity which made Europe and North America by 1870 clearly the greatest concentration of wealth on the face of the globe; its origin lay in agriculture. People have spoken of an 'agricultural revolution' and no word much less strong can do justice to the huge surge in world output achieved between 1750 and 1870 (and, later, even surpassed). But it was a process of great complexity, drawing on many different sources and linked to the other sectors of the economy in indispensable ways, and it was very slow and long-term. It was an aspect, too, of worldwide economic change; it involved in the end not merely Europe, but the Americas and Australasia as well.

In 1800, advanced agricultural technique – even the first employment of steam-power in ploughing – was most evident in the United Kingdom. But it had already spread beyond that country, and was to spread further. Unsurprisingly, changes came by many routes and, except by comparison with earlier centuries of quasi-immobility, progress was sometimes slow. In parts of Calabria or Andalusia, it may have been almost imperceptible over a century. The battle against the inelasticities of food-supply was in the end won, but it was the outcome of hundreds of particular victories over fixed crop rotations, out-dated fiscal arrangements, poor standards of tillage and husbandry, and sheer ignorance. The gains were better stock, more effective control of plant blight and animal disease, the introduction of new species, and much else. Change on so comprehensive a basis often had to work against social and political obstacles, too.

The French had formally abolished serfdom in 1789, but there were few serfs left in France by that date. The abolition of what they called the 'feudal system' in that year – the mass of traditional and legal usages and rights which stood in the way of the exploitation of the land by individuals as an investment like any other – was more important, though a change made confusing and difficult to measure by the fact that there took place at the same time a big redistribution of property. Within a few years much land previously belonging to the Church was sold to private individuals. The consequent increase both in the number of people owning land outright and in the average size of properties might have been expected to lead to a period of great agricultural advance and rising productivity in France, but it did not. There was for a long time only very slow progress and little consolidation of properties on the English pattern, though important restraints had been removed.

This suggests, rightly, that generalization about the pace or uniformity of what was happening should be cautious and qualified. For all the enthusiasm Germans were showing for travelling exhibitions of agricultural machinery in the 1840s, theirs was a huge country and one (France was another) of which a great economic historian commented that 'broadly speaking, no general and thorough-going improvement can be registered in peasant agriculture before the railway age'[1]. Yet the dismantling of medieval institutions standing in the way of agricultural improvement was going on before that and prepared the way for it. It was accelerated in some places by the arrival during the Napoleonic period of French laws on property and legal status and after this by institutional reforms such as those promoted in Prussia by the reforming statesman Stein. By 1850 peasants tied to the soil and obligatory labour had disappeared from most of Europe west of the Russian frontier. Yet even much later, Prussian, Magyar and Polish landlords seem, for good and ill, to have maintained much of their patriarchal authority over their tenants. Conservative aristocratic values survived in the east in a much more intense and concentrated way than in western Europe. The Junker could accept the implications of the market in planning his estate management, but not in his relations with his peasants.

The longest resistance to change in traditional legal forms was shown in Russia. Serfdom persisted there until abolished in 1861. This act did not at once bring Russian agriculture entirely under the operation of individualist and market economy principles, but with it an era of European history had closed: the agricultural Middle Ages were over. From the Urals to Corunna there no longer survived in law any substantial working of land by those who were legally serfs, even if conditions not easy to distinguish from serfdom in practice could be found in the Balkans. Nor were peasants any longer bound to landlords whom they could not leave (though there remained restrictions on the movement of Russian peasants away from their villages while the costs of emancipation were worked off). It was the end of a system which had been passed from antiquity to western Christendom in the era of the barbarian invasions and had been the basis of much of European civilization for centuries. After 1861, Europe's rural proletariat everywhere worked for wages or keep; the pattern which had begun to spread in England and France with the fourteenth-century agricultural crisis had become universal. Two European nations overseas, the United States and Brazil, were soon to follow suit and to abolish slavery in 1865 and 1888, respectively.[2]

---

[1] J.H. Clapham, *The Economic Development of France and Germany 1815–1914*, 4th edn. (Cambridge, 1945) p.52.

[2] The Emancipation Proclamation of 1 January 1863 applied only to those States of the Union 'the people whereof shall then be in rebellion against the United States'. Slavery was only abolished throughout the Union by the Thirteenth Amendment to the Constitution, December 1865.

New European lands

For centuries, agricultural output in Europe had been slowly pushed up by taking in new land for cultivation. This continued to happen in the nineteenth century, but faster than ever, though most of the new land was in fact overseas – indeed, transoceanic. The United States, Canada, Australia and New Zealand, the Argentine and Uruguay were soon able to show they could grow food more cheaply than Europe herself. One explanation was the immense natural resources of these new lands. The American plains, the huge stretches of pasture in the South American pampas and the temperate regions of Australasia provided vast areas for the growing of grain and the raising of livestock. Another was a revolution in transport. As steam-driven railways and ships came into service in increasing numbers from the 1860s, transport costs quickly fell, and did so all the faster as lower prices bred growing demand. Thus further profits were generated to be invested in the ranges and prairies of Europe's overseas estates. On a smaller scale the same phenomenon would be seen inside Europe, too. From the 1870s the eastern European and German farmers began to see that they had a competitor in Russian grain, able to reach the west much more cheaply once railways were built in Poland and western Russia and steamships could bring it from Black Sea ports. By 1900 the context in which European farmers worked, whether they knew it or not, was the whole world; the price of Chilean guano or New Zealand lamb could already settle what went on in their local markets.

Industrialism

After creating civilization in the first place and then setting a limit to its advance for thousands of years, agriculture had in the nineteenth century become its propellant. It suddenly demonstrated that many more people than ever before could be fed. Growing cities, railway-building, the investment of capital, all point to its inseparable interconnexion with other sides of a growing trans-oceanic economy between 1750 and 1870. Though it came first, and provided much of the investment capital for other developments, the story of agriculture in this period is at the heart of the appearance of a new kind of society, based on large-scale industrialization. This is a colossal subject. It is not even easy to see just how big it is. Industrialization brought about the most striking change in European history since the barbarian invasions; it has been seen as even more important, as the biggest change in human history since the coming of agriculture, iron or the wheel. Within a fairly short time – a century and a half or so – societies of peasants and craftsmen turned into societies of machine-tenders and book-keepers. Ironically, industrialism ended the ancient primacy of agriculture which had made it possible. It was one of the major facts turning human experience back from the differentiation produced by millenia of cultural evolution to common experiences and cultural convergence.

Even to define it is by no means easy. Although it embodied countless conscious decisions by countless entrepreneurs and customers, industrialization resembles a blind, self-animating force sweeping across social life with transforming power. One thread in the story is the replacement of human or animal muscle-power by machines driven by energy from other sources. Another is the organization of production in larger units. Another is increasing specialization in manufacturing. One of its most important long-term characteristics is the spread of the phenomenon of wage-dependency among producers to become the normal pattern. But all these things have implications and ramifications which quickly take us far beyond them.

Like those of agricultural change, the pre-conditions of industrialization can be traced back far beyond the early modern age. Capital for investment had been accumulated slowly over many centuries of agricultural and commercial innovation. Knowledge had been built up, too. Charlemagne had built a canal; though only in the eighteenth century did they begin to be built as never before in Europe so as to rival even the Chinese achievements centuries earlier. Startling technical innovations had roots deep in the past. The innovators stood on the shoulders of innumerable craftsmen and artificers of pre-industrial times who had slowly built up skills and experience for the future. Fourteenth-century Rhinelanders had been the first Europeans to learn how to cast iron; by 1600 the gradual spread of blast furnaces had begun to remove the limits hitherto set to the use of iron by its high cost and in the eighteenth century came the inventions making it possible to use coal to end the age-old dependence on wood as fuel in some processes. Cheaper iron, even in what were by later standards small quantities, led to experiment with new ways of using it; further changes then followed. New demand meant that areas where ore was easily mined became important. The location of supplies of coal and iron untapped for millenia began to fashion the later industrial geography of Europe and North America and to reveal the importance of Europe's geological history. Areas such as the Ruhr and Silesia acquired new significance.

Steam

Better metal and richer fuel contributed to early industrialization above all through the perfecting of a new source of energy, the steam-engine. Again, the technological lineage goes deep; that the power of steam could be used to produce movement was known in Hellenistic Alexandria. But little followed until, around 1700, a demand arose in Europe for more power to work bigger pumps needed in mines being driven to deeper levels than ever before. The first commercially successful steam-engines were produced to meet it, and though an improvement on pumps driven by animal or water power, they were very inefficient. The eighteenth century brought new investment in development, technical refinements and in the end fundamental innovation. James Watt's invention of the condenser was of revolutionary importance. It not only made possible the conversion of heat to energy at a whole new order of efficiency, but quickly led to the production of an engine which could provide rotary motion, and therefore drive machinery as well as pumps.

The new steam-engines consumed coal and iron directly, both as fuel and as material used in their own construction. Indirectly they made possible other processes which led to increased demand for these minerals. The most obvious and spectacular by mid-century was in railway-building. This was unanticipated. The manner in which steam-operated trains operating over long distances displaced animal-drawn carriage on short private tracks has been well described as 'sleep-walking'[3]. Railways consumed huge quantities of iron (and later steel) for rails and rolling-stock, and burnt coal as fuel. They

---

[3] S. Lilley, in *The Fontana Economic History of Europe*. Vol. 3. *The Industrial Revolution*, ed. C. Cipolla (London, 1970), p.206.

were built to move things at lower cost than before and what the new trains moved was also often coal or iron ore, thus allowing these materials to be used cheaply far from where they were easily found and dug. New industrial areas followed the lines, from which the railway could carry away goods to distant markets.

The first steamship put to sea in 1809. By 1870, though there were still many sailing-ships at work, and some navies were still building battleships with a full spread of sail, regular ocean sailings by 'steamers' were commonplace. The economic effect was dramatic. The real cost of shipping goods across the Atlantic in 1900 was then a seventh of what it had been a 100 years earlier. The shrinking of time spent in transit, and of space, which steamships and railways produced also overturned men's ideas of the possible. Since the domestication of the horse and the invention of the wheel, people and goods had been conveyed at speeds which might vary according to the local roads available, but always only within limits of probably no more than four or five miles per hour over any considerable distance; water transport could do better than this (and had speeded up somewhat over millenia in which ships had indeed undergone quite considerable modification). But all such slow improvement was dwarfed when in a man's lifetime he could experience the difference between travel on horseback and in a train capable of forty or even fifty miles an hour for long periods.

Industrial societies

Some who lived through early industrialization came to speak of it as the 'industrial revolution', a phrase invented by a Frenchman in the 1830s, though perhaps usefully applicable only to the 75 years or so of British development down to 1850, when the first industrial society came into being with a startling rapidity unmatched anywhere else. The 'revolution' was made visible in the menacing aspect of the new industrial towns, dominated by factories with smoking chimneys as the pre-industrial towns had been by the spires of church or cathedral. So dramatic and novel was the engine-driven factory, indeed, that it is frequently forgotten that it was a rare sight in the early nineteenth century. Even in its middle decades most industrial workers in England, the most advanced manufacturing nation in the world, worked in enterprises employing fewer than fifty. Great agglomerations of labour were long to be found only in textiles; the huge Lancashire cotton mills which first gave that area a visual and urban character distinct from earlier manufacturing towns were startling because they were unique. Yet by 1850 it was apparent that the trend in manufacturing was towards centralization under one roof. Economies of transport, specialization of function, the use of more powerful machinery and the imposition of effective work discipline all made this attractive.

At mid-century Great Britain was still the only mature industrial economy. Many explanations have been put forward. Domestic peace and less rapacious government than on the continent had bred confidence for investment among its most enterprising natives. Agriculture had provided new and greater surpluses earlier than elsewhere. Mineral resources were easily available for exploitation by the new technology resulting from two or three generations of remarkable invention. An expanding overseas commerce generated profits for investment, as well as the basic finance and banking structure and machinery, so that it was already in being before industrialization needed to call on it. Perhaps commerce readied society psychologically for further change;

observers already said they detected an exceptional sensitivity to pecuniary and commercial opportunity even in early eighteenth-century England. Finally, the country had a rapidly growing population to provide both labour and a rising demand for manufactured goods. All these forces flowed together. The result was unprecedented and continuing industrial growth.

Germany, France, Switzerland, Belgium and the United States soon joined Great Britain in showing the capacity for self-sustained economic growth but she remained for a long time first among them both in the scale of her industrial plant and in her world primacy. The inhabitants of the 'workshop of the world', as the British liked to think of themselves, were fond of running over the figures which showed how wealth and power had followed upon industrialization. In 1850 the United Kingdom owned half the world's ocean-going ships and contained half the world's railway track. On those railways trains ran with a precision and regularity and even a speed not much improved upon for a 100 years to come. They were regulated by the first 'time-tables' and their operation was assisted by electric telegraph. They were used by men and women who had a few years before ridden only in stage-coaches or carters' wagons. In 1851, a year when a great international exhibition at London advertised her new supremacy, Great Britain smelted 2,500,000 tons of iron. It does not sound much, but it was five times as much as the United States of America and ten times as much as Germany. At that moment, British steam-engines could produce more than 1.2 million horsepower, more than half all Europe's total.

By 1870 a change in relative positions had already begun to appear. Great Britain was still in most ways economically in the lead, but less decisively. Nor was she long to remain there. She still had more steam horsepower than any other European country, but the United States had been ahead of her even in 1850 and Germany was coming up fast. In the 1850s both Germany and France had followed Great Britain in making the important transition from smelting most of their iron by charcoal to smelting with mineral fuels. British superiority in manufacturing iron was still there and her pig-iron output had gone on rising, but now it was only three and a half times that of the United States and four times that of Germany. By 1900, Great Britain would no longer be in front, even in Europe; Germany would be in many more ways ahead of her, and the world manufacturing supremacy of the United States was much more obvious.

A *world economic system*

Europe's economic history cannot be separated from that of the rest of the world. Europe's factories sucked in raw materials – cotton, jute, timber, minerals – from overseas. By 1850 more than half the wool used in English mills came from Australia; France was taking more than half of hers from outside Europe, too, by 1914. Some raw materials were suddenly discovered to have new uses – rubber, towards the end of the nineteenth century, was an outstanding instance – and this transformed economic life in the places which produced them. As more such materials, as well as food and manufactured goods, were moved about the world, there was a dramatic increase in world trade.

The greatest trading nation of all was Great Britain and the total value of her exports and imports together rose from about £55,000,000 a year in 1800 to over £400,000,000 in 1913. Although her gross output had by then been overtaken in important respects by that of the United States and Germany, the bulk of the world's shipping and carrying trade was in British hands, she was the main importing and exporting nation and the only one which sent more of her manufactures to non-European nations than to European. As the biggest exporter of capital she drew a huge income from overseas investments, notably those in the United States and South America. Her special role underpinned a roughly triangular system of international exchange. The British bought goods, manufactured and otherwise, from Europe and paid for them with their own manufactures, with cash and with overseas produce. To the rest of the world they exported manufactures, capital and services, taking in return food, raw materials and cash. This complex system meant that Europe's economic relationships with the rest of the world cannot be schematized as a simple exchange of raw materials for manufactured goods.

Though Europe, on the whole, imported raw materials (both for food and industrial requirements) from other countries and exported manufactured goods in exchange, this was far from the whole story. Europe was the power-house of world trade; the growth of European population, its increasing wealth and its ever more voracious factories sucked huge quantities of food, minerals and timber, but also manufactured goods from one part of the world to another. In the 1860s, Great Britain still produced most of the food she consumed, but by 1900 she imported 80 per cent of her wheat and 40 per cent of her meat. Nonetheless, manufacturing countries were one another's best customers and in 1914, she was the best customer of Germany, another industrial giant, and one second only to India as a customer for British goods. Great quantities of goods were exchanged between European countries and the United States (which also, of course, supplied much farm produce). By 1914 Europe took over 60 per cent of the world's imports and supplied about 55 per cent of its exports.

By 1914 virtually all mankind directly or indirectly formed part of the same great trading community, whether they knew it or not. For the first time, there existed a true world-wide market. People could buy and sell round the world at world prices; what grain cost in Chicago, or meat in Buenos Aires, or steel in Essen could change other prices right round the world. At least in an economic sense, in the nineteenth century, 'One World' and a measure of a single world economic history already existed. The last steps had been taken as China, Japan and Africa were at last opened up to trade with Europe and North America. A huge global web of markets was serviced by long-established credit and exchange arrangements of which the most important was a system of paying for goods anywhere with bills 'on' (that is, to be settled by) European bankers and merchants. This had grown out of the credit transactions first set up between a few big European commercial centres in the Middle Ages. In its fully developed form the system was centred, above all, in London, which was by 1914 the centre of the world network of trade, and concentrated financial institutions as did no other city. Paper – in the forms of bills authorized for settlement, bank notes, cheques – kept the whole system going. Such paper was always redeemable in credit for other goods or paid off in the last resort in gold. All civilized nations based their currencies on gold. Exchange rates did not much fluctuate, therefore. With a bag of gold sovereigns, twenty-dollar, or hundred-mark pieces you could go anywhere in the world and pay your way. International business was easier than ever before.

Governments sometimes interfered with the flow of trade across their frontiers for what they thought were good reasons. During slumps, they would try to protect their own manufacturers and farmers by imposing 'tariffs' of duties on foreign goods. Great Britain was virtually the only big nation which refused to do this, and stuck to the 'Free Trade' practices which (it was believed) had done so much to make her a great trading nation and gave her cheap food. But even the tariffs of the late 1890s still left plenty of elbow room for merchants to do international business.

Europe was also the world's main exporter of capital, usually in the form of loans, which could be used to buy needed materials or to pay labour for agricultural or industrial development in capital-importing countries. This was how many of the railways of the United States and South America were built, how mining was expanded in Africa and how tea and rubber plantations were set up in Asia. The interest on the capital was paid with the profits from the enterprises thus launched. As time passed, this could become an irritant. It looked more and more as if Europeans – or, rather, European banks and merchants – owned too much of the business of non-European countries, which depended more and more on European capital. Local businessmen tended to think that it was unreasonable that the profits of these countries went to the benefit of Europeans.

For a few European countries, income from such overseas investment made up a big part of their overseas earnings. This was so, above all for Great Britain. Huge sums from these and other 'invisible exports' – not only dividends from overseas investments, but charges for shipping, or services such as insurance, and financial commissions of all kinds – were needed in order to balance the British imports and exports accounts. Such invisible exports made it possible for the British to pay for the imports which gave them a high standard of living. This was one reason why their governments were always keen to preserve international peace and normal business conditions; more than any other nation, the British depended on selling huge quantities of goods on other people's behalf, re-exporting much that they imported, and on the freedom of their merchant ships to plough the seas and that of their bankers and insurance brokers to take calculated risks abroad. The implications of this very complex system went far beyond the merely economic. Bringing down prices and stimulating innovation and investment advanced the sort of civilization which Europeans had created. In many ways it made the world a better place. But it was also true that when everyone's affairs were more closely tied up with everyone else's, a glut of grain in America could ruin European farmers and the collapse of a bank or merchant house in London could throw people out of work in Valparaiso or Rangoon.

The ups and downs of trade – the patterns of boom and slump called the 'trade cycle' which were first pointed out in Europe in the early nineteenth century – began to have a world impact as time went on. The search for 'protection' through tariffs was always liable to undermine the great world trading system. Yet it was strong enough to weather the storms, and it came to be assumed that the complex world of international trade was a natural state of affairs. It was such a success that it came by 1914 to be taken for granted and was not seen as the extraordinary achievement it really was.

It is perhaps less surprising that by 1900 most British economists thought that the prosperity and increasing wealth which their country enjoyed demonstrated the truth of Free Trade doctrine. That doctrine had even been used to justify the use of force to secure the opening of China to British trade. In the middle of the nineteenth century there had been for a time hopes that other European governments would adopt Free Trade policies. For a time, tariff barriers seemed to be coming down and the comparative advantage of the British, first among trading and manufacturing nations, had continued. But this era passed in the 1870s and 1880s and by 1900 Great Britain was again the only major nation without tariffs for protection and even in that country questioning of the old Free Trade dogmas was beginning to be heard as foreign competition (especially from Germany) grew fiercer and more alarming.

Even now, the economic world of 1914 still seems to be one of astonishing economic freedom and confidence. A long European peace between great powers had provided the soil for trading connexions to mature. Stable currencies assured great flexibility to a world price system; exchange control existed nowhere in the world. Russia and China were by then as completely integrated into this market as were other countries. Freight and insurance rates had steadily come down, food prices had followed suit and wages had risen in real terms in the long-term. Interest rates and taxation were low. It seemed as if a capitalist paradise might be achievable.

Cities

Among the first countries to industrialize, only Great Britain and Belgium had a majority of their population already living in urban areas in the middle of the nineteenth century. The census of 1851 showed that agriculture was still the biggest single employer of labour among British industries, (it was rivalled only by domestic service). Even then, though the growing numbers engaged in manufacturing industries, the rise of new concentrations of economic wealth and a new scale of urbanization all made the pace of change very visible in the spectacular growth of British towns, particularly after 1850, when the appearance of big centres that would be the nuclei of what a later age would call 'conurbations' was especially marked. This was soon also the case on the continent. Soon, European cities no longer depended on rural immigration for their growth.

There are difficulties in measuring urbanization, largely because in different countries urban areas were defined in different ways, but the main lines of what was happening are clear. In 1800 London, Paris and Berlin had, respectively, about 900,000, 600,000 and 170,000 inhabitants. In 1900 the corresponding figures were 4.7 million, 3.6 million and 2.7 million. In that year, Glasgow, Moscow, St Petersburg and Vienna also had more than a 1,000,000 inhabitants each. These were the giants; just behind them were sixteen more European cities with over 500,000; a century earlier, only London and Paris had so many. These great cities and many lesser ones (which were themselves immeasurably bigger than the older towns they overshadowed) reflected the marked tendency to urbanization in the countries where industrialization first made headway; it was the wealth and employment generated by industry which first drew people to them. Of the twenty-three cities of more than a 500,000 inhabitants in 1900, thirteen were in four countries, the United Kingdom (6), Germany (3), France (3) and Belgium (1).

Across the centuries, Europeans' opinions about cities have undergone many changes, but have often been unfavourable. As the eighteenth century ended, something like a sentimental discovery of rural life had been under way, and it coincided with the first phase of visible industrialization. The nineteenth century opened with the tide of aesthetic and moral comment already flowing against a city life which was indeed about to reveal a new and often unpleasant face. That urbanization was seen as an unwelcome, even unhealthy, change by many people, was in part a tribute to the subversive force of what was going on. Conservatives distrusted and feared cities. Conditions in many of the new metropolitan centres were often harsh and terrible for the poor. The East End of London could present appalling evidence of poverty, filth, disease and deprivation to anyone who chose to penetrate its slums. A young German businessman, Friedrich Engels, wrote in 1844 an influential book, *The Condition of the English Working-Class*, to expose the appalling conditions in which the poor of Manchester lived, and many writers were drawn to similar themes. In France the phenomenon of the 'dangerous classes' (as the Parisian poor were called) preoccupied governments for the first half of the century, and misery helped to fire a succession of revolutionary outbreaks. It was not unreasonable to fear that the growing cities could breed resentment and hatred of society's rulers and beneficiaries, and that this was a potentially revolutionary force.

It was also reasonable to guess that the city made for ideological subversion. It was a great destroyer of traditional patterns of behaviour, a crucible of new social reforms and ideas, a huge and anonymous thicket in which men and women could escape the scrutiny of the priest, squire and neighbours which regulated rural communities. In this new sense, like that of medieval towns, city air, foul though it might be, made men free. In the city (and this was especially true as literacy slowly spread downwards) new ideas came to bear upon long-unchallenged assumptions. Upper-class nineteenth-century Europeans were particularly struck by the seeming tendency of the urban masses to atheism and irreligion. More was at stake in that, they felt, than religious truth and sound doctrine (about which the upper classes themselves had long comfortably tolerated disagreement). Religion was still seen as the great sustainer of morals and the support of the established social order. In the 1840s one revolutionary writer had asserted that religion was 'the sigh of the oppressed' but also 'the opium of the people'.[4] The possessing classes would hardly have put it in the same terms, but they believed religion was good social cement. One result was a long-continued series of attempts both in Catholic and Protestant countries to find a way of recapturing the towns for Christianity. Such attempts were probably misconceived in so far as they presumed that the churches had ever had any footing in the urban areas which had long since swamped the traditional parish structures and religious institutions of the old towns and villages at their hearts. But they led to the building of new churches in industrial suburbs and the creation of missions combining evangelism and social service which taught priests and pastors the facts of modern city life. By the end of the century the religious-minded were at least well aware of the challenge they faced.

---

[4] Karl Marx, 'Contribution to the critique of Hegel's philosophy of law' in *Karl Marx, Friedrich Engels. Collected Works*, Vol.3 (London, 1975), p.175.

CHAPTER THREE A new sort of civilization

New patterns of life

It is almost impossible to strike a satisfactory balance in summarizing the impact of industrialization. It was too wide, deep and rapid. Even the rhythms of daily life changed. For the whole of history down to modern times, most economic behaviour had been regulated by nature. In the countryside, natural phenomena imposed a pattern on the year which dictated both the work which had to be undertaken and the work which could be. Operating within the framework set by the seasons were the subordinate divisions of light and darkness, fair weather and foul. Men lived in great intimacy with their tools, their animals and the fields in which they won their bread. Even townsmen lived, in large measure, lives shaped by the forces of nature. Weather was still a key factor well after 1850, a bad harvest could then still blight a whole year's business. Yet by then many people were living lives whose rhythms were dictated by quite different pacemakers. They were set by the methods of production, by the need to keep machines economically employed, by the cheapness or dearness of investment capital, by the availability of labour. The symbol of this was the factory whose machinery set a pattern of work in which accurate time-keeping was essential. Yet all this took place while most Europeans still lived on the land as peasants.

As well as imposing new rhythms, industrialism related the labourer to his work in other new ways. It is difficult, but important, to avoid sentiment in talking about what this meant. The disenchantment of the factory worker with a monotonous routine, with its exclusion of personal involvement and its background of the sense of working for another's profit has inspired much regret for a craftsman's world that has vanished, and much wringing of hands over the alienation of the worker from his product. But the life of the medieval peasant was monotonous, too, and for most it was spent working for another's profit. Nor is an iron routine necessarily less painful because it is set by sunset and sunrise instead of a factory clock, or more agreeably varied by drought or tempest than by commercial slump and boom. It may be safest simply to recognize that large-scale industry transformed the ways in which men won their livelihood, however we may evaluate the quality of the change.

A less troublesome example to assess can be found in child labour. Its abuse soon became notorious as a persistent evil of early industrialism. A generation of Englishmen morally braced by the abolition of slavery and by the exaltation that accompanied it, was also one intensely aware of the importance of religious training – and therefore of anything which might stand between it and the young. It was a generation, also, many of whose members were disposed to be sentimental about children in a way earlier generations had not been. All this helped to create an early awareness of this problem in the United Kingdom which perhaps distracted attention from the fact that the brutal exploitation of children in factories was only one part of the transformation of employment which was going on. That children should labour was not in itself new. They had for centuries provided adult Europeans with swineherds, birdscarers, gleaners, maids-of-all-work, crossing-sweepers, prostitutes and casual drudges, roles they still perform in many non-European societies. The terrible picture of the lot of unprotected children in the great novel of the French author Victor Hugo, *Les Misérables* (1862), is a picture of their life in a *pre*-industrial society. The difference made by industrialism was that their exploitation acquired new regularities and new harshnesses. Whereas the work of children in an agricultural society had perforce been clearly differentiated from that of adults by their inferior strength, the tending of machines offered opportunities for children's labour to compete directly with that of adults. In a labour market normally over-supplied, this meant well-nigh irresistible pressures upon the parent to send the child into the factory to add to the family income as soon as possible, sometimes at the age of five or six. The consequences were not only often terrible for the victims, but also revolutionary, for both the relations of children to society and the structure of the family were blighted.

Such evils were too pressing to remain long without attention. By 1850, British law had begun to intervene to protect women and children in mines and factories and other European states soon followed. It is worth recalling that in all the millennia of the history of agriculturally-based economies, it had still been impossible by that date to eradicate slavery, even in the Atlantic world. Given the unprecedented scale and speed with which social transformation was upon them, there is little to be gained (except self-satisfaction) by blaming the law-makers of early industrial Europe without qualification for not acting more quickly to remedy ills whose outlines they could only dimly grasp, and for not casting off more readily the blinkers imposed on them by their own share in the benefits of what was going on. To try to understand why they acted in some ways rather than others is more helpful.

Industrialization and ideology

It is temptingly easy to relate consciousness – the way people think and feel – to circumstances, especially those which are material and economic. Done badly, this is dangerously misleading, but gross 'reductionism', as it is called (the explaining-away of ideas and attitudes as mere expressions or consequences of some determining social and material reality) is fairly easy to detect and discount. Yet there is a large, ill-defined zone of human activity where connexions between thought and society in its more material aspects seem evident, though to pin down those connexions is hard. In talking about it, the simplest cases to approach are the most ideologically self-conscious, where men and women put forward complex, sometimes coherent or even systematic, ways of thinking which deliberately draw attention to the historical ground in which they are rooted. One of the most important of these in the early nineteenth century was evident in wide European support for a body of thinking and teaching often summed up in a phrase made famous by Frenchmen in the eighteenth century: *laissez-faire*. It was notably advocated in the leading industrial nation, Great Britain, but intellectuals in many countries were attracted to the ideas associated with it.

Though it is almost impossible to find economic theorists and publicists of the early industrial period who would in the last resort advocate absolute non-interference by government with the economy, there was a broad, sustaining current of support for the view that good would result if the market economy was left to operate without the help or hindrance of politicians and civil servants. Broadly speaking, economists after the great Adam Smith had said with growing consensus that the production of wealth would be accelerated, and therefore the general well-being would increase, if the use of economic resources followed the 'natural' demands of the market. This trend was easily accommodated to the individualism embodied both in the assumption that individuals knew their own business best and in the increasing organization of society around the rights and interests of individuals.

In these ideas lay the sources of a long-enduring political association between industrialism and liberalism; they were deplored by conservatives who mourned and idealized a hierarchical, agricultural order of mutual obligations and duties, settled ideas and religious values, and did not welcome the onset of what one of their seers called the age of 'sophists, economists and calculators'.[1] Yet those who welcomed the new age did not take their stand on a purely negative and selfish principle; the creed of 'Manchester' (as the liberal movement was often called in England because of the symbolic importance of that city in the nation's industrial and commercial development), was for those who articulated it most bluntly more than a matter of mere self-enrichment. A great political battle which for years preoccupied Englishmen in the early nineteenth century made this clear. Its focus was a campaign for the repeal of what were called the 'Corn Laws', a tariff system originally imposed to protect the British farmer from imports of cheap foreign grain. The 'repealers', whose ideological and political leader was a (none-too-successful) businessman, Richard Cobden, argued that much more was at stake. To begin with, retention of the duties on grain demonstrated the grip upon the legislative machinery of the agricultural interest, the traditional ruling class, who ought not to be allowed such power. Opposed to that class were the dynamic forces of the future, self-righteously and public-spiritedly seeking to liberate the economy from such distortions in the interest of particular groups. The anti-repealers rejoined that the manufacturers too were a particular interest who only wanted cheap food imports in order to be able to pay lower wages; if they wanted to help the poor, said Manchester's opponents, the way to do so was to regulate more firmly and humanely the conditions under which they employed women and children in their factories. There, the inhumanity of the production process showed a callous disregard for obligations towards the weak which (it was alleged) would never have been tolerated in rural England. To this, the repealers could again respond – that cheap food would mean cheaper goods for export, an outcome in which, for someone like Cobden, much more than profit was involved. World-wide Free Trade untrammelled by the interference of mercantilist governments would, he thought, lead to international progress both material and spiritual; trade brought peoples together, exchanged and multiplied the blessings of civilization and increased the power in each country of its progressive forces. On

---

[1] The phrase is Burke's and is to be found in his *Reflections on the Revolution in France*.

one occasion Cobden even committed himself to the view that Free Trade was the expression of the Divine Will (though he did not go as far as the British consul at Canton who had proclaimed that 'Jesus Christ is Free Trade, and Free Trade is Jesus Christ').

There was much more to the Free Trade debate (of which the Corn Law issue was the focus) than any brief summary suggests. The more it is expounded, though, the more it becomes clear that industrialism involved creative, positive ideologies and intellectual, social and political challenge to the past. It was not only a matter of simple moral judgements about exploitation, though at the time both conservatives and liberals thought it could be. The same man might resist legislation to protect the workman against long hours while proving himself a considerate employer, actively supporting educational and political reform and fighting the corruption of public interest by privileged birth. His opponent might struggle to protect the children working in factories while proving a model squire and benevolent parish patriarch to his tenants, and bitterly resisting the extension of the franchise to those outside the established Church or any reduction of the political influence of landlords. It was all very muddled. In the specific issue of the Corn Laws the outcome was paradoxical, too, for it was a conservative prime minister, Sir Robert Peel, who was in the end convinced by the arguments of the repealers, and persuaded parliament in 1846 to authorize their repeal.

Only in England was so big an issue fought out so explicitly and to so clear-cut a conclusion. In other countries, paradoxically, protectionists soon turned out to have the best of it. In Germany, in particular, the idea that a national economy might combine internal economic liberalism with a protection like that of old-fashioned mercantilism was well received.[2] Though a period of expansion and prosperity in the middle of the century won Free Trade ideas some support outside the United Kingdom, this did not last. The prestige of British economic primacy helped to give them a brief popularity elsewhere, but the prosperity of the era in fact owed much to other influences, and when these faded, international competition prompted a reversion to protective policies – operated largely through 'tariffs' of duties on imported goods – in most European countries by 1900. Yet economic liberals retained their confidence in the merits of competition and the potential of the individual.

The solid grounds for their optimism can nowadays be too easily overlooked. Circumstances favoured them, Europe was doing well out of its increasing mastery of first its own and then the world's resources. In the nineteenth century, Europeans went on, almost without reflexion on why they were able to do so, taking for themselves and consuming a growing share of the world's goods, usually after paying for them (but not at very high prices, because they did not need to). Rich when the nineteenth century began, they grew richer still as it went on. Compound interest and a certain self-feeding process was at work; new wealth in one part of the world helped to generate power to appropriate wealth in others. Congo rubber, Burmese teak and West African palm oil produced profits which for the most part were not reinvested in their countries of origin. Even poor Europeans benefited from falling prices for raw materials and food. European peasants could buy cheaply manufactured clothes and tools while African and Asian contemporaries still lived undisturbed in the Stone Age.

---

[2]   Ideas set out, especially, by the economist Friedrich List.

For all the apparent poverty of the new industrial societies, we labour under the handicap of not having before us the squalor of the past it left behind in trying to assess them. For all the filth and the slums, European city-dwellers in 1900 (and the very worst was over by then) consumed more and lived longer than their ancestors. This did not, of course, mean that by later standards they were either tolerably off or should have been contented. But they were often, and probably for the most part, materially better off than their predecessors or most of their contemporaries in the non-European world. Amazing as it may seem, they were part of the privileged minority of mankind. Their longer lives were the best evidence of it. They were the 'new rich' of the world; their grandparents had known nothing like such abundance.

Socialism

Distributing the new abundance nevertheless threw into relief stark contrasts within the European societies which were the first to be blessed with it. These in due course led to more and more governmental intervention in society and the economy. Contrasts of wealth were, of course, not new. There had also always been some who deplored or denounced them from the pulpit, for example. Now, though, differences were becoming more noticeable, partly because such evils were concentrated very visibly in the new cities and in new and unfamiliar forms. One outcome was the emergence of a new ideology of social criticism, and new political terms.

'Socialism', like the related 'socialist', was one of these. It has come to cover many different things. Both words first appeared in France round about 1830 to describe theories and men opposed to a society run on market principles and to an economy operated on *laissez-faire* lines, of which the main beneficiaries (they thought) were the wealthy. Most socialists have been able to agree that economic and social egalitarianism is fundamental to the socialist idea. All socialists could also agree that there was nothing sacred about property, whose rights usually buttressed injustice; some sought its complete abolition and were called communists.

Ideas like these might be frightening, but in some respects were not very novel. 'Property is theft' was a slogan coined in the French Revolution. Egalitarian ideas have fascinated men throughout history. The Christian rulers of Europe managed for centuries to reconcile social arrangements resting on sharp contrasts of rich and poor with the practice of a religion one of whose greatest hymns praised God for filling the hungry with good things and sending the rich empty away. What happened in the early nineteenth century was that these and similar ideas seemed to become at once more dangerous and more widespread. One reason for this was, paradoxically, the ambiguous success of liberal political reform itself. It appeared to show that civic and legal equality was not enough, if that equality was deprived of content by dependence on other men's economic power, or denatured by poverty and attendant ignorance. Another was that already in the eighteenth century a few thinkers had seen big discrepancies of wealth as irrationalities in a world which could and should (they thought) be regulated to produce the greatest good of the greatest number. In the French Revolution some thinkers and agitators pressed forward specific demands in which later generations would see socialist ideas. Egalitarian ideas none the less only became socialism in a modern sense when they began to grapple with the problems of the new epoch of economic and social change, above all with those presented by industrialization.

These changes only slowly made themselves felt outside Great Britain. Yet perhaps because the contrast they presented with traditional society was so stark, even the small beginnings of concentration in capitalist finance and manufacturing were easily noticed. This was all the more true in countries whose transition from the *ancien régime* was, as a result of the French Revolution, much sharper. One of the first men to grasp their potentially very great implications for social organization was a French nobleman, Claude Saint-Simon, who argued that technological and scientific advance not only made planned organization of the economy and society imperative, but implied (indeed, demanded) the replacement of the traditional ruling classes, aristocratic and rural in their outlook, by élites representing new economic and intellectual forces. Such ideas influenced other thinkers (most of them French) who in the 1830s advocated greater egalitarianism; they argued that on rational as well as ethical grounds greater economic equality was desirable. As most of them willingly identified themselves with the tradition of the French Revolution, picturing the realization of their ideals as its next phase was easy. It was also easy for the French possessing classes to see the 'June Days', a great Parisian uprising of 1848, as a 'socialist' revolution since it emerged from the withdrawal from Parisians of relief payments which they had been told represented 'socialism' by those who had advocated them.

It was in that year, too, that there had appeared a pamphlet which is the most important document in the history of socialism. It is always known as *The Communist Manifesto* (though this was not the title under which it appeared). With it the point is reached at which the prehistory of socialism can be separated from its history. It was largely the work of a young German Jew from the Rhineland, Karl Marx, who proclaimed a complete break with what he called the 'utopian socialism' of his predecessors. Utopian socialists attacked industrial capitalism because they thought it was unjust; Marx said this was beside the point. Nothing, according to Marx, could be hoped for from arguments to persuade people that change was morally desirable. Everything depended on the way history was actually going, towards the inevitable creation of a new working class by industrial society, the rootless wage-earners of the industrial cities whom he termed the industrial proletariat. This class was bound, according to him, to act in a revolutionary way. History would work upon it so as to generate revolutionary capacity and mentality. It would present its members with conditions to which revolution was the only logical outcome and that revolution would be, by those conditions, guaranteed success. What mattered was not that capitalism was morally wrong, but that it was historically out-of-date and therefore doomed. Marx asserted that every society had its own system of property rights and class relationships, and that these accordingly shaped its particular political arrangements. Politics were bound to express economic forces. They would change as the particular organization of society changed under the influence of economic developments, and therefore, sooner or later (and Marx seems to have thought sooner), the revolution would sweep away capitalist society and its forms as capitalist society had already swept away feudal.

This striking and encouraging message and his own combativeness, energy and intellectual ascendancy gave Marx domination of the international socialist movement which emerged in the next twenty years. The assurance that history was on their side was a great tonic to revolutionaries. They learnt with gratitude that the cause to which they were impelled anyway by motives ranging from a sense of injustice to the promptings of envy was predestined to triumph. This was essentially a religious dogma. For all its intellectual possibilities as an analytical instrument, Marxism came to be a mythology, resting on a view of history which said that men were bound by necessity because their institutions were determined by the evolving methods of production, and on a faith that the working class were the Chosen People whose pilgrimage through a wicked world would end in the triumphal establishment of a just society in which necessity's iron law would cease to operate. Social revolutionaries could thus feel confident of scientifically irrefutable arguments for irresistible progress towards the socialist millennium while clinging to a revolutionary activism it might have seemed to make unnecessary. Marx himself seems to have followed his teaching more cautiously, applying it only to the broad, sweeping changes in history which individuals are powerless to resist and not to its detailed unfolding. Perhaps it is not surprising that, like many masters, he did not recognize all his pupils: he came later to protest that he was not a Marxist.

This new religion provided further inspiration for working-class mobilization. Trades unions and co-operatives already existed in some countries; the first international organization (soon known, for short, as 'the International') of working men appeared in 1863. Though it included many who did not subscribe to Marx's views (anarchists, among others), his influence was paramount within it (he was its secretary). Its name frightened conservatives, and their instinct was right. In the years after 1848 socialism captured the revolutionary tradition from the liberals, and a belief in the historical role of an industrial working class which was still barely visible outside England (let alone predominant in most countries) was tacked on to the tradition which held that, broadly speaking, revolution could not be wrong. Forms of thinking about politics evolved in the French Revolution were thus transferred to societies to which they would often prove inappropriate.

Intellectual and cultural change

It is an immensely complicated problem to distinguish how and when modern civilization – the first, so far as we know, which does not have some formal structure of religious belief at its heart – came into being. So much depends on our definition of what we are looking for. Perhaps we cannot separate the role of the city or factory in breaking down traditional structures of belief from, say, that of science and philosophy in changing (or corrupting) culture, or from that of political radicals teaching that religion was a mask for social oppression. Yet a new future was visible already in the European industrial population by 1870. Much of it was literate, alienated from traditional authority, secular-minded and beginning to be conscious of itself as an entity. This was a different human basis for civilization from anything yet seen.

At the higher levels of intellectual activity, moreover, the nineteenth century was one of immense intellectual ferment. Both old and new ideas were constantly challenged. For that age, it is harder than ever to say what 'society' on the whole 'thought', and perhaps to try to do so is not sensible. People have pointed out, for example, that the things which often seemed most to dwarf the individual and remove his power to run his life – the growth of huge, anonymous cities, the building-up of industrial empires in which people were only little cogs in big machines, the increase in the power of government – were all likely to create feelings of passivity, apathy and helplessness. But it could equally well be argued that millions of people already and actually had more freedom of choice in much of their day-to-day life than in the past because science and technology gave them greater control than ever before over their environment and they had a little money in their pockets. Electricity and piped gas offered them better use of their time by providing cheaper, cleaner and simpler methods of lighting houses and workshops. Once the bicycle had been invented, millions of people had a new freedom of movement which they used both in leisure and in work. As the idea of contraception spread, men and women could shape their family lives as they pleased and not in accordance with chance.

Such freedom in very down-to-earth, practical matters must surely have told towards the general change in outlook in advanced societies which has been labelled 'materialism'. It was not just a matter of a growing taste for material comforts and pleasures; in every age such scarce goods as have been available have always been sought after by all ranks of society who thought they could get at them. The nineteenth century indeed marked an advance of materialism in this sense, because, as it proceeded, more and more goods were advertised as being available, and more and more pleasures came within reach of more and more people. But materialism at a deeper level was also a phenomenon of the age and perhaps more important as a register of cultural change.

One sign of it was a slow ebbing of belief in the overriding importance of the supernatural; church-going was declining in several countries already in the first half of the century. By the end of the century many people – at all levels of society – would have been willing to look to material explanations, often drawn from natural science, for explanations of the natural and human worlds and to reject whatever traditional religions might say about such matters. This was, from one point of view, a belated triumph of Enlightenment ideas. But no fruitful phase of a culture is without its contradictions and inner tensions, and such materialism clashed with other legacies of Enlightenment whose practical working-out only came in the nineteenth century. Materialism, for instance, was taken by some to imply that since certain material facts often determine what will happen in the long run and that individual efforts will not be able to affect this in any important degree, the fate of individuals was settled not by their rational choices and informed will – far less, by acts of God – but by mindless natural processes. The Enlightenment vision of the self-determining rational individual could have no place in such a world. In identifying such determining processes, some stressed the importance of geography or climate, others of race, others of economics. Official Marxism, in particular, tended as the century went on to seem more and more to boil down to saying that the world was bound to be the way it was because of material forces shaping economic life, with a happy outcome in sight in the inevitable triumph of the proletariat over its predecessors; whether this seemed comforting or depressing depended on where you sat to watch the drama of history unfold.

Determinist theories all had nonetheless one important feature in common: they tended to weaken the feeling that people have responsibility for their own lives and can freely take the decisions which shape them in accordance with chosen goals. This made them very different from the Christian ideas which lay at the root of European civilization, or from the vision of the free, enquiring individual dreamed of by the thinkers of the Renaissance and Enlightenment, and even from the attitudes of the men who made the break-through to industrial society: all of these believed that what individuals decided to do mattered very much and could, indeed, change the world. The popularity of determinist ideas showed that something very fundamental was shifting at the deepest levels of an inherited culture.

Science

All civilizations have contributed to mankind's growing management of nature. The greatest instrument ever brought to bear to that end is modern science and it is another easily acceptable truism that 'no people or group of peoples has had a monopoly in contributing to the development of Science'[3]. But it is also a truism that all the science now practised throughout the world can be traced back to roots in the transformation of attitudes towards the natural world which manifested itself in Europe in the sixteenth and seventeenth centuries. However much had been absorbed into European thinking about the natural world from other cultures before that time – above all in the form of observations – what is now world science is the product of the experimental method, the institutional arrangements and the techniques and the instrumentation whose evolution began in the European 'Scientific Revolution'.

By 1800 that had already created an international community with a distinctive scientific culture (and it already spanned the Atlantic). The next 100 years enlarged it worldwide, but above all in the old and new Europe. This was both a part and a reflexion of a huge and complex growth in scientific endeavour. Big books have been written even about some of its secondary manifestations, so rapid was an exponential growth in discovery, technique and scale. As a part of the story of the general history of Europe, though, all that can be indicated here are three topics which appear to have over-riding importance. One is psychological and cultural: the growing public esteem enjoyed by science and its own practitioners' growing self-confidence. One is the accomplishment itself and the accelerating and diversifying nature of what was done. The third is the impact made by science on the lives of those who were not engaged in it.

Words can be useful guides to status; the 1830s and 1840s brought the now familiar word 'scientist' into the English language. The usual term before that for those who studied nature and its workings had been 'natural philosophers'. People had begun to feel, though, that there was a need to distinguish more clearly between the rigorous experimental investigation of nature and speculation about it through abstract reason. There was also a growing sense of difference between true science and the work of those who sought to apply its knowledge in what men and women in 1800 still called the 'useful and mechanical arts'. This change was associated with the clarification of the nature of 'scientific' as opposed to other kinds of truth. One man who did much to urge the need for this revaluation of science as a unique form of knowledge based only on observable phenomena, also spoke of it as 'positive' truth. This was Auguste Comte, a Frenchman who based a philosophy of 'positivism' on the distinction; it enjoyed some vogue for a considerable time among intellectuals and was based (like the views of Marx) on a conception of the way history was moving. Comte's view was that history had reached in his day the final stage in the evolution of civilization, its positive or scientific stage after earlier phases in which the human intellect had looked to superstition and religion for guidance.

Positivism did not have a very long life as philosophical system but helped, as the century progressed, together with the practical fall-out from the work of scientists and much popular misunderstanding and ignorance of what they actually did, to win the confidence of the educated public to science and its methods. This, in turn gave scientists self-

---

[3]   Joseph Needham, *Science and Civilization in China*, I (Cambridge, 1954), I, p.9.

confidence. Such developments were part of the background of the way science became a mythology, or even a religion, for many Europeans as time passed. The pronouncements of scientists began to influence the way men and women looked at the world as the teachings of priests had once done. It came to be as influential in this way as through its explanation and manipulation of nature. In its grossest form, such credulity has been called 'scientism' by some historians of culture. One of its expressions was a greatly increased willingness to extend the scientific method into new areas as the only sure road to truth. Saint-Simon envisaged a reconstruction of society on the basis of science and industry. Karl Marx also exemplified the wish to found a science of society, and a name for one was provided by Comte – 'sociology'. In particular, some sought to establish 'social sciences'. The utilitarian followers of the English reformer and philosopher Jeremy Bentham were among these. He had hoped to base the management of society upon calculated use of the principles that men responded to pleasure and pain, and that pleasure should be maximized and pain minimized, it being understood that what was to be taken into account were the sensations of the greatest number and their intensity. These (and many other) attempts to emulate the natural sciences proceeded on a basis of a search for general and quasi-mechanical laws; that the natural sciences were at that moment moving away from the search for such laws does not signify here; the search by non-scientists still testified to the scientific model's prestige. The insight of the Enlightenment that man himself might be a subject for study as a determined natural object was taken up with enthusiasm and little concern for what might be the implications or consequences.

Major scientific advances of the nineteenth century were cumulative and came with increasing rapidity. Broadly speaking, when it began the horizons of natural science were still set by the physics of Newton, the mathematics of Laplace, and the chemistry of Lavoisier. In addition, the reliable observation of and experimentation with electrical phenomena had begun, as had the systematic investigation of heat; much solid and specific observational knowledge had also been acquired of the botanical and animal worlds, as of geology and anatomy in the previous century. In the nineteenth, the landscape changed dramatically and by 1900 the physical universe looked very different. Physics had been revolutionised. Chemistry had by then become a bundle of sciences rather than a single field and its applications to living substances were enthusiastically under examination. A new science, genetics (though not its name; the word 'gene' was only invented in 1909), had emerged from the hybridization experiments of the Austrian monk, Gregor Mendel, while from biology had also come a hypothesis whose possible application was seemingly so broad that it might be reckoned to be as important as had been the ideas of Newton two centuries earlier.

To explain comprehensively how this happened, and by what precise steps, is impossible in the compass of this book, and any attempt to trace the process is liable to degrade the story into an inadequate catalogue of names. Some, though, cannot be omitted, and must include those of Michael Faraday, the great experimentalist who began as a chemist, and James Clerk Maxwell, for their contribution to the discovery and understanding of electro-magnetism and thermodynamics; their work opened the way to a new view of the universe as more than a collection of lumps of matter in various combinations. They made possible a revolution in physics still gathering pace in the 1890s, with the discovery of X-rays and the phenomenon of radioactivity. Chemistry was revolutionized almost as sweepingly by men among whom the leading names were at first German, above all that of von Liebig, the architect of organic chemistry, though

wider public attention was won later by the Frenchman, Louis Pasteur. Through micro-
biology he produced the evidence to formulate and sustain the theory of infection, a
landmark in medical history. It was soon put to use, notably by the surgeon Lister, who
introduced antisepsis to the operating theatre (by, among other things, spraying it with
carbolic acid, thus, to the great man's chagrin, provoking chants of 'let us spray' from his
irreverent students).

The rapid deployment in agriculture, industry and medicine of the work of Pasteur
is well-known, but that of Faraday, Maxwell and Liebig, too, like that of hundreds of
other scientists, was also soon put to practical use. Application was one of the ways in
which science made its fastest and most striking impact on the imagination of the lay
public. But this was not the only way the European mind was changed by science. This
is clear in, above all, the instance of a man who, if the general effect of his work is considered, was probably the most influential scientist of the century.

In 1859 Charles Darwin, an English naturalist, published a book usually known for
short as *The Origin of Species*. It was in fact a follow-up to a paper he and another naturalist, Alfred Russell Wallace, had presented to the Royal Society the previous year, and
set out more completely and comprehensively an evolutionary theory of zoology
sketched in that paper. Its central proposition, confirmed by observation, was that living
beings were what they were because their species had undergone evolution through
selection, often over very long periods, from earlier ones, changing physically in the
process. Though the word 'evolution' did not appear in the book until its fifth edition,
ten years later, it was already in use before Darwin wrote[4]; his special contribution and
clarification of it was to identify the way in which physical evolution happened. Drawing on botanical and geological data as well as zoology, he argued that those qualities
which made it possible for animals to succeed and survive in hostile environments were
likely to be passed on by them to their descendants because they enabled them to survive to breed. Those with less appropriate qualities would be unable to pass those particular qualities on, because they would not survive to do so. Thus occurred a 'natural
selection' of creatures with certain characteristics. Later (not by Darwin) there was
coined a striking phrase, 'the survival of the fittest', words which vulgarized his views
and were often to be misunderstood, but which were also picked up and widely misused
to summarize his message.

Darwin had put into circulation what was to prove the most fruitful scientific idea
of the century. In 1871 he published another book, *The Descent of Man*, in which he
made it explicit that his hypothesis about natural selection and evolution applied to
humans. The relevance beyond biological science was obvious. His ideas were soon
being applied, with little regard for close understanding of them, to those who wished
to justify political or social success (as shown, for example, by the rule of white men over
other races) as that of those 'fittest' to enjoy it. They influenced arguments about economic life, by satisfying people that the supposedly free competition of the marketplace
would assure that those with brains and acumen would come to the top naturally in
commerce and industry. These were comforting ideas for those who had been successful in the battles of life. They were usually taken to imply that not much good could be
done by interference to alleviate the lot of those unsuccessful in them. The noisiest

---

5   The major exposition of another theory of evolution as the basis of animal differentiation had been by
the French scientist Lamarck in his *Philosophie zoologique* of 1809.

impact of Darwinian thinking, nonetheless, was made (first in England) among the religiously minded. Natural selection was a blow delivered not only against the biblical account of creation (already weakened by geological science) but against the fundamental assumption that humankind enjoyed a special and God-given status among living creatures. Darwinian ideas made it impossible for any conscientious and thoughtful person to accept – as had still been possible when the century began – that the Bible, the central text of Christianity, was literally true.

Science probably struck its heaviest blows against religious belief and the institutions which upheld it by undermining the authority of scripture and traditional religious teaching. Yet it was not the only damaging influence at work to do so, nor did it operate solely by providing what seemed to be direct and convincing contradictions of the things religion had traditionally taught. It was influential also through a growing prestige. As scepticism spread beyond the élites which could debate (or at least had heard of) what Darwin said, the mythology which surrounded science grew steadily, but for reasons very different from conviction by argument. Thousands who knew nothing of the work of Lister or Faraday (or even their names) knew by 1900 nonetheless that the medicine they could turn to was different from and better than that available to their grandparents and were familiar with the operation of the mysterious force of electricity at work around them. Material progress imperceptibly drew the man-in-the-street to worship at new shrines, whether at first consciously or not. It was in the nineteenth century that science at last came to play not only an important but an obvious role in the maintenance of society and in its daily life. Chemistry, for example, through its importance to dyeing, then for the first time showed its industrial potential to those who had not grasped the importance of chemical reactions in an ancient practice like brewing. The investigation of the chemistry of dyes led into other areas of manufacturing – drugs, antiseptics, explosives – with huge effect. As for the new 'fast' dyes themselves, they had their own psychological and social importance. They made possible somewhat less drab cheap clothing for the industrial working class. In medicine it was epoch-marking that aspirin should be produced at the very end of the century as a relief for pain, something hardly available either to rich or poor in the past except through opium or alcohol.

In such seedbeds, the mythology of science flourished. It is now a familiar fact that science, with its vast and accumulating mass of knowledge validated by experiment, shapes the way men look at the world, just as great religions have done in the past. Some have sought from it guidance about metaphysical questions, or about the aims men ought to pursue, or the standards they should employ to regulate behaviour. All this, of course, has had no intrinsic or necessary connexion with science as the pursuit of scientists, but was a result of informal, inferential perceptions about things ordinary people did not understand. The ultimate outcome was to be a civilization with, except vestigially, no essential religious belief or transcendent ideals. They did not seem to be needed in order to understand the world – or at least not needed by the masses. The core of modern European civilization for them, whether or not made explicit, lay (and still lies) in belief in the promise of what can be done by manipulating nature. In principle, modernity preached that no problem need be regarded as insoluble, given sufficient resources of intellect and money; there was room in modern life for the obscure, but not for the essentially mysterious. Many scientists have drawn back from this conclusion, of course. All its implications are still far from being grasped. But it is the assumption on which a world view now rests and it was formed in essentials before 1900.

CHAPTER FOUR A new
European order

Legitimacy and its challengers

The revolutionary and Napoleonic years had demolished much of the European *ancien régime*, as well as shaking or setting aside still more of it for a time, but above all had called it in question. It could never again be seen as the only, the necessary, way in which Europe could live and be governed. It was henceforth known to be challengeable and changeable; whether that was thought to be a good or a bad thing. A new sense of the fragility of the established order was strengthened, too, by the slow but fundamental social and economic changes just beginning to be visible in one or two places in Europe in 1815. Such facts as these would not go away. It was to be among the deepest sources of the disappointments of conservative statesmen in the next half-century or so, that they grew larger and larger. They came even to dominate the political landscape in many countries. Added to the specific changes in political arrangements, and to the ideas and aspirations which were left over from an unprecedented era of revolution and war, it is hardly surprising that far from the return to a near-static normality to which some aspired, 1815 marked in fact the beginning of another turbulent era.

The scope of what that brought can most easily and quickly be grasped through the way the map of Europe changed in the next eighty or so years. By 1871, when a newly-united Germany took its place among the great powers, most of Europe west of a line drawn from the Adriatic to the Baltic was organized in states based on the principle of nationality, however qualified that principle was in practice. Even to the east of that line there were some states already identified as nations. By 1914 most of the Balkans would be organized as nation-states, too, and after that the triumph of nationalism was to go yet further.

The changes in the map were inseparable from the acceptance of a new framework of political thought and action. Over time, and over more of Europe, it came to be recognized during the nineteenth century that a public interest existed which was superior to that of individual rulers or privileged hierarchies. Governments came to accept that they had at least to appear to govern on behalf of that interest. Competition within the state to define and protect it came to be seen as legitimate. Such competition was thought increasingly to require special arenas and institutions; old juridical or courtly forms no longer seemed adequate to settle its outcome. These new politics were not merely a matter of a new language and new devices, moreover. There was also a change in political thinking at the deepest level, the assertion of the politics of will. Constitutional and good government ceased to be simply a matter of assuring people the enjoyment of what they were entitled to by law or tradition, and political struggle came instead increasingly to be directed towards satisfying wants. For centuries a huge weight of respect for the historic past had overhung what we somewhat anachronistically think of as European 'politics', transactions of power very little like our own. In the sixteenth century, Dutchmen and Belgians had resisted their legal sovereign in defence of their legal and historic privileges — those of towns, provinces, individuals. In the seventeenth century, some Englishmen resisted the king in defence of the historic (they said) privileges of parliament, and others fought for the Crown to protect the historic rights of its holder. At about the same time Catalonians talked the language of the old constitution of the Kingdom of Aragon while they rebelled against government from Madrid. Even Americans began in the 1760s by saying they were claiming rights to which they were as entitled as other subjects of the crown who enjoyed them. Finally the breakdown of the old order in France in 1789 came about and revolution was detonated when aristocrats and the judiciary opposed the monarchy's wish to interfere with traditional privilege.

In this sense, the words 'We the People' can serve as a marker for the beginning of change. After the experiments in France in the 1790s the mode of European political thinking was already having to take account of something new, the search for what was *willed*, as well as for what was due. This transformed old arguments about obedience and obligation: the question became one of identifying the people whose wishes

EUROPE IN 1815
—— German Confederation boundary

should be attended to, the group entitled to exercise sovereignty. What could properly legitimize authority was continually argued and re-argued as the century went on. Appeal to historic right alone was insufficient. Even if it deserved some respect — or if, at least, sympathy might be shown to those claiming its protection — in every country the leading political question became, in the end, one about whose wishes ought legitimately to prevail. The answers to it were increasingly to be given in terms of nationality and democracy, but the institutional framework for such a transformation and formal recognition of it took much longer to emerge in some countries than others. In the restoration era after 1815 nationalism was evidently still a force struggling against older principles — that of dynasticism, for instance. Moreover, although it was more and more a commonplace of European political debate as the nineteenth century went on that the interests of those recognized to be 'historic' nations should be protected and promoted by governments, this was wholly compatible with bitter and prolonged disagreement about which 'nations' or peoples claiming to be nations were historic, about how their interests could be defined, and about who should speak for them and to what extent they could and should be given weight in statesmen's decisions.

The process was sometimes violent, for the idea of legitimate opposition was for many people an unacceptable paradox: in the half-century after 1780 perhaps only the United Kingdom (and, across the Atlantic, the United States) actually accepted it. In interpreting slow but crucial change, therefore, there is a danger of anachronism: terms like democracy and liberalism are not easy to define, and now carry associations they did not have in the early nineteenth century. What can be said is that a general trend towards accepting representative institutions as a way of associating (even if only formally) more and more people with the government operated over the long run. Liberals and democrats almost always asked for more people to be given votes and for better electoral representation. More and more, too, the individual became the basis of political and social organization in economically advanced countries. Membership of communal, religious, occupational and family units was coming to matter less than individual rights. This led in some ways to greater freedom, in some ways to less. The state was to go on growing more powerful both practically and juridically in relation to its subjects in the nineteenth century.

Besides having enormous importance in actually launching such changes, the French Revolution was a continuing influence and source of mythology. For all the hopes and fears that the Revolution was over by 1815, its full Europe-wide impact had then still to be felt. In many countries ancient institutions invited criticism and demolition and were becoming more vulnerable as economic and social change got to work. This gave radicals and revolutionaries new hopes and opportunities. There was a widespread sense that all Europe, for good or ill, faced revolution, at least potentially. This encouraged upholders and would-be-destroyers of the existing order alike to sharpen political issues and to try to fit them into the frameworks provided by the principles of 1789. By and large, these ideas dominated the history of Europe down to about 1870 and provided the dynamic of its politics, though they did not achieve all their advocates hoped and their realization in practice had many qualifications. Yet they made nineteenth-century Europe a political laboratory whose experiments, discoveries and explosions shaped the history of the rest of the world.

Foundations of peace

The foundation deed of the nineteenth-century international order was the Treaty of Vienna of 1815. It closed the era of the French wars and was intended to prevent their repetition. The peacemakers sought the containment of France and the avoidance of revolution, using as their materials the principle of legitimacy which was the ideological core of conservative Europe and certain practical territorial arrangements against future French aggression. Thus Prussia was given large acquisitions on the Rhine, a new monarchy (constitutional, and with a reasonably large electorate) appeared under a Dutch king ruling both Belgium and the Netherlands, Genoa was given to the kingdom of Sardinia, and Austria not only recovered her former Italian possessions, but kept Venice and was allowed a virtually free hand to keep the other Italian states in order. In some of these cases legitimacy can be seen to bow to expediency; those despoiled during the years of upheaval did not all obtain restoration. But the powers talked legitimacy all the same, and (once the arrangements were complete) did so with some success. For nearly forty years the Vienna settlement provided a framework within which disputes were settled without war. Most of what was set up in 1815 was still there, even if somewhat shaken, forty years later.

This owed much to a salutary fear of subversion. In all the major continental states the years after 1815 were a great period for policemen and plotters alike. Secret societies proliferated, undiscouraged by failure after failure which showed that they presented no revolutionary threat that could not be handled. Austrian soldiers dealt with attempted coups in Piedmont and Naples, a French army restored the power of a reactionary Spanish king hampered by a liberal constitution, the Russian empire survived a military conspiracy and a Polish revolt. The Austrian predominance in Germany was not threatened (though the imperial government feared it was) and it is difficult in retrospect to discern any very real danger to any part of the Habsburg monarchy before 1848. Russian and Austrian power, the first in reserve, the second the main force in central Europe and Italy from 1815 to 1848, were the two rocks on which the Vienna system rested.

Mistakenly, liberalism and nationalism were usually supposed to be inseparable; this was later to be shown to be terribly untrue, but in so far as a few people did seek to change Europe by revolution before 1848, it is broadly true that they wanted to do so by advancing both the political principles of the French Revolution — representative government, popular sovereignty, freedom of the individual and the press — and those of nationality. Many confused the two; the most famous and admired of those who did so was Mazzini, a young Italian. By advocating an Italian unity most of his countrymen did not want and conspiring unsuccessfully to bring it about, he became an inspiration and model for other nationalists and democrats in every continent for over a century and one of the first idols of radical chic. But the age of the ideas he represented had not yet quite come.

West of the Rhine, where the writ of the Holy Alliance (the name often used for the group of three conservative powers, Russia, Austria and Prussia) did not run, the story was different; there, legitimism did not last long. The very restoration of the Bourbon dynasty in 1814 had itself been a compromise with the principle. Louis XVIII was supposed to have reigned like any other king of France since the death of his predecessor,

THE MAKING OF THE ITALIAN NATIONAL STATE 1815–71

1815	Jan	Italy organized as	– Kingdom of Sardinia (Savoy, Piedmont, former republic of Genoa, and the island of Sardinia)
			– Duchies of Modena, Lucca and Parma
			– Grand-duchy of Tuscany
			– The Papal States
			– Kingdom of Naples
			– Republic of San Marino
		Lombardy and Venetia are given to Austria.	

1820 and 1831   Waves of temporarily successful risings and coups in Naples, Turin, Modena, Parma, Papal States all put down in the end with Austrian help. Mazzini fails to bring off insurrection in Piedmont (1832) and Savoy (1833).

1846   Election of Pius IX, believed to be a 'liberal' pope.

1847   Foundation of newspaper *Il Risorgimento* at Turin by Cavour.
Austrian occupation of Ferrara (Papal States).

1848   Jan –Mar   Constitutional and patriotic (anti-Austrian) risings in Sicily, Naples, Tuscany, Piedmont, Romagna, Milan, Venice, and Sardinian declaration of war on Austria.

       Apr   Pius IX pronounces against war with Austria as a Catholic power.
       Aug   Sardinia forced to an armistice by defeat.
       Nov   Rising in Rome and the pope flees from the city followed by:

1849   Feb   Proclamation of a Roman Republic.
       July   French expedition suppresses Roman Republic and restores Pius.
       Aug   Sardinia resumes war with Austria and is defeated; forced to pay indemnity and king abdicates (but consitution granted in 1847 is maintained). Venice surrenders to Austrians.

1850   Cavour enters Sardinian government (prime minister in 1852). Promotes anti-clerical legislation.

1855   Sardinia joins in Crimean War against Russia and Cavour uses peace congress to publicise Italy's plight.

1856   National Society founded to work for Italian unity under Sardinian monarchy.

1858   Secret agreement of Cavour and Napoleon III for a new war with Austria.

1859   Apr   Austria provokes war with Sardinia.
      May–June   Revolutions in Tuscany, Modena, Parma, Papal States; defeat of Austrians by French in Lombardy.
            Peace of Villafranca between France and Austria.

1860   Napoleon III agrees to Sardinian annexation (after plebiscite) of Parma, Modena, Tuscany, Romagna, in return for cession to France of Nice and Savoy. With covert support from Cavour, Garibaldi invades Sicily with the 'Thousand', crosses to Italy, overthrows Naples monarchy. Rising in Papal States provides excuse for Sardinian invasion which then blocks Garibaldi's advance on Rome. Naples, Sicily, Umbria and Papal Marches vote for annexation to Sardinia.

1861   17 Mar   Proclamation of Kingdom of Italy under Vittorio Emmanuele II.

1862   Italian forces halt expedition by Garibaldi, who is wounded and captured by them at Aspromonte (29 August).

THE MAKING OF THE ITALIAN NATIONAL STATE 1815–71 (continued)	
1866	Italo-Prussian alliance and transfer of Venetia to Italy after Austrian defeat in Seven Weeks' War with Prussia.
1867	Garibaldi's invasion of Papal States halted by papal and French forces at Mentana (3 November).
1870	Withdrawal of French garrison from Rome during Franco-Prussian war, and (20 September) Italian forces enter the city after bombardment and assault. After plebiscite, Rome annexed and becomes capital of Italy
1871	Law of Guarantees defines Italo-Papal relations, assuring income and independence of the pope, and extra-territoriality of Vatican State.

Louis XVII, in a Paris prison in 1795. In fact, as everyone knew but legitimists tried to conceal, he came back in the baggage train of the Allied armies which had defeated Napoleon and did so only on terms acceptable to the French political and military élites and, presumably, tolerated by the mass of Frenchmen. The restored regime was a constitutional monarchy, albeit with a limited suffrage. The rights of individuals were guaranteed in a formal charter and the land settlement resulting from revolutionary confiscations and sales was undisturbed; there was to be no return to 1789. Napoleon's Concordat continued to regulate the Church and France's new departmental divisions and prefectorial system were left intact.

Nevertheless, there was some uncertainty about the future; battle between Right and Left began with arguments about the charter — was it a contract between king and people, or a simple emanation of the royal benevolence which might therefore be withdrawn as easily as it had been granted? — and went on over a whole range of issues which raised questions of principle (or were thought to do so) about ground won for liberty and the possessing classes in the Revolution. What was implicitly at stake was to establish what the Revolution had actually achieved. One way of describing that would be to say that those who had struggled to be recognized as having a voice in ruling France under the *ancien régime* had won; the political weight of the 'notables', as they were sometimes called, was assured. Whether drawn from the old nobility of France, those who had done well out of the Revolution as Napoleon's lackeys and soldiers, or simply substantial landowners and businessmen, they were the real rulers of France. Another change had been the nation-making of the 1790s; no person or corporation could now claim to stand outside the operative sphere of the national government of France. Finally and crucially, the Revolution had transformed the terms in which French public affairs could be discussed and debated. Wherever the line was to be drawn between Right and Left, conservatives or liberals, it was on that line that political struggle now focused, not over the privilege of counselling a monarch by Divine Right. When the last king of the direct Bourbon line, Charles X, failed to see this and by what was virtually a *coup d'état* foolishly attempted in 1830 to break out of the constitutional limitations which bound him, Paris rose against him. Liberal politicians hastily put themselves at the head of the 'July Revolution'. To the chagrin of republicans, they made sure that a new king replaced Charles, but 'legitimists' saw him as a usurper.

GERMANY'S CONSOLIDATION: BEFORE 1815

1785	Frederick II of Prussia organizes League of German Princes to oppose plans of the emperor Joseph II to negotiate absorption of Bavaria into Habsburg dominions.
1790	Prussia supports Ottoman empire in resisting Austro–Russian pressure.
1801	Treaty of Lunéville between France and Austria gives France the left bank of the Rhine with provision for compensation of the German princes there from territory inside Germany. This opens way to:
1803	Decision of deputies of Holy Roman Empire (Reichsdeputationschluss) to reorganize Germany. All major princes gain territory, but only one former ecclesiastical principality and six free imperial cities survive.
1804	Francis II, Holy Roman Emperor, takes title of Francis I, emperor of Austria.
1805	By treaty of Pressburg with France (after battle of Austerlitz, 2 December) Austria concides territories to Bavaria, Wurtemberg and Baden.
1806	Confederation of Rhine set up (July) by France (it eventually embraces all German princes except those of Austria, Prussia, Brunswick and Hesse) and (August) end of Holy Roman Empire. In October, French defeat Prussia at Jena, Auerstadt and in:
1807	Napoleon sets up new kingdom of Westphalia and a duchy of Warsaw under king of Saxony, with land taken from both Prussia and Russia.
1809	Further Austrian territorial losses after abortive appeal for German support in rising against the French (Tyrol responds).
1812	Prussia and Austria both again go to war with France. Battle of Leipzig (October) and crumbling of French hegemony in Germany begins. Allies offer France peace on basis of Rhine frontier but this is not taken up.
1814–15	Vienna settlements provide for territorial gain in Germany by both Austria and Prussia and set up a new Germanic Confederation of 39 states, including four free cities, with a federal diet presided over by an Austrian representative.

The July Monarchy

The new king, Louis Philippe, was head of the junior branch of the French royal house, the Orléans family, and to many conservatives the Revolution incarnate, though he hardly struck radicals as anything of the sort. But his father had voted for the execution of Louis XVI (and went to the scaffold himself soon after) while Louis Philippe had fought as an officer in the republican armies and had even been a member of the notorious Jacobin club in the 1790s. To liberals Louis Philippe was attractive because he reconciled the Revolution with the stability provided by the monarchy. For eighteen years his governments acted constitutionally and preserved the essential political freedoms in the interests of the well-to-do. They vigorously suppressed urban disorder (of which poverty produced plenty in the 1830s) and this made the regime unpopular with the Left. One prominent politician told his fellow-countrymen to enrich themselves — a recommendation much ridiculed and misunderstood, though all he was trying to do was to tell them that the way to obtain the vote was through the qualification which a high income conferred (at the outset of the 'July Monarchy' only about a third as many Frenchmen as Englishmen had a vote in national elections, while the population of France was about twice that of England).

Nevertheless, the regime rested in theory on popular sovereignty, the revolutionary principle of 1789.

This gave it a special international stance, too. In the 1830s differences between a constitutional Europe — England, France, Spain and Portugal — and the legitimist, dynastic states of the East, bound together by the crime of Polish partition, and their domination of Italian and German satellites, were sharply evident. The dynastic empires had not liked the July revolution. They were alarmed when the Belgians rebelled against their Dutch king in 1830, and broke away, but could not support him because the British and French favoured the Belgians and Russia soon had a Polish rebellion on her hands. It took until 1839 to secure an independent Belgium; this was the only important change in the state system created by the Vienna settlement before 1848, though the internal troubles of Spain and Portugal caused much diplomatic concern.

The new Eastern Question

In south-east Europe, the pace of change quickened more visibly. A new revolutionary era was opening there just as that of western Europe moved to its climax. In 1804 a well-to-do Serbian pork dealer had led a revolt by his countrymen against the undisciplined Turkish garrison of Belgrade. At that moment, the Ottoman regime was willing to countenance his actions in order to bridle its own mutinous soldiers. But the eventual cost to the empire was the establishment of an autonomous Serbian princedom in 1817. By then the Turks had also ceded Bessarabia to Russia, and had been forced to recognize that their hold on much of Greece and Albania was little more than formal, real power being in the hands of the local Pashas.

This was, though hardly yet visibly so, the opening of the Eastern Question of the nineteenth century which after more than a century and two world wars, still remains unsolved: who or what was to inherit the fragments of the crumbling Ottoman empire? Both in Europe, North Africa and Asia, wars of the Ottoman Succession were to go on for the next two centuries. The Vienna settlement had not included Ottoman territories among those covered by guarantees from the great powers. Racial, religious, ideological and diplomatic issues were entangled from the start. When what was soon represented as a 'revolution' of 'Greeks' (by which were meant Orthodox Christian subjects of the Sultan, many of them bandits and pirates) began against the Turks in 1821, Russia favoured the rebels; this cut across conservative principles, but public opinion (there was much sympathy for the Greeks), religion and the old pull of Russian imperialist interests to the south-east made it impossible for the Holy Alliance to support the sultan as it supported other rulers. In the end, the Russians alone went to war with the Ottomans and defeated them. It was now evident that the nineteenth-century Eastern Question was going to be further complicated by other national rebellions, for the independent kingdom of Greece which emerged in 1832 was bound to give ideas to other peoples of the Balkans.

1848

The 1840s were in many places years of economic hardship, food shortages and distress, particularly in Ireland where, in 1846, there was a horrifying famine, and then in the following year in central Europe and France, where commercial slump brought unemployment. This bred social violence which gave new edge to radical movements everywhere. One disturbance inspired another; example was contagious and weakened the capacity of the international security system to deal with further outbreaks. The outcome was a continent-wide explosion of revolution which for a time seemed to endanger the whole Vienna settlement.

The symbolic start came in February 1848, in Paris. Louis Philippe quickly abdicated when it suddenly appeared that he no longer had middle-class support for his continued opposition to extension of the suffrage. This was the 'February Revolution'. When a republic then appeared in France, every revolutionary and political exile in Europe took heart. For a little while it seemed that the whole 1815 settlement might crumble. The dreams of thirty years' conspiracies seemed realizable. The *Grande Nation* would be on the move again and the armies of the Revolution might once more march to spread its principles. This, of course, was a correspondingly terrible prospect for conservatives. As it turned out, hopes and fears were both unrealized. France made a diplomatic genuflexion in the direction of martyred Poland, the classical focus of liberal sympathies, but the only military operations she undertook were to be in defence of the pope against Roman revolutionaries. Without French help, though, by the middle of the year government had been swept aside or was at best on the defensive in every major European capital except London, Madrid and St Petersburg. Politics almost everywhere else were, for a little while, internationalized.

This was only superficial. The revolutionaries of 1848 were provoked by very different situations, had many different aims, and followed divergent and confusing paths. In most of Italy and central Europe townsmen rebelled against governments which they thought oppressive because they were illiberal; their great symbolic demand was for constitutions to guarantee essential freedoms. When such a revolution occurred in Vienna itself, the chancellor Metternich, an architect and the most enduring upholder of the conservative order of 1815, fled into exile. Successful revolution at Vienna meant the paralysis of government throughout much of central Europe. Germans were now free to have their revolutions without fear of Austrian intervention. The *ancien régime* collapsed in the smaller states. Elsewhere in the Austrian dominions, Italians (led by an ambitious but apprehensive conservative king of Sardinia) turned on the Austrian armies in Lombardy and Venetia. A republic appeared at Rome and the pope fled the city. Hungarians revolted at Budapest, and Czechs at Prague. But some of these revolutionaries sought national independence rather than constitutionalism, though constitutionalism seemed for a time the way to independence because it attacked dynastic autocracy. If the liberals were successful in getting constitutional governments installed in all the capitals of central Europe and Italy, then it would be likely that there would actually come into existence nations hitherto without state structures of their own, or at least without them for a very long time.

Soon, discouraging prospects appeared; this promising scenario lost some of its charm. If, for instance, Slavs (or Pan-Slavs) achieved their national liberation, then states previously thought of as German would be shorn of huge tracts of their territory, notably in Poland and Bohemia. It took some time for this to sink in. The German liberals suddenly fell over the problem in 1848 and the eventual outcome was the failure of the German revolutions. Essentially, they decided that German nationalism required the preservation of German lands in the east. Hence, they needed a strong Prussia and would have to accept its terms for the future organization of Germany.

1848–49: MAJOR EVENTS

1848	Jan	Popular rebellion in Sicily, spreading through kingdom of Naples.
	Feb	Constitution granted in Naples. Revolution in Paris, Louis Philippe abdicates and Second Republic proclaimed. Granting of constitutions in Piedmont and Tuscany.
	Mar	Uprising in Vienna. Demands for Czech and Hungarian autonomy, Venetian and Lombard independence. Uprising in Berlin, King Frederick William IV grants constitution in Prussia. Other German states follow suit.
	Apr	Hungary separates from Austria within the Habsburg empire. Constitution granted in Austria.
	May	Frankfurt Parliament, dominated by German liberals, opens debate on a new constitution for Germany as a whole.
	June	'Pan-Slav' congress meets in Prague. Uprising in Prague crushed by Habsburg forces: first recovery of the reaction. Radical Parisian revolt suppressed in 'June Days'.
	Sept	Serfs freed in Austria.
	Oct	Insurrection in Vienna suppressed by Windischgrätz.
	Nov	Berlin occupied by troops and Prussian revolution ends.
	Dec	Abdication of Emperor Ferdinand of Austria. Franz Joseph succeeds him. Louis Napoleon elected president of France.
1849	Feb	Proclamation of the Roman Republic; pope flees.
	Mar	Austrians defeat Sardinian army at Novara, Charles Albert abdicates and Victor Emmanuel succeeds him. Frankfurt Parliament completes constitution making and offers crown of a united Germany to Prussian King Frederick William IV – he refuses it.
	Apr	Hungary claims independence from Austria after centralist constitution is adopted in Vienna.
	June	Frankfurt Parliament (German National Assembly) forcibly dispersed by Prussian troops.
	July	French troops suppress the Roman Republic.
	Aug	Russian forces crush Hungarian resistance. Venetian Republic surrenders to Austrians.

There were other signs, too, that the tide had turned before the end of 1848. The Austrian army mastered the Sardinians in northern Italy. In Paris a rising which might have given the Revolution a further shove in the direction of democracy was crushed with great bloodshed in 'the June Days'. This settled that the French republic would be conservative. In 1849 came the end. The Sardinian army had been the only shield of the Italian revolutions, and after its defeat monarchs all over the peninsula then began to withdraw the constitutional concessions they had made while Austrian power was in abeyance. German rulers did the same, led by Prussia. The Croats and Hungarians kept up pressure on the Habsburgs but the Russian army came to its ally's help. By the end of 1849 the formal structure of Europe was once again much as it had been in 1847.

Liberals had seen 1848 as a 'springtime of the nations'. If it had been one, the shoots had not lived long before they withered. Nationalism had been a popular cause in 1848, but had been shown to be neither strong enough to sustain revolutionary governments nor necessarily enlightened. Its failure shows that the charge that the statesmen of 1815 'neglected' to give it due attention is false; no new nation emerged from 1848 for none was ready to do so. The basic reason for this was that over most of Europe nationalism was for the masses still an abstraction; only a relatively few and well-educated, or at least half-educated, people cared much about it. Nations, it was to appear, would in future be made after independence, by government and education, rather than emerge fully-grown. Where national differences also embodied social issues there was sometimes effective action by people who felt they had an identity given them by language, tradition or religion, and significant local changes followed, but they did not lead to the setting up of new nations. The Ruthene peasants of Galicia in 1847 had happily murdered their Polish landlords when the Habsburg administration allowed them to do so. Having thus satisfied themselves they remained loyal to the Habsburgs in 1848.

There were some truly popular risings in 1848. In Italy they were usually in the towns rather than the countryside; the peasantry of Lombardy cheered the returning Austrian army, because it saw no good in a revolution led by the aristocrats who were its landlords. In parts of Germany, over much of which the traditional structures of landed rural society remained intact, the countryside was sometimes disturbed. German peasants behaved as French peasants had done in 1789, burning their landlords' houses, not merely through personal animus but in order to destroy the hated and feared records of rents, dues and labour services, but that was all. Yet such outbreaks frightened urban liberals as much as the June Days frightened the middle classes in France. There, because the peasant was since 1789 (speaking broadly) a conservative, the government was assured the support of the provinces in crushing the Parisian poor who had given radicalism a brief success. But conservatism could be found within revolutionary movements, too. German working-class turbulence alarmed the better-off, because the leaders of German workers spoke of 'socialism'. Yet they actually sought a return to the past. They had the safe world of guilds and apprenticeships in mind, and feared the new machinery, the factories, the Rhine steamboats which put boatmen out of work, the opening of unrestricted entry to trades — in short, the all-too-evident signs of the onset of market society. Almost always, liberalism's lack of appeal to the masses was shown up in 1848 by popular revolution.

It was probably in the countryside of eastern and central Europe that revolution changed society most. There, liberal principles and the fear of popular revolt went hand in hand to force concession from the landlords. Obligatory peasant labour and bondage to the soil was abolished as a result of 1848 everywhere outside the Russian empire. The rural social revolution launched sixty years earlier in France had been carried to central and much of eastern Europe. The way was now open for the reconstruction of agricultural life in Germany and the Danube valley on individualist and market lines. Though many of its practices and habits of mind were still to linger, the medieval economic order had in effect now come to an end. The political components of French revolutionary principles, though, would have to wait longer for their expression.

The Crimean War

Though hardly anything at once changed, 1848 nonetheless punctuates the story of international relations, and divides (though it was hard to see this at the time) a period of prolonged international peace from one of intermittent war. In the next quarter-century there were wars between Great Britain, France, Turkey and Sardinia on the one side, and Russia on the other (the 'Crimean' war, 1854—6), between France allied with Sardinia against Austria (1859), and three others fought by Prussia against Denmark (1864), Austria (1866, Italy joining in on the Prussian side) and France (1870). The last four were about nation-building. The first was about another Eastern question: should Russia dominate and perhaps overthrow Turkey?

A dispute over Russian influence in the Near East, as the tsar sought to safeguard his country's interests in a time of declining Ottoman power, ended in 1854 the long peace between great powers. The Crimean War, in which the French and British fought as allies of the Turks against the Russians, was in many ways a notable struggle. Fighting took place in the Baltic, in southern Russia and in the Crimea. The last theatre attracted most attention. There, the allies had set themselves to capture Sebastopol, the naval base which was the key to Russian power in the Black Sea. Some of the results were surprising. For the British, whose army was especially distinguished by the inadequacy of its administrative arrangements, one outcome was the launching of an important wave of radical reform at home. It was another, connected but almost incidental, result of the war that there was founded a new profession for women, that of nursing, for the collapse of the British medical services had been particularly striking. Florence Nightingale's work launched the first major extension of the occupational opportunities available to respectable European women since the creation of female religious communities in the Dark Ages. The conduct of the war is also noteworthy in another way as an index of technological modernity: it was the first between great powers in which steamships and a railway were employed.

Yet these things, however portentous, mattered less in the short run than the war's impact on international relations. Russia was defeated and her power to intimidate Turkey was bridled for a time. A step was taken towards the establishment of another new Christian nation, Rumania, which was finally brought about in 1862. Once more, nationality triumphed in former Turkish lands. But the crucial effect of the war was that the Holy Alliance had at last disappeared. The old rivalry of the eighteenth century between Austria and Russia over what would happen to the Turkish inheritance in the Balkans had broken out again when Austria warned Russia not to occupy the Danube principalities (the future Rumania) during the war and then occupied them herself. Yet only five years before Russia had helped to restore Habsburg power by crushing the Hungarian revolution. It was the end of the anti-revolutionary friendship between the two powers. The next time Austria faced a revolutionary threat she would have to do so without the Russian policeman at her side.

Re-shaping the map

In 1856, when peace was made, few people can have anticipated how quickly that time would come. Within the next ten years Austria lost in two short, sharp wars her hegemony both in Italy and in Germany, countries both united five years later in new national states. Nationalism had indeed triumphed, and at the cost of the Habsburgs, as had been prophesied by enthusiasts in 1848, but in a totally unexpected way. Not revolution, but the ambitions of two conservative and traditionally expansive monarchies, Sardinia and Prussia, had led each to set about improving its position at the expense of Austria, whose isolation was at that moment complete. Not only had she sacrificed the Russian alliance, but after 1852 France was ruled by an emperor who again bore the name Napoleon. He was the nephew of the first, and had in 1848 been elected presi-

---

THE CONSOLIDATION OF GERMANY: PRUSSIAN TRIUMPH 1815–71

1815	Prussia and Austria join with Great Britain and Russia in Quadruple Alliance to uphold Vienna decisions.
1819	Common customes tariff for all Prussian territories.
1829	Enlargement of Customs Union (Zollverein) under Prussian leadership begins (it soon includes most German states).
1830	July Revolution in Paris has repercussions in Germany; some abdications and granting of constitutions.
1833	Radical attempt to seize Frankfurt; new reactionary wave of precautions, led by Austria.
1848	February revolution in Paris catalyzes wave of revolution in Germany and Austria provinces. Self-constituted assembly (Vorparlament) arranges for a National Assembly, which meets at Frankfurt 18 May, appoints a national executive and begins to debate a national constitution.
1848–9	Gradual restoration of monarchical authority in Berlin and Vienna while Frankfurt assembly argues over Grossdeutsch (Germany including Austria's German possessions) and Kleindeutsch (non-Habsburg Germany solutions to unity problem).
1849 21 Apr	King of Prussia refuses offer of crown of a new federal Germany and collapse of Frankfurt assembly follows.
1850	Prussian attempt to unify Germany on Kleindeutsch lines supported by most German rulers thwarted by Austrian threat of war (the 'humiliation of Olmütz'). Old Germanic confederation re-established.
1862	Bismarck becomes first minister of Prussia.
1865	Bismarck engineers quarrel with Austria over Schleswig-Holstein.
1865	Prussian alliance with Italy;
June–Aug	Seven Weeks' War between them and Austria. Prussian victory at Sadowa (Königgrätz).
3 July	Peace of Nikolsburg then excludes Austria from Germany, provides for organization of Germany north of the Main under Prussian leadership and independence of southern states. French claims for 'compensation' rebuffed.
1867	North German Confederation inaugurated with Prussian king as president, Prussian control of armed forces, Prussian preponderance in federal council. southern German states join Zollverein and new Customes parliament (Zollparlament) set up with limited powers but for all Germany.
1870	France provoked to declaration of war on Prussia over possible Hohenzollern candidacy to throne of Spain; German states all join in defeating her. Winter negotiation of a new German empire based on constitution of North German Confederation.
1871 18 Jan	Inauguration of German empire at Versailles (Alsace and Lorraine incorporated in it).

dent of the Second Republic, whose constitution he then set aside by *coup d'état*, at the end of 1851. The name Napoleon was itself terrifying. It suggested a programme of international reconstruction — or revolution. Napoleon III (Napoleon II was an honorific fiction, *l'Aiglon* who had never ruled, the son of the great emperor) stood for the destruction of the anti-French settlement of 1815 and therefore of the Austrian predominance which propped it up in Italy and Germany. He talked the language of nationality with less inhibition than most rulers and seems to have believed in it. With French arms and diplomacy he forwarded, not always by design, the work of two great diplomatic technicians, Cavour and Bismarck, the prime ministers respectively of Sardinia and Prussia.

In 1859 Sardinia and France fought Austria; after a brief war the Austrians were left with Venetia as their only Italian province. Cavour now set to work to incorporate other Italian states into Sardinia, a part of the price being that Savoy had to be given to France. He died in 1861, and debate continues over what was the extent of his real aims, but by 1871 his successors had produced a united Italy under the king of Sardinia, who was thus recompensed for the surrender of Savoy, the ancestral duchy of his house. In that year Germany, too, was united in a new empire. Bismarck had begun by rallying German liberal sentiment to the Prussian cause once again in a war engineered against Denmark in 1864. Two years later Prussia defeated Austria in a lightning campaign in Bohemia, thus at last ending the Hohenzollern-Habsburg duel for supremacy in Germany begun in 1740 by Frederick II. This was something of a registration of accomplished fact. Since 1849 (when German liberals had offered the German crown not to her emperor, but to the king of Prussia who refused it) Austria had been much weakened in German affairs. Those states which had still looked to Vienna for leadership and patronage were now left alone after 1866 to face Prussian bullying. The Habsburg empire was now to be predominantly Danubian, preoccupied with south-east Europe and the Balkans. It had retired from the Netherlands in 1815, had given up Lombardy in 1859, Venetia had been exacted from it by the Prussians and given to the Italians in 1866, and now it left Germany to its own devices, too. Immediately after the peace the Hungarians seized the opportunity to inflict a further defeat on the humiliated monarchy. In the 'Compromise' of 1867 they won virtual autonomy for their half of it. The Habsburg empire thus became the 'Dual Monarchy' or 'Austria-Hungary', divided rather untidily into two entities linked by little more than the dynasty itself and the conduct of a common foreign policy. Franz Joseph was emperor in one half of his lands and king in the other.

German unification required one further step. It had gradually dawned in Paris that the assertion of Prussian power beyond the Rhine was not in the French interest; instead of a disputed Germany, France now faced one dominated by one important military power. The era opened by Richelieu had crumbled away unnoticed. Bismarck used this new awareness, together with Napoleon III's weaknesses at home and international isolation, to provoke France into a foolish declaration of war in 1870. Victory in this war set the coping-stone on the new edifice of German nationality, for Prussia had taken the lead in 'defending' Germany against France — and there were still Germans alive who could remember what French armies had done in Germany under the first Napoleon. The Prussian army destroyed the Second empire (France's last monarchical regime) and created the second German Reich, an empire very unlike its medieval predecessor. In practice, it was a Prussian domination cloaked in federal forms, but as a German national state it satisfied many German liberals. It was formally (as well as dramatically and appropriately) inaugurated in 1871 when the king of Prussia accepted the crown of united Germany (which his predecessor had refused to take from German liberals) from his fellow-princes in the palace of Louis XIV at Versailles.

Thus closed a revolution in European relations. In fifty years Germany had replaced France as the dominant land-power in Europe as France had replaced Spain in the seventeenth century. This fact was to encumber international affairs until 1945. The over-riding of legitimacy and the Vienna settlement had, it turned out, owed hardly anything to the much-feared revolutionary politics of the Left except in so far as they were nationalist. The much-feared conspirators had achieved nothing comparable with the work of Cavour, Bismarck and, half in spite of himself, Napoleon III. This is very odd, given the hopes entertained by revolutionaries in this period, and the fears they had awoken. Social revolution had even begun to show signs of flagging. Down to 1848 there had been plenty of revolutions, to say nothing of plots, conspiracies and *pronunciamientos* which did not justify the name. After 1848 there were very few. Another Polish revolution took place in 1863, but this was the only outbreak of note in the lands of the great powers until 1871.

An ebbing of revolutionary effort after 1848 is understandable. Revolutions seemed to have achieved little outside France and had there brought disillusion and dictatorship. Revolutionary goals were being achieved in other ways. Cavour and his followers had, after all, created a united Italy, using plebiscites to give it a new sort of legitimacy, but they had done so greatly to the chagrin of Mazzini. Bismarck had done what many of the German liberals of 1848 had hoped for by creating a Germany which was indisputably a great power. That the motives of both statesmen were deeply conservative did not much matter except to their irritated radical opponents. Other ends were being achieved by economic progress; for all the horrors of the poverty which it contained, nineteenth-century Europe was getting richer and giving more and more of its peoples a larger share of its wealth. Some short-term factors helped. The year 1848 was soon followed by the great gold discoveries of California which provided a flow of bullion to stimulate the world economy in the 1850s and 1860s; confidence grew and unemployment fell in these decades and this was good for social peace.

A more fundamental reason why revolutions were less frequent was, perhaps, that they became more difficult to carry out. Governments were finding it easier to grapple with disorder. The nineteenth century created modern police forces and national gendarmeries. Better communications by rail and telegraph gave new power to central government in dealing with distant disturbance. Above all, armies had a growing technical superiority to rebellion. Even in 1795 a French government showed that once it had control of the regular armed forces, and was prepared to use them, it could master Paris. During the long peace from 1815 to 1848 some European armies in fact became much more instruments of security, directed potentially against their own populations, than means of international competition, directed against foreign enemies. It was the defection of important sections of the armed forces which permitted successful revolution in Paris in 1830 and 1848; when such forces were loyal to government, battles like that of the June Days ('the greatest slave-war in history', as one observer put it) could only end with the defeat of the rebels. After that year, no popular revolt was ever to succeed in a major European country against a government whose control of its armed forces was unshaken by defeat in war or by subversion, and which was determined to use its power.

Conservatism and modernization: Russia

Like the medieval struggles of Church and State, like Renaissance and Reformation, the French Revolution was another of those European historical experiences which passed Russia by. Alexander I, the tsar under whom Russia met the 1812 invasion, had toyed with liberal ideas and had even thought of a constitution, but nothing came of this after 1815. Liberalism and revolutionary ideologies did not quite leave Russia untouched and a few critics of the regime found models to admire in western Europe. Some of the Russian officers who went to Paris with the armies which pursued Napoleon were led by what they saw and heard to make comparisons unfavourable to their homeland; this was the beginning of a continuous political opposition in Russia. In an autocracy opposition had to mean conspiracy. A few officers organized secret societies which attempted a *coup* amid the uncertainty caused by Alexander's death in 1825; this was called the 'Decembrist' movement. It collapsed but only after giving a fright to Nicholas I, the new tsar. This mattered. Above all because of the immobility which he imposed upon her, Nicholas' reign deeply and negatively influenced Russia's destiny. A dedicated believer in autocracy, he was all the more willing after the Decembrists to confirm the Russian traditions of authoritarian bureaucracy, the management of cultural life, and the rule of the secret police just when other conservative powers were, however unwillingly, beginning to move in the opposite direction. There was, of course, much to build on. History had long since differentiated Russian autocracy from western European monarchy. But there were also great challenges to be met, and for the most part Nicholas' reign was a sterile but immediately effective response to them. What Russia got was a simple deployment of the old methods of despotism by a man more determined than his predecessor to use them. As late as 1848 they were still effective enough to give Russia the domestic security enabling her to play the role of Europe's policeman.

Although outside her Polish lands Russia seemed immune to political revolution such as troubled other countries, the ethnic, linguistic and geographical diversity of the empire in fact already posed serious problems in the nineteenth century. By the outbreak of the Crimean War, she was beginning to have to face others. Many of them outran the capacity of Muscovite and autocratic tradition to deal with them. They were above all problems of modernization — of generating and using resources effectively, so as to enrich society and provide the strength needed if Russia was to continue in the front rank of powers. The population of the empire more than doubled in the forty years after 1770. An ever-diversifying and growing society none the less remained overwhelmingly backward; its few cities were hardly a part of the vast rural expanses in which they stood and often seemed insubstantial and impermanent, more like huge temporary encampments than settled centres of civilization. The greatest expansion had been to the south and south-east, into Asian lands where new élites had to be incorporated in the imperial structure. As the conflict with Napoleon had compromised the old prestige of things French and the sceptical ideas of the Enlightenment associated with that country, a new emphasis had been given to religion in the evolution of a new ideological basis for the Russian empire under Nicholas. 'Official Nationality', as it was called, was Slav-centred, religious in doctrine and bureaucratic in form, and gave Russia an ideological unity it had tended to lose with expansion beyond its historic centre in Muscovy. The tiny intellectual class was divided in its view of what the country needed. 'Westerners' looked to ideas and institutions drawn from western Europe, 'Slavophiles' to tapping the sources of renewal they saw in Orthodoxy, tradition and indigenous institutions.

Ideology was to be of growing importance as the source of differences between Russia and western nations. Until 1991 Russian governments never gave up the promotion of ideology as a unifying force. Yet this did not mean that daily life in the mid-nineteenth century, either for the civilized classes or the mass of a backward population, was much different from that of other parts of eastern and central Europe. This was one reason why Russian intellectuals argued about whether Russia was or was not a European country. A decisive emphasis was given to her distinctiveness under Nicholas. From the beginning of his reign possibilities of change which were at least being felt in other dynastic states in the first half of the nineteenth century (and had faintly and briefly appeared to flicker into life under Alexander I) were simply not allowed to appear in Russia. To be the land *par excellence* of censorship and police implied the denial of certain possibilities of modernization (though other obstacles rooted in Russian society seem equally important in settling that).

In the short run, the policy could be thought successful. Russia passed through the whole nineteenth century without revolution; revolts in Poland in 1830–1 and 1863–4 were ruthlessly suppressed, the more easily because Poles and Russians cherished traditions of mutual dislike. But the other side of the coin was almost continuous violence and disorder of a savage and primitive rural society, and a mounting and more and more violent tradition of conspiracy which perhaps incapacitated Russia even further for civilized politics and the shared assumptions they require. A number of famous summaries of Nicholas' reign as an 'ice age', a 'plague zone' and a 'prison', suggest it could not silence its critics.

Not for the last time in Russian history, though, a harsh and unyielding despotism at home was compatible with a strong international role. Russia had a huge military potential. When armies contended with muzzle-loaders and no important technological differences distinguished them from one another, her vast numbers were decisive. On them rested the anti-revolutionary international security system, as 1849 showed, and they appeared adequate until the Crimea. Meanwhile, imperial Russia had its extra-European successes, too, mainly at the expense of the central Asian khanates, Persia, and on China. There were even efforts to pursue Russian expansion in North America; until the 1840s Russian forts survived in Alaska and there were settlements in northern California. The major thrust of Russian foreign policy, nevertheless, continued to be directed to the south-west, towards Ottoman Europe.

Wars in 1806–12 and 1828 had carried the Russian frontier across Bessarabia to the Pruth and the mouths of the Danube. The fate of the Ottoman empire in Europe would be even more crucial to nineteenth-century diplomacy than the partition of Poland had been to that of the eighteenth, for more powers would be involved in it. It did not, though, lead to great power conflict until the Crimean War, and a peace which obliged Russia to renounce for the foreseeable future some of her traditional goals in the Black Sea area.

In the middle of the war Nicholas I had died. This simplified the problems of his successor, Alexander II. Defeat made it obvious that change had to come. The Crimean War mattered in Russia's internal affairs more than in those of any other country, for the military colossus of the 1815 restoration had been shown now no longer to enjoy an unquestioned superiority even on her own territory. Modernization of Russian institutions was indispensable if Russia was again to generate a power commensurate with her vast potential, a task now shown to be unrealizable without changing her traditional framework. When the Crimean War broke out there was still no Russian railway south of Moscow. Russia's once important contribution to European industrial production had hardly grown since 1800 and was now far outstripped by others'. Her agriculture remained one of the least productive in the world and yet her population steadily rose, pressing harder upon its resources. It was in these unpropitious circumstances that Russia began again to modernize.

What happened was in fact more of a revolution than much that went by that name elsewhere. Nicholas' reign had been marked by increasingly frequent rural insurrections, attacks on landlords, crop-burning and cattle-maiming. Even he had agreed that serfdom was the central evil of Russian society. It took away any incentive for better cultivation by the peasant, and prevented the free movement of labour which would have provided workers for new factories. Poverty kept down the peasant's demand for goods, too. On the other hand, it had to be conceded that serfdom was embedded so deeply in Russian society, that sudden abolition might mean the breakdown of much of government itself. The autocracy relied upon the estate-owner to carry many of the burdens of what would elsewhere have been called local government. Yet it was appallingly difficult for the rider to get off the elephant. The vast majority of Russians were serfs and could not be transformed overnight by mere legislation into wage labourers or smallholders. Nor could a whole property-owning class be impoverished by confiscation. Nor could the state at once take the strain of the administrative burden which would suddenly be thrown upon it if the manorial system should collapse.

Though Nicholas had not dared to proceed, the one card Russian government could play was the unquestioned authority of the autocrat. It was now put to good use. After years of study of the evidence and possible advantages and disadvantages of different forms of abolition, the tsar issued in 1861 an edict which marked an epoch in Russian history and won him the title of the 'Tsar Liberator'. It gave the serfs personal freedom and ended bonded labour. It also gave them allotments of land. But these were to be paid for by redemption charges to pay the compensation needed to make the change acceptable to the serf-owners. To secure the repayments and offset the dangers of suddenly introducing a free labour market, the peasant was to remain subject for years yet to the authority of his village community, which was given the charge of distributing the land allotments on a family basis.

Much was later to be said about the shortcomings of this settlement. Yet in retrospect it seems a massive achievement. When a few years later the United States emancipated its black slaves, there were far fewer of them than there were Russian peasants. They lived in a country of much greater economic opportunity, yet throwing them on the labour market, exposed to *laissez-faire* economic liberalism, exacerbated a problem with whose ramifying consequences Americans are still grappling. In Russia the largest measure of social engineering in recorded history down to this time was carried out without comparable dislocation and opened the way to modernization for what was potentially one of the strongest powers on earth. It was the indispensable first step towards making the peasant available for industrial employment, and to the modernization of Russian agriculture.

Liberation also opened an era of reform; by 1870 Russia had a representative system of local government and a reformed judiciary. Reforms did not, though, touch the central principle of autocracy. However much liberals might welcome them, such changes were not recognized as the right of the Russian people or even as a concession to legitimate demands; they might be withdrawn as they had been granted, at the will of the tsar. This was one reason why some critics of the regime continued to refuse to compromise with it and went on plotting and struggling to overthrow it. Some of them blew up the Tsar Liberator in 1881, on the day he had approved the beginnings of a new policy of constitutional concession. It was swept aside by his successor who inaugurated a much more reactionary regime. Perhaps, after all, Russia was not firmly on the road to modernization.

Ten years earlier, a warning of what Russian modernization might mean if it was ever achieved had been given to Europe. The Russians had then taken advantage of the Franco-Prussian War to denounce some of the restrictions placed in 1856 on their freedom in the Black Sea. It was a symbolic step as well as a practical one. After tackling her greatest problem and beginning to improve her domestic institutions Russia was announcing not only that she would again be master in her own house, but that the resumption of the most consistently and long-pursued policies of expansion in modern history was only a matter of time.

Conservatism and modernization: the United Kingdom

The pace-setter of European social and economic development in the first half of the nineteenth century was the United Kingdom (as it had been since 1801, when an Act of Union abolished the Irish parliament and gave Ireland representation at Westminster). Yet, paradoxically, it also showed (thought close and informed continental observers) an astonishing constitutional and political continuity. It was surprising that this continuity was apparently undisturbed by the revolutionizing force of industrialization, or by the country's pre-eminence after 1815 as a European and world power at the head of a greater empire than had ever been seen.

For most of the nineteenth century, the word 'democracy' tended to alarm many Britons. At first, it still reminded them too readily of the French Revolution and military despotism. The growing numbers of the urban masses gave point to the association, and suggested new dangers as well. Another association of the word was with the United States, the home of republicanism and other undesirable tendencies. Yet the democratization of British politics is a central institutional thread to the British nineteenth century. Though universal, adult male suffrage would not come until 1918, the process was long before that past the point of irreversibility. Though it had deeply libertarian features — equality at law, legal safeguards of personal liberty, a representative legislative system based on an electorate large by any European standard and a bias against executive authority — the British constitution of 1800 in no sense embodied the democratic idea. Its basis was the sovereignty of the Crown in parliament, parliament itself resting upon the representation of a variety of individual and historic rights and the Crown upon a conditional and statutory tenure.

The first changes in principle came in the later 1820s, when religious restraints on political rights were removed. In 1832, though, came the most important step of the century towards British democracy, the passing of a Reform Act which, though not itself democratic (it was, indeed, intended by those who supported it to act as a barrier to democracy) brought a great revision of the representative system. It removed anomalies (such as tiny constituencies controlled by private patrons), provided parliamentary constituencies which better (though still far from perfectly) reflected the needs of a population balance tilting from country to the industrial cities, and above all regulated the franchise on a more coherent and defensible basis. The model elector was the man with a stake in the country, through property or a modestly adequate income, although dispute about exact qualifications still left some oddities. The immediate result was an electorate of about 650,000 and a House of Commons whose members did not look very different from their predecessors. None the less, dominated by the aristocracy as it still was, the first 'reformed' House of Commons marked the beginning of nearly a century in which, the constitution having been once changed in this way, it would be changed again. The House of Lords remained untouched, but the Commons would more and more have the last word.

The incomplete democratizing process brought other changes as the century went on. Slowly, and somewhat grudgingly, the traditional political class began to take account of the need to organize parties which were something more than family connexions or personal cliques of members of parliament. This was much more obvious after 1867, when another Reform Act produced an electorate of about 2,000,000 and after the adoption of voting by secret ballot in 1872. The implication that there was a public opinion to be courted which was more than that of the old landed class had nonetheless been grasped earlier than this, as the Corn Laws debate had shown. All the greatest English parliamentary leaders in the nineteenth century were men whose success rested on their ability to catch not only the ear of the House of Commons, but that of important sections of society outside it. The first and possibly most significant example was Sir Robert Peel, who, by accepting the verdicts of public opinion gave English conservatism a pliability which saved it from an intransigence such as that shown in some European countries. Almost incidentally, though, he broke his party in the process. His conservative followers had been brought by him to accept parliamentary reform in 1832 and in 1846 he was just able to make them swallow repeal of the Corn Laws, but the champions of the agricultural interest turned on Peel soon afterwards and rejected him. The whole tendency of what he had done had been directed to the triumph of the new class which they identified with the middle-class manufacturers.

The redirection of British tariff and fiscal politics was part of a general alignment of British politics towards cautious liberalization, practical reform and more active government in the central decades of the century. A beginning was then made with local government reform (significantly, in the towns, not in the countryside where the landlords were still the masters), a new Poor Law was introduced to tackle the relief of poverty in a rapidly-growing population, factory and mining legislation was passed and began to be effectively policed by inspection, the judicial system was reconstructed, what was left of religious disabilities (on Protestant nonconformists, Roman Catholics and Jews) were reduced still further, the ecclesiastical monopoly of matrimonial law which went back to Anglo-Saxon times was ended, a postal system was set up which became a model for the world, and a beginning was even made in tackling the scandalous neglect of public education. It was a wonderfully constructive age, accompanied by unprecedented growth in wealth, whose confident symbol was the holding in 1851 of a Great Exhibition of the world's wares in London under the patronage of the queen herself and the direction of her consort.

British institutions and the country's economy had never looked healthier, though, of course, not everyone was pleased. Some moaned about a loss of economic privilege; others about the United Kingdom's extremes of wealth and poverty. There was fear of creeping centralization, that the country might be going the way of France, a country whose structurally centralized government was taken to be sufficient explanation of the failure to achieve liberty which had accompanied the French success in establishing an equality many Englishmen deplored. Yet the United Kingdom continued unscathed with huge reconstructions of her institutions, in spite of revolutionary fears lingering from the turbulent first half of the century. She emerged from it with her power and wealth enhanced and the principles of liberalism even more apparent in her politics. Many foreigners admired, wondering how, in spite of the appalling conditions of her factory towns, she had managed to navigate rapids of popular unrest fatal to other states. Her statesmen and historians gloried in reiterating that the essence of the nation's life was freedom, in a famous phrase, 'broadening down from precedent to precedent'[1]. Englishmen seemed fervently to believe this, yet it did not lead to licence. To ask how they did it is a leading question, and some historians still ask it without querying the implicit presupposition that certain conditions make revolution likely and that British society fulfilled them. It may be that no such propositions need to be conceded. Perhaps there never was a revolutionary potential in this rapidly changing society.

Much of what the French Revolution brought to Europe, after all, had already existed in Great Britain for centuries. However rusty or encrusted with inconvenient historic accretion her fundamental institutions might be, they offered large possibilities. Even in unreformed days, the House of Commons and House of Lords were not closed corporate institutions such as were all that many European states had on offer as representative bodies. Already before 1832, they had shown they could meet new needs, even if slowly and belatedly; the first Factory Act (not, admittedly, very effective) had been passed as early as 1801. There were good grounds after 1832 for thinking that if parliament were only pressed hard enough from the outside, it could carry out any reforms that were required. There was no legal restraint on its power to do so. Amid the many outbreaks of desperate violence in the 1830s and 1840s (which were especially hard times for the poor) the 'Chartists' the most radical popular movement of the day, gathering up a great spectrum of protest, demanded measures to make parliament more responsive to popular needs, not its abolition.

Yet parliament would not have provided reform had not other factors been at work. The great reforms of Victorian England were (with the possible exception of factory legislation) all likely to appeal to the middle classes as much as to the masses. The English *bourgeoisie* came to an early share in political power as their continental counterparts did not. They could use it to obtain change they wanted and were not likely to ally with revolution, the recourse of desperate men to whom other avenues were closed. Nor does it seem that the English masses were very disaffected. Contemporary visitors noted English deference to social superiors. There were working-class organizations which provided alternatives to revolution which were very 'Victorian' in their admirable emphasis on self-help, caution, prudence, sobriety. Of the elements making up the great English Labour movement, only the political party which bears that name came into existence after 1840. The 'friendly societies' for insurance against misfortune, the cooperatives and, above all, the trades unions, all provided channels for personal participation in the improvement of working-class life, even if at first only to a few and only

---

[1]   The phrase is that of Lord Tennyson, poet laureate.

slowly. This early maturity was to underly the paradox of English socialism, its later dependence on a conservative and unrevolutionary trade-union movement, long the largest in the world.

Once the hungry 1840s were over, too, economic trends may have favoured social peace. At any rate some radicals said so, almost regretfully; they, at least, thought that betterment told against a revolutionary outcome in England. As the international economy picked up in the 1850s good times came to the industrial cities of a country which was not only the workshop of the world but its merchant, banker and insurer, too. As employment and wages rose, the support which the Chartists had mustered crumbled away. Soon they were only a reminiscence.

The symbols of the unchanging forms which managed change were the central institutions of the kingdom: parliament and the Crown. When the Palace of Westminster was burned down and a new one was built, a mock-medieval design was chosen to emphasize the antiquity of the Mother of Parliaments. The most revolutionary era of British history continued to cloak itself in the robes of custom and tradition. Already when Queen Victoria ascended the throne, the monarchy was second only to the papacy in antiquity among European political institutions; yet it had long been changing, for all that. Victoria and her husband were to make monarchy for a time all but unquestioned. In part this went against the grain for the queen herself; she did not pretend to like the political neutrality appropriate to a constitutional monarch and a Crown withdrawn above the political battle. None the less, it was in her reign that this withdrawal was seen to be made. She also domesticated the monarchy; for the first time since the days of the young George III the 'the Royal Family' could be seen to be such. It was one of many ways in which her German husband, Prince Albert, helped her, though he got little thanks for it from an ungrateful English public.

Only in Ireland did the capacity for imaginative change seem always to fail the British. They successfully weathered rebellion there in 1798. In the 1850s and 1860s things were quiet, but largely because of an appalling disaster which had fallen on Ireland in the 1840s when the failure of the potato crop was followed by famine, disease and thus, brutally, a Malthusian solution of Ireland's over-population by death and emigration. For the moment, nationalist demands for the repeal of the Act of Union were muted, the dislike of a predominantly Catholic population for an alien and established Protestant Church was in abeyance and there was no serious disturbance among peasants feeling no loyalty to absentee English landlords. Problems nonetheless remained. In the 1870s a new Irish nationalist movement emerged, demanding 'Home Rule'. That demand was to haunt British politics and overturn their combinations and settlements for the rest of the century and beyond.

CHAPTER FIVE World hegemony

Europe's new global role

The most conspicuous single fact of nineteenth-century history was the maturing of European hegemony worldwide. This had many expressions. In 1900 peoples of European stocks dominated the globe in more ways and to a degree startlingly greater than a 100 years earlier. The world for the most part responded to European initiatives and marched to European tunes; many of its non-European inhabitants did so quite literally, and under European flags, too. It was a unique moment in world history; for the first time one civilization among many was accepted universally as a model. In the long run, this would prove even more important than political or military power (which was, in any case, beginning to be qualified). European values went round the world on the powerful wings of aspiration and envy.

It was certainly to prove far more influential than mere formal empire, the outright European possession of overseas territories. In some places that was a fairly recent phenomenon. It was only relatively late in the day, for example, after a period of economic aggression, that European nations other than Russia or Portugal actually began to acquire territory in China. Even within individual European 'empires', too, there were always important distinctions to be drawn about the exact degree of control exercised by the metropolitan power and the exact nature of its links with its subjects; less formal relations might be just as important as outright dominion. It is to the point also that even when other continents were for practical purposes, or indeed, legally, independent – the Antipodes or the Americas, for example – their dominating cultures were European in origin and essence, even if slowly modulating into something else under the influence of local conditions. European power, moreover, could operate (in economic matters, for example) even where there was no overt control. It was not always to the disadvantage of non-European countries that this was so, but it meant that they tended almost always to adapt to the world the Europeans had made, rather than the other way round. Sometimes they did so eagerly, when they succumbed to the attractive force of Europeans' progressive ideals or formulated, almost unconsciously, new expectations under their influence.

The Great Resettlement

One expression of European hegemony was a diaspora of Europeans sometimes called, because of its demographic importance, the Great Resettlement. It had

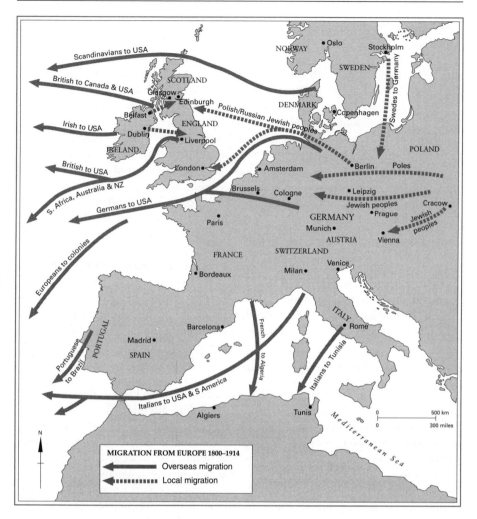

MIGRATION FROM EUROPE 1800–1914

Overseas migration
Local migration

already been well under way in 1800. The most numerous transplantations of Europeans overseas by then were to the Americas, North and South. To this in the nineteenth century was added migration to other new countries of British settlement, colonial in origin, but in fact self-governing, hybrid, not quite independent nations, but soon not really colonies either. Before 1800, most European emigrants had come from Iberia, the British Isles, Germany and France (all to the Americas) or Russia (to Siberia). In the nineteenth century something like another 60,000,000 Europeans went overseas, the tide beginning to flow strongly in the 1830s. Most of them went to North America, to Latin America (especially Argentina and Brazil), to Australia and South Africa. Substantial emigration across land continued also within the Russian empire. The peak of European emigration overseas came in 1913; over a 1,500,000 Europeans left in that year, over a third of them Italians, nearly 400,000 British, and 200,000 Spanish. 50 years earlier, Germans and Scandinavians had loomed larger and Italians had figured only to a minor degree. The British Isles always contributed a steady flow; between 1880 and 1910, 8,500,000 British subjects went overseas, many from Ireland (the Italian figure for this period was just over 6,000,000). Most of them (especially the Irish) went to the United States and two-thirds of them between 1815 and 1900, but large numbers went also to the 'self-governing' colonies which received after 1900 a majority of the British emigrants. The United States remained the greatest single recipient of Europeans (over 33,000,000 between 1820 and 1950).

Many sources fed this torrent. Politics was one of the first, notably in Germany after 1848. Rising population in Europe was always fundamental, especially in the 1880s and 1890s as 'unemployment' came to be a phenomenon to be reckoned with, and European farmers began to suffer from overseas competition. Strongest was the draw of opportunity; for the first time in human history, labour was short in certain places at a moment when there were suddenly new, easier and cheaper ways of getting to them. Steamships and railroads changed demographic history. They permitted greater mobility within Europe, too. The United Kingdom sent Irish peasants, Welsh miners and steelworkers and English farmers overseas; she also took in Jews from eastern Europe, and the Italian waiters and ice-cream salesmen who came to be part of British folk-lore. Poles crossed Europe to work in French coalmines. Once conquest made North Africa available for settlement it, too, was changed by migration from Europe; Italians, Spaniards and Frenchmen who were drawn there created the first European communities in Islamic lands since the thirteenth century, distinct both from the places from which the settlers had come and from the native societies among which they settled.

The civilized world

Standing, as they did, in a variety of relationships with Europe, the countries of European settlement overseas long remained psychologically tied to it, even dependent. They made up, with Europe itself, what was often called the 'civilized' world and sometimes already the 'western' world. Nowadays, 'civilized' is too debatable and elastic a term for an age of growing awareness of cultural variety, and 'western' is now geographical nonsense. Neither is satisfactory except as a matter of subjective identification. Nonetheless, each expresses an important fact: consciousness of similarities in ideas and institutions[1]. In different environments and unique historical circumstances, ideas and institutions drawn from the same origins helped the men and women of those societies to deal with the challenges they faced and to manage their worlds. It mattered that for a long time those societies were all formally Christian; new lands were never settled in the name of atheism until the twentieth century. They all regulated their lives by European laws, and sought to preserve the cultures of Europe and its languages.

Those who confidently talked of the 'civilized world' did not, as they looked about them, find much beyond Europe and its transplants worthy of inclusion (though by the twentieth century, the Japanese were recognized by some to have come to share in the dominant 'civilization'). Almost everywhere else, the world seemed to Europeans full of heathen, backward, benighted peoples, among whom a few were striving to join those who had achieved 'civilization'. This attitude, blinkered and unattractive as it was later to come to appear, was an important ingredient of European cultural and political suc-

---

[1] The earliest use of the word 'western' in more or less the modern sense which I have come across is in Gibbon, Bury edn., I., p. 368, where in a footnote he speaks of 'intercourse between China and the Western countries'.

cess. What were taken to be demonstrations of the inherent superiority of European ideas and values nerved men to fresh assaults on the world and inspired fresh comprehension and mis-reading of it. The progressive values of the eighteenth century provided new arguments for superiority to reinforce others originally stemming from religion. By 1800, Europeans had already lost most of their sometime respect for other cultures. Their own social practice seemed obviously superior to the unintelligible barbarities found elsewhere. They could look back upon centuries of conflict with Islam, its expulsion from Iberia and the beginnings of its retreat in central and south-eastern Europe, and regard successful contest with it as the advance of true civilization. Or they could contemplate the inexplicable unresponsiveness of China and its seemingly consequential decay. The European overthrow of American Indian empires was seen as the extirpation of barbarism and meaningless cruelty.

In their own day, they heard of countries where cannibalism was still practised, of child-marriage and widow-burning in India, and itched to obliterate them as the slave trade had been obliterated. Such a selective view left all but a tiny minority of Europeans long unable to see anything on the other side of the coin. For all the efforts of the Spanish clergy to defend the American Indians, or of the anti-slavery campaign enthusiasts of the eighteenth century, they were not seeking to protect other cultures. Even they, too, were sure that among what Europeans had to offer the world was unquestionably the greatest benefit of all: Christianity. Later, more secular ideals – individual rights, education, universal suffrage, the protection of women, children and animals from exploitation – would be advocated and actively promoted right down to our own day in other lands by later Europeans (and Americans). Even when they opposed colonialism, the philanthropists and progressives who did so long continued to be confident that the values of European civilization should be universalized along with its medicine and sanitation. To promote them was increasingly seen as a universal right and duty. Science, when its day came, seemed to point in the same direction of ideological universalism, to the destruction of superstition and the bringing of the blessings of a rational exploitation of resources, the provision of formal education and the suppression of backward social customs by a universal culture. There was not much left by 1900 of the romantic idea of the noble savage. What was much more obvious was the well-nigh universal assumption of Europeans that the values of their civilization were superior to those of others (as they often were) and a large obliviousness to any disruptive effects they might have.

The direct impact

Many of the peoples of lands over which 'thick darkness brooded yet' (as the Victorian hymn put it) were by 1900 ruled directly by Europeans. Enlightened colonial administrators were among those who strove to bring the blessings of railways, Western education, hospitals, law and order to peoples whose own institutions had clearly not been able (it was taken as evidence of their inadequacy that it was so) to stand up to the challenge of superior civilization. Even when native institutions were protected and preserved, it was from a position which assumed the superiority of the culture of the colonial power.

Such consciousness of cultural superiority is no longer admired or admitted. In one specific respect, nevertheless, it achieved an end which the most scrupulous critics of colonialism still accept as good, even when they throw doubt on the motives behind it. This was the abolition of slavery wherever European rule existed. Nor was this all. Force and diplomacy was then deployed by European states to contain and reduce it beyond their territories. The crucial steps were taken in 1807 and 1834, when the British parliament abolished first the trade in slaves and then slavery itself within the British empire. This action by the major naval, imperial and commercial power was decisive; similar measures were soon enforced by other European governments. By the middle of the century the Royal Navy was pressing hard on the operations of Arab slave-traders in the African continent and the Indian Ocean. Many forces, intellectual, religious, economic and political, went into the great achievements of emancipation. Debate about their precise individual weight continues. It is worth recalling, however, that though abolition came about only after 300 years and more of large-scale slave-trading, Europe's is the only civilization which has ever eradicated slavery for itself, without external pressure to do so. Though in the present century slave-labour again briefly reappeared in Europe, it could not be sustained except by force, nor was it avowable as slavery. It cannot have been much consolation to their unhappy occupants, but the Soviet forced-labour camps of our own century were run by men who had to pay the tribute of hypocrisy to virtue by disguising their slaves as the subjects of re-education or judicial punishment, while Nazis did their best to conceal what they did, rationalizing it for themselves (when they felt the need) by bogus science.

Slavery had itself shown how the lives of non-European societies could be shaped and manipulated by European civilization, but there were other ways in which this happened. One was the corrosion of values and institutions, which could then lead to indirect European political interference and the weakening of traditional authority. This happened in the Chinese and Ottoman empires. Sometimes such contacts were stimulating but Japan was the only nineteenth-century example of an important nation exploiting such contact as a stimulus to success. What was virtually impossible was to remain untouched by Europe. The busy, bustling energy of the European trader would alone have seen to that. Geographical remoteness was almost the only security (and even Tibet was invaded by the British in 1904). Ethiopia is virtually the solitary example of successful independence without modernization; it survived both British and Italian invasion in the nineteenth century (besides terrain, it had on its side the moral advantage of an at least intermittent Christian history of some fourteen centuries).

Christianity, because of its concern with all sides of human behaviour, as well as with belief had always been one of the most important agencies bringing European civilization to the rest of the world. The territorial spread of the organized churches and the growth in their numbers of official adherents in the nineteenth century made it the greatest age of Christian expansion since apostolic times. Much of this was the result of a renewed wave of missionary activity; new missionary orders were set up by Roman Catholics, new societies for the support of overseas missions appeared in Protestant countries. The paradoxical outcome was the intensifying of the European flavour of what was supposedly a creed for all sorts and conditions of men. In most of the receiving countries, Christianity was long presented in a way which encouraged non-Christians to see it as just one more aspect of European civilization, rather than as a spiritual message which might equally well be expressed in local idiom. Missionaries were, for example, often much concerned with dress. Jesuits in seventeenth-century China had discreetly adopted the costume of their hosts, but their nineteenth-century successors set to work with zeal to put Bantus and Solomon Islanders into European garments often of almost freakish unsuitability. In such ways Christian missionaries diffused more than a religious message – as they did when they brought food in time of famine, agricultural techniques, vaccination, hospitals and schools. Through such things filtered the assumptions of a progressive civilization, sometimes disruptively.

Europeans, missionaries and non-missionaries alike, could not be kept away. In the end, there seemed to be no part of the inhabited world where they could not, if they wished, impose themselves by their armed strength, in spite of occasional disasters (like that of the Italian army wiped out at Adua, in Ethiopia, in 1896). Advances in communications and weapons in the nineteenth century gave Europeans much greater relative advantage than they enjoyed when the first Portuguese broadside was fired at Calicut. Even when advanced devices were available to other peoples, they could rarely deploy them effectively. At the battle of Omdurman in the Sudan in 1898 the masses of the Mahdist army never reached the British line; in that short action 10,000 of them were killed for a loss of 48 British and Egyptian soldiers. Not only a technical, but a mental transformation was required before non-European cultures could turn the instrumentation of the Europeans against them.

There was also one other way, less disagreeable, in which European civilization rested upon force. Throughout the whole nineteenth century the *Pax Britannica* stood in the way of European nations fighting each other for mastery of the non-European world. Though the greatest extension of direct colonial rule in modern times was then going on, and was richly productive of diplomatic squabbles, there was no repeat performance of the colonial wars of the seventeenth and eighteenth centuries. Traders of all nations could move without let or hindrance on the surface of the seas. British naval supremacy was a precondition of the informal expansion of European civilization and the competition of a world market, goals implicitly cherished by many Britons.

New European nations overseas

In the eighteenth century, the British and the French had lost empires. The subsequent crumbling of the Spanish, and the breakaway of Brazil from Portugal tempted some to expect that other British colonies would soon throw off the shackles of London, too. In a way, this was what happened, but not as expected. 1783 had been a major lesson for British statesmen, with whom settler colonies went out of fashion as a consequence. They had learnt that colonies were tricky things, costing the mother-country money and bringing her few benefits not more cheaply and readily available through trade. They were liable to engage her in fruitless strife with other powers or native peoples; settlers were likely in the end to turn round to bite the hand that fed them. Colonial entanglements were to be distrusted – especially when profits could be made in East Asia by trade with no implications of European settlement nor any need for expensive protection which could not easily be met by the Royal Navy.

Broadly speaking, this attitude prevailed in British official circles during the nineteenth century. It led them to tackle the affairs of existing colonies with an eye, above all else, to cheapness and avoidance of trouble. In the huge spaces of Canada and Australia this road led, through disputes and quarrels, but almost entirely without bloodshed, to the eventual uniting of individual colonies in federal structures with responsibility for their own government. The Dominion of Canada came into existence in 1867, and in 1901 the Commonwealth of Australia. In each case, union had been preceded by the granting of responsible government. Each was a huge, thinly populated country which could only gradually be pulled together to generate a sense of nationality and the process by which that came about was slow. In the end, their nationalism was assisted by the growth of awareness of potential external dangers – United States economic strength in Canada, and Asian immigration in Australia – and, of course, by bickering with the British. New Zealand also achieved responsible government in the nineteenth century. Europeans had arrived there from the 1790s onwards to find a native people, the Maori, with an advanced and complex culture, whom they set about corrupting. Missionaries followed, and did their best to keep out further settlers and traders. But they arrived just the same. When it seemed that a French entrepreneur was likely to establish a French interest, the British government at last reluctantly gave way to the pressure of some of the settlers and proclaimed British sovereignty in 1840. Only sixteen years later the colony was given responsible government, though wars with the Maori delayed the withdrawal of British soldiers until 1870. New Zealand achieved full self-government in 1907, the year after a Colonial Conference in London had decided that the name 'Dominion' should in future be used for all the self-governing dependencies, which meant, in effect, the colonies of white settlement, a club joined in 1910 by a Union of South Africa.

The new Union looked back on a pre-history much more troubled than that of any of the other Dominions. There had been no British in South Africa until after 1815, when Great Britain for strategic reasons annexed the Dutch colony founded in the seventeenth century at the Cape of Good Hope. 'Cape Colony' soon drew some thousands of British settlers. They remained outnumbered by the Dutch but had the backing of the British government in introducing British assumptions and law. Cape Colony was also distinctive in that, unlike North America or the future Australia, there was a large native population which did not go away or die out. It had been there when the Dutch arrived, and grew in numbers as time passed. In 1900, even after many more settlers (mainly British) had gone to South Africa, the white population was only about one quarter of the black. Different views about the treatment of the native Africans always made it difficult for the British governors and Dutch farmers (the 'Boers', as they were called) to come to terms. But there were other difficulties, too. The Dutch were closely-knit by custom, language and religion, and did not want their ways to be contaminated by alien influences. Yet English became the official language instead of Dutch, and the old judicial arrangements were replaced by British. To the additional annoyance of the Boers, British missionaries almost at once took up the defence of the rights of the natives, whom they sought to convert. When slavery was abolished throughout the British empire, there was much grumbling over the terms of compensation.

All in all, it is scarcely surprising that in 1835 some 10,000 Boers went north with their families, cattle and possessions, across the Vaal river in the 'Great Trek' which was the origin of the later Boer republic of the Transvaal. It was also the foundation of a national myth. A few years later, another British colony was established in Natal, replacing a Boer republic there – and so more settlers of Dutch stock went north in search of their own kind. Thus opened decades during which Anglo-Saxon and Boer struggled to live sometimes apart, sometimes together, but did so always uncomfortably. Their decisions dragged in their train others about the fate of the black Africans. These included peoples otherwise likely to present a continuing security problem (as the Zulus had already shown the Boers).

By mid-century, alongside the Boer Orange Free State and the Transvaal republic in the north, Cape Colony and the Natal were under the British flag, with elected assemblies for which the few black men who met the required economic tests could vote. There were also some native kingdoms under British protection. From 1872, the Cape had its own responsible government. Then, the discovery of diamonds led to further British advance north of the Orange which angered the Boers. British support for the Basutos, whom the Boers had defeated was a further irritant. Finally, the governor of Cape Colony foolishly annexed the Transvaal republic. This had to be reversed in 1881, but from this moment Boer distrust of British policy in South Africa was probably insurmountable. Within twenty years it led again to war. By then a small-scale industrial revolution had taken place in the Transvaal, where gold was found in 1886. With a huge influx of miners and speculators Johannesburg grew in a few years to become a city of 100,000 – the only African city of that size south of the Zambezi. It seemed possible that the Boer republic might acquire the financial resources to escape from British suzerainty. At that time, other parts of Africa were being swallowed by other European powers. The British government deemed that a secure British presence at the Cape was essential to the control of sea-routes to the East. The possibility of the Transvaal obtaining independent access to the Indian Ocean and a sea-port which might someday be used by a hostile European power was disturbing.

An oddly-assorted crew of idealistic imperialists, Cape politicians, English demagogues and shady financiers provoked a confrontation with the Boers in 1899 and a second Boer War. Of the outcome there could be no doubt; as Queen Victoria remarked, (with better strategical judgement than some of her subjects) the possibilities of defeat did not exist. South Africa was isolated by British sea-power. No other European power could help the Boers and it was only a matter of time before superior numbers and resources were brought to bear. Nevertheless, victory was costly. Over a quarter of a 1,000,000 soldiers were sent to South Africa, much bitterness was aroused in British domestic politics, and British prestige fell in the eyes of the world. The Boers were regarded as an oppressed nationality; so they were, but the nineteenth-century liberal obsession with nationality in this case as in many others blinded observers to some of the shadows it cast, in this case over black Africans. The British conceded a generous treaty to end the war in 1902 when the Boers had been beaten in the field. Though this was the end of the Boer republics, futher concession soon followed and by 1906 the Transvaal had a responsible government of its own which the Boers controlled after an electoral victory the following year. Almost at once they began to legislate against Asian immigrants, mainly Indian. When, in 1909, a draft constitution for the Union of South Africa was agreed, it prescribed equality for the Dutch and English languages and, all-important, provided for government by an elected assembly to be formed according to the electoral regulations decided in each province. In the Boer provinces the franchise was reserved to white men. At the time, the settlement seemed a good one. Its defects would take time to appear.

Humanitarian and missionary sentiment in England and the well-founded Colonial Office tradition of distrust of settler demands had made it hard to forget the native populations in South Africa. Yet in all the British colonies, unlike the Indian sub-continent, modernity confronted very vulnerable and primitive societies, some of them at a very primitive level of achievement. The Canadian Indians and Eskimos were relatively few; they presented no such important obstacle to the exploitation of the west and north-west as had done the Plains Indians' struggle to keep their hunting grounds from the Americans (who swept them ruthlessly aside). The story in Australia was bloody and there was perhaps no other native population inside former British territory whose fate was so like that of the American Indian. In New Zealand, the Maoris, too, declined in numbers, though not so violently or irreversibly as did the Australian aborigines. In South and British East Africa the story was more mixed. A few peoples survived into the twentieth century living lives on their ancestral lands which changed only slowly. Others were driven off or exterminated. Many were sucked into a growing and mod-ernizing economy, and the new roles and assumptions that went with it. In all cases, though, the crux of the situation in the European empires, was that the fate of the native inhabitants was never in their own hands. In the short run they could sometimes pre-sent formidable military problems (as did the Zulus of Cetewayo, or the guerrilla war-fare of the Maoris), but they could not in the end generate from their own resources the means of effective resistance any more than had the Aztecs. For non-European peoples to do that, they had in some measure to Europeanize.

Europeans who witnessed what was happening were hardly troubled. It is too simple to explain this by saying they were all bad, greedy men (and, in any case, the work of the humanitarians among them makes the blackest judgement untenable). The answer must lie somewhere in mentality. Europeans able to see that native popu-lations were damaged by contact with the whites, even when it was benevolent in inten-tion, could not for a long time understand the full corrosive effect of their culture. That required an anthropological knowledge and insight Europe had still to achieve. The missionary confidence of the European settler was strong. He *knew* he was on the side of Progress and Improvement. The belief that he embodied a higher civilization was not only a licence for predatory habits, as Christianity had been in twelfth-century cru-sading, or sixteenth-century Portuguese and Dutch piracy, but the nerve of an attitude which easily blinded men to the actual and material results of substituting individual freehold for tribal rights, of turning hunters and gatherers whose possessions were what they could carry, into wage-earners.

Empire-building

The word 'imperialism' appears to have come into use in English only in the 1850s. That no doubt registers the recognition of something special about the age. Overwhelmingly, the nineteenth century was an age of European imperialism in the sense of expanding direct rule. The United States was also a great imperial power in this sense, but something of a special case. Since Japan was the only other expanding power, this sort of empire-building was above all the work of white peoples of European stocks or culture. Its nineteenth-century heyday divides into two distinguishable phases, one running down to about 1870, one after.

Some of the nations acquiring new territories – Russia, Great Britain, France – had long been in the business of empire. On the other hand, one of the oldest European imperial powers, Spain, though she picked up a little new real estate, lost much more than she gained after 1800; she was really no longer in the race by the end of it, when she lost most of what was left of her empire in a war with the United States. The Portuguese and Dutch, were in much the same position, though undefeated in war. But two European states which had only recently come into existence, Germany and Italy, were acquiring new territory overseas by 1900, and so was Belgium, only a little older than they. The tendency to expansion struck some as irresistible.

Russia's territorial growth has at first sight something in common both with the North American experience of filling up a continent and bullying weaker neighbours and backward aborigines, and something with that of the British in India in seeking strategical frontiers. Yet it was in fact a special case. To the west Russia faced matured, established European states where there was no hope of or wish for further territorial gain. The same was only slightly less true of the Danubian region, where the interests of other powers were always likely to come into play and check Russia in the end. Her main freedom of action long lay southwards and eastwards, where the century brought her great acquisitions. A successful war against Persia (1826–9) led to the establishment of Russian naval power on the Caspian and the seizure of territory in Armenia. In central Asia an almost continuous advance into Turkestan and towards the central oases of Bokhara and Khiva culminated in the annexation of the whole of Transcaspia in 1881. In Siberia, aggressive expansion was followed by the exaction from China of the left bank of the Amur down to the sea and the founding in 1860 of Vladivostok, the Far Eastern capital. Soon after, Russia liquidated her commitments in America by selling Alaska to the United States; she was going to be an Asian and Pacific, but not an American, power.

In the first half of the century, the two powers which showed most expansionist dynamism overseas were France and Great Britain. Many British gains were made at France's expense in the victorious peace in 1815. This buttressed British maritime strength with the retention of such scattered stations as Malta, St Lucia, the Ionian islands, the Cape of Good Hope, Mauritius and Trincomalee. In 1839, the internal troubles in the Ottoman empire gave the British the opportunity to take Aden, once Portuguese, and a base of strategic importance on the route to India. Others were to follow as steamships were added to the Royal Navy and coaling had to be taken into account. No other European power could successfully challenge such action after Trafalgar. It was not that resources did not exist elsewhere which, had they been assembled, could not have wrested naval supremacy from Great Britain; it had been done, briefly, in 1781, and Yorktown was the result. But it would have demanded an unimaginable effort. No other nation found it worthwhile to challenge this thalassocracy. There were, too, international advantages in the maritime *Pax Britannica*. The policing of the seas was a benefit to all. As for Great Britain herself, her naval supremacy guarded the trade which ensured her colonies participation in the fastest-growing commercial system of the age. Already before the American Revolution British policy had been more successful in encouraging trade than Spanish or French; as the old colonies themselves had grown in wealth and prosperity, so the later Dominions were to benefit.

Geography and history shaped British imperialism's internal logic. A new concern about imperial communication with Asia can be traced even before 1783, in the exploration of the South Pacific and in a growing Asian trade. War with the Netherlands, when it was a French satellite, had promoted new British enterprise in Malaya and Indonesia. Above all, there was a steadily-deepening British involvement in India. By 1800 the importance of the Indian trade was a central axiom of British commercial thinking. By 1850, it has been urged, much of the rest of the empire had only been acquired because of the strategical needs of India. It was the centre-piece of British imperialism.

India: the growth of responsibility

The possession of India was one of the shaping facts of modern British history. The responsibility of British government there continued to grow after the beginnings in 1784 of a 'Dual Control' shared with the Company, and the role of the Company to decline. The Company lost its monopoly of trade with the sub-continent in 1813, towards the end of the wars with France which had further extended British power in South India. Sometimes this was by annexation, sometimes by securing British control of the foreign policy of native rulers. When the Company's charter was again renewed in 1833, it was only in the north-west of the sub-continent that there survived a substantial area of India not under direct or indirect British rule. After the annexation of the Punjab and Sind in the 1840s, and the establishing of paramountcy in Kashmir, the British held sway over virtually all of it.

The Company had by then become solely a government. The 1833 charter took away its trading functions and its monopoly of trade with China; in sympathy with current thinking, Asian trade was henceforth to be free trade. The way was open to the consummation of many real and symbolic breaks with India's past and the final incorporation of the subcontinent in a modernizing world. Symbolically, the name of the Moghul emperor was removed from the coinage, and it was more than a symbol that Persian ceased to be the legal language of record and justice. It not only marked the advance of English as the official language (and therefore of English education), but also disturbed the balance of forces between Indian communities. Anglicized Hindus would prove to do better in British India than less enterprising Moslems. In a subcontinent so divided in so many ways, the adoption of English as the language of administration was complemented by the decision to provide primary education in it.

At the same time the enlightened despotism of successive governors-general began to impose material and institutional improvement. Roads and canals were built and the first Indian railway followed in 1853. Legal codes were introduced. English officials for the Company's service began to be trained specially in the college established for this purpose. The first three universities in India were founded in 1857. There were other educational structures, too; as far back as 1791 a Scotchman had founded a Sanskrit college at Benares, the Lourdes of Hinduism. Much of the transformation which India was gradually undergoing arose not from the direct work of government but from the increasing freedom with which these and other agencies were allowed to operate. From 1813 the arrival of missionaries (the Company had hitherto kept them out) had gradually built up another constituency at home with a stake in what happened in India – often to the embarrassment of official India. Two philosophies, in effect, were competing to make government act positively. Utilitarianism looked for the promotion of happiness, and evangelical Christianity to the salvation of souls. Both were sure they knew what was best for India and judged its cultures equally arrogantly. Both subtly changed British attitudes as time passed, and therefore the importance of India in British public opinion.

Steamships made India seem nearer to home. As more Englishmen and Scotchmen sought careers there, the nature of the British presence changed. The comparatively few officers of the eighteenth-century Company had been content to live as exiles, seeking rewards in their commercial opportunities and relaxation in a social life sometimes closely integrated with that of the Indians. They often lived much in the style of Indian gentlemen, some of them taking to Indian dress and food, some to Indian wives and concubines. After 1800, reform-minded officials, intent on the eradication of backward and barbaric custom – and in such practices as female infanticide and *suttee* they had good cause for concern – together with missionaries preaching a creed corrosive of Hindu or Moslem society, and the Englishwomen who came out to make homes in India while their husbands worked there, all changed the temper of the British community in India. It lived more and more apart from the natives, with a growing sense that its cultural and moral superiority sanctioned its rule over them. The rulers consciously grew away from those they ruled. One British official defined his countrymen's task in the early 1870s as 'the introduction of the essential parts of European civilization into a country densely peopled, grossly ignorant, steeped in idolatrous superstition, unenergetic, fatalistic, indifferent to most of what we regard as the evils of life and preferring the response of submitting to them to the trouble of encountering and trying to remove them'[2]. This robust creed was far from that of the eighteenth-century 'nabobs', most of whom had innocently sought to do no more in India than make fortunes. Now, while making new laws which antagonized powerful native interests, those who shared this creed had less and less social contact with Indians; more and more they confined the educated Indian to the lower ranks of the administration and withdrew into an enclosed, though conspicuously privileged, life of their own. Earlier conquerors had been absorbed by Indian society in greater or lesser measure; the Victorian British, thanks to a modern technology which continuously refreshed their contacts with the homeland and their confidence in their intellectual and religious superiority, remained immune, increasingly aloof, as no earlier conqueror had been. Many legacies to the English language and the English breakfast and dinner-table still testify that they could not remain untouched by India, but they created a civilization which was not Indian, even if it was not wholly English. 'Anglo-Indian' was a word applied in the nineteenth century not to a person of mixed blood, but to an Englishman who made his career in India. It indicated a cultural and social distinctiveness.

India: the Mutiny and after

The alienation of Anglo-Indian society from India was made virtually absolute by the rebellions of 1857 called the Indian Mutiny. Essentially, these were a chain reaction of outbreaks, initiated by mutinying Hindu soldiers who feared the polluting effect of using a new type of cartridge, greased with animal fat. This detail is significant. Much of the rebellion was the spontaneous and reactionary response of traditional society to innovation and modernization. The irritations of native rulers, both Moslem and Hindu, sometimes helped it along; they regretted the loss of their privileges and thought that the chance might have come to recover their independence. The British were very few. Yet the response of those few was prompt and ruthless. With the vital help of loyal Indian soldiers the rebellions were crushed, though not before there had

---

[2]   Fitzjames Stephen, q. by J.M. Brown, *Modern India. The Origins of an Asian Democracy*, 2nd edn. (Oxford, 1994), p. 105.

been some massacres of British captives and a British garrison had been under siege at Lucknow, in rebel territory, for some months.

The Mutiny and its suppression were psychological disasters for British India. It did not much matter that the Moghul empire was at last formally brought to an end by the British (the Delhi mutineers had proclaimed the last emperor their leader). Nor was what happened (as later Indian nationalists were to suggest) a crushing of a national liberation movement. Like many episodes important in the making of nations, the Mutiny was to be important as myth and inspiration; it contributed to later Indian nationalism, but was not an expression of it. What it was later believed to have been was more important than the jumble of essentially reactionary protests it actually was. Its deepest effect was the wound it gave to British goodwill and confidence. Whatever the expressed intentions of British policy, the consciousness of the British in India was from this time suffused by the memory that Indians had once proved almost fatally untrustworthy. Among Anglo-Indians as well as Indians the mythical importance of the Mutiny grew with time. The atrocities actually committed were bad enough, but others which had never occurred were also alleged as grounds for a policy of repression and new social exclusiveness. Immediately and institutionally, the Mutiny also marked an epoch, for it ended the government of the Company. The governor-general now became the queen's viceroy, responsible to a British cabinet minister. This settled the framework of the British Raj for the rest of its life. If the Mutiny changed Indian history it did so by thrusting it more firmly in a direction to which it already tended.

The nineteenth-century flowering of India's economic connexion with Great Britain had more directly revolutionary results. Commerce was the root of the British presence in the subcontinent and it continued to shape its destiny. India became the essential base for the China trade which rapidly expanded in the 1830s and 1840s and at about the same time there began a rise in British exports to India, notably of textiles, so that, by the time of the Mutiny, a big Indian commercial interest existed involving many more Englishmen and English commercial houses than the old Company had ever done. The story of Anglo-Indian trade was henceforth locked into that of the general expansion of British manufacturing supremacy and world commerce. The opening of the Suez Canal in 1869 brought down the costs of shipping goods to Asia by a huge factor and by the end of the century the volume of British trade with India had more than quadrupled. Paradoxically, this development delayed India's modernization. Her industrialization might have gone ahead more rapidly without British competition. But by the end of the century the Raj and the stimulus of the cultural influences it released and protected had already made impossible the survival of an India untouched by modernization.

The structure and style of government did not greatly alter. When in 1877 Parliament bestowed the title of 'Empress of India' on Queen Victoria a few Englishmen disapproved, some laughed and most probably did not think it mattered much: they took it for granted that British supremacy in the subcontinent would be permanent or near-permanent and were not much concerned with its nomenclatures. They would have agreed (as one of them said) that 'we are not in India to be pleasant' and that only firm government could prevent another Mutiny. Others would also have agreed with the British viceroy who declared as the twentieth century began that 'As long as we rule India, we are the greatest power in the world. If we lose it, we shall drop straightaway to a third-rate power'.

The exact truth of that judgement, though, is still hard to gauge. The Indian tax-payer certainly paid for the Indian army and therefore not only for the defence of India but of some of the rest of the empire, too. It was also true that Indian tariff policy was long managed in the interests of British merchants, industrialists and factory hands. But this was not the whole story. There were British inputs, too, often with important mate-rial consequences. Human beings need myths to justify collective purposes and the British in India did not find it possible to do without them. They wanted to believe they were doing good there. Some made personal sacrifices, stoically bearing the burden of exile in an alien land so as to bring peace to the warring and law to peoples without it. Most of them probably never formulated clear views but were simply convinced that what they could offer was better than what they found and therefore what they were doing was good. At the basis of all these views there was a conviction of superiority, rein-forced as the century went on by fashionable racialist ideas and muddled reflexions about the survival of the fittest.

A second great fact is that viewed as a whole the Raj was a huge complicity between rulers and ruled. This was not quickly apparent. Although there was a modest intake of nominated Indian landlords and native rulers into the legislative branch of government after the Mutiny it was not until the very end of the century that these were joined by elected Indians. Though Indians could compete to enter the civil service, there were important practical obstacles in the way of their entry to the ranks of the decision-makers. In the army, too, Indians were kept out of the senior commissioned ranks. The largest single part of the British army was always stationed in India, and its reliability and monopoly of artillery combined with the officering of the Indian regiments by Europeans to ensure that there would be no repetition of the Mutiny. The coming of railways, telegraphs and more advanced weapons favoured government in India as much as in any European country. But armed force alone does not explain the self-assuredness of British rule. The Census report of 1901 recorded that there were just under 300,000,000 Indians. They were governed by about 900 European civil servants. Usually there was about one British soldier for every 4,000 Indians. As one Englishman once put it, had all the Indians chosen to spit at the same moment, his countrymen would have been drowned.

The Raj could not in fact rest only on force; it demanded carefully administered policies and Indian collaboration. One influential assumption after the Mutiny was that Indian society should be interfered with as little as possible. Female infanticide, since it was murder, was forbidden, but there was to be no attempt to prohibit polygamy or child marriage (though after 1891 it was not legal for a marriage to be consummated until the wife was twelve years old). The line of the law was to run as far as possible out-side what was sanctioned by Hindu religion. Conservatism was also reflected in a new attitude towards the native Indian rulers. In the Mutiny they had usually proved loyal; those who turned against the government had been provoked by resentment against British annexation of their lands. The rights of native rulers were therefore scrupulously respected after the Mutiny; the princes ruled their own states independently and virtu-ally irresponsibly, checked only by the British political officers resident at their courts, and those states included over a fifth of the population. This was part of a search for sup-port from key groups of Indians.

Yet no more than any other imperial government could the Raj insulate itself from change. Its very successes told against it. Since the suppression of warfare favoured the growth of population, more frequent famine would follow. But the provision of ways of earning a living other than by agriculture in an over-populated countryside was made very difficult by the obstacles in the way of Indian industrialization, arising in part from tariff policy. A slowly emerging class of Indian industrialists did not, therefore, feel warmly towards government, but tended to be antagonized by it. There was also a growing number of Indians who had received an education along English lines and had subsequently been irritated to compare its precepts with the practice of the British in India. Some who had studied at Oxford, Cambridge, or the Inns of Court found the contrast especially galling: as the century moved to its close, there were in England Indian members of parliament, while an Indian graduate at home might be insulted by a British private soldier. Some, too, had pondered what they read in their studies; John Stuart Mill and Mazzini were to have a huge influence in India.

Ironically, it was British orientalists who, at the beginning of the nineteenth century, had begun the rediscovery of classical Indian culture which was to give Hindu nationalism self-respect. It was under European guidance that Indian scholars began to bring to light the culture and religion embedded in the neglected Sanskrit scriptures. By the end of the nineteenth century the recovery of the Aryan and Vedic past – Islamic India was virtually disregarded – enabled Hindus to meet with greater confidence the reproaches of Christian missionaries and offer a cultural counter-attack. But a new national consciousness was for a long time confined to a few, an élite defined by education as much as wealth. Its backbone was provided by Hindus, often Bengali, who felt especially disappointed when their educational attainments failed to win them a share in the running of India and respect in British eyes.

The Indian National Congress was founded against this background. The immediate prelude was a flurry of excitement over government proposals, subsequently modified because of the outcry of European residents, to equalize the treatment of Indians and Europeans in the courts. An Englishman, a former civil servant, took steps which led to the first conference of the Congress in Bombay in December 1885. Vice-regal initiatives, too, had played a part, and Europeans were long to be prominent in the administration of Congress and to patronize it with advocacy and advice from London. It was an appropriate symbol of the complexity of the European impact on India that some Indian delegates attended its first conference in morning-suits and top-hats of comical unsuitability to the climate, but the formal attire of their rulers.

France overseas

British imperialism was only the outstanding instance of a European fact. The French had, too, within a few decades of 1815 made substantial additions to their empire. The first clear signal of a reviving French imperialism came in North Africa, newly vulnerable to imperial predators because of the decay of the formal Ottoman overlordship of the southern and eastern Mediterranean coasts. French interest was natural and unsurprising; it went back to a great extension of the country's Levant trade in the eighteenth century and Bonaparte's expedition to Egypt in 1798.

Nonetheless, the French conquest of Algeria began uncertainly in 1830. A series of wars followed, not only with its native inhabitants but with the sultan of Morocco, and by 1870 most of the country had been subdued. The French had by then turned their attention to Tunis, too, which had accepted financial control by an Anglo-French-Italian administration after the bankruptcy of the government in 1869. While the Bey of Tunis remained under the suzerainty of the Ottoman sultan, the French and Italian governments quarrelled over concessions to their nationals; to the irritation of the latter a French invasion (the excuse was provided by raiders crossing the frontier from Tunis into Algeria) was followed by the Bey's acceptance of French protectorate in 1881. The Turks and Italians protested, to no avail. To both sometime Ottoman dependencies there now began a flow of European immigrants and the building up of European populations in a few cities. This was to complicate the story of French rule. The day was past when the African Algerian might have been exterminated or all but exterminated, like the Aztec, American Indian or Australian aborigine. His society, in any case, was more resistant, formed in the crucible of an Islamic civilization which had challenged Christendom. None the less, Algerians suffered, notably from the introduction of European land law which broke up traditional usages and impoverished the peasant by exposing him to the full blast of market economics.

French imperial activity in the Mediterranean was not limited to the Maghreb. At the eastern end of the African Mediterranean coasts there had been early in the nineteenth century an essay in modernization in Egypt initiated by the first great indigenous modernizer of a non-European country, Mehemet Ali, pasha of the Ottoman sultan. An admirer of Europe, Mehemet Ali sought to borrow its methods while asserting his independence. As ever, the problems of an empire in decline offered temptations and opportunities and when he had helped the Ottoman regime against the Greek revolution, Mehemet Ali tried to claim Syria as his reward. This provoked an international crisis, for it endangered Ottoman stability, and not all European powers were pleased by that. The French took Mehemet Ali's side – unsuccessfully. But this renewed French interest in the Levant and Syria and its eventual outcome would be the brief establishment of French government in both Syria and the Lebanon.

French imperialism in Asia was a different matter, (though decaying empires were again involved) and must be understood in a broader context. Though India was the largest single mass of non-European population and territory under European rule in Asia, other areas of dense populations long of interest to Europeans and theatres of their activity lay to the south-east and in Indonesia. Few generalizations are possible. One negative fact was observable; everywhere modernization was soon corroding native cultures. In 1880 most of mainland South-East Asia had still been ruled by native princes who were independent rulers, even if they had made concessions in 'unequal treaties' to European power. In the following decade this was changed by the British annexation of Burma and French expansion in Indo-China. The sultans of Malaya acquired British residents at their courts who directed policy through the native administration, while the 'Straits Settlements' were ruled directly as a colony. By 1900 only Siam was still independent among the kingdoms of this region, though Vietnam, that part of Indo-China known in the early stages of French Asian expansion as Annam, also stood somewhat apart from the general picture.

Vietnam was special in its close cultural links with China (which claimed suzerainty over it). It also had the longest tradition of national identity in the region and a history of rebelliousness long before the European imperial era. French interest in the country also had deep roots, going back to Christian missions in the seventeenth century. In the 1850s the persecution of Christianity led the French (briefly assisted by the

Spanish) to intervene in south Vietnam, then known as Cochin China, thus bringing on diplomatic conflict with China. In 1863 the emperor of Annam ceded to France part of Cochin China under duress, and Cambodia accepted a French protectorate. This was followed by further French advance and Indo-Chinese resistance. In the 1870s the French occupied the Red River delta; soon, other quarrels led to a war with China, the paramount power. But this confirmed the French grip on Indo-China. In 1887 a *Union Indo-Chinoise* was set up which disguised a centralized regime behind a system of protectorates. The emperor of Annam and the kings of Cambodia and Laos remained on their thrones, but cultural assimilation was the aim of French colonial policy. French culture was to be brought to new French subjects whose élites were to be gallicized as the best way to modernization and civilization.

Further south, too, French history had at least an indirect impact. By the end of the nineteenth century there were some 60,000,000 Indonesians; population pressure had not yet produced there such strains as were to come, but it was the largest group of non-Europeans ruled by a European state outside India. Indonesians had nearly two centuries of sometimes bitter experience of Dutch rule before the French Revolution led to the invasion of the United Provinces, and the dissolving of the Dutch East India Company. Another consequence soon followed, the occupation of Java by the British, who troubled the waters further by making important changes in the revenue system. Other disturbing influences also were now at work. Though originally an outcropping of the Hindu civilization of India, Indonesia was also part of the Islamic world. Many Indonesians were at least nominally Moslem. There were important and long-established commercial ties with Arabia. In the early years of the nineteenth century all this had new importance. Indonesian pilgrims, among them men of birth and rank, went to Mecca and sometimes on to Egypt and Turkey where they made acquaintance with ideas from further west. The instability of the situation was revealed when the Dutch returned and had, in 1825, to fight a 'Java War' against a dissident prince. It lasted five years and so damaged the island's finances that the Dutch were constrained to introduce further changes. The result was an agricultural system which enforced the cultivation of crops with an eye solely to the fiscal interests of colonial government.

The 'imperialist wave' and international relations

If we set aside the slightly notional claims made in Antarctica, more than four-fifths of the world's land surface in 1914 belonged to European empires or new nations of European settlement. Of the fraction of it which remained formally independent, few indigenous regimes enjoyed total autonomy, as the fate of the Chinese, Persian, Moroccan and Ottoman empires showed. Two nations, Great Britain and Russia, counted about a third of the world's land area as part of their empires. The contrast with 1800 was startling empires. Much of the formal extension of European empire which had brought this about occurred only in the last quarter of the nineteenth century. Between 1880 and 1900 the population of the British empire grew by a third. In the same period France added about 3.5 million square miles to hers and Germany about 1,000,000. It was the last and greatest surge in a process begun 400 years earlier and before long – though no-one could have known it – it was to come to an end.

People have often debated the reasons for the 'imperialist wave' as the century approached its close, but it has always been easier to recognize than to explain. Its rapidity and extent demanded special explanations. There seemed for a while to be no area of the world so unattractive that someone did not want to annex it, and more nations than ever had begun empire-building. Not only the new Italy and Germany, but new Europeans overseas, notably those of the United States and Australia, entered the game as 1900 approached. Contemporary explanation often took the form of advocacy and justification. (It is interesting, of course, that justification was thought to be needed.) Some, stressing one side of imperial expansion overseas, argued the need to relieve population pressure at home. They stressed the dangers presented by the ills of industrial society and the impact of the trade cycle on employment; emigration to colonies might provide safety-valves against discontent at home. Others used arguments which echoed and distorted those of the Darwinian biology; they urged that imperialism was inevitable because of the racial superiority of the whites, genetically destined to rule the world. Science, understood or misunderstood, was said to lend support to such ideas through the evidence it allegedly supplied of the greater efficiency of the white races in a struggle among the human animals for access to resources; they were said to be more intelligent, morally better braced for competition, mentally and perhaps physically superior. With time, more was heard of explanations (less of justification, though) in terms of economic competition unrelated to implausible speculation about innate racial quality and the natural competition that flowed from it. It was alleged that European nations were driven by internal and structural forces to compete for new markets and new sources of cheap raw materials and primary products and therefore to seize lands overseas. This was developed into more overtly political criticism of 'capitalism' as a system whose essential nature drove governments to seek investment opportunities through political control (even if indirect) of countries where the return on investment would be better than could be found at home.

In retrospect practical and technical facts must be given much weight. The powers at the disposal of Europeans were no longer restricted to the superiority in weaponry and sailing skills exercised by their ancestors who had launched the European onslaught on the world in the fifteenth century. Science, for example, eased European access to Africa, long an interesting and 'dark' continent; its full exploitation became possible at last in the 1870s when medicine began to make tropical disease easier to resist and permanent bases easier to maintain. At the same time, steamboats began to make it easier to penetrate an unknown landmass. Such possibilities rekindled economic hopes which were often ill-founded and usually disappointed, but which accelerated further exploration and sometimes led to political outcomes in annexations or the negotiation of commercial treaties with native peoples.

Imperial expansion was so complex that in the end the notion of 'causes' is not very helpful. Part of the explanation were the sheer momentum, new forms, and the infectious example of accumulating power. Ambitions and visions changed as new goals seemed to become achievable. Economic interest alone certainly cannot be the sole explanation, for it was itself stimulated by other changes. Overtly economic imperialism, too, was often far from successful. Whatever the appeal of what one British politician called 'undeveloped estates' in Africa, or the supposedly vast market for consumer goods constituted by the penniless millions of China, industrial countries still found other industrial countries their best customers and trading partners. As for overseas investment, former or existing colonies of settlement rather than new possessions attracted most of it. British money invested abroad went for the most part to the United States and South America or to the 'old' settler colonies; French investors preferred Russia to Africa, and German money went to Turkey.

It is true that economic expectation excited individuals to act, but they are another random factor hard to generalize about. Explorers, traders, soldiers and adventurers sometimes took steps which led governments, willingly or not, to act. Some of them became popular heroes, for this most active phase of European imperialism coincided with a great growth of popular participation in public affairs. By buying newspapers, voting, or cheering in the streets, the masses felt more and more involved in politics which (among other things) found imperial competition good copy. Much as in sport today, it was presented in terms of national rivalry in an age of vulgarized romanticism about nationhood. The new cheap press and popular novelists pandered to this by dramatizing exploration and colonial warfare. Some cynical politicians, thought, too, that voters might be soothed by the contemplation of the extension of the rule of the national flag over new areas even when the experts knew that nothing was likely to be forthcoming except expense. Slum-dwellers could get a little pleasure out of feeling superior to 'heathen' peoples far away ruled by their governments. But cynicism is no more the whole story than are the profit motive or the over-stimulated egos of visionaries. The idealism which drove some imperialists salved the conscience of many more. Men who believed that they possessed true civilization were bound to see the ruling of others for their good as a duty. Kipling's famous poem did not urge Americans to take up the White Man's Booty, but his Burden.

After 1870, these elements, much tangled together, had to find a place in a context of changing international relationships which imposed its own logic on colonial affairs. Two continuing facts stand out. One is the centrality to it of Great Britain. As the only truly worldwide imperial power, she quarrelled with more states over extra-European matters than anyone else. She had possessions everywhere, though more than ever preoccupied with India as the century went on, acquiring African territory to safeguard the Cape route (and a new one via Suez) and frequently uneasy over dangers to the central Asian lands which were India's glacis. Between 1870 and 1914 the only crises in which Great Britain seemed in danger of going to war with another great power arose over places as remote as Afghanistan and the upper Nile valley. She had a running quarrel with France over Egypt and others only slightly less bitter in south-east Asia and the south Pacific. Not only with France, but with Germany, too, she disputed boundaries in West Africa and the Congo. There was further dispute with Germany over New Guinea and over Persia, Central Asia and Afghanistan with the Russians. This wide range of concerns often made it easy for other powers to co-operate against the United Kingdom.

A second and much more paradoxical fact is that, although European diplomats quarrelled for forty years or so about what happened overseas and though the United States went to war with Spain, the continuing partition of the non-European world was remarkably peaceful. Even after 1900 quarrels over non-European affairs tended to be a positive distraction from the more dangerous rivalries of Europe itself; in the nineteenth century they may even have helped to preserve European peace. When a Great War at last broke out in 1914, Great Britain, Russia and France, the three nations which had quarrelled with one another most over imperial and colonial issues would be on the same side. Only a few months earlier, the British and Germans had been negotiating amicably about a possible partition of the Portuguese empire. Overseas colonial rivalry no longer took Europe to war as is had in the eighteenth century.

The Scramble for Africa

The most striking instance of the competition-driven, self-feeding, complex nature of the last high phase of European imperialism was to be seen in Africa. Explorers, missionaries, and the campaigners against slavery early in the nineteenth century had encouraged the belief that extension of European rule in the 'Dark Continent' was justified by spreading the blessings of civilization there. On its coasts, centuries of trade had shown that desirable products other than slaves might be available in the interior. The whites at the Cape were pushing further inland (thanks in part to Boer resentment of British rule). Africa was already unstable when in 1881 a British force was sent to Egypt to secure that country's government against a nationalist movement whose success (it was feared) might threaten the safety of the Suez Canal. The corrosive power of European culture – for that was the source of the ideas of the Egyptian nationalists – thus touched off another stage in the decline of the Ottoman empire of which Egypt was still formally a part. It also launched what was called the 'Scramble for Africa'.

The British had hoped to withdraw their soldiers from Egypt quickly; in 1914 they were still there and British officials were by then virtually running the country. Elsewhere, Anglo-Egyptian rule had pushed deep into the Sudan, Turkey's western

provinces in Libya and Tripolitania had been taken by the Italians (who had felt unjustly treated over Tunisia's French protectorate), Algeria was more emphatically French than ever and France was enjoying a fairly free hand in Morocco, except where the Spanish were installed. But this was far from all. Southwards from Morocco to the Cape of Good Hope, the coastline had been entirely divided between the British, French, Germans, Spanish, Portuguese and Belgians, the only exception being the isolated and backward black republic of Liberia. The empty wastes of the Sahara had been left to the French, as well as the basin of the Senegal and much of the northern side of that of the Congo. The Belgians were installed in the rest of the Congo basin on what was soon to prove some of the richest mineral-bearing land in Africa. Further east, British territories ran from the Cape up to Rhodesia and the Congo border. On the east coast they were cut off from the sea by Tanganyika (in 1914 German) and Portuguese East Africa. From Mombasa, Kenya's port, another belt of British territory stretched through Uganda to the borders of the Sudan and the headwaters of the Nile. Somalia and Eritrea (in British, Italian and French hands) isolated Ethiopia, the only African country other than Liberia still independent of European rule and the only one which averted European conquest by military victory. Other Africans did not have the power to resist successfully, as the French suppression of Algerian and Tunisian revolts, the Portuguese mastery (with some difficulty) of insurrection in Angola in 1902 and in 1907, the British destruction of Zulu and Matabele power in South and East Africa, and, worst of all, the German massacre of the Herrero of South-West Africa in 1907, all showed.

This colossal extension of European power was, for the most part achieved after 1881 and it was a remarkable achievement to have settled it without war between imperial powers. It transformed African history. The bargains of European negotiators, the accidents of discovery and the convenience of colonial administrations in the end settled the ways in which Africa entered modern history. Here, though, the complex, varied and fascinating story of what followed that division of Africa is relevant to Europe only in so far as it absorbed European energies, attention and resources, and in what it left of European entanglement when the empires at last went away.

Europe itself was little changed by the African adventure. It meant that Europeans could and did seize yet more easily exploitable wealth, but it may be that only Belgium drew from Africa resources making a real difference to it. Sometimes, too, the exploiting of Africa touched off political disputes at home. The atrocities in the Congo under the Belgian King Leopold and the forced labour of Portuguese Africa were notorious examples, but there were other places where Africa's natural resources – human and material – were ruthlessly exploited or despoiled in the interests of profit with the connivance of imperial authorities. Most imperial nations recruited African soldiers (though only the French hoped to employ them for service in Europe, to offset the weight of German numbers). There were hopes of finding outlets for emigration which would ease social problems, but the opportunities presented by Africa for European residence were very mixed. The two largest blocks of settlement were those of the Boers and British in the south, and Kenya and Rhodesia would later provide lands suitable for white farmers. Apart from this, settler Africa consisted of the cities of French North Africa, and the small but growing community of Portuguese in Angola. Italian hopes of Africa were disappointed, and German emigration was tiny and almost entirely temporary.

Imperial Europe and the Far East

The Pacific was partitioned less dramatically than Africa but in the end no independent political unit survived among its island peoples. Few diplomatic difficulties comparable to those posed in Africa arose there. The expansion of British, French and Russian territory in Asia was a different matter. When the French established themselves in Indo-China, the British followed suit in Malaya and Burma, as a means of safeguarding the approaches to India. Siam retained its independence because it suited both powers to have a buffer between them. The British also asserted their superiority in Central Asia, threatening war with the Russians over Afghanistan in 1885, and later, in 1904, by an expedition to Tibet, still with Indian security in mind. Most of these areas (like many of those in the zone of Russian overland expansion) were formally under Chinese suzerainty. Their story is part of that of another imperial decline reflecting corrosion by European influence. It had, though, greater importance for world history then what happened to Ottomans and Persians. At one moment it looked as if a scramble for China might follow the partition of Africa, with the extra complication that the United States of America might take part.

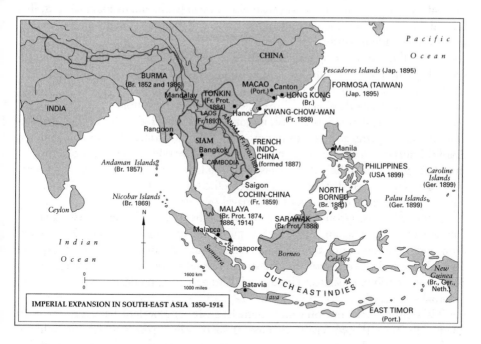

IMPERIAL EXPANSION IN SOUTH-EAST ASIA 1850–1914

China: the barbarian onslaught

China had once been, for many centuries, the greatest land-power in Asia and probably in the world. Confrontation with Europeans in the nineteenth century led to her temporary eclipse. Engaged for some centuries with European commerce and, mildly, European cultural influence, the Chinese empire in 1800 was still a powerful state. It faced a number of testing domestic problems, but was ruled by a cultural élite confident of its values, contemptuous of 'barbarians' from Europe and their offerings. A

100 years later, in contrast, the imperial government was semi-paralysed, many of China's ports were in alien hands, many Chinese intellectuals and administrators were alienated from their tradition and demoralized. Some thought the empire was on the eve of disintegration.

The historical logic leading to this conclusion can be conveniently taken up in the episode which became notorious as the 'Opium War'. Ever since the sixteenth century, trade between China and Europe had been bedevilled (from the European point of view) by Europe's inability to produce goods which the Chinese wanted. European traders in China had, therefore, to pay for what they bought in silver, the basis of the Chinese currency. The British East India Company shipped silver bullion out to the East to pay for the tea and other goods its ships picked up in eighteenth-century Canton. In the first years of the nineteenth century, though, this situation changed.

Opium, a drug made from poppies, is a useful pain-killer. It has also been used by some cultures rather as others have used alcohol, though the parallel is not exact because whereas alcohol can provoke not only physical collapse, but excitement and obstreperousness, opium usually brings on a drowsy, foggy contentment ending in sleep and happy dreams. In opium, the British at last found a commodity which the Chinese wanted, and it could be grown in India. Unfortunately, like many another drug, it is addictive – people become dependent on it, and will then break many of the ordinary rules of social life to satisfy their craving for it. Other effects of opium (lethargy, care-lessness of the future, irresponsibility) also seemed very undesirable to Manchu officials. They therefore forbade the drug's importation (it was also disadvantageous in their eyes in that it came from abroad and so might make China dependent on foreigners). So began the awakening of China and its slide into the European sphere.

In 1839, a great outcry by British merchants was provoked by the official destruction of a large quantity of opium imported by them at Canton. Reasonably enough, Lord Palmerston, in charge of foreign affairs in London, told them that his government could not intervene to help its subjects break the laws of the country where they were seeking to do business. But British officials on the spot thought otherwise. Attempts to patch up the quarrel on the spot failed; naval operations followed and British troops were landed to occupy some southern ports and other places. Outright bullying forced on China a peace treaty in 1842 which required the opening of five of her ports to foreign trade, the levying of a single rate of fixed duty on imports, and the cession of Hong Kong to Britain. It was the end of the restriction of foreign traders to Canton and of their tributary status. These were Europe's first interferences with China's internal sovereignty.

The episode is not one on which many Englishmen now look back with pride. To many at the time, though, civilization meant not only lining one's pocket but overcoming backwardness. Free trade was not only expected to benefit both sides, but to enable Christianity and humanitarianism to be brought to bear on the barbarities of a pagan society – China's oppression of women, for example, or use of judicial torture. The government of Queen Victoria may have launched the Chinese Revolution unwittingly, but some of her subjects entertained views with large and revolutionary implications.

Within ten years, the Americans and French walked through the door the British had kicked open and signed their own 'unequal treaties' (as they were later called). They won rights of trade and diplomatic representation, too, and special legal protection for their citizens, and these led in due course to further concessions, the arrival of missionaries and the toleration of Christianity. Thus began the undermining of the authority and prestige of the empire, though that had not been the aim of the treaty-makers. But they had forced the Manchu to acknowledge the ending of the age-old principle that all foreign peoples were really tributaries of the 'Middle Kingdom'; Chinese diplomacy had to come to terms with western ideas about the sovereignty of individual states. Worse still, the arrival of foreign merchants and missionaries in increasing numbers and their immunity from prosecution before Chinese courts showed that the imperial government could not resist the barbarians it officially despised.

Missionary influences were particularly insidious. Not only did they undermine the Confucian tradition and social system (to preach the idea that all human beings were equal in the sight of God was itself revolutionary in China), but the missionaries' converts began to claim the protection of the European consuls and courts. They tried to live in European areas where they could not be harassed by Chinese officials. Even when the missionaries met popular hostility, too, as they often did, this did not help the officials much. If they protected them, then they would become unpopular, if they did not, the missionaries might get killed, the local European consul would send for a gunboat or some soldiers to seize the murderers, and the imperial administration would be shown up as unable to protect its subjects against the foreigners.

Almost coincidentally, these strains appeared against the background of deepening social distress and a growing danger of rebellion. But China's rulers took a long time to recognize an approaching crisis, remembering that China had often faced difficulties in her long history. She had always come through them. The superiority of Chinese culture was such (they were sure) that China would, in due course, resume her rightful position in the world, however bad things might look for a time. A few, meanwhile, thought it might be wise to find out from the barbarians some of the secrets of their steamships and cannon so that they could be put to use by the empire. Even educated Chinese, though, could not yet believe that traditional ways might have to be changed in very deep ways. Yet this was the case. The 1840s opened a period of upheaval and revolution which took a century to come to completion. It would slowly reveal itself as a double repudiation, both of the foreigner and of much of the Chinese past. Yet it was increasingly to express itself in the modes and idioms of the European world. Because such ideological forces could not be contained within the traditional framework, they would in the end prove fatal to it, when the Chinese sought to remove the obstacles to modernization and national power, and shattered for good a social system which had been the foundation of Chinese life for thousands of years.

China: concessions and decline

Deeply-entrenched attitudes made it difficult for China to react effectively to the vigorous and pushful Europeans. Half-hearted borrowing was one response; Europeans were employed as military help (rather as Romans of the late western empire enlisted barbarians to defend them) in mastering the Taiping rebellion, a huge upheaval which raged from 1850 to 1864, under a leader who drew his ideas in part from American missionaries' teaching. In the end the rebellion was crushed, but not before the Ch'ing had been forced to make yet more concessions to the foreigners in order to buy time and support, and only at the cost of about 20,000,000 lives. Amid its disorders, French and British armed forces were engaged every year against the Chinese between 1856 and 1860, and on one occasion jointly seized Peking, sacking and burning the Summer Palace.

There were other humiliations. In 1858 Chinese provinces north of the river Amur were surrendered to Russia, and the Ussuri peninsula (on which the Russians were to build Vladivostok) was handed over two years later. Big surrenders of Chinese territory were also made to Russia in Central Asia, beyond the frontier of Sinkiang. Russia's appetite was great; she was the power with the longest land frontier with China and had been pressing forward in Central Asia for decades before this and on the Amur, since the days of Peter the Great. But other European states also nibbled away. The Chinese had always claimed overlordship over Burma and Indo-China but now they lost both. Before the end of the century, perhaps encouraged by a Japanese seizure in 1895 of Formosa (Taiwan) and the Pescadores, and spurred on somewhat by the fear that rivals might get ahead of them in the race if China collapsed altogether, the Europeans turned again to land-grabbing in China itself. The Russians installed themselves in Port Arthur; England, France and Germany took other seaports on long leases, and the Portuguese in Macao turned their old lease there into outright ownership (they said). Even the Italians made a bid, but unsuccessfully. In the background, moreover, was a continuing stream of concessions, loan agreements and interference in the Chinese administration all of which made China look a country increasingly under foreign control, one which, even if still legally independent, was nevertheless beginning to undergo a measure of colonization.

This was why many Europeans in 1900 thought China would break up as the Ottoman empire seemed to be doing. It was hardly surprising that when a British prime minister spoke of two classes of nation, the 'living and the dying', China was envisaged as the outstanding example of the second. Far from the sleeping giant against whose awakening Napoleon had warned, China seemed to be likely to undergo the death of a 1,000 cuts – a legendary but still exacted Chinese punishment – sliced up bit by bit by the predators from the west. By the end of the century, though, some Chinese were determined this should not happen. They noted the efforts of Peter the Great and contemporary efforts to modernize another Asian society, Japan. Students were for the first time officially sent abroad to study in Europe and the United States. Yet even those who sought reform found it hard to shake off the idea that they should root it in the Confucian tradition. In 1898, in any case, they were swept aside by a palace coup.

At about the same time, the strength of popular conservatism produced an outbreak of troubles in the provinces, under the influence of a widespread and secret society called (somewhat oddly to western ears) the 'Society of Harmonious Fists'; its members were therefore labelled 'Boxers', for short. They were violently anti-foreign, attacking Christian Chinese converts and, soon, missionaries. The Manchu officials and the court secretly favoured and hoped to use them, a bad miscalculation. There were diplomatic protests and demands that they be suppressed by the government. When a full-scale Boxer rebellion broke out, egged on by the dowager empress and her agents, European troops seized Chinese forts in order to secure the route to Peking, where there was a foreign community to be safeguarded. The empress declared war on all foreign powers, the German minister at Peking was murdered and the legations besieged; elsewhere, more than 200 foreigners – mainly missionaries – were killed. Retribution was swift. An international expeditionary force fought its way to Peking and the Russians occupied southern Manchuria. The court fled from the capital, but after a few months had to accept terms; the punishment of responsible officials, the payment of a huge indemnity, the razing of forts, and foreign garrisons. The Boxer rising had not only failed, but had further undermined the already shaky Manchu regime.

Japan: qualified hegemony

In 1800 there was little to suggest that the isolated empire of Japan might adapt more successfully than China to challenge from the Europeanizing world. To all appearances just as conservative, Japan had behind her two centuries of isolation which had sheltered division within her ruling classes, the decay of her military system and the growth of social instability. Some Japanese knew that insulation against western ideas had long since ceased to be possible. A few learned men had interested themselves in books which entered Japan through the narrow aperture of the Dutch trade at Nagasaki. Yet Japan was very different from China. Many Japanese were eager to learn from Europeans, as unhampered by their traditions as the Chinese seemed bogged down in theirs. Japan's posture when she suddenly had to face a new and unprecedented challenge from the outside was less disadvantageous than that of China.

It was becoming clearer in the 1840s, while Japan's rulers observed with increasing alarm events in China, that Europeans and North Americans seemed both to have a new interest in breaking into Asian trade and new and irresistible strength to do it. The king of the Netherlands warned the shogun that exclusion was no longer a realistic policy. But there was no quick agreement among Japan's rulers about whether resistance or concession was the better. It was therefore the president of the United States who took the decisive step by sending the first foreign squadron to sail into Japanese waters to Edo Bay in 1853. In the following year it came back and the first of a series of 'unequal' treaties with foreign powers was made by the shogunate. This was a warning. No doubt some Japanese saw it as such, but there were still a few years of somewhat muddled response to the barbarian threat (there was even one further attempt to expel foreigners by force) and a new course was not set until well into the 1860s. Before that, commercial privileges, extra-territoriality for western residents, the admission of diplomatic representatives, and restrictions on the Japanese export of opium had all been won by the United States, Great Britain, France, Russia and the Netherlands. Soon afterwards the shogunate came to an end and the imperial court and administration resumed control in 1868 in the so-called 'Meiji Restoration'.

Its symbolic opening was the transference of the court to Edo (the modern Tokyo) from the old capital at Kyoto. There followed the abolition of feudalism and the surrender of land by the great clan in return for government lands. Then came, within five years, the adoption of a prefectorial system of administration, postal services, a daily newspaper, a ministry of education, military conscription, the first railway, religious toleration, and the Gregorian calendar. All were deliberate imitations of Europe. A representative system of local government was inaugurated in 1879 and ten years later a new constitution set up a bi-cameral parliament for which a peerage had already been created in preparation for the organization of the upper house.

Although the innovatory passion was beginning to show signs of flagging in the 1880s, and much of old Japan was to survive the Meiji revolution, much, too, had gone, never to be restored. For the modernized army and navy foreign instruction was sought. Significantly, French military advisers were dropped and Germans were employed after the Franco-Prussian War; the British provided instructors for the navy. Young Japanese were sent abroad to learn at first hand the secrets of the wonderful and threatening puissance of Europe and North America.

It is still hard not to be moved by the ardour of many of these young men and their elders, and impossible not to be impressed by their achievement. Its impact was felt far beyond Japan and their own time. It inspired national leaders across Asia from India to China. Meanwhile, the success of the reformers was rapidly evident. The borrowing of western technology and expertise was not the whole reason for the release in Japan of a current of economic growth long unrivalled in any other non-western state. The country was lucky in being already well-supplied with entrepreneurs who took for granted the profit motive. Increase in agricultural production was maintained, though the peasants, who made up four-fifths of the population in 1868, benefited little from it. Japan managed to feed a growing population, nonetheless, and the land taxes helped to pay for the further protection from the foreigner which came with Japan's swift rise to international power and status. Paradoxically, its first great demonstration was against China, whose forces were shattered by the Japanese in the war of 1894–5.

That war was also a demonstration of another outcome of European world hegemony: that the hegemony was itself already passing. It was already qualified when European states could no longer behave as the sole players who mattered on the world stage. Japan's assertion of her own interests in the Far East was, indeed, so alarming that it produced a coalition of European powers which prevented her from picking up all her winnings from the table after her victory over China. The United States, too, was another non-European world player: her hegemony in the western hemisphere had long been tacitly recognized by European states. When one of them, Spain, was stripped by the United States of her Far Eastern and Pacific possessions in 1898, American policy had already been unrolling for nearly a half-century in the Far East and Pacific. Finally, there were already the first stirrings of a new nationalism all over Asia.

CHAPTER SIX International order and disorder

New patterns of power

The central fact of 1871 was that a new German empire replaced France as the major European land power west of Russia. This was a great change in the dynamics of international relations. It was at an obvious level a matter of military numbers. The size of armies was not the only factor which mattered in assessing military power, but was in the end a good rough indicator, at least if other factors were equal. Even in 1900 most senior officers in European armies would also probably have agreed that the best material to provide those numbers was to be found in the countryside, from peasants presumed to be hardy and unlikely to question authority once in uniform – and it became easier to enforce conscription as the century went on. France still had a large peasant population in 1900 but over the nineteenth century as a whole her share of the rising total population of Europe fell from 15 to 10 per cent of the enlarged total, while Germany's after unification went up to 14 per cent of it by 1900. Another of the losers in the mid-century wars, Austria-Hungary, also saw her share go down, though in 1900 it was still larger than that of France, at 12 per cent. Russia remained in that year a still-growing demographic giant, with a population which had gone up from 21 to 24 per cent of the European total since 1800.

Statesmen had to think about such changes, and sometimes came to different policy conclusions. The German government chose to discourage emigration because it feared a loss of military manpower; French statesmen came increasingly to think about ways of encouraging the national birth-rate. Meanwhile, population growth and worries over unemployment and the rising numbers of the poor in the United Kingdom had encouraged emigration (not for the first time in England's history), and that had in turn influenced sentiment and policy towards settler colonies. The British, though, were not concerned about keeping up a large army; the one they had was expensive, but they remained down to 1914 the only great power without military conscription. Nonetheless, they had a huge navy and showed no disposition to give up the independence of action around the world which it gave them.

Great Britain could afford such strength; she was in these years the richest of European countries and still in 1871 its leading industrial power, though Germany was coming up fast and would in many respects overtake her by 1900. Such facts had to be taken into account as another factor in assessing military capability. Although industrial strength was primarily of importance in generating wealth to sustain power, it also had an increasingly direct bearing on the terms of conflict. The tactical lessons of the American Civil War (1861–65) had largely been overlooked or ignored by Europeans but to those who wished to consider it, that struggle showed the importance of manufacturing capacity, modern communications and technological modernity in obtaining victory. The part played by the availability of railways, in particular, in European military planning was striking after 1871. But so was the development of better weapons, of artillery of greater range and power, of rifled small-arms, machine-guns, better armour and engines for warships. Germany became by far the best-prepared country for competition in such matters as her industrial strength grew rapidly after unification. Austria-Hungary and Russia were unlikely to catch up with her for a long time, large though their armies were. Commitments, too, had to be considered. All three of the eastern empires were multi-ethnic, but in the case of Germany this implied less of a burden on military resources and less internal weakness than for the other two. As for expensive distractions, Russia was the only European great power whose imperial interests rivalled those of Great Britain in extent.

Nationalism

Some soldiers were less reliable than others. In the multi-national empires, it could no longer be taken for granted by the end of the century that all could be disciplined to the same degree of reliability. Those who led the Habsburg army had to consider, for example, the likely reactions of Slav regiments if certain operations were contemplated. Their forces did not even have a common language; German was used for command, but a vocabulary of less than a hundred words was all that an Italian-speaking or Croat recruit had to be able to recognize. As the decades passed, the question of loyalties became more troubling, thanks to the continuing and growing potential of nationalism in these years as a factor in international relations.

Nationalism has now behind it at least two centuries as the most successful revolutionary force of modern politics. In 1871 it was still, after easing the path to Italian and German unity, a long way from demonstrating all it might do, and new forces were coming into play to feed it. In developing societies where old social ties and loyalties were breaking down in great cities and wide anonymous markets, there was a vacuum to be filled. Personal and collective identities had to be redefined, new emotional foci established. This, though, was happening when a new and more immediate sharing of information and emotion than ever before was becoming available through greater literacy, more popular newspapers, speedier world communication of information. National self-conciousness was seized upon by the politicians of order and liberty alike: conservatives lauded it in the name of tradition, liberals as the ground of self-determination. It was also used as a smokescreen for vested interests and demagogy.

Nationalism rested at bottom on the assumption, still by no means universally accepted in 1871, that Europe should be organized as a system of states whose legitimacy derived from the fact that they represented identifiable nations. This could be, and had sometimes been, arranged peacefully. Habsburg concessions to Hungary in 1867 had not been made as a result of civil war (though they would not have been easily imaginable without the defeat inflicted on the Habsburgs by Prussia) and in 1905 Norway was to separate itself from Sweden peacefully and by agreement. But it could not be said in 1871 that the omens were good. The century's history down to that year had been studded with revolution and war in the name of nationalism. With three European great imperial powers and another empire, the Ottoman, resting on different principles, the future looked unpromising, given the evident problems ahead.[1]

For all the success of German and Italian nationalism in the mid-century decades, and in spite of the establishment of new national states in Serbia, Greece and Rumania by 1870, the threat national aspirations posed to European peace did not go away. There was no flagging in patriotic efforts to establish other new nations inside the Ottoman empire. Two more, Bulgaria and Montenegro, emerged in the 1870s, and in 1913, Albania for the first time made its appearance on the map in a final spasm of nation-making from the remains of European Turkey. Even Crete had by then at least obtained the Sultan's recognition of an autonomous form of government under a Greek governor. Broadly speaking, for forty years the nationalities of the Ottoman or former Ottoman empire in the Balkans raised more questions for European statesmen to solve than any other force. All European diplomats knew they presented great potential danger to peace because they threatened always to drag great powers into their quarrels.

Inside the Russian empire, though Poles, Jews, Ukrainians and Lithuanians all felt oppressed, and Finland had lost such autonomy as she had enjoyed under Alexander II, unrest had few international implications. The more reactionary regimes of Alexander III and Nicholas II seemed quite able to contain disorder and to maintain the de facto domination of the Russian peoples over other subjects of the empire. It became increasingly clear, though, that a danger of war between the great powers might be presented one day by strains within the Dual Monarchy. In Hungary there was fear of a growing revolutionary threat; Slavs who formed local majorities in some of the Hungarian lands felt oppressed and activists among them looked to Serbia as a possible future protector against Magyar domination. Hungary also had a large Rumanian population in Transylvania, which might grow more responsive to encouragement from compatriots in the new independent Rumanian kingdom. In the Austrian lands of empire – in Bohemia, for example – feeling was less intense, but even there nationalism was an issue. Plans were canvassed at Vienna for possible constitutional structures which would satisfy other nationalities – federalist and 'trialist' solutions were at different times in vogue – but which nonetheless always ran into bitter opposition from the Magyars, stake-holders in the Dualist outcome of 1867.

Another imperial power, Great Britain, also had two intransigent European nationalist movements of her own to deal with, both in Ireland. The more obvious for most of the nineteenth century was that of the Catholic Irish and by 1900 important concessions had been made in attempts to buy it off, though all fell short of the solution of autonomy or 'Home Rule', to which one of the two great political parties, the Liberal, was committed by 1900. Progress towards that goal was opposed by the Protestant nationalism of Ulster, encouraged by the Conservative (or 'Unionist') Party, and paradoxically directed not towards independence, but to maintenance of the existing constitutional connexion with England. Its leader encouraged talk of violence if the

---

[1]   Though an (unfriendly) writer on democracy (Maine, *Popular Government*, 1885) pointed out that 'Russia and Turkey are the only European states which *completely* [my italics] reject the theory that governments hold their power by delegation from the community.' By 1900, Montenegro was the only other European state which did not have a parliament.

parliament at Westminster should concede Home Rule to a united Ireland. This turned out to have European implications; when Home Rule legislation was finally passed in 1914, the resulting uproar in Ulster led some foreign observers to think (erroneously) that the United Kingdom was about to be paralysed by revolution.

National feeling among the populations of the great powers themselves – or what was claimed to be such feeling in the first age of mass newspapers – was another potentially disturbing force. France and Germany were psychologically sundered by the German seizure of Alsace and Lorraine as spoils of victory in 1871 and many Frenchmen could be easily agitated by bemoaning the lost provinces. French politicians whom it suited to do so were long able to cultivate and exploit the seductive theme of *revanche*. Nationalism in France became entangled, too, in more domestic issues. It could raise questions about loyalty to the great national institutions, even loyalty to the Republic itself. The British, too, supposedly more sober as a people (or so they alleged and liked to think), were tainted by 'Jingoism' (a word invented in the 1870s), and grew excited from time to time about national symbols; as the end of this century approached, this expressed itself especially in enthusiasm for the empire and the supremacy of the Royal Navy. The British were also encouraged to feel antagonism to Germany over her commercial success in world markets and the danger it was supposed to present; the fact was that the two countries were each other's best customers, but this mattered less than the appearance of opposed interests in an era of awakening patriotic excitement.

Some extra plausibility was given to British popular sentiments (and sometimes apprehension) by the increasing stridency and vociferousness with which German national feeling was expressed during the reign of William II, the emperor of Germany and king of Prussia, who came to his double throne in 1888. It was unfortunate that because no united Germany had existed thirty years earlier, even Bismarck had found it easy to exaggerate the divisive dangers confronting a new nation as he sought support from nationalist politicians. He thought, and preached, that German Catholics who looked to ultramontane Rome and Socialists who talked about the international working class were equally 'enemies of the empire' (*Reichsfeinde*) and he viewed internal politics accordingly as a battleground of ideologies. William II (after a brief enthusiasm for conciliation of the working-class) became even more excited over the dangers of revolution and also looked to nationalist and chauvinistic feeling for support.

Bismarck had nonetheless been cautious; after he had been sent into retirement, German foreign policy began to show more concern for the slippery prizes of respect and prestige (a term the old chancellor had disliked) – a 'place in the sun', as some put it. With the emperor's approval, Germany's 'new course' in the 1890s led not only to a new assertiveness about Germany's role in Europe, but evolved into the promotion of a global vision of the country's proper standing, a 'World Policy' (*Weltpolitik*). This was warmly welcomed by some, among them industrial interests growing in importance since 1871. One symbolic expression of it was the beginning of the building of a big navy. At first British opinion was not much alarmed (British official policy was in the 1890s much more concerned to assure supremacy over the combined French and Russian fleets than by German aspirations) but in the early years of the twentieth century, it began to be asked against whom the German High Seas fleet was likely to be employed unless it was against Great Britain. There was by then a growing impression in several European countries, far from unjustified, that the German empire tended to throw its weight about too much in international affairs. The emergence of this view is hard to summarize in its complexity, but it fed the simplifications of public opinion. It was an important instance of the disturbing and unintended effects which nationalist sentiment could have as the twentieth century began, for, in constitutional states at least, governments could not ignore public opinion.

The management of danger

Nonetheless, the European powers seem in retrospect to have been remarkably successful in running their relations with one another in the last decades of the century. For all the rows which broke out from time to time, they managed to avoid fighting one another. There was even room for optimism. International violence had abated since the turbulent 1850s and 1860s and acceptance of international arbitration had become more frequent. The meeting in 1899 of the first international congress to set up better arbitration arrangements and to limit armaments failed in its aim of permanent armament reductions, but from it emerged the international court at the Hague, which could be thought a promising sign. The congress had also done something to limit the brutality of conflict (it was agreed that for a period there should be no use of poison gas, dum-dum bullets or even bombing from the air). When the German emperor sent off the German contingent to the international expeditionary force to China in 1900 he was much stirred by reports of Boxer atrocities against Europeans and urged his soldiers to respond by behaving 'like Huns'. The phrase was striking and was not to be forgotten; it was thought to be going too far. Just in that, though, lay its symptomatic importance; by 1900, no-one expected European soldiers to behave in a barbaric way, even if they sometimes did. The humanizing of war had come far enough for William II to think he needed to tell his soldiers to cast aside the restraints of 'civilized warfare' and to behave barbarically.

A different facet of the fundamental optimism over European diplomacy in these years appears also in the fact that it was almost never suggested that Europe would not continue to be the centre of the world's affairs and the real maker of its destinies. Except (and it was an important qualification) in the western hemisphere, and (beginning in the 1890s) in a measure in the Far East, European statesmen rarely worried about anything except their relations with other Europeans. Their relationships with one another mattered most to them and the record, in terms of settling conflict without going to war, was by 1900 impressive. Yet real dangers persisted.

These mattered most, but not solely, to the eastern monarchies, whose internal constitutional arrangements seemed increasingly out of tune with the movement of history. Germany had a written constitution, representative parliamentary institutions, universal suffrage, and protection of individual rights by independent courts; her institutions had permitted the emergence of the strongest parliamentary socialist party in Europe. Yet she was ruled by men uneasily aware – perhaps in the emperor's case, almost hysterically aware – that the country's outstanding economic progress had generated social and political forces harder and harder to reconcile with social conservatism. These forces found little space to operate and had no voice in the management of the country. Much real, often decisive, power was still wielded informally by the crown, the conservative agrarian aristocracy of Prussia, and the soldiers. German conservatives could still speak at times as if they still believed in the old assumption of the era of the Holy Alliance that governments were the natural opponents of their subjects.

This proposition was perhaps even more acceptable among the directing élites of the Dual Monarchy, in spite of its parliamentary institutions. Though the adoption of its new and hyphenated constitution had itself registered a triumph of a national (Magyar) idea, there were growing signs by 1900 that it was going to be hard to keep its structure intact without provoking subject peoples in the empire beyond endurance. Social change in the Austrian lands, too (industrialization in Austria and Bohemia, for example), was adding new tensions to the problems of dynasty. By and large this was tackled by a combination of social bribery – workers' protection in the workplace, insurance, and regulation of the working-day – and repression of socialist organizations, a somewhat sharper version of what had been done by Bismarck in Germany.

Russia was meanwhile changing more deeply and rapidly still. Autocracy and terrorism had between them blighted the promise of the reforming years of Alexander II, but had not hindered the onset of economic revolution. Fiscal policies extracted grain from the peasants which provided exports to pay the interest on foreign loans of capital for investment in infrastructure, above all, in railways. But even primary industrialization created problems. An industrial proletariat began to accumulate in the manufacturing cities. Meanwhile, the conditions for liberalizing society and the state remained weak. Autocracy remained in the saddle. Rural disturbance never ceased, though it fluctuated in intensity, and terrorism always found new recruits. Russian socialism was marked by it from the start. Some of the tensions thus created were to explode in revolution in 1905.

These very visible facts seemed increasingly incongruous in a Europe most of whose other states were undergoing peaceful (if occasionally excited) change towards more democratic, and sometimes even liberal, styles of politics. The widespread tendency to enlarge the suffrage for national elections was a clear sign of the trend[2]. Others were the sapping of the privileges of established religion, greater equality before the law, evident gain in freedoms of association, speech, and publication. Political parties proliferated and acquired refined techniques of organization and agitation. All this went with much continuing distrust of democracy and liberalism, but it indicated the dominating currents of the age – and they were to win further successes in the early years of the next century.

The fears of conservatives in virtually every European country were, of course, inflamed by the often violent rhetoric of the Left. Constitutional states, too, had to face social and conspiratorial violence. Yet the state machine everywhere grew stronger than ever. This was vividly and bloodily demonstrated in France in 1871. In the aftermath of the Prussian siege of Paris a popular régime which drew to itself a wide range of radicals and reformers set itself up in the capital as a 'Commune', a name evocative of traditions of municipal independence going back to the Middle Ages and, more important, to 1793, when the Commune (or city council) of Paris had been the centre of revolutionary fervour. The Commune of 1871 took power when the provisional government of France was unable to disarm the capital of the weapons with which its inhabitants had successfully withstood a siege, because defeat had inflamed many Parisians against men they believed to have let them down and perhaps to be ready to restore the monarchy.

---

[2] By 1900 male adult universal suffrage existed in France, Germany, Spain and Norway. The British electorate of 1871 had been much enlarged in 1885, the Italian in 1881 and the Dutch twice, in 1887 and 1896.

There were a few weeks of quiet while the government prepared its riposte, during which the Commune did little, though it stimulated much left-wing rhetoric. It came to be seen as the embodiment of social revolution – as many of its supporters wished – and was suspected by some to be the outcome of plotting by the notorious International (it was not).

This gave additional bitterness to repression when it came. When the government had reassembled its forces from returning prisoners of war, Paris became the scene of brief but bloody street-fighting. Once again, trained armed forces soon overcame workmen and shopkeepers manning hastily improvised barricades. If anything could do so, the ghastly failure of the Paris Commune (over 20,000 men, women and children were killed and over 300,000 arrested) should have finished off the revolutionary myth, both in its power to terrify and its power to inspire. Yet it did not. If anything, it strengthened it. Conservatives found the Commune a great standby in evoking the dangers always ready to burst out from under the surface of society. Revolutionaries had a new episode of heroism and martyrdom from which to extend an apostolic succession of their predecessors running already from 1789 to 1848. But the Commune also revivified the association of socialism with the revolutionary myth.

Socialism

Marx quickly snapped up the drama and exaltation of the Paris Commune for socialism. In a powerful tract he annexed it to his own theories, though it had been the product of many complicated and differing forces and had expressed in its actions very little in the way of egalitarianism, let alone 'scientific' socialism. It emerged, moreover, in a city which though huge, was not one of the great manufacturing centres in which he predicted proletarian revolution would mature. These remained stubbornly quiescent. The Commune was, instead, the last and greatest example of traditional Parisian revolutionary radicalism.

Marx nonetheless made it central to socialist mythology, and this was of importance as, after 1871, socialism became institutionalized as never before. The first International of working-class associations had embraced a wide range of views and doctrines, both on fundamentals and on tactics. It had been more important as an inspiration than as an effective agency and disappeared in the 1870s, after Marx transferred its secretariat formally to the United States as part of his struggles to keep it under his own control. Far more important was the foundation in 1889 of what became known as the 'Second International'. It united socialist political parties and groups across Europe with trades unions and other working-class organizations. It was ideologically Marxist, though not to such a degree as would impede membership by non-Marxists; anarchists could belong to it. Nonetheless, what was called 'Marxism' both by its opponents and by socialists, a body of dogma drawn, allegedly, from Marx's teaching and writing, was officially accepted by socialists almost everywhere by the end of the century, though they sometimes differed about its application. Marx himself protested in his later years that he was not a 'Marxist', and seems to have disapproved of what many of his disciples were saying, but confident assertions that history would inevitably generate the overthrow of capitalism and, in the end, inaugurate a rationally ordered society in which individuals could at last be truly free, became for many socialists the heart of a new religion (and one not unlike older faiths in its capacity to generate elaboration, exigesis and heresy).

The Second International benefited from the growth in the previous thirty years of socialist political parties, above all in constitutional states, and of trades unions. The latter, unsurprisingly, had prospered (sometimes in the teeth of official opposition) in the most developed industrial countries. Socialism by 1900 had no effective competitor on the Left. But its success was a curious phenomenon, for though, broadly speaking, socialist leaders talked revolution, they increasingly used their power in the work-place or polling-booth to win advantages for their followers from capitalist society – and so helped to blunt the edge of the misery which could fuel revolution. This was another source of piecemeal improvement in standards of living and expectations.

Changing opinions

It was a source of dismay to traditionalists and conservatives that political and social trends seemed for most of the century to go hand in hand with changes in intellectual culture in an alliance to weaken established structures, traditions and customs important as social preservatives. The reality of their perception is doubtful, but of the sincerity of their concern there can be no doubt. Much was going on – and had been going on for a long time (some said since the Protestant Reformation, and, a few extremists, since the expulsion from the Garden of Eden) which weakened the grip of traditional ideas. Those who felt endangered by intellectual innovations which questioned the foundations of religion, nevertheless probably exaggerated the degree to which the ideas of scholars and philosophers had much to do with the growing paganism of the masses. It is not easy to establish direct correlations between belief (or lack of it) and even the most obvious changes in material life, and the expectations and assumption to which they gave rise. It really mattered to intellectuals, on the other hand, that biblical scholars had been from the 1840s onwards demolishing many simple assumptions about the value of the Bible as historical evidence. In the longer run this made it possible to regard the Bible simply as a historic text, to be approached as critically as any other. An immensely successful (and scandal-provoking) *Life of Jesus*, published in 1863 by a French scholar, Ernest Renan, brought such an attitude before a wider public than ever before. The book which had been the central text of European civilization since its emergence in the Dark Ages would never recover its position among the sceptical élite.

Yet it is hard to believe that the damage done among the thinking classes by philology and textual criticism to Christian belief equalled that done by science. This, too, was first felt through attacks on the historical record scripture provided. Charges against internal and logical inconsistency in the teaching of the Church became much more alarming when empirical evidence could be produced to show that things said in the Bible (and therefore based on the same authority as everything else in it) plainly did not fit observable fact. The starting-point had been in geology; ideas which had been about since the end of the eighteenth century were given a much wider public in the 1830s by the publication of *Principles of Geology* by a Scotch scientist, George Lyell. This book explained landscape and geological structure in terms of forces still at work and not as the result of a single act of creation, but of wind, rain and so on. If this were correct, then the presence of fossils of different forms of life in different geological strata implied that the creation of new animals had been repeated in each geological age and the biblical account of creation would not do. That a chronology based on the Bible was simply untrue in relation to man was also suggested by discoveries of stone tools in British caves along with the fossilized bones of extinct animals – clearly, man was much older than the biblical account allowed. What followed with the publication of Darwin's views was an even heavier blow against the biblical account of creation (as well as against the assumption of the unique status of Man) which was to win wider publicity than any earlier one. In combination with biblical criticism and geology, his book made it impossible for a conscientious and thoughtful man to accept – as he had still been able to do in 1800 – the Bible as literally true.

The undermining of the authority of scripture remains the most obvious single way in which science affected formulated beliefs. Yet just as important, if not more so, was the growing prestige which science was coming to have among a broader public than ever before because of its new status as the supreme instrument for the manipulation of nature, which was seen as increasingly powerless to resist. While the great achievements of seventeenth-century or even eighteenth-century science had not often resulted in changes in the lives of ordinary men and women, those of the nineteenth century increasingly did. The authority of science was more and more evoked by those who sought social and political change, too. A much larger place was given to science in education, and professional studies (not only in medicine) came to incorporate larger scientific components. The sum effect was to carry further a long-established growth of society's investment in science. Since about 1700 the world population of scientists has doubled in number roughly every fifteen years, and in the nineteenth century other measurements of the growth of science also provide exponential curves. The cultural outcome in the sense of effects on the conduct and belief of large populations remains hard to weigh. Perhaps it will never be possible to estimate it exactly. Yet it is unimaginable that there was no connexion.

Rome and modernity

Protestant and Catholic alike, the churches tended to emerge from the period of the Revolution with few notions of adaptation to the post-revolutionary environment except by putting up more buildings. They also showed an exaggerated sense of the dangers of false doctrine, impiety and 'Voltairean' principles: the *Index* of prohibited books and the Inquisition were both re-established at Rome after the return of Pius VIII from his detention since 1812 in France. An encyclical of Gregory XVI in 1832 condemned freedom of conscience and liberty of the press. For much of the next forty years, the papacy was to take a similar line, and found it all the easier to do so while the forces of liberalism and nationalism were deployed against it in the cause of Italian unity. For many Italians who welcomed it, the ending of the Temporal Power and the occupation of Rome itself by Italian troops in 1870 had been a logical consequence of the *Risorgimento*. With the important difference that he did not think it welcome, this was a view shared by Pius IX, who retired to the Vatican City (from which he and his successors were not to emerge even to visit the pope's cathedral church as bishop of Rome, St John Lateran, for the next sixty years).

Before that, the reign of Pius IX had already provided even more dramatic symbolic evidence of what seemed to be the widening gulf between the Church and the spirit of the age. In 1854, Pius promulgated as dogma (and therefore a belief requiring the assent of all Catholics) a belief in the Immaculate Conception of the Blessed Virgin

Mary, the mother of Christ – that is, that she was born free of the stain of original sin which tainted every other human being save Christ himself. This was the first addition to the dogmas of the Church since the Council of Trent, and it was made on the pope's sole authority. The doctrine had a long history, having been sustained by Franciscans against Dominicans in the Middle Ages (Aquinas had been against it), and was in many places the object of popular devotions. Its meaning remains, except to the eye of faith, arcane and complex, but it carried a ringing implication of opposition to the public mind of a modernizing Europe.

Ten years later, there appeared appended to an encyclical letter a 'Syllabus of Errors' which made such opposition explicit and detailed. In it the pope not only condemned (among many other things) such notorious innovations as rationalism, socialism and freemasonry, but declared it also to be an error 'to believe that the Roman Pontiff can and ought to reconcile himself to, and agree with, progress, liberalism and contemporary civilization'. Then, at the first ecumenical council since Trent, summoned to the Vatican in 1869 and sitting for ten months, it was proclaimed that the pope was infallible when speaking *ex cathedra* on faith and morals. It was evident that whatever the diminished worldly power of the papacy and the loss of its territories, its claims to authority over Christians had been re-asserted with a pretension unprecedented since the Middle Ages (and, to many, all too reminiscent of them).

The Austrian government had made a concordat with the papacy in 1855, which marked the end of what was called 'Josephinism', the assertion of state power over the Church which had begun under the eighteenth-century emperor, Joseph II. Now, within a few days of the promulgation of the infallibility dogma, it cancelled it. Infallibility, though, was not the sole reason why the Church soon found itself engaged in several countries in quarrels with lay authority. Church and State, co-operative for decades after the Restoration, were once more, it seemed, often ranged on opposite sides. Particular reasons often lay behind this. The circumstances which led to papal denunciation of the new Italy and to a declaration that it was not expedient for Italian Catholics to take part in its constitutional life by voting in its elections are clear. A major struggle in Germany which lasted over a decade, the *Kulturkampf* (cultural struggle), was formally detonated by infallibility, but actually involved a political struggle between German parties; Catholic voters who supported a Centre party organized to protect Catholic interests in the new German empire were predominantly representative of areas within the federation which sought to defend their particular interests against (Protestant) Prussia. The result over the next decade was a series of punitive measures against Catholic interests, including the expulsion of the Jesuits and lay interference with ecclesiastical discipline over clergy. Only after 1879 did the temperature begin to fall, when Bismarck, again for reason of domestic political tactics, began to relax the repressive laws. In France, too, the religious issue was complicated by internal politics. For years after the defeat of 1870, the future of the *de facto* Third Republic which emerged from that year was uncertain. The legitimists who sought to restore the old house of Bourbon were deeply tainted in the eyes of republicans by historic association with clerical causes and even with the ultramontane clergy who accepted the most extreme papal pretensions. Other conservatives, backing other pretenders to the throne, also tended to be respectful of the Catholic tradition of France and what was believed to be the Catholic loyalty of the rural masses. Conversely, republicanism was enthusiastic in linking itself with the tradition of the Revolution; the few liberal

Catholics had never enjoyed any success which might have blurred this great division – one, too, tragically stained with blood; two archbishops of Paris had died at the hands of Parisian revolutionaries, in 1848 and 1871. The Right did not need to go back to 1793 for atrocities. When, after ten years, the republic at last seemed safe for the republicans (although monarchists continued to seek its overthrow) their legislation (notably in education) often had a pronounced anti-clerical content, although relations with the Church continued to be regulated by the concordat of Napoleon I.

Issues of Church and State relations in Catholic countries must also be seen in the perspective of the tendency of the age to draw more power to the national state. Civil marriage and divorce, the regulation of fiscal matters which raised questions of charitable and clerical immunity, the control of the press and free speech, the content of education – these were issues increasingly difficult to debate in an atmosphere of intransigence. Education, above all, posed problems, as new nations sought to make Italians and Germans through their schooling, and older ones (like France) fought out in their schools ideological battles from the past. Such issues of the age were hard to manage under Pius IX, associated as he was with the most ultramontane claims for papal authority and what his critics saw as obscurantism.

Leo XIII, who succeeded him in 1878, brought a very different personality and intellect to the papacy. His views and actions did much to recover influence on governments for the papacy by promoting changes in the behaviour of clerical politicians (in France, they were told to support the republic). In some measure he operated in a more favourable political climate than his predecessor, since anxiety over socialism (notably in Germany) tended to bring together conservatives and liberals; Catholic parties began to appear during his pontificate which were committed to upholding constitutional processes and to the use of the ballot-box to bring their weight to bear. The word 'liberal' had too many anti-clerical connotations for him to adopt it, but Leo has been called a liberal pope, not only for his discernment of the possibilities of democratic and constitutional machinery in providing protection for religion, but also for the first pronouncements by the papacy (notably in the encyclical *Rerum novarum*, of 1891) on the proper treatment of labour questions in a capitalist society. But he did not soften his predecessor's attitudes towards united Italy and continued to insist overtly on the duty of Italian Catholics to abstain from participation in politics.

Bismarck's Europe

The new German *Reich* of 1871 had not been welcomed by its first ruler, the emperor William I. A true conservative, deeply opposed to innovation, he believed that it was better to be king of Prussia than emperor of a collection of historic states submerged in a new federal union acclaimed by German liberals. His irritation had been expressed to his chancellor, Bismarck, the engineer of German unification and whom he blamed for it. They agreed, though, that Prussia (and the new Germany) was now a satisfied power; no more alterations in the map or acquisitions of territory like that of Alsace and Lorraine were desirable. As a conservative and representative of conservatives – the squirearchy of east Prussia – Bismarck's aim henceforth was to preserve European peace. War might threaten the stability of monarchies as it had done in the days of Napoleon; there was evidence of latent revolutionary danger in the violence of the Commune and the agitation of socialists. What was necessary was that France, the power above all dissatisfied with the outcome of the revolutionary Cavour–Bismarck era, should be kept isolated, without the ally she would need before she had even a prospect of successfully fighting a war of revenge.

In more specific terms, isolating France boiled down to keeping alive the old Habsburg antagonism towards her (the latest affront of the French to the dynasty, after all, had been to encourage Sardinia to despoil it of its Italian provinces), to maintaining Prussia's traditional friendship with Russia, and, later, to encouraging the new Italy to quarrel with France whenever possible. Great Britain was never likely to be the ally of any power, let alone France, and needed only to be prodded occasionally into a state of irritation with her; opportunities would occur to do this from time to time by inflaming Anglo-French differences outside Europe. The only likely difficulties about ensuring peace would arise over an old and enduring, if temporarily quiescent, issue, the rivalry of Romanov and Habsburg in south-eastern Europe.

Its origins lay deep in the east European revolution of the eighteenth century. The issue had then been stimulated anew after 1800 by ideological influence stemming from the French Revolution, by the opportunities offered by the turbulence of international affairs in the Napoleonic years and by the seemingly growing and irredeemable incapacity of the Ottoman government to satisfy its subjects or control its nominal servants. With the Crimean War (which had destroyed the conservative sympathy and goodwill that had brought Russia to the help of the Habsburgs in supporting revolution in 1849), a watershed had been crossed. It had been made evident that a standing danger now existed of future armed conflict over who or what would take the place of the Ottomans if and when their European empire crumbled further. The Austrians did not want the Russians (or Russia's satellites), to bar their route to the south down the Danube. The Russians did not want it to be the Austrians (or their satellites), who might block their advance to the Straits, the mouth of the Black Sea. The British and French traditionally feared unencumbered Russian access to the Mediterranean more than Austrian domination of the Danube valley, and had shown it by going to war, but they preferred to either the preservation of the Ottoman empire in Europe for as long as possible, and, as second-best, the construction of new national states in the Balkans in its place.

In 1876 Russia again invaded Ottoman territory, in support of the Bulgarian subjects of the sultan, who were in rebellion. After the imposition by the Russians on the Turks of a victorious peace settlement which set up a large and independent Bulgarian state with an Aegean coast, it looked for a moment as if Austria and Great Britain might both go to war to hold Russia in check. The Concert of Europe was once again brought into existence at a great Congress held in Berlin in 1878. It was the master performance of Bismarck's diplomatic career. He managed – by somehow rewarding everybody – to ensure that peace was maintained without sacrificing the friendship of either St Petersburg or Vienna. The Treaty of Berlin generated a new settlement of the Eastern Question replacing that agreed at the end of the Crimean War. In due course, a 'League of the Three Emperors' of the eastern monarchies was renewed in 1884.

The Balkans themselves did not at once settle down quietly. There was another Bulgarian crisis in 1885, essentially because of the volatility of Bulgaria's internal politics. A lack of sympathy between the Russian Tsar Alexander III and the young German king of the new Bulgaria gave opportunities to Bulgarians left outside the kingdom in provinces still under Turkish rule. When they proclaimed eastern Roumelia a part of

Bulgaria the Berlin settlement faced its first major challenge. What followed rapidly revealed the extent to which settlements imposed by the powers in concert might be wrecked on the reefs of the politics of Balkan nations. At one moment Greece was at war with Turkey, Serbia with Bulgaria. Despite Russian disapproval, a new king was found for Bulgaria and at the end of the whole episode that country appeared to have become an Austrian rather than Russian satellite. Peace between the great powers was maintained, but only just, and Bismarck had found it much harder than in 1878 to avoid a choice between Germany's two friends.

International relations in the 1890s

Though Austrian and Russian policy settled down again after a few years following the troubles of the 1880s (and indeed in the 1890s the two monarchies came to something like an understanding not to rock the boat), to control events in south-eastern Europe was not forever in their power. The old concert of Europe was slowly broken apart by revolutionary nationalism. This was not just a matter of the Habsburgs' subject peoples. There were also Slavs under Ottoman rule, some of whom yearned to emulate the Serbs, who had been the first to shake it off. Under pressure from the Magyars, though, government in Vienna was bound to be wary of Serbia. Some Austrians and many Magyars saw it as a standing menace, the nucleus of a potential future state embracing all South Slavs, with rulers not only unable but probably unwilling to restrain the revolutionary nationalists who used Serbia as a base for terrorism and subversion in Bosnia. This Ottoman province was occupied by Austrian forces and administered by Vienna since the Treaty of Berlin. Not for the first or last time, it was tempting to draw dangerous lessons from history; in Vienna it was too readily assumed that Serbia might (and wanted to) play in the Danube valley the role which Sardinia had played in Italy. At the same time a new influence had begun to affect Russian policy, the rise of the phenomenon of 'Panslavism' expressed as support for other Slav nations. Its first evident effects had been seen in the agitation in favour of Russian support for the Bulgarians in 1876.

A more complex and subtle problem remained implicit: the senior partners in the Triple Alliance which Bismarck had created in 1882, Germany and Austria (the third power was Italy), were in many ways ill-matched. The outcome of a century of Habsburg-Hohenzollern rivalry in 1866 had left them unequal and Germany's military and economic strength had grown even greater since. This did not matter much during the Bismarck era; it was to matter much more when, under his successors, bad advice from Berlin was urged upon Vienna. Bismarck had been able to maintain – though with increasing difficulty – friendship with both Russia and Austria, expressed until 1887 by the personal league of the three emperors, the *Dreikaiserbund*. That had enabled him to secure European peace, a far from negligible achievement. But to muffle forever Austro-Russian antagonism was beyond even his powers. Nevertheless, after the lapsing of the *Dreikaiserbund* he kept open the line to St Petersburg with a Reinsurance Treaty between Germany and Russia. When he retired in 1890 it was already clear that this might be more difficult to keep up and his successors did not renew it when it lapsed in June that year.

They were less able and wise than he, perhaps, but also had more complicated political situations to deal with at home, where new interests were clamouring for attention.

Internal change in Germany was beginning to affect the international situation – and not only because of the excitable young William II. Even Bismarck had in his later years given way to popular agitation over colonial expansion. Yet though he continued to subordinate such matters to the aims of his European policy, he increasingly felt unfitted to grapple with the implications of an industrial society, and its advocates both of global adventure and of advance in eastern Europe. Once he had gone their arguments had more scope. So had the fantasies of the new emperor, now unchallenged at the head of a nation over which he believed he had almost absolute power.

The 1890s thus brought a seemingly accelerating abandonment of the caution of the previous twenty years of German foreign policy, but the most important change in the structure of European international relations in those years had nothing immediately to do with Germany, though its eventual implications for her were immense. This was the ending of French isolation by an alliance with Russia, worked out between 1891 and 1894. It was for many Frenchmen and a few Russians the realization at last of a long-cherished dream. It was made easier too, by continuing concern in each country over relations with Great Britain. Both had long-standing quarrels in zones of conflict and friction with her. Russia had them in Central Asia, China and Persia, and France in Siam, west Africa and, above all, Egypt. But the emphasis of their policies towards *rapprochement* with one another was different. For France, the point of an alliance was to win a measure of protection against German attack. The Russians' attention was focused on the Straits of Constantinople, whose closure to Russian warships the British still regarded as essential. In 1891 the French first promised Russia diplomatic support against the British; it was agreed that measures should be 'concerted' if either power were threatened by foreign aggression. In the following year a military convention was agreed (but not given formal effect) which registered that the French view had prevailed. In the first week of 1894 the agreement was formalized (for reasons of French domestic policy, as a military convention, not a treaty). It was to operate as a counterweight to the Triple Alliance: Russia agreed to come to the help of France if she were attacked by Germany, and the French to the help of Russia if she were attacked by Germany, or by the Dual Monarchy supported by Germany (the French were not obliged to come to the help of Russia if she were attacked solely by the Dual Monarchy). As a consequence of the leaking of incomplete knowledge of this agreement, German strategical planning was henceforth based on the assumption that in any future war with the two powers, Germany had best first settle with France – the seed of other future developments of major importance.

Yet so far as Anglo-German relations were concerned, the decade had opened promisingly, with a colonial agreement covering many issues at stake between the two countries. Connexions between their ruling families helped (at least on the English side) to prolong a policy of benevolence towards the new regime (Bismarck had not been popular at Windsor, nor had he liked English influence at the German court). Unfortunately, there were soon signs that benevolence might meet rebuffs at Potsdam. The onset of *Weltpolitik* and the opportunities it gave for misunderstanding and misrepresentation in the press, together with the temperament of the emperor Wilhelm II heightened the psychological tension felt in Berlin. An act of folly by British adventurers in 1896 (the Jameson Raid on the Transvaal republic) was followed by a rank gesture of support for the Boers (the so-called 'Kruger Telegram'). The building of the Franco-Russian alliance therefore took place against the background of the jeopardizing by Germany of her hitherto good relations with Great Britain and the failure of her statesmen to maintain the old triangular relationship between Berlin, Vienna and St Petersburg.

Such implications, nonetheless, took a long time to surface. In the second half of the decade, renewed Austro-Russian cordiality made possible agreement on Balkan issues between the old rivals. Great Britain was meanwhile faced with disputes (particularly with Russia and France) in many parts of the world. Although they might blow up into armed conflict, she appeared diplomatically effectively isolated in face of this possibility. For the remainder of the century this could be taken as a datum. Continued irritation with Great Britain over imperial friction helped to disguise the extent to which France and Russia had, by their alliance, taken a further step towards the division of Europe into two camps. But the British government was increasingly disposed to liquidate diplomatic differences whenever she could do so, and had more obvious differences with these two than with any other power. When in the middle of the 1890s Great Britain failed completely to obtain support for further intervention in the Ottoman government's misman-agement of its subjects (the term is hardly strong enough for the wave of officially tolerated massacres of Armenian Christians which had at that moment enraged British public opinion – though not that in any other country) there followed a major strategic decision. It was accepted that to defend the route to India by attempting to uphold Ottoman power in the Straits was no longer necessary; a British garrison in Egypt to pro-tect the Suez Canal would be better.

This implicitly reduced the chance of conflict with Russia. On the other hand, it increased British sensitivity over the importance of Egypt, where British and French policy had been in conflict since the early 1880s. A French government's unwillingness to co-operate had then led to British influence preponderating in the Khedive's admin-istration (which was still nominally subject to Constantinople) and a British military presence. One French response was to seek to extend French control of central Africa and of the upper Nile valley before the British seized that, too. In 1896, a British and Egyptian army advanced up the Nile, entered the Sudan and in 1898 defeated the Moslem forces of its ruler, the Mahdi, at Omdurman. A smaller expedition pushed on, in the hope of meeting other British forces from Uganda further up the valley. Instead, they found a French expedition flying its flag at Fashoda. Claiming the territory for Egypt, the British refused to discuss French claims until the French had withdrawn. Russian support was not forthcoming for France, although there was a clear danger of war. The French withdrew and in the following year gave up all claims on the Nile. Anglophobia reached new heights in Paris.

The war in South Africa with the Boer republics which began in 1899 threw into vivid relief both the disadvantages and strengths of Great Britain's international isola-tion. On the one hand, her conduct was regarded (and commented upon) unsympa-thetically by almost every other power. On the other hand, given her strategic aims at that moment, that did not much matter. Like Fashoda, the Boer War showed that where the vital theatre was to be reached only by sea, Great Britain could in the end do much as she liked in imperial and colonial matters outside the western hemisphere. It was up to those who thought it worthwhile to do so to make satisfactory agreements with her about their own interests.

As the century ended, there were still good grounds, then, for thinking peace could be maintained between the great European powers. The prospects of avoiding trouble in the Balkans remained at least as good as they had been for the last five years, and

Russia's primary attention seemed likely to go on being fixed upon the Far East rather than that area. In 1895 she had completed a railway across Siberia as far as Lake Baikal. In that year, too, she had found it easy to make common cause with the French and Germans in order to prevent Japan from reaping the benefits she expected from a victory won over China over Korea; France was happy to do something to oblige her ally and in any case sought diplomatic support for her own forward policy in south-east Asia, while Germany saw prestige and perhaps strategical advantage in acquiring a coaling-station on Chinese soil. Some European statesmen began to speculate about potential Chinese spoils for peaceful and amicable distribution in any future 'scramble'. It was not an unhopeful prospect.

BOOK FIVE

Europe's twentieth century: the era of European civil war

Europe is a term like 'Asia' or 'Africa' – or, for that matter, at a different level of scrutiny, 'Bologna' or 'Bournemouth' – identified by those talking about it for particular reasons, sometimes those of political study, sometimes quite other. It refers to a part of the world, not always defined in exactly the same way, where special things happened. It is not an entity, or a collective personality with enduring content; it indicates a place of shared experience. Nevertheless, this book has already called attention to several instances of the fact that some of those who lived in Europe (however specifically defined) were at some times also aware that they shared those experiences (which we can choose to call 'European'). This has tended to be more and more the case in the last couple of centuries. It may be that by 1900 there was a majority of them who could feel they were unlike people who lived in other parts of the world. A few among them would have had some sense that their forbears had grappled with shared experiences and the events which gave rise to them in a particularly satisfactory way. They and their parents, to go back no further, could actually see a growth in Europeans' collective and individual power. This is sometimes overlooked because of the forms in which it was expressed. Nonetheless, greater wealth and power were made available to individuals through, say, piped water in their dwellings and the ability to turn on a gas-tap or even an electrical switch as they were to their rulers through, say, dividends and battleships. Many Europeans had access to material privileges in 1900 which were unknown to most inhabitants of the rest of the globe. Some Europeans also noted a certain success in managing public affairs which had resulted in their living together peaceably; there had, after all, been no armed conflict between great powers for thirty years (and, indeed, European nations had been able to avoid fighting one another for nearly two-thirds of the previous century).

In the next fifty years such grounds for confidence were, metaphorically speaking, blown away in two European wars which turned into world wars. To call them 'civil' wars is another metaphor, but one whose limits can easily be recognized and understood. The description draws attention to the breakdown, in one particular part of the world, of self-contained systems which had long been able to manage that region's tensions. They proved unable at last to do so longer. Europe fell into internal conflict in spite of all that its peoples shared. Thanks to huge accumulated wealth, these conflicts were conducted on an unprecedentedly colossal and ferocious scale. They destroyed faith in accumulated beliefs and exposed illusions which had underpinned past successes. By 1945 Europeans looked out from their ruins on a world transformed. They could no longer play their former role and no other was visible. It could be said that European history as an identifiable and autonomous process was over.

CHAPTER ONE Pressures and strains

European identity in a changing world

In many ways, the gap between the world of Europe and European lands overseas, on the one hand, and the non-European world, on the other, was wider in 1900 than ever before. Europeans had never known so much about other civilizations and cultures and therefore knew how different they were whenever they thought about them. They rarely felt that alien cultures had anything to teach them. As for material life and expectations the difference was probably greater than it would ever be again, although it is hard to be conclusive. Yet the corrosive power of European ways had already begun to infringe the lives of millions in Asia and Africa, just as European power already settled many of the practical circumstances of their lives.

Not all thoughtful Europeans were confident or complacent, even if many (and not only the unreflective among them) were. As the new century began, there were signs of pressure and strain inside European civilization, even if they were not much noticed in societies still publicly confident and redolent of a sense of continuing progress. In so far as they thought at all about the world and its history, Europeans were, to a remarkable degree, self-conscious and self-congratulatory. They were, in their own eyes, the heart of the 'civilized world', an ill-defined notion which combined reminiscences of Christendom, racial ideas about the superiority of European stocks (whatever distinctions might in practice be drawn between them), shared historical experiences and myths, similar institutions and ideas. They were, of course, themselves divided in many ways, and above all by nationality. A few institutions transcended Europe's national boundaries – the European Postal Union, or the Scandinavian or Latin monetary unions were matters of agreement and convenience, as were international bodies for the regulation of great rivers, or of European interests outside Europe. Only a few enthusiasts occasionally mused that federal Germany or federal Switzerland might provide models for a future federal Europe. Yet, subjectively, Europe was in 1900 a familiar, if vague, idea.

Europe's large share of the world population was to be reduced dramatically in the next century as death-rates fell and the expectation of life lengthened in Asia, Africa and South America. The long perspective is helpful here. Although Europe's population had continued to rise strikingly, that of the world was to treble between the beginning of the century and 1990. It had reached 2,500,000,000 by 1950 and then in the next forty years more than doubled to over 5,000 millions. Of that huge total, Europe's share was at the end of the century between a ninth and a tenth; in 1900 it had been between a quarter and a fifth.

A slowing was already beginning to be visible in 1900 in Europe's rate of population growth, most obviously in the major developed countries. They already showed the consequences of conscious efforts to limit family size. The nineteenth century had provided first the better-off and then poorer families with better devices and techniques to supplement traditional contraceptive knowledge (or superstition). As these were more widely taken up, their impact on population structure would be in due course be very great, and it would affect much more than simple numbers. Rising expectations would follow, and growing differences in those expectations, not only between one class and another, but, very importantly, between men and women.

There were already significant regional differences. Mediterranean and eastern Europe in 1900 barely showed new demographic trends. Their rapidly growing populations were then already somewhat younger than those of northern and western Europe – though they, of course, had proportionately many more young people than today. Some of the strains this produced were alleviated by emigration. There was to be an unsurpassed outpouring of Europeans overseas in the years before 1914; even in the early 1920s, though, many would still follow them, notably to the Americas. Changing conditions – legal restrictions on entry to the United States were notable – then brought about a dwindling of the flow particularly during a great worldwide depression in the 1930s. Even then there was still European emigration, notably to French North Africa and the British dominions (while attempts by the Italian government to populate its African empire with settlers were strikingly unsuccessful) and of German Jews. After 1945, patterns again changed, largely because Europe's own need for labour was growing; it was to stimulate before long the new phenomenon of immigration to Europe, especially from the Caribbean (to Great Britain), North Africa (to France), Asia (to Great Britain and the Netherlands) and Turkey (to Germany). This promoted tensions soon evident in most of the receiving 'host' countries; it might also have been expected to provoke renewed concern about the balance of numbers between continents. In a list of the ten most populous states of the world drawn up in 1988 only one 'European' country, the USSR, found a place – and she had a large non-European population. Agencies which had already cut death-rates in Europe, were beginning to operate in Asia and Africa.

In the nineteenth century the Malthusian crisis of over-population had ceased to be a bogey for Europeans. Agricultural productivity and better communications had turned famine and dearth into only local and occasional scourges in all except the poorest countries, and it had been possible to set Malthus' warnings aside while Europeans enjoyed the greatest increase in wealth the world had ever known in so short a time. In most countries a growing population had been carried on output growing even faster; between 1871 and 1900, for example, Germany's population rose by about a third, but her production of pig iron increased sixfold. In 1900 few doubted that economic growth would continue, whatever hiccups there might be. New energy sources were being tapped: oil and electricity had joined coal, wood, wind and running water. A chemical industry existed which could not have been envisaged a century before. Railways, electric trams, steamships, motor-cars and bicycles had given to millions new possibilities of movement; it was the greatest increase in transport resources since animals had first been harnessed to carts thousands of years before. In terms of consumption, the services to which they had access, or even health, the overwhelming majority of people in developed countries were much better off in 1900 than had been their predecessors a century before. If such improvements still passed by, say, the Russian or Andalusian peasant (though generalities about such categories are by no means easy to formulate), a key to prosperity seemed to have been found which could benefit all Europeans in the end.

Yet in spite of this cheerful picture, doubts would break in. The costs of getting the new wealth and protests about the social justice of its distribution were both troubling. Most Europeans in 1900 were still by today's standards very poor. If they lived in rich countries, then the incongruity of this was beginning to be thought less tolerable than in earlier times. Poverty became more afflicting to endure – and witness – when society had such obvious power to create wealth. A shift in expectations was on the way, and it implied many other changes. Further doubts arose when men (and a few women) thought about their condition and reflected on their ability to earn a livelihood at all. It was not new that they should find themselves sometimes without work. What was new was that the operation of blind forces of boom and slump should suddenly take away the work of millions of men concentrated in great towns. This was 'unemployment', a new phenomenon for which a new word had been needed and invented in the nineteenth century. Some economists thought it might be an inevitable concomitant of industrial capitalism's huge productive power.

Privilege and democracy

Such insecurities troubled those among Europe's ruling classes who had experienced a nineteenth century overhung by the threat of revolution. The composition and nature of those ruling classes varied from country to country. The Swiss bourgeois was very different from the Prussian Junker. Everywhere, though, they still included substantial components from the old hereditary hierarchies of blood and noble status, as well as representatives of the plutocracy and professions. This presented a rich variety of social custom and many internal distinctions within the ranks of the ruling élites. The conduct of some of them was still governed by conventions which would today be regarded as strange. Land still played a large part even in the most developed countries in sustaining the incomes of the wealthy. Yet when all such facts are given due weight, we can only fall back on some such bland generalization as the statement that Europe in 1900 was ruled by a combination of aristocracy and the higher *bourgeoisie*.

That does not tell us very much that is helpful in looking at any country in detail. There were parts of Europe where the dominant classes could still be said to be living in a mental world which was pre-nineteenth rather than pre-twentieth century, though those parts might be easily accessible by railway. At one extreme of the spectrum, in much of eastern Europe, quasi-patriarchal relationships and the traditional authority of the landowner over those who lived on his estates were still intact. Such societies still produced aristocratic conservatives who were opposed in spirit not merely to encroachments upon their material privilege, but also to the values and assumptions of what was to be called 'market society'. At the other extreme were examples such as could be found in the United Kingdom, where the aristocracy were long used to the idea of equality before the law, whatever the realities of social and economic power, and the landowners, though disproportionately influential still in politics and society, yet exercised their influence alongside and even through democratically elected institutions, and shared it with businessmen, bankers, and even a few trades unionists.

The ruling classes everywhere in Europe took one dogma for granted: the sanctity of property. Distinctions between them remained important for certain (mainly social) purposes, but they tended to become more blurred as time went by and, for the most part, conservative thinking western Europe in the early twentieth century narrowed and increasingly fell back upon the defence of capital, a position which, of course, would in many places half a century earlier have been regarded as radically liberal, because individualist. A new form of capitalist, industrial conservatism opposed itself more and more vigorously to state interference with wealth, an interference which had grown as the state took a larger and larger role in the regulation of society (a crisis in England over the issue led to a revolutionary transformation of what was left of the 1688 constitution in 1911 when the power of the hereditary House of Lords to restrain an elected House of Commons was at last broken). By 1914, though, even France had accepted the principle of an income tax (though not its actual imposition).

Such concessions were part of the logic of the democratizing of politics. By 1914, universal adult male suffrage existed in France, Germany and several smaller European countries; Great Britain and Italy had electorates big enough to come near to meeting this criterion. Many among the better-off feared, in consequence, that despoliation and social revolution lay ahead. The gains already made by liberalism and democracy were ominous; further and more radically threatening advances might demand resistance, if necessary, by force.

Women in politics and society

Perhaps because of its psychological dimensions, one political question which emerged with irresistible logic from the advances of democracy in Europe to trouble the early years of the century was especially notable: if men, why should not women take part in national politics? The issue was to remain open in many countries for another thirty years. It had already caused uproar in English politics; but it was only the most spectacular embodiment of a new assertion of women's role in European society, one also expressed in debates over their education, employment and legal status. Political rights were only part of a vast question.

The overall bias of Europe's civilization, like that of every other which had preceded it, was determined overwhelmingly by the interests and values of men. Serious questioning of women's traditional roles had begun in Europe only in the eighteenth century. Women's rights to education, to employment, to control of their own property, to moral independence, even to wear more comfortable clothes, were increasingly debated as the nineteenth century went on. Ibsen's play, A Doll's House, was interpreted as a trumpet-call for the liberation of women (instead of, as the author intended, a plea for the individual). A real revolution was by then under way. The claims of women in Europe and North America threatened assumptions and attitudes with not merely centuries, but even millenia, of acceptance and familiarity behind them. They awoke complex emotions, linked as they were to deep-seated notions about the family and sexuality. Because of this some people – men and women alike – were more deeply troubled by them than even by the threat of social revolution or political democracy. They were right to sense a truly revolutionary force, and it was to have worldwide effect. In the early European and North American feminist movements lay the seed of something whose explosive content would be transferred soon to other cultures and civilizations.

For a long time, the politicization of women and even their successful political attacks on the legal and institutional structures which were felt by them to be oppressive, did less for most women than did other changes. Three were of slowly growing but, eventually, gigantic importance in undermining the fixity of tradition. The first was the growth and elaboration of the advanced industrial economy. By 1914 this had already in some countries created great numbers of new women's jobs – as typists, secretaries, telephone operators, factory hands, department store assistants and teachers. Almost none of them had existed a century earlier. They brought a huge practical shift of economic power to women: if they could earn their own living, they were entering a road which would eventually lead to new family structures, new social roles. Paradoxically, the demands of warfare in the industrial societies of the twentieth century would accelerate this advance as the need for labour opened an even wider range of occupations to them. For growing numbers of girls and women, even by 1900, a job in industry or commerce already meant a degree of liberation from parental regulation and a chance to escape the trap of married drudgery. Most women did not so benefit by 1914, but a cumulative process was at work, because such developments would stimulate other demands, for example, for education and professional training.

Contraception was the second great force transforming women's lives. It, too, was far from showing its full potential by 1914, and perhaps even further from doing so than were the new employment possibilities. It had nonetheless already begun to affect European demography. What lay ahead was a revolution in outlook as more women absorbed the idea that they might control the demands of childbearing and rearing which hitherto had throughout history dominated and structured the lives of their sex; beyond that lay an even deeper change, only beginning to emerge in 1914, as a few women came to see that they could pursue sexual satisfaction without necessarily entering the obligation of lifelong marriage.

To the third great tendency moving women imperceptibly but irresistibly towards liberation from ancient ways and assumptions it is much harder to give an identifying single name, but if one force governs it, it is technology. The general tendency of many innovations, some already accumulating slowly for decades before 1900, was to cut into the iron timetables of domestic routine and drudgery, and was to continue after that date in a swelling flood. The coming of piped water, or of gas for heating and lighting, had been among the first examples; electricity's cleanliness and flexibility had even more obvious effects. Better shops were the advance guard of mutations in retail distribution which not only gave a notion of luxury to people other than the rich, but also made it easier to meet household needs. Imported food, better processed and preserved, slowly changed family catering routines once based – as they are still today often based in Asia or Africa – on daily (or twice or thrice daily) visits to the market. The world of detergents and easily cleaned artificial fibres still lay ahead in 1900, but soap and washing soda were by then easily and cheaply available, while the first domestic machines – gas cookers, vacuum cleaners, washing machines – were appearing, at least in the homes of the rich. Historians who would recognize at once the importance of the introduction of the stirrup or lathe in earlier times have strangely neglected the cumulative influence of such humble agencies. They implied a revolution. It is more understandable that their long-term implications interested fewer people at the beginning of this century than the antics of 'suffragettes', as women who sought the vote were called in England. One immediate stimulus to their often violent activity was the evident democratizing of political institutions for the benefit of more men. This was the background which their campaign presupposed. Logically, there were indeed grounds for pursuing democracy across the boundaries of sex even if this meant doubling the size of electorates. But in 1914, Finland and Norway were the only European countries when women had votes in national elections.

The politics of mass society

Voting rights and formal and legal representative structures were not the whole story of the way politics was given more and more of a 'mass' or democratic quality. The masses had to be organized. By 1900 there had appeared to meet this need the modern political party, with its simplifications of issues in order to present them as choices, its apparatus for the spread of political awareness, and its cultivation of special interests. From Europe and the United States the idea, the language and the institution of party politics spread round the world. Old-fashioned politicians deplored the new mass model of party and by no means always did so insincerely, because it brought with it the corruption of public debate as well as a need for traditional élites to adapt their politics to the ways of the man in the street.

The beginnings of change had been implicit in the new nineteenth-century discovery of public opinion. It had been thought decisive in England in the struggles over the Corn Laws. In 1870, Napoleon III felt he could not resist popular clamour for a war which he feared (and was to lose). Even Bismarck, the quintessential conservative statesman, had in the end come to feel that he must give way to public opinion. Its manipulation, was seeming to have become possible in any case (or so, at least, many newspaper owners and statesmen believed) thanks to spreading literacy. It had been urged that investment in mass education was necessary in order to civilize the masses for the proper use of the vote, but one of the most visible consequences seemed to be a role for a new cheap press in pandering to emotionalism and sensationalism, and an opportunity for the devisers of advertising campaigns, another invention of the nineteenth century. Early in the twentieth century both the English *Daily Mail* and the French *Petit Parisien* had circulations of over a 1,000,000.

There were, for all that, only two states in Europe in 1914, with constitutions both democratic and republican. These were France and Switzerland. Elsewhere (a few curious fossils such as Andorra or San Marino excepted) hereditary monarchy was still the prevailing constitutional form of the state, sometimes in countries which also had a broad franchise and what could be reasonably termed democratic institutions. As late as 1914 a new state (Albania) was given a monarchy as a matter of course on its emergence from the Ottoman heritage. Uniformity nonetheless concealed much variety; few monarchs regarded the institution with the consistency of Edward VII, whose respect for it extended to the native rulers of the South Pacific, while the Kaiser, at least, did not believe the British monarchy really to be one at all. Broadly, a distinction can be made between two kinds of monarchic states. There were on the one hand the constitutional monarchies, of which the British was the leading example. Others were to be found in Belgium, the Netherlands, Scandinavia, Italy, Spain, Portugal and some of the new Balkan creations of the nineteenth century, the oldest being that of Greece. Within this group, the realities of power varied a lot, whatever the formal constitutional arrangements. There were some unpromising examples of the *genre* among the newer creations (especially in the Balkans). Constitutional monarchy was nonetheless a successful, recognizable and recognized European reality in 1900.

The other major monarchical form may still best be called dynastic. While a network of marriage alliances tied together the constitutional monarchies and many old-fashioned attitudes could still be found in their courts, the old subordination of national and social interest to the continuing interest of the ruling house was much more evident in two of the three major multi-ethnic empires, and, slightly more ambiguously, in the third, too. The Habsburg empire (the Dual Monarchy) and Romanov Russia were the two unambiguous examples embodying the dynastic principle. In Hohenzollern Germany much adulation was heaped on the monarch and his authority was the subject of much rhetorical exaggeration (not least by himself), but William II was legally the head of a constitutional and federal monarchy, made up of states with their own rulers and interests. The reality was that the *Reich* was dominated by Prussia and that the real rulers of Prussia were the Prussian aristocrats. The internal reality of the Prussian monarchy, for all the incense burnt to the 'War-Lord' (as William II liked to term himself), was that he could not move far outside the parameters which the Prussian ruling class would tolerate (an illustration of the potential for strain in this relationship had been seen during the brief three-month reign of the emperor Frederick III, whose early death brought evident relief to some of his subjects who had feared what he might attempt). In all three dynastic empires, the personality and temperament of the monarch was likely to be a decisive factor, as well as his incapacity or capacity.

Two political Europes thus differed in the assumptions on which their component states were based. Not everyone, and few other monarchs, would have put it as did William II in a private letter to his cousin, the Tsar: 'the democratic countries governed by Parliamentary majorities, against the Imperial Monarchies'[1], but there was a grain of truth even in so excited a mis-interpretation. Everyone knew that monarchical power had more weight in the three great multi-ethnic empires than elsewhere. Almost everywhere, though, the words 'democratic' and 'democracy' could still arouse alarm among ruling classes still dominated by hereditary nobility and memories of the Commune, and even some Englishmen seemed to have obtained a special *frisson* of loyal excitement in toasting the 'king-emperor' of India.

Social fear

By 1900 the majority of western Europeans were town-dwellers. By 1914 there were more than 140 European cities of over a 100,000 inhabitants. Life in them was far from rid of evils which had struck earlier observers and critics of industrial society. Many millions were ill-housed, under-provided with fresh air, let alone with education and amusement (other than that of the streets), though they were sometimes well within sight of the wealth their efforts helped to produce. The 'slums' (a word the nineteenth century felt it needed, and had therefore invented) often inspired fear. It fed a

---

[1]   *The Kaiser's letters to the Tsar. The Willy-Nicky Correspondence*, ed. N.F. Grant (London, 1920), pp. 98–99, 19 Nov. 1903.

long tradition of distrust of cities as centres of crime, wicked men and revolution. To others, of course, this brought hope: cities seemed so provocative of discontent that revolution against social and economic injustice would surely be more likely as time went by. This optimistic and revolutionary view in the event turned out to be as exaggerated as the gloomy predictions of conservatives. In spite of alarming outbreaks of disorder, evidence accumulated that in the most economically developed countries successful revolution, or even insurrection, was becoming less and less likely.

It could be allowed that among the great powers, Russia was a special case, though her endemic social disorder had always been rural rather than urban. Though increasingly sharing in Europe-wide developments, she lagged behind in all kinds of economic and social advance. Her autocracy had been unchanged in principle by nineteenth-century administrative and governmental reform. One consequence was an inability to stifle a continuing revolutionary movement, often divided in aim, but spawning terrorists who murdered officials and had killed a tsar. The subversive threat was continually refreshed by upheaval in the countryside; attacks on landlords and their bailiffs reached a peak in the early years of this century. When, in 1904 and 1905, rural disorder was followed by a shaking of the regime's confidence as a result of defeat in war at the hands of the Japanese, the result was for the first time a city-based resistance leading to revolution. It forced more substantial constitutional concessions out of the government than anything earlier. They still left the principle of autocracy untouched, nonetheless.

Further west, Italy, too, had something which to some looked like barely-contained revolution both in 1898, when, for the first time in fifty years artillery opened fire in the streets of Milan, and again in the 'Red Week' of 1914, when a number of departments (Italy had adopted the French system of local administration) slipped briefly out of control by Rome. Barcelona, one of the great cities of Spain, erupted into bloody street-fighting in 1909 (this was part of an episode which went down in the history of the Spanish Left as the 'Tragic Week'; perhaps the name says something about differences between the Spanish and Italian temperament – or even the outcomes). Elsewhere, too, strikes, and demonstrations were often violent. France had plenty of experience of the deployment of soldiers in industrial disturbances in the decade before the war (a future saviour of the Republic, Clemenceau, won notoriety as a strike-breaker in 1908 when he was prime minister for the first time) and even in Great Britain violent deaths were not unknown in riots before 1914. The public imagination meanwhile continued to be impressed by anarchists whose bombings and assassinations had won them publicity in the 1890s. Not all anarchists shared the same aims, but they were all the more suspect for that, and because they protested against a whole society which they saw as unjust in its essence and not just against the governmental structures of particular countries.

The spectre of socialism

Undoubtedly, though, socialist propaganda and rhetoric did more to frighten the possessing classes. Socialism long seemed very successful, even if not in the provocation of revolution. Success was more evident in the organization of the working classes for political combat through the ballot-box and for industrial struggle through trades unions. After 1871 and until 1950 or so, socialism, however loosely defined,

enjoyed a long ascendancy over the culture of the Left; in one form or another, collec-
tivist, egalitarian, materially-based distributive solutions came to be accepted as never
before by those who believed in the progressive amelioration of society, and sought to
achieve it. Almost everywhere, too, socialism came to mean some form of Marxism,
diluted or pure (there was much debate about interpretation). Important alternative traditions existed only in France, Spain and Italy (where anarchist and revolutionary syn-
dicalism flourished in propitious circumstances) and, above all, in England, where the
early appearance of a legal and numerous trade-union movement and the possibility of
achieving change through established political parties and processes produced an
effective non-revolutionary radicalism.

The well-established hostility between anarchism and Marxism for a time dominated socialist organizations. Marxism's victory on the continent (by contrast with England) was formally expressed in 1896 when the 'Second International', set up seven
years before to coordinate socialist action in all countries, expelled the anarchists who
had until then belonged to it. Four years later, the International opened a permanent
office in Brussels. German numbers, wealth and doctrine were preponderant in the
movement the International led. Thanks to Germany's rapid industrialization, the
Social Democratic Party had prospered in spite of police persecution and by 1900 was
an established fact of German politics, its first truly mass party. Numbers and wealth
alone would have made it likely that Marxism, the official creed of the German party,
would be that of the international socialist movement, even had Marxism not had its
own intellectual and emotional appeal.

Yet for all the fears it aroused in the established order, some intelligent socialists had
already noticed that after 1880 or so the facts by no means obviously justified Marxist
mythology and language. Manifestly, great numbers of people were beginning to enjoy
a higher standard of living within the capitalist system. The unfolding of that system in
all its complexity was not simplifying and sharpening class conflict in the way Marx had
predicted. Capitalist political institutions had served the working class; in Germany
and in England, above all, important legal advantages were won for it through parliaments. The vote was a weapon some socialists were not disposed to ignore while waiting for the revolution. This led to attempts to restate official Marxism so as to take
account of such trends; they were called 'Revisionism'. Broadly speaking, revisionists
advocated an advance towards the transformation of society by non-violent struggle. If
people liked to call that transformation, when it came, a revolution, then only an argument about usage was involved. Inside this theoretical position and the conflict it provoked was a practical issue which came to a head at the end of the century: should
socialists or should they not sit as ministers in 'capitalist' governments?

The debate took years. What emerged in the end was explicit condemnation of revisionism by the Second International while national parties, notably the Germans, continued to act on it in practice, doing deals with the existing system as suited them. Their
rhetoric continued to be about revolution. Many socialists even hoped that this might
be made a reality if war broke out and conscripts refused to fight for capitalist governments. One socialist group, the majority in the Russian party, continued vigorously to
denounce revisionism; no doubt this recognized the peculiarity of the Russian situation, where there was little opportunity for effective parliamentary activity and a deep
tradition of revolution and terrorism. It was called Bolshevik, from the Russian word
meaning a majority.

Religion in European public life

By 1900 Christianity had long lost any plausibility as a potential check to violence in the international sphere. Restraint arising from religious belief or affiliation had never exercised decisive or continuous control over Europe's rulers in their dealings with one another; even the hope of such a check was virtually non-existent by 1900. The idea of Christendom no longer had any political content. Already in the nineteenth century religion had been at most a palliative or mitigation of conflict, and at worst had sometimes played an inflammatory role; Orthodox Russians (and even evangelical Englishmen) could be excited more easily against the Turk when he was massacring Christians.

In 1882, the German seer and prophetic philosopher Friedrich Nietzsche had already announced that 'God is dead': religious faith, he was saying, was no longer possible for the intelligent human being, and the spirit-and-body dualism so long at the centre of European culture could no longer be sustained. Whether this was true, and, if it were, whether it was the result of a general loss of religious belief or of a changing view of what religion might be thought to imply and require is a harder question to clarify. Many millions of Europeans still regularly attended religious worship in 1900, most of them in Christian churches and chapels. What this meant for the effective power of ecclesiastical organizations is hard to discern. That their authority was not what it had once been was much remarked at the end of the nineteenth century, whether with approval or regret. Already fifty years earlier, Charles Dickens had pointed out that it was not the workers of Coketown who filled its many churches and chapels. Yet many Europeans still retained simple and literal beliefs in the dogmas of their faiths and the narratives of the Bible, even as others more and more vigorously contested the claims of revelation and questioned the authority of priest and pastor. Traditional belief may indeed well have been most consciously threatened and challenged among Europe's élites. Many of them had long held 'Voltairean' ideas of a generally irreligious and sceptical nature. The nineteenth century had witnessed the impact of other ideas corrosive of faith which were also at first the concern only of such élites but which gradually reached wider audiences thanks to cheap printing and the spread of mass literacy.

Most of the established churches were affected by such intellectual competition, the Orthodox and Roman Catholic churches the most obviously. The second was also embarrassingly involved in politics in many countries. Jurisdictional, fiscal and educational issues had emerged in states newly conscious of the respect due to national sovereignty. They led politicians to denounce long-accepted views of the proper relations of Church and State. The Roman Church, too, had made growing ideological and intellectual demands on the credulity of the age as the century went on. Like other churches (despite the example of a few such innovatory successes like the Salvation Army), it did not seem able to exploit new devices – the new mass-circulation newspapers, for instance – which might have helped it. Indeed, the Roman Catholic Church long positively proclaimed its distrust of such developments.

Under Leo XIII, who succeeded Pius IX in 1878, there was some improvement in some countries in the political position of the Roman church, but anti-clericalism and priest-baiting continued in France, Italy and Spain, while governments continued to encroach upon areas where the Church had previously been paramount – above all, education. Quarrelling bred intransigence. In France, the eventual outcome was the ending of the old concordat and the separation of Church and State in 1905 (and a consequent further inflammation of ideological divisions inside French political life). The Vatican's relations with the Italian state, on the other hand, improved *de facto* under Pius X. In conflict, it also emerged that whatever view might be taken of the teachings of the Roman Church, it could still draw on vast reservoirs of loyalty among the faithful. Moreover, these were still being recruited by conversion in the mission field overseas where they would soon be added to in still greater numbers by demographic trends. Though the Church might not make much progress among the new city-dwellers of Europe, untouched by an inadequate ecclesiastical machine and paganized by the slow stain of the secular culture in which they were immersed, it was far from dying, let alone dead, as a political and social force. Indeed, the liberation of the papacy from its temporal role had made it easier for many Catholics to feel uncompromised loyalty towards it.

Changing mentalities

It has already been argued that one of the most effective, though often indirect, forces undermining mass support for traditional religion was science, hard to measure though its effects are. Science certainly became more visible than ever in its applications by 1914. Radio messages could then be sent across the Atlantic, flying-machines which did not rely upon support by bags of gas (aeroplanes) were common, petrol-driven motor-cars were familiar objects in city streets, and educated Europeans (at least) took for granted anaesthetics, steam turbines, harder and specialized steels, telephones, and many more marvels which had not existed even half a century before. Cheap electrical power was already changing the layout and working of cities through electric trams and trains, work in factories through electric motors, and electric light in streets and homes. Even animal populations were affected: the 36,000 horses pulling trams in Great Britain in 1900 had become only 900 in 1914. Most of such changes were due ultimately to the practical application of science. While there had never been a time since the seventeenth century when there had not been some obvious technological fall-out from scientific activity, it had been for a long time confined largely to ballistics, navigation and map-making, agriculture and a few elementary industrial processes. By the twentieth century it was hard to imagine life without science.

Although respect for it usually grew in proportion to spectacular results in engineering or manufacture, fundamental science went on making important progress which had longer-term implications. One group of effects easy to assess came in medicine. Though European medicine in 1914 may today be regarded as still primitive, advances had been made which were huge by comparison with a century earlier. Antiseptics and anaesthetics had been absorbed into practice (Queen Victoria herself had been a pioneer in the publicizing of new medical methods; the use of anaesthetics during the birth of a prince or princess had helped to win social acceptance for them). There had been pharmacological advances such as the discovery in 1909 of Salvarsan, a landmark in the development of selective treatment of infection, the carrier of malaria had been identified by pathologists, and the discovery of X-rays had been followed by their introduction to medical practice.

Yet, paradoxically, science was by 1914 contributing not only to the confidence of a civilization in its growing mastery of nature, but also to an ill-defined sense of strain.

This showed most obviously in the problems posed to traditional religion, without doubt, but it also operated in the determinisms its discoveries often encouraged, or through the relativism suggested by anthropology or the study of the human mind. Science was itself a force sapping confidence in the values of objectivity and rationality so important to science itself. By 1914 there were signs that liberal, rational, enlightened Europe was under strain just as much as traditional, religious and conservative Europe. Some people already found it hard to be sure that there were such things as absolute values. What this meant in terms of changes in the minds of most people nonetheless remains hard to say.

Cracks in the European world hegemony

At the beginning of the century there was talk in some European circles and in the popular press of an ill-defined 'Yellow Peril', its source seen variously in China or Japan. Contemporaneously, in other, far more restricted, circles there was noisy appreciation of the stimulus and variety brought to European art by awareness and enjoyment of Japanese prints, or of African sculpture. One major attraction of the great international exhibition held in Paris in 1900 was its revelation to Frenchmen of the exotic variety of the French colonial empire and its diverse peoples. All such growing awareness, nonetheless (and there were many more instances of the same receptiveness to impressions, menacing or agreeable, from the non-European world) hardly adds up to any general fear, sense of burgeoning threat, challenge or competition from the non-European world or of any fundamental change in Europe's relations with it. Signs and seeds of menacing change were there, nevertheless, slight as they might seem.

Most of the non-European world's surface was governed outright or through puppet rulers by Europeans or those of European stock. Even when, in 1898, one of the oldest imperial powers, Spain, lost its last major colonies, it did so to the United States, a transatlantic power of reassuringly European origins which was clearly part of the 'civilized world', and could be regarded as achieving in that struggle the consummation of its own imperialist nineteenth century. Among the assumptions of the civilized world was the almost universally held belief that an innate superiority, whether cultural and temporary, or ethnic and permanent, justified the rule of Europeans over non-Europeans. There was even a feeling that Spain had somewhat let the side down, and that the United States might take up the 'White Man's Burden' of ruling Filipinos and discharge the duties of doing so rather better than had the Spanish. The end of the nineteenth and the first decade of the twentieth century, indeed, showed little decline in the self-confidence of European imperialism, even if official circles might be sceptical about its practical value and real cost (notably illustrated by the Boer War). There was concern about the proper management and humanitarian treatment of European colonies (the acquiescence of the Belgian king in the misgovernment of the Belgian Congo particularly shocked opinion when the atrocities practised there came to light) and there were 'anti-colonial' organizations already active in many countries. Nonetheless, imperialism was still acceptable and, indeed, assumed to be the normal state of affairs.

The structures embodying it in 1914 were undeniably impressive. Great Britain had nearly 400,000,000 subjects outside its borders in 1914, France over 50,000,000. Germany and Italy were far behind with about 14,000,000 each, but these were populations larger than those of some European states. True the likelihood that these huge structures would be enlarged much further was remote. There were not many 'undeveloped estates' left to acquire. The Spanish-American war was a hint that empires might in future grow only at the expense of one another; at one time the Germans and British discreetly discussed the possibility of sharing the Portuguese possessions in Africa between them. Elsewhere, China had proved a disappointment. Even if Russia still envisaged total partition of the country as the appropriate conclusion of her two centuries of encroachment upon it, the Chinese seemed at last to be stirring into a real possibility of modernization. The only major area for further predation after 1900 seemed to be the decaying Ottoman empire.

New competitors: Young Turks

The first European political crisis of the new century occurred in 1908. The Habsburg monarchy then formally annexed the Ottoman provinces of Bosnia and Herzegovina which it had already occupied for nearly forty years. This much irritated Russia, but had other important repercussions, too. Among these were changes in the Ottoman regime itself. Exasperated by its failures and weakness, there had already taken place in 1907 a successful revolution by a group calling themselves 'Young Turks' (a name echoing the language of Mazzini's 'Young Italy' and 'Young Europe' of the 1830s). The Young Turks strove to promote reform and modernization, taking European practice as their model – ironically, much on lines European powers in the nineteenth century had urged upon the Sultan. They sought constitutional rule on the European model less for its own sake than as a means of revivifying the empire and making its modernization possible. Like the Meiji reformers, the Young Turks wanted modernization in order to resist European interference in their country's affairs (for example, in the management of finance which had tied down the Egyptian government), and what the Young Turks saw as a long history of European bullying which lay behind the Ottoman retreat in Europe. Modernization through a measure of Europeanization was to be a way to power.

Liberals abroad at first smiled on the constitutional aspirations of the Young Turk programme; it seemed that at last the long story of Ottoman misrule might be ending. Then, an attempted counter-revolution led the Young Turks in 1909 to stage a coup which deposed Abdul Hamid and installed a dictatorship behind a façade of constitutional monarchy. A new tone and, indeed, programme, announced another fundamental change. 'We glory in being Ottoman' said one Young Turk leader, proclaiming there were no longer Bulgars, Rumanians, Jews, Moslems. The old multinational empire of tribute from many peoples was to turn itself into a national state.

European powers were bound to be deeply interested in such developments. For some of them, the possible implications and repercussions of events at Constantinople might be felt far afield. The Ottoman empire was, in the first place, the world's major Islamic state and the seat of the caliphate. More than this, though little was left of it in Europe even in 1900, the empire still ruled non-European areas which covered a large and strategically very important zone. The imperial boundaries ran from the Caucasus along the frontiers with Persia to the Gulf near Basra, at the mouth of the Tigris. On the southern shore of the Gulf they ran round Kuwait (whose sheik was under British protection) and then back to the coast as far south as Qatar. From here the coasts of Arabia

round to the entrance of the Red Sea were in one way or another under British influence, but the whole interior and Red Sea coast were Ottoman. Under British pressure
the Sinai desert had been surrendered to the Khedive of Egypt (still nominally subject
to Constantinople) a few years before, but the ancient lands of Palestine, Syria and
Mesopotamia were still under direct Ottoman rule. Even within the historic Islamic
heartland, though, there were signs before 1914 that new political forces were at work,
stemming partly from old-established European cultural influences, which operated in
Syria and the Lebanon much more strongly than in Egypt. French influence had been
joined in those countries by American missionary efforts and the foundation of schools
and colleges to which there came Arab boys, both Moslem and Christian, from all over
the Arab world. The Levant was culturally advanced and literate. On the eve of the
world war over a 100 Arabic newspapers were being published in the Ottoman empire
outside Egypt.

It was against this background that in 1912, the Italians seized Tripoli, (in part, in
what they saw as compensation for the Habsburg gains of 1908). For a little while, it
seemed as if the death-knell of the empire had been rung, for in 1912 a coalition of
Balkan states assembled which within a year seized from the Ottoman government
almost all of its remaining European territory. Division of the booty and the exact identity of the successors to Ottoman rule was not easy to establish, though, and a second
Balkan War between the victors followed. Austria-Hungary and Russia stood off, but this
was a warning of the dangers attending the collapse of empires.

The Young Turks resented these losses, but their own Ottomanizing tendencies had
provoked new ferment in the Asiatic empire, too. In 1913 there was a meeting (in
Persia) of Arabs to consider the independence of Iraq. Secret societies and open groups
of dissidents were formed among Arab exiles, notably in Paris and Cairo. In the background, the allegiance of the rulers of the Arabian peninsula to the sultan looked shaky.
The Young Turks had, in fact, provoked fresh difficulties for themselves. Yet they were
on the side of the future. They represented nationalization and modernization, the
future for a Turkey as yet unknown. They had even, having lost by then most of what
was left to the Ottomans in Europe, and Tripoli and Libya in North Africa, actually
made some of their goals easier to achieve, though they were unaware of that. But their
heritage still encumbered them, and in 1914 they had done nothing to turn back the
encroachment of European nations. It was not altogether surprising that when what
seemed a favourable conjuncture appeared in 1914, they would choose war as a way
out from the empire's problems.

New competitors: the Far East

The ambiguous outcome in the Ottoman empire of the combination of a wish
to resist European pressures and bullying with aspirations arising from European ideas
had some similarities with what happened in China. At one time, it looked as if a
'scramble' for that country might well be on the cards. Well before the end of the nineteenth century some Chinese intellectuals and civil servants saw that the traditional
order would not generate the energy necessary to resist the new barbarians. But reform
had failed and so had reaction (in the form of the Boxers) to regenerate the empire.
Some Chinese now turned to revolution. The Japanese (who had great prestige in the
eyes of the young Chinese radicals as Asians who had escaped from the trap of tradi-

RETREAT OF OTTOMAN POWER IN EUROPE
- Turkish Empire 1880
- International boundary 1880
- International boundary 1914
- *1885* Date of aquisition from Turks
- **1913** Date of independence

tional backwardness) were happy to encourage subversive movements which might weaken their neighbour. Support from discontented exiles and Chinese businessmen abroad helped a young Chinese radical, Sun Yat-sen, to form in 1905 in Japan a revolutionary alliance aiming at the expulsion of the Manchus, a republican constitution, and land reform. When in 1911 a revolt at last turned into a successful revolution, though, Sun Yat-sen, whose name the rebels used, was abroad and taken by surprise. On 12 February 1912 the last Manchu emperor abdicated. A republic had already been proclaimed. China still had far to travel to reach the goal of true national independence, let alone restore the once-great sway of the empire. She had none the less begun the long march towards that goal and towards modernization.

Paradoxically, China's most bitter opponent as she did so was to be not European, but Asian. Japan's success in war with China had been followed by national humiliation, when Russia, France and Germany together forced her to accept a peace treaty much less advantageous than the one she had imposed on the Chinese. Resentment of Europe now fused in Japan with enthusiasm for expansion in Asia. Popular dislike of the 'unequal treaties' had been running high and this disappointment brought it to a head. It soon became clear to the western powers that dealing with Japan was a very different matter from bullying China. Japan was increasingly a candidate for consideration as a 'civilized' state, not like other non-European nations; significantly, in 1899 extra-territoriality, a humiliating sign of European predominance, came to an end. Soon, Japan joined in the international action against the Boxers. Then, in 1902, came the clearest acknowledgement of Japan's new international standing, an alliance between her and Great Britain, the European state which had not joined the others in imposing the shame of 1895. Japan, it was said, had joined Europe.

Russia had been decisive in thwarting Japan in 1895; her subsequent advances made it clear to the Japanese that one longed-for prize, Korea, might elude them if they did not anticipate a Russian threat there. Railway-building, the development of Vladivostok, and Russian commercial activity within Korea – where politics was already little more than the struggle of pro-Russian and pro-Japanese factions – were alarming. Ominously, the Russians had leased the naval base of Port Arthur from the enfeebled Chinese. In 1904 the Japanese struck, in a surprise attack on the Russian base. After a year's fighting, the Russians accepted defeat. It was the end of tsarist pretensions in Korea and South Manchuria, where Japanese influence was henceforth dominant. Other territories passed into Japanese possession to remain there until 1945. But there was more to the Japanese victory than that. If we exclude the special instance of Ethiopian victory over an Italian expedition, this was the first time since the Middle Ages that non-Europeans had defeated a European power in a major war.

Japan's annexation of Korea in 1910, and the Chinese Revolution of the following year, can now be seen as milestones. They mark the end of the first phase of Asia's response to western aggression. Not surprisingly, different Asian countries had shown very differing reactions to challenge. Japan had inoculated herself against the threat by accepting the virus of modernization. China had long striven not to do so. In each case, the direct and indirect stimulus to change had come from Europe – or, more accurately, given American involvement, the 'West'. In one case it was successfully contained and in the other it was not. In each case, too, the fate of the Asian power was shaped not only by its own response, but by the relations of the Western powers among themselves. Their rivalries had generated a fresh scramble for ports and concessions in China in the 1890s which had alarmed and tempted the Japanese. Alliance with Great Britain had made it possible for them to strike at Russia, whom they feared most, and find her unsupported. A few years more and Japan and China would both be participants in a European war. Meanwhile, Japan's example and, above all, its victory over Russia, were an inspiration to other Asians, the greatest single reason for them to ponder whether European rule was bound to be their lot. In 1905 an American scholar could already speak of the Japanese as the 'peers of western peoples'; what they had done, by turning Europe's skills and ideas against her, might not other Asians do in their turn?

Troubled empires

Everywhere in Asia European agencies had already launched or helped to launch changes which led in the end to the dissolving of Europe's political hegemony. Those agencies had brought with them ideas about nationalism and humanitarianism, the Christian missionary's dislocation of local society and belief, and a new sense of exploitation not sanctioned by tradition. Primitive, almost blind, responses like the Indian Mutiny or the Boxer rebellion had been the first and obvious outcomes, but there were others, with more important futures ahead of them. This was first apparent in India. Soon after its foundation, Congress had committed itself to clearly European goals: national unity and regeneration. Yet there had never been an Indian nation or Indian national idea. Congress did not then aspire to Indian self-government and it still proclaimed its 'unswerving loyalty' to the British Crown. It saw its role, rather, as one of communicating Indian views to the viceroy in the hope notice would be taken of them. It took another twenty years during which Congress' attitude had been soured and stiffened by the vilification it received from British residents who declared it unrepresentative, and the unresponsiveness of an administration which preferred to work through more traditional and conservative social forces, for it to begin to discuss the possibility of independence.

In 1905 a new administrative division of Bengal produced a West Bengal where there was a Hindu majority, and an East Bengal with a Moslem one. Rage over this partition detonated a mass of explosive materials long accumulating. Extremists were heartened by anti-partition riots. A new weapon was deployed against the British, a boycott (the term had not long before first entered the English language from another cradle of imperial difficulty, Ireland) of goods. Congress hoped to extend it to other forms of passive resistance. By 1908 the extremists were excluded from Congress (which was by then seeking a measure of self-government such as that enjoyed by the British white dominions) and it was apparent that they were turning to violence. Russian terrorism now joined the doctrines of Mazzini and the example of Garibaldi, the guerrilla leader hero of Italian independence, as a formative influence on an emerging India. It was argued that political murder was not ordinary murder. Assassination and bombing followed, and were met with special repressive measures.

More momentously still, the partition brought out into the open the political division of Moslem and Hindu India. For reasons which went back even before the Mutiny, Moslems had become more and more distinct from Hindus. Distrusted by the British after attempts to revivify the Moghul empire in 1857, and perhaps obstructed by cultural heritage, they had little success in winning posts in government or on the judicial bench. Hindus had responded more eagerly than Moslems to the educational opportunities offered by the Raj; they had more commercial weight and more influence on government. But Moslems too, had found British sympathizers and patrons, who had established an Islamic college, providing the English education they needed to compete with Hindus, and had helped to set up Moslem political organizations. Some English civil servants began to see a potential which this could give the Raj for balancing Hindu pressure.

In 1905, the split became, as it remained, an assumption of Indian politics. Anti-partitionists campaigned with a strident display of Hindu symbols and slogans. A British governor of eastern Bengal who favoured Moslems against Hindus was dismissed, but the inoculation had taken: Bengal Moslems deplored his removal. It looked as if an Anglo-Moslem *entente* was in the making. This further inflamed Hindu terrorists. To make things worse, all this was taking place during a period of economic strain and rising prices. Political reforms conceded in 1909 did not help, though they provided further elected places for Indians in the legislative councils. But the elections were to be made by electorates which had a communal basis; the division of Hindu and Moslem India, that is to say, was institutionalized.

In 1911, for the first and only time, a reigning British monarch visited India. A great imperial durbar was held at Delhi, the old centre of Moghul rule, to which the capital of British India was now transferred from Calcutta. The princes of India came to do homage and Congress did not question its loyalty to the throne. The accession of George V that year had been marked by real and symbolic concessions, of which the most politically significant was the reuniting of Bengal. If the Raj had an apogee and climax, this was it. Even at that moment, though, it was notable that British governments had already set out on a road leading away from post-Mutiny despotism towards effective representation of Indians in government, had reversed an unpopular measure (the partition) after experience of the hostility it aroused, and had implicitly (by alliance with an Asian power) conceded that they might not be able single-handed to sustain British empire in Asia if faced with major challenges nearer home. The year after the Durbar, the viceroy was wounded by a terrorist's bomb.

The French had their difficulties in Indo-China. Administration in the Napoleonic tradition soon made it clear that native government there was a sham, but the French sapped local institutions without replacing them with others which might win the loyalty of the people. This was a dangerous course. French presence also brought with it French tariff policy, which was to slow down industrialization. The inspiring motto to be found on official buildings and documents of the Third Republic, 'liberty, equality and fraternity' led Indo-Chinese businessmen, like their Indian equivalents, to reflect in whose interests their country ought to be run. The conception of an Indo-China which was integrally a part of France, whose inhabitants should be turned into Frenchmen, brought problems to a deeply Confucian Indo-Chinese dominant class, while French law and notions of property broke down the structure of village landholding and threw power into the hands of money-lenders and landlords. With a growing population in the rice-growing areas, this was to build up a revolutionary potential for the future.

Traditional Vietnamese nationalism soon made itself felt. The Japanese victory over Russia led several young Vietnamese to go to Tokyo, where they met Sun Yat-sen and the Japanese sponsors of an 'Asia for the Asians'. After the Chinese Revolution of 1911, one of them organized a society for a Vietnamese Republic. None of this much troubled the French who were well able to contain such opposition before 1914, but it paralleled conservative opposition to them among the mandarin class. Though they opened a university in 1907, the French had to close it almost at once because of fears of unrest (it remained closed until 1918). An important section of Vietnamese opinion was deeply alienated from French rule within a couple of decades of its establishment.

Indonesia did not form part of the historic Chinese cultural sphere, but of the Hindu. There, some Dutchmen had begun by the end of the century to feel uneasiness about the conduct of their colonial government. This culminated in an important change of attitude; in 1901 a new 'Ethical Policy' was announced which was expressed in decentralization and a campaign to achieve improvement through village administration. But this proved so paternalistic and interventionist that it, too, sometimes stimulated a hostility utilized by the first Indonesian nationalists. In 1908 they formed an organization to promote national education. Three years later an Islamic association appeared (though its early activities were directed as much against Chinese traders as against the Dutch). By 1916 it had gone so far as to ask for self-government while remaining in union with the Netherlands. Before this, a true independence party had been founded in 1912 in the name of native-born Indonesians, of any race; a Dutchman was among its three founders. In 1916 the Dutch took the first step towards meeting the demands of these groups by authorizing a parliament with limited powers for Indonesia.

European ideas of nationalism were all too visibly at work throughout Asia in the early years of this century. They had different expressions and faced different possibilities; not all colonial regimes behaved in the same way. The British encouraged nationalists in Burma, while the Americans doggedly pursued a benevolent paternalism in the Philippines after an ugly suppression of an insurrection begun against their Spanish predecessors. Those same Spanish, like the Portuguese elsewhere in Asia, had for centuries vigorously promoted Christian conversion, while the British Raj remained cautious about interference with native religion. History had shaped the future of colonial Asia through different colonial styles. What the effect of historical possibilities and historical inertia might be appeared most clearly in Japan and China, where European influence was just as dramatic but inevitably less direct in its effects as in India or Vietnam. The international context was also decisive in shaping the future in China and Japan.

Nationalism was proving by 1914 the most successful of all ideologies exported by Europe. In this connexion, it may seem particularly symbolic that among the last converts to it were European Jews. The history of that diverse people, concentrated above all in Europe, had taken a new turn when, in 1897, there appeared a Zionist Congress whose aim was the securing of a national home. In the long history of Jewry, assimilation to local society, still barely achieved in many European countries even after the liberating impact of the French Revolution, was now challenged as an ideal by that of territorial nationalism. A desirable location was not at once obvious; Argentina and Uganda were suggested at different times, but by the end of the century Zionist opinion had come to rest finally on Palestine. Jewish immigration to it had begun by 1914, though still on a small scale.

CHAPTER TWO The breakdown of international order

Attitudes and expectations

One of the most difficult imaginative leaps required in order to understand the Europe of 1900 is to accept that no-one then knew that the era in which they lived would come to an end fourteen years later. We are handicapped by hindsight. What happened in 1914 and the years that followed left so deep a mark on European's memories that even now it overshadows our reading of the early twentieth century's history. The great war which destroyed the old Europe seems inescapably *there* in advance; effort is needed to realise that down to almost the last moment the end of the story would have been unimaginable for most Europeans. Later historians long concentrated upon events and facts which demonstrated – or seemed to demonstrate – the logical inevitability with which they led towards war between the Great Powers. Yet circumstances created the logic, and many of those circumstances were not in place until a very late stage indeed.

A preoccupation with the approach to war as the central theme in the relations of European nations with one another was still evident in 1939, when another great European war began. It was not confined to historians. Just because the experiences of 1914–1918 had been so terrible and their revolutionary effects so vast, many in 1939 were deeply distressed at what they thought lay before them. In the event, the second great European war was to prove even more awful than its predecessor, which it was to deprive of its dreadful distinction as the bloodiest war in history. Nevertheless, the war which began in 1914 was the bloodiest, most intensely fought and greatest in geographical extent to have occurred to that time. Nations in every continent took part. It was also costlier than any earlier war; it ate up resources at an unprecedented rate, requiring the mobilization of whole societies on a new scale to provide them. It was also the first war to show the full impact of science and modern technology. Such facts justify its claim to uniqueness and help to explain its unprecedented psychological and cultural effects. They also explain the simple name given to the struggle by those who fought it: the *Great* War.[1]

To bear in mind what was to come in 1939 also helps us to understand another fact about the war which qualifies its claim to uniqueness. Like other great international struggles, it incorporated many initially distinct conflicts. Some have argued that it

---

[1] A name for a time also given in Great Britain after 1815 to the war with Napoleonic France.

might be called another 'Balkan War' (the third, after those of 1912 and 1913). In another perspective it was one more of the wars of the Ottoman Succession. But at its heart lay a question about Germany. As was to be the case a quarter of a century later, the central issue of the war in Europe was the position of Germany in Europe and the control of German power, and in other senses, too, the Great War began as a German war. It would take a Second German War to settle the question.

The damage inflicted in fighting both wars finally robbed Europe of her hegemony. Perhaps that would have come about without war, anyway; it seems likely, though, that it would have taken longer. But that is hypothesis: the wars were decisive. This is why it is possible to think of the whole era as one of European civil war, provided we remember that it is a metaphor. The containment of internal disorder is the fundamental pre-supposition of a state; Europe had never been united in that sense and could not therefore in the strict sense have a civil war. Europe had never been free from wars in the past. But it was the source and seat of a world system of power and of a civilization which, for all its variety, was an organic unity. It had in 1914 just experienced a longer period of peace between its leading nations than ever before. Educated Europeans at least felt they had something in common with other Europeans which they did not recognize when they looked at the mysterious, sometimes menacing millions formed by other cultures. All these facts were to vanish by mid-century; that makes the metaphor of civil war acceptable as shorthand for the internecine, self-destructive madness of the years from 1914 to 1945.

This destructiveness began to be released when enough influential and interested Europeans had come to feel that a war (though not one like that which actually took place between 1914 and 1918) and its chances might offer them more than would continuing peace. This disturbed the balance which had kept the international system working for nearly forty years. Such people were especially, but not solely, important in ruling circles in Germany, Austria-Hungary and Russia, but they were also to be found in other countries. When this happened, it did so in a particular context, shaped in the first place by complicated diplomatic ties, obligations and agreements. These made it unlikely that international conflict could easily be limited to only a few nations. Another element in that context was a public psychology grown more volatile and uncontrollable in its nature and more powerful in its influence upon politicians than in any earlier generation. 'Public opinion' had come to matter a lot by 1914; the war of that year was not only made by élites. Mass emotion was easily aroused (as many individual episodes had shown in the last forty years or so) by nationalist and patriotic stimuli. The dangers of war and its potential consequences were masked by ignorance, too. Even the soldiers – who should have known better – for the most part thought about war in terms of France in 1870 and Bohemia in 1866. They should have considered modern war's first battlefield demonstration of its real nature and costs in the slaughter done by breech-loaders and rifled guns in Virginia and Tennessee only a few years earlier. Nor were the businessmen, bankers and economists usually other than complacent; they found it difficult to believe that the costs of war could be sustained by civilized states for any prolonged period and, at best, envisaged 'modern' wars as brief affairs. A deep incapacity to imagine what a new war would be like was not shaken by the very few who saw further: it was probably more important in the long run than the noisy positive welcome to war given, when it came, by a few intellectuals who saw it as an emotional release, a purging of feelings of sterility, purposelessness, a chance to express their dislike of bourgeois materialism and decadence. As for revolutionaries, some of them, too, actually hoped for a war which, they believed, would offer them opportunities for transformations, whether national or social; it must be said, though, that they did little to offset the widespread confidence that nothing so disastrous could actually occur.

The efforts of diplomats and statesmen have to be understood against this background. For the most part, they were not incompetent or unintelligent men, and only a few of them were wicked or foolish enough positively to court disaster. They were seriously concerned with many awkward and difficult problems. None of them, however, would have recognized until a very late moment that among them was the question which later came to obsess historians, that of the origins of the Great War.

Alliances and entanglements

Convention and good diplomatic manners recognized all sovereign states as formally equal, but also that there were six major European powers in 1900: the United Kingdom, France, Russia, Germany, Austria-Hungary and Italy – that is, the great powers of 1815 plus two. Of Italy, Bismarck had rudely remarked that she had a big appetite but poor teeth. Spain and Portugal were still treated courteously as ancient states and were still to some extent imperial nations, but they carried little weight when it came to fighting-power or wealth.

From time to time, groupings came and went among these six powers and gave some semblance of organized structure to the system they formed. One such, historically, had been the conservative tie between the three eastern empires whose last manifestation had been the *Dreikaiserbund*, but this had disappeared by 1900 even if two of three emperors (Wilhelm II and Nicholas II) personally liked to think they still had some shared common anti-liberal and anti-democratic interest which ought to influence their countries' policy. Two crucial groupings had cut across this old ideological notion; they were the Triple Alliance of Germany, Austria-Hungary and Italy, and the Franco-Russian alliance. The first associated two strongly dynastic states with the constitutional Italian monarchy, a state with a long history of anti-Austrian policy, while the other linked the most reactionary and autocratic of all monarchies with Europe's only republican power, France, the self-conscious heiress of the Revolution. Necessity makes strange bed-fellows. Not all the terms of these alliances were known to the world. Each had arisen in special circumstances to meet different needs, and they did not imply at first any automatic or necessary division of Europe in two camps. If, though, circumstances developed in some ways rather than others, they might tend to produce that in the end.

This diplomatic framework had to be taken into account by others than the rulers of the alliance powers themselves, but was by no means all that shaped the diplomatic calculations of Europe. The participants in the alliances each had other interests formally unaffected by these treaty commitments and understandings. So, too, had other nations which were not members of the alliances, or even European; the United States, the British Dominions, Japan and even China might at times have to be taken into account. Many historic facts seemingly remote from those of the five major European land powers affected the way international relations worked.

The United Kingdom in particular had special interests; they had long been known, as had the deep historic (indeed, prehistoric) roots which shaped her policies. As one of her prime ministers put it, her concerns were oceanic, *'nous sommes des poissons'*[2] . In 1900, because of these, she was fighting her greatest colonial war for over a century in South Africa, to the almost universal disapproval of the other European powers, who, nonetheless, could do nothing about it; Britannia ruled the waves. None of the European states had been directly involved in the issues which had brought about the Boer War, but elsewhere in the world there were still many British imperial interests which had given rise to conflict and confrontation with some of them. Yet for a long time, the United Kingdom found she could remain clear of European entanglements; this was an advantage, though it might not last. The oldest industrial nation was increasingly troubled, too, by uncertainty about her economic position. By 1900 some British businessmen were clear that Germany was a major commercial rival; there were plenty of signs – in scale and volume of production; in technology and method – that German industry was greatly superior to British. Old certainties were giving way; Free Trade itself was called in question. In politics, the violence of Ulstermen and suffragettes and embittered struggles over social legislation with a House of Lords determined to safeguard the interests of wealth, led some by 1914 to wonder if parliamentarianism itself were not threatened. The sustaining social consensus of mid-Victorian politics had gone. Yet there was also a huge solidity about British institutions and political habits. Parliamentary monarchy had proved able to carry through and adapt itself to vast changes.

The French, too, had a great empire, as farflung if not as large as the British. But the major focus of French foreign policy had to be in Europe. 1898, in retrospect, can be seen to have been something of a turning-point. When the French government decided not to press matters to war with Great Britain after the confrontation at Fashoda, it was implicitly recognizing that forward imperial policies in remote places might jeopardize France's freedom of action in Europe, where the over-riding obsession of many (politicians said a majority of) Frenchmen was the recovery of Alsace and Lorraine. Since their seizure by Germany in 1871, the disparity between French and German power had further increased; it was clearer than ever by 1900 that France could not challenge her neighbour over that (or any other question) if she stood alone. She could not produce the numbers of soldiers to do so with the certainty of victory. France was also dwarfed by her neighbour's industrial growth. Just before 1914, she was raising about one-sixth as much coal as Germany, made less than a third as much pig-iron and a quarter as much steel. If there was ever to be a return match for 1870, Frenchmen knew they needed allies. This was the central datum of French policy. She was an unsatisfied power, even if weakness bound her to quiescence. She was also politically turbulent, though what looked like instability was superficial; it reflected a tradition of bitter exchanges between politicians who strove to keep alive the myths of 1789 and the rhetoric of revolution and reaction. The working-class movement was weak. The Third Republic was socially conservative and probably as stable socially as any other regime in Europe.

Russia had been the obvious candidate for French courtship. She was also the only power comparable with France and Great Britain in the range of her imperial interests and the concern they awoke, particularly since the 1880s, when Russian policy had been given a new expansionist emphasis in the Far East, and had begun to turn away from the Balkans. Imperial Russia had long pursued great ambitions in Manchuria and China (no country had taken more territory from the Chinese empire in the nineteenth

---

[2]   Lord Salisbury. See *German Diplomatic Documents*, ed. E.T.S. Dugdale (London, 1928), I, p.249.

century), and cherished a long-standing rivalry with the British in the Central Asian bufferlands between her and India, and over their respective degree of influence in Afghanistan and Persia. On the other hand, the imperial government could never forget Slav Europe and the Straits. Should further revolutionary changes occur there, then the Habsburg monarchy might become the undisputed dominant power in the Danube valley and at Constantinople. As Panslavist agitation had already shown, too, public opinion had to be taken into account even in Russia, and the ambitions of fellow-Slavs in the Balkans might well confront the tsar's ministers with circumstances not of their own making which would require Russian responses. If that happened, it would inevitably antagonize the Dual Monarchy.

A shadow on the future was thrown by the Magyars of Hungary, who were assuming a much more influential role in the foreign affairs of the Dual Monarchy in the early years of this century. Ruling as they did, in their half of the Monarchy, large populations of non-Magyars to whom they denied equitable treatment, the Magyars wanted above all to assure that Habsburg foreign policy would oppose Slav national ambitions. Serbia, a Russian satellite and client, was the focus of the hopes of South Slavs for unification in an enlarged Serbia. The Magyars feared their own Slav subjects would respond to this. They were anxious to show them that they could hope for nothing from Serbia by demonstrating her powerlessness to effect change. The role that Cavour's Piedmont-Sardinia had played in the unification of Italy forty years before was never forgotten.

Nevertheless, in 1900 Austro-Russian relations were good. They had recently been managed with some care, in spite of the lapsing of the *Dreikaiserbund* and the making of a German-Austrian alliance without Russia and in the 1890s neither power wished to disturb the *status quo* of the already modified Berlin settlement. The Russians were prepared to tolerate Austrian occupation of the formally Ottoman provinces of Bosnia and Herzegovina (where particularly vociferous pro-Serb nationalists were to be found) and (if ever such a description can be properly used), Russia seemed a satisfied power in Europe at the beginning of the century, with no inclination to rock the diplomatic boat.

Some Balkan nations created in the past century nonetheless felt much dissatisfaction and anguish. Serbians deplored the Austrian occupation of Bosnia-Herzegovina and the disfavoured position of Slavs under Magyar rule. A few of them also aspired to a Greater Serbia as the key to the future organization of the Danube valley. Romanians felt strongly about the position of 3,000,000 of their countrymen in Transylvania, another part of the Kingdom of Hungary. Macedonia, still under Ottoman rule and chronically disordered, was coveted by Bulgarians and Greeks. But dangers posed by Ottoman weakness were familiar to European diplomats and were therefore usually carefully monitored. They had been handled safely so far by concerted action among the powers; there was in 1900 no special cause for concern. If anything, the indirect results of earlier Ottoman decline seemed to matter more; conflict between the Balkan succession states seemed more likely to cause trouble than great power interests in the region.

Italy was another dissatisfied nation. The occupation of Rome had ended the period of her constitutional and territorial organization. Her rulers now faced formidable social and political problems at home. Abroad, no Italian government could think of quarrelling with the British, the old friends and patrons of Italian unity and possessors of naval power of which long coasts made Italians especially aware. But Italy bickered with another former patron, France, over North Africa and cherished ambitions on the Dalmatian coast which encouraged her to tinker with the Ottoman empire, too. Above all, for many Italians the *Risorgimento* was not complete. There remained Italians under Habsburg rule, in Venezia Giulia, Croatia and Trentino. These areas formed the 'unredeemed' Italy *(Italia irredenta)* of patriotic rhetoric. Fortunately, many Italians, too, knew that their country's teeth were poor.

Prussia had helped Italy towards unity, in 1866. Formally the new Germany was Italy's ally, in the Triple Alliance. But by 1900 she was no longer the Germany of Bismarck, carefully conservative, assiduous in preserving, if possible, good relations with Russia, and intent on avoiding war. Germany increasingly provided an element of instability in the European system. The 'New Course' in foreign policy had by no means obviously brought her solid benefits, and had caused strains where they might have been easily avoided, in, for instance, relations with the United Kingdom. Much of the seeming restlessness in German foreign policy had its roots in psychological facts, some collective, some personal, rather than in calculated national interest or *Realpolitik*. The ambiguities which surrounded the actual location of power and decision-making in Germany made matters worse. Nevertheless, no particular issue of interest to Germany was in agitation in 1900 which presented a potential threat to European order.

In the chancelleries of Europe in that year, in fact, little attention was being paid – because there was no reason to pay it – to any of the matters in which might be discerned the origins of conflict fourteen years later. Far from prefiguring the collapse of the European system, a renewed Franco-Russian military convention in 1900 still envisaged the possibility that the two allies might find themselves fighting a war against Great Britain. Russia was still busy in the Far East, and other European powers, too (even Italy), had their eyes on the possibilities in China. The French were consolidating in North Africa. The Balkans were quiet. But perhaps long success in negotiating grave crises without war (and diplomats continued to show their skill in doing so for many years yet) was itself a danger. The diplomatic machinery had worked so many times that when it was presented with facts more than ordinarily recalcitrant, their significance for a time seemed to escape many of those who had to deal with them. On the very eve of conflict, in July 1914, statesmen found it hard to see why another conference of ambassadors or even a European congress should not extricate them from their problems as so often before.

The beginnings of international change

The dynamic which drove the next phase of international relations between the European powers originated in the first place outside Europe. The first sign of the significance of this for European powers came with the important change in British imperial and foreign policy represented by alliance with a non-European power, Japan. Both countries had been alarmed in the 1890s by the Russians' success in extending their influence in the Far East, notably in Manchuria, and felt the danger it presented in Korea. This was the background for the Anglo-Japanese alliance of 1902, the first alliance made by the United Kingdom in peacetime for over a century. It provided for the benevolent neutrality of each partner if the other found itself obliged to defend by war its interests in the Far East; should a third power enter such a war, it committed the non-engaged partner to come to the other's assistance. The possible enemies in mind, clearly, were Russia and her ally, France.

By 1902, though, in spite of strident anglophobia in France during the Boer War, a way had been opened to better relations between her and Great Britain. Fashoda's importance was clear to Delcassé, who, as cabinets came and went, was foreign minister of France from 1898 to 1905. It showed, he believed, that quarrels over secondary issues outside Europe should be subordinated to the improvement of France's diplomatic position there. She should seek, for example, to ease Anglo-Russian relations and reduce the dangers of conflict between her ally and the British. But this meant forgetting old antagonisms. Popular feeling in London and Paris was flattered by an exchange of personal visits by the French president and the English king. Meanwhile officials settled down to consider a wide range of business of mutual interest. The outcome was an Anglo-French agreement in 1904. Its core was the assurance of British approval and goodwill towards the development of French interests in Morocco where the French had ambitious ideas of future possibilities on the one side, and a French undertaking that there should be no further efforts to hinder and embarrass the British in Egypt on the other. Friction caused by the long British occupation of Egypt could now be laid to rest.

The Anglo-French agreement went further than this, though. It wound up a number of other long-running disputes. West Africa, the Newfoundland fishing grounds, Siam, Madagascar and the South Pacific all provided causes for resolution; the British were especially pleased to heal so many running sores. Yet even this does not exhaust the importance of the convention which registered the agreement. It was a seed from which would grow *entente* – understanding on other matters, or, as a later generation might put it, a special relationship – the implications of which were to remain vague, undefined and unincorporated in treaty form, and perhaps more powerful for that reason. But that all lay in the future; it was not part of the intention of the makers of the convention, and it would require the actions of others to make the possibility a reality.

Perhaps it should not have come as a surprise to its negotiators that William II and some of his officials felt that the settlement of Morocco's fate without consulting Germany (or, indeed, any other government except the Spanish) had slighted their country. It was decided in Berlin that a gesture must be made; Germany should show France that she expected to be taken into account in such matters. The emperor was happy to make it. The French at that moment were pressing reforms upon the Sultan of Morocco. On a visit to Tangier in March 1905 William made a provocative speech, stressing Germany's commercial interests in Morocco (they were far less substantial than those of Great Britain, let alone France) and the importance of maintaining the independence of the Sultan. This caused consternation, perhaps all the more because no-one was quite sure what he meant. Out of what was intended as a re-assertion of out-raged dignity and an exercise in prestige, grew a crisis. In its resolution, Germany won a Pyrrhic victory. An international conference met at Algeciras, thus implicitly conced-ing that Europe had a collective interest in management of the fate of Morocco. But Germany obtained nothing else of substance and was unsupported at the conference except by the Austrians.

An important conclusion was drawn by officials in the British foreign office; they – and, in some measure, British public opinion – had awoken to the United Kingdom's interest in supporting France, if the balance of European power was to be maintained and Germany was not to assert her right to a decisive voice in every question that arose. A corner had been turned; on one side of it lay the 1904 agreement on specific issues and on the other, *entente*. Groundlessly, Germany had already suspected a secret Franco-British alliance; she had now driven the two countries closer together and had perhaps made one more possible. On the day after the Algeciras conference opened, Anglo-French military conversations had begun between representatives of the two general staffs. The first Morocco crisis (there was to be another) was not the point of no return on the road to 1914, but it was one of the moments at which certain conjunc-tures became more likely. As a British foreign secretary was still insisting in 1914 a few days before his country went to war, military conversations were not an alliance; they bound the British government in no way to any specific course of action. But they reg-ister the end of what had seemed to be a period of British isolation in Europe and in the assumptions of British policy. The 1902 and 1904 agreements had sought to look after British interests overseas. Morocco brought British policy back to the European bal-ance of power.

Another rapprochement over non-European issues took place in 1907, again arous-ing suspicion in Berlin of what it was now fashionable there to term 'encirclement'. This was an Anglo-Russian convention. In effect it divided Persia, nominally indepen-dent, into Russian and British spheres of influence, provided for the neutrality of Afghanistan, an old area of competition, and assured that neither government should (as the British had just done) interfere in the affairs of Tibet (which was in any case claimed by the Chinese empire, whose suzerainty both governments recognized). This range of decisions, like those of 1904, offered limited but real advantages to each par-ticipant. It was an additional cloud over Anglo-German relations, all the more unset-tling because it accompanied increasingly blatant and acknowledged naval competition between the two countries.

Germany had for some years advertised her intention to build a battle-fleet which could challenge the British – there was no-one else there to challenge – in the North Sea. In 1907 the British offered to cut construction and so save both countries money. The British naval estimates of 1908 were actually reduced, but Germany would only agree to give up her building plans in return for an unconditional promise of British neutrality in the event of a war between France and Germany. This was impossible after

Algeciras. Yet a threat to British naval hegemony was bound to alarm British public opinion, deepen the often uncomprehending exasperations of British politicians and officials with German policy, and increase the financial burdens of tax-payers in each country.

The re-emergence of Balkan questions

In this more poisoned atmosphere tensions revived in the Balkans which finally opened the way to 1914. After 1900 there had been for some years reasonably settled conditions and only slow and undramatic internal change in what was left of the Ottoman empire in Europe. At Constantinople itself, Germany's influence was growing, perhaps imprudently in the light of the canons of Bismarckian diplomacy. Macedonia, where Ottoman government faced an enduring revolutionary movement, had not settled down and this, besides reflecting badly on Ottoman rule, encouraged Balkan states to dabble in its troubles. Then came the Young Turk revolution, and with it a new phase. It was quickly apparent that if one possible outcome was a revivified and reformed Ottoman empire, then new assumptions were required in Balkan diplomacy.

The potential destabilization might still have been avoided and adaptation managed without disaster had both Habsburg and Russian policy still been focused on the preservation of the *status quo*. The two empires had co-operated to contain the Macedonian question when smaller nations were willing to rock the boat. Unfortunately, Habsburg policy veered away from its cautious stance in 1906, when a tariff war began with Serbia. At this moment Russia, after the disaster of defeat by Japan in the Far East, was turning back to take a renewed interest in south-east Europe. In this, there was a new element. Interest in the Straits was for Russia no longer a matter of the historic dream of a new 'Greek' empire which would revive the splendours of Byzantium, but of concern for the conduit through which Russian grain exports from the Black Sea passed to their markets further west.

Hardening Habsburg policy towards Serbia reflected Magyar political weight at Vienna. Instead of concessions which might meet the aspirations of its Slav subjects the foreign ministry now offered a new solution to the South Slav problem. Serbia, long suspected of encouraging South Slav nationalists, still hoped one day to acquire Bosnia and Herzegovina and perhaps an outlet in the Adriatic if the Ottoman empire ever gave up its legal sovereignty over them; formal annexation by the Dual Monarchy, therefore, would end any Serbian hopes of acquiring them. This would deal a blow to Serbia's prestige as the champion of South Slav hopes, while enabling the Habsburg administration seriously to take in hand the real terrorist problem there. If the provinces were incorporated in the Austrian half of the Monarchy, Habsburg rule could show its ability to manage Slavs properly when Magyars were not involved. The successful Young Turk coup made it desirable that annexation should take place soon; it would not do for a reformed and effective Ottoman administration to establish itself in the provinces.

In principle, Russia was not against Habsburg acquisition of Bosnia and Herzegovina. All she required was visible and adequate compensation to balance the gain to the Dual Monarchy. The Russian foreign minister believed he had obtained a promise from his Habsburg opposite number which would assure such compensation. At the international conference which would be needed to legitimize and agree any modification of the 1878 settlement, Russia would ask for a strengthening of her position at the

Straits, and the Dual Monarchy (as the most interested power) would support her. Unfortunately, the two statesmen had left their crucial meeting with different ideas of what had actually been agreed – or so they later said. A diplomatic disaster followed.

Austrian annexation of the province took place on 5 October 1908, shortly after they met. The Russians protested strongly when it became clear that they were not to have the *quid pro quo* they had expected. Thanks to the annoyance it felt over the Anglo-Russian convention, the German government gave unconditional support to the Austrians, forcing Russia to recognize that she could not fight Germany and the Habsburg empire if they stood together. In such a war the French would not wish to take part and there was a likelihood that Serbia, Russia's *protégé*, would disappear altogether. The Russians had to give in; they formally acknowledged the validity of the annexation without obtaining compensation. But they were enraged. Their foreign minister was soon advocating a Balkan league, including the Ottoman government, to resist further encroachments.

After over a decade of good relations and co-operation there had in fact now re-emerged the old danger of outright conflict between the Dual Monarchy and Russia in the Balkans. The South Slav problem remained unsolved. It was soon further inflamed when in 1909 a group of Croat leaders was convicted at Zagreb on the basis of forged evidence from the Austrian foreign office of plotting with Serbia: the forgery was exposed and they were acquitted on appeal. The terrorists began to get more clandestine help from Belgrade; Habsburg officials were attacked. Russian officialdom was deeply wounded by the demonstration that the old Berlin-St Petersburg connexion was finally gone and increasingly worried about German influence in Constantinople. A major programme of reorganization and re-equipment of the Russian army was begun so that no such disaster for the autocracy's prestige as 1908 could ever occur again, nor any doubt arise that Russia could not in a future crisis stand up for her Slav brothers.

Russian recovery and Russian power

Important as they were, the defeat by Japan in 1905 and the moral defeat (as it was seen) of 1908 do not by themselves provide a deep enough perspective to understand the course of Russian policy in the remaining years of peace. Well before those events the slow process of modernization was at work in the empire. By 1900 it was evident that Russia was a great industrial power in the making. The essential step had been emancipation. Forty years after it, it was true that most Russians were still peasants living in poverty, but their taxes had produced the money to pay for essential infrastructure, railways, and primary plant. Businessmen and farmers with a stake in the growth of the economy were slowly growing in numbers. Things could have moved faster, but Nicholas II was one of the most unimaginative tsars. Revolution broke out in 1905 after defeat in the war with Japan. For a time, liberals inside and outside Russia felt hopeful about constitutional progress. A consultative council called the Duma emerged from the revolution and it looked as if the long-delayed training of Russians in self-government could begin at last. Unhappily, the Duma was to have only a few years of life, and those studded with frustration. Meanwhile, Russian economic development quickened.

In 1914 Russia's great power status was again unquestionable. She was well on the road to importance as an economic power. Though well behind Germany or Great Britain – she produced only about a quarter as much steel as the former and a third as

much pig-iron as the latter – her rate of growth was faster than that of either. More important, there were signs that at long last Russian agriculture might have turned the corner
and become capable of producing grain harvests which grew faster than the population.
New legislation had accelerated the emergence of a new class of peasant-farmers –
kulaks – whose self-interest improved productivity. They registered the disappearance of
the restraints on individualism imposed at the time of serf emancipation. Stolypin, the
minister who presided over this hopeful development, characteristically, was strongly
disliked by the tsar and tsarina, and they hardly minded when he was assassinated in
1912. His murder was one more sign of the continuing inability to extinguish the revolutionary and terrorist tradition, and, therefore, of the political failure of the regime.

In 1914 Russia's rulers could again be confident that the army's numbers and
modern weapons, supported by a growing railway network and expanding industrial
base, could sustain her great power role. Yet there were still enduring weaknesses. A
European power in name, Russia still displayed poverty of Asiatic horror, experienced
recurrent famine, and had a largely illiterate population. In that year less than ten per
cent of Russians lived in towns and only two per cent of them worked in industry. She
was still a country dependent on foreign capital (most of it from France). Liberal tradition was stinted and puny. The Orthodox Church was still mixed up in government and
society in a way unknown for a century or so past in most of western Europe. Russia had
one or two good universities and schools and some distinguished scientists and scholars,
but the overwhelming majority of the tsar's subjects were ignorant and superstitious
peasants. Above all, she was still a country where government rested in the last resort on
what was regarded as the god-given power of the autocrat. It was a consequence of all
these things that she was also the only great power in which there existed a seriously
menacing revolutionary movement quite happy to overthrow the regime by force.
Russia was not yet a modern state.

The end of peace

No nation in 1914 felt more menaced by Russia's growing and potential
strength than Germany. By then her military planners took the view that Russia might
become militarily invincible in another three or four years with the completion of her
strategic railway systems. But German action against Russia had already contributed
greatly to the damage done by the Bosnian crisis six years before that. Whether international relations were then irreversibly set on a path to general war is, though, doubtful.
It took those six years to show it, if it were true. Much could have happened otherwise
in that time.

Unfortunately, one of the things that did happen was another Morocco crisis, precipitated once again by Germany. Morocco seemed another 'dying' empire. The
French had consolidated their position and special influence there since 1905, and
economic initiatives by other European nations (among them Germany) had followed.
There were hopes of significant developments in Morocco's mining potential. This
kept European interest in the country alive. There was much interest and speculation
when a rebellion against the Sultan prompted the French to send an expedition to
occupy Fez, the capital. The German government decided to establish a position from
which it could make a strong claim for compensation if a permanent extension of the
French role in the country followed. The means chosen was to send a German warship

to the Moroccan port of Agadir, ostensibly to protect German nationals (there were none there). The real aim was to show that Germany meant business and to frighten France into agreeing to compensation for her. On 1 July 1911 the gunboat *Panther* dropped anchor at Agadir.

Gratuitously provocative, the gesture was ham-fisted as well. A government in Paris disposed to be conciliatory to Germany almost at once found it very difficult to make any concessions because of the feeling aroused among Frenchmen by the *Panther's* leap; it could not allow itself to appear to be weak in defending French interests. Agadir had also startled the British. Although the Admiralty did not seem much concerned, the Foreign Office was troubled and the Press excited by the alleged danger of a German naval base being set up on the Moroccan coast (in fact, the Germans had no intention of creating one). It was felt that a gesture was needed in reply and the outcome was a speech by a British minister which was taken to be a warning that if France found herself at war with Germany, Great Britain would support her.

In due course, diplomacy negotiated the second Moroccan crisis. Germany got a little more territory out of it (in the Congo). But the importance of the crisis was that it had occurred at all. It had much strengthened the *entente* and won more support for it among the French and British publics. The British again became agitated over the German naval threat, for the gap in size between the two fleets was narrower in 1911 than it had ever been (or was to be again). German anglophobes, on the other hand, believed Germany had suffered 'humiliation' as a result of British threats. When this bore fruit in the following year in an announcement of an even larger German building programme, the British increased their own capital ship building and, more significantly, withdrew the Mediterranean Fleet to home waters, while later in the year the French fleet was moved to Toulon. Clearly, British naval strategy now envisaged only one potential enemy, Germany. The result of this and increased building was that British naval superiority in the North Sea was by 1914 greater than it had been at the time of Agadir.

These were not the only repercussions of the crisis. Italy had been made uneasy by the Bosnian annexation as a gain for the Habsburgs. Perhaps imitatively, she too now began to seek 'compensation' for the French ascendancy in Morocco. The obvious place to seek it was the Ottoman empire. In September 1911, after declaring war on the Sultan, Italian troops landed in Tripoli; later they opened another front in the Ottoman islands of the Dodecanese. When the Turks announced the closure of the Straits, the Russians felt bound to take precautions and, after failing to get agreement with the Turks, began to look for help elsewhere. The Italians had launched a new Balkan crisis. By setting about the further demolition of the Ottoman empire in Africa they now provoked others to think the time had come for its possible final elimination in Europe. Contradictory but cumulative doubts (about the Ottoman capacity to survive) and fears (that the Young Turks might succeed in making survival possible) led to an alliance between Serbia and Bulgaria in 1912. The Russians found this promising; it would discourage further Habsburg adventures in the Balkans and give the Turks something to think about and so check German influence at Constantinople. The new allies were joined by Greece, and began to plan their 'compensations'. This further suggested to Russian diplomats that the outcome might help to maintain Russian interests in the Straits. They did not want to appear to be failing to support other Slav nations, either. So, Russia found herself drifting into the position of under-writing a possible war against Turkey by the smaller nations.

In the end, the First Balkan War was started by Montenegro on 8 October 1912. Facing Montenegrins, Bulgars, Serbs and Greeks, the Turks hastily made peace with Italy by ceding territory in Africa. The Great Powers began to fear dangers nearer home. The Dual Monarchy believed it could not allow Serbia to acquire an Adriatic port (just as the British felt the Boers could not be allowed one on the Indian Ocean in the 1890s). The Russians were soon alarmed by fears that the Bulgars intended to fight their way to Constantinople and take it for themselves. Such reflexions made concerted action easier. A conference of ambassadors met in London and averted the danger of the war spreading further. To cut off Serbia from the sea, an independent Albania was created, the last new nation to emerge from Ottoman Europe. This reassured Austria, and as the Bulgarians had not after all been able to get to the Straits, Russia found this acceptable. Unfortunately, the victors soon fell out over the spoils.

This caused the Second Balkan War. Serbia was attacked by Bulgaria in order to turn her out of part of Macedonia invaded by Serb forces. Then followed a further Bulgarian attack, this time on Greece, again over claims to Macedonia. Once again, it seemed a good moment for others to speculate on the chances of war; Rumania chose the moment to attack Bulgaria while she was preoccupied in the west, with the aim of detaching from her the Dobrudja, and the Turks quickly retook Adrianople. When the great powers did not intervene, Bulgaria lost almost everything she had gained in the First Balkan War. Only Germany felt obliged to make a gesture: William II insisted that the Austrians send an ultimatum to Belgrade over a Serbian incursion into Albania. The Serbs withdrew.

These episodes in faraway countries, of which most of the newspaper-readers and inhabitants of the capital cities of the great powers knew nothing or almost nothing that was detailed or wholly true, exhibited the potential for future trouble. Obstreperous smaller states had taken the initiative in a further despoiling of the Turks after the Italian lead, and the great powers had not been able to prevent further infringement of a territorial settlement they had authorized. Serbia had gained a 1,500,000 more inhabitants but the thwarting of her hopes to reach the Adriatic left that country more embittered against Vienna than ever. Meanwhile, Vienna's worries about Serbian ambitions were further increased; there was something of a parallel, though not a complete one, between her nervous desire to settle with the Serbians and that of a British government fifteen years earlier to settle with the Boers (the crucial difference was that Africa was not Europe, and no other power in 1899 thought its vital interests involved, so the British could act without danger to international peace). The Bulgarians now had new grudges to nurse against their neighbours and an unsupportive Russia. It was a small off-setting factor that there at last appeared to have been a slight improvement in Anglo-German relations as the two powers worked together in the London Conference. They negotiated secretly over a possible disposition of another seemingly crumbling empire, that of Portugal (it was in the end to prove almost the longest-lived of all), and a proposed railway from Berlin to Baghdad. This should have reassured the Germans. Unhappily, German officials did not read the situation in this way; taking British responsiveness on these matters to indicate a lack of confidence, they hopefully speculated that Great Britain might not, after all, be serious about backing France, should Germany attack her.

Such an attack had by this stage long been an essential element in German strategical planning. By 1913, when German politicians began to talk among themselves of the 'coming world war'[3] and in an atmosphere of excited patriotism (it was the centenary of the 'War of Liberation' with Napoleonic France) a special army bill was introduced into the *Reichstag*. It is clear that Russian modernization (above all, of her railways) and rearmament (to be completed by 1917) alarmed the German soldiers. But by itself this can hardly explain the psychological deterioration in Germany which had brought about so dangerous a transformation of German policy as the acceptance of the inevitability of conflict with Russia – and therefore with France – if Germany's due weight in Europe was to be assured. Many Germans felt an 'encirclement' which frustrated the exercise of German power, and which they believed should be broken, if only for reasons of prestige. Other Germans thought more positively of possible territorial and material gains in the east. Few thought of the colonial possibilities which had been contentious and prickly in the 1880s and 1890s, but which had proved so disappointing in the outcome; colonial rivalry played no part in the final approach to war.

The crisis and after

By 1914, the Russians were less preoccupied with Balkan than with Ottoman issues. German influence was clearly ascendant at Constantinople. She alone among the great powers had never taken an inch of former Ottoman territory for herself. In 1913 a German general had been appointed to command the Ottoman forces at the Straits, and a German military mission had reorganized the Ottoman army. Comparatively, the old rivalry with the Dual Monarchy had receded somewhat in Russian thinking. But to Germany, the acceptance of the inevitability of war with Russia gave new importance to her ally. It meant that at the very least the long Austro-Hungarian frontier with Russia would pin down large Russian forces in the event of a war. Her leaders did nothing to restrain Vienna from renewing confrontation with Russia, but, rather, actively encouraged it. Of course, this still did not by itself imply a great European war. Neither Germany nor any other power envisaged such a thing until the last few hours of the final crisis. But the nature of military planning already made the development of one likely if any conflict were actually to begin, and there were plenty of dangerous materials lying about.

By June 1914, indeed, they were being added to. Magyar administration was still posing problems to Vienna. Not only were there many discontented Slavs in the Kingdom of Hungary, but also 3,000,000 Rumanians. When a Russian minister on a visit to Rumania ostentatiously crossed the frontier to Transylvania to see how these subjects of the Dual Monarchy lived, it caused alarm in Budapest and Vienna. The planning of a royal visit to Sarajevo, the Bosnian capital, for the end of the month, went ahead, therefore, against the background of heightened feeling in Vienna that Serbia and Rumania should both in some way be shown the danger of backing irredentist movements inside the Monarchy.

On 28 June, when the visit by the Archduke Franz Ferdinand and his wife to Sarajevo had barely begun, both of them were shot dead by a young Bosnian Serb terrorist. He was part of a gang which had already that day failed to carry out the assassination in the manner it had planned; it was an accident that he suddenly found himself able to

---

[3] Words used by the German secretary of state in confidential discussion with parliamentary deputies in April 1913. See F. Ficsher, *Germany's Aims in the First World War* (London, 1967), p. 37.

remedy his colleagues' failure. It was at once felt in Vienna that the moment had come for a reckoning with Serbia. Her agents were presumed to be behind the murder (some were indeed in touch with the terrorists, but not necessarily with the authorization of the Serbian government). Counsels of prudence were silenced when enthusiastic German support was at once forthcoming for an ultimatum to Belgrade (characteristically, William II and his chancellor offered this support without consulting the German foreign minister). It was hoped that Russia would not feel able to support her Slav brothers – and, as in 1909, would accept the outcome – but, if she did not, the German generals were ready to fight. On 23 July the Austrians presented a humiliating ultimatum to the Serbian government which demanded action against South Slav terrorism amounting to intervention in Serbia's internal government. Russia had advised the Serbs not to resist. Great Britain had offered to act as a go-between. Serbia accepted most of the terms. Without waiting, though, for further clarification, the Dual Monarchy, determined now to crush Serbia once and for all, declared war on her on 28 July.

German encouragement to the Austrians had made this outcome inevitable. The uncertainty which remained was over who would join in. German military planning had always taken it for granted that if Germany went to war with Russia, the Franco-Russian alliance would operate sooner or later. The German generals had drawn the reasonable conclusion that if Germany had to fight on two fronts, it would be desirable for her to overthrow France before Russia's slow mobilization could provide effective help to her ally. In the east, space and Russia's administrative and material backwardness would for a time favour Germany. The chief of the German general staff from

1891 to 1905 had planned, therefore, an immediate sweep into France with the aim of defeating her even more quickly than in 1870. But this required a huge outflanking movement through Belgium, whose neutrality was under international guarantee. It raised the possibility of a British intervention to defend Belgian neutrality. The 'Schlieffen Plan' (named after the German Chief of Staff in 1895, when it was adopted) accepted this danger, and the German general staff therefore accepted the risk of a widening of the war.

Once the Austrians had declared war on Serbia, Russian mobilization began. Nonetheless, it was deliberately restrained; only those armies which might be needed to intervene against the Dual Monarchy were put on a war footing. Even with this self-imposed handicap, though, it was too much for Berlin. German mobilization was ordered on 31 July and on the following day Germany declared war on Russia – although her ally, Austria-Hungary, was still only at war with Serbia and not with Russia. The Germans asked France for a declaration of neutrality. The French reply was considered insufficiently provocative; an alleged French air raid on Nuremberg was therefore said to justify a German declaration of war on France on 3 August. Germany was now at war – on her own initiative – with two great powers, Austria-Hungary with none.

Great Britain at once warned Germany that naval operations in the Channel against France would not be permitted, but that was all. Though some thought that the country should go further in standing up to Germany, many did not. The French were dismayed. A German ultimatum to Belgium on 3 August demanding unobstructed passage for her armies across that country, resolved the British government's difficulty. On the following day, it demanded that Belgian neutrality, of which Great Britain was a guarantor, be respected. This was ignored and a British declaration of war on Germany followed. Thus Germany acquired a third great power as an antagonist, while Austria still had none.

Tragic though this sequence of events was, it was rich in paradoxes. In the end, the Franco-Russian alliance never actually came into effect at all; the Germans had declared war on France before it could. The British on 4 August still had no treaty obligations to France or Russia, whatever their moral commitment to the first; the Anglo-French military conversations had only been given reality by German military planning which gave the British government a chance to enter the war without serious discussion and at the head (in so far as these things are ever possible) of a united public opinion, in defence of international law and the rights of small nations. These were grounds wholly unconnected either with the colonial and naval rivalries which so often in the past had seemed to bedevil the possibility of friendship between England and Germany, or with the alliance system. Finally, the central issue of so much of forty years' worried diplomacy dropped out of sight as the final crisis unrolled. It was not until 6 August that the Dual Monarchy at last declared war on the Russians. Only on 12 August did the British and French go to war with the Austrians. In the last analysis the Great War was made in Berlin.

CHAPTER THREE European revolution

The Great War

The twentieth century swept away the European domination which was the basis of international order in 1900, a gigantic historical change, the end of a phase in both global and European history. That process was accompanied by revolution in Europe itself, a ragged and untidy business, but one whose effects justify the term, not merely in the sense of transformations in politics and society, but in ideas and culture, too. Paradoxically, while the twentieth century had been notable for wider and wider, and more and more enthusiastic adoption of European ideas, institutions and standards in non-European parts of the world, it also deprived Europeans of their confidence in many of the assumptions and beliefs which lay at the roots of their civilization.

In these huge transformations, whose origins in some cases have already been shown to lie very deep indeed, the Great War was a major catalyst, if not the most important one. Geographically, it had quickly spread. Japan and the Ottoman empire soon joined in, the former on the side of the Allies (as France, Great Britain and Russia were called) and the Ottoman empire on that of the Central Powers (Germany and Austria-Hungary). Italy abandoned her former co-signatories of the Triple Alliance and joined the Allies in 1915, after securing promises of Austrian territory from them. It was not the only effort by combatants to pick up new supporters by offering cheques to be cashed after a victorious peace; Bulgaria joined the Central Powers in September 1915 and Romania the Allies in the following year. Greece became an Ally in 1917. Portugal's government had tried to enter the war in 1914, but though unable to do so because of internal troubles was finally faced with a German declaration of war in 1916. By the end of that year, the original issues had been thoroughly confused by other contests, therefore. The Balkan states were fighting the third Balkan war (or, from another point of view, the last war of the Ottoman succession in Europe), the British a war against German hegemony and, it came to appear, naval power, the Italians the last war of the *Risorgimento*. Meanwhile, British, Russians and Arabs had begun a war of Ottoman partition in Asia and the Japanese were initiating another cheap and highly profitable episode of imperial expansion in the Far East.

One reason why there was much searching for allies in 1915 and 1916 was that the war by then showed every sign of bogging down in a stalemate no one had expected. The nature of the fighting had surprised everyone. The planned German sweep into northern France did not achieve the lightning victory which was its aim though it gave the Germans possession of all but a tiny scrap of Belgium and of much of north-eastern France, too. In the east, early Russian offensives had been stopped by the Germans and Austrians. Thereafter, though more noticeably in the west than the east, the battlefields settled down to siege warfare on an unprecedented scale, thanks to the huge killing-power of modern weapons. Magazine rifles, machine-guns and barbed wire could stop any infantry attack not preceded by pulverizing bombardment. The casualty lists showed this. By the end of 1915 the French army alone had lost 300,000 dead; that was bad enough, but in 1916 one seven-month battle before Verdun added another 315,000 to this total and killed 280,000 Germans. While it was going on, another struggle further north, on the Somme, cost the British 420,000 dead, wounded, and missing and the Germans about the same (on the first day of the battle alone, the British army suffered 60,000 casualties, more than a third of them killed).

Pre-war assurances that the cost of modern war would be bound to make any struggle a short one and the policies governments had based on that assumption were soon shown to be nonsense. In July 1914, on the eve of war, Germany was still exporting grain; there were no food regulations or plans for the management of industry: 'even our ammunition was not planned for a large-scale war' said one German politician[1]. Yet there followed a revelation of the enormous wealth and war-making power of industrial societies. By the end of 1916 the warring states had amply demonstrated a capacity far greater than had been imagined to conscript and organize themselves as never before in history and to provide unprecedented quantities of arms and recruits for new armies. Not every country found the means to fight in the same ways; the British army was still a volunteer force at the beginning of 1916, and when conscription (traditional in all the continental powers before 1914) was adopted, it was not applied to Ireland, for political reasons. Great Britain, on the other hand, had income tax at the beginning of the war while France had not, and its standard rate of application rose from just under 6 per cent in 1914 to 25 per cent in the course of the war. Whole societies were mobilized against one another; the international solidarity of the working class might never have been thought of for all the resistance it opposed to this, nor the international interests of ruling classes against subversion. One British civil servant spoke of the British Ministry of Food as 'suppressing private enterprise entirely'[2]. That was exaggerated, but war gave much of Europe its first taste of socialism in practice.

Inability to batter one another into submission on the battlefields was one reason why diplomats had sought new allies and generals new fronts. The Allies in 1915 mounted an attack at the Dardanelles in the hope, not to be realized, of knocking the Ottoman empire out of the war and opening up communication with Russia through the Black Sea. The search for a way round later produced a new Balkan front at Salonika to replace the one which had collapsed when Serbia was overrun. Colonial possessions, too, had ensured from the first that there would be fighting all round the globe, even if on a smaller scale than in Europe. The German colonies were for the most part picked up fairly easily, thanks to the British command of the seas, though those in Africa provoked some lengthy campaigning. The most important and considerable extra-European operations were in the eastern and southern parts of the

[1]   F. Henry Cord Meyer, *Mitteleuropa in German Thought and Action 1815–1945* (The Hague, 1955), p. 123.
[2]   W.H. Beveridge, *British Food Control* (London, 1928), p. 338.

Ottoman empire. A British and Indian army entered Iraq (then still known as Mesopotamia). Another force advanced from the Suez canal towards Palestine. In the desert, an Arab revolt against the Turks provided some of the few romantic episodes to relieve the brutal squalor of industrial war.

By 1916, the mills, factories, mines, and furnaces of Europe were working as never before. So were those of the United States and Japan, the former neutral but accessible to the Allies and not to the Central Powers thanks to British sea power. The maintenance of millions of men in the field required not only arms and ammunition, but food, clothing, medical equipment, and machines in huge quantities. Though the war used up millions of animals, it was also the first war of the internal-combustion engine; trucks and tractors swallowed petrol as avidly as horses and mules ate their fodder. The repercussions of this vast increase in demand rolled outwards through society, leading in all countries in varying measure to inflation, government interference with the economy, direction and sometimes conscription of labour, the revolutionizing of women's employment, and the introduction of new health and welfare services. They also rolled across the oceans. The United States ceased to be a debtor nation as the Allies sold their investments there to pay for what they needed and became debtors in their turn. Indian industry received the fillip it had long required. Boom days came to the ranchers and farmers of the Argentine and the British Dominions. The latter also shared the military burden, sending soldiers to Europe and picking off German colonies.

Technical innovation made war all-consuming. This was not just because machine-guns and high explosive made possible terrible slaughter, nor even because of new weapons such as poison gas, flame-throwers or tanks, all of which made their appearance as soldiers strove to find a way out of the deadlock of the battlefield. It was also because the engagement of whole societies in warfare brought with it the treatment of

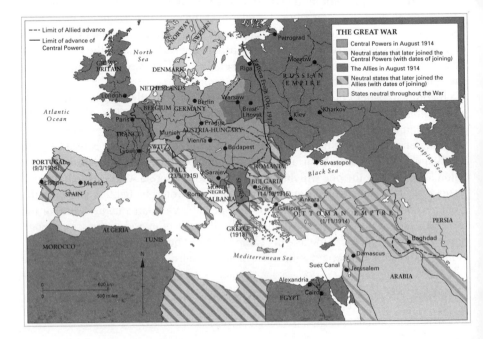

whole societies as targets for war-like operations. Attacks were mounted on the morale, health and efficiency of civilian workers and voters by blockade and, occasionally, direct bombardment and bombing from the air. When such acts were denounced, the denunciations themselves became blows in another campaign, that of propaganda. The possibilities of mass literacy and the recently created cinema industry supplemented and overtook such old standbys as pulpit and school in struggles for public opinion. To British charges that the Germans who carried out primitive aerial bombing raids on London were 'babykillers', Germans retorted that the same could be said of the sailors who sustained the British blockade. The rising figures of German infant mortality bore them out; both were right.

In part because of the slowly tightening but apparently irresistible stranglehold of the British blockade and because of its unwillingness to risk the battle-fleet whose building had done so much to poison pre-war feeling between the two countries, the German High Command devised a new use for a weapon whose power had been underrated in 1914, the submarine. It was launched at Allied merchant shipping and the ships of neutrals who were supplying the Allies, attacks often being made without warning and on unarmed vessels. This happened first in early 1915, though the few submarines then available did not do much damage. After an outcry when a great British liner was torpedoed that year, with the loss of 1,200 lives, many of them American, the unrestricted sinking of shipping was called off by the Germans. By the beginning of 1917, though, it was clear that if Germany did not starve Great Britain first, she herself would be choked by the British blockade. During that winter there was famine in Balkan countries and starvation in Vienna. The French had already suffered 3,350,000 casualties, the British over a 1,000,000, and the Germans nearly 2,500,000. Germany was still fighting the war on two fronts that the Schlieffen Plan had been meant to avoid, and strikes were becoming more frequent; infant mortality was nearly 50 per cent higher than in 1915. There was no reason to suppose that the German army, divided between east and west, would be any more likely to achieve a knockout than had been the British and French. It was better placed than they to fight on the defensive in the west, though, and in these circumstances the German general staff chose to resume unrestricted submarine warfare.

This brought about the first revolutionary transformation of the war. Unrestricted submarine warfare was a direct threat to American interests and the safety of her citizens. The Germans knew it would bring in the United States, but gambled on bringing Great Britain to her knees – and thus France – before American weight could be decisive. When the American government also learnt that Germany hoped to negotiate an alliance with Mexico and Japan against the United States, the hostility aroused by the submarines was confirmed. Soon, an American ship was sunk without warning and the United States declared war shortly afterwards, on 6 April 1917.

Revolutionizing the war

The impossibility of breaking the European deadlock by means short of total war had sucked the New World into the quarrels of the Old. The Allies were delighted; victory was now assured. Yet a struggle of a different kind was now to overtake the plans of 1914. Immediately Great Britain and France faced an even blacker year than 1916 had been. Not only did the submarine take months to master (only in May 1917 did the adoption of convoy at sea open the way to securing the Atlantic sea-lanes) but a terrible series of battles in France (usually lumped under one name, Passchendaele) inflicted an ineffaceable scar upon the British national consciousness and cost another 400,000 men to gain five miles of mud. The persistence of the British generals in what seemed unrewarded squandering of their armies was partly to be explained by their wish to take pressure off their allies. Worn out by its earlier heroic efforts, the French army had to master and recover from a series of mutinies in 1917. Worst of all for the Allies, the Russian empire collapsed.

In January 1917, Lenin, the leader of the Bolshevik socialists and in exile in Switzerland said that his generation would not live to see revolution in Russia. Yet that empire had by then been mortally wounded. The makers of revolution in Russia were the German armies. The fighting in the end broke the hearts of even the long-enduring Russian soldiers. Their families were starving (because of the breakdown of the transport system rather than falling production, though that had occurred). They were ruled by an incompetent and corrupt government which feared constitutionalism and liberalism as much as defeat. At the beginning of 1917 the security forces themselves could no longer be depended upon. In February, food riots were followed by mutiny. The autocracy was suddenly seen to be powerless. A provisional government of liberals and socialists was formed and the Tsar abdicated. The new government faltered and failed, in the main because it was attempting the impossible, the continuation of the war. Russians wanted peace and bread, as Lenin (who had by now been helped by the Germans to return to Russia from exile) saw. His determination and readiness to take power by force from the moderate provisional government was the second reason for its failure. Presiding over a disintegrating country, administration, and army, still facing the unsolved problems of privation in the cities, the provisional government was itself swept away in a second change, the *coup* called the October Revolution which, together with the American entry into the war, marks 1917 as a fault-line of European history. Previously, Europe had settled its own affairs; now the United States would be bound to have a large say in its future and in Russia there had come into being a state committed by the beliefs of its founders to the Marxist goal of destruction of the whole pre-war European order, a truly and consciously revolutionary centre for world politics. It was something which pre-war socialists had never dreamed of.

The immediate and obvious consequence of the establishment of the new Russia (the Union of Soviet and Socialist Republics or USSR, as it was to be called from 1923), was a new strategic situation. The Bolsheviks consolidated their success by dissolving (since they did not control) the only freely-elected representative body based on universal suffrage Russia ever had until 1990, and by winning the peasants' support with promises of land and peace. This was essential if they were to survive; the backbone of the party which now strove to assert its authority over Russia was the small industrial working class of a few cities. Peace negotiations began, but at first the terms demanded by the Germans were thought so objectionable that the Russians withdrew; they then had to accept a much more punitive outcome. In March 1918, the Treaty of Brest-Litovsk imposed severe losses of territory, but gave the new order the peace and time it desperately needed to tackle its internal troubles.

The Allies were furious. They saw the Bolsheviks' action as a treacherous defection. Nor was their attitude towards the new regime softened by the revolutionary propaganda it directed towards their citizens. The Russian leaders expected a working-class revolution in the advanced capitalist countries. This gave an extra dimension to a series of military 'interventions' in Russia by the Allies which began in August 1918 with British landings at Archangelsk and Japanese advances in Siberia. Their original purpose was strategic, in that they hoped to stop the Germans exploiting the advantage of being able to close down their eastern front, but they were quickly interpreted by many people in the capitalist countries and by all Bolsheviks as anti-communist crusades. Worse still, they became entangled in the civil war which was harshly testing the new regime. Even without the doctrinal filter of Marxist theory through which Lenin and his colleagues saw the world, these episodes would have been likely to sour relations between the new Russia and her former allies for a long time; in Marxist terms they seemed a confirmation of an essential, unpredictable and ineradicable hostility. Their recollection long dogged Soviet attitudes. They also helped to justify the Russian revolution's turn backward into authoritarian government. Fear of the invader as restorer of the old order and patron of the landlords combined with Russian traditions of autocracy and police terrorism to stifle any possible liberalization of the regime.

Revolution and strategy

The Bolsheviks' conviction that revolution was about to occur elsewhere in Europe was in one sense correct, yet crucially wrong. In the war's last year, Europe's revolutionary potential indeed became plain, but in national, not social, forms. The Allies were provoked (in part by the Bolsheviks) to a revolutionary strategy of their own. The military situation looked bleak for them at the end of 1917. It was obvious that they would face a German attack in France in the spring and would do so without a Russian ally to draw off their enemies. It would be a long time, too, before American troops arrived in numbers to help them in France. In these circumstances, an appeal to the subversive potential of the nationalities of the Austro-Hungarian empire looked attractive; revolution was to be part of Allied strategy, too. This had the additional advantage of further emphasizing in American eyes the ideological respectability of the Allied cause now that it was no longer tied to tsardom. Accordingly, in 1918, propaganda was directed at the Austro-Hungarian armies and patronage was given to Czech and South Slav dissidents in exile. As a result, the Dual Monarchy was dissolving under the combined effects of reawakened national sentiment and a Balkan campaign which at last began to provide allied victories, already before Germany gave in. This was the second great revolution in the old Europe. The political structure of the whole area bounded by the Urals, the Baltic and the Danube valley was now put in question as it had not been for centuries. There was even a national Polish army again, patronized by the Germans as a weapon against Russia, while the American president announced that an independent Poland was an essential of Allied peacemaking. All the political certainties of the eastern and central Europe of 1914 seemed to be in the melting-pot.

The Ottoman collapse

Also already subject to question was the future of the Ottoman empire. Its rulers had entered the war because of Young Turk optimism, the Germans' long cultivation of military and diplomatic influence at Constantinople and the unplanned arrival of a couple of German warships in the Straits in September 1914. The Allies had declared war on the Ottoman government a few weeks later, after those vessels had bombarded Russian ports. Once Great Britain was committed to war, the last remnants of her historic support for the Ottomans against Russia evaporated. Turning their backs on nearly a century and a half of diplomacy, the British and French had joined in secret agreements with Russia that she should have Constantinople at the peace. Other harsh consequences for the Ottoman empire followed. Though French preoccupations over Egypt had diminished with the making of the *Entente* and successes in Morocco, French patriots liked to recall the tradition of a special French role in the Levant. The evocations of St Louis and the crusaders with which some enthusiasts fondly toyed did not matter much but French governments had, undeniably, exercised for a century or so a special protection of Roman Catholicism in the Ottoman lands, especially Syria (to which Napoleon III had sent an army in 1860) which excited some Frenchmen and gave diplomatic leverage. The cultural presence evinced by a wide use of the French language in the Levant, and a large investment of French capital were also matters not to be overlooked.

In 1914, though, Turkey's main military antagonists outside Europe were likely to be Russia in the Caucausus, and Great Britain in the Sinai desert. It rapidly became clear that the Suez Canal was not threatened by Ottoman armies. But events soon followed which indicated that other, and new, factors were entering the equations. They implied revolution for the whole Near East. At the end of 1914 an Indian-British army landed at Basra to safeguard oil supplies from Persia (the Royal Navy's new ships were now all being built with oil-fuel engines), the beginning of an interplay of oil and politics in the historical destiny of this area whose full implications would not appear until well after the Ottoman empire had ceased to exist. Another new factor was the British decision to exploit Arab nationalism, or what might pass for it.

The attraction of striking a blow against Germany's ally became all the greater as fighting went on bloodily but indecisively in Europe. The attempt in 1915 to force the Dardanelles by combined naval and land operations, in the hope of taking Constantinople and opening a new route to Russia, bogged down. There was a limit to what could be offered to win Arab allies but agreement was reached with Hussein, sherif of Mecca, at the beginning of 1916. The French had to be consulted, because of their interest in Syria. When an agreement was made between the British and French on spheres of influence in a partitioned Ottoman empire it left many questions still unsettled for the future, including the status of Iraq, but that there should be an Arab national state after victory was now agreed by both allies. An Arab nationalist political programme had become a reality.

The success of that undertaking, though, was soon in doubt. The Arab revolt was never more than a distraction from the main theatres of war, though it prospered and became a legend. Soon the British felt they must recognize Hussein as king of the Hejaz. British and imperial troops pressed forwards in 1917 into Palestine, taking Jerusalem. In 1918 they were to enter Damascus together with the Arabs. Before this, though, came the American entry into the war; in a statement of war aims President Wilson said he favoured 'an absolute unmolested opportunity of autonomous development' for the non-Turks of the Ottoman empire[3]. Another embarrassment was

---

[3]   See the 'Fourteen Points', no. xii, e.g. in *Speeches and Documents in American History*, IV. 1914–39, ed. R. Birley (Oxford, 1942), p. 41.

the Bolshevik publication of Russian records of their predecessors' secret diplomacy and its revelation of Anglo-French proposals for spheres of influence in the Middle East.

One part of these had been agreement that Palestine should be administered internationally. Another irritant to Arab feeling was added when it was announced that British policy favoured the establishment of a national home in Palestine for the Jewish people. The 'Balfour Declaration' of November 1917 can be accounted the greatest success of Zionism down to this time. It was not strictly incompatible with what had been said to the Arabs, but it was hard for Arabs to see that. The American president joined in the good work of muddying the waters by introducing qualifications to protect the non-Jewish Palestinians. The nature of what would replace Ottoman rule was very confused and uncertain as the war came to an end. What was certain was that, once again, the 'Eastern Question' had a new shape.

The end of the first German war

The crucial battles in the west were fought against this increasingly revolutionary background. By the summer, the Allies had managed to halt the last great German offensive. It had made huge gains, but not enough. When the Allied armies began to move forward victoriously in their turn, and the German army to crumble, the German leaders sought an end; they too thought they saw signs of revolution, and at home. When the Kaiser abdicated, the third of the dynastic empires had fallen; the Habsburgs had already gone, but the Hohenzollerns had only just outlasted their old rivals. A new German government requested an armistice; it was rapidly granted and the fighting came to an end.

The cost of the Great War has never been exactly computed. Its scale, though, is clear enough: about 10,000,000 men had died as a result of direct military action. As for disease, typhus probably killed another 1,000,000 in the Balkans alone. Many of these died in Serbia, the country over which, ostensibly, Europe had gone to war and which suffered the highest proportionate loss of any participant – a quarter of her 1914 population. Nor do even these horrible figures indicate the physical cost in maiming, blinding, the loss to families of fathers and husbands, of their children and their children's sweethearts, the spiritual havoc in the destruction of ideals, confidence and goodwill. Europeans looked at their huge cemeteries and hospitals, and were appalled. The economic damage was immense, too. Over much of Europe people were starving. A year after the war manufacturing output was still nearly a quarter below that of 1914; Russia's was only a fifth of what it had then been. Railway or river transport was in some countries almost impossible to procure. The complicated, fragile machinery of international exchange was smashed and some of it could never be replaced. At the centre of this chaos lay, exhausted, a Germany which had been the economic dynamo of Europe. 'We are at the dead season of our fortunes', wrote a young British economist who attended the peace conference. 'Our power of feeling or caring beyond the immediate questions of our own material well-being is temporarily eclipsed ... We have been moved beyond endurance, and need rest. Never in the lifetime of men now living has the universal element in the soul of man burnt so dimly'[4].

---

[4] J.M. Keynes, *The Economic Consequences of the Peace* (London, 1919), p. 278.

The peace settlements

Delegates to the Peace Conference were already assembling in Paris by the end of 1918. Their failures were to be great and manifest, but perspective and the recognition of the magnitude of the tasks facing them should impose a certain respect for what they did. It was the greatest settlement since 1815 and presented huge challenges. It had to reconcile great expectations with stubborn facts. The power to make the crucial decisions was remarkably concentrated: the British and French prime ministers and the American president dominated the negotiations. These were between the victors; the defeated Germans were subsequently presented with their terms. In the diverging interests of France, aware above all of the appalling danger of any third repetition of German aggression, and of the Anglo-Saxon nations, conscious of standing in no such peril, lay a central problem of European security, but many others surrounded and obscured it. Not least, the peace settlement had to be a world settlement. It not only dealt with territories outside Europe – as earlier great settlements had done – but many non-European voices were heard in its making. Seventeen of the twenty-seven states whose representatives signed the main treaty lay in other continents. The United States was the greatest of these; with Japan, Great Britain, France and Italy she formed the group described as the 'principal' victorious powers. For a world settlement, nevertheless, it was ominous that no representative attended from Russia, the only great power with both European and Asian land frontiers.

Technically, the peace settlement consisted of a group of distinct treaties made not only with Germany, but with Bulgaria, Ottoman Turkey and the 'succession states' which replaced the Dual Monarchy. Of these a resurrected Poland, an enlarged Serbia and an entirely new Czechoslovakia were present at the conference as allies, while a much reduced Hungary and the Germanic heart of old Austria were treated as defeated enemies. All of this posed difficult problems. But the main concern of the Peace Conference was the settlement with Germany embodied in the Treaty of Versailles and signed in June 1919.

The Versailles treaty was deliberately punitive. It also explicitly stated that the Germans were responsible for the outbreak of war. This was to be a misleading and unfortunate conjunction, for the harshest terms actually arose not from any presumption of moral guilt but from the French wish, if possible, so to tie Germany down that any third war between the two countries would be impossible. Boundaries were re-drawn not only to redress the injustice of 1871, but in order to weaken the defeated. This was also the purpose of economic reparation, the payments which, it was stipulated, Germany was to make to the allies for years. Reparations were the most ill-considered part of the settlement, economic nonsense which angered Germans and made their acceptance of defeat even harder, because of the personal economic hardship they brought. Nor was it likely that arrangements could be made to ensure that Germany might not one day try to reverse the decision by force of arms, if the victorious powers were not to maintain a long occupation. The armistice had been granted too swiftly for the Germans to feel the reality of military defeat in fighting on German soil and the evident destruction of their army. Germany's territorial losses, it went without saying, included Alsace and Lorraine, but were otherwise greatest in the east (to Poland); in the west the French did not get much more reassurance than an undertaking that the German bank of the Rhine should be 'demilitarized', and temporary allied occupation of certain zones. They did not feel it was enough.

THE END OF THE GREAT WAR AND THE PEACE SETTLEMENTS

1918	Mar 3	German-Soviet treaty of Brest-Litovsk.
	Apr 10	Congress of Austrian subject peoples in Rome.
	May 7	German-Romanian treaty of Bucharest.
	June–Sept	Allies recognize independence of Czechoslovakia.
	Sept 30	Allies grant armistice to Bulgaria.
	Oct 29	Yugoslav independence proclaimed.
	Oct 30	Allies grant armistice to Ottoman empire.
	Nov 3	Armistice between Allies and Austria-Hungary.
	Nov 9	German republic proclaimed.
	Nov 10	Romania re-enters war on Allied side.
	Nov 11	30-day Armistice ends fighting on the western front.
	Nov 13	Austrian republic proclaimed.
	Nov 16	Hungarian republic proclaimed.
1919	Jan 18	Peace Conference opens at Paris.
	June 28	Signature of Treaty of Versailles with Germany.
	Sept 10	Treaty of St Germain with Austrian republic.
	Nov 27	Treaty of Neuilly with Bulgaria.
1920	June 4	Treaty of Trianon with Hungary.
	Aug 10	Treaty of Sèvres with Ottoman monarchy.
1921	Mar 16	Kemalist government of Turkey makes treaty with USSR.
1923	July 24	Treaty of Lausanne and final peace terms between new Turkish government and allied powers.

The second leading characteristic of the peace was its acceptance of the principles of self-determination and nationality. Sometimes this simply meant recognizing existing facts; Polish and Czechoslovak governments already existed before the peace conference met, and the future Yugoslavia was built round the core of pre-war Serbia and Montenegro. By the end of 1918, these principles had already triumphed throughout much of the area of the old Dual Monarchy (and were soon to do so also in the former Baltic provinces of Russia). After outlasting even the Holy Roman Empire, the Habsburgs were gone; their successor states, though not uninterruptedly, were to survive them for most of the century.

Unfortunately, nationality was not always helpful, though the principle of self-determination allowed certain zones to settle their destiny by plebiscite. Geographical, historical, cultural and economic realities cut across the national idea. When it prevailed over them – as in the destruction of the Danube's economic unity – the results could be bad; when it did not, they could be just as bad because of the aggrieved feelings left behind. Eastern and central Europe were studded with minorities embedded resentfully in states to which they felt no allegiance. A third of Poland's population did not speak Polish; more than a third of Czechoslovakia's consisted of Poles, Russians, Germans, Magyars and Ruthenes; an enlarged Romania now contained over a 1,000,000 Hungarians. In some places, the infringement of the principle was felt with especial acuteness as an injustice. Germans resented the existence of a 'corridor' across old German lands to connect Poland with the Baltic, Italy was disappointed of Adriatic spoils promised by her allies when they had needed her help, and the Irish had still not got Home Rule after all.

There was another important innovation in dealing with former German colonies. Old-fashioned colonialism was not acceptable to the United States; instead, tutelage for non-European peoples formerly under German or Ottoman rule was provided by the device of trusteeship. 'Mandates' were given to the victorious powers (the United States declined any) to administer those territories while they were prepared for self-government. The mandate system was one of the better ideas to emerge from the settlement, even though it was in some instances used to drape with respectability the last extensions of European imperialism. This happened most obviously in former Ottoman lands. Mandates in Syria, the Lebanon, Palestine and Iraq settled the fate (for a time) of millions of Arabs caught in the contradictions of French and British policy. After the awakening of the political ambitions of Arab subjects of the Ottomans, the Balfour Declaration had increased these complexities, and the uncertainties of many Arabs – notably the Palestinians – but for the moment the problems they posed were left to the mandatory powers.

The League of Nations and Europe

From Paris there also emerged the institutionalizing of a great creative idea and the most imaginative of the settlement: a League of Nations. It owed much to the enthusiasm of Woodrow Wilson, who ensured the League's Covenant – its constitution – pride of place as the first part of the Treaty of Versailles. The name was significant; it was a further registration of the nationalist principle as a foundation of world order. The League transcended Europe; it is another sign of a new age that twenty-six of its original forty-two members were non-European countries. Unfortunately, the United States was not among them, and this was the most fatal of the League's several grave weaknesses. Perhaps, though, it never could have met all the expectations it aroused.

Another absentee from the League was the new Russia. She, too, had been unrepresented at the peace conference, and hers may have been an even more important absence than the American. The political arrangements shaping the next stage of European history were entered into without consulting Soviet opinion, though in eastern Europe they required the drawing of boundaries in which any Russian government was bound to be vitally interested. It was true that the Bolshevik leaders did all they could to provide reasons for their own exclusion. They envenomed their relations with the major powers by revolutionary propaganda, for they were convinced that the capitalist countries were determined to overthrow them. The British prime minister, Lloyd George, and Wilson were in fact more flexible – even sympathetic – than many of their colleagues and electors in dealing with the new state. The French prime minister Clemenceau, on the other hand, was passionately anti-Bolshevik and had the support of many French investors in being so (Versailles was the first great European peace to be made by statesmen continually aware of the dangers of disappointing democratic electorates). But however the responsibility is allocated, the outcome was that the European power which had, potentially, the greatest weight of all in the affairs of the new continent, was not consulted in the making of a new Europe. Though for the time

LOSERS OF 1919-23
- Territories passing to states existing before 1914
- Territories subject to plebicites
- International boundaries 1914
- International boundaries 1921

being weak, the USSR would join the ranks of the dissatisfied who wished to revise the settlement or overthrow it, under rulers who detested and renounced the social system that settlement was meant to protect.

Huge hopes had been entertained of the peace. They were often unrealistic, yet in spite of its manifest failures, the settlement had its good points. When it failed, it was sometimes for reasons which were beyond the control of the men who made it. In the first place, the days of a European world hegemony in the narrowest political sense had been ended by the Great War. The peace makers of 1919 could effect little beyond Europe, except in the former Ottoman territories, and there only for a few decades. The old imperial policemen had now either disappeared or were too weakened to do their job inside it, let alone outside. The United States had been needed to ensure Germany's defeat but now she was about to immerse herself in a period of unrealistic isolation. Nor did Bolshevik Russia ever wish to help stabilize Europe. The withdrawal upon itself of the one power and the sterilization of the other by ideology left the continent to its own inadequate devices. When no revolution broke out in Europe, the Soviet leaders turned in on themselves; when Americans were given the chance by Wilson to be involved in Europe's peace-keeping, they refused it. Both decisions are comprehensible, but their effect was to preserve an illusion. European statesmen for the most part presumed an autonomy in running their affairs which was no longer a reality and could no longer be an adequate framework for handling its problems.

The settlement's gravest immediate weakness lay in the economic fragility of the new structures it presupposed. The complex but remarkably efficient economic system of 1914 had been irreparably damaged. Post-war international exchange was hampered by a huge increase of restrictions as new nations strove to protect their infant economies with tariffs and exchange control, and bigger and older nations tried to repair their shattered and enfeebled ones. Inflation swept away healthy currencies. The Versailles treaty made things worse by saddling Germany, the most important of all the European industrial states, with an indefinite burden of reparation in kind and in cash. This not only distorted her economy and delayed its recovery for years, but also took away much of the incentive to make it work, while adding to the problems presented by an appalling inflation. To the east, Germany's greatest potential market, Russia, was almost entirely cut off behind a frontier which little trade could penetrate; the Danube valley and the Balkans, another great area of German enterprise, was divided and impoverished. These difficulties were to be gradually overcome by the availability of American money, which Americans were willing to lend (though they would not take European goods for it, and retired behind their tariff walls). But this brought about a dangerous dependence on the continued prosperity of the United States.

Self-determination had the disadvantage that it often made nonsense of economics. But it is difficult to see on what grounds self-determination could have been set aside. Allied victory and the rhetoric of peace-making made many think that there had been a great triumph of liberalism and democracy. Four autocratic or undemocratic, antinational illiberal empires had collapsed, and to this day the peace settlement retains the distinction of being the only one in history made by great powers all of which were democracies. Liberal optimism also drew strength from the ostentatious purity of Wilson; he had done all he could to make it clear that he saw the participation of the United States as essentially different in kind from that of the Allies, being inspired (he irksomely reiterated) by high-minded ideals and a belief that the world could be made safe for democracy if other nations would give up their bad old ways. Some thought that he had been shown to be right; new states (above all the new Germany) adopted liberal, parliamentary constitutions and often republican ones, too. Finally, there was the illusion of the League; the dream of a new international authority which was not an empire seemed at last a reality.

All this was rooted in fallacy and false premise. Principles had been much muddied in practice. Peace-making had left much unsatisfied nationalism about; in Germany it had created new and fierce nationalist resentment. Perhaps this could not be helped, but it was soil in which things other than liberalism could grow. Further, the democratic institutions of the new states – and the old ones, too for that matter – were being launched on a world where poverty, hardship and unemployment exacerbated political struggle and in many places were made worse by the special dislocations produced by the worship of national sovereignty. The crumbling of old economic patterns of exchange in the war made it much more difficult to deal with problems like peasant poverty and unemployment within states; Russia, once the granary of much of Europe, was now inaccessible to it economically. This was a background which revolutionaries could, and would, try to exploit.

Their opportunities were all the greater because so many countries nursed ambitions to revise the peace treaties, or at least contained important minorities wishing to do so. Many Italians saw the new Yugoslavia as a barrier to the realization of satisfying old dreams of Adriatic and Balkan expansion, and others had hoped for formerly Turkish territory in Asia Minor. The Greeks had similar hopes. Lithuanians and Poles quarrelled over their claims to Vilna. A plebiscitary solution to Polish and German claims to Silesia gave more time for hatreds and passions to mount there before a settlement was arrived at which neither side thought satisfactory. Hungarians bitterly resented their huge losses of territory from the ancient kingdom. To make matters worse, over the countries of eastern and central Europe there hung, also, the shadow of the new Russia.

Revolution and the new Russia

'Bolshevism', as the revolutionary creed proclaimed by the new Russian state created by the October revolution of 1917 was often called, appeared as a double threat to many Europeans in the post-war years. Every European country soon found it had a revolutionary communist party proclaiming loyalty to the international cause of the working-class, and the leadership provided for it in Moscow. The communists effected little that was positive, but caused great alarm. They also did much to prevent the emergence of strong progressive political forces. The circumstances of their birth decided this. A Third International, the 'Comintern', was set up by the Bolshevik leaders in Moscow in March 1919 to provide leadership for the international socialist movement which might otherwise, they feared, rally again to the former leaders whose lack of revolutionary zeal they blamed for a failure to exploit the opportunities of the war. Lenin's test of socialist movements was adherence to the Comintern; its policies were deliberately rigid, disciplined and uncompromising, in accordance with his view of the needs of an effective revolutionary party. In almost every European country this divided socialists into two camps which competed for working-class support, thus gravely weakening the Left in most countries. Some adhered to the Comintern and usually took the name communist; others, even when claiming still to be Marxists, remained in the rump national parties and trades unions which emerged from schisms and splits. The most conspicuous among the latter were the German Social Democrats and the French Socialists.

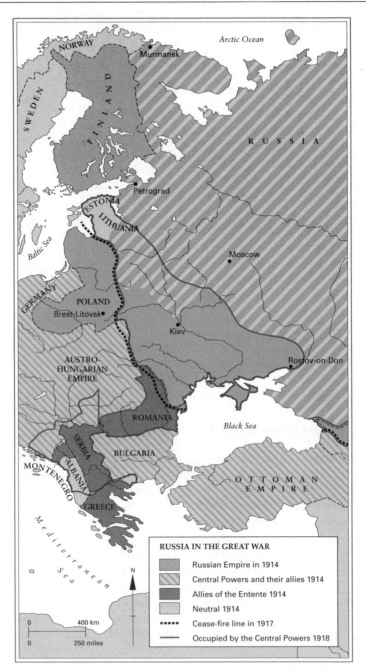

Many Europeans nonetheless found even moderate socialism alarming, for there seemed to be plenty of revolutionary possibilities to exploit in the wake of the war. A Bolshevik government actually took power for a short time in Hungary, but more startling, perhaps, were a scatter of attempted communist risings in Germany, some briefly successful. Ironically, even before the founding of the Comintern, this forced back the socialist-dominated government of the new German republic which had emerged in the aftermath of defeat to reliance upon conservative forces – notably the professional soldiers of the old army – in order to avert revolution. It gave a special bitterness to the divisions of the Left in Germany. But everywhere, communist policy made united resistance to conservatism more difficult, frightening moderates with revolutionary rhetoric and conspiracy.

The deliberate division of international socialists, and the new Soviet-inspired ideological alienation of some of them from constitutional government – and, indeed, from any government which appeared to uphold a capitalist economic regime – split Europeans culturally and politically as they had not been since the Reformation. The fact that the committed communists were often a minority was to be masked for many years by the skills of manoeuvre they showed in taking leadership of the Left in country after country. They were, in an 'objective' sense (as Marxist terminology had it), agents of a foreign power, for they owed allegiance to what was now, at least ideologically, one half of a divided world – to which Europe did not belong. Europe once again, in fact, had a new boundary to the east. The old question about whether Russia was European or not, was now to be answered in a new way, for the USSR emphatically claimed that, in the most important respects, she was not.

That this was by no means always clear was because it was never easy to distinguish communist from traditionally Russian themes in the conduct of Soviet foreign policy. This was especially true in the east. The tendency of its neighbours after 1918 had been to fear a combined social and national threat from the new Russia. In the long run, international communist aims were used and manipulated by the Bolsheviks to serve national Russian interests in a rational and justifiable way, given the assumption that the future of world revolution depended upon the preservation of the first socialist state as the citadel of the international working class. In the early years of civil war and slow consolidation of Bolshevik power throughout the country, that belief led to the deliberate incitement of disaffection abroad in order to preoccupy capitalist governments. But in eastern and central Europe there was more to it than this, because the actual territorial outcome over much of the area was in doubt long after the Versailles treaty. The First World War did not end there until in March 1921 a peace treaty between Russia and the new Polish Republic defined frontiers which were to last until 1939. Poland was the most anti-Russian by tradition, the most anti-Bolshevik by religion, as well as the largest and most ambitious of Europe's 'new' eastern nations. But all of them would feel threatened by any recovery of Russian power, all the more when tied to social revolution as the Bolsheviks now proclaimed. Fears aroused by this connexion helped to turn many of these states before 1939 to dictatorial or military governments with a strong anti-communist line.

Fear of communist revolution in eastern and central Europe was most evident in the immediate post-war years of economic collapse and uncertainty about the outcome of the Polish-Soviet war (at one time, Warsaw itself appeared threatened). After 1921, with peace at last and, symbolically, the establishment of orderly official relations between Russia and Great Britain, the first west European state to seek them, there was a noticeable relaxation. This owed something to the Soviet leadership's own sense of emerging from a period of acute danger in civil war. It did not produce much in the way of better diplomatic manners, and revolutionary propaganda and denunciation of capitalist countries did not cease, but the Bolsheviks could now turn to the rebuilding of their own shattered land. In 1921 Russian pig-iron production was about one-fifth of its 1913 level, that of coal a tiny three per cent or so, while the railways had less than half as many locomotives in service as at the start of the war. Livestock had declined by over a quarter and cereal deliveries were less than two-fifths of those of 1916. On this impoverished economy there fell in 1921 a drought in south Russia. More than 2,000,000 died in the subsequent famine; even cannibalism was reported. Liberalization of the economy brought about a turnround. By 1927 both industrial and agricultural production were nearly back to pre-war levels.

The regime in these years experienced some uncertainty in its leadership. It had already been apparent before Lenin died in 1924, but the removal of a man whose acknowledged ascendancy had appeared to keep forces within it in balance opened a period of evolution and explicit and implicit debate. No leading Soviet Bolshevik questioned the centralized, autocratic nature of the regime. None of them considered that political liberation was conceivable or that the use of secret police and the party dictatorship could be dispensed with in a world of hostile capitalist states. But they could disagree about economic policy and tactics. Personal rivalry sometimes gave great edge to this.

Broadly speaking, two viewpoints emerged about the route the USSR might take to modernization and communism. One emphasized that the revolution depended on the goodwill of the mass of the peasants. They had first been allowed to take over the land (because they could not be prevented doing so, and Bolshevik acceptance of this had won their support for the revolution), then antagonized by attempts to feed the cities at their expense, then conciliated again by the liberalization of the economy and what was known as 'NEP', a 'New Economic Policy' which Lenin had approved as expedient. Under it, peasants had been allowed to make profits for themselves; they therefore began to grow more food and to sell it to the cities. The other viewpoint accepted the same facts but set them in a longer perspective. To conciliate the peasants would slow down industrialization, which the Soviet Union needed to survive in a hostile world. The party's proper course, argued those who took this view, was to rely upon the revolutionary militants of the cities; it should exploit the still non-Bolshevized peasants in the interest of the industrial proletariat while pressing on with economic development and the promotion of revolution abroad. The communist leader Trotsky took this view. These were alternative routes to modernization.

The story can conveniently be pursued a little further. Roughly speaking, Trotsky was shouldered aside, but his view prevailed. From the intricate politics of the party there emerged eventually the ascendancy of a member of its bureaucracy, Joseph Stalin, a man far less attractive intellectually than either Lenin or Trotsky, equally ruthless, even more personally unpleasant, and of greater historical importance. As Commissar of Nationalities, Commissar of the Workers' and Peasants' Inspectorate, member of the Politburo and, finally, general secretary of the Communist Party of the Soviet Union, he had radically but silently armed himself with a power which he used against former colleagues and old Bolsheviks as willingly as against his enemies. Two years after the end of the civil war, it has been said, Soviet society lived under his 'virtual rule, without being aware of the ruler's name'[5]. It was to become the most famous name in the Soviet Union.

Stalin, it may be said, finally carried out revolution to which the Bolshevik seizure

---

[5] I. Deutscher, *Stalin*, 2nd. edn. (Oxford, 1966), p. 228.

of power had opened the way and created a new Soviet élite in the process. For him a drive to industrialize was paramount. The road to it lay through finding a way of forcing the peasant to pay for it by supplying the grain he would eat if not offered a good profit. Two 'Five Year Plans' carried out an industrialization programme from 1928 onwards, and their basis was the collectivization of agriculture.

At last, the Party conquered the countryside. In what was in all but name a new civil war millions of peasants were killed or transported and grain levies brought back famine. But the towns were fed, though consumption was held down as far as possible, and there was a fall in real wages. It was more significant that by 1937 80 per cent of Soviet industrial output came from plant built since 1928. The price in suffering of making the Union a great power was enormous. Collectivization was only made possible by brutality on a scale far greater than that of the tsars; Stalin presided over a state machine far more effective and totalitarian than the old autocracy had been. He was a somewhat paradoxical claimant to Marxist orthodoxy, which taught that the economic structure of society determined its politics. Stalin precisely inverted this, he demonstrated that if the will to use political power was there, the economic substructure could be revolutionized by force. Although a Georgian, Stalin is perhaps best understood as that very Russian figure, the autocratic tsar, an Ivan the Terrible or Peter the Great, rather than an ideologue. Yet critics of liberal capitalist society in other countries often held up Soviet Russia, of which they had a very rosy picture, as an example of the way in which a society might achieve progress and a revitalization of its cultural and ethical life. The establishment of the USSR and the dividing of Europe in a new way was in fact the preliminary to a new ideological division of the world, which was to remain for seventy years part of the context in which Europe had to work out its fate. The single civilized world of 1914, with its shared assumptions at many levels, and seemingly irresistible progressive tendency to spread the pursuit of the same goals, had gone.

It may appear that it was in this way that the Russian revolution should be reckoned to have left its deepest mark on the age and here that its largest significance lies. It created a citadel and chief place of arms (as well as providing many of the leaders and general staff) for world revolution. That there should be such a centre at all was a new fact in world history. Another new fact at that level was the provision by the USSR of a mythology to sustain the process of modernization and industrialization in other backward societies as an alternative to the other available, that of liberal, capitalist society (both, of course, were European products).

This was one of the reasons why European history was becoming more difficult to separate from world history. The Russian revolution affected Europe indirectly through its effects in other parts of the world, as well as directly through the new shape and context it gave to purely European politics. It left very few existing political forces unaffected and every European country was in some degree changed by the quarrels and fears it aroused. In Europe's international relations, it was only a small change that Russian foreign policy lost, for a time, its old pan-Slavist and vestigially religious overtones; within Europe's power relationships, though, the Russian revolution may well have delayed other changes which would have been likely to come about more quickly without revolution. The potential of imperial Russia was such that had she escaped defeat and been among the victorious allies of 1918, with their old rival Austria-Hungary in a state of disintegration and Germany disarmed, she would then at once have assumed the continental predominance which the USSR was to display only in 1945.

It had been hinted at, after all, already in the pre-industrial era of the Holy Alliance. It may be (to take speculation just a little further still) that the failure of the Dardanelles campaign cost Russia a quarter-century of exclusion from the European role it might have expected to play, for failure to overcome isolation from the Allies' material support accelerated the military and economic defeat which made possible the Bolshevik seizure of power. Undoubtedly, too, the revolution slowed down Russia's recovery from the damage done by war to its economy by closing the USSR to foreign investment and so delaying the onset of rapid industrialization until the 1930s. Stalin then put the country back on the road to it with more ruthless energy than the tsarist regime had ever shown, but even by 1941, though, it is hard to be sure whether the Soviet Union could have survived the German onslaught single-handed. Certainly there is no indisputable evidence that Soviet development had made that possible, or that another regime could not have done so more rapidly.

Locarno

In 1922 the German and Russian governments surprised Europe by suddenly coming to an agreement with one another at Rapallo to exchange ambassadors and to co-operate in some economic matters. This registered the natural interest of both powers in revisionism; each was registering its emergence from diplomatic isolation. The sensation in other countries was immense, especially in France. Meanwhile, Great Britain and France had drifted apart over French efforts to enforce economic reparation rigorously on Germany, which reached their climax in 1923 with a Franco-Belgian military occupation of the Ruhr, and the virtual closing-down of Germany's greatest industrial region.

This was the worst moment of the early post-war years. The Ruhr occupation, though, did not give France what she wanted, and soon French financial stability, too, was endangered. A change of government in France led to a gradual rapprochement with Germany and American financial action to ease the reparation problem. A new flow of American investment to Germany began. Statesmen began to talk of 'appeasement' of Germany, and 'reconciliation' with her and by a series of gradual steps the way was opened to agreements made at Locarno at the end of 1925 which ended the distinction of 'enemy' and 'allied' powers and reconciled France and Germany – formally – in guarantees of the frontiers of France and Belgium with Germany against attack from either side. Significantly, nothing was said about Germany's eastern frontiers. When Germany was admitted to the League of Nations in the following year, it seemed that the way was open at last to the new world of peace, optimism and prosperity which western Europe had dreamed of in 1918 and which had proved so hard to achieve. It was one of the last illusions of the inter-war years to take shape.

CHAPTER FOUR Crumbling foundations

Attitudes and ideas

The Great War fell on cultures already undergoing profound change. It is hard to speak confidently or precisely about them. It is obvious, nonetheless, that the declining years of European world hegemony were accompanied by the questioning and qualifying within Europe of established ideas and values as never before. A connexion is hard to establish, but the presumption that there was one also seems hard to argue away. The trend seems to accelerate after 1918; as old systems of thought and old values were increasingly undermined, new claimants for adherence and intellectual acceptance appeared. Scepticism about the past grew refusal to admit the possibility of absolute standards at all.

For all the difficulty of distinguishing between the explicit utterances of intellectuals and educated minorities on the one hand, and attitudes and behaviour of society at large, signs of what was to come were already apparent before 1914. Disintegrating forces were already at work within the intellectual and liberal culture which was the product of the high civilization of the European age. Even in the nineteenth century there were those troubled by a sense that the traditional culture was too limited because of its exclusion of the resources of emotion and experience which lay in the unconscious. One man, more than any other, had at the beginning of this century begun to set out a language in which to explore this area and to promote confidence that it was there that the key to much of life lay: Sigmund Freud, the founder of psychoanalysis. He deserves a place in the history of culture beside Newton or Darwin not because he was of their intellectual stature or because of the difference he made to science, but because, more than any other person, he changed the way educated people thought of themselves. He provided a new cultural mythology, a way of understanding and an idiom in which to express it. Several of his ideas quickly made their way into ordinary discourse: the special meanings we now give to the words 'complex', 'unconscious' and 'obsession', and the familiar terms 'Freudian slip' and 'libido' speak for his achievement. His influence quickly spread into literature, personal relations, education, politics. What he said was often distorted. What he was believed to have said was vastly more important than his specific clinical studies.

Like the impact of Newton and Darwin, Freud's went beyond science, where his influence was more questionable than theirs. Like them he offered a new vision, and like those of Marx and Darwin, it was to prove highly corrosive. The message taken by laymen from his teaching was that the unconscious was the real source of much behaviour, that moral values and attitudes were projections of the influences which had moulded this unconscious, that, therefore, the idea of responsibility was at best a myth and probably a dangerous one, and that perhaps rationality itself was an illusion. It did not matter much that Freud's own assertions would have been nonsense had this been true or that this left out many of his qualifications. This was what many people believed he had proved, and some still believe. Such ideas called in question the very foundation of liberal civilization, the idea of the rational, responsible, consciously motivated individual. It was another sort of determinism.

Moreover, he appeared also to say that much previously thought good was, in fact, bad. Conscience (by whatever name you might call it) had always been thought of as a fundamentally good force, regulating and checking not only conscious wickedness, but evil impulse; now people were asked to confront the idea that self-control might be a source of danger to mental health. We need not exaggerate. Freud's teaching was not the only intellectual force contributing to the loss of certainty and the sense that men had little firm ground beneath their feet[1]. But along with Marxism it was the most obvious in the interwar period. From grappling with the insights he brought, or with the chaos of the arts and the feebleness of twentieth-century Christianity, or with the incomprehensibility of a world of science which, as the name of Einstein became famous, seemed suddenly to have abandoned Laplace and Newton, men plunged all the more worriedly into the search for new bearings. Politically, this led many to new irrationalisms, or more violent statements of older ones (such as nationalism); there was little excitement about tolerance, democracy, and the old freedoms set up to protect the exercise of the rational will of the individual. Or so, at least, the conscious intellectual life of Europe seemed to indicate.

The arts, too, offered obvious symptoms of fundamental cultural change. For three or four centuries, since the age of humanism, Europeans had believed that they expressed aspirations, insights and pleasures accessible in principle to ordinary men, even though they might be raised to such an exceptional degree of fineness in execution, or be so especially concentrated in form that sometimes only educated men could enjoy them. But it had always been thought possible for the whole of that time that a cultivated man, given time and study, could discriminate with taste among the arts of his time because they were expressions of a shared culture with shared standards. True, this idea was somewhat weakened when the nineteenth century, in the wake of the Romantic movement, had come to idealize the artist as genius – Beethoven was one of the first examples – and formulated the notion of the *avant-garde*. But far greater fragmentation of artistic culture was to follow. By the first decade of the twentieth century, it was already very difficult for even trained eyes and ears to recognize art in much of what was offered to them by contemporary artists, poets and musicians.

One instance of this was the dislocation of the image in painting. Here, the flight from the representational still kept a tenuous link with tradition as late as Cubism, but by then that link had long ceased to be apparent to the average 'cultivated man' – if he still existed. Artists retired into a less and less accessible chaos of private visions, whose

---

[1]   His fundamental publications had come before 1914; it was, though, only in 1923 that Freud published *The Ego and the Id*, a study which more obviously than any of his others promoted the psycho-analytic study of the moral life.

centre was reached after 1918 in Dada and Surrealism. The twentieth century had achieved new disintegration; in Surrealism even the notion of the objective disappeared, let alone its representation. Through chance, symbolism, shock, suggestion and violence many artists, writers and musicians sought to go beyond consciousness itself.

Art in the 1920s and 1930s showed that though many people still clung to old shibboleths, many in the élites which led thought and opinion found the old foundations no longer firm. People still regularly attended religious services – though only a minority, even in Roman Catholic countries – but the masses of the industrial cities lived in a post-Christian world in which the physical removal of the institutions and symbols of religion would have made little difference to their daily lives and in which a mass-entertainment industry had destroyed much of the structure of the traditional calendar with its festivals and commemorations. References long understood were becoming incomprehensible. Intellectuals faced perhaps an even greater problem than that of loss of religious belief, because many of the liberal ideas which had helped to displace Christianity since the eighteenth century were by now being displaced in their turn. In the 1920s and 1930s, sweeping changes could be sensed on every side. The liberal certainties of the autonomy of the individual, objective moral criteria, rationality, the authority of parents, and an explicable mechanical universe all seemed to be going under together.

The last age of formal empire

For a variety of reasons, some arising from causes similar to those sapping European confidence in cultural certainties, and others from evident and empirical facts, some Europeans also no longer felt so sure as their nineteenth-century predecessors about the foundations of Europe's world power. Liberal certainties and claims that their values were universal had long encouraged doubts about the right to rule subject populations, even for their own good, without regard to the implications of democratic and nationalist ideology. But there was also, among a few at least, a sense of changing world realities. As the century opened there had been talk of a 'Yellow Peril' as well as of 'dying empires'. In a few years, the emergence of Japan showed that Europe was no longer the only focus of the international power system.

Although the German colonial empire, a relatively recent creation, had disappeared in 1918, the empires of other European powers did not. For a little a few of them were actually to grow bigger. But Europe's troubles in the years before 1939 came to cramp further the ability of her governments to operate effectively in other parts of the world; it was another sign that European history was no longer an autonomous process, to be narrated in purely European terms.

The first and clearest evidence came in Asia. In the perspective of world history, Europe's power there was to prove to have been only briefly unchallengeable and unchallenged. Its greatest and most spectacular age was over by 1914. The greatest imperial power, Great Britain, had made an alliance with an Asian nation because she needed to do so. Russia, with greater Asian territories than any other power had been the first 'white' power so to go down before an Asiatic power in war, and had turned back to her traditional European interests by 1914. China itself, dying empire *par excellence*, had no longer to surrender territory to European imperialists after the Boxer rebellion, though she had long been seen by then as a possible candidate for partition, and had begun at last to take the first steps towards modernization. There had been many signs, too, before 1914, of difficulties within the European Asian empires.

British India

In India political opposition to the British Raj had not died away after the concessions of 1911. Perhaps they had made things worse. Sedition and terrorism continued. Favours shown to Moslems had made Hindus more resentful. Moslems felt the government had gone back on understandings with them by cancelling the Bengal partition. The strain grew as Moslem élites which had favoured co-operation with the British felt themselves threatened by Moslems more susceptible to the appeal of pan-Islamic agitation. They felt the British had stood by, while (in 1911 in Tripoli, and in the following years in the Balkans) Christian states were attacking the Ottoman regime, seat of the caliphate: Great Britain had done nothing to support the spiritual leader of the religion of so many millions of its subjects. When the Ottoman government decided to go to war with Great Britain in 1914, a few Indian Moslems plotted revolution.

Nonetheless, most Indian politicians rallied to the Crown in the war; India contributed men and money to the imperial war effort (one among those who did so, believing that it would in time bring Indians their due reward, was Mahatma Gandhi, later to be revered as the father of the Indian nation). In 1917 the British government announced it favoured steady progress towards 'responsible' government for the whole of India (Home Rule, as it were), though this fell short of the Dominion status for which some Indians were now asking. Though it is possible to write the story of British India from this point as one of continuous decline, therefore, it is an over-simplification to do so. There were ups as well as downs in the next twenty years; the British never had their backs to the wall.

Yet management of political opposition in India was becoming harder. Besides continuing substantial and vociferous opposition in England (particularly in some sections of the Conservative party) to any concession of imperial power in India, the utterances and behaviour of members of the British community in India were psychologically influential – for good and ill. Amongst other misconceptions, most of that community tended to take the view that Indian nationalism was only a matter of a few ambitious and self-interested intellectuals. They urged British governments to rely on police measures against conspiracy and sedition; support for this view was not only unduly influenced by the revolutionary threat from Bolshevik Russia (in fact, an Indian communist party was not founded until 1923) but by confident and out-dated racial judgements.

In 1919 the first suspension (against the wishes of all Indian members of the Viceroy's legislative council) of normal legal process in dealing with conspiracy provoked Gandhi's first campaign of strikes and civil disobedience. He had by now a substantial following in the Indian National Congress. In spite of his efforts to avoid violence, there were riots and bloodshed. Englishmen were attacked and some killed in the Punjab. At Amritsar there took place an incident which may well have done more moral damage to the Raj than any other. An Indian army officer of hitherto unblemished and even distinguished record, decided to show his countrymen's determination to master disorder by dispersing a crowd by force. When the firing stopped, nearly 400 Indians had been killed and over a 1,000 wounded. The effect on Indian opinion was disastrous and was made worse by further actions Brigadier-General Dyer took. Though he was soon obliged to resign, an irreparable blow had been dealt to British prestige and reputation. To make things worse, some members of parliament and British residents in India expressed noisy approval for what Dyer had done.

Further civil disturbance followed. Gandhi's programme was adopted by Congress, and in spite of his insistence that his campaign should be non-violent it could not but provoke disorder. In 1922 he was arrested and imprisoned for the first time. Nonetheless, there followed some years of signs of flagging enthusiasm and rifts within Congress. More alarmingly, the division between Hindu and Moslem deepened. There was communal rioting and bloodshed. By 1930 the political leader of Moslem India was already envisaging a sub-continent divided after independence, with a separate Moslem state in its north-west.

In the 1930s civil disobedience was resumed and excitement rose as the international economic situation deteriorated. The rural masses were now readier for mobilization by nationalist appeals; thanks in part to the communications and educational policies of the Raj, Gandhi became the first Indian politician who could plausibly claim an all-India following. In spite of setbacks, too, the lessons of events since 1917 had been learnt in London. In 1935 a Government of India Act became law which provided for a real further devolution of power and patronage. It left virtually only defence and foreign affairs in the viceroy's sole control, provided for full local representative government, and for a transfer of power to a representative and responsible national assembly (a building for which was now begun). The outbreak of war in 1939 overtook the last, but the British had now effectively set up a framework for national politics.

With hindsight it now seems clear that by then the tide was set irreversibly towards Indian independence, even though, to the rage of many Indians, the viceroy committed the country to war in that year without any pretence of consulting Indian opinion. Nearly twenty years' actual working of representative institutions in local government and the steady Indianization of the Indian Civil Service already meant that the subcontinent was governable only with the consent and help of native élites. Education and experience had begun to prepare them for future self-rule. The Raj would prove still able to maintain its grip in wartime, but not without difficulty and embarrassment. India had been revolutionized by British rule; there as elsewhere empire had brought with it the germs of its own overthrow.

A new Asia in the making

In the background to changes in any individual imperial possessions, a wider revolutionizing of Asia was under way, driven by cultural interplay, economic power and the promise of modernization which had produced anti-European reactions in many countries, above all, in Japan. Though indirectly, that country set the pace of the final phase of the Hundred Years' War of East and West which had opened with the Opium Wars. Japanese dynamism was crucial to the undermining of European ascendancy in Asia.

The Russo-Japanese war had shown that Asian history was moving again to rhythms marked increasingly by events whose significance for European history was rarely at once apparent. It is therefore necessary to break out of the framework of European chronology to understand them. In 1911, for instance, a year when majestic ceremonies at Delhi set out the formal message of imperial domination as never before, a revolution in China provides a chronological marker of hugely greater import than the Durbar. The 1911 revolution which brought the Chinese empire to an end marked an epoch in the history of a civilization eclipsed during the nineteenth century. It was to lead to more fundamental change than the French or Russian revolutions; it closed more than 2,000 years of history during which the Confucian state had held China together and Confucian ideals had dominated Chinese culture and society. Yet for European powers with possessions or interests in China, so momentous a change did not at once seem of great importance. Divisions among the revolutionaries soon intensified the dislocation of the country. There lay ahead a brief golden age for soldiers who had arms and men at their disposal, the 'warlords'.

Abroad, the Japanese were the main beneficiaries of China's prolonged weakness. Japan's allies could hardly object to her seizure of the German ports in China during the Great War; even if they would have liked to do so, they could do nothing about it. They needed Japanese ships and manufactures and always hoped that the Japanese might send an army to help them in Europe. This never happened. Instead, the Japanese finessed, arousing fears that they might make a separate peace with the Germans, and continued to press ahead in China. At the beginning of 1915 they presented the Chinese government with a list of twenty-one demands amounting to a proposal for a Japanese protectorate over China; much of what they asked was conceded. Next, in 1916, Japanese pressure was brought to bear on the British to dissuade them from recognizing a Chinese general who proposed to make himself emperor; in the following year came another 'unequal' treaty with China, extending the recognition of Japan's special interests as far as Inner Mongolia. It was now clear that Japan was as much a predator as the European barbarians had ever been. In August 1917 the Chinese government went to war with Germany, partly in the hope of winning goodwill and support which would ensure her an independent voice at the peace.

Versailles in fact deeply disappointed Chinese and Japanese alike. Indisputably a power (she had in 1918 the third largest navy in the world), Japan won solid gains. She retained the former German rights in Shantung (promised to her by the British and French in 1917), and was granted a mandate over many of the former German Pacific islands and a permanent seat on the Council of the League of Nations. But these gains were offset in Japanese eyes when a declaration in favour of racial equality was not written into the Covenant of the League. The Chinese, offered only the ending of German and Austrian extra-territoriality and the concession of delay in paying the Boxer indemnities, had even more to feel aggrieved about. They refused altogether to sign the treaty.

One consequence was the 'May 4th Movement' of 1919, an upheaval to which some commentators have given an importance as great as that of the 1911 revolution itself. A student demonstration in Peking against the peace escalated, at first into a riot and the resignation of the head of the university, and then into a nationwide student movement which spread to embrace others than students and provoked strikes and a boycott of Japanese goods. It was the strongest evidence yet of widespread and mounting rejection of Europe by Asians.

Whatever the practical benefits western liberalism had brought, it had never had mass appeal in China, and now intellectuals felt drawn to another western but rival ideology, Marxism. At the moment of disillusion with the peace, Soviet Russia was very popular among young Chinese intellectuals. One of the first acts of the Bolshevik government had been a formal renunciation of all extra-territorial rights and jurisdictions enjoyed by the tsarist state. In the eyes of the nationalists, they had clean hands. Moreover, Russia's revolution, a revolution in a great peasant society, suggested lessons for China. With the formation in 1921 of the Chinese Communist Party (CCP) began the last stage of the Chinese Revolution and a new twist of the curious dialectic which has run through the relations of Europe with Asia. The western idea of Marxism, born and shaped in a European context, was now to play its most disturbing and dynamic role in undermining European power elsewhere in the world.

Japan's dynamism meanwhile continued to show itself. Well before 1914, cheap Japanese imports had worried European manufacturers. The Great War gave Japan new opportunities: markets (especially in Asia) in which she had faced heavy western competition were open to her when their former exploiters found they could not meet the war's demands at home. Allied governments ordered munitions and supplies from Japanese factories; a world shipping shortage gave her new shipyards the work they needed. The Japanese gross national product went up by forty per cent during the war years. Though interrupted in 1920, expansion was resumed later in the decade and in 1929 the Japanese had an industrial base which (though still engaging less than one in five of the population) had in twenty years multiplied its steel production almost tenfold, tripled its textile production, and doubled its coal output. This could still be seen as part and parcel of an overall process of 'westernizing'. In 1925 universal male suffrage was introduced; in spite of much European evidence that this had no necessary connexion with liberalism or moderation, it looked like the continuation of steady constitutional progress begun in the nineteenth century.

By 1931, Asia could feel the impact of a world slump. In that year, half Japan's factories were idle; the collapse of European colonial markets and the entrenchment of what remained of them behind new tariff barriers had a shattering effect. Japanese exports of manufactures went down by two-thirds. The position of the Japanese masses deteriorated. Grave political consequences were soon manifest, though less in intensified class conflict than in nationalist extremism. Japan's markets on the Asian mainland were now crucial. Anything that seemed to threaten them provoked alarm and irritation. Circumstances seemed propitious for response by further Japanese aggression on the mainland. European colonialism was clearly on the defensive, if not in retreat. The Dutch faced rebellions in Java and Sumatra in the 1920s, the French a Vietnamese revolt in 1930; in both places there was the sinister novelty of communist help to nationalist rebels. In China, the British wanted only a quiet accommodation with the nationalist government (they agreed in 1922 to give back one of their ports), if possible, without loss of face.

In 1922, China's territorial integrity was guaranteed as part of a complicated set of agreements made at Washington to which, besides the United States, China and Japan, six other nations, all European, subscribed[2]. Other decisions about limitations on naval strength (there was great uneasiness about the cost of armaments) left Japan relatively stronger, but the United States, Great Britain, France and Japan also guaranteed one another's possessions. This provided a decent burial for the Anglo-Japanese alliance, whose ending had long been sought by the Americans. Meanwhile, foreigners continued to administer the customs and tax revenues on which the Chinese government

---

[2]   Great Britain, France, Belgium, the Netherlands, Italy and Portugal.

depended, and foreign agents and businessmen dealt directly with the warlords when it suited them.

By 1927 something of a semblance of unity had been restored to China under the leadership of the Kuomintang (KMT), the nationalist party founded by SunYat-sen. A successful boycott of British goods led the British government, alarmed by the evidence of growing Soviet influence on the KMT, to give up some of its concessions; the United States had already renounced its share of the Boxer indemnity. In the 1920s, in fact, the only European power making serious efforts to direct China's national development was the USSR. On more than one ground, its interest was predictable. Not only was it self-proclaimedly revolutionary and anti-colonialist but it was a great Asian empire in its own right. Soviet policy was bound to be especially concerned about Japanese expansion in the Far East; Japanese troops had only left Siberia in 1922. The USSR shared with China the longest international boundary in the world, and its rulers could hardly forget that imperial Russia had once held even more Chinese territory than they did. Furthermore, though no great power had greater territorial interests in the Far East, she had not been invited to participate in the Washington Conference.

Moscow sought to co-operate with the KMT, both to safeguard Soviet interests in Mongolia and to stiffen Chinese resistance to the Japanese. The KMT was also standing up to the British, whose power as the central supporters of the whole imperialist system was much exaggerated in Moscow. The Soviet line had not changed with the appearance of the CCP; orthodox Marxism argued that bourgeois nationalist revolution had to precede proletarian revolution, and Chinese communism would have to await its turn. Although he had sent advisers and money to the CCP, Stalin did not protect it from proscription and the savage repression of its urban cadres by the KMT in 1929. Soviet advice and patronage was then withdrawn from the CCP, which went underground. Chinese nationalism had done better out of Soviet policy.

The success of the KMT gave further food for thought to the predatory Japanese. They were especially concerned about Manchuria where they had prospered since 1905; investment had buttressed their presence during the Great War and Chinese governments had acquiesced in the presence of Japanese garrisons, not being able to do otherwise. Yet although in the eyes of the world the responsible agency, the Japanese government was not in fact in control in Manchuria. When in 1931 the Japanese military commanders there staged an incident at Mukden as an excuse to take over the province outright, more cautious men in Tokyo could not restrain them. There followed the appearance of a new puppet state (Manchukuo), consternation in China (and Moscow) and an ineffectual outcry at the League of Nations. When the Chinese organized a boycott of Japanese goods, Japanese troops were landed at Shanghai, China's greatest port and the seat of European commercial power and European-administered 'concessions'. Then, in 1933, Japanese forces invaded China. An imposed peace left them occupying a large area of the country.

China had been unable to resist imperialist aggression, even when it was not European. Although the KMT government had whittled away at the 'unequal' treaties and the western powers had showed themselves a little more accommodating (they were beginning to see the KMT as an ally against communism in Asia), it was at once on the defensive when a new full-scale attack was launched by the Japanese in 1937. The 'China incident', as the Japanese continued to call it, was to drag out to eight years of fighting and has been seen as the opening of the Second World War. Yet the western powers felt unable to intervene, though the Soviet Union supplied some aircraft to the nationalists and the League formally condemned Japan. Protests, even on behalf of United States and European nationals, were brushed aside. The Japanese made it clear that they were prepared to blockade the foreign settlements in China if recognition of their new order in Asia was not forthcoming. For weak British and French responses there was an obvious explanation: they had troubles enough elsewhere not to be able to return to old-fashioned imperial assertiveness. American ineffectiveness after a gunboat was sunk by Japanese bombers reflected a long-established fact – that the United States might talk about mainland Asia, but Americans would not fight for it. Perhaps this was wise.

By 1941, China, much damaged and half-occupied, was all but cut off from the outside world. In the long struggle Japan so far looked like the winner. Her international position had never seemed stronger as she showed by humiliating western residents in China and in 1940 by forcing the British to close the Burma Road by which supplies were reaching the KMT government (now driven back to Chungking), and the French to admit a Japanese army to Indo-China. Temptations to further adventure were not likely to be resisted while the prestige of the Japanese military and their power in government remained high, as it had been since the mid-1930s. For all her aggression against China, too, it was with the window-dressing slogan of 'Asia for the Asians' that Japan had first advanced on the crumbling western position in Asia. Just as her defeat of Russia in 1905 marked an epoch in the psychological relations of Europe and Asia, so did the independence and power which she showed in 1938–41, as the one successfully modernized Asian power.

European empire in the Middle East[3]

The Great War opened a period of turbulence in the Arab lands of the former Ottoman empire. Hussein, the ally of the British, was recognized by them in 1918 as 'king of the Arab peoples', but the title proved not to mean much. The British and French, with the help of the League, had the power to settle the new shape of the Arab lands, not the Arab rulers, nor, except by the difficulties they created, even the Arab peoples. In this sense it was the last age of imperial power in an area which had long shaped the history of European states and their relations with one another. In one respect it posed slightly less complex diplomatic problems than in earlier times. Old tsarist ambitions to succeed the Ottoman at Constantinople had no longer to be taken into account, and it was some time before they were replaced by the disturbing force of international communism. For most of the inter-war years, only two great powers,

---

[3] The term 'Middle East' appears in the early years of this century, exactly when, I do not know. There had earlier been in use the terms 'Near East' – indicating, substantially, the lands from Egypt to the Straits formerly in Ottoman hands – and the 'Far East' – which indicated a zone whose central core was China. 'Middle East', when it came into use was, logically, intended to cover those countries forming the approaches to India from the west – Persia and Afghanistan, with the somewhat odd addition of Tibet. By the 1920s, though, 'Middle East' experts in the British colonial affairs were expected to deal also with what was previously known as the 'Near East'. 'Middle East' thus took over Turkey, the Arab lands of the former Ottoman empire and Egypt. It became normal to confine it to these lands and so it is used here. It does not seem necessary to identify regional groupings further east other than in the case of the Persian Gulf (as in the 'Gulf region' or 'the Gulf states').

France and Great Britain, mattered in the Middle East, and though they distrusted one another, they could agree, roughly on the basis of the zones of influence constituted by the League's award of mandates. These had given Palestine, Transjordan and Iraq to the British, Syria and the Lebanon to France.

The French from the start governed Syria somewhat high-handedly, perhaps because they had to install themselves there by force after a national congress had asked for independence or at any rate a British or American mandate instead of a French. After evicting a king chosen by the Syrians they faced a full-scale insurrection. In the 1930s they were still holding their own, but there were signs by then that they were preparing to make concessions to the nationalists. The complexities of the area were then made apparent when the Kurds of north Syria revolted against the prospect of submergence in an Arab state. As for the British, they were handicapped by strife between Arab rulers while they moved as fast as they dared towards liquidating the mandate over Iraq. Having secured British strategic interests by preserving a military and air force presence there, they were content to see Iraq assume full independence in 1932 and join the League as a sovereign state. Earlier, in 1928, they had already recognized Transjordan as independent, again with some military and financial powers retained in British hands. Palestine was a more difficult case.

From 1921, when anti-Jewish riots by Arabs alarmed over Jewish immigration and Jewish acquisition of Arab land took place, that unhappy country was never long at peace. More was at stake than merely religious or national feeling. Jewish immigration meant the irruption of a new, for the most part westernizing and modernizing, influence, changing economic relationships and making new demands on a traditional society. The British mandatory power was caught between the outcry of Arabs if it did not restrict Jewish immigration, and the outcry of Jews if it did. Arab governments now had to be taken into account, too, and they occupied lands economically and strategically important to British security. Finally, world opinion was becoming involved. The question was inflamed by another order of magnitude when in 1933 there came to power in Germany a regime which soon began to persecute Jews and to remove the legal and social gains they had been making since the French Revolution.

By 1937 there were pitched battles between Jews and Arabs in Palestine. Soon a British army was trying to hold down an Arab insurrection. The collapse of paramount power in the Arab lands had usually in the past been followed by a period of disorder. What seemed less likely this time was that it would be followed – as earlier periods of anarchy had eventually been – by the establishment of a new imperial hegemony. The British wanted an imperial role only with strict qualification; after a brief spell of intoxication in the aftermath of victory, they desired only to secure what they regarded as their essential interests in the region, the protection of the Suez Canal route to India and the swelling flow of oil from Iraq and Iran. By 1934 a great pipeline had been built from northern Iraq across Transjordania and Palestine to Haifa. This gave new significance to these territories, though the consumption of oil in Europe was not yet so large that there was any general dependence on it, nor had very great discoveries of new deposits yet been made.

Keeping forces in Egypt caused the British increasing trouble. The war had intensified Egyptian national feeling. Armies of occupation are rarely popular; when the war sent up prices the foreigner was blamed. Egyptian nationalist leaders attempted in 1919 to put their case to the Paris Peace Conference but were prevented from doing so; there followed a rising against the British. It was quickly put down but the British protectorate was ended in 1922 in the hope of getting ahead of nationalist feeling. Yet the electorate of the new constitutional Egypt returned nationalist majority after nationalist majority, and it was impossible for any Egyptian government to come to terms which any British government would find acceptable as safeguards of British interests. The result was pro-longed constitutional crisis and intermittent disorder until in 1936 the British finally agreed to be content with a right to keep a garrison solely in the Canal Zone and a naval base at Alexandria for eight years. An end was also announced to the jurisdictional priv-ileges of foreigners, though mixed courts of European and Egyptian judges were main-tained.

The British retreat from empire reflected an awareness that British power and resources were over-stretched. British foreign policy in the 1930s was beginning to be preoccupied by Europe and the Far East. Changes literally worldwide thus helped to shape post-Ottoman developments in Islamic lands. Soon, Marxist communism was also doing so. During the whole of the years between the wars, Russian radio broad-casting to the Arab countries supported the first Arab communists[4]. But for all the worry they caused, communism showed no sign of being able to displace the strongest revo-lutionary influence of the area, still that of Arab nationalism, whose focus had come by 1938 to be Palestine. In that year a congress was held in Syria to support the Palestinian Arab cause. Arab resentment of the brutality of the French in Syria was beginning to be as evident, too, as the outcry of the Egyptian nationalists against the British. In pan-Arab feeling lay a force which some thought might in the end override the divisions of the Hashemite Kingdoms.

Europeanizing Islamic societies

Allied agreements during the Great War were the departure point for the post-war history of the Ottoman homeland. The British, French, Greeks and Italians had all agreed in advance on their shares of the booty; one simplification brought by the war had been the elimination of the Russian claim to Constantinople and the Straits. Faced with Greek and Italian invasion, the sultan signed a humiliating peace renouncing all non-Turkish territory. Under the Treaty of Sèvres, Greece was given large concessions, Armenia became an independent state, while what was left of Turkey was divided into British, French and Italian spheres of influence. The Straits were to be placed under international control. To drive home the point, European financial control was re-established. This was the most blatant imperialism, and enormously strengthened the position of any patriotic Turkish politician who denounced it.

The first successful revision of the peace settlements quickly followed, largely thanks to one man, a former Young Turk and an outstanding soldier, Mustafa Kemal. He defeated French and Greek armies, and with Bolshevik help crushed the Armeni-ans. The British, unsupported by their former allies, decided to negotiate and so a second treaty was made with Turkey at Lausanne in 1923. This triumph of nationalism over the decisions at Paris was the only part of the peace settlement which was negoti-ated between equals and not imposed on the defeated, and the only one in which Russ-

---

[4]   Though it was broadcasting from Italy to the Arabs which led the British government to allow the BBC to begin its first regular broadcasting in a foreign language, Arabic.

ian negotiators took part. It was to last better than any of the other peace treaties. Under it, the capitulations and financial controls disappeared. Turkey gave up her claims to the Arab lands and the islands of the Aegean, Cyprus, Rhodes and the Dodecanese. The Straits were demilitarized. A big exchange of Greek and Turkish population followed and the hatred of these peoples for one another was refreshed by new grudges. So, after six centuries, the Ottoman empire outside Anatolia (except for Constantinople and a small part of Thrace) was wound up. A new republic of Turkey came into existence in 1923 in Asia Minor as a national state, and the sultanate was abolished. The caliphate followed it in the following year. This was the end of Ottoman history; and a new beginning for Turkish. The Anatolian Turks were now for the first time in five or six centuries the majority in a national state.

The old Ottoman empire had provided a boundary which had helped to differentiate civilizations. Many generations of Europeans had been deeply affected by this. Now a new problem was to emerge: should Turkey itself be regarded as a part of Europe? Both republicanism and nationalism were European imports to the Islamic world. Kemal, as he tended to call himself (the name meant 'Perfection'), was a passionate modernizer on European lines. Turkish law was secularized (on the model of the Napoleonic code), the Moslem calendar abandoned, and in 1928 the constitution was amended to remove the statement that Turkey was an Islamic state. Polygamy was forbidden. In 1935 the weekly day of rest (formerly Friday, the Islamic holy day) became Sunday and a new word entered the language: *vikend* (the period from 1.00 p.m. Saturday to midnight Sunday). Schools ceased to give religious instruction. The fez was forbidden; although originally from Europe it was considered to be too Moslem. Kemal was conscious of the radical nature of the modernization he wished to achieve and such symbols mattered to him. They were signs of something very important, the replacement of a traditional Islamic society by a European one. The alphabet was latinized; education in it was henceforth obligatory at the primary level. A national past was written into the school-books; it was said that Adam had been a Turk. A much greater break with the past than in Europe was involved in giving a new role to women, but in 1934 Turkish women received the vote and they were encouraged to enter the professions[5]. Right down to his death in 1938 Kemal seemed determined not to let his revolution congeal. The result was the creation of a state in some ways among the most advanced in the world at that date.

Persia, had been ruled before 1914 neither by Europeans nor Ottomans. The British and Russians had both gone on interfering in Persia's affairs after agreeing their spheres of influence in 1907, but Russian power had lapsed with the Bolshevik Revolution, while British forces had continued to operate there until the end of the war. Resentment against the British was excited when a Persian delegation, like the Egyptian, was not allowed to state its case to the Peace Conference. There could be no question of retaining Persia by force, given the demands on British strength, and for a confused period the British struggled to find a way of holding off the Bolsheviks after withdrawal of their forces. Reza Khan, a Persian officer, carried out a *coup d'état* in 1921 and then used the Bolshevik fear of the British to get from them a treaty conceding all Russian rights and property in Persia and the withdrawal of Russian forces. Reza Khan then went on to defeat separatists who had British support. In 1925 he was given

---

[5]   The women of France waited until 1945 for the suffrage, and those of Switzerland until 1971.

dictatorial powers by the national assembly and a few months later was proclaimed 'Shah of Shahs'. He was to rule until 1941 (when the Russians and the British, having returned, together turned him off the throne), somewhat in the style of an Iranian Kemal. Secular aims were not pressed so far as in Turkey but the capitulations were abolished, an important symbolic step, in 1928. In 1933 the Shah won the first notable success in a new art, the diplomacy of oil, when he cancelled the concession held by the Anglo-Persian Oil Company. When the British government took the question to the League of Nations, another and more favourable concession resulted: this was Reza Shah's greatest victory and the best evidence of his country's new independence. A new era had opened in the Gulf, even if the British presence there remained dominant.

Economic disaster: the world slump

In many ways, Europe's world position was dealt its heaviest blows after 1919 by economic forces. After the immediate post-war years, with which victors and vanquished alike found it so difficult to grapple, there had begun a gradual recovery of prosperity shared by most of Europe outside Russia. The years from 1925 to 1929 were, in economic life, on the whole good ones. In 1925 the production of food and raw materials in Europe for the first time passed the 1913 figure and a recovery of manufacturing was under way. This encouraged political optimism. Currencies emerged from appalling inflations of the first half of the decade (when money prices in Austria, for example, went up by a multiple of 14,000 – and those in Germany by a multiple of 1,000,000,000) were once more stable; the resumption by many countries of the gold standard was a sign that some still thought the old pre-1914 days were returned. With the help of a worldwide recovery of trade and huge investment from the United States, now an exporter of capital, European trade reached in 1929 a level not to be reached again until 1954. Yet collapse followed. Economic recovery had been built on insecure foundations. When faced with a sudden crisis, the new prosperity crumbled rapidly. There erupted into history not merely a European, but a world economic disaster which was the most influential single event in world history between the two world wars. Though its effects in the most developed European countries were in fact less harrowing than in Europe's rural slums, it shattered such basis as there existed for the preservation of international order and opened the door to further revolution.

The role of the United States in the world economy had radically changed. Before 1914 she had mainly exported agricultural produce and had been a major importer of capital, a debtor nation. After the war her much increased manufacturing capacity was more than able to meet domestic demand; in the 1920s the United States produced nearly 40 per cent of the world's coal and over half the world's manufactures. She was a creditor nation, whose rich men and institutions looked for opportunities to lend money abroad. American domestic prosperity, because of this, was crucial to the rest of the world. On it depended the confidence which provided American capital for export and the re-equipping of Europe.

In 1928 there began to be signs that the end of the long boom and a swing in the business cycle might be approaching. Short-term money began to be harder to get in the United States. American loans were called back from Europe. Soon some European borrowers were in difficulties. Meanwhile, demand continued to slacken in the United States as people began to think a severe slump might be on the way. Almost accidentally, this detonated a particularly sudden and spectacular stock market collapse in October 1929. The end of American business confidence meant the end of American overseas investment. After a last brief rally in 1930 it dried up, and the flywheel of world prosperity ceased to turn. A world slump began.

The story was one of accelerating and spreading disaster. As debtor nations tried to put their accounts in order, they cut imports. This brought down world prices. But primary producers could not afford to buy manufactures as their incomes fell. Meanwhile, at the centre of things, both the United States and Europe went into a financial crisis; as countries struggled, unsuccessfully, to keep the value of their currencies steady in relation to gold (an internationally acceptable means of exchange – hence the expression 'gold standard') they adopted deflationary policies to balance their books. This further cut their domestic demand. By 1933 all the major currencies, except the French, were 'off' gold, that is, they were no longer equally convertible to it. This dethronement of one old idol of liberal economics was a symbol of the tragedy now under way. Part of its reality was unemployment on an unimagined scale. It may have reached a level of 30,000,000 in the industrial world, many of them, of course, in Europe. In 1932 (the worst year) the index of industrial production for the United States and Germany was in each case only just above half of what it had been in 1929.

The effects of economic depression rolled on with a ghastly and irresistible logic. The social gains of the late 1920s, when European standards of living had improved almost everywhere, were wiped out. No country had a solution to unemployment. It appeared to be at its worst in the United States and Germany but existed in a virulent but sometimes semi-concealed form all round the world in the villages and farmlands of the primary producers, with even worse social effects. Its psychological impact may, though, have been even more tragic than the material consequences, or even the actual physiological outcome in sickness and under-nourishment for millions. The morale of whole societies plunged as unemployment and idleness infected the workforces with the feeling that they were unwanted, unesteemed, rejected. National incomes and the prices of manufactured goods fell, but raw material and foodstuffs prices had fallen faster. Everywhere, poorer nations and the poorer sectors of the mature economies suffered disproportionately. They may not always have seemed to do so, because they had less far to fall; an eastern European or an Argentinian peasant may not have been absolutely much worse off for he had always been badly off. An unemployed German clerk or factory hand certainly was worse off and knew it.

Countries cut themselves off more and more behind tariffs and this made things still worse. Some strove to achieve economic self-sufficiency by an increasing state control of their economic life. Some did better than others at this, some did very badly. The disaster was a promising setting for those who desired, expected or advocated the overthrow of democracy and liberal civilization; vultures now began to flap expectantly about enfeebled and apparently foundering new constitutional states. The end of the gold standard and the abandonment of belief in non-interference with the economy mark the collapse of a world order in its economic dimension as strikingly as the onset of social unrest and the new stridency of nationalist resentments mark it in its political. Liberal civilization, frighteningly but evidently had lost its power to control events. This was for some further evidence of the contingent, relative nature of its values; while the political and economic hegemony which had sustained them was now in decay all round the world.

Europeans who found it hard to see this continued to dream of restoring an age when their civilization enjoyed unquestioned supremacy. This was not to happen. Though world economic recovery was to come, it would be only in another great war, a paradox and another clear demonstration that the European age was at last over. Unlike the Great War it would demonstrate (or appear to demonstrate) through its horrific nature and effects that the liberal assumptions about human nature, its capacity for rational self-control, and its potential for improvement had all to be abandoned together with the optimism about material progress which had evaporated in the depression.

CHAPTER FIVE The last years of European illusion

New politics

So easily can the changing global context and its constraining force now be seen to have been at work in shaping European history between 1919 and 1939, that it can seem odd that this was not better recognized in those years. Many statesmen and politicians, for much of the time, went on behaving as if what happened in Europe and its diplomatic chancelleries was all that mattered. Only when particular issues arose – an initiative of Soviet foreign policy, a domestic demand for economic protection, or the need to toe a line in Asia actually (if not admittedly) set by the Japanese – would they for a time give much notice to how the world outside had changed. It was, of course, increasingly true that the most urgent and pressing problems they had to face were concentrated in Europe. But even there many politicians found it hard to recognize that much of the pre-1914 world had gone, never to be restored, while others of its realities – that Germany and Russia would be bound to enjoy again one day the power and standing to which their populations, economic potential and geographical position entitled them, for instance – would return.

Power relationships were not the only relevant facts, though. There were other important and changing political realities. One was the apparently irresistible involvement in politics of the masses. It was not limited to the enlargement of electorates and the advance of universal suffrage, important as these were (the United Kingdom at last achieved universal adult suffrage in 1928 – peers, lunatics and convicted felons alone being excluded). Mass action could express itself in other ways than through the ballot box. Existing political parties had to adapt themselves to this trend. They adapted, too, to the political effects of mass literacy achieved through compulsory education, the deployment in politics of a mass press and – only beginning in the 1920s – the introduction of 'wireless' broadcasting, and the growing cheapness and availability of receivers. In the 1930s this last was to put new power in the hands of those who controlled access to radio, as the experience of (notably) Germany and the USSR was to demonstrate. Another mass medium which had been available more quickly for political use during the Great War was the cinema, first silent and then with sound. Mass communication had, of course, cultural, economic, social implications which by far transcended even its important political influence. Fittingly, when in 1937 the man who first sent messages by radio, the Italian Marconi, died, British broadcasting stations paid him the unique tribute of two minutes' silence after making the announcement.

Another new political fact was communism in its novel scale and guise. Its role varied from country to country. In the economic depression which soon followed the peace many socialists who had been active in political parties and trades unions in existence well before 1914 were encouraged to intensify their efforts. This contributed to a wave of political and social turbulence of a kind which was not new. Though the communists rapidly produced fragmentation within the Left, they did not at first seem to many politicians to register a change in the whole context of politics, but merely to intensify existing struggles. The fact that so much of the Left could so plausibly be categorized as 'Marxist' even before the Bolsheviks made an explicit claim to lead the way to international revolution, helped to feed a generalized anti-Marxist reaction detectable in many countries in the 1920s. Some of this reaction also embodied revolutionary elements and ideas.

The most important and earliest of these movements which challenged the liberal presuppositions of constitutional politics emerged in Italy. The Great War had badly strained that young constitutional state. Poorer than other countries regarded in 1914 as great powers, Italy's share of fighting had been disproportionately heavy, often unsuccessful, and virtually all on Italian territory. Inequalities of suffering had accentuated social divisions as the war went on. With peace came even faster inflation. The owners of property, whether agricultural or industrial, and those who could ask higher wages because of a labour shortage, were more insulated against it than the professional classes and those who lived on investment or fixed incomes. Yet these were on the whole the most convinced supporters of the unification completed in 1870. They had sustained the constitutional and liberal state which conservative Roman Catholics and revolutionary socialists had opposed. Many of them had seen Italy's entrance to the war as an extension of the *Risorgimento* struggle to unite Italy as a nation, a crusade to remove Austria from the last soil inhabited by those of Italian blood or speech which she ruled. Such ideas were muddled and unscientific, but powerful.

Peace, though, brought disappointment and disillusion; such nationalist dreams were left unrealized. Moreover, as the immediate post-war economic crisis deepened, the socialists grew stronger in parliament and seemed more alarming now that a Marxist state existed in Russia. Disappointed and frightened, tired of speeches by socialist anti-patriots and pacifists, many Italians lost faith in liberal parliamentarianism and began to look for a new way out of Italy's disappointments. They were sympathetic to intransigent nationalism abroad (for example, to an adventurer who seized the Adriatic port of Fiume which the Peace Conference had failed to give to Italy) and violent anti-Marxism at home; the second had extra resonance in a Roman Catholic country. It was not only from the traditionally conservative Church, though, that the new leadership against Marxism came, but from a new movement, 'fascism'. The name came from the Italian word for a 'bundle' (among other things, of rods carried by the ancient Roman lictors): *fascio*. It was used in the 1890s by Sicilian revolutionaries to mean a 'band' or 'group'. It was then taken up early in the Great War by Italians urging on the government that the country should enter that struggle. The name was later to be extended to a number of other and only loosely related radical movements in other countries which had in common a rejection of liberalism and strong anti-Marxism[1]. The first was in

---

[1] The word is now so broadly applied that it has lost much of its usefulness. A helpful summary of what it meant in the 1920s is H.W. Fowler's: 'notions of co-operative, riotous behaviour, revolutionary activities, dislike of pacifism, scorn of neutrality, reaction from socialism, hatred of communism, and belief in physical force and dictatorship'. Foligno and Fowler, in *S.P.E. Tract no XIX* (Oxford, 1925) p.32.

Italy, where, in 1919 a journalist, ex-serviceman and ex-socialist (of extreme views before the war), Benito Mussolini, joined a group of discontented young men to form the first *fascio regionale di combattimento*, which can be roughly translated as 'regional union for struggle'. It sought power by any means, among them violence (already deployed in the streets by communist 'Red Guards'). Groups of young fascist thugs harassed socialists and working-class organizations, and then began to turn against elected authorities. The movement prospered.

Italy's constitutional politicians could neither control fascism nor tame it by co-operation; some of them seemed not to wish to do so, seeing fascist squads as invaluable allies against socialist newspapers and assertive trades unions. Soon the 'fascists' (as they came to be called) were in some places enjoying official or quasi-official patronage and protection from local officials and police. Gangsterism was semi-institutionalized, and the cudgel and castor-oil (with which fascists dosed their victims) became a familiar part of street politics. In 1921 a national fascist party was formed to unite existing local *fasci*. By 1922 the fascists had not only achieved important electoral success but had in some places virtually made orderly government impossible. Other politicians having failed (or shown themselves unwilling) to master the fascist challenge, the king called on Mussolini to form a government. A coalition under him took office, and the violence came to an end. The episode became famous in later fascist mythology as the 'March on Rome', but it was not quite the end of constitutional Italy. Mussolini only slowly turned his position into a dictatorship. In 1926 government by decree began; elections were suspended. There was little opposition.

For all the terrorism at its roots, and its explicit denunciation of liberal ideals, Mussolini's rule fell far short of totalitarianism and was much less brutal than that of the Bolsheviks of whom he at times spoke admiringly. He undoubtedly had aspirations to revolutionary change, and many of his followers much clearer and more radical ones, but his 'revolution' turned out in practice to be mostly window-dressing; Mussolini himself showed temperamental impatience with an established society from which he felt excluded, but Italian fascism in practice and theory rarely achieved coherence. Once in power, indeed, it came more and more to reflect the weight of established Italy. Its greatest domestic achievement (and a true break with the liberal past) was a diplomatic agreement with the papacy, the Lateran treaties of 1929. In return for substantial concessions to the authority of the Church in Italian life (which persist to this day) the pope at last officially recognized the legitimacy of the Italian state. The agreement was a victory for the greatest conservative force in Italy. 'We have given back God to Italy and Italy to God', said the pope. Less epoch-making, but equally unrevolutionary was the outcome of fascist criticism of free enterprise and fascist rhetoric about subordinating individual interest to the state. It boiled down in practice to depriving trades unions of their power to protect their members' interests. Few checks were placed on the freedom of employers. For the rest, Fascist economic planning was a mockery. Only agricultural production notably improved while efforts to encourage emigration and the colonization of Italian Africa were wholly unsuccessful.

A new authoritarianism

Similar divergence between style and aspiration on the one hand and achievement on the other was marked in other movements which have been called fascist.

Though indeed reflecting something new and post-liberal – and they were inconceivable except as expressions of mass society, and new emphasis on youth, energy and revolution – such movements almost always in practice compromised with conservative interests. This makes it difficult to speak of the phenomenon of 'fascism' at all precisely. Many countries threw up regimes which were authoritarian, intensely nationalist, and anti-Marxist. But fascism was not the only possible source of such ideas. In Portugal and Spain, for example, there appeared regimes built upon traditional and conservative forces; they had little to do with the new phenomena of mass politics, except in technique. In them, real fascists often became discontented at concessions to conservatives; they hoped to transform the existing social order. Only in Germany, in the end, did a revolution sometimes called 'fascist' succeed in mastering historical conservatism. For such reasons, the label of fascism sometimes confuses as much as it clarifies.

Perhaps it is best merely to distinguish two phenomena of the twenty years after 1918. One is the appearance of ideologists and activists who spoke the language of a new, radical politics, used a rhetoric of energy, idealism, will-power and sacrifice, deployed physical violence against their opponents, and looked forward to rebuilding society and the state on new lines without respect to vested interests or concessions to materialism. They stressed their modernity and their ideas were often rooted in *avant-garde* ideas canvassed before 1914. Though widespread, such forces triumphed in only two major states, Italy and Germany. In each, economic collapse, outraged nationalism and anti-Marxism helped them to success, which in Germany did not come until 1933. If one word is wanted for this, let it be fascism.

In other countries, often among the poorer of Europe, it might be better to speak of authoritarian rather than fascist regimes. Large, poverty-stricken agricultural populations, huge social inequalities, underdevelopment, and a troubling succession of boundary changes had all inflamed their politics and led to a search for someone to blame. Sometimes the presence of alien minorities appeared to threaten new nations, where liberal institutions were only superficially implanted and traditional conservative social and religious forces were strong. In many of them a brief period of constitutionalism tended to give way sooner or later to the rule of strong men and soldiers; the words of the Yugoslav king who set aside constitutional government in 1929 might have been used by many of these limping democracies: 'the machine no longer works'[2]. This happened before 1939 in the new Baltic states, Poland and all the other successor states of the Dual Monarchy except Czechoslovakia, the one effective democracy in central Europe or the Balkans. The need of these countries to fall back on such regimes demonstrated both the unreality of the hopes entertained of their political maturity in 1918 and fears of the new threat of Marxist communism, especially acute on Russia's borders. Similar pressures operated also – though less acutely – in Spain and Portugal, where the influence of traditional conservatism was even stronger and Catholic social thinking counted for more than fascism. Finally, both the reversion to traditional forces and fascist revolution were responses to an underlying fact apparent everywhere with differences only of degree: the waning of the attractive power of the liberal assumptions of the world before 1914. Both also, like all political trends, attracted support from time-servers and careerists, wherever they prospered.

---

[2] He was speaking to a French newspaper correspondent and the phrase appeared in *Le Matin*, 15 January 1929; I take it from A. Polonsky, *The Little Dictators* (London, 1975), p.99.

The re-emergence of the German question

Though for a time obscured in the later 1920s, the role of Germany was bound to be the most important theme (and question) of international relations in Europe in the inter-war years. She had been defeated, had undergone political revolution and she had lost much territory. But she had not been destroyed. It was a logical consequence that Germany would one day again exercise the weight given her by geography, population and industrial power. In one way or another a united and economically rebuilt Germany would certainly dominate central Europe and overshadow France. What was at issue at bottom was whether this could happen without war. Only a few cranks thought it might be disposed of by dividing yet further the Germany united in 1871. Only the French briefly toyed with military sanctions (though a British garrison stayed in the Rhineland until 1929 and a French until 1930). For the most part, diplomats approached the problem with the assumption that the starting-point had to be an attempt to make the terms of the peace treaty work. It took some time for the inadequacy of this to become apparent.

Germans soon began to seek revision of the Versailles settlement. In the 1920s their demands were listened to and the problems of realizing them were still tackled in a hopeful spirit. The real burden of reparations was gradually whittled away. The treaties of Locarno at the end of 1925 were seen as a great landmark. Through them, Germany acquiesced in the Versailles territorial settlement in the west, while France was reassured by guarantees of her frontiers by Great Britain and Italy. It left open the question of revision in the east, over which it was clear that the British wanted no commitments. Behind this loomed the larger question: how could a country potentially as powerful as Germany be related to its neighbours in a balanced, peaceful way, given the particular historical and cultural experience of its people? One step could be taken, and was: Germany entered the League of Nations in the following year.

Many people hoped that the potential danger of a Germany once again asserting itself would prove to have been averted by the creation of a democratic German republic whose institutions would gently and benevolently re-educate German society and once more allow to flourish the many and widely-admired qualities of German culture. It was true that the constitution of the Weimar Republic (as the new Germany was called after the place where its constituent assembly had met) was liberal and democratic, but too many Germans were out of sympathy with it from the start. That Weimar had solved the German problem was revealed as an illusion when economic depression shattered the narrow base of consensus on which the German republic rested and set loose the destructive nationalist and social forces it had masked.

When this happened, the containment of Germany again became an international problem, but for a number of reasons, the 1930s were a very unpromising decade for containment. One was the effect of the world economic crisis, especially on the relatively weak agricultural economies of eastern and south-eastern Europe, where France had sought allies against German revival. Those allies were now much enfeebled and troubled with internal quarrels. Furthermore, the very existence of some of them made it doubly difficult to involve Russia, by the mid-1930s seen again as an indisputable (if mysterious) great power, in the containment of Germany. Her ideological distinction presented barriers enough to co-operation with the United Kingdom and France, but there was also her strategic position. No Russian force could reach central Europe without crossing one or more of the east European states whose short histories were haunted by fear of Russia and communism: Romania, Poland and the Baltic states, after all, were built from, among other things, former Russian lands.

The Americans would not help and, indeed, it is difficult to see why the ordinary American voter should have wanted to do so. The whole trend of American policy since Wilson had been back towards a self-absorbed isolation. When Americans were not confusedly blaming Europe for their troubles – the question of inter-allied debts from the war years had great psychological impact because it was believed to be tied up with international financial problems (as indeed it was, though not quite as most Americans thought) – they felt distrustful of further entanglement. Anyway, the depression left them with enough on their plate. Even in 1939 the 'New Deal' of the Roosevelt administration which took office in 1933 had still not solved the country's economic problems. As for foreign policy, though Roosevelt was more aware than most of his fellow-citizens of the dangers of persistent American isolation from Europe's problems, he could reveal his own views only slowly; he was a democratically-elected national leader.

If the Soviet Union and the United States were unavailable, only the western European great powers remained to confront Germany if needed. Great Britain and France were badly placed to be the policemen of Europe. They had vivid memories of the difficulty of containing Germany even with Russia on their side. They had been much at odds with one another since 1918. They were militarily weak. France, conscious of her inferiority in manpower should Germany ever rearm, had invested in a programme of strategic defence by fortification which looked impressive but effectively deprived her of the power to act offensively. The Royal Navy was no longer without a rival, nor was it, as in 1914, safe in concentrating its resources in European waters. British governments long sought to reduce expenditure on armaments at a time when worldwide commitments were a growing strain on British forces, all the more so in the depression; it was feared that the costs of rearmament would cripple recovery and cause inflation. Many British voters, too, believed that Germany's grievances were just. They were disposed to make concessions in the name of German nationalism and self-determination, even by handing back German colonies. Both Great Britain and France were also troubled by Italy, whose strength they over-rated. Italy was something of a joker in the European pack. Hopes that she might be enlisted against Germany had disappeared by 1938.

This was the outcome of a belated attempt by Mussolini to participate in the Scramble for Africa. In 1935, Italian forces invaded Ethiopia, an action clearly in breach of the Covenant of the League of Nations of which both countries were members. France and Great Britain were embarrassed. As great powers, as Mediterranean powers and as African colonial powers, they had to oppose Italy at the League. But they did so feebly and half-heartedly, for they did not want to alienate a country they would like to have with them against Germany if it ever came to struggle. The result was the worst possible one. The League failed to check aggression and Italy was alienated. Ethiopia lost its independence, (though, it later proved, only for a few years). This was one of several moments at which it later looked as if a fatal error was committed. But it is impossible to say in retrospect at what stage the situation which developed from these facts became unmanageable and irreversible. Certainly the emergence of a much more radical and ferociously opportunist regime in Germany was the major turning-point. But the depression had preceded this and made it possible. Economic collapse also had another important effect. It made plausible an ideological interpretation of events in the 1930s and thus further embittered them. Again, the decisive fork in the road is hard to identify.

Ideology in international relations

The infection of foreign policy by ideology was probably unavoidable. It derived ultimately from the emergence of international communism and a potential great power to promote it. But the intensification of class conflict by economic collapse encouraged the interpretation of international relations in terms of Marxism versus anti-Marxism, fascism versus communism, and even of Right versus Left, or Democracy versus Dictatorship. This was easier still after Mussolini, offended over Ethiopia, allied Italy to Germany and talked of an anti-communist crusade. All this was not only misleading, but damaging and distracting. It obscured the central nature of the German problem – and, therefore, made it harder to tackle.

Events inside the Soviet Union in the 1930s made matters worse. As the decade opened the internal situation there was precarious. Industrialization was imposing grave strains and sacrifices. These were weathered – but at huge cost to millions of Soviet citizens – by a savage intensification of dictatorship. It expressed itself not only in a war against the peasants in the name of collectivization, but from 1934 in a terror now turned against the cadres of the regime itself. In the next five years millions were executed, imprisoned or exiled, often to forced labour. The world looked on amazed as batches of defendants grovelled with grotesque confessions before Soviet courts. Nine out of ten generals in the army disappeared, and, it has been estimated, half the officer corps. A new communist élite replaced the old one; by 1939 over half the delegates who had attended the Party Congress of 1934 had been arrested. It was very difficult for outsiders to be sure what was happening, but it was clear (as many had always said) that the USSR was by no means a civilized, liberal state whatever its fascinated admirers might say; some also wondered if it was, in fact, a strong potential ally, a more important point for statesmen and strategical planners.

More directly, this also affected the international situation through Soviet propaganda, much of which appeared to reflect a deliberate promotion by Stalin of a siege mentality; far from being relaxed, the habit of thinking of the world in terms of Us versus Them which had been born in Marxist dogma and the interventions of 1918–22 was encouraged again in the 1930s. As this notion took hold, so, outside, did the preaching of the doctrine of international class-struggle by the Comintern. The effects were predictable. The fears of conservatives everywhere were intensified. Those sceptical of co-operation with Russia had only to point to the words of its rulers. It became easy to think of any concession to left-wing or even mildly progressive forces as a victory for the Bolsheviks. As attitudes thus hardened on the Right, so communists were given new evidence for the thesis of inevitable class-conflict and revolution.

Yet there was not one successful socialist or communist revolution in Europe between the wars. Such revolutionary danger as there had been had subsided rapidly after the immediate post-war emergencies. Labour governments peacefully and undramatically ruled Great Britain for part of the 1920s, to be followed in the next decade by conservative coalitions which had overwhelming electoral support and governed with remarkable fidelity to the tradition of progressive and piecemeal social and administrative reform tempered by financial prudence which had marked Great Britain's advance into what a later generation called the 'Welfare State'. The Scandinavian countries went even further; they were often extolled for their combination of political democracy, social provision and egalitarianism, and as a contrast to communism. Even in France, where there was a large and active communist party, it could not win over the majority of the electorate even after the depression, and social reform was begun in the second half of the decade. The tradition of revolutionary militancy on the left was still alive, and its rhetoric alarmed some of the *bourgeoisie*, but the split between communist and socialist persisted even within the 'Popular Front'. In Germany the communist party before 1933 had been able to poll more votes than the Social Democrats, but was never able to displace their control of the working-class movement. In less industrialized countries, communism's revolutionary success was smaller still. In Spain it had to compete on the left with socialism and anarchism; Spanish conservatives certainly feared it and may have been right to fear also the tendency to slide towards social revolution and national division which they felt and feared under the democratic republic established in 1931. In the end, though, the quarrels between Spanish communists, socialists and anarchists, were to help conservatives to destroy the republic so many of them hated.

Hitler's revolution

The successful revolutions (or sham-revolutions, like that of Mussolini) of these years were not left-wing, though often enjoying popular support. They tapped ideological obsession in other ways. In Germany a new ruler, Adolf Hitler, came to power in 1933. His astonishing success makes it very difficult to deny his political genius, despite his pursuit of goals which also make it hard to believe him wholly sane. In the early 1920s he was only a disappointed agitator who had failed in one attempt to overthrow an elected government (the Bavarian), pouring out his obsessive nationalism and anti-semitism in hypnotically effective speeches and a long, shapeless, semi-autobiographical book which few people read. In 1933, the Nationalist Socialist German Workers Party which he led ('Nazi' for short) was strong enough for him to be legally appointed chancellor (that is, prime minister) by the president of the Republic. Politically, this was one of the most momentous decisions of the century. It opened the way to the revolutionizing of Germany, and its subsequent redirection upon a course of aggression which ended by destroying itself and the rest of the old Europe too in another German war. Hitler's appeal was complex, his messages were simple. He preached that Germany's troubles had identifiable sources. The Treaty of Versailles was one. International capitalists were another. German Marxists and Jews and their supposedly anti-national activities were others. He also said that the righting of Germany's political wrongs must be combined with the renovation of German society and culture, and that this was to be done by purifying the biological stock of the German people, by excising its non-Aryan components.

At first such themes had taken Hitler very little way, but in 1930 his followers won 107 seats in the German parliament – more than the communists' 77. The Nazis were the beneficiaries of economic collapse, and it was to get worse. There are several reasons why the Nazis reaped this political harvest. It helped that the communists spent as

THE APPROACH TO THE WAR OF 1939

1932	11 Dec	British, French, German and Italian governments declare they will not resort to force in resolving differences between them.
1933	30 Jan	Hitler becomes German chancellor.
	Feb	Disarmament Conference fails to win German acceptance for proposals opening way to German rearmament on a basis of eventual equality with other powers.
	28 May	Nazi success in Danzig (Free City) elections and beginnings of Nazi takeover of city administration.
	June–July	Failure of London International Economic Conference after American repudiation of proposals to settle war debts and reparation questions.
	14 Oct	Germany withdraws from Disarmament Conference.
	23 Oct	Germany withdraws from League of Nations.
1934	26 Jan	German–Polish treaty breaches French alliance network in eastern Europe.
	25 July	Assassination of Austrian Chancellor Dollfuss and attempted Nazi coup in Vienna.
	19 Aug	Hitler becomes president of Germany.
	18 Sept	USSR joins League of Nations.
	19 Dec	Japan denounces naval agreements, including those of 1922.
1935	13 Jan	Saar plebiscite for reunion with Germany.
	16 Mar	Germany denounces disarmament clauses of Versailles treaty and reintroduces conscription.
	2 May	Franco–Russian alliance for mutual aid to resist unprovoked aggression against either.
	18 June	Anglo–German naval agreement.
	3 Oct	Italian invasion of Ethiopia.
	18 Oct	League votes imposition of economic sanctions of Italy.
1936	7 Mar	Germany denounces Locarno pacts and reoccupies demilitarized Rhineland.
	9 May	Italian annexation of Ethiopia.
	18 July	Spanish civil war begins with military revolt in Spanish Morocco.
	25 Oct	German–Italian pact establishes Berlin–Rome 'axis'.
	25 Nov	German–Japanese pact against communism.
1938	12–14 Mar	German invasion and absorption of Austria.
	May–Sept	Prolonged and deepening Czech crisis resolved finally by Munich agreements of 29 Sept, the culmination of 'appeasement' efforts in western policy, which give territory to Poland, Hungary and Germany from former Czechoslovakia leaving rump 'Czecho–Slovakia' and effectively ends French alliance system in eastern Europe.
1939	10–16 Mar	Germany absorbs remainder of Czech lands; Ruthenia passes to Hungary.
	21 Mar	German annexation of Memel.
	31 Mar	Anglo–French guarantee of independence and integrity to Poland.
	7 Apr	Italian invasion of Albania.

THE APPROACH TO THE WAR OF 1939 (continued)		
1939	13 Apr	Anglo–French guarantees to Romania and Greece.
	June–Aug	Negotiations between USSR, Great Britain and France.
	23 Aug	Nazi–Soviet pact.
	24 Aug	Anglo–Polish mutual assistance pact.
	1 Sept	German invasion of Poland.
	3 Sept	British and French declarations of war on Germany.

much energy fighting the socialists as their other opponents, a fatal handicap for the German Left all through the 1920s. Another reason was that under the democratic republic anti-semitic feeling had grown, inflamed by economic collapse. Anti-semitism, like nationalism, had an appeal which cut across classes as an explanation of Germany's troubles, unlike the equally simple Marxist explanation in terms of class war which, naturally, antagonized some potentially powerful groups as well as (it was hoped) attracting others.

The Nazis were as the 1930s opened already clearly a power in the land. They attracted more support, winning backing from those who saw in their street-fighting 'storm troopers' an anti-communist insurance, from nationalists who sought rearmament and revision of the Versailles peace settlement and from conservative politicians who thought that Hitler was a party leader like any other and might now be used in their own game. The manoeuvres were complicated, but in the 1932 elections the Nazis became the biggest party in the German parliament, though not with a majority. After Hitler's acceptance of the chancellorship in January 1933 further elections were held. The government's monopoly of the radio and unhesitating use of intimidation still did not secure the Nazis a parliamentary majority but subsequent support from some right-wing members of parliament gave them the opportunity to vote special enabling powers to the government. The most important was that of governing by emergency decree. So ended Weimar and parliamentary sovereignty. Armed with legally acquired powers, the Nazis proceeded to carry out a revolutionary destruction of democratic institutions.

Like Stalin's Russia, the Nazi regime used terror mercilessly against its enemies. It was soon unleashed especially against the Jews and an astonished Europe found itself witnessing revivals in one of its most advanced societies of the pogroms of medieval Europe or tsarist Russia. More important to the stability of the regime, though, was the fear of violence, informers and the secret police. Together with patriotic enthusiasm, an end to unemployment and effective positive propaganda it gave Nazi Germany an astonishing resilience. By 1939, there was virtually no institution of German society except the Roman Catholic Church not controlled or intimidated by the Nazis. The conservatives, too, had lost. They soon found that Nazi interference with the independence of traditional authorities was likely to go very far, even in the rebuilt German army.

Not only Germans, but many foreigners long found it difficult to believe what was happening. Confusion over the nature of the regime made it hard to deal with. Some saw Hitler simply as a nationalist leader bent, like an Ataturk, upon the material and psychological regeneration of his country and the assertion of its rightful claims, if somewhat careless towards traditional values. Others saw him as a crusader – against Bolshevism, moral degeneration, biological contamination of the race and many other things. Even people who only thought he might be a useful protector against the left, by doing so increased the likelihood that the left would see him as a tool of capitalism, another half-truth. No simple formula will contain Hitler or his aims – and there is still disagreement about what these really were – and probably a reasonable approximation to the truth is simply to recognize that he expressed the resentments and exasperations of German society in their most negative and destructive forms and embodied them to a monstrous degree. When his personality was given scope by economic disaster, political cynicism and a favourable arrangement of international forces, he released these negative qualities at the expense of all Europeans, his own countrymen included. That meant war.

The path to war

The path by which Germany came to be at war again in 1939 is easy to trace, though still cluttered with controversy. Argument goes on about when, if ever, there was still a chance to avoid war, whether or not the particular war which came about. One important moment was when Mussolini, formerly wary of German ambitions in central Europe, became Hitler's ally. Already alienated by British and French reactions to his Ethiopian adventure, a civil war which broke out in Spain in 1936 appeared to offer a prospect of adventure and advantage. Hitler and Mussolini both sent contingents to support the man who emerged as the leader of generals who had mutinied against the left-wing republic, General Franco. More than any other single international development, Spain gave ideological colour to Europe's diplomatic divisions. Hitler, Mussolini and Franco (who in fact carefully manipulated the Spanish fascists who looked to him) were all now labelled 'fascist' by the Left. Soviet diplomacy began to co-ordinate support for Spain within western countries by leading local communists to abandon their attacks on other left-wing parties and encouraging 'Popular Fronts'. Spain came to represent the conflict between Right and Left in its purest form; this was a distortion, but it made it easier to think of Europe as divided into two camps.

British and French governments were by this time only too aware of the difficulties of dealing with the new Germany. Hitler had already in 1935 announced that the German rearmament forbidden at Versailles had begun. Until their own could be completed, France and Great Britain would remain weak; France had a big army, but no strategy of using it offensively, and though the Royal Navy was still (just) the largest in the world, it could not guarantee successful maintenance at the same time of British interests in the Far East, Mediterranean and home waters. The first consequence of this was apparent when Hitler denounced Locarno and German troops re-entered the 'demilitarized' zone of the Rhineland from which they had been excluded by the Treaty of Versailles. No attempt was made to eject them. After the civil war in Spain had thrown public opinion in Great Britain and France into further disarray, Hitler then in 1938 seized Austria. It was not easy to argue for upholding the Versailles provision which forbade the fusion of Germany and Austria; to the French and British electorates the *Anschluss* (as it was called) could be presented as a matter of the legitimately aggrieved nationalism of those of German blood and speech, seeking peaceful and fraternal unification. The Austrian republic had also long had internal troubles. In the autumn came the next German aggression, the seizure of part of Czechoslovakia. Hitler was gradually fulfilling the old dream which had seemed to fade away when Prussia beat Austria in 1866 – the dream of a united Great Germany, defined as all lands of those of German blood.

In retrospect, nevertheless, the dismemberment of Czechoslovakia can be seen as something of a turning-point. It was brought about by agreement at Munich in September 1938 as a result of the last British foreign policy initiative to try to satisfy Hitler. The British prime minister, Neville Chamberlain, was still too unsure of what had been achieved by British rearmament to resist Hitler's demands, but hoped that the transference of the last substantial group of Germans under alien rule to that of their homeland might deprive Hitler of the motive for further revision of Versailles – a settlement now somewhat tattered, in any case. The justification was found in the specious claims of self-determination; but the areas involved, because of their large German populations, were important and their loss crippled the prospect of future Czechoslovak self-defence.

Chamberlain was wrong. Hitler went on to inaugurate another old dream, expansion into non-German Slav lands. The first step was the absorption of what was left of Czechoslovakia, in March 1939; the British declared a guarantee of it which they had given the previous autumn inoperative because, they said, Czecho-Slovakia (hyphenated since Munich) had broken up from within. Almost at once the largely German city of Memel, awarded by the League to Lithuania in 1924, was seized by the Nazis. Feeling a threat, Poland mobilized, ready to defend the frontier settled in 1919. Hitler resented the 'Polish Corridor' which separated East Prussia from Germany and contained Danzig, an old German city given an independent and internationalized status in 1919. At this point the British government, though hesitatingly, changed tack and offered a guarantee to Poland and other east European countries against aggression. It also began a wary negotiation with the USSR.

Soviet policy remains hard to interpret. It seems that Stalin kept the Spanish civil war going by helping the republic as long as it seemed likely to tie up German attention, but then looked for other ways of buying time against the attack from the west which he always feared. To him, it seemed likely that the Germans might be encouraged to attack the USSR by those in Great Britain and France who would see with relief the danger facing them turned against the workers' state. No doubt they would have done. But there was in any case little possibility of the USSR working with the British or French to oppose Hitler, even if they wanted to do so, because no Soviet army could reach Germany except through Poland – and this the Poles would never permit. Accordingly, for the USSR there was now nothing for it but another partition of Poland; this was arranged in the summer of 1939. After all the propaganda each had directed respectively against Bolshevik-Slav barbarism and fascist-capitalist exploitation, Nazis and Communists agreed in August to divide Poland between them; authoritarian states enjoy great flexibility in the conduct of diplomacy. Armed with this, Hitler attacked Poland on 1 September 1939.

The second German war

Two days later the British and French government honoured their guarantee to Poland and declared war on Germany, though with no enthusiasm. It was obvious

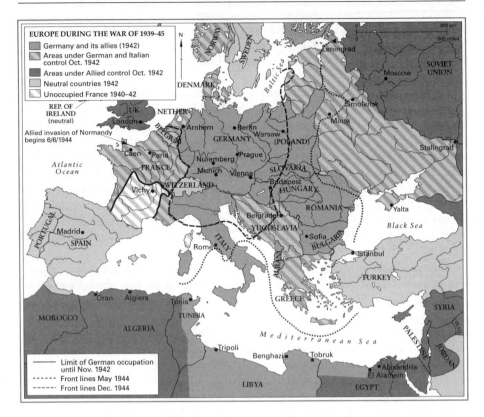

EUROPE DURING THE WAR OF 1939–45

- Germany and its allies (1942)
- Areas under German and Italian control Oct. 1942
- Areas under Allied control Oct. 1942
- Neutral countries 1942
- Unoccupied France 1940–42

Allied invasion of Normandy begins 6/6/1944

———— Limit of German occupation until Nov. 1942
------ Front lines May 1944
------ Front lines Dec. 1944

that they could not save Poland and that unhappy nation disappeared once more, divided by Russian and German forces about a month later. But not to have intervened would have meant acquiescing to the German domination of Europe, for no other nation would have thought British or French support worth having. So, uneasily, and without the popular enthusiasms of 1914, the only two constitutional great powers left in Europe faced Germany alone, and a totalitarian regime, to boot. Neither their peoples nor their rulers had much keenness for this role. Their position was relatively much inferior to that of their predecessors in 1914, but exasperation with Hitler's long series of aggressions and broken promises made it hard to see what sort of peace could be made which would reassure them. The basic cause of the war was, as in 1914, German aggression. But whereas then Germany had gone to war because *she* felt threatened, now Great Britain and France were responding to the danger presented by her expansion. *They* felt threatened this time. Hitler had hoped merely for a campaign, but he had in fact touched off a war like many earlier ones, about the balance of power in Europe. But it was to be much more, too, and like its predecessor of 1914, a world war.

To the surprise of many observers, and the relief of some, the first six months of the war were almost uneventful once the short Polish campaign was over. It had shown that mechanized forces and airpower were to play a much more important part than in the Great War. The memory of the slaughter of the Somme and Verdun was too vivid, though, for the British and French to plan anything but an economic offensive; they hoped blockade would be effective while they sat behind a western front believed to be impregnable. For the first few months of war, Hitler was unwilling to disturb them, because he was anxious to make peace. This deadlock was only broken when the British sought to intensify the blockade in Scandinavian waters, an initiative which coincided, remarkably, with a successful German offensive to secure ore supplies from Norway and Denmark. Its launching on 9 April 1940 opened an astonishing period of further German success on land but severe losses at sea. Only a month later there followed a German invasion first of the Low Countries and then of France. A powerful armoured attack through the Ardennes opened the way to the division of the Allied armies and the capture of Paris. On 22 June the French government, now led by the French marshal, Pétain, a hero of the First World War, signed an armistice. By the end of the month, the whole European coast from the Pyrenees to the North Cape was in German hands. Italy had joined in on the German side ten days before the French surrender. The French government (now at Vichy, after German occupation of half France) broke off relations with Great Britain after the British had seized or destroyed French warships they felt might fall into German hands. The Third Republic came to an end with the installation of Pétain as Head of State. With no ally left on the continent, Great Britain faced a strategical situation worse by far than that in the struggle against Napoleon.

She was not quite alone. The Dominions had all entered the war on her side, and she sheltered a number of governments in exile from the overrun continent, some of which commanded forces of their own; Norwegians, Danes, Dutchmen, Belgians, Czechs and Poles were to fight gallantly in the years ahead. The most important exiled contingents were those of the French, but at this stage they represented a faction within France, not its legal government. Their leader was a junior general who had left France before the armistice and was condemned to death *in absentia*: Charles de Gaulle. He was recognized by the British as leader of the 'Free French'. He saw himself as constitutional legatee of the Third Republic and the custodian of France's interests and honour. He soon began to show (not always wisely) the independence which was in the end to make him the greatest servant of France since Clemenceau.

Africa was the first continent other than Europe to be sucked into the war. Italy's entry assured this, her African possessions and the Mediterranean sea-lanes becoming operational areas as a result. In addition, uncertainties about what might happen to parts of the French empire, where he hoped to find sympathizers who would join him to continue the fight, led De Gaulle to unsuccessful initiatives there. Another strategic change followed from German victories in Europe. The availability of Atlantic and Scandinavian ports to Germany meant that what was later called the 'Battle of the Atlantic', the German struggle to sever British sea communications by submarine, surface and air attack, would become much fiercer.

Immediately, the British Isles faced direct attack. The hour had already found the man to brace the nation for the challenge; Winston Churchill, after a long and chequered political career, had become prime minister when the Norwegian campaign collapsed, because no other man commanded support in all parties in the House of Commons. To the coalition government which he immediately formed he gave conspicuous and vigorous leadership, something hitherto lacking. More important than this, he called forth in his people, whom he could address by radio, qualities they had forgotten they possessed. It was soon made clear that only starvation or military defeat following direct assault was going to get the British out of the war. This was even more certain after a great air battle over southern England in August and September had been won by British science (deployed in a chain of 'radio-location' stations built before the outbreak of war) and the Royal Air Force. For a moment, Englishmen knew the pride and relief of the Greeks after Marathon. The victory made a German seaborne invasion impossible (though a successful one was always unlikely). It also established that Great Britain could not be defeated by air bombardment alone. The islands had a bleak outlook ahead, but this victory changed the direction of the war. It opened a period in which a variety of influences, among them the British refusal to make peace, turned German attention elsewhere. In December 1940 planning began for a German invasion of the Soviet Union.

During that winter, the USSR made further territorial gains, apparently with an eye to securing a glacis against a future German attack. A war against Finland won her some of them. The Baltic republics of Latvia, Lithuania and Estonia, already occupied by Soviet forces, were swallowed in 1940. Bessarabia, which Romania had taken from the Bolsheviks in 1918, was now recovered, together with the northern Bukovina. In this case, Stalin was going beyond old tsarist boundaries. The timing of Hitler's decision to turn on him arose in part because of concern about possible future Russian expansion: Germany sought to keep Soviet power away from the Balkans and the Straits. A quick overthrow of the USSR would not only achieve this but would show the British that further war-making was pointless. But there was also a deep and essentially personal element at work. Hitler had always sincerely and fanatically detested Bolshevism and believed that the Slavs, whom he saw as a racially inferior group of peoples, should provide Germans with living-space and raw materials in the east. Many Germans responded to this perverted vision of the old struggle of the Teuton to impose western civilization on the Slav east. It was to justify greater atrocity than any earlier crusading myth.

A brief spring campaign provided an overture to the coming clash of titans. The Germans overran Yugoslavia and Greece (with the second of which Italian forces had been unhappily engaged since October 1940). Once again British armies were driven from the mainland of Europe, to which they had been sent, in inadequate force, to help new allies. Crete, too, was then taken by a spectacular German airborne assault. Now all was ready for 'Barbarossa', as the great onslaught on the Soviet Union was named, after a crusading German emperor of the Middle Ages. It was launched on 22 June 1941. In huge early successes vast numbers of prisoners were taken and the Russian armies fell back hundreds of miles. The German advance guard came within a narrow margin of entering Moscow. But that margin was not quite eliminated and by Christmas the first successful Soviet counter-attacks announced that in fact Germany was pinned down. Germany had lost the initiative. A great mistake had been made, after all. If the British and Russians could hold on and keep up their alliance, then, failing a radical technical modification of the war by the discovery of new weapons of great power, their access to American production by sea would inexorably increase their strength. This did not, of course, mean that they would inevitably overthrow Germany, only that they might bring her to negotiate terms.

The Second World War

The Second World War has usually been agreed to have been already under way before the launch of Barbarossa; among favoured dates for its beginning are 1937 (in China) or 1936 (in Spain). What can truly be said was that it was an assemblage of wars, and that some of them were going on even before 1939. The first to come together were the war in western Europe against German power and the Nazi-Soviet (or Teuton-Slav) struggle in the east. 1941 entangled these with other struggles.

The American president Franklin Roosevelt had believed since 1940 that in the interests of the United States Great Britain had to be supported up to the limits permitted by American public opinion and the law of neutrality (and he went beyond both at times). By the summer of 1941, Hitler knew that to all intents and purposes the United States was an undeclared enemy. A crucial step was the American Lend-Lease Act of March that year which provided production and services to the allies without payment (and would be in due course extended to the USSR). Soon afterwards, the American government extended naval patrols and the protection of its shipping further eastward into the Atlantic. After the invasion of Russia, the first meeting between Churchill and Roosevelt resulted in a statement of shared principles – the Atlantic Charter – in which one nation at war and another formally at peace spoke of the needs of a post-war world 'after the final destruction of the Nazi tyranny'. Such language was a long way from isolationism. It helps to explain Hitler's second fateful and foolish decision of 1941, a declaration of war on the United States on 11 December, after a Japanese attack on British, Dutch and American possessions four days earlier. Hitler had earlier promised the Japanese he would join them. The war thus became global, and a great chance had been thrown away. The British and American declarations of war on Japan could have left two separate wars to rage, with only Great Britain, Australia, New Zealand and the Dutch government in exile engaged in both; Hitler's decision ignored the possibility that American power might be kept out of Europe and deployed only in the Pacific. Few single acts have so marked the end of an epoch, for he had ensured the eclipse of European power. The continent's future would now be settled not by its own efforts but by the two great powers on its flanks, the United States and Soviet Russia.

Japan's alliance with Germany and Italy turned out not to amount to much in practice. The Japanese struggle was essentially against the United States. The prospects of rapid gains, above all in raw materials and oil, by conquering European possessions in the Far East were decisive in the timing and manner of the Japanese attack. But to go to war with the United States was the crucial decision, and startlingly rapid and widespread though the early Japanese successes were, it was a gamble which failed. Once the initial victories came to an end, the Japanese faced a prolonged war such as they were bound to lose. Pearl Harbor united Americans as little else could have done. Isolationism could be virtually ignored after 8 December; Roosevelt had a nation behind him as Wilson never had. Hitler's decision made that decisive for European history, as well as Asian.

The war was now much more truly a world war than that of 1914–18 had ever been. By the time of Pearl Harbor German operations in the Balkans left in Europe only five neutral countries outside the European struggle – Turkey (with only very little European territory), Spain, Portugal, Sweden and Switzerland. The war in North Africa which raged back and forth in Libya and Egypt had by then been extended to Syria and to Iraq where a nationalist government supported by German aircraft was removed by a British force. Iran was occupied by the British and Russians in 1941. In Africa, Ethiopia was liberated and the Italian colonial empire destroyed. Other European empires faced their demolition at the hands of the Japanese who had within a few months in early 1942 seized Indonesia, Indo-China, Malaya, and the Philippines. They pressed through Burma towards the Indian border and were soon bombing Australia from New Guinea.

Meanwhile, the naval war went on. German submarines, aircraft and surface raiders ranged over the Atlantic, the Arctic, the Mediterranean and the Indian Ocean. Soon, only a tiny minority of countries were left outside this colossal struggle.

Its demands carried social and economic mobilization much further than had the First World War. The role of the United States was decisive. Her huge manufacturing power made the material preponderance of the 'United Nations' (as the coalition of states fighting the Germans, the Italians and Japanese was called from the beginning of 1942) incontestable. None the less, the way ahead was still very hard in the first months of 1942. Four great and very different battles were turning-points. In June a Japanese fleet attacking Midway Island was broken in a battle fought largely by aircraft. Japanese losses were such that she never regained the strategical initiative and a long American counter-attack in the Pacific now began to unroll. Then, at the beginning of November, the British army in Egypt decisively defeated the Germans and Italians and began to march west to join Anglo-American forces landed in French North Africa in the total defeat of the enemy and his eviction from all North Africa by May 1943. Six months earlier, at the end of 1942, the Soviet army had bottled up at Stalingrad on the Volga a German army rashly exposed by Hitler. Its remnants surrendered in February in the most demoralizing defeat yet suffered by the Germans in Russia, and one which was only part of three splendid months of Soviet winter advance which marked the turning-point of the war on the eastern front.

The other great Allied victory was in the Battle of the Atlantic to maintain sea-communications with the United Kingdom. Its peak came in the early months of 1942. In March nearly 850,000 tons of shipping were lost and six U-boats were sunk; six months later, the figures were 560,000 tons and eleven U-boats. The tide had turned, though there was still hard fighting ahead. At the end of the year nearly 8,000,000 tons of shipping had been lost for eighty-seven U-boats sunk. In 1943 the corresponding figures were three and a 250,000 tons and 237 U-boats. This was the most crucial battle of all for the United Nations, for on it depended their ability to draw on American production and to re-enter western Europe. It owed most to a British superiority in signals intelligence which was almost continuous from 1941 onwards.

Roosevelt had agreed to give priority to the defeat of Germany, but an invasion of France could not in the end be mounted before 1944, and the delay angered Stalin. When it came, the invasion of northern France in June that year was the greatest seaborne expedition in history. Mussolini had by then been overthrown by Italians and Italy had been invaded from the south; now Germany was fighting on three European land fronts. Soon after the landings in Normandy, the Russians entered Poland. Going faster than their allies, it still took them until April 1945 to reach Berlin. Allied forces in the west had by then broken out of Italy into central Europe and from the Low Countries into northern Germany. Almost incidentally, terrible destruction had been inflicted on German cities by a great air offensive, though until the last few months of the war it probably had no decisive strategic effect. It helped to ensure, though, that much of historic Europe was literally as well as figuratively in ruins when, on 30 April, the man who had ignited this conflagration killed himself amid the ruins of Berlin. On 8 May, those who had inherited from Hitler the nominal government of Germany surrendered unconditionally.

The war in the Far East took a little longer but the decisive moments came when two nuclear weapons of a destructive power hitherto unknown were dropped by the

Americans with terrible effect on two Japanese cities. Between the explosions, the Russians declared war on Japan. On 2 September the Japanese government signed an instrument of surrender. The Second World War had come to an end.

The meaning of victory

It was difficult in 1945 to measure the colossal extent of what happened. There was visible only one immediately obvious and unambiguously good outcome: the overthrow of the Nazi regime. As the Allied armies had advanced into Europe, the evils of an unprecedented and hitherto unimaginable system of terror and torture had been revealed. The prison camps for slave labour and political prisoners and the revelations of what went on in them were only part of an appalling story. It was suddenly apparent that Churchill had spoken no more than the bare truth when he told his countrymen that 'if we fail, then the whole world, including the United States, including all that we have known and cared for, will sink into the abyss of a new Dark Age made all the more sinister, and perhaps more protracted, by the lights of perverted science'. The reality of this threat could suddenly be seen in places like Belsen and Buchenwald, but it had been lived by thousands of slave-labourers or victims of the Gestapo torture-chambers in the previous six years. Distinctions could hardly be meaningful between the degrees of atrocity inflicted throughout Europe and revealed at last.

Rightly, though, as more evidence emerged, the world's imagination was transfixed by something even worse: the systematic attempt which had been made to wipe out European Jewry. This was the so-called 'Final Solution' sought by Germans and initiated at a conference in a Berlin suburb in January 1942. In the next three years the attempt was carried far enough to change the demographic map of Europe. The three and a 250,000 Polish Jews who had made up about a tenth of the whole Jewish population of Europe in 1939 were all but obliterated. Dutch, Czech, Baltic, Greek and Austrian Jews, too, suffered terribly in proportion to their numbers; but Jews were safe virtually nowhere in Germany's occupied territories or those of her allies. Overall, though complete figures may never be available, it is probable that between 6,000,000 and 7,000,000 Jews died, whether in gas-chambers and crematoria, in the special extermination camps, by shootings and extermination on the spot in east and south-east Europe, or from overwork, disease and hunger. A chapter of European and world history came to an end as the demographic base which had made Europe for centuries the centre of world Jewry was shattered.

There had never before been an attempt to wipe out so large a group of Europeans supposedly defined only by genetic inheritance. Nor had murder ever been carried out on such a scale, so systematically or with such bureaucratic orderliness; the full resources of the mature bureaucratic state were employed, even if the task was ultimately irrational (and it may actually have wasted resources which would have been better employed otherwise to sustain the German war effort). It should not be overlooked – perhaps it is the only touch of relief in the whole dreadful canvas – that even the Nazi regime was never to acknowledge publicly its extermination policies and what flowed from the much-touted rubbish of racial purity and bogus 'science' on which those policies rested. No doubt ancient myths of Jewish conspiracy and collective guilt fed the process – there was nothing new about anti-semitism in itself – but the Holocaust (as Jews came to call it after the war) was a horrifyingly modern fact, bringing together attitudes, ideas, and possibilities which arose from the mature European civilization of the last century or so. It was also a shocking novelty that so much scope had been given to inadequate and psychopathic men and women whom most societies would have striven to repress and control; many of the Nazi hierarchy themselves were psychologically warped, sometimes disturbed, credulous, ignorant creatures (but others were highly intelligent) and below them were deployed as in no other country the nation's criminals and sadists, authorized by rank and uniform to work out their hatreds and destructiveness on victims provided by a mad but methodical social engineering. This was a feature of the Holocaust even more dreadful than the silence of the many who actually knew or could guess the nature of what was going on.

Many others than Jews also died in the extermination and labour camps. Yet the Holocaust was a unique atrocity. It led to doubt about the validity of a civilization, of any meaning to European history, to a withering of beliefs about human nature, its capacity for rational self-direction, benevolence, and its potential for progressive improvement. In many ways, thoughtful Germans had for decades believed their country to be one of the most civilized in Europe, and so, indeed, it had been. It embodied much of what was best in the European heritage. That Germany should fall prey to collective derangement as she had done seemed to argue that something had been at the root of that civilization itself. Hitler had not been a new Genghis Khan, revelling in the ravaging of what he did not understand, but a man working within a deranged logic which he had persuaded others to share. The crimes of Nazism had been carried out not only in a fit of barbaric intoxication with conquest, but in a way about which there was little that was irrational except the appalling ends which it sought. In this respect the Asian war was importantly different. Its fearful but unsystematic cruelties and brutalities were limited, mainly affecting only the British and Dutch among European peoples. Japanese imperialism replaced the old western imperialisms for a time, sometimes harshly, but the subject peoples did not always regret the change.

It was in retrospect distressing, but perhaps an unsurprising fact that relatively few people and no governments had actually engaged in the war because they saw it as a struggle against Nazi wickedness, even if many of them were heartened as it proceeded by a growing sense that the conflict had a moral dimension. Propaganda contributed to this, before the full evil of Nazism was revealed. Even while England was the only nation in Europe still on her feet and fighting for her survival, a democratic society had sought to see in the struggle positive ends which went beyond survival. Hopes of social and economic reconstruction and a new world of co-operation between democratic great powers were embodied in the Atlantic Charter and new international organizations already in being in 1945. These were entities significantly transcending European history in their importance. They were encouraged by goodwill towards allies, a sense of comradeship in an unequivocally righteous cause, and a tragic blurring of differences of interest and social ideals which were only too quickly to re-emerge. Much wartime rhetoric was to boomerang badly with the coming of peace; disillusionment began soon to follow inspection of the world after the guns were silent. Yet for all this, the war of 1939–45 in Europe had turned out in the end to be a moral struggle in a way, perhaps, in which no other has ever been. Too much would be heard in due course of the regrettable consequences of Allied victory; it should never be forgotten that it crushed the worst challenge to liberal civilization which has ever arisen, even if that challenge was, somehow, also the monstrous creation of that civilization.

Europe in 1945

The most obvious immediate legacy of the war in Europe was the sheer and unparalleled destruction it had caused. It was most visible in the devastated cities of Germany, where mass aerial bombing, a major innovation of the struggle, was much more brutal and costly to those who underwent it than had been the bombing of Spanish cities in the Spanish civil war, terrible as that had seemed at the time. But not only had whole cities been flattened. Economic life and communications had also been grievously stricken, especially in central and eastern Europe. In late 1945, millions of refugees were still wandering about in it, trying to get home. There was a grave danger of famine and epidemic because of the difficulty of supplying food. The tremendous problems of 1918 were upon Europe again, and in even more threatening ways. This time they confronted nations demoralized by defeat and occupation; only the neutrals and Great Britain had escaped those scourges. There were abundant arms in private hands, and revolution was feared in some countries. The connexion with the political impact of the war was obvious. The power structure which had been a reality until 1914 and had an illusory prolongation of life between the two world wars, had been doomed since 1941. Two great peripheral powers dominated Europe politically and were established militarily at its heart.

This was evident at a meeting of the Allied leaders at Yalta in February 1945 which provided a basis for agreement, and what would have to serve as the basis of a peace settlement in Europe for decades. Europe was to be divided into eastern and western halves. Once again an Adriatic-Baltic division became a reality; new differences were to be layered on top of old. At the end of 1945 there lay to the east a Europe of states all of which, except for Greece, had governments in which communists shared power or were dominant. The Soviet army had proved itself a far better instrument for the extension of international communism than revolution. The pre-war Baltic republics did not emerge from the Soviet embrace which had enfolded them in 1939, and the borders of the Soviet Union now also included parts of pre-war Poland and Rumania.

A phase of European history which Germany had dominated was at an end. Once the centre of the old European power structure, she had effectively ceased to exist. Hitler's creation had been fragmented by the liberation of Poland and Czechoslovakia and the institution of distinct and separate occupation arrangements for Austria. Even Bismarck's smaller Germany (with the exception of Alsace and Lorraine, resumed again by France) was now partitioned into zones occupied by the Russians, Americans, British and French and reduced by losses of territory in the east. The other major political units of continental western Europe had reconstituted themselves after occupation and defeat, but were still feeble (though France had a substantial army in the field again at the end of the war); Italy, which had changed sides after Mussolini had been overthrown, had, like France, a much strengthened and enlarged communist party which, it could not be forgotten, was still committed to the revolutionary overthrow of capitalism. Franco's Spain survived, suffering from the prolongation, in effect, of the economic misery of her own civil war by wartime blockade, isolated by world opinion. Only Great Britain retained in the world's eyes her stature, morally enhanced by her stand in 1940 and 1941. She remained for a while the formal equal of the USSR and the United States, as did France and China, too. Yet this was unreal. Great Britain's moment was past. By mobilizing her resources and society to a degree unequalled out-

THE EUROPEAN WAR 1939–45

1939	Sept 1	German invasion of Poland.
	Sept 17	Soviet invasion of Poland.
	Sept 27	Polish resistance comes to an end.
	Nov 30	Soviet attack on Finland.
1940	Mar 12	Finns make peace with USSR.
	Apr	British and French mine Norwegian waters to hinder German shipping.
	Apr 9	Germans invade Norway and Denmark.
	May 10	German invasion of Netherlands, Belgium, Luxembourg.
	May 14	Dutch army lays down arms .
	May 26	Belgian forces ordered to capitulate.
	May 28–June 4	Evacuation of bulk of British forces and 140,000 French from Dunkirk.
	June 3–7	Allied forces withdraw from Norway.
	June 10	Italy declares war on France and Britain.
	June 22	French armistice with Germany (and June 24 with Italy).
	July 9	End of French Third Republic and formal initiation of new regime at Vichy.
	Aug 8–Oct 10	Battle of Britain.
	Oct 8	German troops enter Romania.
	Oct 28	Italian attack on Greece from Albania.
	Nov	Hungary and Romania join German-Italian-Japanese pact.
1941	Mar	Bulgaria joins Axis.
	Apr 6	German invasion of Yugoslavia and Greece.
	Apr 17	Yugoslav capitulation.
	Apr 23	Greek armistice with Germans; British forces withdrawn.
	May 20	Successful German airborne attack on Crete begins.
	June 22	German invasion of USSR. By the end of October German forces have occupied Odessa and Kharkov, entered the Crimea, and are on the outskirts of Moscow.
1942	July 2	Opening of German summer offensive – capture of Sevastopol and advance into northern Caucasus.
	Oct 25	Start of battle of El Alamein.
	Nov 8	Anglo-American landings in North Africa provoke occupation of Vichy. France by Germans and scuttling of French fleet at Toulon.
	Nov 19	At furthest extent of German success, Russian counter-offensive begins.
1943	Jan	Russians raise siege of Leningrad.
	Feb 2	German surrender at Stalingrad.
	Mar	German spring offensive begins.
	July	Soviet summer offensive opens.
	July 10	Allied landings in Sicily.
	Sept 3	Allied invasion of Italy and armistice with new Italian government.
	Nov 6	Russian recapture of Kiev.
	Dec 31	Russian recapture of Zhitomir.
1944	Feb	Soviet forces enter former Estonia.
	Mar	Crimea retaken by Soviet forces.
	June 4	Anglo-American forces enter Rome.

THE EUROPEAN WAR 1939–45 (CONTINUED)

1944	June 6	Anglo-American landings in Normandy open the invasion of northern Europe.
	Aug	Soviet forces enter Poland, Romania and East Prussia.
	Aug 15	Allied landings in south of France.
	Aug 24	Surrender of Rumanian government.
	Sept 2	Liberation of Brussels.
	Sept 12	American forces enter German territory near Eupen.
	Sept 25	USSR declares war on Bulgaria: surrender three days later.
	Oct 20	Russians enter Belgrade.
	Dec 16–25	German counter-offensive in France defeated.
1945	Jan–Apr	Battle of Germany.
	Jan 17	Soviet forces take Warsaw.
	Feb 7	Yalta Conference.
	Feb 13	Final Russian mastery of Budapest.
	Feb 20	Russians near Berlin.
	Mar 7	Allied forces cross the Rhine.
	Apr 20	Russians enter Berlin.
	Apr 25	US/USSR forces meet on the Elbe.
	Apr 28	German forces in Italy surrender.
	May 1	Death of Hitler announced.
	May 7	German surrender.
	May 8	VE day – the end of the war in Europe.
	June 5	Allied Control Commission takes control of German territory as of 31 Dec 1937.

side Stalin's Russia, she had been able to survive. But she had been let out of strategic impasse only by the German attack on Russia, and kept afloat only by Lend-Lease. Such aid, too, had been costly: the Americans had insisted on the sale of British overseas assets to meet the bills before it was forthcoming. The sterling area was dislocated and American capital was now to move into the old Dominions on a large scale. Those countries had learnt new lessons both from their new wartime strength and, paradoxically, from their weakness, in so far as they had relied upon the 'mother country' for their defence. From 1945, they more and more acted with full as well as formal independence. As for the colonial empire, it had not only been strained by the war, but had lost more of its moral authority when it proved unable to defend many of its subjects.

This huge change in the position of the greatest of the old imperial powers was, for the perceptive, already clear. When Great Britain made her last great military effort in Europe in 1944, the expedition in which she joined was commanded by an American. Though British forces in Europe still for a few months afterwards matched the Americans, they were by the end of the war outnumbered. In the Far East, too (though the British reconquered Burma, destroying there the largest Japanese army to be overcome in a single theatre by any of the allies), American naval and air power drove Japan to surrender. For all Churchill's efforts, Roosevelt was by the end of the war negotiating over his head with Stalin, proposing *inter alia* the dismantling of the British empire. Great Britain, in spite of her victorious stand alone in 1940 and the moral prestige it gave her, could not escape the shattering impact on Europe of the war. Indeed, she was in some ways the power (other than Germany) whose condition illustrated it best.

BOOK SIX Europe in the
Cold War and after

Historical acceleration is a metaphor. It is very hard to measure what it means; though many statistical indexes might be employed to calibrate the pace of change, its most important aspect may well be subjective, inexpressible in numbers or measurements, a reality in the minds of men and women who more and more experienced disorientation, a sudden absence of familiar mental landmarks and psychological supports, a startling awareness that the world was not as it used to be. In this sense, it is impossible to exaggerate the acceleration of change since 1945. Men and women whose parents lived in societies still not much unlike those of their remote Stone Age ancestors have seen children grow up with a familiarity with the world of the computer incomprehensible to them. People born before the first heavier-than-air man-carrying flight have watched men walk about the surface of the moon. Scores of new nations have come into being within a few years of one another, and as they did old empires swiftly crumbled.

The last multi-national empire crumbled very fast indeed between 1989 and 1991, and with it what had long been for Europeans (and many non-Europeans, too) a central fact of life for nearly half a century: the Cold War. That supreme fact more than any other casts doubt upon the feasibility of writing an intelligible history of Europe in the post-war years, for it was a global struggle, determining much of Europe's fate, but always transcending it. There has to be more account taken of the non-European world in this last Book than in any of those which precede it. The ending of the Cold War does not remove that difficulty. Strenuous efforts have been made to construct an entity which can be meaningfully called 'Europe' in recent years, but the history of the continent however it is defined cannot after 1945 be separated comprehensibly from the history of the rest of the globe.

CHAPTER ONE Europe in the aftermath of war

The dwarfing of Europe

In 1945 thoughtful and well-read Europeans might have contemplated with admiration the prescience of a prophecy made by the French political philosopher and historian Alexis de Tocqueville over a century earlier about the Americans and the Russians whom, he noted, seemed each marked out 'to sway the destinies of half the globe'[1]. At the end of a second World War the destinies of the world did, indeed, at last appear to be likely to be dominated by two great and very differing systems of power, one based in what had been Russia, one in the United States of America. The fate of Europe was for decades to come to be shaped irresistibly by decisions taken in Moscow or Washington. Hitler's decisions of 1941 to go to war with the USSR and USA were to turn out to be the last taken by a European for many years which would change the history of the whole continent. Whatever historic Russia and the USA owed to Europe or reflected of it in their behaviour (and both were at least formally founded on ideologies European in origin) their concerns were also different and global. Geography alone settled that. Much of their behaviour towards Europe in the next few years can only be understood in a global setting; this is another reason why European history is difficult to separate from world history in the years after 1945, besides those arising from old colonial and economic connexions.

Diplomatic niceties, national psychologies and practical politics were bound for a time to limit public awareness of this consummation to the shift in world power relationships which had been going on at least since 1905. New international arrangements set up even during the Second World War to secure the rational management of international affairs and (as the League had been meant to do) to maintain international peace nevertheless reflected it. The name adopted during the war by the victorious allies, the United Nations, was given by them to a new creation, the United Nations Organization (later usually and universally known by its initials, UNO, or just UN). After careful negotiation, this organization was inaugurated at San Francisco in 1945 in a conference which opened, by apt coincidence, on the day that American and Soviet

---

[1] The quotation comes from Tocqueville's *Democracy in America*, whose original French edition appeared in two parts, published respectively in 1835 and 1840. The passage cited, from which my quotation is taken, appears on the last page of the first part, and can conveniently be found in Phillips Bradley's edition of Reeves' translation of the book (New York, 1948), I, p. 434.

soldiers met on the Elbe. There was one conspicuous and encouraging difference between its constitution and that of the old League; the USSR and USA were members from the start. Of the other forty-nine original members (there are now over 180) a majority lay outside Europe. The international hierarchies which had buttressed Europe's old ascendancy were none the less recognized in other aspects of the new organization's structure. The General Assembly contained representatives of all member states, all of whom had equal voting rights, but the Security Council had only eleven members of whom six were chosen in rotation from the member states for a month at a time, and five were permanent.

The USSR and USA each had one of these five seats but two of the others went to European nations, one to the United Kingdom, the only former European great power to survive the war unsubdued and uninvaded, and one to France (on the insistence of Winston Churchill). The fifth member, less plausibly, was China, still, under its nationalist KMT government, in no sense able to act as a great power. Each of these permanent members had a veto – a necessary concession if the USA and USSR, let alone the other three permanent members, were to accept the UNO at all. It was decided, too, that the General Assembly should sit in New York and it did so permanently from 1952 onwards – another sign of a shift in world power relationships – though its first ordinary meeting (in January 1946) was held in London. At that meeting, the first veto was cast, by the delegate of the USSR, and it was after bitter debate about the continuing presence months after the war was finished, of Soviet soldiers in Iranian Azerbaijan and of British in Greece.

The new balance of power

The presence of the United Kingdom, France and even China in the quintet of permanent members of the Security Council is hard to justify logically even if historically easy to understand. In terms of relative strength there were really only two great powers left in 1945, a fact informally recognizable long before they came to be called 'superpowers'. For all the legal and diplomatic fictions, British power was badly overstretched and overstrained. France had barely risen from the living death of occupation and was stricken by internal division, likely to be exploited by a strong and well-disciplined French communist party. Of other European pre-war 'great powers', Italy was discovering that the last two years of the war had bred new quarrels among Italians to inflame older ones not yet assuaged. Germany was in ruins and under the heel of occupation armies, no-one knew for how long.

All the nations of Europe except perhaps the former neutral states of Sweden and Switzerland, but including Spain (which, though neutral during the war, had been deprived by it of the possibility of economic recovery from her own civil war) faced grave problems, and some of them were appalling. The material ones were the most obvious. Only the United Kingdom, Sweden and Switzerland had in 1945 a higher agricultural production than in 1939. Coal output everywhere – and above all in Germany – was far below 1934–8 averages. Europe had suffered more physical and economic damage than any other continent, and the cost of the war's direct destruction there has never been accurately measured. Outside the USSR 14,000,000 Europeans were dead; of the unhappy peoples of that great country it is likely that over 20,000,000 died, perhaps 13,000,000 of them as soldiers or prisoners. In the most stricken countries those who survived lived amid ruins. Factories and communications were shattered in many places – above all, Germany. There was nothing with which to pay for the imports Europe needed except dollars from American aid or expenditure in Europe and currencies had collapsed; Allied occupation forces found that cigarettes, Spam and bully-beef were better than money. Civilized society had given way not only under the horrors of Nazi warfare, but also because occupation had transformed lying, swindling, cheating and stealing into acts of virtue; they were not only necessary to survival, but were legitimized as acts of 'resistance'. That phenomenon had itself bred new hatreds; as countries were liberated by the advancing Allied armies, the firing squads got to work in their wake. Old scores were wiped out and new ones run up (it was said that in France more perished in the 'purification' of liberation than in the great Terror of 1793, but even that comparison is dwarfed by the vengeance taken in Yugoslavia, where old enmities between communities opened up by wartime decisions to co-operate with or fight the Germans were now driven home yet more deeply by new massacres).

Much more than in 1918, European economic life had disintegrated, and that may have been more important than the physical damage. The flywheel of economic Europe had once been industrial Germany. But even if the communications and the productive capacity to restore equipment had been there, the Allies were at first bent on holding down German industrial production. Their first aim was to prevent, not encourage, Germany's recovery of her economic strength. Furthermore, Germany was divided. From the start the Russians had been carrying off capital equipment as 'reparations' to repair their own ravaged lands (as well they might after what fighting and occupation had done in the USSR; the Germans had destroyed 39,000 miles of railway track alone in their retreat). It is against this background that the power balance stands starkly in relief. In Europe, let alone outside it, the Americans and Russians enjoyed in 1945 an immense military superiority over all possible rivals. All other victorious states had, at best, won survival or resurrection; the USA and the USSR were the only real victors. What was unknown was the extent to which the might of the Red Army might mask weaknesses behind it.

The post-war USSR

Right to the end, the Soviet Union was, like its tsarist predecessor, to remain a great multinational empire, and, indeed, the last of the breed. With indispensable help from her allies, but above all at huge cost to her own peoples, she had won by 1945 a position which was stronger than the tsarist empire had ever known. In Europe, her armies dominated a broad western glacis, much of which was sovereign territory newly acquired from Germany, Poland, Czechoslovakia and Romania. The rest was soon to be organized almost completely as a system of satellites, some with Soviet garrisons. The eastern part of Germany, one of the most important areas, was potentially a major industrial entity, if it could be got on its feet again. Further west, beyond the glacis, lay Yugoslavia and Albania, the only communist states which had appeared without the help of Soviet occupying forces. In 1945 both seemed assured allies of Moscow.

Decisions taken by western governments in consultation with their allies and their military commanders had contributed to the great strategical success of the USSR. General Eisenhower, in particular, the supreme allied commander in the west, had resisted political pressure to seize Prague and Berlin before Soviet forces could get there. The outcome was a strategic preponderance of Soviet land power in eastern and central Europe all the more menacing because the barriers which had faced Russian power in 1914 (the old Habsburg empire and a united Germany) had gone. In 1945 an exhausted Great Britain and convalescent France could not be expected to stand up to the Red Army, and the only other conceivable military counterweight – the American army – was soon beginning to go home.

There were also Soviet armies on the borders of Turkey and Greece. British statesmen recalled nineteenth-century nightmares about direct Russian access to the Mediterranean; it made things look worse that a communist rebellion was under way in Greece, where a restored monarchy looked shaky. Meanwhile, outside Europe, Soviet forces occupied northern Iran and in the Far East held much of Sinkiang, Mongolia, northern Korea and the naval base of Port Arthur. They had also liberated the rest of Manchuria, though the only territory they took from Japan itself was the southern half of the island of Sakhalin and the Kuriles. The rest of these gains, like those made in the Far East by tsarist Russia, had been in the old style, that is to say, effectively at China's expense. What is more, in China there was already visible at the end of the war the possibility of a new communist success, so there, too, a new Soviet satellite might be in the making.

On the other hand, the real strength of the USSR as the war came to an end still remains hard to assess. Its peoples had clearly suffered appallingly, more, possibly, than even the Germans. Besides its huge manpower losses, probably a quarter of the Union's gross capital equipment was destroyed. In 1945, Stalin may well have been less aware of strength than of weakness. Although his governmental methods and the prestige of victory relieved him of any need, such as faced the western allies, to demobilize the huge land forces which gave him supremacy on the spot in Europe, the USSR had no atomic bomb nor a significant strategic bomber force. Stalin's decision to develop nuclear weapons (ten 'Atomgrads' were rapidly built) put a further grave strain on the Soviet economy at a time when general economic reconstruction was desperately needed. The years immediately after the war were to prove as grim as had been those of the industrialisation race of the 1930s. Yet in September 1949 an atomic explosion was achieved. In the following March it was officially announced that the USSR had an atomic weapon; the American monopoly of it no longer existed.

The United States and post-war Europe

In 1945, American world power rested much less on territorial occupation than did that of the USSR. The United States, too, had at the end of the war a garrison in the heart of Europe, but American electors wanted it brought home as soon as possible. American naval and air bases round much of the Eurasian land mass were another matter. Russia might be a greater Asian landpower than ever, but the Pacific Ocean had become an American lake. Above all, Hiroshima and Nagasaki had demonstrated the power of the atomic bomb, the new weapon which only the United States possessed.

The deepest roots of American empire lay, though, in her economic strength. Together with the Red army, the overwhelming industrial power of the United States had been the decisive material factor behind the Allied victory in Europe. America had equipped not only her own huge forces but much of those of her allies. Moreover, by comparison with them, victory had cost her little. American casualties were not few, but they were far fewer than those of her allies; those of the United Kingdom were heavy by comparison and the USSR's were colossally so. The home base of the United States had been immune to any but trivial enemy attack and was undamaged; her fixed capital was intact, her resources greater than ever. Her citizens had actually seen their standard of living rise during the war. Finally, the United States was a great creditor country, with capital to invest abroad in a world where no one else could supply it and in which her old commercial and political rivals were staggering under the troubles of recovery. Their economies drifted into the ambit of the American. The result was a world-wide surge of indirect American power, its beginnings visible even before the war ended.

In Europe this already presented a problem rapidly emerging in the last months of the war. Effectively, the United States dollar was the indispensable source of international liquidity. Through lend-lease, relief channelled through UNRRA (the United Nations Relief and Rehabilitation Administration; an agency set up in 1943) and direct expenditure on services overseas by the American armed services and other governmental agencies, Europe relied in 1945 on a dangerously contingent source to fund its imports. In effect, the United States had become Europe's banker unnoticed by millions of Europeans, however uneasy some of its officials might be.

Cold War origins

If the assertions of Lenin and his colleagues on the one hand and of Woodrow Wilson and his successors on the other are to be taken seriously, a fundamental ideological antagonism between the United States and the Soviet Union was inevitable. In this sense the Cold War might be traced back as far as 1917. Ideology was specially important on the Soviet side, for the state was founded on it; if the Soviet ruling elite and their indoctrinated subjects had not always had deep preconceptions about the behaviour of capitalist societies, their attitude towards their wartime ally would certainly have been different. It is also true that some Americans never ceased to distrust the USSR and always saw it as the revolutionary threat the early Bolsheviks had proclaimed, a threat vigorously denied by other Americans on the left. But those who consistently distrusted the USSR and feared communism were relatively few. They had no major impact on the making of American policy during the war. When the war ended, the more suspicious and wary of the two victorious allies was the Soviet Union.

When, before the end of the war, a future political division had began to appear in Europe between east and west, the British, not the Americans, had been most concerned. Soviet behaviour over Poland was, it is true, hardly what Americans had envisaged as freedom for eastern Europeans to choose their own rulers. Nonetheless, while the war went on neither the American government nor, it seemed, those who voted for it ceased to hope for reasonable agreements with the USSR about such matters. Broadly speaking, Roosevelt remained confident that the two powers could get on; they should, he thought, be able to agree, given the common ground they shared in preventing a revival of German power, and supporting the anti-colonialism which the war had released in the former European empires (the USSR he did not regard as an empire). Neither he nor his countrymen were much aware of the historic tendencies of Russian policy while, on the other hand, they had a strong historical view, and strongly disapproved, of the British empire. As the war ended, many Americans deeply distrusted British action in liberated Greece against the communist guerrilla movement which sought to overthrow the monarchy there (Stalin, interestingly, showed he was willing to let the British get on with it; he had easily agreed with Churchill that in return for leaving the Soviet Union a free hand in Rumania, the British should have one in Greece). In spite of the Monroe doctrine and their own Caribbean record, Americans in 1945 still disliked talk of explicit spheres of interest; the Soviet Union was always readier to take them as a working basis for negotiations.

When President Roosevelt died on the eve of victory, in April 1945, there was no important change in American policy or psychology. The most powerful nation on earth was, after victory, strangely unwilling to use its power in Europe; interestingly, it had shown more concern to secure important cities in China from the Chinese communists than to occupy European capitals before the Red Army could arrive. The first concern of the American military was to achieve as rapid a demobilization as possible. Even before the Japanese surrender, President Truman had cut off the Lend-Lease arrangements with America's allies which had been so important in winning the war; the USSR was among them, but, more importantly, this actually somewhat reduced the international leverage of the United States, by weakening other old friends whose help she might soon need again. Given their economic burdens, they could nowhere replace American strength with a new security system. As for the ultimate weapon, the atomic bomb, it was already clear that it was so powerful that it could only be used in the last resort – and, in any case, it took time to make such weapons; the only two available in August 1945 had been dropped on Japan.

A change in American attitudes and policy only came about with time and experience won, above all, in Germany. The Soviet forces had punctiliously carried out their agreement to set up occupation zones, to admit British and American (and later French) garrisons to Berlin, a city deep inside the Soviet zone, and to share its administration with them. There is every indication that Stalin wished, as he, Churchill and Truman had envisaged at their Potsdam meeting in July 1945, that Germany should in the end be governed as a unit; this would give the USSR a hand in the future of the Ruhr, potentially a treasure-house of reparations. At the same time a unified, occupied Germany was to be a diminished Germany; much of Silesia passed with Pomerania and East Prussia to Poland (from these new lands, and from other countries some 7,000,000 Germans were to be expelled to be resettled further west), and, once more, Alsace and Lorraine were returned to France.

Soviet efforts to ensure security against German recovery led to an increasing practical separation of the eastern zone from those of the other three occupying powers, so far as was compatible with the occupation agreements. This divergence may well have been motivated at first by a wish to provide a solid and reliable (that is communist) core for a future united Germany. It was to lead, though, in the end to a solution of the German problem by partition for forty-five years, something no one had envisaged. Economic considerations, though, were equally divisive. Soon, the western zones were for economic reasons integrated with one another. Meanwhile events inside the Soviet zone aroused growing suspicion. Steps taken in east Germany seemed to reflect a pattern already seen elsewhere. In 1945 only Yugoslavia and Bulgaria had governments supported by communist majorities; in other eastern European countries the communists shared in coalition governments, yet they, too, increasingly seemed to have to dance to the Soviet tune. Something like a communist bloc was already crystallizing in 1946. Whatever his exact motives, Stalin obviously feared any reunification of Germany unless it was under a government he could control; Russian historical memory was haunted by onslaughts from the west, by the Teutonic Knights, by the Swedes of the seventeenth century, by the 'interventions' of 1919. If not ruled by allies or, better still, creatures, of the USSR, a united Germany would always be a danger. This was always likely to be a fact of international life, whatever the ideological nature of the regime in Moscow; it would make it all the more threatening if a united Germany were also to be capitalist.

Elsewhere, there were other signs to worry former allies about Soviet policy. If in China the USSR still officially supported the non-communist – indeed, anti-communist – and nationalist KMT, it showed reluctance to withdraw Soviet forces from Iran as agreed. When they did go they left behind a satellite communist republic in Azerbaijan (to be obliterated later by the Iranians, who were by 1947 receiving military aid from the Americans). In the Security Council the Soviet veto was employed more and more frequently to frustrate former allies, and west European communists gave clear signs of their manipulation in the Soviet interest. Yet Stalin's calculations remain in doubt; perhaps he was waiting for, expecting, or even relying upon a new economic collapse in the capitalist world.

When Winston Churchill spoke in the United States in 1946 about the increasing division of Europe by an 'iron curtain' from Trieste to the Oder, many condemned him, for he by no means spoke for all his countrymen, far less for many Americans. The USSR still enjoyed much goodwill among her old allies. Yet though many of the British Labour supporters who had won a general election in 1945 had been hopeful that 'Left could speak to Left', ministers in the new Labour government quickly became sceptical. British and American policy began to converge during 1946 as American officials thought more about the tendency of Soviet policy and as it became clearer, almost incidentally, that British intervention in Greece had at least the merit of having made free elections possible there – they had not taken place in Poland, after all. The British, moreover, had by then already announced they were going to leave India, and that counted with official American opinion. Finally, President Truman had no fixed perceptions or prejudices in favour of the USSR to overcome or shed.

In the next few years, the decisive choices settling Europe's destiny for decades were taken in Washington, sometimes as a result of others taken in Moscow. One of the most momentous, was occasioned in February 1947 by a communication from the British government which implicitly conceded that Great Britain was no longer a world power. The British economy, gravely damaged by the huge efforts made during the war, urgently needed more investment at home. The first stages of decolonialization were expensive. That was not the only reason British military expenditure abroad was high, but was an important contributory fact[2]. There were new domestic costs associated with the expansion of the welfare state. A big American loan of 1945 had been used up by 1947; in the previous year, bread rationing had been introduced in the United Kingdom (it had not been found necessary during the war). By 1947 the British balance of payments was such that it could only be maintained if British forces and aid were withdrawn from Greece. In that event, that country's security would be precarious. President Truman at once decided that the United States must fill the gap. Financial aid was

---

[2]   Military expenditure abroad in 1947 was £209,000,000; the annual average of all British government expenditure abroad 1934–8, including administrative and diplomatic as well as military costs, had been £6 millions. A.S. Milward, *The Reconstruction of Western Europe 1945–51* (London, 1984), p. 41.

given to Greece and to Turkey, to enable them to survive Soviet pressure. In his personal appearance before Congress the President deliberately drew attention to the implication; much more than propping up two countries was involved. 'No government is perfect', he said, (and went on to acknowledge that the Greek was not), but, nevertheless, it was a virtue of democracy 'that its defects are always visible and under democratic process can be pointed out and corrected'[3]. The ideological challenge was explicit. Although only Turkey and Greece were to receive aid, he offered the 'free peoples' of the world American leadership to resist, with American help, 'attempted subjugation by armed minorities or by outside pressures'.

This overt decision to 'contain' Russian power, as it was called, though primarily through economic and financial aid, may well be thought the most important in American diplomacy since the Louisiana Purchase. It was a public reversal of the apparent return to isolation from Europe which the United States had seemed to hanker for in 1945, and announced an enormous break with the historic traditions of American foreign policy. In the end this would lead to unrealistic assessments of the effective limits of American power, and, critics were to say, to a new American imperialism, as the policy was extended outside Europe, but this could not be seen at the time. It was provoked by Russian behaviour and the growing fears Stalin's policy had aroused over the previous eighteen months as well as by British weakness; few decisions by American politicians and officials have ever had such great consequence for the domestic history of Europe.

The Marshall Plan

A few months later, the 'Truman Doctrine' was completed by another much more pondered step, now favoured by political conjunctures, an offer of American economic aid to European nations which would come together to plan jointly their economic recovery. This was the Marshall Plan, named after the American Secretary of State who announced it. Its roots lay in the politics of European reconstruction. The United States' interest had by now come to be seen by many American officials as one of securing the survival of democratic and friendly regimes in Europe. They may have exaggerated the political dangers facing France and Italy, but this was a new perception. The way chosen to do this was by relieving the chronic European balance of payments problems, thus assuring the economic recovery of Europe and so achieving a non-military, unaggressive form of containment of the USSR.

The British foreign secretary, Ernest Bevin, was the first European statesman to grasp the implications. With the French, he pressed for the acceptance of the offer by western European nations. It was made to all Europe. But the USSR neither wished to participate, nor would it allow its satellites to do so; the plan was bitterly attacked in Moscow. Soon (though with obvious regret) the Czechoslovakian coalition government also declined to join up; the only country in eastern Europe still without a fully communist government and not regarded as a Russian satellite, it was obviously having to toe the Soviet line. Residual belief in Czechoslovakia's independence was then

---

[3]   The President's message was delivered on March 12 (the British were to shut down their Greek commitment on March 31). See *Public Papers of the Presidents of the United States – Harry S. Truman. Jan 1 to Dec 31 1947* (Washington, 1965), pp. 176–180 for the full text.

removed by a communist *coup* in February 1948. Another sign of Russian intransigence was the revival of an old pre-war propaganda device, the Comintern, under the name of the 'Cominform' in September 1947. It at once began the denunciation of what it termed a 'frankly predatory and expansionist course ... to establish the world supremacy of American imperialism'. Finally, when western Europe set up an Organization for European Economic Cooperation (OEEC) to handle the Marshall Plan, the Russians replied by organizing their own half of Europe in Comecon, a Council for Mutual Economic Assistance which was window-dressing for the Soviet domination of the command economies of the east.

The Cold War (as it came to be called) had in fact begun. The first phase of Europe's post-war history was over. The next, a phase in global history, too, was to continue well into the 1960s. In it, two groups of states which spanned the globe, one led by the United States and one by Soviet Russia, strove throughout a succession of crises to achieve their own security by all means short of war between the principal contenders.

For all the simple brutalities of the language it generated, what followed now looks somewhat like the tangled struggles of religion in sixteenth- and seventeenth-century Europe, when ideology promoted violence, passion, and even, at times, conviction, but could never wholly accommodate all the complexities and cross-currents of the day. Above all, Cold War could not contain national interest. There was soon every sign, though, that although specific quarrels might die down and disaster be avoided, rhetoric and mythology would go rolling on, complicating and embittering issues long after they ceased to reflect reality (this too, of course, was reminiscent of the religious struggles of the European past). In some countries of what came to be a western bloc, the Cold War appeared as civil war or near-war, and generated moral debate about values such as freedom, social justice and individualism. Some of it was fought in marginal theatres by propaganda and subversion or by guerrilla movements, both subsidized and sponsored by the two great competitors. The Cold War was also an economic struggle, a competition conducted by bribery of satellites, ex-colonial politicians and uncommitted nations. Inevitably, in the process much opportunism got mixed up with doctrinaire rigidity. Probably unavoidably, Cold War was a blight which left little of the world untouched, and became a seeping source of crime, corruption and suffering for more than thirty years. But it was also the source of a protection for western Europe behind which it could grow a new future.

The liquidation of empire

One of the early complications to cut across Cold War affected Europe directly much less than a number of states in other continents. This was the emergence of nations which did not feel committed to one side or the other. Many were new nations which came into existence within a few years of 1945 as a result of decolonization, a process which, though posing little danger of nuclear conflict between superpowers, caused upheavals in international relations just as great as did the Cold War. The United Nations General Assembly was to prove much more important as a platform for anti-colonial than for Cold War propaganda (though they were often confused). Other than the USSR, six European states still had empires in 1945: Great Britain, France, Belgium, the Netherlands, Portugal and Spain. For all the vigour and rapidity with which they reassumed control after the war (the French, uniquely, carrying out bombardments of two capital cities – Hanoi and Damascus – in the process of returning) they all, in the next quarter-century, had to accept the liquidation of their colonial holdings.

With all due allowances for many differences of degree, circumstance and timing, the Asian nationalist movements had already by and large been assured eventual success when the war flattened the card castles of European imperialism in south-east Asia and Indonesia. The surrender of 60,000 British, Indian and Dominion troops at Singapore in 1942 had been the signal that European empire in Asia was doomed; no efforts could retrieve a disaster far worse than Yorktown. The repercussions were colossal even in areas (such as the Indian subcontinent) where the imperial power had not been displaced by the Japanese. The loss of face had compromised the confidence and prestige of every European in the Far East. It did not matter that the Japanese sometimes behaved badly to their new subjects. By 1945 there was a big potential for change and the former Asian empires were to be all but swept away within a few years.

In India even before 1939 it was already plain that the ending of imperial rule had become merely a question of timetable and form. Englishmen who favoured Indian independence hoped to keep it linked to the British Commonwealth of Nations, the name usually given to the empire since the Imperial Conference of 1926, which produced the first official definition of 'Dominion Status' as independent association to the Commonwealth in allegiance to the Crown, with complete control of internal and external affairs. Dominion status set a conceivable goal for India, though not one which British governments conceded as an acceptable aim until 1940. By 1941, when Japan entered the war, the tide in India was running fast both on and under the surface. Different Indian interests saw different opportunities. The Japanese attack forced the hand of the British government, which offered the Congress nationalists autonomy after the war and a right of secession from the Commonwealth. This was too late; the demand was now for immediate independence, campaigned for under the slogan 'Quit India'. Congress leaders were arrested and the British Raj continued. Rebellion in 1942 was crushed much more rapidly than had been the Mutiny nearly a century earlier, but the sands were running out if the British wanted to go peacefully. President Roosevelt discussed confidentially with Stalin the need to prepare for Indian independence (as well as that of other parts of Asia, and the need for trusteeship for French Indo-China); the entry of the United States to the war implied revolutionary change for Europeans just as it had done in 1917.

The Labour Party had long had the independence of India (and Burma) as part of its programme. On 14 March 1946 the British government offered it. Nearly a year later, (and just before announcing to President Truman its decision to withdraw from Greece) it put a pistol to the head of the Indians by announcing that it would hand over power not later than June 1948. This made it necessary to cut through the tangle of communal rivalries, already the cause of much bloodshed. The partition of the subcontinent followed. The only governmental unity it had ever enjoyed was ended on 15 August 1947 when two new Dominions of the Commonwealth appeared within it, Pakistan and India. The first was Moslem and consisted of two slabs of land on either side of northern India; the second was officially secular but overwhelmingly Hindu in its leadership and inspiration. Huge massacres followed as hundreds of thousands of refugees strove to flee across the new frontiers to find refuge from communal violence.

Outright territorial rule was not all that was at stake in Asia. Though Russian and American spheres of influence in Europe were (with the possible exception of Berlin) clearly enough demarcated in 1948 to remain virtually unchanged for forty years, the settlement of great power relationships in the Far East was to be in doubt for much longer because of the role of China. She had for over a century been trying to fight off more than merely territorial imperialism. The Second World War made it possible for her to survive the Japanese threat and to complete her long revolution. For that reason too 1941 is a key date. The merging of Sino-Japanese in world conflict, sapped Japan's freedom of action and gave China powerful allies and a new importance. Significantly, the last vestiges of the 'unequal treaties' with Great Britain, France and the United States were then swept away. This was almost more notable than any military help the Allies could give; for a long time they were too busy extricating themselves from the disasters of early 1942 to do much for China. Instead, a Chinese army was sent to help the British defend the Burma Road against the Japanese. Still hemmed in to the west, though supported by American aircraft, the Chinese had for a long time to hold out as best they could, in touch with their allies only by air or the Burma Road. None the less a decisive change had begun in the elimination of the western grip on China. It was consummated with the inauguration in 1949, on 1 October, of the People's Republic of China, a national regime formally committed to a European ideology, Marxist communism.

As in India and China, in south-east Asia and Indonesia the Second World War was decisive. The pace of change was sometimes faster in Dutch and French colonies than British. The grant of representative institutions by the Dutch in Indonesia before 1939 had not checked the growth of nationalism and communism there. Some of the nationalist leaders collaborated with the Japanese when they occupied the islands in 1942. They were in a favourable position to seize power when the Japanese surrendered, and proclaimed an independent Indonesian republic before the Dutch could return. Fighting and negotiation followed for nearly two years. Agreement was then reached for an Indonesian republic still under the Dutch Crown; this did not work. Fighting began again, the Dutch pressing forward vainly with their 'police operations' in one of the first campaigns by a former colonial power to attract the full blast of communist and anticolonial stricture at the United Nations. Both India and Australia (a country which had concluded that she would be wise to conciliate the independent Indonesia which must eventually emerge) took the matter to the Security Council. Finally the Dutch gave in. The story begun by the East India Company of Amsterdam three and a half centuries before thus came to an end in 1949 with the creation of the United States of Indonesia. A vague union with the Netherlands survived, to be dissolved five years later.

For a time the French seemed to be doing better than the Dutch. Indo-China's wartime history had been somewhat different from that of Malaysia or Indonesia because although the Japanese had exercised complete military control there since 1941, French paramountcy was not formally challenged until early 1945. The Japanese had amalgamated Annam, Cochin-China and Tongking to form a new Vietnamese state under the Emperor of Annam. As soon as the Japanese surrendered, Ho Chi Minh, the chief of the local communist party, (the Viet Minh), installed himself in the government palace at Hanoi and proclaimed a Vietnamese republic. The revolutionary movement supporting him spread rapidly. It was soon evident that for the French to re-establish themselves would not be easy. A large expeditionary force was sent to Indo-China. The French conceded the recognition of Vietnam as an autonomous state within the French Union; over the question of giving Cochin-China separate status all attempts to agree broke down. Meanwhile, French soldiers were being sniped at and their convoys ambushed. At the end of 1946 there was an attack on foreign residents in Hanoi and many deaths. Hanoi was relieved by French troops and a war began in which the communists struggled essentially for the nationalist aim of a united country, while the French tried to retain a diminished Vietnam which, with the other Indo-Chinese states, would remain inside the French Union. By 1949 they had come round to including Cochin-China in Vietnam and recognizing Cambodia and Laos as 'associate states'. But new outsiders were now becoming interested. Ho Chi Minh's government was recognized in Moscow and Peking, and that of the Annamese emperor (whom the French had set up) by the British and Americans.

Thus Asian decolonialization had quickly burst out of the simple processes envisaged by Roosevelt. Meanwhile, Burma and Ceylon had become independent in 1947. In the following year, communist-supported guerrilla war began in Malaya; though it was to be unsuccessful and not to impede steady progress towards independence in 1957, it was one of the first of several post-colonial conflicts which were to torment American relations with European states. Growing antagonism with the communist world cut across the simplicities of anti-colonialism.

The post-war Middle East

In the Middle East, stability had not yet proved too difficult to assure between the two world wars, for all the excitement the region had from time to time occasioned. In 1939 the French still held mandates in Syria and the Lebanon and the British retained theirs in Palestine while exercising varying degrees of influence or power in other Arab lands after negotiations with local rulers. The most important British interests were in Iraq, where a small force, mainly of air force units, was maintained, and Egypt, where a substantial garrison still protected the Suez Canal. After Italy's entry to the war in 1940, the Canal Zone became one of the most vital (and at times most threatened) concerns of British strategy. Egypt suddenly found herself with a battlefront on her western border (and the Sudan, where Egypt and Great Britain shared responsibilities, briefly provided another in 1940–41). Egypt remained neutral almost to the end of the war, but was in effect a British base and little else. The war also required assurance of the supply of oil from the Gulf, especially from Iraq. This led to British intervention there when Iraq threatened to move in a pro-German direction after a nationalist *coup* in 1941. A British and Free French invasion of Syria to keep Syria out of German hands in the same year in due course produced another new nation. Soon afterwards the Lebanon proclaimed its independence. The French tried to re-establish their authority at the end of the war, bombarding both Damascus and Beirut, but unsuccessfully, and during 1946 their garrisons left. The French also had difficulties further west, in Algeria, where fighting broke out in 1945. Nationalists there were at that moment asking only for autonomy in federation with France. The French made gestures in this direction in 1947, but this was not to be the end of the story.

Where British influence was paramount, anti-British sentiment was a good rallying-cry for local politicians. In both Egypt and Iraq there was much popular hostility to British occupation in the post-war years. In 1946 the British announced that they were prepared to withdraw from Egypt, but negotiations towards a new treaty broke down so badly that Egypt referred the matter (unsuccessfully) to the United Nations. By this time, though, the whole question of great power roles in the Middle East had been transformed by new forces.

Israel and the Cold War

A Palestine question and therefore uncertainty over the post-colonial fate of the Arab lands was born with a Jewish decision to establish a national state in Palestine, if necessary, by force. The catalyst was European: the Nazi revolution. At the time of the Balfour Declaration 600,000 Arabs had lived in Palestine beside 80,000 Jews. That number was already felt by some Arabs to be threateningly large. In some years between the World Wars, though, Jewish emigration from Palestine actually exceeded immigration and there appeared still to be ground for hope that the problem of reconciling the promise of a 'national home' for Jews with respect for 'the civil and religious rights of the existing non-Jewish communities' (as the Balfour Declaration had put it) might be resolved. Hitler changed this, for with the launching of Nazi persecution the numbers of Jews seeking to come to Palestine began to rise.

Some extremists always saw the British as the main enemy, rather than Hitler. Then the extermination policies began to unroll in the war years, British attempts to restrict immigration made British policy for Palestine unacceptable to more and more Jews. One side of that policy – partitioning – was also rejected by the Arabs. The issue was dramatized as soon as the war was over by a World Zionist Congress demand that a 1,000,000 Jews should be admitted to Palestine at once. British policy was increasingly denounced as a simple expression of imperial reluctance to give up territory. Other new factors now began to appear. The British had looked benevolently on the formation of an 'Arab League' of Egypt, Syria, Lebanon, Iraq, Saudi Arabia, the Yemen and Transjordan in 1945. British policy long fostered a strand of illusion that pan-Arabism might prove the way in which the Middle East could be persuaded to settle down and that the coordination of the policies of Arab states would provide a start to the solution of its problems. In fact the Arab League was soon preoccupied with Palestine to the virtual exclusion of anything else.

The other new factor was the Cold War. In the immediate post-war era, Stalin seems still to have taken the old communist view that Great Britain was the main imperialist prop of the international capitalist system. Attacks on her position and influence in the Middle East therefore followed, though the Soviet government had shown little interest in the area between 1919 and 1939. After the war, Soviet pressure was brought to bear on Turkey and Soviet support was ostentatiously given to Zionism, the most disruptive element in the region. It did not need extraordinary political insight to recognize the implications of a resumption of traditional Russian interest in the fragmented Ottoman legacy. Yet at the same moment American policy for the region turned anti-British, or, rather, pro-Zionist. In the 1946 mid-term congressional elections Jewish votes were important; a Democratic president could hardly even envisage an anti-Zionist position.

The British faced both Jewish and Arab terrorism in Palestine from 1945 onwards. They sought to disentangle themselves and leave the Holy Land. Unhappy Arab, Jewish and British policemen struggled to hold the ring while the British government tried to find a way acceptable to both sides of bringing the mandate to an end. American help was sought, but to no avail; Truman wanted a pro-Zionist outcome. In the end the British took the matter to the United Nations, which recommended partition. This was still a non-starter for the Arabs. Fighting between the two communities grew fiercer and the British decided to withdraw without more ado. On the day that they did so, 14 May 1948, the state of Israel was proclaimed. Sixteen minutes after the act of foundation it was recognized by the United States. Soon afterwards the USSR did the same. They were to agree about little else in the Middle East for the next quarter-century.

Almost at once, Israel was attacked. Egyptian armies invaded a part of Palestine which the United Nations proposal had awarded to Jews; Jordanian and Iraqi forces supported Palestinian Arabs in the territory which had been proposed for them. But David fought off Goliath, and a truce followed. In 1949 the Israeli government moved to Jerusalem, a Jewish national capital again for the first time since the days of imperial Rome, though half the city was still occupied by Jordanian forces and the move was in defiance of the United Nations which wanted the Holy City to be internationalized. With American and Russian diplomatic support and American private money, Jewish energy and initiative had successfully established a new national state where no basis for one had existed twenty-five years before.

The cost was to prove very heavy. The disappointment and humiliation of the Arab states assured their continuing hostility to the new nation and therefore opportunities for great power intervention in the future. Increasingly, Israel looked to them like another European or western implant – the first since the Crusader states – in the Islamic Middle East. Victims for centuries, the Jews were now seen by Arabs as persecutors and exploiters. For their part, Jewish leaders spoke of the danger of new Holocausts. The old quarrels of the area were thus further poisoned. In the background lay the dissolution of centuries of Ottoman power, the rivalries of successor imperialisms, the rise of two new world powers which dwarfed these in their turn, the interplay of nineteenth-century European nationalism and ancient religion, and the first effects of the growing dependence of industrial nations on oil. There are few moments in twentieth-century politics so soaked – so unhappily soaked – in history as the establishment of Israel. It was truly a moment in world history; the preponderance of European Jewry had come to an end with the Holocaust and emigration in the next quarter-century would confirm this. World Jewry, if it had a centre, would now have to look for it to Israel, with all the complicated implications that commitment to a state focus brought with it.

Europe divided: the first crisis

In Europe, the primary expression of the Cold War between the two superpowers was the *de facto* division of the continent. This overshadowed all other historic developments for more than thirty years, stimulating some, tainting others. In 1947 Hungary, Romania and Poland all ceased to have non-communists in their governments. The following February, there had followed the *coup* in Czechoslovakia with the same outcome. After this clarification there came the first true battle of the Cold War, over Berlin.

The British and Americans had begun by merging their occupation zones for economic purposes, an act which prompted a Soviet withdrawal from the joint Allied Central Commission for Germany. In June 1948, without Soviet agreement, all three western occupying powers introduced a currency reform in their own zones, with gal-

POST-WAR GERMANY AND CENTRAL EUROPE

- - - - Pre-war boundary of Germany and Poland

Post-war USSR

Warsaw Pact member-states 1955

German zones occupied by the Allies (1945–55)

UK

USA

France

USSR

The three western zones constitute the former Federal Republic, the Russian zone being the German Democratic Republic (East). Berlin remained under four-power occupation.

vanic effect, releasing the process of economic recovery in western Germany, and, more than any earlier step, cutting Germany in two. Following Marshall Aid, available (thanks to Soviet decisions) only to the western-occupied zones, it meant that the recovery of eastern Germany would not be integrated with that of western Europe. A strong western Germany might now emerge by itself, and the western powers had already made it clear that they envisaged one under its own government. That they should get on with the business of putting German industry on its feet undoubtedly made economic sense, but it also meant that eastern Germany would be thenceforth decisively on the other side of the Iron Curtain.

Currency reform divided Berlin, too, and thereby prejudiced communist chances of staging a popular putsch in the city. The immediate Soviet response was to disrupt communication between the western zones of Germany and Berlin, isolated inside the Soviet zone. Whatever their original motives, the dispute escalated. Some western officials had already had it in mind that a severance of eastern Berlin from the three western occupation zones might be attempted before this crisis; the word 'blockade' had been used and Soviet acts were now interpreted in this sense. The rights of the western allies to have access to their own forces in Berlin were not touched or questioned by the Soviet occupation forces, but they interfered with the traffic which ensured other supply to the western sectors. To nourish West Berlin, the British and Americans organized an airlift to the city. The Soviet aim was to show West Berliners that the western powers could not stay there if the Russians did not want them to; thus they hoped to remove the obstacle which elected non-communist municipal authorities presented to Soviet control of Berlin. So, a trial of strength was quickly under way. The western powers, in spite of the enormous cost of such a flow of food, fuel and medicine as would just keep West Berlin alive, announced they were prepared to keep it up indefinitely. The implication was they could only be stopped by force; for the first time since the war ended American strategic bombers moved back to English bases.

West Berliners were not in the end intimidated, because allied supply was shown to be indefinitely sustainable unless interrupted by force. After a year, the blockade was defeated. This achievement was costly, and technically remarkable; Berlin's one airfield had to handle for most of the time over a 1,000 aircraft a day (the average daily delivery of coal alone was 5,000 tons). Yet the blockade's real significance was at a higher – indeed, the highest – level. Its defeat established that at a certain point the United States was prepared to risk fighting the USSR in order to preserve the post-war settlement as it stood in 1948. Soviet policy-makers do not seem to have anticipated this outcome.

They made the best of defeat, introducing new barriers to movement between their sector of Berlin and the three western sectors (between which movement was unimpeded) and refusing the city's elected mayor access to his office. The major Soviet aim was unchanged – that there should be no reunited and economically powerful German state independent of Soviet control and embracing German national territory; this aim was now to be secured by other means than agreement between the victors. But the western allies were now able to get on with quickening the German economy in the greater part of the country without waiting for Germany's political future to be settled; and that had major implications for western Europe as a whole.

The beginnings of European political integration

The great events both inside and outside Europe which moulded the history of the continent after 1945 had unrolled against a background of opinion which, more than at any earlier time, had begun to show the significant influence not only of fears, but of feelings and thoughts about the nature of Europe as a whole, its destiny and the possibilities of shaping it, and, even, of idealism. The disaster of the war was the primary stimulus for many politicians; it could not be argued that Europe had benefited in any sense at all except in escaping an even more barbaric fate than the one she had in fact undergone. It was understandable, too, that nationalism should be identified and stigmatized as a fundamental source of European weakness which had demonstrated its power again in 1939 as in 1914. Some felt that European history in an even longer run, too, showed it to be a matter of life and death to overcome the continent's disunion.

Many other sources – some of them running back well before 1939 to the aftermath of the Great War – also contributed to what can be called the 'European Movement'. But the special circumstances of 1945 and the next few years were crucial; they each encouraged and gave opportunities to Europeans who sought a new way of organizing Europe and threw themselves enthusiastically into doing so.

Governments responded in varying degree both to such currents and to the circumstances of the day. Broadly speaking, their views, in so far as they were not circumstantial and pragmatic tended to take one of two directions in the late 1940s and early 1950s on questions of European integration. One was fairly consistently that of British governments – usually with support from Scandinavia and Ireland – and it focused on inter-governmental co-operation for defined and specific ends. In contrast, some continental European governments tended to be more willing to listen to plans for more far-reaching, supra-national integration, perhaps even going so far as federal structures and a European Parliament. Even by 1948, this had already led to important divergences and disputes. The British deeply opposed the development in that year of what became a 'Council of Europe' (formally inaugurated early in 1949) on any but the most minimalist lines – even to the extent of defeating the Franco-Italian proposal that the new body should be called the 'European Union'.

The Marshall Plan had meanwhile been followed in the following year by a specific and local defence arrangement, when Great Britain, France, Belgium, the Netherlands and Luxembourg signed the Brussels Treaty. But this was practically transcended in April 1949, a few weeks before the formal ending of the blockade, by a new international alliance, the North Atlantic Treaty Organization (NATO). This was the first Cold War agreement to link continents in its membership. Both the United States and Canada belonged to it. It was a further break with the isolationist tradition in American foreign policy, an entangling alliance providing for the mutual defence of any member attacked. Of the western European states, only Sweden, Switzerland and Spain did not become members.

On 23 May the same year, a new Germany emerged from the three western zones of occupation, the Federal Republic. In September its first government was formed, and Konrad Adenauer, a leading Catholic (Christian Democrat) politician, became the German Federal Republic's first Chancellor. A riposte followed in October when a new German Democratic Republic (GDR) took over administration from the Soviet army in the eastern zone. Under the name of the Socialist Unity Party, communists controlled its government. For the foreseeable future, then, there were to be two Germanies. The Cold War would run along the line dividing them. A dangerous and uncertain phase had been brought to a close. It was to turn out that this had been mainly at the cost of the East Germans, now tightly linked to Soviet policy and interest.

<u>CHAPTER TWO</u> Europe and
global Cold War

A new East Asia

In 1949 it had begun to appear that history might have in store not just two
Europes, but two worlds, and Europe could hardly escape the effects of that. Though of
vast consequence, the abandonment of India and other British far eastern possessions
and the mortal weakening of French and Dutch colonialism were dwarfed in importance by the inauguration of the new, communist, People's Democratic Republic of
China. In Cold War perspective, this added to the communist camp the largest population under one government anywhere in the world.

Within a year, the possibility of two worlds looked even more plausible. Korea was
another country divided by occupation after the Japanese defeat. The UN had tried to
grapple with the reunification of the two halves of the country defined by American and
Russian armies, but, after many efforts, failed to get agreement to elections covering the
entire country. In 1948 it had therefore recognized as the lawful government of all
Korea one elected in the south under American protection. This government claimed,
but could not enforce, sovereignty over the whole peninsula. A Korean People's Democratic Republic had meanwhile been set up in the north. It now appears that it was with
the foreknowledge and approval of Stalin that its armies invaded the southern republic
in June 1950. Within two days, the Security Council had voted to resist the aggression
against a member state of the UN and President Truman had sent American forces to
help the south Koreans in its name. Because the USSR was at that moment boycotting
meetings of the Council, the Soviet delegation had not been able to exercise its veto,
and the UN was consequently to achieve its only major success in imposing international discipline on an aggressor.

The bulk of the UN forces in Korea were always to be American, but other nations,
including some European, sent contingents to help; the British did so as part of a Commonwealth division, supported by naval and air forces. The allied army was successful;
within a few months it crossed into the territory of North Korea, across the 38th parallel. Then, as fighting drew near the Manchurian border, Chinese forces intervened.
The UN armies were thrown back and the danger of a much greater war, possibly
involving the use of nuclear weapons by the Americans, now loomed up. And behind
China, possibly, there stood the USSR. Prudently, and after moderating advice (from,
notably, the United Kingdom) the United States did not provoke a major war in Asia.
Soon, further fighting showed that the Chinese could not overturn South Korea against

the wishes of the Americans. In demonstrating their will and capacity to uphold South Korean independence, the Americans had won another Cold War battle, this time in Asia. An armistice was signed in July 1953, and talks began with the aim of turning it into a definitive peace; they are still going on.

The war had brought at last China's clear re-emergence as a great power. Though not able to achieve all her own aims, she had demonstrated that she could not be defeated except at the cost of a major war, and possibly of a nuclear confrontation with the USSR. The next evidence of her use of a renewed independence came when she began to supply arms to the communist guerrilla forces in Vietnam. These were less to

---

DECOLONIZATION IN ASIA

Indian sub-continent

1942   British offer of autonomy after the war refused by Indian independence movement.

1946   **Mar 14** British offer of full independence to India.

1947   **Feb 20** British set terminal date for withdrawal.
June Endorsement of partition by Hindu and Moslem leaders
Aug 15 Inauguration of Dominions of India and Pakistan.

1948   Ceylon (Sri Lanka) becomes a Dominion.

1950   Inauguration of Republic of India within Commonwealth.

1956   Inauguration of Islamic Republic of Pakistan within Commonwealth.

South-East Asia

1945   Independence of Vietnam, Cambodia, Laos all proclaimed, but French slowly regain control of each country.

1948   Burma becomes independent republic.

1949   Independence of Vietnam within French Union conceded by French.

1954   France concedes complete independence of South Vietnam, Laos, Cambodia. Vietnam divided by internal agreement.

1957   Federation of Malayan states, independent within Commonwealth.

1959   Self-government for Singapore.

Indonesia

1945   Independence of new Republic of Indonesia proclaimed, followed by re-establishment of Dutch authority.

1949   Dutch transfer sovereignty to new United States of Indonesia.

1954   French dissolution of all links with Netherlands.

East Asia

1943   UK and US relinquish extra-territorial rights in China.

1945   Division of Korea between USSR and USA occupation.

1946   Inauguration of Republic of Philippines.

1948   Republic of Korea (South) and Korean Peoples' Democratic Republic (North) set up; UN recognizes only the former.

support a struggle against colonialism – that was decided already – than to help settle what should follow it. In 1953 the French had given up both Cambodia and Laos. In 1954 they lost at a base called Dien Bien Phu a battle decisive both for their prestige and for the French electorate's will to fight. After this, it was impossible to maintain French ascendancy in the Red River delta. A conference at Geneva agreed to partition Vietnam between a South Vietnamese government and the communists who had come to dominate the north, pending elections which might reunite the country. The elections never took place. Instead, there was soon to open in Indo-China what was to become the fiercest phase since 1945 of the Asian war against the West begun in 1941. The western contenders were no longer the former colonial powers but the Americans; the French had gone home and the British had problems enough elsewhere. On the other side was a mixture of Indo-Chinese communists, nationalists and reformers supported by their Chinese and Soviet patrons. American anti-colonialism and the belief that the United States should support indigenous non-communist governments led it to back the South Vietnamese as it backed South Koreans. Unfortunately neither in Laos nor South Vietnam, nor, in the end, in Cambodia, did there emerge regimes of unquestioned legitimacy in the eyes of those they ruled. The domestic interests of their peoples, though, were to be increasingly lost to sight in the next few years as more and more Indo-Chinese history was forced into the mould of the Cold War.

The Europeans were closing down their colonial business in Asia. At times, they moved less rapidly than they themselves wished. The British, in particular, experienced several delays arising from factors beyond their control. Their forces had to come back into action again in south-east Asia as late as 1964 when Sukarno, the strong man of the new Indonesia, turned on the new federation of Malaysia which had emerged in 1957 (and was enlarged in 1962) from fragments of the colonial empire. For many Asians, though, the end of European rule now seems less of a turning-point than once thought, and less influential than Cold War rivalries. Realities conceded by imperial facades began to appear. Europeans had swayed the fate of millions of Asians and had influenced their lives for centuries, tying them into new, international special relationships, but their civilization had touched the hearts and minds of few except the ruling élites with whom they had co-operated, or which they had helped to create. In Asia it had to contend with deeper-rooted and more powerful traditions than anywhere else in the world. Asian cultures had not been (because they could not be) swept aside like those of pre-Columban America. As in the Islamic world outside Asia, both the direct efforts of Europeans and the indirect diffusion of European culture through self-imposed modernization faced formidable obstacles. The deepest layers of thought and behaviour often remained undisturbed even in Asians who believed themselves most emancipated from their past, the most 'Europeanized'.

The Middle East and North Africa

The survival of Israel had revolutionized politics in the Middle East. To these destabilizing forces was added an accelerating rise after 1948 in the demand for oil and the impact of the Cold War. Israel focused Arab feeling more sharply than Great Britain had ever done (though there was still a British garrison in Suez, as well as British forces in other 'friendly' Arab states). It even for a time made pan-Arabism look plausible. On the injustice of the seizure of what were regarded as Arab lands (and promised to Arab rulers in the Great War), on the plight of the Palestine refugees and the obligations of the great powers and the United Nations to act on their behalf, Arabs brooded bitterly. Their rulers were able to agree over these grievances as on nothing else. None the less, after the defeat of 1948–9, the Arab states were not for some time disposed again to commit their own forces openly.

A series of armistices which established Israel's *de facto* borders with Jordan, Syria and Egypt lasted until 1967. There was continuing friction in the early 1950s, and raids were carried out upon Israel from Egyptian and Syrian territory by bands of young guerrilla soldiers recruited from the refugee camps, but immigration, hard work and money from the United States steadily consolidated the new state. As the gap between Israel's *per capita* income and that of the more populous Arab states widened, this was an extra irritant for the Arabs. Foreign aid to their countries produced nothing like such dramatic change. Egypt, the most developed, faced particularly grave problems thanks to rapid population growth. Contrasts deepened between different Arab states, and between rich and poor within them. Most of the oil-producing countries were ruled by small, wealthy, often traditional and conservative, occasionally nationalist and westernized, élites, usually uninterested in the poverty-stricken peasants and slum-dwellers of more populous neighbours. Yet nationalists and pan-Arabists alike faced difficulties in pulling together anti-Israeli, anti-British and anti-western feeling.

More hopeful prospects seemed to open after a revolution in Egypt brought to the front a young soldier, Gamal Abdel Nasser, who for a time seemed likely both to unite the Arab world against Israel and to open the way to social change. In 1954 he became the leader of the military junta which had overthrown the Egyptian monarchy. The British government, at a time of strong hostile feeling, tried always to co-operate with Arab rulers; the Middle East was not thought to matter less after withdrawal from India. In 1951 a British ally, the king of Jordan, had been assassinated; in order to survive, his successor had to make it clear that he rejected the old ties with Great Britain. Further west, the French, who had been forced to recognize the complete independence of Morocco and Tunisia soon after the war, faced more trouble. In 1954 an Algerian national rebellion began; no French government could easily abandon over a 1,000,000 settlers of European stock. Moreover oil had just been discovered in the Sahara.

Against this background Nasser's rhetoric of social reform and nationalism appealed to Arabs outside Egypt. His anti-Israeli feelings were not in doubt and he quickly had to his credit an agreement with Great Britain for the evacuation of the Suez base. The Americans, too, increasingly aware of Russian menace in the Middle East, looked on him for a while with favour as a spotless anti-colonialist and potential client but he soon came to appeal to them much less. In 1950, the British, French and Americans had agreed to try to calm the area by providing only limited supplies of arms to old customers in the Middle East and to do so only on such terms as would keep a balance between Israel and the Arabs. When Nasser carried off an arms deal with Czechoslovakia on the security of the cotton crop and Egypt gave diplomatic recognition to communist China, second thoughts about him hardened. To show displeasure, an American and British offer to finance a cherished project of internal development, a dam high on the Nile, was withdrawn. As a riposte, Nasser seized the assets of the private company which owned and ran the Suez Canal, saying its profits should finance the dam; this touched an old nerve of British imperial sensibility. Instincts only half-disciplined by imperial withdrawal seemed for once to be coherent both with anti-communism and with friendship towards more traditional Arab states whose rulers were beginning to look askance at Nasser as a revolutionary radical. The British prime minister, too, was obsessed with a false analogy: he identified Nasser as a new Hitler, to be checked before he embarked upon a career of successful aggression. As for the French, they were aggrieved by Nasser's support for the Algerian insurrection. Both nations formally protested over the Canal's seizure and, in collusion with Israel, began to plot Nasser's overthrow.

In October 1956, the Israelis suddenly invaded Egypt to destroy, they announced, bases from which guerrillas harassed their borders. The British and French governments at once announced that freedom of movement through the Canal was in danger. They called for a cease-fire; when Nasser rejected this they launched (on Guy Fawkes' Day) first an air attack and then a seaborne assault on Egypt. Collusion with Israel was denied but the denial was preposterous. It was a lie, and, still worse, a lie always incredible. Soon, the Americans were thoroughly alarmed; they feared the USSR would benefit from this renewal of imperial adventure. Their financial pressure forced the British to accept a cease-fire negotiated by the United Nations. The Anglo-French intervention ended in humiliation.

The Suez affair looked (and was) a western disaster, but its main importance was immediate, moral and psychological. The British suffered most; it cost them much goodwill, particularly within the Commonwealth, and squandered confidence in the sincerity of their retreat from empire. It confirmed the Arabs' hatred of Israel; the suspicion that she was indissolubly linked to the west made them yet more receptive to Soviet blandishment. Nasser's prestige soared still higher. Some thought, too, that Suez had badly distracted the west at a crucial moment from eastern Europe (where a revolution in Hungary against its Soviet satellite government was crushed by the Soviet army while the western powers quarrelled with one another). Nevertheless, the essentials of the region's affairs were left by the crisis much as before. Suez did not change the balance of the Cold War, or of the Middle East, where the British and French were never again to risk burning their fingers so badly. They watched the later collapse of friendly governments with more sorrow than anger, though in the 1960s British forces were summoned to Jordan to sustain its ruler, ironically, against pro-Nasser forces. The most important development in the Arab world came in Algeria, to which Suez had been only indirectly connected.

In that decade, the Algerian national revolution proved uncontainable. It was embittered by the complexities of civil war, for 'Algerians' included both the indigenous peoples of the Maghreb (who were divided among themselves) and those of European descent (who were only somewhat less divided). The intransigence of settlers and the bitterness of many soldiers who felt they were asked to do an impossible job there nearly brought about a *coup d'état* in France itself. General de Gaulle, who had become president under the new constitution of the French Fifth Republic in 1958, nevertheless opened secret negotiations with the Algerian rebels and in July 1962, after a referendum, France formally granted independence to a new Algeria. Libya having already emerged from United Nations trusteeship to independence in 1951, the entire North African coast outside the tiny Spanish enclaves was now rid of European supremacy.

European interests had in fact changed. In the Middle East they were no longer dominated by old preoccupations. The USSR continued to see the area in terms of Cold War. It dropped its early support of Israel as soon as it ceased to be useful against the British and subsequently took a steady pro-Arab line, assiduously fanning Arab resentment over survivals of British imperialism, while, at the margins, earning on its own behalf a cheap bonus of Arab approval in the later 1960s by harassing Soviet Jews. The major factor now changing the terms of the Middle Eastern problem, though, was oil. In the 1950s there were two important developments. One was a much greater rate of oil discovery than hitherto, in particular on the southern shores of the Persian Gulf, in the small sheikdoms then still largely under British influence, and in Saudi Arabia. The second change was a huge acceleration of energy consumption in industrial countries. The prime beneficiaries of the oil boom were Saudi Arabia, Libya, Kuwait and, some way behind, Iran and Iraq, the established major producers. Countries dependent upon Middle Eastern oil – the United States, Great Britain, Germany and, soon, Japan – would have to give greater weight to Arab views in their diplomacy.

Growing oil revenues had another significance, too, in that they led to social change – in many different ways, some intended, more unintended – in the oil producing countries. This was by no means of interest only to them. Widening contrasts between Middle Eastern and Gulf region economies, increasing immizeration in some as population rose, improved internal security systems for conservative rulers, new access to western luxuries for the rich, the accumulation of large immigrant workforces in some places – these were some of many more developments all tending in the end to destabilization or at least growing problems of social and cultural cohesion. It is true that since 1919, the major state structures of the Middle East have proved durable and able to survive ambitious revolutionary schemes of pan-Arab consolidation and unification more or less intact. They were strained by, but survived, the creation and survival of Israel. The internal politics of these states, nonetheless, have been studded since the end of the World War by violence and assassination. What the oil revolution was to do was to involve the Arab masses in politics, even if only as a menacing background factor, as never before in modern times. In the context of the Cold War, and external interest in maintaining the existing regimes, this took time to appear. But when it did, it was to be of the first concern to all 'western' countries, not just Europe.

Europe and sub-Saharan Africa

Simply in terms of colouring the map, nineteenth-century European imperialists had done better in Africa than anywhere else. The First World War eliminated German possessions there, and the Second the Italian, but this did not affect the general European hegemony in sub-Saharan Africa. In 1945, its only independent countries were Liberia, and the Union of South Africa (which was a member of the British Commonwealth). All the rest was under direct or indirect British, French, Belgian or Portuguese rule (Spain had a tiny island colony off West Africa). Decolonization in this area was to be rapid, but fraught with greater difficulties and would have even more ambiguous outcomes than in Asia. But it was also surprisingly bloodless as a process: only in Algeria did the making of a decolonized Africa cost many lives (though there was plenty of bloodshed in the post-colonial era, when African set about African). Portugal only gave in after domestic revolution, but colonialism elsewhere in Africa was replaced fairly peacefully. French and British governments were anxious to retain, if they could, some sort of influence by ostentatiously benevolent interest in their former subjects; settlers, rather than imperial rulers, were the usual brake on withdrawal.

The end of empire came more rapidly than most had anticipated. There had not been in 1945 any solid ground of expectation such as there had been in India, but by 1961, (when South Africa became a fully independent republic and left the Commonwealth), twenty-four new African states were already in existence. Ten years later, Portugal was the only former colonial power still hanging on to black African possessions and by the end of 1975 they had gone, too. The Iberians who had led the adventure of overseas European dominion were almost the last to abandon it.

Imperial withdrawal was followed by Balkanization. Africa lacked the unifying influence of great indigenous civilizations such as those of Asia to offset colonial fragmentation. The doctrine of nationalism which appealed to the westernized African élites (Senegal, a Moslem country, provided an unusually distinguished example in a president who wrote poetry in French and was an expert on Goethe) confirmed the continent's inherent lack of cultural integration and often ignored important realities which colonialism had contained or manipulated. As a result, black Africa owes its present form in the main to decisions of nineteenth-century Europeans (just as much of the Middle East owes its framework to their successors in this century). New African 'nations' were usually defined by the boundaries of former colonies; they often enclosed peoples of many languages, stocks, and customs, for whom colonial administration had provided little more than a formal unity.

In spite of the continent's great economic potential, the economic and social foundations of new African nations were often shaky. This tended to encourage the persistence of European economic influence after the disappearance of formal empire. Once again, the imperial legacy was significant, both negatively and positively. Colonial regimes in Africa left behind feebler cultural and economic infrastructures than in Asia. Rates of literacy were low and trained cadres of administrators and technical experts were small. They were unevenly distributed between states. Africa's important economic resources (especially of minerals) required for their exploitation skills, capital and marketing facilities which could only come in the near future from the world outside (and white South Africa counted as 'outside' to many black politicians). What was more, some African economies had only recently undergone disruption and diversion because of European needs and in European interests.

Ghana, formerly British, was in 1957 the first ex-colonial new nation to emerge in sub-Saharan Africa. In the next 27 years twelve wars were fought in Africa; thirteen heads of state would be assassinated. There were two especially bad outbreaks of strife. In the former Belgian Congo an attempt by the mineral-rich region of Katanga to break away provoked a civil war in which Soviet and American influences quickly became entangled. Belgian soldiers returned there, while the United Nations strove to restore peace. Then, at the end of the 1960s, came a distressing civil war in Nigeria, hitherto one of the most stable and promising of the new African states, which again drew non-Africans to dabble in the blood-bath (one reason was that Nigeria had joined the ranks of the oil producers). With only one or two exceptions, though, African states for the most part were spared overt manipulation by outsiders in the cause of Cold War politics, whatever other non-African interests might be seen at work in them. Formally Marxist regimes appeared only in Ethiopia, one of the most traditional states, and in the former Portuguese colonies. Former French and British colonies, sometimes enjoying or suffering a measure of patronage by former colonial masters, were hardly affected by super-power rivalry. But Europeans were not uninvolved in the demonologies of

African politics. Scapegoats were needed for the sometimes abysmal performance of newly independent regimes, and there were two major European settler countries on the continent – potential Algerias, some thought.

The Union of South Africa mattered most. By 1945 it was dominated by Afrikaans-speaking Boers whose cherished grievances against the British went back to the Great Trek, had been intensified by defeat in the Boer War, and had motivated the progressive demolition of ties with the British Commonwealth after the First World War. This had been made easier by the concentration of voters of Anglo-Saxon origin in the provinces of Cape Town and Natal; the Boers were entrenched in the Transvaal and the major industrial areas as well as the rural hinterland. South Africa, it is true, entered the war in 1939 on the British side and supplied important forces to fight in it, but even then intransigent 'Afrikaners', as they increasingly called themselves, supported a movement favouring co-operation with the Nazis. Its leader became prime minister in 1948, after defeating South Africa's senior statesman, Jan Smuts, in a general election. As the Afrikaners had steadily engrossed power inside the Union, and had built up their economic position in the industrial and financial sectors, the prospect of imposing a policy towards the black African which diverged from their deep prejudices was soon inconceivable. The eventual result was the construction of a system of separation of the races: *apartheid*. It systematically embodied and reinforced the reduction of the black African to the inferior status he occupied in Boer ideology. Its aim was to guarantee the dominant position of the whites in a land where industrialism and market economies had done much to break down the regulation and distribution of the growing black population by the old tribal divisions.

Apartheid appealed – on even less excusable grounds than the primitive superstitions or supposed economic necessities of the Afrikaners – to white people elsewhere in Africa. The only country with a similar balance of black and white population to that of South Africa and a similar and consequential unequal distribution of wealth was Southern Rhodesia. To the great embarrassment of the British government, it seceded from the Commonwealth in 1965. The aim of the white secessionists, it was feared, was to move towards a society more and more like South Africa's. The British government of the day dithered and missed its chance. There was nothing that the black African states could immediately do about Rhodesia, and not much that the United Nations could do either, though 'sanctions' were invoked in the form of an embargo on trade with the former colony; many black African states ignored them and the British Labour government winked at the steps taken by major oil companies to ensure their product reached the rebels. In this shameful episode Great Britain's stock sank in the eyes of Africans who, understandably, did not see why the British could not suppress a colonial rebellion as flagrant as that of 1776. Many Britons reflected that precisely that precedent made the outlook for intervention by a remote and militarily weak imperial sovereign look very discouraging. It was another marker of the ebbing of British power.

European recovery

The disappearance of European empire mattered at home most to former colonial nations, but they showed fewer effects than might have been anticipated. Perhaps the most apparent were sociological – the return (or first arrival) in a few countries of substantial numbers of former inhabitants, settler or indigenous, from former colonies – and psychological, as familiar assumptions slowly dropped away and old ties withered. It usually took a long time for the full impact of either to appear. Meanwhile, the recovery of Europe east and west from post-war poverty went ahead, and with it the further shaping of its divisions. Changes in former relations with overseas territories mattered very little in that process. Existing economic ties with them indeed proved quite durable (as they had done in 1783, the historically-minded could note).

Europe's economic and social history since 1945 has nonetheless to be understood in a global context. With big temporary setbacks (notably, that of the world economic depression of the 1930s) humanity's wealth has increased during the twentieth century almost continuously and by a huge degree. Since 1945, overall economic growth has never ceased. Moreover, in spite of huge disparities and differences and setbacks which some countries more than others, this growth has been widely shared throughout the world. Yet in *per capita* (and usually in gross) terms, the developed world undoubtedly did best out of this. Europe, of course, for a long time contained most of the countries in it.

The beginnings of a general explanation of growing abundance must lie in the long preservation of peace between major states. The facts that the decades since 1945 have been studded by smaller-scale or incipient conflicts, that men and women have been killed in warlike operations on every day of them, that great powers have often had surrogates to do their fighting for them, and that there have been long periods of international tension and costly expenditure on arms does not affect this. No such destruction of human and material capital as that of 1914–18 and 1939–45 has taken place – above all, in Europe. Almost as surprising, though, in view of the precedents of the years after 1918 (and, indeed, those after 1815), was that the re-stocking boom which came with peace after a great war was not after 1945 very soon overtaken by slump.

A part of the explanation of this was political. Even before the Marshall Plan, politics had made possible American provision of dollars needed for European reconstruction. The Cold War influence did not go away. International rivalry was to sustain economic activity in Europe, and to provoke more than simple recovery. Huge sums were involved. In 1948 and 1949 no less than 3 per cent of the United States' GDP came to Europe. The life of the Marshall Plan was extended past its planned ending in 1951 and under it, no less than $17 billion in all was given outright to its recipients, who also absorbed $3 billion of World Bank loans. Such transfers provided beneficial technological spin-off and major capital investments which increased Europe's real wealth. They also made possible in 1949 a series of devaluations of European currencies which for two decades or so gave a huge boost to European competitiveness.

The recovery of Europe as a major world centre of industrial production thus predicated the existence of the American dynamo; its precondition lay outside Europe. Thanks to the combination of American economic support and the efforts of European countries themselves, the western half of the continent was substantially rebuilt and restored by 1953, and it was by then embarked on what has been called a 'golden age of economic growth' lasting until the early 1970s. Figures drawn from twelve western European countries (which include Finland) show an average annual growth rate of 4.6 per cent real GDP and of 0.7 per cent in population between 1950 and 1972 (the comparable figure for 1913–50 had been 1.4 and 0.5, respectively).[1] But it is still difficult to identify specific reasons for this, or for the variations between individual countries. Economists are still debating why it happened.

Eastern Europe also experienced economic growth, but to a less striking degree. The reasons, again, are complex. Undoubtedly they must go back beyond 1945. The comparative backwardness of some east European countries (and in particular that of their agricultural sectors) had been notable in the inter-war years. Commercial relations between the USSR and other countries had been encumbered on and off by politics ever since the October Revolution. In the huge disruption and net decrease of world trade after 1931 as the capitalist economies plunged into recession and sought salvation in protection (or, even, autarky), and the USSR grappled with other disasters (some of its own making), opportunities to overcome barriers evaporated. Then came the destruction of the war years after which all earlier divisions of the world market were transcended as two methods of organizing the distribution of scarce resources increasingly divided the world, and more sharply, Europe. The essential determinant of one system, the capitalist, was the market – though a market very different from that envisaged by the old liberal Free Trade ideology and in many ways a very imperfect one, tolerating a substantial degree of intervention through international agencies and agreement; in the communist-controlled group of nations (and some others) political authority was intended to be the decisive economic factor. Trade went on between the market and command (or would-be command) systems, but in a severely restricted way.

Contacts between the two systems multiplied as the years passed, but without bringing them significantly closer to one another. They offered alternative and politically competing models for economic growth, their competition inflamed by the political struggles of the Cold War and actually helping to spread its antagonisms. This could not be a completely static situation. In the 1960s one system was to be much less completely dominated by the United States and the other somewhat less completely dominated by the Soviet Union than was the case ten years earlier. Both shared (though in far different degree) in the continuing economic growth of the 1950s and the 1960s, but diverged as the market economies moved ahead more rapidly. Comecon, like the OECD, expanded outside Europe (Mongolia, Cuba and Vietnam all in the end belonged to it) but it proved comparatively ineffective in increasing the trade between its member states, in spite of attempts to encourage national economic specialization. Given the divergences of east and west, to seek to identify an overall economic position for Europe, and to relate that position to other parts of the world is unrealistic and artificial. Nonetheless, Europeans, east and west, were for the most part among the richer part of humanity.

Those in the west, though, experienced an unprecedented and prolonged surge of prosperity. Most of them lived in the industrialized countries which enjoyed the highest standards of living in 1950 and still, by and large, enjoy them today, though they have been joined (and are still being joined) by others. In 1970 three of the great industrial agglomerations of the world were still, as they had been in 1939, the United States, Europe and Russia, but they had been joined by Japan.

Modern industrial economies do not much resemble their nineteenth-century predecessors, and this was in the 1960s beginning to be as evident in Europe as elsewhere. The old heavy and manufacturing industries, long the backbone of economic strength,

---

[1] These figures are taken from a table in a somewhat technical (though the author says 'selective and non-technical') but informative article by N.F.R. Crofts, 'The Golden Age of Economic Growth in Western Europe, 1950–1973', in *Economic History Review* XLVIII (1995), pp. 429–47.

were declining in importance. Here, a long perspective helps. Of the three major steel-making countries of 1900, the first two were still among the first five world producers eighty years later, but in third and fifth places respectively; these were the United States and Germany (counting West Germany as her replacement). The United Kingdom (third in 1900) came tenth in the same world table – with Spain, Romania and Brazil close on her heels. In 1982, Poland made more steel than the USA had done in 1900. What is more, new industries had appeared as much more than simple extrapolations in technology and structure from the past. Much economic growth in recent years has been in industries – electronics and plastics are obvious examples – which barely existed even in 1945. Coal, which overtook running water and wood in the nineteenth century as the major source of industrial energy, was long before 1939 joined by hydro-electricity, oil and natural gas; very recently, power generated by nuclear fission has been added to these. Continuity is easier to discern in effects than in such processes. As in the nineteenth century, but on a much increased scale, industrial growth has raised standards of living. Cheaper power and materials for the production of goods have offset rising costs of labour. Improving transport has further lowered costs. An enormous growth in the production of commodities directly for the use and pleasure of the European consumer has been the outcome.

Such changes, like others, were symptoms of more than an economic trend. They reflect also the major theme already apparent in the political sphere: the increasing difficulty of distinguishing between European and world history. Niceties of timing are hard to establish, but it appears broadly true that the new abundance was first to be seen in American life, then in Europe, and was later to spread to other continents. Its importance was immediately apparent in a growing flow of material goods and an improving standard of life, but those facts in themselves implied and promoted other changes, also to be shared among developed societies round the globe. A certain level of material life brought with it changes in attitudes and ideas - in part, this was the last belated triumph of Europe as a global cultural influence, the end of the story which had begun with the export of the European state, European religion and European culture four centuries earlier. Such changes went beyond the superficialities of taste and fashion (which, in any case, often reflected the impact of Europe's American derivatives). For example, for all the cultural variety of European countries, virtually all had to confront notable changes in the attitudes and behaviour of their young people in the 1960s and 1970s. The supreme accolade was given to the young: commercial acknowledgement in the form of targeted merchandising, entertainment and journalism. For the first time, something like an international youth culture made its appearance. In some places for a time this produced a certain turbulence. Attention-catching though this was, it was largely froth, the least profound manifestation of a great change. A new internationalising of taste, values and assumptions among young people was much more important. It was based on the new prosperity and the wealth to which it gave access (in many ways: to survive without employment was in some countries much easier than in earlier times, thanks to increasing the readiness of democratic electorates to vote for social welfare). Wealth brought privileges in leisure and movement, as well as cheaper and more material goods. But the stirrings of youth also reflected new communications. By the 1960s 'mass' communication no longer meant just the popular newspapers which had done so much to educate and mould the early twentieth-century European towndweller, newly literate as a result of mass schooling. Change began with radio broadcasting in the 1920s and 1930s, though it had barely begun to indicate what was coming before the sweeping aside of Gutenberg's world came about through the even more powerful (because so much more immediately and irrationally persuasive) medium of television.

Political reorganization

The political rivalry of the USA and USSR continued to harden after Berlin. In 1953, Stalin died (shortly before the Korean armistice). This was clearly very significant – but exactly of what it was difficult to say. His closest colleagues were for some hours terrified that he might not really be dead, and so did nothing immediately. In due course, it was to look as if the leader's departure had brought a change in method, if not in aims, of Soviet policy. Immediately, President Eisenhower (who had succeeded Truman in 1953) and his advisers remained distrustful of Soviet intentions; they continued to see Europe as the centre of the Cold War and the likeliest target of a direct Soviet threat. Soon, too, Stalin's successors revealed that they had the improved – that is, even more powerfully and indiscriminately destructive – weapon known as the hydrogen bomb (the Americans had exploded the first in 1952). It was Stalin's last gift, from the grave, to his subjects, guaranteeing the status in world affairs which he had given the USSR. It crowned his achievements, greater than those of Lenin; Stalin had carried through the logic of his predecessor's actions, giving the country the industrial and military strength to survive (just) the worst threat it ever faced from abroad. After the war, he rebuilt the tsarist empire and more and made the USSR a superpower. What can never be proved is that only his terrible methods could have done this. Russia, since the days of Peter the Great, had been bound to be a great European and Asian power; whether by 1917 communism and Stalinism was the price which had to be paid for modernization is an insoluble question. Unhappily, many other modernizing regimes tended to find the Soviet model attractive because it appeared to have done the trick, and to ignore the other side of the coin. The Soviet people had been rewarded with precious little but survival for their sufferings; indeed, after 1945 consumption was held down in the USSR and both the propaganda to which the Soviet citizen was submitted, and the brutalities of the police system seem, if anything to have been intensified after some relaxation during what was called (interestingly) the Great Patriotic War.

One consequence of Soviet policy was that the German Federal Republic and the GDR continued to move further and further apart. On two successive days in March 1954 Moscow announced that the eastern republic now possessed full sovereignty and the West German president signed a constitutional amendment permitting the rearmament of his country. In 1955 West Germany entered NATO; the Soviet riposte this time was the Warsaw Pact, an alliance of its satellites. Berlin's future was still in doubt, but it was clear that the NATO powers would fight to resist changes in its status except by agreement. In the east, the GDR agreed to settle with old enemies: the line of the Oder-Neisse was to be the frontier with Poland. Hitler's dream of realizing the greater Germany of the nineteenth-century nationalists had ended in the obliteration of Bismarckian Germany and what was left of historic Prussia was now ruled by revolutionary communists, while the new West Germany was federal in structure, non-militarist in sentiment, where Catholic and Social Democratic politicians whom Bismarck would have seen as 'enemies of the state' competed for power. Sometimes with the help of the

German Liberal party, the Christian Democratic Union was to dominate the Federal Republic and exclude the Social Democrats from power until 1969. In this framework, without a peace treaty, the problem of containing the German power which had twice devastated Europe by war was to be managed for thirty-five years.[2] The CDU was a European as well as a German fact; for over the moderate Catholic Right everywhere in Europe it exercised an ascendancy faintly reminiscent of that of the German socialists over the international Left before 1914.

A last settlement by a agreement of land frontiers in central Europe came in 1955, when occupying forces were withdrawn from Austria, which re-emerged as an independent state. At the same time, a long-running Italian-Yugoslav border dispute was settled, and the last American and British troops were withdrawn from Trieste. Two Europes were settling down. This no doubt helped to sustain the position of a few countries which did not take their place in a Cold War alignment. In 1948, Soviet advisers had been recalled from Yugoslavia, which was expelled from the Cominform. Yugoslavia's treaties with the USSR and other communist countries were denounced. There opened five years of vitriolic attacks on 'Titoism'. Yet Tito survived. Yugoslavia had frontiers with Warsaw Pact countries but none with the Soviet Union. Albania, for a long time violently loyal to Moscow's leadership, and a founder-member of the Pact, nonetheless fell out with the USSR in 1961, but continued to show its traditional hostility to Yugoslavia.

New structures in western Europe

After 1945, Portugal and Spain, countries which, with certain nuances and compromises dictated by circumstance, had remained neutral during the war, were ruled by dictators. Both were often designated 'fascist', but this is over-simplified. It was easier for Portugal than for Spain under Franco to take its full place in international life (a resolution of 1946 barring Spain from entry to the UNO was not rescinded until 1950) but both were by the 1950s clearly on the western side of Europe's great divide. That divide mattered more than their constitutional or ideological orientation in the organization of western Europe on a more coherent basis. Aspirations to European unity went back at least to the end of the first World War, and had been given renewed vigour in the second. The horror at what Europe's quarrels had led to between 1939 and 1945 was a powerful stimulus to fresh thinking. Then came the growing sense of a Soviet threat and the needs of economic reconstruction and recovery. Some statesmen sensed a re-discovery of shared civilized values which they believed were 'European', as they grappled with a growing awareness of the decline of the power of individual European states in global affairs and the loss of the nerve or taste for colonial power. Such differing influences, and others, help to explain why, in the late 1940s, western Europe had begun to show some of the earliest signs, feeble though they were, that nationalism's grip on the human potential for large-scale organization might be loosening in the very place where nationalism as a political doctrine had been born.

Enthusiasts have enjoyed going back to the Carolingians in search of legacies of common experience for Europeans, but 1945 seems far enough. When the outcome of

---

[2] Peace treaties had been signed, it may be noticed, between the victorious powers and Italy, Romania, Bulgaria, Hungary and Finland, in February 1947.

the war (and later Soviet policy) ended the German problem and partition emerged as an institutionalized durable solution, old fears in France were quietened but not altogether removed. The likelihood of another great civil war in the West over Germany's place in Europe seemed remote, it is true. Soviet policy then gave western European countries new reasons to co-operate more closely; what happened in eastern Europe in the late 1940s was seen as a warning of what might happen if the Americans ever went home leaving western Europe divided. The Marshall Plan and NATO therefore turned out to be only among the first of several milestones on a road leading to a new Europe. The initiation of the Marshall Plan had been followed by the setting-up of an Organization (at first of sixteen countries, but later expanded) of European Economic Cooperation (OEEC) in 1948, but the following year, a month after the signing of the treaty setting up NATO, the first political bodies representing ten different European states were also set up under the new Council of Europe. Economic forces making for integration developed more rapidly than the political. Customs Unions had already been created in 1948 between the 'Benelux' countries (Belgium, the Netherlands, and Luxembourg), and (in a different form) between France and Italy ('Francital'). The most important of the early steps towards European economic (and, in due course, political) integration, though, emerged from a proposal about specific industries.

A proposal by the French foreign minister, Robert Schumann, for the international organization and management of Europe's main industrial resource, coal and steel production, came to fruition in 1951. France, Italy, the Benelux countries and, most significantly, West Germany, then signed an agreement to set up a European Coal and Steel Community (ECSC) which brought together the political aim of providing an insuperable obstacle to future Franco-German conflict with a measure of economic rationalization. Coal and steel resources in western Europe were to be administered by a supra-national authority. This was likely to improve the market by removing tariff and technical barriers to integration and (it was hoped) to allow better management of fluctuations and mismatches in coal and steel supply. But the ECSC also opened the way to broader political horizons; it was significant that it brought with it the settlement of the problem of the control of the Saar basin which had broken out so soon after 1918. Jean Monnet, the mastermind of the French Planning Commission, saw ECSC as the first supranational organization embodying significant European integration.

The most important immediate diplomatic consequence of the ECSC had been the formal incorporation of western Germany into a new international structure. It provided one means of containing while reviving a new country, West Germany, whose strength, it was becoming increasingly clear, would be needed in a western Europe menaced by Soviet land-power. To the consternation of some (above all, the French), American official opinion rapidly came round under the influence of events in Korea to the view that Germany had to be rearmed.

The subsidence, thanks mainly to economic recovery, of the political weakness symptomized by large numbers of communist voters in both France and Italy also helped to ease the way for supra-nationalist ideas. Communists had ceased to take part in government in those two countries as early as 1947 and the danger that their democracies might go under as Czechoslovakia's had done disappeared by 1950. Anti-communist opinion tended there, and elsewhere in western Europe east of the Pyrenees, to coalesce about parties whose integrating forces were either Roman Catholic politicians or social democrats vividly aware of the fate of their comrades in eastern Europe (though this did not prevent vigorous campaigning against them by opponents who insisted that all Marxist roads led, in the end, to Moscow). Broadly speaking, these changes meant that western Europe governments of a moderate right-wing complexion pursued similar aims of economic recovery, welfare service provision, and western European integration in practical matters during the 1950s. Christian Democracy in its various national manifestations drew upon a hitherto neglected current in European politics, the Catholic social ideas first set out authoritatively in the encyclicals of Leo XIII. It produced economic and social regimes comfortable with the idea of intervention in the economy in the interests of the weak and providing substantial welfare benefits.

Between 1952 and 1954 efforts were made to form a European Defence Community to supersede the Brussels treaty arrangements and through it to formalize West Germany's military position. French suspicions frustrated these attempts. In 1955, though, the Federal Republic was admitted to NATO and arguments about European defence organization died away (West Germany had joined the Brussels Treaty group – renamed Western European Union or WEU in 1954 as a preliminary). The main thrust towards greater unity, as before, remained economic. The crucial steps came in 1957: the European Atomic Community and (more importantly), the European Economic Community (EEC or 'Common Market') then came into being and France, Germany, Belgium, the Netherlands, Luxembourg and Italy joined in the signing of the Treaty of Rome. Its first significant outcome was the institution of a Customs Union, whose shape was substantially completed in the next ten years, but the Treaty did much more than this. It provided for a system of Commissions presiding over a bureaucracy to monitor the treaty and promote further integration, for a Council of Ministers as a decision-making authority, for a Court of Justice and, finally, for a European Parliament with advisory (not legislative) powers. There was talk of the reconstitution of Charlemagne's heritage; a geographical correspondence of sorts could, indeed, be detected. The Treaty of Rome spurred countries which had not joined the EEC to set up their own, looser and more limited, European Free Trade Association (EFTA) two and a half years later. By 1986, the six countries of the original EEC (by then it had become simply the EC – the word 'Economic', significantly, had been dropped) were twelve, while EFTA had lost all but four of its members to it. Five years later still, and what was left of EFTA was envisaging a merger with the EC.

Western Europe's complicated, slow but accelerating movement towards greater unity demonstrated (among many other things) the confidence of those who made the arrangements that armed conflict could never again be an acceptable alternative to co-operation and negotiation between their countries. The era of war between western European powers, rooted in the beginnings of the national state system, seemed to be over. Tragically, though recognizing that fact, Great Britain's rulers did not seize at the outset the chance to join in giving it institutional expression; their more imaginative successors were twice to be refused admission to the EEC before finally being allowed to join. Meanwhile the Community's interests were steadily cemented together by a Common Agricultural Policy (CAP) which was, to all intents and purposes, a huge bribe to the farmers and peasants who were so important a part of the German and French electorates, and, later, to those of poorer countries which sought to become members.

Economic matters had been from the outset of the first importance in European integration. Concern with them and their technical demands had produced institutions from the inauguration of 'Benelux' and 'Francital' in 1948 onwards and although some disappeared with time, others endured (together with some functional non-economic bodies). The outcome was somewhat confusing and was bound to create some new tensions, as well as bringing about an unprecedented surge of true trans-national experience among European élites. A truly focused European self-consciousness was for the first time a reality, beginning even in the 1950s to be visible among civil servants, industrialists and businessmen. Its emergence of course also provoked very hostile and nationalist feelings in some places.

The evolution of institutions, many overlapping in function and membership continued to complicate the notion of what 'Western' Europe ought to be or in fact was. For instance, the OEEC of 1948 was in due course joined by the new Federal Republic of Germany, Spain and Finland before becoming in 1961 the Organization of Economic Co-operation and Development (OECD) – of which the United States and Canada, too, were members. The ten members of the Council of Europe of 1949 grew to twenty-three by 1990. All the time, though, any notion of how western Europe might be organized (and therefore defined) always tended to be overridden by American perceptions of Cold War realities. Above all, it was never to be identified solely with the EEC or its successors – which disappointed some enthusiasts.

East European rumblings

Eastern Europe proved no exception to the rule that the simplicities of Cold War propaganda always obscured complicated reality. Within a couple of years of Stalin's death upheavals within the Soviet leadership had occurred and other changes appeared likely now to follow. The most important was the emergence of Nikita Khrushchev. In 1956 he made a speech at a secret session of the Soviet communist party's twentieth congress which quickly became known. It caused a sensation by denouncing the misdeeds of the Stalin era and declaring that 'coexistence' should now be the goal of Soviet foreign policy. Earlier in the year it had already been announced that reductions in Soviet armaments were planned; this added to a sense of hopefulness. But the atmosphere of 1956 was then doubly fouled. The Suez episode was one source of renewed bitterness, leading to Soviet threats to Great Britain and France; Khrushchev was not going to put Arab goodwill at risk by failing to proclaim his support for Egypt. The Americans did not like that. The other episode which had done great damage to the international climate had been a Soviet suppression of revolution in Hungary.

Ever since 1948, the year when Stalin's quarrel with Tito had begun, Soviet policy had been almost morbidly sensitive to any signs of deviation or dissatisfaction among its satellites. The fact that both Tito himself and the Yugoslavian socialist state had survived the massive vilification which had been directed at them by the Cominform, had simply left the Soviet government more alert than ever for tremors among its allies. Anti-Soviet riots in east Berlin in 1953 were crushed by the Soviet army; more than 300 citizens of the GDR were killed (the West Germans took the chance to make the day of the insurrection – 17 June – a national day of commemoration for the next thirty-five years, under the name of Day of National Unity). Three years later, in the summer of 1956, there were riots in Poland which, again, were brusquely put down.

In October of the same year, while the Suez expedition was in preparation, a series of disturbances in Budapest blew up into a nationwide movement. This time, Soviet forces withdrew from the capital, and a new Hungarian government took office, promising free elections and the end of one-party rule. Perhaps unwisely, it soon went further. It announced Hungary's withdrawal from the Warsaw Pact, declared its neutrality and asked the United Nations to take up the Hungarian question. At this, the Soviet forces returned (accompanied by those of other Warsaw Pact countries) and the Hungarian revolution was obliterated. The UN General Assembly twice condemned the intervention, without effect. This episode much hardened psychological attitudes on both sides of the Cold War. Western Europe was once more reminded of the realities of Soviet power. On the other side, the Soviet leadership was made aware more vividly than ever of how evanescent the supposed friendship of the peoples of eastern Europe could prove to be; Moscow easily became alarmed when Americans talked of 'liberating' them.

The tensions of 1960–62

Scenting danger in a rearmed West Germany, the Soviet leadership was more than ever anxious to strengthen its satellite, the GDR. In the late 1950s that country was undergoing a prolonged and worsening economic strain. West Berlin, independent and capitalist, but located in its territory, was a weakness. The city's internal sector boundaries were easily crossed eastward and westward. Across them, prosperity and freedom, both very visible in the western sectors of the city, drew many East Germans – especially skilled workers, who could easily find jobs there – to the Federal Republic. In 1958 the Soviet authorities denounced the arrangements under which Berlin had been run for the last ten years; they said they would hand over their sector to the GDR if better ones could not be found. Two years of drawn-out diplomacy and mounting tension followed. Then in August 1961, the East Germans suddenly put up a wall, soon fortified with mines, barbed wire and armed guards, to separate physically the Soviet and western sectors of Berlin.

As the atmosphere of crisis over Berlin had deepened, there had been a huge rise in the numbers of those fleeing to the west while they could. 140,000 had crossed in 1959, 200,000 in 1960. More than 100,000 fled in the first half of 1961. The stemming of this flow by building the wall raised tension in the short run, but probably lowered it in the end since it effectively finished off illegal emigration. The wall remained in place for twenty-eight years and while it did so more than 150 east Germans were killed trying to cross it and many more were injured in or imprisoned for making the attempt. It was a notable symbol of difference between two worlds and a gift to western Cold War propagandists. As for any claims to change in the legal status of Berlin, Khrushchev quietly dropped them when it was clear that the United States was willing to contemplate war rather than permit it.

This was nonetheless only the beginning of a period during which Soviet policy appeared to be willing to test American resolve much further than before. Before long, there was a new crisis, though this time focused not in Europe but in the Caribbean. After the Great War, European interests there, as well as in Central and South America, were comparatively few. The substantial pre-war British investments in Latin America had been largely run down. No European nation was now likely to challenge the Monroe doctrine in order to look after its remaining territorial possessions in the western hemisphere (the British, French, Dutch and Danes all had some surviving

Caribbean and Central American colonies). The United States' political predominance in the hemisphere was more evident than ever, as was American economic weight, after 1945. This makes it all the more paradoxical that when a European power attempted a trial of strength with the United States in the Americas, it should be the USSR, which had never had either territorial or investment interests in the area. The crisis over Cuba was a purely Cold War creation.

The influence of the United States in Cuba was strong and evident (there was an American naval base there) since the beginning of this century. In the 1950s what this might mean was seen when American favour and support were withdrawn from the local dictator. The United States government looked on with benevolent approval while his regime was overthrown by a young and patriotic guerrilla leader, Fidel Castro. In 1959, when he became prime minister, Castro described his regime as 'humanistic' and, specifically, not communist. At first, he was idolized by many Americans as a romantic figure (beards became fashionable among American radicals). But official relationships rapidly soured when Castro began to interfere with American business interests and denounced those Americanized elements in Cuba which had supported the old regime. Anti-Americanism turned out to be a rewarding theme; Cubans responded to it by uniting behind the revolution. American opinion now began to turn against Castro. Soon, the United States broke off diplomatic relations with Cuba; the administration was convinced that Castro's increasingly obvious dependence on known communists meant that the island was about to fall into their hands. Thus, the Cold War arrived in the western hemisphere.

It did not improve matters when Khrushchev warned the United States publicly of the danger of retaliation (from Soviet rocket forces) if it took military action against Cuba (he also announced that the Monroe doctrine was dead; the State Department quickly assured the world that reports of its demise were greatly exaggerated). Meanwhile, the United States had decided to promote Castro's overthrow indirectly, by financing and arming Cuban exiles to carry it out. This was the policy inherited by President Kennedy when he took office in 1961. Perhaps understandably, he was neither cautious enough nor sufficiently informed to impede it. The outcome was a fiasco, the so-called 'Bay of Pigs' operation, a miserable end to an expedition of dissident Cubans. Disapproval for an attack on a popularly-based government was almost worldwide, even among European allies of the United States. Castro now turned in earnest for support to the USSR. At the end of 1961 he declared himself a Marxist-Leninist.

The Soviet government must have believed it faced a golden opportunity. It is not known why exactly it took the decision to exploit it in the way it did, by deciding to install in Cuba missiles with the range to reach any target in the United States (thus roughly doubling the number of American bases or cities which were potential targets). Nor is it known whether the initiative came from Havana or Moscow, but the second seems likeliest. The outcome was the most serious confrontation of the Cold War and perhaps its turning-point.

In October 1962 American photographic reconnaissance confirmed that missile sites were being built for Soviet weapons in Cuba. President Kennedy waited until this could be incontrovertibly demonstrated and then announced that the United States navy would stop any ship delivering further missiles to Cuba and that those already in the island would have to be withdrawn. One Lebanese ship making for the island was boarded and searched. Soviet ships were closely observed and photographed. The American nuclear striking force was made ready for war with the Soviet Union. After a few days and an exchange of personal letters between Kennedy and Khrushchev, the latter agreed that the missiles should be withdrawn.

There had briefly seemed to be a danger that Europe might again become a battle-field – or an incinerated desert – and this time over a matter of no direct concern to any of its peoples. America's allies were not as anxious over Cuba as they had been over the preservation of the status quo in Germany; they had been within range of Soviet mis-siles for years. The European allies of the USSR should have been more ideologically interested, since the Cuban regime proclaimed itself to be Marxist, but it is unlikely that this was a widely felt tie. What was really at stake for the European nations which took sides was that the credibility of the will and power of their particular superpower patron should be confirmed without a nuclear war. In the end, after something as near to a pure confrontation as is easily imaginable, the USSR appeared to have been forced to give way. Its missiles were withdrawn from Cuba. President Kennedy had avoided action or language which might have been dangerously provocative and had left a simple route of retreat open to Soviet diplomacy by confining his demands to essentials (and discreetly agreeing to the reciprocal withdrawal of American missiles from Turkey after a few months).

With hindsight's advantage, it is now not difficult to believe that the prospect of nuclear war as the ultimate price of geographical extension of the Cold War had been faced and found unacceptable. If so, Cuba was a true turning-point. It was also clear that in spite of Soviet boasting to the contrary, American preponderance in weapons was as great as ever. What mattered for purposes of direct conflict between the two superpowers was the inter-continental ballistic missile (ICBM); at the end of 1962 the Americans had a superiority in this class of weapon of more than six to one. The choice was made of rockets before butter and once again the Soviet consumer was to bear the burden as the USSR set to work to reduce this disparity. Meanwhile, the Cuban con-frontation had probably helped to achieve the first agreement between Great Britain (at that time the only European state with nuclear weapons of its own), the United States and the Soviet Union on the restriction of testing nuclear weapons in space, the atmosphere or underwater. Disarmament would still be pursued without success for many years, but this was the first positive outcome of negotiations about nuclear weapons.

Change in the USSR

In 1964, Khrushchev was removed from office, after being head of both gov-ernment and party for six years. Colleagues whom he had offended or alarmed did this with the connivance of the army. Yet he was not killed – or even sent off to an undigni-fied exile running a power-station in Mongolia. This alone showed much had changed in Soviet politics. Khrushchev's historical contribution seems likely to have been the major shaking-up he provided within the system. The speech he gave at the twentieth congress could not be unsaid (copies of it had eventually circulated freely) and it had at least launched 'de-Stalinization', qualified though that might be. He had also presided over a huge failure in agricultural policy, but it may have been that foreign policy, above all the Cuban adventure, counted most in his removal. His ascendancy had coincided with a cultural relaxation; some called it a 'thaw'. Marginally greater freedom of expression was allowed to writers and artists, while the regime appeared briefly to take a little more notice of what the world thought over such matters as its treatment of Jews. But this was personal and sporadic; liberalization depended on who had Khrushchev's ear. It seems clear only that after Stalin's death, particularly during the era of Khrushchev's ascendancy, the party had re-emerged as a more independent factor in Russian life, no longer the creature and tool of one man. The fundamentally authoritarian nature of the Russian government, though, seemed unchanged – which is what might have been expected.

Even so, some came to think that the United States and Soviet Russia were growing more and more alike, and that this would make Russian policy less menacing. This mirage of 'convergence' gave a distorted emphasis to an undoubted truth: the Soviet Union was a developed economy and much richer than in 1945. In the 1960s, because of that, some still thought socialism a plausible road to modernization. The inefficiency and lopsidedness of the Soviet economy was often overlooked. Soviet industrial growth, though allegedly faster than that of the United States in the 1950s, had continued to be overwhelmingly a matter of heavy industry. The private consumer in the Soviet Union remained poor and would have been even more visibly so but for a costly system of subsidies. Russian agriculture, which had once fed the cities of Central Europe and paid for the industrialization of the tsarist era, had been a continuing failure; paradoxically, the Soviet Union often had to buy American grain. The official Soviet communist party programme of 1961 proposed that by 1970 the USSR should outstrip the United States in industrial output, but the proposal was not made reality (unlike President Kennedy's of the same year to put a man on the Moon by the end of the decade). Yet the USSR, in comparison with many undeveloped countries, was undoubtedly rich and millions of its citizens were deeply grateful for the benefits available in the 1960s when they recalled the stricken and impoverished life of 1945.

Such comparisons, which fall easily over the line from quantitative to qualitative judgement, nevertheless do not alter the basic fact that the *per capita* GDP of the Soviet Union at the end of the 1960s still lagged far behind that of most western European nations. If Soviet citizens had at last been given old age pensions in 1956 (nearly half a century after the British), they also had to put up with health services which fell further and further behind those available in the west. Real wages in Russia got back to their 1928 level only in 1952. The theory of 'convergence' was always too optimistic. The USSR had, none the less, a scientific and industrial base which in scale and quality was by 1970 in its best sectors comparable with that of the United States. Its most obvious expression, and a great source of patriotic pride to the Soviet citizen, was the exploration of space. By 1970 there was so much ironmongery in orbit that it was difficult to recapture the startling impression made in 1957 by the first Soviet satellites. Although American successes had speedily followed, Soviet space achievements remained of the first rank. There seemed to be something in space exploration which fed the patriotic imagination and rewarded patience with other aspects of daily life in the USSR. It is not too much to say that for some Soviet citizens their space technology justified the Revolution; historically backward Russia, modernized by communism, was shown by it to be able to do almost anything another nation could do, and much that only one other could do, and perhaps even one or two things which, for a while, no other could do. She was, they thought, thoroughly modernized at last.

That the USSR had become a satisfied nation, with leaders more confident and less suspicious of the outside world and less prone to disturb the international scene, seemed less evident. Soviet responses to Chinese resurgence were not encouraging; quarrels in the 1960s had led to talk of pre-emptive nuclear attacks on China. Soviet society was by 1970 beginning to show other signs of strain, too. Dissent and criticism, particularly of restraints upon intellectual freedom, had become more audible and visible. Increasing anti-social behaviour showed itself in hooliganism, corruption and alcoholism. But such defects probably held both as much and as little potential for significant change as in other large countries. Meanwhile, the Soviet Union still remained a police state where the limits of freedom and the basic privileges of the individual were defined in practice by an apparatus backed up by administrative decisions and political prisons. The real difference between the Soviet Union and the United States (or any west European nation) was still best shown by such yardsticks as that, or by her enormous expenditure on jamming foreign broadcasting.

Complications

The terrible simplifications of the Cold War (apparently institutionalised in NATO and the Warsaw Pact) had nevertheless begun to require qualification well before 1960. That the great fact in Asia – the appearance of communist China – might have implications other than for the Cold War had soon appeared. Almost inevitably a Soviet-Chinese treaty in 1950 and years of Marxist rhetoric had been taken to mean that China was a clearly aligned participant in that struggle. But there was soon evidence that this might be too simple, and in the end China's re-emergence as a power in her own right did not accentuate the dualist Cold War system, but made nonsense of it, though at first only in a limited sphere.

In 1955 representatives of twenty-nine African and Asian states meeting in Bandung in Indonesia declared their countries 'non-aligned' in the Cold War. One of the delegations was from China; most of the rest were from the former colonial empires. Yugoslavia was soon to join them. Most of these nations were poor and needy, more suspicious of the United States than of Russia, and more attracted to China than to either. These came to be called the 'Third World', a term apparently coined by a French journalist in a conscious reminiscence of the legally-underprivileged French 'Third Estate' of 1789 which had provided much of the driving-force of the French Revolution. The implication was that such nations were both disregarded by the great powers, and excluded from the economic privileges of the developed countries. Plausible though this might sound, the expression 'Third World' actually masked important differences between such nations and the coherence of Third World politics was not to prove very enduring. Nevertheless, ten years after the end of the Second World War Bandung forced the superpowers to recognize that the weak had power if they could mobilize it. Bearing this in mind, they looked for allies.

By 1960 there were already clear signs that Russian and Chinese interests might diverge and each sought the leadership of the underdeveloped and uncommitted. At first this emerged only obliquely in shadow-boxing over differing attitudes to Yugoslavia; later, it was to be a worldwide contest. That brought paradoxes; in the 1960s Pakistan drew closer to China (in spite of a treaty with the United States) and the USSR closer to India. A new fluidity began to mark international affairs. Early in 1963 a startled world suddenly heard bitter denunciation of the Soviet leadership by the Chinese.

In Europe, the violence with which Albania, the tiniest of Europe's communist countries, condemned the Soviet Union and applauded China when the two fell out showed (as had Tito's survival) that not even all European Marxists thought alike and that this was a fact which would have to be endured in Moscow; Albania had no frontier with other Warsaw Pact countries and so was not likely to have to take account of the Red Army. It was more striking when Rumania, with Chinese support, successfully contested the direction of her economy by Comecon, asserting a national right to develop it in her own interest. She even took up a vaguely neutralist position on questions of foreign policy – though remaining inside the Warsaw Pact – and did so, oddly enough, under a ruler who imposed on his countrymen one of the most rigidly dictatorial regimes in eastern Europe. But Rumania had no land frontier with a NATO country (Albania had one with Greece), and one 800 kilometres long with the USSR; Rumanian skittishness did not have to be, but could be, tolerated, for limits to it could easily be enforced.

The reality of such limits to any weakening of the old monolithic unity of communism was clearly shown in 1968. When a communist government in Czechoslovakia set about liberalizing its internal structure and developing trade relations with West Germany, a series of attempts was made to bring it to heel. Finally, Czechoslovakia was invaded in August 1968 by Warsaw Pact forces. To avoid a repetition of what had happened in Hungary in 1956, the Czech government did not resist and a brief attempt to provide an example of 'socialism with a human face', as one Czech politician put it, was obliterated.

West of the Iron Curtain, the USSR must by then long since have given up any hope of revolutionary leadership from the indigenous communist parties, and had been obliged to face the virtual eclipse of communism as a politically revolutionary force in the West. In the 1960s its power to win votes visibly declined, above all in France and Italy. The Italian party even produced a new ideological idea, 'polycentrism', which implied a liberation of national communist parties from the discipline of Moscow.

De Gaulle and Gaullisme

Some thought the major western states increasingly reflected a similar tendency in their political evolution and similar commitments to social provision, in what had come to be known in the United Kingdom as the 'welfare state', and the achievement of economic well-being (which meant, above all, the maintenance of full employment). Two old nation states nonetheless stood somewhat apart. The United Kingdom was one. In the 1960s she completed a successful, virtually bloodless and almost total decolonization. Unhappily, the British retained (and their elected representatives encouraged) illusions. The economy chronically performed less well than those of other European countries. Illusion also hung over the fundamental direction of her foreign policy, which registered the outstanding failure of remaining outside the process of integration going on across the Channel, notably in 1967 when the 'European Community' came into being by merger of the EEC, ECSC and Euratom. In so far as this integration had political, and not just economic or moral dimensions, though, there had been a slowing-down of its advance. This owed much to another important exception to generalities, France under the presidency of General de Gaulle.

He had returned to politics in 1958 when the Fourth republic was threatened with civil war over Algeria. His first task after becoming president was to negotiate these rapids by carrying through important constitutional reforms. His next service to France was as great as any in his wartime career, the liquidation in 1961 of her Algerian commitment. The legions came home, some disgruntled (there were plots and attempts against De Gaulle's life). The act freed both him and his country for a more vigorous international role, though a somewhat negative one.

The general's view of the way European consolidation should proceed was clear. Sweeping aside the dream of those who envisaged a sovereign Europe based on a European parliament ('the Council of Europe', he once said, was 'dying on the shore where it was abandoned') he wanted integration to be limited to political action based on agreement between independent states. He saw the EEC as above all a way of protecting French economic interests and was quite prepared to strain the new organization to get his way. Further, he in effect twice vetoed British application to join it. Wartime experience had left de Gaulle with a deep distrust of the 'Anglo-Saxons' and a belief, by no means ill-founded, that British statesmen still hankered after integration with an Atlantic community embracing the United States, rather than with continental Europe. In 1964 he annoyed the Americans by exchanging diplomatic representatives with communist China. He insisted that France go ahead with her own nuclear weapons programme, declining to be dependent on American patronage. Finally, after causing much trouble within it, he withdrew from NATO.

What might be termed the Gaullist ascendancy in Europe reached its climax in 1966 in a 'Luxembourg compromise' which institutionalized a national right to veto within the EEC's Council of ministers. This substantially offset the further degree of formal integration which was achieved in the following year. When, two years later, de Gaulle resigned after an unfavourable referendum on further constitutional change in France, a major political force making for uncertainty and disarray in western Europe disappeared. Those who led France for the next couple of decades, while trying to sound like him, and sometimes feeling like him (notably in their suspicion of British attitudes towards Europe: six centuries of national consciousness do not easily evaporate) were to prove less intransigent, although French policy still hesitated between evolution towards a true Common Market, free from internal restraints on trade, or towards a politically united Europe on terms which sacrificed national independence to cohesion. For many Frenchmen, the construction of Europe still meant, in the last resort, the paying of a necessary price to contain Germany. Increasingly, though, Germany's economic strength was driving up that price.

Germany: Ostpolitik

Meanwhile, German policy, too, was undergoing subtle changes. Goals which could not have been dreamt of in the 1950s were becoming thinkable. Old landmarks disappeared, notably when at their congress at Bad Godesberg in November 1959 the Socialists accepted free enterprise and competition as appropriate (they used the word 'important') features of the economy they envisaged; this was a tacit renunciation of the Marxist tradition of the party. Ten years later a coalition government of liberal and socialist politicians took power under a new chancellor, Willy Brandt; for the first time since 1930 Germany had a socialist chancellor (and for the first time since 1925, also a socialist president).

Brandt introduced his government's programme to parliament in a statement which made special reference to the GDR, while stating that its international recognition was impossible, as one of 'two German states within one German nation'. This mysterious formula excited interest. It was clear (and other facts soon confirmed this) that the German chancellor was willing to soften West Germany's tone towards her neighbour, and to extend to it a measure of informal recognition it had not earlier received. Without abandoning the goal of reunification he sought to make sure the two Germanies did not move further apart and to bring about real contacts which might eventually help to change the GDR. This was both idealistic and pragmatic, given an international tendency to move towards some measure of *détente* in the Cold War. It frightened some, nonetheless, that the Federal Republic might be moving towards independent relations with the eastern states and the USSR. Its implications for further European integration were that its advocates would in future have to take account of the possibility of embracing German re-unification and a special role for Germany in the east. It was also certain that the new government was less enthusiastic about any advance towards supranational European integration, if that were confined only to western Europe, than its predecessors had been.

CHAPTER THREE The end of the European post-war order

A search for stability: the 1970s

By the end of the 1960s there were plentiful signs of difficulties in the USSR. It had to face the truism that Marxism itself proclaimed: that consciousness evolves with material conditions. Among other troubling outcomes of the real but limited rewards Soviet society had given its citizens were an evident dissidence, trivial in scale, a matter of individuals rather than significant groups, but suggesting a growing demand for greater spiritual freedom, and a less explicit, but real, ground-swell of opinion that further material gains should be forthcoming. The Soviet Union nevertheless continued to spend colossal sums on armaments and it appeared that advances in technology might mean their continuing escalation into the indefinite future. What change might follow from that was debatable. That there would have to be change, though, seemed more and more likely.

The deepest pressures towards new accommodations between the superpowers came from a compelling tie between them which had grown more evident since the Cuba emergency. The Americans, with their gift for the arresting slogan, concisely summed up the situation as MAD; that is to say, both countries had the weapon capacity to produce 'Mutually Assured Destruction', or, more precisely, a situation in which each of two potential combatants had enough striking power to ensure that even if a surprise nuclear attack deprived it of the cream of its armoury, what remained would be sufficient to ensure a reply so appalling as to leave an opponent's cities smoking wildernesses and his armed forces capable of little but attempting to control the terrorized survivors.

This bizarre possibility turned out to be a great conservative force. Even if madmen (to put the matter over-forcefully) are occasionally to be found in seats of power, Dr Johnson's observation that the knowledge that you are to be hanged wonderfully concentrates the mind is as applicable to collectivities threatened with disaster on this scale as to individuals: the knowledge that a blunder may be followed by extinction is a great stimulus to prudence. Here may well lie the most fundamental explanation of a new degree of co-operation which began to be shown by the United States and the Soviet Union in spite of specific quarrels.

Nevertheless, the two powers had, inevitably, very different notions of what *détente*, a popular word at the time, might mean. Many of the efforts to make it a reality grew out of circumstance as much as design. It had long been a Soviet aim, put forward more than once in the 1960s, to hold a European conference to achieve an agreed settlement of European boundaries which would give international sanction to the realities established in 1945 and, in effect, to a peace settlement for Germany. In the 1970s talks began on further arms limitations and upon the possibility of a comprehensive security arrangement in Europe, which bore fruit at last when there met in 1974 a Conference on Security and Co-operation in Europe (CSCE) in Helsinki. The United States and Canada also took part. Its conclusions were embodied in a 'Final Act' signed the following year and were very important. In return for the implicit recognition of Europe's post-war frontiers (above all, that between the two Germanies), Soviet negotiators finally agreed in 1975 at Helsinki to increase economic intercourse between eastern and western Europe, to join in recognition of the principle of self-determination, and to sign a guarantee of human rights and political freedom. The last, of course, was unenforceable. Yet in a decade when it was to become increasingly difficult to exclude access by east Europeans and Soviet citizens to information and messages from and about the West (thanks to improved television broadcasting and a virtual cessation of radio jamming), Helsinki gave much encouragement to dissidents. The agreement had silently set aside restraint on what had hitherto been deemed interference in the internal affairs of communist states, by encouraging campaigning publicity about what were seen as infringements of rights. Very slowly, there began to flow more freely a generalized public criticism which was to challenge long-held assumptions in the communist states.

It may not at first have been clear to the Soviet leaders that this was part of the price to be paid for Helsinki; as it became clearer, they did not like it. Yet what they had desired they had secured: the nearest thing to a peace treaty ending the Second World War and recognizing the territorial consequences of military victory. This was a great foreign policy success. It could be reasonably argued that the position of the USSR after 1975 was diplomatically stronger than ever and much more favourable than for some time when compared with that of the United States on the global stage. But there was another side to the equation. While the USSR saw the Final Act as a factor telling for stability in territorial arguments and non-interference in the affairs of eastern Europe, western European and Americans stressed the CSCE's symbolic and practical value (there were to be a number of follow-up conferences) as a source of legitimized interest in human rights and a reminder of Europe-wide ties transcending a divided Europe. Significantly, they spoke of a Helsinki 'process'.

To American voters, though, potential advantage in the Cold War was hardly interesting while immediate gains seemed hard to seek in the middle of a bad decade. Over the first half of it had hung a national psychological disaster: defeat in the long Vietnam entanglement after heavy casualties, and the liquidation of the commitment with huge loss of face and the sacrifice of Asian allies. Emotion and trauma was prolonged in the turmoil over the fall from office in 1974 of President Nixon, whose diplomatic achievements were lost to sight in uproar over his illegal and grossly improper acts in domestic politics. Then, in the second half of the decade the United States had to face another setback when revolution overthrew its ally, the Shah of Iran, and replaced him by a hostile regime. This was the most explicit evidence yet to be seen of the unpredictable instabilities introduced by modernization, industrial expansion and the growth of oil wealth in Islamic countries. It is fair to remark that the Iranian Islamic republic was soon denouncing the USSR as strongly as the USA; it had no time for either side in a

Cold War which it saw as between what Islamic rhetoric picturesquely described as two 'Great Satans'. When, in 1979, though, Soviet forces were sent to Afghanistan to support a puppet regime there against Moslem rebels, the United States had to stand helplessly by while the USSR extended its own reach in Asia. This did not in the end turn out so satisfactorily as Soviet planners had hoped, but it was in striking contrast to the powerlessness the United States showed in the following year when it could not obtain by force or diplomacy the release of American diplomats held as hostages by Iranians.

Given this background, the American presidential election of 1980 was, for understandable if not easily avowable domestic reasons, fought in a way which played on the voters' sense of national weakness and on their fears of the USSR; the hopes of *détente* had soon soured. A conservative Soviet leadership showed renewed suspicion of the trend of American policy as the new President Reagan prepared to take office. In the event, his administration was to show in the next few years a remarkable pragmatism in foreign affairs, as well as bringing about a remarkable recovery in the confidence and morale of Mr Reagan's fellow-citizens.

The oil crisis and western Europe

One grave shock in the early 1970s had been shared by Europeans with Americans, and, for that matter by all industrial countries except the USSR. It originated in another attack by Egypt and Syria on Israel, in October 1973 on the Jewish holy day of Yom Kippur. The Israelis for the first time faced the prospect of military defeat by the greatly improved and Soviet-armed forces of their opponents. Once again they won, though only after the Russians were reported to have sent nuclear weapons to Egypt and the Americans had put their forces on the alert round the world. Clearly, the Middle East retained all its alarming potential to detonate crises which went far beyond it, and this may have eased the way to Helsinki. More immediately obvious was the impact of the announcement of restrictions on oil supply to Europe, Japan and the United States by other Arab states, led by Saudi Arabia.

The impact of the new 'oil diplomacy' was immediate: prices shot up. This suddenly made evident the historic implication of twenty years of change which had gone largely unnoticed by most Europeans. Throughout the 1950s and most of the 1960s the United States and United Kingdom had enjoyed stable and cheap oil supplies assured by their informal influence in the Gulf States and Saudi Arabia, and in Iraq until 1963, when a Ba'ath regime seized power there. In the 1970s this assurance broke down under the strain, primarily, of the Israeli question. Overnight, economic problems which had gone grumbling along but were still tolerable in the 1960s became acute. Dependence on oil imports played havoc with balance-of-payment problems. The United States, a huge consumer of oil, was badly shaken. There was talk of a new world depression like that of the 1930s. The golden age of economic growth which had begun with post-war recovery seemed to have come to an end.

In a long-term perspective, and with hindsight, this salutary shock brought with it much froth which obscured a decades-long trend of world importance, Europe's continuing advance in wealth and share of world trade since 1958. At the time, though, the effect of the oil crisis was very violent in most European countries. Exchange problems, as the dollar fluctuated violently, drove France and Germany to seek liberation from the hitherto benevolent despotism of the dollar which had endured since 1948 by form-

ing in 1979 the European Monetary System (EMS). Institutional bickering and squabbling (particularly on economic and financial matters) reminded Europeans of the
limits to any transcendence of bipolarity so far achieved. Difficulties continued into the
1980s and were coupled with uneasiness about the success of the Far Eastern economic
sphere, dominated by Japan; this distracted attention from other significant developments. By the middle of the 1980s two-thirds of foreign investment in the United States
(which had resumed its pre-1914 status as a major recipient of investment) was European.

A growing realization that other nations would wish to join, had led to renewed
efforts to crystallize to a greater degree ideas about the Community's future. More and
more Europeans saw that greater unity, a habit of co-operation and increasing prosperity were the prerequisites rather than the likely consequences of Europe's political independence. Some felt that independence would always remain hollow unless Europe,
too, could turn herself into a superpower. Comfort could therefore be drawn from further progress and integration by those thinking on such lines, though it alarmed some
others. In 1979, the first direct elections to the European parliament were already being
held. Greece in 1981, Spain and Portugal in 1986, were soon to join the Community.
In the latter year the Single European Act brought the first steps towards permitting
majority voting (instead of requiring unanimity) for some matters. In 1987 the foundations of a common European currency and monetary system were laid (though the
United Kingdom did not accept them) and it was settled that in 1992 there should be
inaugurated a genuine single market, across whose national borders goods, people, capital and services were to move freely. Members even endorsed in principle the idea of
European political union, though the British and French had notable misgivings. This
hardly made at once for greater psychological cohesion and comfort as the implications
emerged, but it was an indisputable sign of development of some sort.

The United Kingdom

Five years after De Gaulle left office the United Kingdom had joined the EEC
in 1973. This was the climax, though not the end, of an era of uncertainty for a nation
which, alone in Europe, had striven to behave as if the world of 1939 was still alive. For
a quarter-century all British governments had tried and failed to combine economic
growth, increased social service provision and a high level of employment. The second
depended ultimately on the first, which, when difficulties arose, had always been sacrificed to the other two. The United Kingdom was a democracy and its gullible voters had
to be placated. The vulnerability of the traditional British economy's commitment to
international trade was a handicap, too. Others lay in its old staple industries, starved of
investment, and the deeply conservative attitudes of its people. Though the United
Kingdom grew richer (in 1970 virtually no British manual worker had four weeks' paid
holiday a year and ten years later, after an economically disastrous decade, a third of
them did), it fell further and further behind other developed countries in wealth and its
rate of creating it. The British had one great achievement and acceptance of change to
their credit: they had managed rapid colonization humanely, without violence and
domestic division. It remained unclear whether they could shake off the past in other
ways and ensure themselves even a modest prosperity as a second-rank developed
nation.

In Northern Ireland, part of the United Kingdom, Protestant and Catholic hooligans alike seemed bent on destroying their homeland rather than co-operate with their rivals. Lunatic nationalism in Ulster cost the lives of thousands of British citizens – soldiers, policemen and civilians, Protestant and Catholic, Irish, Scotch, and English alike – in the 1970s and 1980s. The only gleam of light was that this did not disrupt British party politics as Irish questions had done in the past. The electorate remained preoccupied, rather, by material concerns. As inflation rose in the 1970s to unprecedented levels (the annualized rate 1970–80 was over 13 per cent) it was accompanied by a new fierceness in industrial relations as the oil crisis bit. There was speculation about whether the country was 'ungovernable'. A miners' strike brought down a government, leaders and interpreters of opinion often seemed obsessed with the themes of social division. Even the question of whether the United Kingdom should remain in the EEC, which was submitted to the constitutionally revolutionary device of a referendum in June 1975, was often put in terms of class interest. Many politicians were surprised when the outcome was unambiguously favourable to continued membership. Perhaps this was the first sign for a decade or so that the views of the country at large were not necessarily represented by those who considered themselves its spokesmen. It may also have been a turning-point, marking a closing off of choices which would have flowed ineluctably from a reassertion of insularity.

Bad times (economically speaking) continued; inflation (in 1975 running at 26.9 per cent) was at last identified by a Labour government as the major threat. Wage demands by trades unions were anticipating inflation still to come and it began to dawn on some that the era of unquestioned growth in consumption was over. There was a gleam of hope; a few years earlier vast oil fields had been discovered under the sea-bed off the coasts of northern Europe and some were British. In 1976 the United Kingdom became an oil-exporting nation. That did not at once help much; in the same year, a loan from the International Monetary Fund was required. When Mrs Thatcher, the country's first woman leader of a major political party (the Conservatives), and Europe's first woman prime minister, took office in 1979 she had, in a sense, little to lose; her opponents were discredited. So, many felt, were ideas which had been long accepted uncritically as the determinants of British policy.

Communist Europe

Whatever Helsinki implied, eastern Europe in 1980 still seemed as frozen into the Soviet security system as ever, with all that meant for the internal life of its individual peoples. What was still also lost to sight behind the carapace provided by the Warsaw Pact were social and political changes which had been going on slowly for thirty years (and more, if one counts the great unwilled changes of the Second World War and its aftermath).

At first sight, the outcome of a long experiment with a particular model of development had been a remarkable uniformity of structure. In each communist-ruled country, the party was supreme; careerists built their lives round it as, in earlier centuries, men on the make clustered about courts and patrons. In each (as above all in the USSR itself) there was also an unspeakable and unexaminable past which could not be mourned or deplored, whose weight overhung and corrupted intellectual life and political discussion, so far as there was any. As for the economies of eastern

Europe, investment in heavy industrial and capital goods had produced a surge of early growth (in some of them more vigorous than in others) and then an international system of trading arrangements with other communist countries, dominated by the USSR and rigidified by aspirations to central planning. Increasingly and obviously, these arrangements, coupled with strict exchange controls, proved unable to meet a growing thirst for consumer goods; commodities taken for granted in western Europe remained luxuries in the east European countries, cut off as they were from the advantages of international economic specialization. In the countryside, private ownership had been much reduced by the middle of the 1950s, usually to be replaced by a mixture of co-operatives and state farms, though, within this broadly uniform picture, different patterns had later emerged. In Poland, for instance, peasants were already moving back into smallholdings by 1960; eventually, something like four-fifths of Polish farmland was to return to private ownership even under communist government. Output remained low; in most east European countries agricultural yields were only from half to three-quarters those of the European Community. By the 1980s all of them, in varying degree, were in a state of economic crisis with the possible exception only of the GDR. Even there, *per capita* GDP stood at only $9,300 a year in 1988, against $19,500 in the Federal Republic.

What had come to be called the 'Brezhnev doctrine' (after a speech in 1968 by Khruschev's successor as general secretary of the Soviet Party in Warsaw) said that developments within eastern bloc countries might require – as in Czechoslovakia that year – direct intervention to safeguard the interests of the USSR and its allies against any attempts to turn socialist economies back towards capitalism. Yet Brezhnev had also been interested in pursuing *détente*. It was not unreasonable, therefore, to interpret his doctrine as a recognition of the possible dangers presented to international stability by breakaway developments in communist Europe, and as an attempt to limit them by drawing clearer lines. Since then, internal change in western countries, steadily growing more prosperous, and with memories of the late 1940s and the seeming possibility of subversion far behind them, had not increased east-west tension. By 1980, after revolutionary changes in Spain and Portugal, not a dictatorship survived west of the Trieste-Stettin line and democracy was everywhere triumphant. For thirty years, the only risings by industrial workers against their political masters had been in East Germany, Hungary, Poland and Czechoslovakia – all communist countries (conspicuously, when Paris was in uproar in 1968 and student riots destroyed the prestige of de Gaulle's government, the Parisian working-class had done nothing).

After 1970, and even more after Helsinki, dissident groups emerged as awareness of contrasts with western Europe grew in the eastern bloc. Gradually, too, a few officials or economic specialists, and even some party members, began to show signs of scepticism about the effects of detailed centralized planning and there was increasing discussion of the advantages of utilizing market mechanisms. The key to stability in the east, nevertheless, remained the Soviet Army. There was no reason to believe that fundamental change was possible in any of the Warsaw Pact countries if the Brezhnev doctrine held, and continued to provide the ultimate support for those subservient to the USSR. Sometimes, though, less spectacular facts than the initiatives and acts of governments turn out to be more important in the long run. Celebrating the fiftieth anniversary of the founding of the USSR, Brezhnev had affirmed in 1972 that 'the national question, as it comes down to us from the past, had been settled completely, finally and for good'. In the same decade an interesting watershed was passed, noticed by only a few perceptive observers: native Russian-speakers for the first time became a minority in the Soviet Union.

Détente *and the Soviet Union*

In the end new attitudes in Moscow were to permit opportunities for exploitation in the satellite states, because they opened the way to greater flexibility in Soviet foreign policy. Leonid Brezhnev, after eighteen years in office, died in November 1982. His immediate replacement (who had been head of the KGB, the Soviet security service) also soon died. After a septuagenarian (whose own death followed even more quickly) succeeded him, a rapid turnover ended with the arrival in office in 1985 of the youngest member of the Politburo, Mr Mikhail Gorbachev, as general secretary. He was fifty-four. Virtually the whole of his political experience had been·of the post-Stalin era. His impact upon his country's, and the world's, history is still hard to assess, but was very great. His initial personal motivation and the conjunction of forces which propelled him to the succession remain unclear. It can be inferred that the KGB, presumably, did not oppose his promotion, and his first acts and speeches were orthodox. In the previous year, though, he had already impressed the British prime minister as someone with whom business could be done.

Mr Gorbachev soon articulated a new political tone. The word 'communism' was heard less in his speeches and 'socialism' was re-interpreted to exclude egalitarianism (though from time to time he reminded his colleagues that he *was* a communist and he never, in fact, left the party). For want of a better term, his aim was seen as liberalization, an inadequate western attempt to sum up two Russian words he used a great deal: *glasnost* (openness) and *perestroika* (restructuring). The implications of the new course were to be profound and dramatic, and for the remainder of the decade Mr Gorbachev grappled with them. What soon appeared was that he, at least, had recognized that without radical modernization the Soviet economy could no longer keep up its former military might (which absorbed a quarter of the budget), sustain its commitments to allies and satellites abroad, improve (however slowly) living standards at home, and assure self-generated technological innovation. The implications of that were vast, even if he did not at once grasp all of them.

It may have been that one psychological contribution to the unrolling of Mikhail Gorbachev's policies was made unexpectedly in 1986 when a frightening accident occurred at a nuclear power station at Chernobyl in the Ukraine. Its breakdown led to the discharge into the atmosphere of huge quantities of radioactive contamination and had appeared, briefly, to threaten the even greater disaster of nuclear explosion. The heroic efforts of a relatively few technicians, soldiers and firemen averted the worst, but enough damage was done to shock all Europe and in some measure the world. Grass eaten by Welsh lambs, milk drunk by Poles and Yugoslavs and the air breathed by Swedes were all contaminated. Such facts drove home the message of Europe-wide interdependence in at least some matters. Overnight and across the continent, the political campaigns of environmentalists benefited. Within the USSR itself, what had happened was surely a startling revelation to government of the potential for disaster in an ageing nuclear power industry and of the huge investment needed once the implications of modernization became clear. Over the whole episode loomed a dreadful uncertainty about the number of Soviet citizens who would fall victims to the long-term effects of the accident.

In foreign affairs, the Soviet leader's new course soon became clear in meetings with the American president. Discussion of arms reduction was renewed. In 1987, the fruits of long negotiation were gathered in an agreement over intermediate range nuclear missiles. This was a watershed. In spite of many shocks and its erosion by the emergence of new foci of power, the nuclear balance had held long enough to make possible the first stand-downs by the superpowers. They had been able to manage their conflicts and the world's crises without all-out war, after all, and they at least, if not other countries seeking to acquire nuclear weapons, appeared to have recognized that nuclear war, if it came, held out the prospect of virtual extinction for mankind. In 1991 there were to be further dramatic developments as the USA and USSR agreed to major reductions in existing weapon stocks.

Agreements were also reached on other issues in the new atmosphere, and this was made easier when the Soviet leadership decided in 1989 to withdraw from Afghanistan. The Soviet army had for years been bogged down there at heavy economic and human cost; the similarity with American experience twenty years earlier in Vietnam was striking and ominous. It was an additionally troubling factor that the anger the Soviet intervention aroused in Iran and other Moslem countries could not be ignored by the large Moslem population of the USSR. The fear with which the 'evil empire' (as Mr Reagan had termed it) of the Soviet Union was regarded by many Americans began to evaporate. Optimism and confidence grew as the USSR showed signs of growing division and difficulty, while Americans were promised wonders by their government in the shape of new defensive measures in outer space. Though thousands of scientists said the project was unrealistic, the Soviet government could not risk facing the costs of having to compete with it.

The United Kingdom in the 1980s

In the atmosphere of economic stagnation of the beginning of the 1980s, there was little reason to expect that the decade would produce important change in western Europe. The outbreak of what may well prove to have been the last war in defence of colonial possessions to be fought by a European nation certainly did not promise it. In 1982 the British prime minister found herself unexpectedly presiding over the reconquest of the Falkland Islands after their brief occupation by Argentinian forces. Her instincts to fight for the principles of international law and territorial sovereignty and for the islanders' right to say by whom they should be governed, were well-attuned to the British popular mood, and the outcome was both a major feat of arms and an important psychological and diplomatic success. After an uncertain start (unsurprising, given its traditional sensitivity over Latin America) the United States provided important practical and clandestine help. Chile, by no means easy with her restive neighbour, was not disposed to object to British covert operations on the mainland of South America. More important, most of the EC countries supported the isolation of Argentina in the UN, and the resolutions which condemned the Argentinian action. Notably, the British had from the start the support (not always so readily available) of the French government, which knew a threat to vested rights under international law when it saw one.

In the United Kingdom, Mrs Thatcher's prestige rose with national morale; abroad, too, her standing was enhanced, and for the rest of the decade this gave her an influence with other heads of state (notably the American president) which British strength could scarcely have sustained by itself. In some ways a comparison with General de Gaulle is to the point, for not everyone agreed that this influence was always advantageously deployed. Mrs Thatcher's personal convictions, preconceptions and prejudices like those of the general, were always very visible. She, like him, was no European, if that meant allowing emotional or even practical commitment to Europe to blur a personal vision of national interest.

The domestic effects of Mrs Thatcher's policies cannot yet be properly evaluated, though they won her the longest tenure of power of any British prime minister in this century. What was clear before that was over was that she had transformed the terms of British politics, and perhaps those of cultural and social debate, dissolving a long *bien-pensant* and implicit consensus about national goals. This, together with her assertive radicalism, awoke both enthusiasm and unusual animosity. Yet she failed to achieve two of her most cherished aims: the reduction of public spending and less government intervention in the national life. Ten years after she took up office, central government was playing a greater, not a smaller, part in many areas of society, and public spending on health and social security had gone up in real terms by a third since 1979 – though without satisfying greatly increased demands. By 1990, many of her political colleagues had come to believe that although she had led the Conservative Party to three general election victories in a row (a unique achievement in British politics), she would be a vote-loser in the next contest. Faced with the erosion of loyalty and support, she resigned. Her successor, Mr Major, was something of an unknown quantity, having not had a long exposure in the front ranks of politics. It seemed likely, though, that British policy might now become less obstructive in its approach to the Community and its affairs (and would certainly be quieter in style). As events turned out, things were to prove otherwise.

Polish revolution

By 1980 there was not a dictatorship left in western Europe. Democracy had triumphed. Now it was to be the turn of eastern Europe. The first clear signs of the con-sequences of softening Soviet attitudes and a slackening of international tension came in Poland. The Polish nation had already in the early 1980s begun the recovery of its independence, though the process was interrupted by setbacks. Poles had retained, to a remarkable degree (but not for the first time in their history) their collective integrity by following their priests and not their rulers. The influence of the Polish Church had not always been exercised benevolently, it must be said. The primate of Poland had in 1946 been willing to pander to traditional prejudices by blaming Jews for the reactions of Poles who in that year indulged themselves in pogroms and murder of Jews who had survived the Holocaust[1]. Nevertheless the Church had an enduring hold on the affec-tions and minds of most Poles as the embodiment of the nation, and was often to speak for them to much better effect – all the more convincingly after a Polish pope had been enthroned in 1978. In the 1970s it had supported workers who protested against eco-

---

[1]   See B. Wasserstein, *Vanishing Diaspora, The Jews in Europe since 1945* (London, 1996).

nomic policy, condemning their ill-treatment. This, together with the worsening of economic conditions and rising food prices, was the background to a series of strikes in 1980 which came to a head in a well-televised struggle in the Gdansk shipyard from which there emerged a new and spontaneously organized federation of trades unions called 'Solidarity'. It added political demands to the economic goals of the strikers, among them one for free and independent trades unions. Solidarity's leader was a remarkable, much-imprisoned, electrical union leader, Lech Walesa, a devout Catholic, closely in touch with the Polish hierarchy. The shipyard gates were decorated with a picture of the pope and open-air masses were held by the strikers.

The world was soon surprised to see a shaken Polish government, troubled by spreading strikes, making historic concessions, above all, by recognising Solidarity as an independent, self-governing trade union. Symbolically, regular broadcasting of the Catholic Mass on Sundays was also conceded. But disorder did not cease. With the winter, the atmosphere of crisis deepened. Threats were heard from Poland's neighbours of possible intervention; forty Soviet divisions were said to be ready in the GDR and on the Russian frontier. But the dog did not bark in the night; the Soviet army did not move and was not ordered by Brezhnev to do so, nor by his successors in the turbulent years which followed, likely as invasion sometimes seemed. It was the first sign of changes in thinking at Moscow which were the necessary premise of what was to follow in eastern Europe.

In 1981, tension continued to rise. The economic situation worsened, but Walesa strove to avoid provocation. On five occasions the Russian commander of the Warsaw Pact forces came to Warsaw. On the last occasion, the Solidarity radicals broke away from Walesa's control and called for a general strike if emergency powers were taken by the government. On 13 December, martial law was declared. There followed fierce repression (opposition may have cost hundreds of lives). But the Polish military's action may also have helped to make Russian invasion unnecessary. Solidarity went underground, to begin seven years of struggle, during which it became more and more evident that the military government could neither prevent further economic deterioration, nor enlist the support of the 'real' Poland, the society alienated from communism, for the regime. A moral revolution was taking place. As one Western observer put it, Poles began to behave 'as if they lived in a free country'; clandestine organization and publication, strikes and demonstrations, and continuing ecclesiastical condemnation of the regime sustained what was at times an atmosphere of civil war.

Although after a few months the government cautiously abandoned formal martial law, it still continued to deploy a varied repertoire of overt and undercover repression. Meanwhile, the economy declined further, western countries offered no help and little sympathy, and, after 1985, the change in Moscow began to produce its effects. Yet the climax came only in 1989, for Poland her greatest year since 1945. It was to be that for other countries, too, thanks to her example. It opened with the regime's acceptance that other political parties and organizations, including Solidarity, had to share in the political process. As a first step to true political pluralism, elections were held in June in which some seats were freely contested. Solidarity swept the board in them. Soon the new parliament denounced the German-Soviet agreement of August 1939, condemned the 1968 invasion of Czechoslovakia, and set up investigations into political murders committed since 1981.

In August 1989 Walesa announced that Solidarity would support a coalition government; the communist diehards were told by Mr Gorbachev that this would be justifiable; the judgement had the more weight because some Soviet military units had already been withdrawn from the country. In September a coalition dominated by Solidarity and led by the first non-communist prime minister since 1945 took office as the government of Poland. It was the first non-communist government in eastern Europe since 1948. Western economic aid was soon promised. By Christmas 1989, the Polish People's Republic had passed from history and, once again, the historic Republic of Poland had risen from its grave.

Contagion and emulation

Poland led eastern Europe to freedom. The importance of events there had quickly been perceived in other communist countries, whose leaders were much alarmed. In varying degree, all eastern Europe was also exposed to two other new factors. The first was a slow, but continuous, growth of east-west trade (including that of the USSR) in Europe, over the 1970s and 1980s. The other was a steadily increasing flow of information about non-communist countries, above all, through television, which was especially effective in the GDR. Helsinki had been reinforced by technology. More freedom of movement, more access to foreign books and newspapers had imperceptibly advanced the process of criticism in other countries than Poland. In spite of some ludicrous attempts to go on controlling information (Romania still required that typewriters be registered with state authorities), a change in popular consciousness throughout almost the whole communist bloc was under way in the second half of the decade. At the same time, Poland's experience was bringing a growing awareness in official circles that an increasingly divided and paralysed USSR would not (perhaps could not) intervene to uphold its creatures in the communist party bureaucracies of the other Warsaw Pact countries. This increasingly shaped events, though its final effect was not felt until the change had received implicit endorsement from Mr Gorbachev himself.

Even before overt political change, the Hungarians had moved almost as rapidly towards economic liberalization as the Poles, but their most important contribution to the dissolution of Communist Europe was indirect. In August 1989 Germans from the GDR were allowed to enter Hungary freely as tourists, though they were known to be seeking to present themselves to the embassy and consulates of the Federal Republic in search of asylum. A complete opening of Hungary's frontiers came in September. Czechoslovakia's followed suit and a flow became a flood. In three days 12,000 East Germans crossed to the west. The Soviet authorities remarked that this was 'unusual'. It was in fact the beginning of the end for the GDR. On the eve of the carefully planned and much-vaunted celebration of forty years' 'success' as a socialist country, and during a visit by Mr Gorbachev (who, to the dismay of the German communists, appeared to urge the East Germans to seize their chance), riot police found themselves battling with anti-government demonstrators on the streets of east Berlin. The government and Socialist Unity Party threw out their leaders, but this was not enough. November opened with huge demonstrations in many cities against a regime whose corruption was daily more evident. On 9 November came the greatest symbolic act of all, the spontaneous breaching of the Berlin Wall. The East German Politburo caved in and the demolition of the rest of the Wall followed. Within a few days more than 9,000,000 east

Germans visited West Berlin and other parts of the Federal Republic, much encouraged by the payment of 100 *Deutschmarks* to each visitor by the Federal Government as 'welcome money'.

More than anywhere else, events in the GDR showed that even in the most advanced communist countries there had been a massive alienation of popular feeling from the regime (and in Germany there was also the special factor of the wish for reunification). 1989 brought this alienation to a head. All over eastern Europe, it was suddenly clear that communist governments had no legitimacy in the eyes of their subjects, who either rose against them or turned their backs and let them fall down. Its institutional expression was everywhere a demand for free elections, with opposition parties freely campaigning. The Poles had followed their own partially-free elections (some seats had still been reserved after them to supporters of the former regime) with the writing of a new constitution; in 1990, Lech Walesa became president. A few months earlier, Hungary had elected a parliament from which emerged a non-communist government. Soviet soldiers began to withdraw from that country, too. In June 1990, elections in Czechoslovakia produced a free government and it was soon agreed that Soviet forces were to leave by May 1991. In none of these elections did the former communist politicians get more than 16 per cent of the vote. Those in Bulgaria were less decisive: there, the contest was won by communist party members turned reformers and calling themselves socialists. Rumania underwent violent upheaval (ending in the killing of its former communist dictator) after a rising in December 1989 which revealed uncertainties about the way ahead and internal divisions which ominously foreshadowed further strife. By June 1990 a government some believed still to be heavily influenced by former communists had turned on some of its former supporters, now critics, and crushed student protest with the aid of vigilante squads of miners at a high cost in lives and some in disapproval abroad.

A new Germany

The GDR was the other formerly communist-ruled country where events took a special, though far less violent, turn. Whatever happened there was always bound to be a special case, because liberalization would raise the question of German reunification, a bogey of Soviet foreign policy since 1945, and, to put it at its least assertive, by no means obviously in the interests of France. It was almost certainly unavoidable in one form or another, though. At the end of 1989 it was already a primary concern of the Christian Democrat German chancellor, Helmut Kohl, whose electoral prospects were likely to benefit from successful reunification, to make sure the process did not run away out of control; international reactions, above all from the four former occupying powers, were still unpredictable.

Ostpolitik, though, had achieved a great deal since 1969, east as well as west. The collapse of the Berlin Wall showed both that there was no political will in the GDR to support communism, and that there was none to preserve the state either. The regime had no general will to legitimize it. When a general election was held in the GDR in March 1990, 48 per cent of the vote and a majority of seats went to a coalition dominated by the Christian Democrats, the ruling party of the Federal Republic, the other Germany. Mr Kohl had accomplished a *volte-face* since the days when Brandt had begun approaches to the GDR as a part of a Social Democrat programme. Before the

GDR election he had already proposed a scheme to progress towards the joining of the two countries. Unity was in principle no longer in doubt, given its huge popular support. But it remained to settle procedure and timetable – and to reassure non-Germans, above all in the USSR. 'We do not want anyone to feel themselves the loser because of German unification' said the Federal Republic's foreign minister in May 1990.

In 1948 currency reform had begun the process of settling on Germany its bipartite division for the next forty-two years; in July 1990 the process of reunification and therefore of the demolition of the formal post-war order began, fittingly, with monetary, economic and social union of the two Germanies. On 3 October they were united politically under a new constitution, the former GDR territories becoming provinces of the Federal Republic. The first elections to the Federal parliament followed in December and confirmed the ascendancy of the Christian Democrats. Helmut Kohl became the first Chancellor of reunited Germany.

The change was momentous. The Americans and the western European states had in the end been brought round without difficulty, and with no open expression of official concern over the reconstitution of a united Germany. What was more surprising was that no serious alarm was officially expressed in Moscow, though it must have been felt there. That the USSR did not oppose German reunification must be accounted Mikhail Gorbachev's second great service to the German nation, after his visit to Berlin in the last months of the communist ascendancy there. It could hardly be gainsaid that with a population of 71,000,000 and the largest economy in Europe west of the USSR itself, the new Germany would be once more capable of playing a great power role as other Germanies had done in the past. Helsinki had undergone its first major modification.

Soviet power was now in eclipse as it had not been since 1918; the halcyon days of victory were forgotten as the Soviet Union (to some extent, like France) appeared at last as the loser of the peace settlement, forty-five years after her armies had stood triumphant in the streets of a ruined Berlin. Mr Gorbachev's compensation was a treaty promising German economic help for Soviet modernization. It might be said, too, by way of reassurance to those who remembered 1941–5, that the new German state was not quite an older Germany revived, but one shorn of the old eastern German lands (indeed, she had formally renounced them) and no longer dominated by Prussia as both Bismarck's *Reich* and the Weimar republic had been. More reassuring still (and of importance to west Europeans who felt misgivings), the Federal Republic was a federal and constitutional state seemingly assured of economic success, with nearly forty years' experience of democratic politics to build on, and embedded in the structures of the EC and NATO. At least for the time being, she was given the benefit of the doubt, even by west Europeans with long memories.

Revolution in the Soviet Union

Mr Gorbachev had come to power during the early stages of the east European revolution. Five years later, it was clear that his assumption of office had released revolutionary institutional change in the Soviet Union too, first, as power began to be taken away from the party, and then as the opportunities so provided were seized by newly emerging opposition forces, above all in the republics of the Union which began to claim greater or lesser degrees of autonomy. Before long, it began to look as if he might be undermining his own authority. Paradoxically, too, and alarmingly, the economic picture looked worse and worse. It became clear that any transition to a market economy, whether slow or rapid, was likely to impose far greater hardship on many Soviet citizens than had been envisaged, and perhaps on most of them. By 1989 it was clear that the Soviet economy was out of control and running down. As always before in Russian history, modernization had been launched from the centre and flowed out to the periphery through authoritarian structures. But the process could now no longer be relied upon, first because of the resistance of the *nomenklatura* and the administrators of the command economy, and then, at the end of the decade, because of the visibly and rapidly crumbling power the centre could exercise. Yet Mr Gorbachev seems never to have abandoned the hope that Soviet communism might be reformed and thus preserved.

By 1990 much more information was available to the rest of the world about the true state of the Soviet Union and its people's attitudes than ever before. Not only were there many overt signs of popular feeling, but *glasnost* had brought to the Soviet Union its first surveys of public opinion through polls. Some rough-and-ready judgements could be made: the discrediting of the party and *nomenklatura* was profound, even if it had not by 1990 gone so far as in some other Warsaw Pact countries (more surprisingly, the long subservient Orthodox Church appeared to have retained more respect and authority than other institution of the Marxist-Leninist *ancien régime*). But it was clear that economic failure everywhere hung like a cloud over any liberalizing of politics. Soviet citizens as well as foreign observers were by 1989 talking of the possibility of civil war.

This threat did not appear only to originate in what looked like economic failure. The thawing of the grip of the past had also revealed the power of nationalist and regional feeling when excited by economic collapse and opportunity. After seventy years of efforts to make Soviet citizens, the USSR was revealed to be a collection of peoples as distinct as ever. Its fifteen republics numbered among them some (above all the three Baltic republics of Latvia, Estonia and Lithuania) which were quick to show dissatisfaction with their lot. Azerbaijan and Soviet Armenia posed problems which were complicated by the fears of Islamic unrest which hung over the whole Union. To make matters worse, some believed there was a danger of a military *coup*; commanders who were as discontented by the Soviet failure in Afghanistan as some American soldiers had been by withdrawal from Vietnam were talked about as potential Bonapartes – a mythical danger long flourished as a bogey of Bolshevism, of course.

The signs of disintegration multiplied, although Mr Gorbachev succeeded in clinging to office and, indeed, in obtaining formal enhancements of his nominal powers (but this had the disadvantage of focusing responsibility for failure, too). One dramatic moment came in March 1990, when the Lithuanian parliament declared the annexation of 1939 invalid and reasserted the country's independence, though this was followed by complicated negotiation to avoid provoking the armed suppression of the revived republic by Soviet forces. Latvia and Estonia also claimed their independence, though in slightly different terms. The upshot was that Mr Gorbachev did not seek to revoke the fact of secession, but in return won agreements that the Baltic republics should guarantee the continued provision of certain practical services to the USSR. Yet this proved to be the beginning of the end for him. A period of increasingly rapid manoeuvring between reforming and conservative groups, in which he allied himself first to one and then, to redress the balance, to the other, led by the end of 1990 to the compromise of the previous summer already looking out of date and unworkable. Connivance at repressive action by the soldiers and KGB in Vilnius and Riga early in the new year did not stem the tide. Parliaments in nine of the Soviet republics had already by then either declared they were sovereign or had asserted a substantial degree of independence from the Union government. Some of them had made local languages official; and some had transferred Soviet ministries and economic agencies to local control. The Russian republic – the most important – set out to run its own economy separately from that of the Union. The Ukrainian republic proposed to set up its own army. In March, elections led Mr Gorbachev once more back to the path of reform and a search for a new Union treaty which could preserve some central role for the State. The world looked on, bemused.

The dissolution of eastern Europe

At the end of 1990, the condition of what had once seemed the almost monolithic east European bloc already defied generalization or brief description. As former communist countries (Czechoslovakia, Poland, Hungary) applied to join the EC, or got ready to do so (Bulgaria), some observers speculated about a potentially wider degree of European unity than ever before. More cautious judgements were made by those who noted the virulent emergence of new – or re-emergence of old – national and ethnic divisions to plague the new east (the first to appear were in Romania). Above all, over the whole area there gathered the storm-clouds of economic failure and the turbulence they might bring. Liberation might have come, but it had come to peoples and societies of very different levels of sophistication and development, and with very different historical inheritances to shape their reactions to it. Prediction was clearly unwise, as was to become clear in 1991.

It was the climax of one of the most startling and important upheavals of European history – and of world history, too, for that matter. Of what lay ahead, no one could be sure – except that it would be a period of danger, difficulty and, for many former Soviet citizens, misery. In other countries, politicians were rarely tempted to express more than caution over the turn events had taken. There was too much uncertainty ahead. Even the USSR's former friends were for the most part silent.

CHAPTER FOUR A new order in the making?

The break-up of Yugoslavia

There is little remarkable about the end or beginning of centuries except people's awareness of them. Anything else which may appear to give years such as 2000 or 2001 special significance arises, (as does all other history) as the consequence of existing facts, some the products of nature, some of human decisions, some of contingent circumstance or of the accidents of the coincidence of all these. It is only psychology which gives a special tone to centenary events, and as 1991 opened, and with it the last decade of the century, the euphoria of the previous few years was already ebbing. That owed much to economic recession which had been apparent already in 1988, though at the time somewhat lost to sight amid the exciting events in eastern Europe. A real deflation of European confidence and euphoria nonetheless only came about with the dissolution of a former communist state, the federal republic of Yugoslavia.

That country's history had always weighed heavily upon it. Its greatest national festival was a commemoration of defeat in a battle fought as long ago as 1389, when the Ottomans overthrew at Kosovo the medieval Serbian kingdom. As late as 1950, the veil was still being worn by some Yugoslav Moslem women, thirty years after Kemal abolished it in Turkey. The country which had emerged in 1918 as the 'Kingdom of Serbs, Croats and Slovenes' (and, after the establishment of a royal dictatorship, had changed its name to 'Yugoslavia' in 1929 in an attempt to obliterate old divisions) had been essentially a manifestation of the old historical dream of a 'Greater Serbia'. The dynasty which had seized back the Serbian throne in 1903 continued on the throne of the new kingdom. Its second king, Alexander, was assassinated in 1934 by a Macedonian who was aided by Croats acting with the support of the Hungarian and Italian governments. This act, which so clearly showed the continuing interest of outsiders in the country's affairs as well as the bitterness of its own divisions, is yet another of those later to be identified as the opening shot of the Second World War.

The divisions within Yugoslavia provide an outstanding example of the (probably inevitable) failures of the peace-makers of 1919 to solve problems whose roots lay far in the past. The census of 1931 classified its peoples as Serbo-Croats, Slovenes, Germans, Magyars, Rumanians, Vlachs, Albanians, Turks, 'Other Slavs', Jews, Gypsies and Italians. 'Serbo-Croats' was itself a misleading category, lumping together as it did Montenegrins, Bosnians, Moslems, Macedonians and Bulgarians, as well as the Serbs and

Croats who gave their name to it. Serbs and Croats speak the same language. But the Croats, being Roman Catholics, use Latin characters to write it, and the Orthodox Serbs use Cyrillic. Catholic and Orthodox, while accounting between them for more than four-fifths of Yugoslavia's supposed believers, had also to live with a substantial minority (11 per cent in 1931) of Moslems, most of them Bosnians[1]. Finally, the kingdom displayed wide disparities of wealth and economic development. Macedonia was one of those backward parts of Europe where the Middle Ages had barely faded away; Slovenia, to notice only one contrast among many, was substantially urbanized and contained significant industry. Yugoslavia's mainly agricultural economy had been weighed down by fast-growing population; pressure on land had produced a proliferation of tiny holdings, whose poverty was made worse by economic depression in the 1930s.

Politics in the kingdom were in the main about Croat-Serb antagonism. By 1939, government from Belgrade was detested by the Croats, who had generated an extremist national movement already making approaches to Hitler. There was also a Croatian fascist movement, the *Ustasa*; much that was bad was to be heard of it during the three-sided civil war which went on after the German invasion and occupation of 1941 between Croatians, mainly Serb communists (led by a Croatian, Josef Broz, or 'Tito') and royalists. It ended in communist victory in 1945, and the containment of the nationalities by Tito's dictatorship.

Forty-five years later (and ten after Tito's death) the old issues were suddenly to show themselves still vigorously alive. They were soon also still clearly of interest to outsiders. In 1990 Yugoslavia faced a double crisis, economic and political. The federal government's attempts to deal with the first were accompanied by increasing evidence of political fragmentation. As Yugoslavs of all nationalities cast about to find ways of filling the political vacuum left by the collapse of communism, parties formed to represent Serb, Croat, Macedonian and Slovene interests. By the end of the year all the governments of the constituent republics except Macedonia's rested on new elected majorities. More ominous still, national minorities had appeared within the republics; Croatian Serbs, for instance, declared their autonomy within Croatia. There was serious bloodshed in Macedonia at Kosovo (four-fifths of whose inhabitants were Albanian); the proclamation of an independent republic there was a major symbolic affront to the Serbians – and of major concern to the Greek and Bulgarian governments, whose predecessors had been ambitious for Macedonian territory since the days of the Balkan wars. Soon, the new republics were quarrelling with one another while the power of the federal government in Belgrade faded away. Serbia re-asserted control over Kosovo, but in March 1991 sporadic fighting began in the north between Serb and Croat villages. It soon drew in the official forces of the republics and led to open conflict between them. The worst areas of fighting lay outside Serbia, in zones of Serb population in other republics.

Precedents for intervention to achieve pacification by outsiders never seemed promising – partly because different views were held by different EC countries – and the prospect became even less attractive after the USSR had uttered warnings about the dangers of spreading local conflict to the international level. Croatia and Slovenia declared themselves independent of the Yugoslav federal republic in June 1991 and by the end of the year Bosnia-Herzegovina had joined them in doing so. Fighting had begun by then between the Moslem and Serb Bosnians, foreshadowing, many feared,

---

[1] See table in A. Polonsky, *The Little Dictatorships*, (London, 1975), p.162.

further spreading of ethnic conflict. It took almost no time for the Bosnian Serbs to fan the flames of wider antagonisms by speaking of their opponents as 'Turks'. Orthodox Serb clergy were only too happy to set the conflict in a context of a supposed renewal of Islamic advance in Europe. Just before Christmas, to the embarrassment of other EC states, Germany gave official recognition to the new Croatia (and was bringing pressure on its partners to follow suit; the EC did so early in 1992).

Serbia had resisted the dissolution of the federal republic, whose continuing unity it had seen as a way of assuring Serbian ascendancy. All that was left of a federal Yugoslavia soon consisted only of Serbia and Montenegro, though. Broadly speaking, the former Yugoslav army had been Serb-dominated and this gave Serbs a military advantage at the outset. Unlike Russia, when confronted with the wish of its former companion-republics to break away from its hegemony, Serbia chose to fight. But the preservation of the former federation soon ceased to be a conceivable goal and a simple battle for the spoils ensued. In the first place, this led to an attempt to seize Dubrovnik by Serbia, hoping thus to achieve her long-sought goal of a port on the Adriatic.

The end of the USSR

The warning over intervention in the former Yugoslavia turned out to be virtually the last diplomatic *démarche* of the Soviet regime and had soon been eclipsed by more startling events. On 19 August 1991 an attempt was made by conservatives (all of them appointed to their positions by Mr Gorbachev) to seize power by *coup d'état*. It failed; three days later Mr Gorbachev was back in occupation of the presidency. Nonetheless, his position had changed; continual manoeuvre in a search for compromise had undermined his political credibility. He had failed to bring about successful economic reform. He had fumbled the nationalities issue. He was tied too much to the past and had clung too long to the Party and the Union; Soviet politics had lurched forward without him.

By the end of August it already looked to many as if the USSR was moving towards civil war or disintegration; nine republics had already declared their independence. The circumstances of the coup had given an opportunity (which he boldly seized) to Mr Boris Yeltsin, the democratically elected leader of the Russian republic, the largest in the Union. The army, the only conceivable threat to his Moscow supporters, did not move against him when he had responded to the *coup* by taking control of all Soviet institutions on Russian territory. He now appeared both as the strong man of the Soviet scene without whose concurrence nothing could be done, and (to some) as a possible standard-bearer for a Russian chauvinism which might threaten other republics. While foreign observers watched uncomprehendingly, the purging of those who had supported or acquiesced in the attempt was developed into a determined replacement of Soviet officialdom at all levels, the redefinition of roles for the KGB, a redistribution between the Union and the republics of control over it, and most strikingly of all, the demolition of the Communist Party of the Soviet Union, after its suspension by the Soviet parliament on 29 August. Almost bloodlessly, at least to begin with, and to the amazement of the world, the huge creation which had grown out of the Bolshevik *coup* of 1917 was coming to an end. There seemed at first good grounds for rejoicing over that, though it was far from clear that only good would follow. As 1991 approached its end, a decision to abandon price controls in the Russian republic in the near future seemed to threaten not only inflation unparalleled since the earliest days of the Soviet system, but perhaps starvation, too, for millions of Russians. By then, in the newly independent Georgia, fighting had already broken out between the supporters of the president elected after the first free elections there and the discontented opposition.

The giant superpower which had emerged from the bloody experiments of the Bolshevik revolution to be, for nearly seventy years and almost to the end, the hope of revolutionaries around the world and the generator of colossal military strength that had fought and won the greatest land campaigns in history, seemed to be helplessly dissolving into a set of successor states. The nationalities question never seems to have been considered by Mr Gorbachev as of more than tactical importance, to be fitted somehow into the struggle for central power, and his dealings with Lithuania, Latvia and Estonia had reflected this. But what was in fact going forward were the death-throes of the last great European multinational empire. On 8 December 1991, Russian, Ukrainian and Belorussian leaders met at Minsk and announced the end of the Soviet Union and the establishment of a new 'Commonwealth' of Independent States (CIS). On 21 December, a gathering of representatives from eleven of the former republics met briefly at Alma-Ata to confirm this. They agreed that the USSR would come to an end formally on the last day of the year. Almost immediately, on Christmas Day, Mr Gorbachev resigned, the first Soviet leader ever to do so voluntarily.

Mr Gorbachev had done much, and had made more possible, even against his own inclinations, but he had outlived the moment when there was still a role for him. 'He wanted to combine things that cannot be combined' said the Russian prime minister[2]. It was the climax of one of the most startling and important upheavals of European history – and of world history, too, for that matter. Of what lay ahead, no one could be sure – except that it would be a period of danger, difficulty and, for many former Soviet citizens, misery. Politicians in other countries were rarely tempted to express more than

---

[2]   Boris Yeltsin was quoted thus in the American magazine *Newsweek*, 6 January 1992, p. 11.

caution over the turn events had taken. There was too much uncertainty ahead, – among other things, about what would happen to the Soviet nuclear arsenal. As for the USSR's former friends, that a few of them had expressed approval or encouragement for the failed coup of August (Libya and the PLO among them) was understandable; the prospect of a return to anything like Cold War groupings was bound to arouse dreams of renewed possibilities of manoeuvre in an international area so radically transformed.

European integration

On New Year's Day 1990 the president of France startled some of his country-men and many non-Frenchmen by speaking of 'one' Europe embracing all its nations excepting, though only for the moment, the USSR. It was perhaps only an aspiration, (or a trial balloon?), as events rapidly showed, but it indicated how far the debate on making Europe had come since the days of Monnet. The next few years were to show how difficult it would be to sustain so generous an interpretation of what further inte-gration might mean; there was a fading of European optimism. It was to prove hard to get beyond the symbolic date of 1992 set in 1985 for the establishment of a single market.

One source of difficulty was that former communist countries were soon wanting to join the Community; to admit them would be bound to pose diplomatic and economic problems to existing members. East Germany had entered the fold *de facto* in 1990 because of reunification but other aspiring entrants would have to wait until western Europeans had themselves settled what kind of Europe they wanted. Unhappily the debate was not to be easily resolved.

The statesmen agreed in 1991 at Maastricht on a new treaty making arrangements for a genuine single European market and a timetable for full economic and monetary union (EMU) not later than 1999. It gave citizenship of the European Union to the nationals of all member states and (a provision from which the United Kingdom secured its exemption) imposed on all members an obligation to impose certain common standards in work practices and some social benefits. Finally, the treaty set out agreement to the principle of 'subsidiarity', a word rooted in Catholic social teaching, which attempted to limit the interference of the Commission or Brussels with the details of national administration – an attempt to reassure the suspicious. In spite of this, the Danes rejected Maastricht the following year in a referendum, a similar test in France produced only a tiny majority in favour, and the British government (in spite of the carefully negotiated special safeguards it had won) was hard-pressed to win the par-liamentary vote on the issue, when a number of 'rebels' in the governing party voted against their leader.

One difficulty in the way of further European integration was, that so far as there was a real debate about the future, it was largely incomprehensible to the majority of west European voters; for them what mattered was perceived very much in terms of tra-ditional sectional and national interests – and in a time of economic difficulty, too. Fur-thermore, national interests tended to lead to a focus of debate in terms of resistance to what was seen as encroachment on them by the Commission at Brussels. It was spe-cially unfortunate that at a delicate moment the frequent tactlessness and triviality of many Commission decisions on matters requiring enforcement by national govern-ments was thrown into relief by the presidency of Mr Jacques Delors, a Frenchman

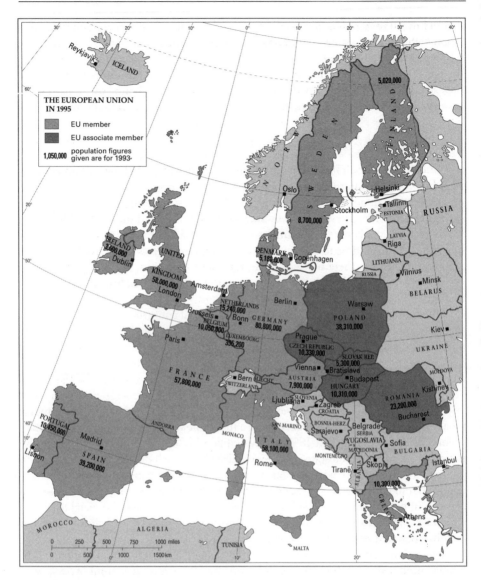

THE EUROPEAN UNION IN 1995

EU member

EU associate member

1,050,000 population figures given are for 1993.

highly articulate and vocal about his ambitions for a Europe which would concentrate still more effective power at Brussels.

Among the practical difficulties also encumbering the European road were some especially affecting Germany, the driving-force, under Chancellor Kohl, of European union. These largely arose from his greatest triumph, re-unification, which had soon proved very costly. Germany had been driven into deficit on its trade account, an unfamiliar experience for West Germans, and one which caused alarm. Political dissatisfaction with re-unification began to be heard as it became obvious that its financial costs would run on for years. As time passed, more was heard of the danger of inflation, an old nightmare for the Germans, and of the load carried by the German tax-payer as a result not only of the movement of former East Germans to the west, but of very large numbers of foreign immigrants taking advantage of the country's liberal attitude to the provision of political asylum. Unemployment, too, was rising.

Economic recession cast shadows in every member state of the EC. It reminded their peoples of disparities and differences of economic strength between them; policies to protect special interests (or what were seen to be such) were therefore pressed more strongly. More fundamentally, in every country fiscal, budgetary and exchange problems came in the 1990s to undermine the power of their governments (which had in some of them come to be taken for granted) to keep up employment and high levels of what may broadly be called 'welfare' spending. In such a context, specific European agreements and allocations of resources – for instance in the regulation of fishing – generated more disturbance than might have been expected.

In such circumstances, it ought to have been unsurprising that even within the European Union (the new name for the Community came into use as the Maastricht Treaty came into force on 1 November 1993) what had been achieved was always in danger of being lost to sight. There were too many misgivings, misinterpretations, ambiguities and even some outright quarrels about what might lie ahead. Economic circumstance made them harder to manage. For instance, a common monetary system set up by the French and Germans in 1987 had been turned in 1989 into a plan for a monetary union. This arrangement, associated particularly with the name of Mr Delors, imposed substantial restrictions on the management of their own currencies by the members by setting up an Exchange Rate Mechanism (ERM). It made revaluation and devaluation to meet domestic needs more difficult, particularly as German domestic concerns drove that country's central bank towards high interest rates. In 1992, Italy and the United Kingdom were both forced out of the ERM. Ireland followed in the next year and then international currency movements put Franco-German relations under major strain and brought about a considerable modification of the system. This cast a long shadow, notably over progress towards the proclaimed goal of European monetary union and a common European currency. By 1996, the timetable for the achievement of these goals was also threatened, probably fatally, by the manifest inability of some countries to achieve the economic conditions laid down as essentials for entrance to the proposed arrangements.

There were too many cross-currents within each country to be easily taken into account by politicians. This was so even in the two countries usually seen as the most consistent supporters of European integration, France and Germany. The fundamentals dictating the position of France did not change much as time went by, although their implications did; for her, the root of the European impulse had always lain in fear of a revived Germany. French statesmen sought to alleviate the danger this would present by tying Germany firmly into first the Common Market, and then the Community. As time went by, and the German economy grew stronger and stronger, French governments were forced to accept greater infringement of their actual independence to act and to recognize that Germany would have the preponderant share in mapping Europe's future. De Gaulle's ideal of a Europe of nation-states had to give way to a more federal view. Making the best of this, some Frenchmen thought that a united Europe could be tolerable if it were consciously built so as to give a maximum of informal and cultural weight in it to France – through, for example, appointments to the Commission. If there had to be a European super-state, France could at least try to dominate it.

Germany's interests in further integration had always had to be interpreted with an eye to her inevitable relations with other central and east European countries. A word which had begun to be heard again in the 1980s was *Mitteleuropa*. It had first been given wide currency in the title of a book published by a German during the First World War which argued for the promotion of the economic cohesiveness of Germany and (under German leadership) the Habsburg empire[3]. It is not an expression adequately translated as 'central Europe', but neither would its full sense be conveyed by 'Germany and its neighbours'. It asserted, nonetheless, a special role for Germany and special relationships deriving from it.

After the collapse of communist Europe the German government had sought to befriend Germany's ex-communist neighbours by taking up the cause of those who sought enlargement of the EC to the east. The rapidity with which German businessmen and investors turned to establishing German economic interest in those countries may have made this easier, though the eagerness with which Germany recognized newly independent Croatia and Slovenia was far from reassuring to other EC countries (besides awakening old cultural fears and memories – notably in Serbia – of historic Slav and Teuton, Orthodox and Catholic antagonisms).

By the mid-1990s, western Europe had come a long way and perhaps further than was always grasped by Europeans born and arrived at maturity since the Treaty of Rome had been signed. There was still an EFTA outside the EU, but one much diminished[4]. The number of other nations now approaching or knocking at the entry door of the Community was at the very least evidence of the material advantages outsiders could see in membership. That there had been some convergences of culture (mainly at the popular level) and even some standardizing of consumption, probably owed less to policy than to progress in international communication and marketing. There may even have been some blurring of differences between social structures. The decline in numbers of German and French farmers showed one slow but shared shift towards a more rational economic structuring. Yet such things had been very costly (and the CAP often irritated non-farming voters). Europe was felt, too, to have failed in its handling of the Yugoslav question, which it saw virtually taken out of its hands by American intervention at the end of 1995, and the deployment of NATO's forces as peace-keepers in a way unanticipated by its founders. There were still then, therefore, major obscurities over the future of European integration.

Having achieved a single European market (albeit with some practical qualification), the EU's next proclaimed goal, a single currency and monetary union, was said to be especially cherished by Chancellor Kohl. It was one to which French governments, too, were believed to be committed, even if after some reluctance. The practicality of the likely timetable, though, looked more and more uncertain as ministers approached an inter-governmental meeting held in Turin in the spring of 1996.

As those attending looked ahead, doubts were likely to multiply. In some countries a strong emotional commitment could be discerned among politicians and administrators to the idea of European policy-making (a sense of the need for it being notably stim-

---

[3]   F. Naumann's *Mitteleuropa* was published in 1915.
[4]   Denmark, the United Kingdom, Portugal and Switzerland had left it by 1995. From 1994 the remaining members had all been united with the EU countries in a common European Economic Area. Austria, Finland, Sweden joined the EU on 1 January 1995.

ulated by the disorder over defence and security policy revealed by the crisis in the Yugoslav successor republics). Some smaller countries were attracted by the idea of reducing or perhaps eliminating the operation of national vetoes. In the more distant future still, some enthusiasts saw a politically united Europe as the inevitable end of a road already entered upon by the component nations of the Union. As all such ideas seemed likely to be realized in terms of conventional political thinking (the implications above all, being that some kind of European sovereign state would emerge), as many were terrified as inspired among those who thought about these things. Politicians brooded over what voters might think when a choice clearly had to be made which would bring home to them the consequences of such an outcome.

Another problem almost as immediately pressing as that of monetary union was that of enlargement of the Union. It was not hard to agree that, were monetary union to slip, and were enlargement not to take place, the EU might well settle back into not much more than a simple customs union dominated by Germany (much as the nineteenth-century *Zollverein* had been dominated by Prussia, as some inclined to historical analogy pointed out). Few outside the ranks of the firm nationalists found this an attractive possibility. But to think of going beyond it meant facing the key question of enlargement: who should be allowed – or encouraged – to join the EU? Of those who wished to be admitted, the longest standing was Turkey. Setting aside the obstacle provided by intransigent Greek opposition to her application, it could reasonably be asked whether Turkey was a European country – and equally reasonably it could be pointed out that if modernity in institutions (representative institutions and a secular state, for example) and a certain level of economic development was the test of Europeanness, then she was. Sweden and Finland among the Scandinavians (the Norwegians rejected the idea in a referendum) had joined the EU and so had Austria; they could hardly have been failed on grounds of insufficient 'Europeanness' and they fitted in as developed economies and countries of liberal political tradition. Greater difficulties arose in central and eastern Europe, perhaps most vividly in what had been Yugoslavia. It might be that not many problems would arise over Hungary and Czechoslovakia; the economic difficulties following reunification with the old GDR were not encouraging, but the passage of time would be likely to have reduced the danger of their repetition in these two countries if they came to join the EU, because of their economic progress since 1990. Other eastern countries seemed much less attractive as potential recruits, whether in terms of political culture or economic preparedness. What is more, they might raise problems for relations between the EU states and members of the CIS, some of whom were as sensitive about their western neighbours' political alignments as had been the USSR. Finally, times were inauspicious for further liberalization of labour flows; the spectre of a potentially immense migration from Russia and the east to the labour markets of the west was frightening.

It was difficult to envisage the resolution of such problems in the middle of the decade, at a moment when the major continental countries were still suffering recession (Great Britain, which, notoriously, had found membership of the EMF impossible to sustain, was the only major state which seemed to be moving out of it). France and Germany faced high and persistent levels of unemployment, and other countries grave budgetary disorder. A tendency to elect conservative governments was one visible response to this. These facts were bound to exercise important influence on the way monetary union and enlargement were dealt with, and that was almost all that could be said about them which was clear at that moment.

They were, though, facts which also made it too easy to forget the overall achievement of the years since the Treaty of Rome. By 1990, what we may for convenience call 'western Europe' was one of the three major players in a new world economy. She accounted by then for some 70 per cent of world trade (much of it between her own member countries) and 40 per cent of the world's Gross Domestic Product. Her own GDP was then larger than that of the USA (and twice as large as that of Japan). She was integrated through world investment flows between the developed world's industrial regions as she had never been even before 1914. Two-thirds of foreign investment in the United States was held by Europeans. Such facts were sometimes overlooked as they worried about their futures.

The Islamic bogy

In 1972 a gang of terrorists from the Middle East seized, held as hostages and then murdered eleven members of the Israeli team competing in the Olympic Games at Munich. This was one of the most spectacular acts of terrorism to disturb Europe (because of the availability of plentiful television coverage) in twenty years. There had already been and would continue to be acts of terrorism by Europeans, too (for example, a bloody massacre when a bomb was set off, apparently by extreme right-wing Italian political groups, at the Bologna railway station in 1980). But those mounted by Arabs or Islamic organizations exercised a growing fascination upon the European (and, for that matter, the North American) imagination and media. In the 1980s this preoccupation was reinforced by the rhetoric of the Iranian revolution, by talk of *jihad* (holy war) by Arab organisations, by dramatic events inside the Arab world itself – such as the murder in 1981 of the Egyptian prime minister who had negotiated peace with Israel, another television spectacular – by the bizarre statements and behaviour of the Moslem dictator of Libya, and by political changes in Moslem countries.

The Iranian revolution had not only raised the international temperature over the chronic issue of Arab-Israeli conflict, but helped to entangle existing economic and political questions with another, vaguer but much larger confrontation. It was sometimes seen – and proclaimed – as one between the western world as a whole and that of Islam. In the early 1990s this even led to talk of a forthcoming struggle of civilizations, an exaggeration too manifest to be taken seriously, but an interesting symptom of the importance which came to be attached to a contrast, and sometimes clash, of cultures. As the Cold War ebbed, what was somewhat inadequately labelled as Islamic 'fundamentalism' (by ill-judged analogy with conservative versions of Christianity in the United States) came to replace the old communist nightmare as the bogy for the western consciousness. The Serbs in Bosnia strove to exploit this (though it turned out not to be a very successful tack for them, since Bosnian Serb atrocities were so much more revoltingly blatant and filled headlines and television screens so much more compellingly than anything Bosnian Moslems did).

The hard anti-western (and occasionally anti-Christian) line of the rulers of the new Iran, and its coupling in that country with a new discipline and austerity in the imposition of Islamic law and custom on the westernized were very striking. So was the successful struggle of the Afghan *mujaheddin* against the Soviet army and the Islamic radicalization of the regime in Afghanistan under the influence of its Iranian neighbour. Afghanistan had never undergone significant modernization (such as had Iran) in spite of communist rule and its religious leaders found plenty of popular support for reaction against what there was and for renewed emphasis on Islamic tradition. This had resonance elsewhere (as well as leading, paradoxically, to clandestine American support for the *mujaheddin*). As the 1980s proceeded, electoral successes for avowedly 'Islamic' parties in several countries led to the installation of more 'Islamic' regimes, notably in the Sudan. The winning of a majority of votes by an Islamic party in the Algerian election of 1990 had an immediate European repercussion, for France felt itself obliged to support the Algerian military regime's attempts to repress the Islamic movement. Everywhere in the Arab lands, the pressure of radical Islamicizing forces was felt in some degree. Everywhere, it could find something to feed on in opposing governments which upheld privileged, sometimes overtly westernized, minorities or showed signs of growing tolerance towards Israel.

In Europe and the United States, such widely scattered phenomena were easy to misjudge; they seemed to form a more coherent pattern than was in fact the case. They looked like a united anti-western movement – or at least one which aspired to unity. Islamic rhetoric often seemed to confirm this. Yet Islamic 'fundamentalism' is full of qualifications and complexities and has obvious limitations as an explanatory term. It is not of equal weight in all Islamic countries. Indonesia and Nigeria have large Moslem populations, but have not displayed the excitement expressed in some Arab countries and Iran. Moreover, the recent expression of Moslem unease in political action (including terrorism) outside Moslem countries, is a more limited phenomenon than is sometimes recognized. Its emergence has in fact aroused new disunity and division within Islamic societies and has brought old problems to the surface.

Most of the Arab lands were once part of the Ottoman empire, which both embodied a claim to spiritual leadership (the caliphate) and gave a framework and measure of order to the zone stretching at one time from the Maghreb to the Sudan, the Yemen, and Mesopotamia. Former Ottoman lands had been the home of the first Islamic peoples to take up western ways in any numbers, sometimes under the influence of European and North American missionary and educational influences in the Near East. They had begun to do so even under the Ottomans, but only after 1918 did serious experiments in westernization begin in any part of it except Egypt (where they had been attempted even early in the nineteenth century under Mehemet Ali). In the inter-war and post-1945 Middle East, western ideas and institutions – the national state and nationalism, socialism and communism, liberal democracy, capitalism – were taken up much more vigorously in several Arab countries. Yet they notably failed to deliver the progress and delivery from humiliation many Arabs hoped for. The western nostrums did not produce the moral and political independence, cultural self-respect, liberal institutions, or the application of material wealth applied to the benefit of the peoples of the region which had been hoped for. Viable national states emerged in some countries, but prosperity and a Europeanized liberal society existed only briefly, in the Lebanon, one of the oldest points of contact between the Arab world and advanced western ideas, and there they were destroyed in the 1970s and 1980s by the careless, the unscrupulous, the exasperated and the disappointed.

By then, of course, exasperation had been enormously increased by the establishment of Israel. Another irritant was the rapid development (begun even before 1914) of the Middle East oil industry, which brought vast new revenues to the area, but without benefiting most Arabs. Westernization failed in its constructive potential, but not in its disruptive and corrosive effect, best-shown in non-Arab and economically well-developed Iran. There (as in Kemalist Turkey) the conservative Islamic clergy had been antagonized into exploiting a confluence of discontents (some people had opposed the Shah because he was not liberal enough, some because he was too liberal) and using the revolution to take power. They had tapped not only resentment of their ruler's misdeeds and errors, but decades of popular frustration outside their country as processes of modernization chipped away at deeply entrenched custom, outraged millions of the poor, and supplied them with reason to look to the Ayatollahs for leadership and inspiration. Success in overthrowing an ally of the Americans and achieving a substantial reduction of overt western cultural influence in Iran was a relief from the humiliation of the powerless so long felt throughout the Middle East.

This promising background was, nevertheless, not to open a decade in which the Islamic peoples of the Middle East and North Africa could feel that the tide of history had turned in their favour. In the first place, nothing had happened which qualified the fundamental flaw in the radical Islamic position, its anti-modernism. Islamic conservatives usually wanted to have the benefits of a selective, controlled modernization. Could they combine their own cultural goals (and rejection of those of the western world) with economic, technological, scientific modernization? There was no sign that this was likely. A second weakness soon became evident, too. In the 1980s division within the Islamic world erupted in one of the bloodiest wars since 1945, between Iraq and Iran. It had a deep historic background and was exacerbated by religious difference going back to the foundation of the Ummayad. The struggle lasted eight years and cost a 1,000,000 lives. Evidently, bitter divisions existed between Islamic countries, whatever their attitudes towards Europeans and Americans. Finally, to the dismay of Moslems all over the Middle East, no progress was made in solving what they saw as the Israel problem (which might mean at a maximum, the elimination of that country, or, at its most modest, satisfaction of reasonable Palestinian demands).

Against this background, another war, much less bloody, revealed more openly still the hidden stumbling-blocks in the way of Islamic co-operation (let alone unity) and brought back European armed forces to the Middle East, although in a subordinate role. Iraq had been favoured by the United States during the war with Iran (given the events of 1979–80, this was not surprising). In 1990, though, Iraqi armies invaded another Arab state, the small but immensely rich oil sheikhdom of Kuwait. Evidently to his surprise, the attempt of the Iraqi dictator, Saddam Hussein, to cover the operation with anti-Israeli rhetoric failed. Only the Palestinians and the king of Jordan (embarrassedly) took his side: Saudi Arabia, Syria and Egypt, on the other hand, joined an alliance against him under American leadership. A well-conducted diplomatic campaign in the UN produced a series of resolutions condemning Hussein's actions and authorizing the use of force to liberate Kuwait. British and French contingents formed part of a multi-national force assembled under American command on Saudi soil (the refusal of the German government – on constitutional grounds – to send one aroused dissatisfaction in Europe). The USSR did not intervene or hinder what was going forward. Iraqi rocket attacks were mounted on Israeli cities, but without military or diplomatic advantage: Israel did not want to enter the war, for that would have presented other Arab countries with grave problems. Finally, in January 1991, the allies struck. Within a month Iraq had given in and withdrawn from Kuwait. It could be said that Israel gained more than anyone else from this display of Islamic disunity. But Europeans and Americans felt better, too. For all the enduring discontents and resentments within the Islamic world, there was less sign than ever that they could be utilized for effective action. Against this background Islamic terrorist activity could be more realistically assessed.

A new development (bearing on relations with Islamic peoples) arousing concern in particular European countries in the early 1990s was the growing and more evident presence in some of them of substantial immigrant minorities. Italy, Spain and France (above all) attracted immigrants from the Maghreb for reasons of geographical proximity and (especially in the case of France) former colonial ties. The German Federal Republic attracted many Turks. Great Britain already had substantial Pakistani and Bangladeshi communities. Europe appeared to offer economic opportunity to countries with fast-growing populations and little chance of providing employment for their young men. When the economic weather turned chilly, though, edge was added to the resentments felt towards immigrants by Europeans who wanted jobs themselves, did not understand the customs and habits of their new neighbours, and read about terrorists. Circumstances varied from country to country and it was not only Moslem immigrants who were harassed, but near-fascist and extreme nationalist politicians and parties exploited the situation when they could. French governments found themselves taking police action against Algerian immigrants as French support for a harsh military regime in Algeria was challenged by its 'Islamic' opponents. Though in the middle of the 1990s, pan-Islamism and fundamentalism showed no sign of being more effective in defending Islamic interests in the global context than earlier responses to European encroachment, it was clear that Islamic factors were exacerbating and complicating other problems facing European governments, too.

The new Russia and the Commonwealth of Independent States

Russia was the biggest and most important state in the CIS. In its affairs, Mr Yeltsin, who had left the Communist Party of the Soviet Union in July 1990, soon stood on ground of more evident legitimacy than Mr Gorbachev. Four times submitting himself to the democratic process, he was four times victorious in elections. When he stood for the presidency of the Russian republic in 1991, he took 57 per cent of the votes cast. In January 1992 he launched a programme of radical economic reform, somewhat on lines tried out earlier in Poland, which led to an almost complete liberation of the economy and the removal of all detailed controls. By that time, inflation in Russia had already gone far, but this bold stroke appears at least to have staved off hyperinflation. Faced, nonetheless, with rising unemployment, savage falls in national income and real wages since 1990, a drop in industrial output by half since 1991, huge corruption in government organs, and widely-ramifying crime, Mr Yeltsin confronted very grave difficulties. Not the least of them were posed by relations with other members of the new Commonwealth, in whose 21 non-Russian republics there lived 27,000,000 Russians (there were 25,000,000 non-Russians in Russia).

The setting-up of the Commonwealth had been followed in 1992 by a treaty signed by 18 out of 20 autonomous republics within Russia, itself a federation. In the next year, a new constitution, for all its doubtful status and approval by narrow majority in a referendum in which only slightly half the electorate voted, completed the formal framework of post-Soviet Russia. The Communist Party, after initial suspension, had been dissolved by presidential decree. This, like the crushing by force of opponents engaged in insurrection against the introduction of the new constitution (in an attack on the so-called Moscow 'White House', the meeting-place of the Russian congress) was seen by some as a symptom of undue presidential high-handedness. Mr Yeltsin's personal style was always unlikely to go too far towards the concessionary and was never emollient, but his impatience with opposition encouraged well-founded attacks on the constitutionality of his actions. It was a dangerous weakness, for, in spite of some successes in handling relations with other members of the CIS which might otherwise have proved dangerous, he had little positive and material gain to offer the Russian people. He had not been able to provide the economic recovery which the man and woman in the street hoped for in the form of employment and lower prices. He was increasingly opposed not only by the often hidden influence of what have been called 'clans' of political interest built around industrial and bureaucratic foci, but openly by ex-communists, fascists, and nationalists with popular appeal, as well as by disappointed ex-reformers (often, after he had sacked them). He continued to enjoy, nevertheless, the ambiguous advantage of moral and diplomatic support from western Europe, notably that of the German chancellor, who urged the priority of restoring stability in Russia upon his fellow-leaders and that they should avoid being distracted into trying to attract former communist countries to membership of NATO, a course bound to alarm Russian nationalism.

It was unfortunate (given these circumstances) that an insurrection in the little land-locked republic of Chechnya in December 1994 quickly turned into a major new problem for the Russian government. Invoking a legend of national struggle against Russian oppression going back to their conquest in the eighteenth century by the armies of Catherine the Great, the rebels proclaimed their independence. A year later, thousands of Chechen civilians were dead, killed by Russian forces sent to restore order, the Chechen capital was in ruins after air and artillery bombardment, both sides had sunk in international esteem because of their bad behaviour (the Russian brutality in operating against civilian targets, and the Chechen practice of taking and using hostages – even on a foreign ship) but the struggle still continued. Many Russians must have seen Chechnya as potentially a new Afghanistan.

This was another part of the context in which elections at the end of 1995 produced a Duma with a majority for reaction and against further reform and Mr Yeltsin; in it, the largest of the group of deputies was communist and the second largest ultra-nationalist. It was not a good start on the road towards June 1996, and the next presidential election which, nonetheless, was won by Mr Yeltsin after a second round of voting. But voting patterns showed that many Russians evidently hankered after the good old Soviet days of secure employment, cheap food and international respect. There seemed little to indicate enthusiasm or even a reluctant willingness in the Russian public mind to accept the opening which had appeared to be present in 1990 towards western traditions and ideas. Less talk was heard abroad of the triumph of liberal democracy and the market society. Russians felt, it seemed, as distinct as ever from other Europeans, as secluded as ever in their own zone of civilization, and just as concerned to preserve that distinction as ever. Unhappily, they also seemed chauvinistically desirous of again playing the international role they felt to be their due, and this was usually seen as a countervailing power to the west. Curiously, China rarely seemed to be considered in the debate this provoked – nor, for that matter, the large Moslem population of Central Asia.

European disorder

National and minority problems remained visibly alive outside the CIS, too, though one of the most ancient among them seemed to have all but gone away, solved by tragic default. The fate of east European Jewry had been determined by the Holocaust; it could never again be the centre of world Jewry. The establishment of Israel provided a new focus. After 1945 many of the survivors of the Holocaust were drawn there and in eastern Europe Communist parties anxious to make use of traditional popular anti-semitism (not least in the Soviet Union) had encouraged emigration by harrying and minor persecution. In some countries the outcome was a virtual elimination of the Jewish population as a significant element in the demography of the region. Poland was the outstanding example; the 200,000 Polish Jews surviving in 1945 had quickly been once more victims of pogrom and harassment (and sometimes murder) and by 1990 their numbers had been reduced to a mere 6,000. Nearly a 1,000,000 Jews, though, then remained in the CIS republics, mainly in Russia (and, paradoxically, France experienced an actual growth in her Jewish population; immigrants from Islamic North Africa raised its numbers to about 500,000).

Elsewhere, nationalist recalcitrance was well alive. Ireland was one instance, though there were some signs that its most destructive effects there might be past. An Anglo-Irish agreement entered into in 1985 had acknowledged the Irish Republic's right to a role in discussion of the future of Ulster and set up new machinery to provide for it. More hopefully still, nine years later there began a period during which there was a cease-fire respected by the terrorist organizations of both sides in the interests of peaceful discussion of Ireland's constitutional future between the interested parties. This hopeful period ended tragically after a little less than eighteen months with another bomb being detonated by the nationalist IRA in London on 1 February 1996. How much moral, psychological and political damage this had done to the peace process remained to be seen.

In many other places, too, old antagonisms between peoples and communities had not disappeared. In 1990, at the time of the collapse of the communist dictatorship in Rumania, there was evident tension between Rumanians and the Hungarian inhabitants of Rumanian Transylvania. It was still there three years later, and surfacing in demands for autonomy within the Rumanian state. But the most tragic evidence of the destructiveness of persistent national feeling still came within the boundaries of the former federal republic of Yugoslavia. What came to be known as 'ethnic cleansing' – a euphemism for the elimination of an indigenous population in a particular locality by means of murder, deportation, terror, rape, arson and starvation – was launched by Serbs living in Bosnia against the Croats and Moslems of that area in 1992. For the next four years, Bosnia's very existence was at stake.

Croatia and Slovenia had quickly established their own independence in resistance to the formally Yugoslav (and actually Serbian) army. The struggle in Bosnia was bound to be more difficult. There were at least three peoples – Moslem, Croat, Serb – in play, and the representatives of these groups were much more mixed up in their distribution, typically in separate villages or separate quarters of towns (among them Sarajevo, the capital), than in any other republic. In March 1992 a referendum which Bosnian Serbs boycotted, but in which Croats and Moslems both voted in favour, decided for Bosnian independence. Bosnian Serbs then took to arms to fight for possession of Sarajevo and other areas they proclaimed to be Serb. They were supported by the Serbian and Montenegrin republics (still officially the constituents of a federal Yugoslavia). This led to the imposition of sanctions on Serbian external trade by the United Nations, the last effective act of that body in the whole sorry business for years.

The European Union, embarrassed by the early commitment of Germany to Croatia's recognition, did little better. Only in 1994 were NATO forces ready to undertake (under UN authorization) offensive (air) action against the Bosnian Serbs who consistently ignored or thwarted attempts to arrive at a settlement. The slow crystallization of American policy was in the end decisive. It brought about the desertion of the Bosnian Serbs by the Serbian government in Belgrade and much more vigorous NATO action. Croats, too, renewed their conflict with the Bosnian Serbs, not so much because they felt friendly towards the Moslems as because of the Croat population's plight in areas Serbs claimed. The Bosnian Serbs, who were at last brought to accept a cease-fire, and the presidents of Serbia, Croatia and Bosnia met for peace negotiations in the United States in November 1995.

Something like 200,000 people had died in four years. The destruction, in countries which were far from rich, was immense. It was easier to fund contingents for the NATO force (60,000 strong) sent to Bosnia to supervise the necessary withdrawals and boundary delimitations than to devise measures and find means for reconstruction, let alone bring criminals to justice. The essentials of the peace agreements were that Bosnia should consist of two entities, one a Moslem-Croat federation, one Serb. The Croatian government had been able to secure all the territory that it wanted in the north; Serbia had failed once again to achieve her port on the Adriatic and had been forced to abandon her hopes of territorial gain elsewhere, but was gratified to be released from the bite of the sanctions which had done her much damage. Moslem Bosnia had survived (which was more than had seemed likely at one or two moments). The Bosnian Serbs, while complying at least at the outset with the terms of partition, bitterly rejected the whole settlement in spirit. They offered no grounds for hope that this example of an old problem of nationalist aspirations had been laid to rest.

Facing the twenty-first century

Recent claims to the contrary notwithstanding, History has not yet come to an End. History has no End so long as there is anyone here to think about it. Individual histories – of nations, churches, religions, cultures, legal institutions, industries, and a thousand and one other things – do, on the other hand, end. In writing about such entities and studying them, historians define their subject implicitly or explicitly in chronological terms. Whatever the definition is, they eventually conclude that they have reached a point at which their arguments or narratives must close, because there is no theme ahead. In this way, to take an example at random, the history of the Holy Roman Empire can be recognized to end in 1806 (whereas the history of the ways in which historians have studied and assessed that empire by no means does so).

Perhaps the history of Europe has now come to an end in such a specific sense. There is no such helpful date as 1806, of course. In considering possibilities we should be clear about what we might mean. Over a period of centuries it is possible to set out a history of Europe as a geographical area fairly distinguishable (for much of the time) from that of the rest of the world. Obviously, though, in the last few centuries more and more non-European history has to be brought into such an account in order to make sense of it. That was true even when the histories of other parts of the world – say, Africa or Asia – can be seen to be much more shaped by what men and things from Europe did to them rather than the other way round. Nonetheless, the influence went both ways; European history was long ago deeply affected by, to take a couple of examples, the introduction of the potato and the flow of silver from the Americas, and this means the non-European history which made them possible is relevant to European.

Nowadays, indeed, the boot seems firmly to be on the other foot. In this century, what has gone on outside Europe has often settled the lives of Europeans. This has become more and more obvious as the end of this century approaches. Decisions taken in Beijing now determine the way in which the last stages of winding-up European empire in Asia will go forward; others taken in Tokyo or Seoul settle job prospects in Wales. At a political level the process has been at work unequivocally since at least 1945, and it is discernible even earlier. Against this background, can the history of Europe go on being written as an autonomous subject, a narrative driven by its own internal dynamic and not dependent on one originating elsewhere in the world? Prudence, at the very least, suggests it cannot.

Before settling the question, though, it is sensible to reflect once more on just what we might mean by speaking of the history of Europe as an autonomous and intelligible field of study. One way of measuring its imperviousness or susceptibility to influence from the outside would be to look at its effect on other parts of the world in which there are many alternative traditions of civilization available. Manifestly, Europe has for a few centuries shown a remarkable powerfulness: it has left a mark on the world. Naming and the knowledge of names have often been understood to be signs and forms of power; much of our world is identified by names given to it by Europeans. Even stars and planets bear names drawn from Europe's inherited mythologies, but the surface of the globe shows it even better. Europe, Africa and Asia were Greek ideas whose vast extension of meaning was given to them by Europeans. The Americas were named after an Italian seaman. Australasia was so called because it lay towards what Europeans called the South Pole. We still concern ourselves with areas called the 'Middle' and 'Far' Easts because of the direction in which they were first reached by Europeans; and all round the world there are names like New York, Nuevo Laredo, Nouvelle France, New Zealand. By naming the world, Europeans organized it intellectually, for themselves and for non-Europeans too.

The world's picture of the globe on which we live is a result of European discoveries was completed only in this century. It has settled the ways in which peoples all round the world see themselves, for Europeans invented names for humanity as well as for places. Just as they created the geographical notion of Africa, so they also created the category 'African'. From the old, vague, 'Moors' – embracing, at first, all non-Christians with dark skins, and in that sense exported as far as India – there emerged as a sub-set 'Africans' (and later came other sub-sets as that term was further subdivided and refined). That made it possible, when the time came, for the inhabitants of the continent of Africa to see themselves as sharing an identity they have never actually possessed and opened the way to other verbal inventions – Pan-Africanism, for instance, or *négritude*. Those notions made easier the borrowing from Europe in due time of others – race, nation, for example. Such ideas were to be very influential all round the world, though they actually cut across and sometimes denied the existence of other, truly native identities.

Europe also gave the world its first world languages. Chinese may be comprehensible to more people than any other, but that has not made it a world language in any of its versions. It has not taken over whole non-Chinese regions, as Spanish took over most of what we now call 'Latin' America (a nineteenth-century inspiration of the French emperor Napoleon III), English the continents of North America and Australasia, or French and English much of Africa. With language (as with representations of geography) go certain determinations of vision and perception, certain emphases, openings in some directions rather than others. The same could be remarked (and there is no space to do more here) of the influence of European games, arts and music the world round.

One can go on and on. Even the most apparently trivial signs reflect the unique impact of a civilization which has, in the most specific sense, been the master-source of most of the major forces shaping the world in the last three hundred years. The phenomenon has been far broader than mere political or military power. It is not even confined to a conscious acceptance of ideas and principles. Indeed, one of the difficulties of weighing European influence is that the process of cultural transference is so often unconscious. Further, it may even at times result in a conscious and noisy rejection of Europe. Finally, it is certainly not a matter only of 'high' culture. It is about nothing less than the shaping (in some degree at every level) of the first civilization with a global spread there has ever been, an influence shaping through and through, from top to bottom, consciously and unconsciously, the whole history of the world in the last few centuries.

Historians (particularly those teaching in universities) are often said to pay too much attention to Europe. Much that they do is described as 'Eurocentric', a symptom of 'Eurocentricity', words which indicate larger, more diffuse targets than simply a pre-occupation with certain topics. Usually, the charge of Eurocentricity seems less to reflect worry that Europe and European themes are given undue attention, than about the reasons which may lie behind such distortion. It tends to imply that not only the rel-ative historical importance but the intrinsic value of what Europeans have done is over-rated. To study European history rather than, say, African, or Chinese, is thought to reflect an assumption that European achievement is, in some crucial sense, more deserving of admiration, more worthy of praise, and therefore 'better'.

It is best to acknowledge that three of four centuries of historical writing have given some plausibility and speciousness to such a charge. Many Europeans have indeed looked down their noses at other cultures. The Chinese civilization which had been admired (more or less uncomprehendingly) by Leibniz and Voltaire came to be regarded with contempt by the Victorians - a 'huge, stationary, unattractive, morose civ-ilization', as one of them put it[1]. Both judgements were superficial, of course. So were many others made across cultures – for instance, the usual judgement of Europeans for centuries that Africans who had been able to master complex techniques in order to sur-vive as ordered communities in the specialized ecological niches provided by their con-tinent could nevertheless be disregarded as 'savages'. Other examples spring easily to mind.

It should also be recalled (for it is a part of European history) that in the great Euro-pean expansion Europeans for centuries assumed that they were in some sense 'better' than those they subjugated, however badly they behaved. Even when they were Chris-tians seeking to save souls of those equal with them in the eyes of God, Europeans thought they possessed the Truth, and that they confronted ignorance, immorality and savagery. Secularized from their Christian originals, such ideas went on to feed Europe's vanity, sustaining the myth of Progress and secular missionary zeal even in this century. But we must not over-simplify. If it is true that for a long time cultivated Euro-peans tended to believe that the only true art was art in the European tradition, it was Europeans who took up the study and collection of the art of other cultures. They did not have to have it forced upon them; they enthusiastically embraced it. It was an Eng-lishman who first promoted a vernacular press in India, not an Indian, and another who launched the study of Indian archaeology which led eventually to the ordered preser-vation of Indian monuments by government, something no previous conqueror had ever attempted. Furthermore (to change tack more sharply), it is a simple fact that the practices of some societies encountered by Europeans *were* often just as beastly, cruel and barbaric as those of the conquering European; it is not easy to argue a case (except on prudential or pragmatic grounds, and even that would be hard) for respecting female infanticide or *suttee*. To be over-impressed by the wickedness of eurocentricity may lead to a pleasurable feeling of rectitude, but certainly also leads to the distortion of historical fact.

---

[1] Cardinal Newman in *The Idea of a University*, ed. I. Ker (Oxford, 1976), p. 213.

World history, if that is the story to be told, and not the history of some parts of it, has in fact to be understood over the last few centuries in eurocentric terms. Europe was the original source of the most powerful of the prime movers of world history for most of that time. The history of other parts of the world or other peoples during those same centuries is obviously worthy of study for excellent reasons quite other than its connexion with European expansion. Chinese, Indian, Japanese history may all well be for any of us just as exciting, enhancing to our sensibilities, enlightening of our judgement or intellectually suggestive as European. As all history always is, it is worth study for its own sake. But so is European, and for a little while, European history's impact on the world was much greater than that of Asia, Africa or the Americas.

What this tells us about the way we should use the word 'Europe' is a different matter, and more difficult to elucidate. Influences emanating from that continent travelled indirectly or directly through the work of Europeans and those whom they met and impressed (whether favourably or violently) and often it is not hard to see what many of them shared with other Europeans. It was usually a selection of the commonplaces of the day, whether these were expressed in words or attitudes. Such shared words and attitudes were outstandingly important and have to be understood as historical facts if those Europeans are to be understood. But they throw no light on any ongoing, persistent civilization we can identify as 'Europe'. In numbers there may now be more Europeans alive than ever before who feel confidence about a growing European institutional unity and some of them feel a real personal interest in advancing that unity or an enthusiasm, or even (in the case of a few) a degree of moral commitment to it. But it took a long time to make Englishmen and Frenchmen and it will take some time yet to make Europeans in a similar sense. That should not be surprising. Different experiences of what they had (or thought they had) in common shaped European thoughts and behaviour in different ways across the centuries.

History should help us to understand, but will not provide off the shelf, definitions of European identity or self-consciousness. Nor will it provide evidence of membership of a continuing common tradition whose own history defines 'Europe' as a historical entity. This suggests that any European loyalty we might feel must mean something quite different from anything that can be discerned in the past. Too many people have tried to attach the idea of a self-conscious tradition to older identities, or at least their embryonic forms. There is no essentially unchanging, enduring European tradition, even if Europe has handed down to us many ideas or attitudes which have roots in the very remote past. I see in the word 'Europe' a historically changing series of meanings, filled out differently as different needs and challenges presented themselves to the European peoples. Europe has produced certain ideas and institutions, has been able, on and off, and with varying degrees of means, to blend them, purify them, make them work effectively, and has been able also to spread them round the world. Those ideas and institutions have been of many sorts. It is their power and effectiveness that links them into a whole at some times and for some purposes.

Europe seems to me best seen, if we have to have an image, as a historical crucible. It is a place – not even an easily defined place – where certain things happened at certain times which turned out – sometimes much later – to have a great impact. That impact is now seen round the globe, for those European events changed world history, and their effect is turned back upon Europe itself. The web of influence – or, if we prefer a more active metaphor, the transmission system – through which the effects of those events flowed to the world, is itself one of the complex consequences of them: it shaped the way things happened. In its turn, it enriched, criticized, modified what was being transmitted: what was European became western. Now, new cultural creations, new determinacies, are appearing which already play on geographical Europe itself. There is no point in seeking to decide the nature of a European heritage still to be transmitted to the world; Europe's work is done.

Some will find this conclusion offensive, some disappointing, and some almost tragic. Yet if there no longer seems to be a world-historical role left for Europe in the future, that is the outcome of a success. Nor does European history cease to be worthy of study because it produced the Holocaust as well as the Rights of Man. All that has happened is that a major civilizing and historical process is over; the parade has gone by. It is a fact, not a cause for regret (or celebration) that the old transmission systems (to use that metaphor again) of imperial rule, confident missionary efforts, economic exploitation, or the speed of technology have gone, for there is little for them to do. Success has removed the chance of a repeat; all that remains is to fill in the last corners of opportunity, to institutionalize yet more ideas and values of European origin, and to watch their steady internalization in other cultures, even when they seem resistant. The inexorable rise of practical and material rivalries in consequence will, of course, follow. There are no untouched, virginal cultural frontiers such as confronted Europe for much of the last five centuries. There will be no new cultural Age of Discovery, no new European age – on this planet, at least – only the hardening of emergent contours and outlines, many of which are already discernible.

But historians should not prophesy. Such visible outlines are very rough. We cannot always trace them aright, and they are still shifting. They may turn out very surprisingly. That is true also of Europe's own future as well as of the world context. Nor is this something which should surprise us, if we look back. The Europe once coterminous with Christendom is now post-Christian and neo-pagan. Its long and fruitful self-criticism and even its self-doubt are now often wholly secular. The nineteenth-century imperialist, for all the occasional superficial similarities, was already in his day cut from a cloth quite unlike that of the *conquistador*. Missionaries today cherish aims far different from those of their predecessors a century and a half ago. It is virtually certain that no western arms dealer today would ever show the prudential caution of that Renaissance pope who wished to prevent the sale of arms to Africans, or that of the British rulers of India who cautiously kept the artillery of their Indian army in the hands of British regiments. All of this – and much more – can be added up to say that the possibilities of cultural transfers have changed out of recognition since the Age of Discovery launched the Europeanization of the globe, and therefore that any notion of a 'Europe' directing cultural influence outwards, as if from a hosepipe, to play upon recipients who may enjoy or dislike the process, but remain essentially passive, is nonsensical; the hosepipes often now play the other way, and Europeans will sometimes have to brace themselves to withstand the showerbath.

It is tempting to think that formal changes in Europe's internal organization will matter less than the enthusiastic and fearful think. The European Union is likely with time to make for greater institutional cohesion, but will probably do so more slowly than we expect, by dealing with specific actual problems, with the need to adjust interests, with the negotiation of arrangements to get round corners and distribute disadvantages and advantages acceptably, and, if possibly, equitably. Some of this may have cultural dimensions: the effect on large numbers of non-European immigrants, for example, who will have at most assimilated only the superficialities of European life. Such a challenge will evoke sharper articulations and definitions of the grounds on which policy should be made. That may clarify the degree of any consensus (whose existence is doubtful, to say the least) about the treatment of aliens. Whether it does so or not, there is likely to be a problem there for attention.

In any case, the EU is for all its logic-defying variety still something which many people will continue to think an incomplete version of Europe. The distinction of western and eastern Europe is the stuff of long-lived debate, and it has cropped up many times in these pages. Two cultural zones east and west have long existed; they were not the creation of the Cold War, of the events of 1939–45 which led to it, or of the October Revolution of 1917. Those events have simply added new constraints to the old, notably in civic culture, economic development, environmental and health realities. The debate will go on about where Europe ends. The Judaeo-Classical roots of historic Christianity grew very different foliage in Catholic and Orthodox Europe. Cesaro-papalism indelibly marked Russian governmental tradition (and recent events suggest there is still a hankering for it) while Ottoman despotism gave government itself a bad name over much of the Balkans. While Poland, the Baltic states, Hungary, Bohemia and Moravia were Catholic, Russia was not: she had no Roman papacy, no Investiture struggle, no medieval immunities and civic liberties, no Renaissance, no Scientific Revolution, no participation in the Discoveries, no native Enlightenment, no French Revolution. She waited until the twentieth century to complete her industrialization, and then did it, surprisingly, within an ideological framework imported from western Europe. Russia has, too, herself been a transmitter of European civilization – for a long time mainly to Asia, but, after 1918, round the world, to which she exported that most European of artifacts, Marxist Communism, paradoxically a great subverter of European power.

The appeal of that creed in many places round the world is further evidence – were it needed – that for good or ill we now look forward to a world made over in the image of the west which emerged from Europe. There is no sign that those who will resist that outcome can hope to hold off for ever the slow encroachment of a civilization whose dangerous gifts are so attractive to so many and so indispensable to the powerful. It may mean first, though, that we shall enter a period when cultural antagonism will give a special tinge to political and economic conflict. Those born in the European traditions are likely to be, for some decades yet, condemned by their cultural opponents as disciples of a 'Great Satan' or something similar, the embodiments of evil principle, as well as political and economic exploiters and aggressors. Yet such personifications are only metaphors. We all, historians included, use such figures of speech, often without recognizing them. Metaphor is a most helpful device, but its seductiveness makes it doubly dangerous. It is too easy to attribute reality, even personality, to the units whose history we choose to argue about or explain, to slip unconsciously into idealization, into thinking that summaries of what happens as the 'mind' of an age is 'enlightened' by new ideas, or that a 'wave' of inflation or disease which we speak of as rolling through a 'society' is in some real or actual sense more than an observer's chosen categorization of thousands of individual events, each of which could be set in quite other contexts, or described in many other ways.

The French historian Braudel used a phrase which seems helpful in thinking of Europe. He speaks of a part of it, Italy, as 'a representation of a historical entity within which events had similar repercussions and effects, and were indeed in a sense impris-oned'[2]. This phrasing recognizes enduring constraints within a framework which is nonetheless not a strait-jacket, and it indicates, above all, a theatre where a certain his-tory unrolled. After all, the name Europe was first given to a place long ago, and although we still cannot assume that we know exactly what the name connotes at any particular time in history without further information, it has usually been possible to agree a minimum geographical content for the term. Within its boundaries, even nar-rowly conceived, certain events built up institutions of certain kinds, peoples became conscious of having histories of their own, some crises were surmounted and others pro-duced disasters, all of which had substantial effect on the lives of millions of people over hundreds of years. The degree to which those Europeans shared common experiences or underwent the impact of the same ideas can (and has to) be argued about; that they shared *something* that was at that time not shared by Asians or Africans is important and can be written about as history; we can still affirm that not all human beings share every-thing, and that sometimes whole groups among them share things they do not share with others.

Self-identification and self-recognition are at any time the product of particular sit-uations. The way the nineteenth-century European, if there was such a typical person, felt about the outside world was bound to be very different from the view Europeans take today. At different times Europeans have been concerned about 'Americaniza-tion' (Hitler made much of it and seems to have been in earnest). Yet alarm about it can hardly play the same part in an age of globally shared 'western' culture as it did in the nineteenth century. For centuries, a fear of Islam shaped Europeans' sense of iden-tity; some elements in their picture of modern Islam now still troubled modern Euro-peans. Yet from the outside, the Islamic picture of Europe and Europeans is over much of the canvas a representation lost in a general response to the 'west' – a materialist, godless, incoherent society already as visible to fervent Moslems in the old Soviet Union as in the United States. Perspectives change, and with them perceptions. 'Europe' is always in the making, *reformanda*. If we find that confusing, an examina-tion even as cursory as this one of the history which shows that, may well be helpful in beginning to deal with it.

---

[2]   Braudel, I, 164.

Index

Maps are indicated by italics; chronologies by bold numbers. Subheadings are in page number order.